ELIZABETHAN ESSAYS

The.holie.Bible.

conteynyng the olde
Testament and the newe.

Non mê pudet Euangely Christi.
Virtus enim Dei est ad salutem
Omni credenti Rom. t. 25.

ELIZABETHAN ESSAYS

PATRICK COLLINSON

THE HAMBLEDON PRESS

LONDON AND RIO GRANDE

Published by The Hambledon Press 1994

102 Gloucester Avenue, London NW1 8HX (U.K.)
P.O. Box 162, Rio Grande, Ohio 45674 (U.S.A.)

ISBN 1 85285 092 2

A description of this book is available from
the British Library and from the Library of Congress

Typeset by Multiplex Techniques Ltd

Printed on acid-free paper and bound in Great Britain by
Cambridge University Press

Contents

Illustrations

Acknowledgements

The essays reprinted in this volume appeared originally in the following places and are reprinted by the kind permission of the original publishers.

1   Inaugural Lecture as Regius Professor of History in the University of Cambridge, delivered on 9 November 1989 (Cambridge University Press, 1990).

2   The J.E. Neale Memorial Lecture for 1986, delivered in the John Rylands University Library of Manchester on 8 May 1986; *Bulletin of the John Rylands Library*, 69 (1987), pp. 394-424.

3   The J.E. Neale Memorial Lecture for 1987, delivered in University College, London, in November 1987; *Parliamentary History*, 7 (1988), pp. 187-211.

4   This essay originated in an Open Lecture given in the University of Kent at Canterbury in February 1982. Versions of it have since been shared with lecture audiences and seminars in the universities of Cambridge, East Anglia, St Andrews, Sheffield and Western Australia, and at the California Institute of Technology. I am grateful for a number of suggestions made on these occasions, some of them incorporated in this final version. I have also benefited from the critical comments of Dr Caroline Litzenberger and Miss Alex Walsham. The essay is printed here for the first time.

5   This essay was read to the Renaissance Society in January 1989 and was subsequently shared with the Church History Seminar in Cambridge; it is printed here for the first time.

6   *Clio's Mirror: Historiography in Britain and the Netherlands* (Britain and the Netherlands, vol. 8), ed. by A.C. Duke and C.A. Tamse (De Walburg Pers, Zutphen, 1985), pp. 31-54.

7   This essay originated in a lecture given at Peterhouse in 1989 to mark the fourth centenary of Perne's death. *Andrew Perne: Quatercentenary Studies*, edited

by David McKitterick, Cambridge Bibliographical Society Monograph no. 11 (Cambridge, 1991), pp. 1-34. This publication also includes the text of a second commemorative lecture by David McKitterick on 'Andrew Perne and his Books' and an edition by Elizabeth Leedham-Green of Perne's will of 1588, together with an earlier will, dated 1581.

8   *William Shakespeare: His World, his Work, his Influence*, i, *His World*, ed. John F. Andrews (Charles Scribner's Sons, New York, 1985), pp. 21-40.

Preface

In the Preface to my *Godly People: Essays on English Protestantism and Puritanism* (Hambledon Press, 1983) I was foolish enough to try to exorcise the ghost of my sometime supervisor, Sir John Neale, who thirty years before had said: 'Collinson, I like to think of you spending the rest of your life on this subject', the subject, that is, of Puritanism. In 1983 I wrote: 'It is time for me to tuck up my articles and occasional pieces in this stout volume and to utter no more on the subject, unless compelled to do so by main force.' But, as I should have known, the main force of the Anglo-American conference industry has prevailed and, for better or worse, there have been more utterances on that subject, described by Dr A.L. Rowse in his review of my very first book as 'rebarbative'. Some of these later essays will appear in a third Hambledon Press collection, *From Cranmer to Sancroft: English Religion in the Age of Reformation*, which is projected to follow this. In the mean time, the present volume presents a rather broader collection of subjects. I cannot get away from religion, but some of the religion in this collection takes us as far back as St Jerome in the fourth century and as far forward as Poland and Ealing in our own century.

The title, *Elizabethan Essays*, indicates where the centre of gravity lies. Sir John Neale, who once published a book with the same title, was the occasion for two of the essays, which are rather more political in focus than the material in *Godly People*. Perhaps Neale might have wished that I *had* spent my entire life on that other, rebarbative topic, since the two lectures which I delivered in his memory, in Manchester and London, and which are included here, present a view of Elizabethan politics which differs significantly from his own. They form a 'trailer' for more substantial publications on the Elizabethan political and social scene.

There are many debts which this little collection of essays incurs, and which it cannot adequately repay. I am indebted to the universities of Manchester and London (University College, London) which did me the honour of inviting me to deliver in each place a Neale Memorial Lecture. My original publisher, Jonathan Cape, and personally Graham Greene, are thanked in connection with the U.C.L. lecture. Two other universities, Sheffield and Cambridge, took me on to their payroll in the years since 1983, and two of the pieces in this collection began life as inaugural lectures. At Cambridge I have been richly blessed with a remarkable cohort of highly gifted postgraduate research students, to whom this book is dedicated. They continually inspire me and materially assist my work in more ways than can be explicitly stated in what follows.

As on an earlier occasion, my most considerable debt is to Martin Sheppard, who is the Hambledon Press. A foreigner, not enjoying perfect familiarity with the nuanced precisions of the English language, might call Martin a great bookmaker. What makes him great is his capacity to turn unpromising materials (I speak only of my own books) into useful and even attractive volumes. And I doubt whether another publisher exists who combines such efficiency with so much unruffled kindness.

I am glad to acknowledge the help of Syndics of the Cambridge University Library in providing many of the illustrations and permitting their reproduction.

Twelfth Night, 1994   Patrick Collinson

Abbreviations

A. & M.   *The Acts and Monuments of John Foxe*, ed. Stephen
                     Reed Cattley (1837-41)

BL   British Library

HMC   Historical Manuscript Commission

Hartley, *Proceedings*   *Proceedings in the Parliaments of Elizabeth I*,
                     ed. T.E. Hartley, i, *1558-1581* (Leicester, 1981)

HP 1558-1603   *The History of Parliament: The House of Commons
                     1558-1601*, ed. P.W. Hasler, 3 vols. (1981)

Neale I   J.E. Neale, *Elizabeth I and her Parliaments, 1559-1581*
                     (1953)

Neale II   J.E. Neale, *Elizabeth I and her Parliaments, 1584-1601*
                     (1957)

Parl. of England   G.R. Elton, *The Parliament of England, 1559-1581*
                     (Cambridge, 1986)

PRO   Public Record Office

Works of Knox   *The Works of John Knox*, ed. David Laing
                     (Edinburgh, 1844-)

To My Postgraduate Research Students,
Past and Present,
in Admiration and with Affection

1

De Republica Anglorum:
Or, History with the Politics Put Back*

A rather bleak biblical text which was hung around my neck as a far from satisfactory child returns to haunt me as the incumbent of this chair: 'Of him to whom much has been given, much shall be required.' But of my predecessor and friend Sir Geoffrey Elton I may well reverse the text and say: 'He who has given so much deserves in return all and more than he has received.' It is not for me to come back after thirty-six years spent elsewhere (and with a certain frisson as I enter this lecture room with its strong undergraduate memories) to tell Cambridge what it owes to Geoffrey Elton, who has been here for the past forty. But it may be that non-historians do not know the full extent of Elton's exertions on behalf of his subject beyond this place, good things done not exactly with stealth but without much self-advertisement: especially in promoting and turning into practical politics and economics a succession of authorial, editorial, biblio-graphical and indexing ventures. And this is not to speak of what is more properly his own, the books from which generations of school and univer-sity students have learned about the sixteenth century. For Elton has never spared himself the stern advice which he imparted in the book called *The Practice of History*: that 'the active labours of teaching and study' should 'fill the year and every day of it'[1] – although I understand that an exception is sometimes made of 25 December. It is an achievement which has not been matched in living memory by any other member of the historical profes-sional. So to Elton himself I extend the elegant turn of phrase which he used in his own inaugural to compliment that other former Regius still happily living among us, and with which I should like to be associated: 'Chadwick rather gave distinction to the Chair than derived distinction from it.'[2]

In that same inaugural, Elton called Sir John Seeley the first truly notable Regius professor, succeeding Charles Kingsley, who was 'the last of the absurdities'. At the risk of inaugurating a new line of absurdities I have to confess to being rather chuffed to sit in a chair once occupied by the author of *Westward Ho!* and *The Water Babies*, which was the second book which I ever read (the first being *Alice in Wonderland*, of course). For I should have

---

* See retrospective note, below, pp.28-9.
[1] G.R. Elton, *The Practice of History* (Sydney, 1967), p. 163;
[2] *The History of England: Inaugural Lecture Delivered 26 January 1984* (Cambridge, 1984).

been on both sides of the Bury – Trevelyan debate about history as art or
science, intuitive or definitive, which followed Bury's inaugural of 1903.
The title of the collection of essays presented to Hugh Trevor-Roper,
another living Regius from another place, *History and Imagination*,[3] does not
suggest to me two distinct entities and activities but one. There can be no
history worth reading without imagination. But imagination has its proper
and improper uses, and the now notorious 'empathy' of some school
history syllabuses is doubtless one of the improper ones. Anyway, 'imagine
that you are Geoffrey Elton or Owen Chadwick' is an examination question
which I should be careful not to attempt.

II

On a day in September 1983, the newspaper *Le Monde* carried as its main
front page headline the announcement that there had to be a reform in the
teaching of history. That was with reference to a government report which
had insisted that the incoherence which had crept into the teaching of the
subject in French schools must give way to a strictly chronological progres-
sion which would ensure that, having begun at a tender age with Pepin the
Short, all children by the time they parted company with formal education
should have reached the 1960s and the reign of Charles the Tall. I was in
France at the time and remember saying that such a headline could never
appear in an English newspaper. Historians should never use the word
never. The Secretary of State for Education and Science, in a letter dated
10 August 1989 (as it happens, my sixtieth birthday), has insisted on a
chronological framework for the teaching of history in our English and
Welsh schools, and that 'the British experience' should be given a 'sharper
focus';[4] and this and other public pronouncements about history have
resonated in the public prints, even if they have yet to reach the top of the
front page. Professional historians are not sure that they agree with
everything or indeed with anything which is being said, but seem gratified
that their subject is a talking point in what must be, at any level beyond the
mythological, the least historically minded of all advanced societies. But we
are also worried, or ought to be. In his inaugural lecture of a quarter of a
century ago, Sir Herbert Butterfield identified one of the factors likely to
determine the future development of historical scholarship as, 'the interest
of government in the subject – a thing which has its dangers as well as its

---

[3]   Hugh Lloyd-Jones, Valerie Pearl and Blair Worden, eds., *History and Imagination: Essays in
Honour of H.R. Trevor-Roper* (1981).
[4]   The Rt Hon. John MacGregor to Commander L.M.M. Saunders Watson, D.L., Chairman,
History Working Group, Schools Branch 3, Department of Education and Science, reproduced in
the *National Curriculum History Working Group Interim Report* (September 1989).

advantages'.[5] I have no idea what these words referred to in 1965 (although I recall that there was a Labour government at the time) but I know what they would mean if uttered now. Government has a legitimate interest in what history is taught in the schools, although I hope that we are entitled to take issue with its judgments. But so far as universities are concerned, one can only endorse what the mistress of Girton has recently written: 'It is absurd to suppose that someone else, not the historians, should dictate what is a proper subject to be taught in their departments.'[6]

Most inaugural lectures delivered from this chair have been general treatments of the subject. Trevelyan spoke in 1927 about *The Present Position of History*, Butler in 1949 on *The Present Need for History*, Butterfield in 1965 on *The Present State of Historical Scholarship*: so many authorities on the past pronouncing on the present! And the future! Sir Geoffrey's theme in 1968 was *The Future of the Past*. As my own title indicates, I had not intended to follow suit. But in the midst of the first national debate on the teaching of history ever staged, something ought to be said by someone who owes his place to the Crown. And I am not forgetting what Elton has told us: that the prince of English and Cambridge historians, F.W. Maitland, turned down the Regius chair in 1902 because he acknowledged that it carried an obligation to 'speak to the world at large', something which Maitland had no inclination to do.[7]

The present debate about history embraces the question of skills versus content which was provoked in the classroom by the Schools History Project but which has spilled over into the universities and even into this faculty, where it is having some impact on the latest episode of that long-running soap opera, tripos reform. For if university entrants have become accustomed to in some sense doing history and not simply learning passively about it, then we must address ourselves to minds which may to this extent be more active and alert than some undergraduate minds of the past, but less well-stocked. So we are talking about work more self-consciously related to the competent handling of primary sources and their secondary interpretation. Meanwhile the Secretary of State has expressed a conservative concern lest the *Interim Report* of the National Curriculum History Working Group, with its interest in skills and methods, may have placed too little emphasis on acquiring knowledge of what Mr John MacGregor calls 'the substance of history', even 'essential historical knowledge'.[8] And can we agree on what *that* is? On this matter I propose to say only that history is *both* an active intellectual skill *and* a body of knowledge.

---

[5] Herbert Butterfield, *The Present State of Historical Scholarship: An Inaugural Lecture* (Cambridge, 1965), p. 3.

[6] *Observer*, 5 November 1989.

[7] G.R. Elton, *F.W. Maitland* (1985), p.14.

[8] *National Curriculum History Working Group Interim Report*.

There can only be limited value in learning about historical skills and even exercising them in a vacuum of content and context. There is *some* value, what the *Interim Report* calls 'benefits beyond the study of history', but not the value of learning about the past. Conversely, there is limited value in acquiring historical information, for example the regnal years of the kings of England, without any thought or attention paid to its status, reliability or meaning. But it is not the value of understanding how the past came to be recorded and how it has been appropriated and applied to the successive presents of human affairs. So history is both a skill and a method and content and context.

As to which skills and methods, the 'which road to the past' debate seems to have subsided of recent years, unless I have been looking the other way. Most historians now seem to favour a latitudinarian position: all helpful roads. At least this is the atmosphere prevailing in this as in most other British history faculties and departments. Not for us the fierce methodological and ideological wars which beset some other subjects, which shall be nameless. Elton has spoken for all of us: 'We are all historians, differing only in what questions interest us and what methods we find useful in answering them.'[9] I am almost wholly innumerate and work from documents and texts. But I have no intention of denigrating the number-crunching cliometricians and can only hope that they will be nice to me.

It is easy to be all things to all men, harder to turn such stifling tolerance into pedagogical practice. Life is short, timetables and national curricula are finite, a three-year degree course is really too short. And history exists in unmanageable profusion, even on a conservative understanding of what it is, and a restrictive doctrine of what kinds of history ought to concern British students of the subject in the 1990s: what Commander Saunders Watson calls 'informed citizens of the 21st century'.[10] This brings me to the question of scope and content on which my predecessor had both heartfelt and provocative things to say six years ago in an inaugural address called *The History of England*.

The *Interim Report* is under fire for what it leaves out from an education in history to be shared by all. It is indeed deplorable that we should lose the middle ages and the Tudors and Stuarts from all but the lowest forms, where such matters can only receive ideographic treatment; that there should be no European history before Napoleon, except, inconsequentially, for the Italian Renaissance – no Reformation, a particular cause of regret for some of us, no Hitler either. More fundamentally, the principle of the Procrustean Bed is regrettable. Why apply to the teaching of history

[9]   R.W. Fogel and G.R. Elton, *Which Road to the Past? Two Views of History* (New Haven, CT, 1983), p. 109.
[10] *National Curriculum History Working Group Interim Report.*

the unnecessary rigidity imposed on the church service by the Tudor acts of uniformity? But at the same time it is awe-inspiring to find what abilities and powers in respect of the past children are now supposed to master at successive stages of their intellectual development. According to the D.E.S. Report entitled *History From 5 to 16*, by the latter age pupils (all pupils) should not only 'know' their world history but should have acquired the capacity 'to distinguish between historical facts and the interpretation of those facts', and 'to understand that events have usually a multiplicity of causes and that historical explanation is provisional, always debatable and sometime controversial'.[11] One wonders what the minority who opt to continue with history beyond the age of sixteen still need to learn about the subject.

At all levels the agenda, or curriculum, is placed under great strain by the near universality of the history which, or so it could be argued, we need to know, and, what is more, to understand. However much we may be inclined to sympathise with the Secretary of State in his concern for the priority of British History (and applaud the determination of the *Interim Report* that this should be properly *British* history and not the history of the Home Counties), there are so many other pressing claims. Are we to follow the example of the British press and pretend that most of South America doesn't exist? Do we believe that the future of those parts of Africa which do not include or impinge upon South Africa already lies in the past and that consequently we do not need to know about that African past? My own answer to both those questions, certainly if they are posed at a tertiary level, is no. We can hardly ignore the U.S.A., still less turn away from Europe at this juncture, nor, in this seismic autumn of 1989, understand by Europe only the member states of the E.E.C. It is also a precious principle that some history should be studied which has no obvious relevance, simply for its otherness, because it is there. So much for breadth. We ought also to applaud Professor Elton's insistence on the need to make students of the subject feel (and suffer?) the sheer *length* of history. History is indeed as long as a piece of string and as broad as we care to make it. And meanwhile the unrelenting accretion of knowledge has produced at all levels that incoherence complained of in *Le Monde* in 1983, the loss of direction which Dame Veronica Wedgwood deplored thirty years ago: 'too many perspectives and too few principles'; in the words of Dr Kitson Clark (who did his fair share of adding to our perspectives): 'a kind of historical nominalism with innumerable accidents and no universals'. There seemed to be less to read when I was an undergraduate. Yet two years before I was born Trevelyan, in his inaugural, had wondered what was to be done with the ever

---

[11] *History from 5 to 16: Curriculum Matters*, 11, Department of Education and Science (HMSO, 1988).

increasing mass of facts which historians were accumulating with such admirable zeal and skill.[12]

III

Historians have acquired a vast empire, Seeley would have said, in a fit of absence of mind. If it happened, or simply existed, the day before yesterday, it is history. Other disciplines, some of them originally fathered by history, others with independent pedigrees, have become colonies of both commerce and settlement: economics, demography, political science, theology, anthropology, psychology, cartography, iconography. To alter the metaphor: I myself am most happy to live next door to the study of literary texts, in a semi- detached house with paper-thin party walls. The environment must surely concern us increasingly. It is too bad that we have no courses in which to prescribe to students the reading of that brilliant book by Sir Keith Thomas, *Man and the Natural World*, a kind of charter document of history's potential green-ness which originated in a course of Trevelyan Lectures delivered in this university.[13] From an absorption with society, some historians have shifted their interest to the human body, defined not only as a social particle but biologically, as an organism. There is no bodily function or dysfunction on which there is not by now a considerable literature claiming historical status: from conception to death, a particularly popular subject, from the ingestion of food and drink to the evacuation of substances, menstruation and the principles and practices of bodily cleanliness – which, we have recently been told, in pre-industrial Europe meant not clean skin but white linen, and when water, and especially hot water, was seen to be life-threatening.[14] Above all, it is a current preoccupation how the body, and especially, it appears, the female body, has been seen in the past, the history of gaze-lines. Every aspect of past sexuality belongs to history; and madness too, or, *homage à Foucault*, the perception of madness. A book on *The Religious Significance of Food to Medieval Women* is by no means a peripheral text.[15]

History has now reached the point where an article on the wearing of earrings in late medieval Florence can occupy sixty pages of a mainstream

---

[12] C.V. Wedgwood quoted by John Kenyon, *The History Men: The Historical Profession in England since the Renaissance* (1983), p. 272.; G.R. Kitson Clark quoted by Arthur Marwick, *The Nature of History* (1970), p. 183; G.M. Trevelyan, *The Present Position of History: An Inaugural Lecture Delivered at Cambridge October 26 1927* (Cambridge, 1927), p. 20.

[13] Keith Thomas, *Man and the Natural World: Changing Attitudes in England, 1500-1800* (1983).

[14] Georges Vigarello, *Concepts of Cleanliness: Changing Attitudes in France since the Middle Ages*, tr. Jean Birrell (Cambridge, 1988).

[15] C.W. Bynum, *Holy Feast and Holy Fast: The Religious Significance of Food to Medieval Women* (Berkeley, CA, 1987).

journal.[16] We are not talking about one of those sub-historical hobbies which constitute a long and honourable tradition of their own, like the history of squash rackets or of trading stamps. Florentine ear-rings were one of those signs which are capable of leading us out along those webs of significance which man has spun for himself and which, according to Clifford Geertz, make up that human artefact, human culture.[17] For as they appear, or fail to appear, on the ears of holy women in Renaissance paintings, ear-rings tell us about a society in which the exotic was also alien and corrupt, where ear-rings were badges of prostitution and Jewishness, where the preaching friars had the power to attribute these significations to otherwise neutral items of personal attire and adornment; but began to lose it, as the evidence takes us from the early to the high Renaissance and as respectable, Christian women began again to decorate their ears. Evidently there are now no limits beyond those indicated by the literary scholar Stephen Greenblatt in the opening sentence of a recent book: 'I began with the desire to speak with the dead.'[18] I want to make it clear that I for one am not prepared to pronounce that any of this is not history. I find mercifully meaningless E.H. Carr's distinction between facts and historical facts.[19] But it remains true, and perhaps mercifully true, that a majority of the doctoral theses in history defended within the last twenty years have not been on the subject of ear-rings but on thoroughly traditional topics in politics and administration, a fact which Sir Keith Thomas has found regrettable.[20]

IV

So on what park bench did we absentmindedly leave Seeley's famous pronouncement that history is 'past politics'? – an aphorism worn into a cliché and also fathered on Edward Augustus Freeman, amongst others.[21] For now history is not so much past politics as past everything. Seeley went on: 'History fades into mere literature when it loses sight of its relation to

[16] Diana Owen Hughes, 'Distinguishing Signs: Ear-Rings, Jews and Franciscan Rhetoric in the Italian Renaissance City', *Past and Present*, 112 (1986), pp. 3-59.

[17] Clifford Geertz, *The Interpretation of Cultures: Selected Essays* (1975), p. 5.

[18] Stephen Greenblatt, *Shakespearean Negotiations: The Circulation of Social Energy in Renaissance England* (Oxford, 1988), p. 1.

[19] E.H. Carr, 'The Historian and his Facts', in *What is History?* (1962).

[20] Keith Thomas, reviewing Lawrence Stone, *The Past and the Present* (1981), *Times Literary Supplement*, 30 April 1982.

[21] The words 'history is past politics' will not be found in Seeley's inaugural, although he is heard in that address to say that 'history is the school of public feeling and patriotism', 'it is the school of statesmanship'. 'The Teaching of Politics: An Inaugural Lecture Delivered at Cambridge', in J.R. Seeley, *Lectures and Essays* (1870), pp. 290-317. 'History is past politics' is attributed to Freeman by Marwick, *The Nature of History*, p. 47, and to Herbert B. Adams by Fogel in *Which Road to the Past?*, p. 15. See Herbert B. Adams, 'Is History Past Politics?', *Johns Hopkins University Studies*, 13 (1895).

practical politics.' His concerns included a local bit of 'practical politics', the need for the still insecure Cambridge history faculty and tripos to anchor itself on some principle and rationale which would make it a success. Seeley's solution to that problem (the solution of someone who was not himself a historian, or at least not a historian's historian cast in the Rankeian mould) led to late nineteenth-century tensions in this place between the interests of history, as it were for its own sake, and Seeley's priorities as a teacher of a kind of political science. But it also led to the alarming success which the History Tripos came to enjoy in early twentieth-century Cambridge, where it occupied some of the time of a quarter of all undergraduates, supplanting the Classics which constituted Seeley's native discipline.[22] Later, Acton's inaugural endorsed his predecessor's dictum. 'The science of politics is the one science that is deposited by the stream of history, like the grains of gold in the sand of a river.' (But it is gratifying for a historian of religion like myself to hear Acton in the same address accord 'some priority' to ecclesiastical history over civil, since 'by reason of the graver issues concerned and the vital consequences of error' (for Acton religion was 'the first of human concerns'), it was more important to get that matter straight, so that ecclesiastical history had attained rigorous standards of scholarship rather earlier than civil history).[23]

It is now nearly twenty years since Sir Geoffrey Elton revived and restated Seeley's dictum in the book called *Political History: Principles and Practice* (1970), one of the most reflective (if I may presume to say so) of all my predecessor's writings: reflective, that is, in the layered depth of the categories and definitions of political history which it acknowledges and deploys, seeing politics as the active expression of a social organism, those dynamic activities which arise from the fact that men create, maintain, transform and destroy the social structures in which they live. But it was also a pugnacious book, pouring scorn on those who supposed that political history was a spent force, 'a very old-fashioned way of looking at the past'.[24] And there were plenty who did say such things in the late 1960s. When the *Times Literary Supplement* published three special issues in 1966, celebrating 'New Ways in History',[25] 'the coming revolution' as Keith Thomas called it, some of the contributors spoke of the preceding sixty or seventy years when, after all, British history had come of age as an academic discipline as a kind of dark tunnel in which historians had 'lost their bearings' (unlike

[22] Peter Slee, *Learning and a Liberal Education: The Study of Modern History in the Universities of Oxford, Cambridge and Manchester, 1860-1914* (Manchester, 1986), p. 58. The fullest account of Seeley and his aspirations is in Deborah Wormell, *Sir John Seeley and the Uses of History* (Cambridge, 1980).

[23] Lord Acton, *A Lecture on the Study of History* (1895), pp. 2-3, 6, 21.

[24] G.R. Elton, *Political History*, pp. 3-11.

[25] The three special issues appeared on 7 April (when Keith Thomas's remarks appeared, p. 275), 28 July and 8 September.

the ensuing twenty years in which, according to diehard traditionalists, their successors proceeded to lose their marbles).

So, on the fashionable denigration of political history, Elton wrote robustly in 1970, in tones reminiscent of Dr Johnson on London and life: 'There is nothing at all to be said for such attitudes: historians who can muster no interest for the active political lives of past societies have no sense of history at all' – in effect, are tired of life.[26] With that it is hard to quarrel. However, another of Elton's propositions seems to me more dubious: that the only political units worthy of study are sovereign and separate states. That was Seeley's view too but it looks no more plausible than Arnold Toynbee's doctrine that the irreducible units of historical investigation consist of a somewhat arbitrary list of past civilisations. I agree with Dr Susan Reynolds when she writes that our task ought to be one of 'disentangling the political ideas and loyalties of the past from those of the present'.[27] Notions of the modern state as a norm or a necessary destination of historical development, especially in the form of the nation state, may distract us in the pursuit of that stringently historical goal. And in any case, on this continent at least, such notions are destined to be overtaken by events: unless, which is possible, state nationalism proves to have the last, or latest laugh. I also try to remember that historians of non-European societies, many of them my colleagues in this faculty, cannot be subject to the Seeley-Elton ruling that political history means the history of states. In many parts of Africa a political history guided by Dr Reynolds's golden rule would not even be about the politics of tribes, for tribes turn out to be one of those pieces of invented tradition, invented, that is, for the convenience of colonial administrations.[28] But from this it does not follow that Africa has no indigenous political history, that its affairs belong exclusively to anthropology.

My title, I admit, is a provocation. It would be absurd to propose that the politics has to be put back into history, and especially absurd in a university which still devotes a series of Tripos papers to the exclusive study of British political and constitutional history, a subject formally separate from social and economic history, and which contains a college which has given its name to the austere study of high political processes, as the Peterhouse School. I may seem to speak for only those prodigals who, having wandered for too long in a far country, eating the husks of social and cultural history, even so-called 'total history', remember that in their father's house, political history, even the servants have food enough and to spare, and decide to come home. The irritation felt by the prodigal's elder brother may well be

[26] Elton, *Political History*, p. 4.
[27] Susan Reynolds, *Kingdoms and Communities in Western Europe, 900-1300* (Oxford, 1984), p. 253.
[28] Terence Ranger, 'The Invention of Tradition in Colonial Africa', in Eric Hobsbawm and Terence Ranger, ed., *The Invention of Tradition* (Cambridge, 1983), pp. 211-62.

shared by those colleagues who are able to say of political history; 'Lo, these many years do I serve thee, neither transgressed I at any time thy commandment.'

I hope that it will be understood that the phrase 'with the politics put back' echoes the third of the notorious Cambridge historical dicta, or clichés, to which it is mandatory to refer, and defer, on such occasions as this. Seeley and Bury have already been quoted. That only leaves Trevelyan's definition of social history as the history of a people with the politics left out. What Trevelyan actually said, on the first page of his best-selling *English Social History*, was that 'social history might be defined negatively as the history of a people with the politics left out'. To quote only the last ten words of this seventeen-word pronouncement is to miss its tentativeness ('might be') and the suggestion that there is, or may be, also a more positive definition of social history. And Trevelyan went on at once to say: 'It is perhaps difficult to leave out the politics from the history of any people, particularly the English people', explaining that he intended only to redress the balance of other history books which had consisted only of political annals, with little or no reference to the social environment.[29] That is reminiscent of Max Weber's careful explanation in his essay on *The Protestant Ethic and the Spirit of Capitalism* that he had no intention of substituting for a one-sided materialistic an equally one-sided spiritualistic interpretation of culture and of history.[30] That did not save Weber from misrepresentation, and Trevelyan too has been misrepresented: but with some justification, since his *English Social History* hardly deserves its title, in the perception of a more recent generation of social historians. Although one must not forget (and Sir John Plumb will not allow us to forget) that several hundred thousand people were happy to read it, that perhaps compounds rather than excuses what Arthur Marwick has called Trevelyan's 'greatest dis-service to historical studies'.[31] In his inaugural, he had defined social history, revealingly and inadequately, as 'everyday things in the past', and doubted whether there was room for such a subject in the Tripos.[32] That was to connect social history with a pre-professional strain of imaginative encounter with the past, mainly through its literary remains, and to confine the rigorous canons of professional, academic history to 'past politics'.

Just as there is now a new social history, a hard-hat area which sometimes seems to threaten us with the kind of intolerant hegemony once exercised

---

[29] G.M. Trevelyan, *English Social History: A Survey of Six Centuries, Chaucer to Queen Victoria* (1942), p. vii.

[30] Max Weber, *The Protestant Ethic and the Spirit of Capitalism*, tr. Talcott Parsons (1930), p. 183 and n. 119, p. 284.

[31] Marwick, *The Nature of History*, p. 59.

[32] Trevelyan, *The Present Position of History*, p. 15.

by political and constitutional history (ecclesiastical historians may feel especially threatened), so we may speak of a new political history, which is social history with the politics put back in, or an account of political processes which is also social. This inaugural can hope to do little more than celebrate the fact that this is currently happening: that, for example, the revival of narrative, which is one of the most discussed departures in current history, involves in almost every case the return of a kind of political history. For what could be more political than the 'thick narrative' comprising *The Return of Martin Guerre*, or *Carnival in Romans*, or the devious village conspiracies disclosed in *Montaillou?*[33] The essence of this new political history is to explore the social depth of politics, to find signs of political life at levels where it was not previously thought to have existed, and to disclose the horizontal connections of political life at those lower levels as coexistent with the vertical connections which depended upon monarchy and lordship and which have been the ordinary concerns of political history, certainly in medieval and early modern Europe. I take as indicative of a current trend the title of a paper not yet published but kindly supplied to me: 'Did Peasants Have a Politics?' The argument concerns English village communities in the fifteenth century and their dealings with the Crown, and it finds that they did indeed have a politics, and not only at the level of village elites but among those whose relative poverty kept them below the local office-bearing class. Even these poor were also political animals.[34]

People's history, working-class history in the socialist tradition, has served as an ideology, or inspiration, for the realisation of a stage of social development achieved only more recently or not yet achieved. It has to do with a future, not with a past, and, to be sure, with a future which we may never live to see. Historians of traditional European society learned some time ago that its popular politics were not at all progressive but, on the contrary, conservative and backward-looking. It has taken rather longer to grasp that they were not necessarily reactive, alternative politics either, but indicative of established and normal cultures and structures, not requiring explanation, still less realisation, by reference to other structures. This lesson was slow to be learned because we have encountered popular politics mainly at those moments of disclosure which were (in conventional terminology) peasant revolts. Without 1381 or 1549 in England, or 1525 in Germany, we might never have suspected that there was a political culture

---

[33] Natalie Davis, *The Return of Martin Guerre* (Cambridge, MA., 1983); E. Le Roy Ladurie, *Carnival in Romans: A People's Uprising at Romans, 1579-1580* (Harmondsworth, 1981); idem, *Montaillou: Cathars and Catholics in a French Village, 1294-1324* (Harmondsworth, 1980). Lawrence Stone writes on the revival of narrative in *The Past and the Present Revisited* (1987), pp. 74-96: 'The Revival of Narrative: Reflections on a New Old History'.

[34] I am grateful to Dr R.B. Goheen of the University of Ottawa for allowing me to read his article 'Did Peasants Have a Politics? Village Communities and the Crown in Fifteenth-Century England', before publication. It is now published in *American Historical Review*, 96 (1991) pp. 42-62.

at relatively submerged levels, well below the apexes of lordship and monarchy. That is as much as to say that a healthy organism, or the organism in a normally healthy state, has been perceived to exist only when it has revealed itself in a somewhat pathological condition.

So Professor Peter Blickle began with the evidence of the so-called Peasants' War of 1525, which he elevated to the status of an early modern Revolution of the Common Man. But he then found that to account for such an abortive revolution it was necessary to understand not only certain extraordinary precipitating circumstances (in a word, the Reformation) but a pre-existent, preconditional culture of communal politics and admin-istration. Late medieval German agrarian society is found to have consisted to a considerable extent of self-governing village communes, with their peasant officers responsible for all the more mundane functions of govern-ment, including the preservation of the peace and law enforcement.[35] Similar discoveries are being made by English students of popular 'commotions' in the sixteenth century,[36] and of the ostensibly democratic movement of the mid-seventeenth century reified by its opponents as the Levellers. As men supposedly born before their time, the Levellers may have enjoyed a vision of things which were yet to be, which accounts for much of the interest taken in them. But that seems inherently unlikely. What is more certain is that the Levellers and their platforms allow historians to see and recognise what already was: the active and indispen-sable involvement in the political and administrative infrastructure of society of thousands of ordinary householders and proprietors. Sir Keith Thomas remarks that the roots of their ostensibly radical proposals lay 'deep in the traditional political structure'.[37]

I am no medievalist but I suspect that one of the more fruitful develop-ments in recent medieval studies has been an enhanced recognition of the communal, associative character of western European political culture in the middle ages, indeed about as far back as it is possible to trace its outlines: which can be expressed as concentration on political horizontality to balance a more traditional preoccupation with verticality. Europe is per-ceived both as a 'network of communities', a mass of local groups acting collectively, and as a series of layers, all involving identification and engagement, up to and including what in England by the thirteenth century it was commonplace to call 'the community of the realm'. Dr Susan Reynolds remarks: 'The collective solidarity of medieval kingdoms has

[35] Peter Blickle, *The Revolution of 1525: The German Peasants' War from a New Perspective*, tr. T.A. Brady Jr and H.C. Erik Midelfort (Baltimore, 1981).
[36] Diarmaid MacCulloch, 'Kett's Rebellion in Context', *Past and Present*, 84 (1979), pp. 36-59; Diarmaid MacCulloch, *Suffolk and the Tudors: Politics and Religion in an English County, 1500-1600* (Oxford, 1986), pp. 315-37.
[37] Keith Thomas, 'The Levellers and the Franchise', in G.E. Aylmer, ed., *The Interregnum: The Quest for Settlement, 1646-1660* (1972), pp. 60-1.

been insufficiently appreciated.'[38]

As an ecclesiastical historian, I take particular interest in the current popularity as a subject for historical research of gilds and fraternities, called by one of their historians 'a form of association as unself-conscious and irresistible as the committee is today' – and, one may add, in all probability more useful and efficient than most committees.[39] The parish, too, is nowadays described as having its roots in similar needs, impulses and circumstances, owing its substance and vitality less to proprietorship and patronage than to the creative input and strong community sense of the parishioners themselves, especially 'parochiani meliores et antiquiores', the village elites.[40]

And here it is necessary to explain that these insights are, or ought to be, stringent, grounded in evidence, and not simply a nostalgic harking back to late nineteenth-century myths about instinctive *Gemeinschaften* in transition towards more purposeful *Gesellschaften*. Community is a potent myth, but it would be a harmful anti-myth to deny that there was any such thing as community in European civilisation.[41] For community was not, as nineteenth-century mythologists supposed, a feature of the social prehistory of Europe but part and parcel of the developing historical process itself. For the horizontal, communal bonding of society was neither unrelated to the vertical ties and demands of lordship nor, except in exceptional circumstances, resistant to vertical ties and demands. Rather it was the case that the growth of government and the imposition of a new range of public functions, initially at least, reinforced local communities and strengthened the hands of local elites and petty office-holders, just as the demands of royal government, and especially its fiscal demands, stimulated at a higher level the development of representative estates and the political culture associated with parliaments. Peasant revolts may have been revolts of the peasants, and in many other cases of other social groups, including townsmen. But they were also forceful protests in extreme circumstances of the lower echelons of government and public service, the medieval

[38] Reynolds, *Kingdoms and Communities*, p. 250.

[39] G.H. Martin, 'The English Borough in the Thirteenth Century', *Transactions of the Royal Historical Society*, 5th ser., 13 (1963), pp. 123-44; Caroline Barron, 'The Parish Fraternities of Medieval London', in Caroline Barron and C. Harper-Bill, ed., *The Church in Pre-Reformation Society: Essays in Honour of F.R.H. du Boulay* (1981); John Henderson, 'Confraternities and the Church in Late Medieval Florence', Richard Mackenney, 'Devotional Fraternities in Renaissance Venice', Miri Rubin, 'Corpus Christi Fraternities and Late Medieval Piety', all in W.J. Sheils and Diana Wood, ed., *Voluntary Religion*, Studies in Church History, 23 (1986), pp. 69-109.

[40] 'The Community of the Parish', in Reynolds, *Kingdoms and Communities*; and C.N.L. Brooke, 'The Churches of Medieval Cambridge', in Derek Beales and Geoffrey Best, ed., *History, Society and the Churches: Essays in Honour of Owen Chadwick* (Cambridge, 1985), pp. 49-76. Important ongoing work on the late medieval and early modern English parish is being done by Dr Clive Burgess of Oxford and Dr Beat Kümin of Cambridge.

[41] Alan Macfarlane et al., *Reconstructing Historical Communities* (Cambridge, 1977).

precursors of N.U.P.E. in action. Dr Reynolds speaks of the collective activities of local communities 'undertaken, as a matter of course, in support of the government, as well as in opposition to it'.[42]

V

It is time to turn away from matters of which I have at best a borrowed understanding and to bring discussion down to the more manageable and defensible scale of the historical smallholding which I myself attempt to cultivate. But nowadays (to press the analogy) senior academics are not so much smallholders as crofters, farming their two or three acres of rocky soil in moments snatched from a variety of other pieces of by-employment, which fill a quite inordinate amount of time with the awesome responsibility of for ever passing judgment on the work of others, as examiner, referee, elector, reviewer, appraiser. So in what follows those who already know my work should not expect to hear something altogether new.

Let me belatedly explain and introduce myself to those who do not know me, which I take to be the purpose of an inaugural. When I am not sitting in that seat of judgment, or professing the whole of modern history (which, according to the terms of my appointment, includes the whole of medieval history as well), I am an early modernist with a prime interest in the history of England in the sixteenth and seventeenth centuries. And, by the way, if nowadays one defines oneself as an early modernist rather than a historian of the Tudors and Stuarts, or of the Reformation, that is some indication that one wishes to be taken as a historian with some social scope, even as a holistic historian, and not as a student only of high politics or of established religion. It also means, as my colleagues well know, that I am irritated and even feel personally inconvenienced by the convention which in the organisation of Part I of the Tripos puts the politics into one set of British History papers and the economic and social history into another. If I had to be classified in any restrictive and exclusive sense, it would have to be as an ecclesiastical and religious historian. But I try to take some interest in politics as well as in social structure and social change.

Sixteenth- and seventeenth-century England was a monarchy, even in some sense, an absolute monarchy, 'farre more absolute', wrote the mid-Tudor intellectual-in-office Sir Thomas Smith, 'than either the dukedom of Venice is, or the kingdome of the Lacedemonians was'.[43] That was in the book *De Republica Anglorum* which has supplied the title for this lecture. Queen Elizabeth I on one occasion expressed astonishment that her cousin and enforced guest, Mary, queen of Scots, should not have known that she

---

[42] Reynolds, *Kingdoms and Communities*, p. 332.
[43] *De Republica Anglorum by Sir Thomas Smith*, ed. Mary Dewar (Cambridge, 1982), p. 85.

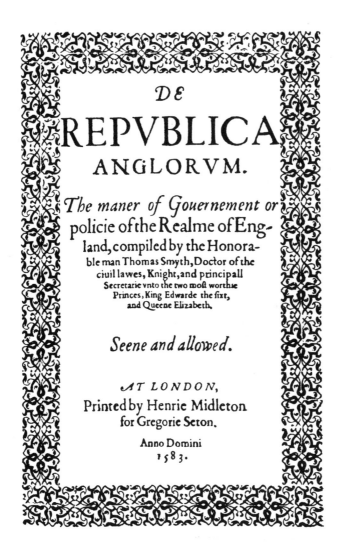

DE
REPVBLICA
ANGLORVM.

The maner of Gouernement or policie of the Realme of England, compiled by the Honorable man Thomas Smyth, Doctor of the ciuil lawes, Knight, and principall Secretarie vnto the two moſt worthie Princes, King Edwarde the ſixt, and Queene Elizabeth,

Seene and allowed.

AT LONDON, Printed by Henrie Midleton for Gregorie Seton.

Anno Domini
1583.

Title-page of Sir Thomas Smith, *De Republica Anglorum*, an anatomy of the social, political and legal fabric of Tudor England. Written in the detachment of a French embassy and posthumously published in 1583, it enjoyed a long after-life. The tenth edition appeared in 1640, at the time of the Short Parliament. (*Cambridge University Library*)

was an absolute monarch. Did Mary 'repute her to be in her minority'?[44]
The sixteenth-century English state had some experience of a royal
minority, but only for six years, not as much as Mary Stuart's Scotland,
where kings and queens usually came to the throne before they could
speak. Minorities and other little local difficulties, when the fiction of
personal monarchy wore thin, are a reminder of what late medieval
political commentators had learned, directly or indirectly, from the political philosophy of Aristotle: that monarchy was, or ought to be, not so much
absolute as mitigated by the principle of the *ius politicum*, supporting a
mixed polity partaking of elements both royal and political, which is to say,
popular and representative. To quote one of Smith's chapter headings:
'Common wealthes or governements are not most commonly simple but
mixt.' In *The Governance of England* (1470), Sir John Fortescue wrote
patriotically of *dominium politicum et regale* as if England had invented the
only constitutional monarchy on earth. In fact, Professor Koenigsberger
assures us, a balanced constitution such as Fortescue described had prevailed, in principle, from Poland to Portugal, Norway to Sicily. '*Dominium
politicum et regale* was the norm, not the exception.' It was a French
parliamentarian who claimed in 1489 that 'history and tradition tell us that
the kings were originally created by the votes of the sovereign people', so
that in the circumstances of a royal minority such as then prevailed in
France, 'the people must resume a power which is their own': which is more
than history and tradition were to tell Sir Thomas Smith.[45]

Our understanding of the political elements of the early modern English
monarchy is currently improving at three levels definable hierarchically as
bottom, middle and top, or, spatially as local community, county community and commonwealth, or community of the realm. Within the formal
framework of a monarchy, and subject always to direct royal intervention
at any of these levels (for personal monarchy was not always what Kantorowicz
called it, 'an abstract physiological fiction),[46] it is apparent that early
modern England consisted of a series of overlapping, superimposed
communities which were also semi-autonomous, self-governing political
cultures. These may be called, but always in quotes, 'republics': village
republics; in the counties, gentry republics; and at a transcendent level, the
commonwealth of England, which Sir Thomas Smith thought it proper to
render in Latin as *Republica Anglorum*. These features of past political
culture appear so ineluctable and obvious that I am almost ashamed to
spend time discussing them. And yet it is not so many years since a leading

[44] Edmund Lodge, *Illustrations of British History* (1791), ii, pp. 276-7.

[45] H.G. Koenigsberger, '*Dominium Regale* or *Dominium Politicum et Regale*: Monarchies and
Parliaments in Early Modern Europe', in his *Politicians and Virtuosi: Essays in Early Modern History*
(1986), pp. 1-25.

[46] Ernest H. Kantorowicz, *The King's Two Bodies: A Study in Medieval Political Theory* (Princeton,
1957), p. 4.

historian of the sixteenth century, having posed the question 'Was There a Tudor Despotism After All?', concluded that there was, and that Tudor England was subject to what he called 'minority rule', the rule of the Crown and of a very small élite.[47] Well, in a sense England was governed by a single person, described by Smith as 'the life, the head and the authoritie of all thinges that be doone in the realme of England'. Meditating on the latest communication from Inland Revenue in its O.H.M.S. envelope, one realises that nothing has changed. But Smith also defined the commonwealth as 'a society or common doing of a multitude of free men collected together and united by common accord and covenauntes among themselves, for the conservation of themselves as well in peace as in warre'.[48] And this 'common doing' evidently took historical precedence over the monarchical office, although Smith, who had not read John Locke, does not tell us how a multitude of free men came to be subject to a monarch who for some purposes was absolute.

More's *Utopia*, a fictive republic, was founded by a conqueror king, Utopus, whereas, according to Smith, England, a real monarchy, originated in some kind of republic, albeit a republic shaped like a family and subject throughout its development to patriarchy: which is to say that Smith anticipated Filmer. (And had he fully integrated Aristotle?) Yet by defining England as a realm, Smith was not denying its political status as a commonwealth, even as a kind of republic, a term not yet incompatible with monarchy. Sir Thomas Elyot, a conservative political commentator, was nervous about the demotic resonances of the word 'commonwealth', and substituted 'public weal' or 'weal public'.[49] But that was to accentuate, at least in my ears, the republican potential of the old constitution. 'Commonwealth', 'common', 'absolute', are all terms in the historical-political lectionary which have been extensively explored. But have we yet paid enough attention to 'public' and to its resonances in the sixteenth century? Did 'the public', in the sense of 'the great British public', already exist?

No less an authority than John Pocock has thought not.[50] What we find in Sir Thomas Smith and comparable texts is merely an ideal, historical-mythical reconstruction of how states, including monarchies, originated: 'a theoretical means of constituting a people as a body intelligent enough to recognise that it had a head'. Pocock calls this a stalagmite of intelligence, rising up towards the descending stalactite of authority: and I suppose, if we pursue the full implications of that metaphor, stalagmites are formed by

---

[47] Joel Hurstfield, 'Was there a Tudor Despotism After All?' in his *Freedom, Corruption and Government in Elizabethan England* (1973), pp. 23-49.

[48] *De Republica Anglorum*, p. 57.

[49] Stanford E. Lehmberg, *Sir Thomas Elyot: Tudor Humanist* (Austin, TX, 1960), pp. 40-1.

[50] J.G.A. Pocock, *The Machiavellian Moment: Florentine Political Thought and the Atlantic Republican Tradition* (Princeton, 1975), p. 334.

drips falling to the floor of the cave from the stalactite above. Fortescue's *corpus misticum* assumed intelligence, but it was not 'a fellowship of action'. Englishmen who had been to school or even to the theatre, perhaps to see *Coriolanus*, were familiar with republican terminology and institutions and knew something of the history of the Roman republic. But it was not open to them to practise active republican virtues. The notion of sixteenth-century intellectuals enduring a kind of internal exile, natural republicans and citizens forced to be subjects, is powerful and appealing; and clearly it applies to More as the author of *Utopia* and to his friend Erasmus, who was a devastating exponent of the irrationality of hereditary monarchy.[51] Erasmus and More were citizens, but of an invisible republic of letters.

But for England to become a *polis* and its inhabitants citizens was dependent, according to Pocock, upon further and extraneous modes of consciousness, such as Puritanism.[52] To me as a historian of Puritanism that does not seem to ring entirely true, although it is certainly true that a biblical, prophetic mode of discourse sharpened the rhetorical edge of what I think we can call public criticism of the Crown, not only in the form of the 'resistance theory' deployed against a catholic ruler like Mary Tudor, but in the reign of her protestant sister.[53] And it cannot be denied, somewhat beyond the sixteenth century, that the sectarian religious experience born out of Puritanism, English Nonconformity, would prove a crucible of radical political consciousness and action. However, I think that Pocock underestimated what I should call quasi-republican modes of political reflection and action within the intellectual and active reach of existing modes of consciousness and established constitutional parameters. These survived the suppression, or at least subsidence, of any public discussion of the principle of mixed government in the later sixteenth and early seventeenth centuries, before the mid-century constitutional crisis revived it. (And already Smith failed to define England as a mixed monarchy, but on the contrary reported that it enjoyed no other government than that of 'the royal and kingly majesty'.)[54]

It is hardly surprising that this perspective should be accessible to a historian (like myself) of the Elizabethan age rather than (as it might be) of the 'despotism' of Henry VIII. For in spite of Elizabeth's absoluteness and charisma, with the stream of Tudor blood running dry (Maitland's phrase),[55]

[51] See especially the adages 'Aut fatuum aut regem nasci oportere' and 'Scarabeus aquilam quaerit', in M.M. Phillips, ed., *Erasmus on his Times: A Shortened Version of the 'Adages' of Erasmus* (Cambridge, 1967), pp. 34-44, 47-72.

[52] Pocock, *Machiavellian Moment*, pp. 338-48.

[53] G.W. Bowler, 'English Protestant and Resistance Writings, 1553-1603' (unpublished Ph.D. thesis, University of London, 1981).

[54] Michael Mendle, *Dangerous Positions: Mixed Government, the Estates of the Realm, and the Making of the 'Answer to the Six Propositions'* (University of Alabama, 1985), pp. 52-6.

[55] F.W. Maitland, in *The Cambridge Modern History*, ii, *The Reformation* (Cambridge, 1907), p. 560.

Elizabethan politicians already lived, proleptically, with their queen's death, and already imagined the dangerous hiatus which that death would leave behind, so long as the succession to the crown was not limited or determined. Already they (and 'they' included the prime minister of the day, William Cecil, Lord Burghley) envisaged themselves conducting business in an acephalous commonwealth in which the great offices of state and the institutions of consultation and government, council and parliament, would continue in being, as if there were no hiatus, no vacancy. For such a hiatus was, in the last resort, intolerable. 'The government of the realm shall continue in all respectes', wrote Burghley, in drafting the terms for an interregnum which was unconstitutional and unprecedented in recent experience, albeit, given the far from smooth operation of the laws of succession in England, not wholly unprecedented. To be sure the realm was still a realm and the interregnum was intended for an emergency device, to last no longer than it was needed. But the capacity and readiness to make plans of this kind is an indication that any degree of political incapacity in the crown, actual or threatened, strengthened rather than diminished the political capacity of the crown's servants, who were also the leading representatives of the commonwealth or public weal, whether in their 'natural' capacity as members of the titled nobility, or as those most recently elevated to positions of trust in court and council. More than that, it tended to suggest that, when it came to the crunch, the realm took precedence over the ruler. So citizens were concealed within subjects. The notion was freely accessible that the crown itself was a public office, which existed only to conserve the public safety: even if the public safety was often spoken of, in terms, as the personal safety of the monarch.[56]

So even under Elizabeth, alive rather than dead, the high political scene is not adequately described as consisting of the crown and its subjects, a stalagmite of intelligent obedience formed by drips from the descending stalactite above it. The active complexity of that scene has, I believe, been obscured (and this is to make a somewhat paradoxical point) by a long-standing and conventional preoccupation with Parliament, which for many (but not for Fortescue) was the embodiment of the political elements of the constitution. The Elizabethan bishop, John Aylmer, having defined 'the regiment of England' as not a mere monarchy, nor a mere oligarchy, nor yet a democracy, but a rule 'mixte of all these', at once observed that 'thimage whereof, and not the image but the thinge in deede', was to be 'seene in the parliament house'.[57] But Smith devoted only two chapters out of fifty-eight to parliament, which he described not as the repository of the political elements of the constitution but as 'the highest court of the realm'.

---

[56] See below, 'The Monarchical Republic of Queen Elizabeth I', pp. 51-5.

[57] John Aylmer, *An Harborowe for Faithfull and Trewe Subiectes* ('at Strasborowe', but *recte* London, 1559), sig. H.3 r.

Recent revisionist parliamentary history tells us that the role of the sixteenth-century parliament was not one of political balance, still less of institutionalised opposition. Parliament was not primarily, or even at all, a political body in that sense but an instrument of government in its legislative expression.[58]

That may go too far. There were Elizabethan parliaments which made their mark as political sounding boards: not, to be sure, for a House of Commons intent on realising its manifest destiny of seizing sovereignty from the crown, but in response to a more broadly based and complex contention between representative elements of the 'political nation' (even, we may dare to say, of the public) and a politically isolated queen. This contention was mostly about the future of a political nation in which the queen, subject as she was to mortality, would not herself have a share.[59]

But parliament was an occasional, even exceptional forum for a contention which continued, in all its implications for policy, both foreign and domestic, elsewhere, not always or often within the earshot of historians. Pocock, following the lead of a half-forgotten book called *The Articulate Citizen and the English Renaissance*, was looking in the right direction when he found the embryonic citizen not so much in the parliamentarian as in the humanist turned statesman, the intellectual in office who possessed 'awareness and skills which the prince did not', so that an almost even balance was struck with the monarch in terms of reciprocal obligations to seek counsel and to give it.[60] In pursuit of this kind of emergent citizen we are not narrowly interested in the small body of sworn counsel usually known from the 1530s on as the privy council, although that body could and did recruit political intelligence of a high order, under Elizabeth men like Sir Thomas Wilson, Sir Francis Walsingham and Smith himself. Of somewhat greater interest are the experts outside the council and of inferior rank who were the think-tanks (if only one-man think-tanks) of the age, the writers of position papers which survive and (we must assume) prolific in verbal advice which has usually not survived. The true significance of these well-informed and often very self-possessed men is not fully conveyed in the phrase 'men-of-business' which it is now the fashion to apply to them. They included not only notable lawyers and 'parliament men' but also mathematical and other specialists in engineering and navigation, and other practical matters. For these too were political animals, using their own initiatives to draw attention to their talents and ideas, operating freely and resourcefully within the constraints of a code of public decorum which they overstepped at some personal risk but which they were also capable of manipulating with sophistication and a heightened sense of the public

[58] G.R. Elton, *The Parliament of England, 1559-1581* (Cambridge, 1986).
[59] 'Puritans, Men of Business and Elizabethan Parliaments', below, chap. 3, passim.
[60] A.B. Ferguson, *The Articulate Citizen and the English Renaissance* (Durham, NC, 1965).

interest, with which they normally claimed to be in true alignment. Men like the learned clerk of the council, Robert Beale, or the engineer Thomas Digges, or the magus John Dee, knew, or thought that they knew, that if the councillors and courtiers to whom they addressed themselves possessed an awareness and skill beyond the capacity of the prince, then their own intelligences operated at a higher level still.[61]

If these experts and intellectuals, who were not very numerous, had communicated only with the monarch or the privy council, and privily, they would have represented a very small body of citizens indeed, hardly enough swallows to make a political summer, and their impact would have been limited. But in fact some of them were also publicists and authors, and in this capacity they are pointers to a much wider body of citizenry, roughly equivalent to what Louis B. Wright, making a virtue of flagrant anachronism, called 'middle-class culture',[62] and which we may dare to identify with public opinion. When John Stubbs opposed the proposed French marriage in the cour-ageously outspoken manifesto *The Gaping Gulf* (1579) and lost his right hand for it, how large was the audience he aspired to address?[63] It was perhaps not quite the same audience which consumed that elaborate fiction *Arcadia*, which Sir Philip Sidney began to compose in that same year, but *Arcadia* too contained coded political messages which its readers were capable of deciphering.[64] The potential and no doubt actual appeal of religion was wider still, and so too the religious public. Preachers in the line established by Hugh Latimer indulged the illusion of apostrophising the entire nation – Oh England! England! – to which they attributed a public intelligence as well as a public conscience.[65] In *The Obedience of a Christian Man* William Tyndale had instructed the mind and conscience of Henry VIII, not privily but in print, for all the world to see and, if it chose, to draw the most critical of conclusions.

I shall not say much on this occasion about the middle-ground politics of what we have begun to call gentry republics, and nothing at all about the government and politics of towns. 'Gentry republic' is not, needless to say, an expression authorised by contemporary usage. But it fits the circum-

[61] M.A.R. Graves, 'The Management of the Elizabethan House of Commons: The Council's "Men-of-Business"', *Parliamentary History*, 2 (1983), pp. 11-38; 'The Common Lawyers and the Privy Council's Parliamentary Men-of-Business, 1584-1601', *Parliamentary History*, 8 (1989), pp. 189-215. See below, pp. 51-3, 72-82, for remarks on Thomas Norton, Robert Beale and Thomas Digges. I have benefited from discussing John Dee as an author of 'position papers' with Dr William Sherman. See Dr Sherman's unpublished Cambridge Ph.D. thesis, '"A Living Library": The Readings and Writings of John Dee' (1992).

[62] Louis B. Wright, *Middle-Class Culture in Elizabethan England* (Chapel Hill, NC, 1935).

[63] *John Stubb's 'Gaping Gulf' ... With Letters and Other Relevant Documents* (Charlottesville, VA, 1968).

[64] Richard C. McCoy, *Sir Philip Sidney: Rebellion in Arcadia* (Hassocks, 1979); David C. Norbrook, *Poetry and Politics in the English Renaissance* (1984), chap. 4 'Sidney and Political Pastoral'.

[65] Patrick Collinson, *The Birthpangs of Protestant England: Religious and Cultural Change in the Sixteenth and Seventeenth Centuries* (1988).

stances especially of those counties where there was no resident lay or
spiritual magnate of consequence, and where ruling gentry consequently
established and operated as it were their own peerage: an aspect of the
alleged rise of the gentry which is more demonstrable than most.[66] Norfolk
and Suffolk after the political extinction in East Anglia of the house of
Howard provide good examples of gentry republics. But a measure of
gentry collegiality, whether stable as (allegedly) in Suffolk or chronically
unstable and factious as (notoriously) in Norfolk, was a general feature of
regional political cultures everywhere, as the institutions of local government were strengthened to bear heavier burdens and as opportunities
increased for political and social interaction.

Twenty or thirty years ago it was a considerable advance on previous
knowledge to grasp that the county existed, as a prime political unit. At first
these provincial worlds were discussed as if they were hermetically sealed
in upon themselves and resistant to the intrusive attention of the centre. My
country, in the sense of my county, right or wrong. The political society of
the county was also described as if it were a thinnish carpet with no
underlay, no social depth. Now we begin to know more about the complex
patterns of social and political alliance among the gentry, across county
boundaries as much as within them, and about those interactions with the
centre which were a principal force in the consolidation of the county
community and its self-consciousness and self-defensiveness; and also
about the verticality as well as the horizontality of county society and county
politics.[67] That very public-spirited Norfolk gentleman Nathaniel Bacon
(Francis Bacon's half-brother) never threw away any of his letters or
accounts. These papers tell us that he had far more to do with his socially
inferior neighbours, in the farmyard, at market, at the sermon, than he had
with his fellow J.P.s, whom he apparently only met on the Bench and at the
Assizes in Norwich.[68] If that was not untypical and eccentric behaviour, we
need to take serious account of it in our unremitting efforts to explain the
English Civil War. In this society, downward deference was an important
principle, almost a way of life, like upward deference. In Suffolk, the landed
gentry made friends with the local townspeople and helped them to pursue

---

[66] A. Hassell Smith, *County and Court: Government and Politics in Norfolk, 1558-1603* (Oxford,
1974); MacCulloch, *Suffolk and the Tudors*; R.H. Fritze, 'Faith and Faction: Religious Changes,
National Politics and the Development of Local Factionalism in Hampshire, 1485-1570' (unpublished Ph.D. thesis, University of Cambridge, 1982).

[67] Alan Everitt, *The Community of Kent and the Great Rebellion, 1640-60* (Leicester, 1966); Clive
Holmes, 'The County Community in Stuart Historiography', *Journal of British Studies*, 19 (1979),
54-73; idem, *Seventeenth-Century Lincolnshire* (Lincoln, 1980); Ann Hughes, 'Militancy and Localism:
Warwickshire Politics and Westminster Politics', *Transactions of the Royal Historical Society*, 5th ser., 31
(1981), pp. 51-68.

[68] I am grateful to Professor A.H. Smith for sharing with me continuing work on Sir Nathaniel
Bacon, reflecting the content of the third and fourth volumes of his edition of *The Papers of Nathaniel
Bacon of Stiffkey*, which are forthcoming.

their lawsuits against other gentry, as a means of pursuing their own private vendettas, and no doubt in the hope of profiting in other ways.[69] According to precious evidence preserved by George Puttenham in *The Art of English Poesie*, the gentry and professional intelligentsia of the sixteenth century were perfectly capable of pronouncing 'received English' but chose to 'condescend' in their speech to the rustic vernacular of meaner persons.[70]

It would be nice to be able to say that this growing depth of knowledge is helping us to an explanatory understanding of the politics of the pre-Civil War years or, for that matter, of the post-Civil War Restoration to which similar methods are being belatedly applied.[71] But in some ways they make an intelligent over-view more elusive than ever. That is the nature of progress in history, which differs from some other subjects where advances in research yield clarification, refinement and simplicity.

It is at a lower, if not quite the lowest, level of the social hierarchies that the opportunities for a new and extended political history are greatest, and where there is most need to undo G.M. Trevelyan's handiwork by putting the politics back into the history of a people, indeed the history of *the* people, who G.K. Chesterton thought never had spoken yet. But to repeat and restate in specific form a point made generally earlier: who ever supposed that the people in the shape of villagers or, if you like to call them that, peasants, had a politics? Who ever suspected that Swallowfield, too, was a republic?

It may be that not everyone has heard of Swallowfield. This was a parish consisting of a number of hamlets, Shepperidge Magna, Shepperidge Parva, Farleigh Hill and Diddenham, geographically part of Berkshire but because of a boundary anomaly administratively a detached portion of Wiltshire, from which it was about twenty miles distant. In 1596, Swallowfield proved that it too could act as 'a society or common doing of a multitude of free men collected together and united by common accord and covenautes among themselves'. On 4 December of that year, the principal inhabitants (very much those 'parochiani meliores et antiquiores' of whom we have already heard) held a town meeting at which it was agreed to hold further regular meetings, under an adopted constitution, 'to the end we may the better and more quyetly lyve together in good love and amytie, to the praise of God and for the better servynge of her Majestie'. And they would keep a book, 'to register all our doynges'.[72]

[69] MacCulloch, *Suffolk and the Tudors*, pp. 321-31.

[70] *The Art of English Poesie by George Puttenham*, ed. G.D. Willock and A. Walker (Cambridge, 1970), p. 145.

[71] Andrew Coleby, *Central Government and the Localities: Hampshire, 1649-1689* (Cambridge, 1987).

[72] Huntington Library, San Marino, CA, MS Ellesmere 6162, fos. 34a-36. The Swallowfield document has no matrix in the volume of Ellesmere papers in which it occurs, which appears to be a miscellaneous *omnium gatherum*.

The purpose of the Swallowfield town meeting was not sociable but administrative and corrective, with a special emphasis on providing remedies for the problems arising from the dearth and hard times prevailing in one of the most arduous decades which ordinary working people in this country have ever had to endure: poverty, bastardy, petty theft, disorderly drunkenness, insubordination. One of the aspirations of the men of Swallowfield was to forestall the marriage of those who lacked 'a convenyent house to lyve in', presumably by preventing the calling of their banns. In that same year, 1596, in neighbouring Oxfordshire, some of the angry young men who found themselves unable to marry, unemployed and so prevented from crossing the threshold into fully adult life (a step they could normally expect to take in their late twenties), tried to organise an armed rising, with some talk of cutting throats. The Swallowfield arrangements help to explain why they failed, why in 1596 there was to be no replay of 1549.[73]

The thoroughly political character of the Swallowfield proceedings is implied first in the field of what may be called foreign relations. So far as possible, Swallowfield would sort out its own problems with its own informal jurisdiction, troubling the justices as seldom as possible. In the second place, politics are implied in the distance created between these 'cheiffe inhabitantes' and their social inferiors, the poor, whether deserving ('the honest poore') or otherwise, who will be made to suffer if they 'malapertly compare with their betters and sette them at nought'. And thirdly, and most significantly, politics is found to be living and breathing in the formal and as it were republican parity which was to prevail among the men of Swallowfield themselves. In their meetings, they were to speak in turn, without fearing interruption or the contempt of open censure from their colleagues: 'synce none of us is ruler of hym sellfe, but the whole Company or the most parte is ruler of us all' – 'as wee wilbe esteemed to be men of discretion, good credence, honest myndes and christian-lyke behaveour, one towards another'. I regard this as expressive of an authentic, indigenous sentiment which also found a voice in the century to follow in the religious movements known as Presbyterianism and Independency, although these experiments in ecclesiastical self-government doubtless owed something, how much would be hard to measure, to what Pocock called 'extraneous modes of consciousness'.

Swallowfield was admittedly a special case. It was partly because the magistrates to whom it was responsible were, as was said, 'far off', in Wiltshire, that it made itself for most practical purposes a self-governing commonwealth. If a murder were to be committed in Swallowfield, somebody would have to ride to Amesbury. Otherwise not. But the desire to

[73] John Walter, 'A "Rising of the People"? The Oxfordshire Rising of 1596', *Past and Present*, 107 (1985), pp. 90-143.

settle less heinous matters informally and out of court, technically the 'non-curial settlement of disputes', was by no means a peculiarity of Swallowfield. Dr Richard Hoyle, who is making a study of this phenomenon, will tell us of the survival from elsewhere of other minute books of the kind which Swallowfield used to record its town meetings. And, more generally, the capacities of the 'chief inhabitants' of this southern English village are not likely to have been exceptional but the kind of qualities which Dr Reynolds and Professor Blickle have attributed to other village communities in other parts of Europe and in other centuries. These were the capacities which the East Anglian yeomanry demonstrated in 1549 in the incident very misleadingly known as Ket's Rebellion. This was without doubt a commotion, but it was entered into with the serious and responsible purpose of taking the king's justice into hands which were thought, not without reason, to be more capable than those of the ruling gentry. Here was no wild lawless *jacquerie* but a well organised system of 'camps' given over to what Dr Diarmaid MacCulloch calls 'fiestas of justice'.[74]

It was a similar instinct for self-governing self-preservation which a hundred years later motivated the Clubmen who took responsibility for the defence of their homes against the depradations of both sides in the Civil War. In Dorset, the Clubmen, meeting in traditional gathering places like Maiden Castle and perhaps with some historical sense of what had been done in such places in earlier generations, were represented from each parish by 'three or four of the ablest men for wisdom, valour, and estate, inhabitants of the same'.[75] Such capacities were taken for granted when the Levellers proposed a general enfranchisement, not so much of the entire population as of male householders of a certain class and standing. It was a capacity proved from day to day, year in and year out, by service on all kinds of juries, juries not merely to find a man guilty or innocent but to determine the responsibility for the clearing of a drain or the repair of a road or river bank; and in the time and effort spent in parish vestries, courts baron and courts leet, all with powers to appoint officers, levy local rates, and fine and otherwise discipline their members. These were the constables, church-wardens and overseers of the poor in nine thousand parishes, the bottom line of early modern government. The orderly distribution of the goods of deceased persons was a matter of concern to almost everyone, and the probate of wills was, in England, business for the spiritual courts. But the courts could do nothing without the numerous private persons who assumed a kind of public responsibility in writing and witnessing wills, and in executing their contents.

In *De Republica Anglorum*, Sir Thomas Smith at first wrote off all these

[74] MacCulloch, 'Kett's Rebellion in Context'.
[75] John Morrill, *Revolt of the Provinces: Conservatives and Radicals in the English Civil War, 1630-1650* (1976), pp. 199-200.

sorts of people (the fourth sort or class amongst us, *proletarii*) as 'onelie to be ruled, not to rule other'. 'These have no voice nor authoritie in our common wealth and no account is made of them.' But then Smith remembered that these despised persons were not to be 'altogether neglected', since they made up juries and filled the parish offices. To save his snobbish face and not to make a total nonsense of what he had just written, Smith then made up a small piece of mythical history. 'At the first', such responsibilities had not been 'imployed uppon such lowe and base persons'.[76]

Such functions were as much political as administrative, since the human material with which these petty officers had to deal (much like the air-raid warden in *Dad's Army*), enforcing the peace, discouraging fornication, distinguishing between the deserving and undeserving poor, consisted of their neighbours and kindred, friends and enemies. Administratively, the churchwarden was under oath to present all offenders. Politically, so far as his oath would allow him, he might exercise his discretion in whom he presented, whom not. He was in office for only a couple of years, and perhaps presentable material himself.

There is something here for all of us, whether we choose to be known as social historians or political historians, and we have hardly started. Historians of crime, like bomb disposal experts, grope for those delicate devices and mechanisms which brought some offenders into court and exempted others.[77] If Stephen Greenblatt wants to talk with the dead, all the dead, ecclesiastical and social historians should have a particular desire to interview the consciences, minds and pockets of extinct churchwardens, complementing work already done on village constables.[78] These are indeed, as Peter Laslett has taught us to call them, so many worlds we have lost,[79] but they are partly retrievable worlds. And since those 'chief men' in their parishes represent what historians of many cultures have learned to call 'brokers', mediating between the higher and lower echelons of an hierarchical society, it is at this level, along this interface, that we can hope

---

[76] *De Republica Anglorum*, pp. 76-7. Since these words were written, the Cambridge doctoral thesis by John Craig (1992) 'Reformation, Politics and Polemics in Sixteenth-Century East Anglian Market Towns', incorporating his work on churchwardens, suggests that Smith may not have been giving an entirely mythical account of changes in the social status of local and petty office-holders. See also the forthcoming Cambridge doctoral thesis by Mr Henry French on office-holding and status in the parishes and townships of Essex and East Anglia.

[77] See 'The Rule of Law', in the introduction to A. Fletcher and J. Stevenson, eds., *Order and Disorder in Early Modern England* (Cambridge, 1985), pp. 15-26; together with J.A. Sharpe, *Crime in Early Modern England, 1550-1750* (1984) and Cynthia B. Herrup, *The Common Peace: Participation and the Criminal Law in Seventeenth-Century England* (Cambridge, 1987).

[78] Joan R. Kent, *The English Village Constable, 1580-1642: A Social and Administrative Study* (Oxford, 1986). This work will be undertaken by the Cambridge historians Dr John Craig and Dr Beat Kümin.

[79] Peter Laslett, *The World We Have Lost* (successive editions).

to understand how nine thousand parishes composed at a higher level a single political society.

'We are all social historians now', as King Edward VII (or was it Sir William Harcourt?) very nearly said; and if social historians, political historians too, whether Sir John Seeley would have acknowledged us as such. And surely this is progressive and hopeful, for history and for this faculty. With all the considerable respect I hold for him as another of the Cambridge greats still living among us, I cannot agree with Sir John Plumb's opinion (expressed only a year or two ago) that 'for decades nothing exciting, nothing original, nothing creative, has been attempted in the teaching of history'.[80] I can agree with Plumb that (as Tory backbenchers are prone to complain) there has been some failure in presentation, academic history failing to offer sustenance to the 'vast and hungry audience, longing to hear about the past', the successors of Trevelyan's countless readers. And in that failure I for one am fully complicit. But the subject itself has surely never been more exciting, more original, more creative. And I am more proud than I can say to profess it and in some measure to represent it, in this, my own university.

---

[80] *The Making of an Historian: The Collected Essays of J.H. Plumb* (Hemel Hempstead, 1988), p. 370.

De Republica Anglorum: A Retrospective Note, 1993

Inaugural lectures are occasional addresses, not affirmations for all time. The date of this lecture was as recent as November 1989, but occasion and context appear now, as 1992 turns into 1993, very remote. At the time, the U.S.S.R. and Eastern Europe were poised on the brink of a disintegrative process of revolution, more ethnic than democratic, the full extent of which we had hardly begun to grasp. Within six weeks the unspeakable Ceascescus would be dead, but we were still two years away from the failed Moscow *coup* and the fall of Gorbachev. Yugoslavia was still intact and for another three years there would still be a state called Czechoslovakia. In 1989 the Desert War and the 'New World Order' had not been heard of. Mrs Thatcher was still in office, resolved to go on and on.

Such has been the unprecedented pace of change that the standpoint from which these retrospective remarks are made, on the first day of 1993, may itself be thoroughly historicised by the time of their publication. What will happen to that limited if expanding portion of Europe which we call the European Community, both in its internal integration and in relation to the remainder of the Continent, is still uncertain, but like most world questions, more sombre in prospect than it was in 1989. The future constitution of the British Isles, and even what to call the archipelago if it is deemed, as it must be, to include Ireland, historically no part of Britain,[1] will not long remain on the back burner, and this too will prove a question as much for historians as for politicians.

The implications of recent events for the study and teaching of history have scarcely been addressed, let alone absorbed. Select groups of historians are currently travelling to Moscow to discuss with their Russian hosts and counterparts how to rewrite their history in the aftermath of Communism. Such are the shifts in our own historiographical perspective that there is no reason why the compliment should not be returned. Russian historians, having become experts in the revisionary reconstruction of their subject, may yet advise us.

1989 was, now it appears, an unsuitable moment at which to set the historical syllabus even in wet concrete. Yet the background to this inaugural lecture was the national debate about the place of history, and what kinds of history, within the National Curriculum for schools which had proceeded with some vigour in the public prints throughout that year, a debate about inclusion and exclusion, method and content, nationality and ecumenicity. How to reconcile the potential infinitude of history with

---

[1]   However there was not much sensitivity on this question in sixteenth-century England, when William Camden called his book *Britannia sive florentissimorum regnorum Angliae, Scotiae, Hiberniae, et insularum adjacantium descriptio* (1586). See also the title of the first English edition: *Britain, or a chorographicall description of the most flourishing kingdoms, England, Scotland, and Ireland.*

the necessary finiteness of any academic history syllabus led in this lecture to more particular reflections on the relation of social history, potentially limitless and holistic in scope, to the more carefully circumscribed bounds of political history, which for my predecessor Sir Geoffrey Elton is a sovereign discipline with some hegemonistic claims. This is a question with local, Cambridge resonances, for in Cambridge undergraduate students of history are confronted with separate examination papers on the social and economic and the political and constitutional history of Britain. It may be, of course, that the point of this dichotomy is to demonstrate the meaning-less of the one without the other, which was the burden of this inaugural lecture.

2

The Monarchical Republic of Queen Elizabeth I

I first met Professor Neale (as he was always content to be known) on a Monday evening in early October 1952,[1] in the England Room of the Institute of Historical Research. I had just come down from Cambridge and Neale seemed pleased with this rare recruit from one of the ancient universities, although most of the new 'Tudorbethans' of that cohort had received a superior education at his own University College. After the regular Monday evening seminar we arranged to meet to discuss a topic. 'Hurstfield!' he said to the late Joel Hurstfield who was standing nearby, 'tell him where my room is. You know where my room is.' One recollects such trivial circumstances in vivid detail, even if one's name is not Richard Cobb. Going down the stairs, an American woman said: 'Don't let him give you something *aw*ful.' This was helpful, for I was in the foolish position of the acolyte researcher who does not know what he wants to research. I only knew that I wanted to work under Neale, and that was because someone had suggested it. But the outcome could not have been happier. Although Dr A.L. Rowse is not unique in regarding the Puritans as a truly *aw*ful subject (my wife shares his view), they have kept me out of mischief ever

---

[1]   The title of this collection has been used at least once before. In 1957 J.E. Neale published his own *Elizabethan Essays*. Neale, who had recently retired from the Astor Chair of English History at University College London, was both the supervisor (from 1952) and examiner (in 1957) of my Ph.D. thesis, 'The Puritan Classical Movement in the Reign of Elizabeth I'. In 1955-6 I was his research assistant, completing the editorial work of Miss Helen Miller on the Elizabethan parliamentary diaries and other materials now in the course of publication by Dr Terry Hartley and the Leicester University Press as *Proceedings in the Parliaments of Elizabeth I*. Neale continued to take a flattering and, as it were, fatherly interest in my work. It was largely thanks to him that my first substantial book was published by the firm of Jonathan Cape with which he was so closely linked. This was *The Elizabethan Puritan Movement* (1967). And but for Neale my biography of Archbishop Grindal, which followed in 1979, would not have been published by Cape or, in all probability, by anybody else. We discussed the desirability of *Archbishop Grindal* seeing the light of day on the last occasion on which we met, at his house in Beaconsfield, in 1974. Sir John Neale has been commemorated in two annual memorial lectures, one at Manchester, where he taught at an early stage of his career, the other at University College London.

The two essays which follow derive from the Neale lectures which I was invited to deliver in Manchester in 1986 and at U.C.L. in 1987. It will be clear from the opening remarks on both occasions that I continue to hold in high regard and even some retrospective affection a scholar and teacher whose reputation since his death has been variously assessed.

since. And but for Jimmy Neale, as everyone called him,[2] it would not have
happened. 'Collinson,' he said, after a while, 'I like to think of you spending
the rest of your life on this subject!' And although I laughed 'within myself',
like Abraham's wife Sarah when the angel announced her pregnancy
(Genesis 18:12), Neale, like the angel, was right. Incidentally, the highest
praise Neale could confer on anyone was that he wrote 'like an angel'. He
liked my style but did not find it angelic.

My topic was not the only thing I owed to Neale. He was not an intrusive
supervisor and to a considerable extent one was left to one's own devices.
The thesis, when at last it came together, was emphatically all one's own
work, not ghosted by the supervisor. But what Neale *did* impart and in
generous manner, pressed down and running over, was enthusiasm and
encouragement. You were made to feel that perhaps tomorrow you would
make that notable discovery which had eluded all earlier historians of the
subject: perhaps another minute book of a clandestine presbyterian classis,
to match the Dedham Minutes which first brought me to Manchester
(Rylands English MS 874). Nowadays, what might be called the 'dark
continent' approach to history – pushing into the interior in the hope of
discovering some hitherto unsuspected tribe, or species, or waterfall – is
denigrated for its conceptual and methodological naivety, and suspect for
its complacent practice of the bourgeois ethic of possessive individualism.
It must be said, with due deference to the late Sir John Neale, that in many
respects it was (and is) a magnificent and fruitful tradition, kept alive and
in good heart by some of Neale's severer critics.

II

The Monarchical Republic of Queen Elizabeth I is a phrase with which
Neale would not have been altogether happy. To explain it it will be helpful
to travel to Swallowfield, a place equidistant from Reading and Wokingham,
physically within Berkshire but by an odd anomaly politically part of
Wiltshire, which meant that the village was almost outside the scope of
normal local government. That was the occasion for a town meeting held
on 4 December 1596, when Swallowfield constituted itself, in effect, a self-
governing republic of the 'chief inhabitants'.[3] Further and regular assemblies were planned, at which those present were to speak in order of rank
and without fear of interruption: for 'none of us is ruler of himself, but the
whole company or the most part is the ruler of us all'. Procedures were

---

[2] I believe that the nickname derived from certain early concert party performances which
became linked with the character of Sunny Jim as depicted on packets containing the breakfast
cereal Force. Not long after the conferment of his knighthood, John Ernest Neale was referred to
in print as 'Sir James Neale', H.J. Habakkuk, 'The Market for Monastic Property, 1539-1603',
Economic History Review, 2nd ser., 10 (1958), p. 363.
[3] Huntington Library, MS EL 6162, fos. 34a-36a.

adopted for dealing with a variety of common offences and abuses: strife between neighbours, bastardy, alehouse disorders, marriage between young people 'before they have a convenient house to live in', and 'malapert' insubordination on the part of the unruly poor. If all else failed, offenders in these and other respects were to be reported to the justices. But in the normal course of events, Swallowfield hoped to govern itself. For 'we will be esteemed to be men of discretion, good credit, honest minds, and christianlike behaviour, one towards another.'

'Self-government at the king's command' was what a great historian taught us to call that kind of thing, whether at the level of Swallowfield or of the gentry republics which comprised the regime in so many Elizabethan counties.[4] It has become a weary cliché, and yet we are far from having exhausted its implications. Swallowfield's ringing affirmation, the voice of all village Hampdens, 'we will be esteemed to be men of discretion', anticipated the voice of the Clubmen who a generation or two later rose in the agony of the Civil War to defend their homes against the marauding armies of both sides. In Dorset the Clubmen resolved to be represented in every parish by 'three or more of the ablest men for wisdom, valour and estate, inhabitants of the same'.[5]

Swallowfield and the Dorset Clubmen demonstrate the vitality in early modern England of traditions of localised self-government, involving men of very humble status. This was a salient feature of its political culture.[6] It could no doubt be demonstrated that in this society more considerable sums of money were collected and disbursed for public purposes locally than ever found their way to the Exchequer in the form of national taxation. When the sea broke through the flood banks at Terrington in Norfolk in 1600, the cost of repairs was put at £2000, a sum equivalent to almost three quarters of one per cent of the annual ordinary revenue of the Crown at that time. The Norfolk bench subsequently reported that the damage could be made good for a mere £700, 'which some, wee are credibly informed,

---

[4]   See Diarmaid MacCulloch, *Suffolk and the Tudors: Politics and Religion in an English County, 1500-1600* (Oxford, 1986); and, on the successful 1553 revolution of this 'local ruling establishment' against Westminster, Dr MacCulloch's edition of '*The Vita Mariae Angliae Reginae* of Robert Wingfield of Brantham', *Camden Miscellany*, 28, Camden 4th ser., 29 (1984), pp. 181-301. Dr MacCulloch's account of a gentry republic which worked pretty well may be contrasted with Professor A. H. Smith's study of neighbouring Norfolk, which indulged more recklessly and openly in factional struggle, *County and Court: Government and Politics in Norfolk, 1558-1603* (Oxford, 1974). On parliamentary aspects of gentry republicanism, see Mark A. Kishlansky, *Parliamentary Selection: Social and Political Choice in Early Modern England* (Cambridge, 1986).

[5]   John Morrill, *The Revolt of the Provinces: Conservatives and Radicals in the English Civil War, 1630-1650* (1976), p. 199. Compare Diarmaid MacCulloch's account of 'Alternative Patterns of Politics', chapter 11 of his *Suffolk and the Tudors*.

[6]   Keith Thomas, 'The Levellers and the Franchise', in Gerald Aylmer, ed., *The Interregnum* (1972), pp. 57-78.

maie be easily borne by the land occupiers of the said towne.'[7] If the little community of Terrington could 'easily' find £700 (and in the end it was obliged to spend £500 on inadequate stopgap repairs) it is not clear why the 9 or 10,000 Terringtons which made up Elizabethan England could not between them have provided the queen with an annual income of 5 or 6 million pounds, 50 times what it in fact was. But Elizabethan England was not that kind of polity. In 1621 James I, who had put a price tag on the coming war with Spain of as much as a million pounds in one year, was told that all England did not contain so much money.[8] Nowadays, central government claims the power through rate-capping to curb expenditure by local government. In the sixteenth century, it was the locality which habitually starved the centre of resources, and had the capacity, through tax strikes, to bring national governments to their knees.

III

When Picasso came to Sheffield to attend a peace rally, he sat on the platform making sketches and dropping them on the floor. Nobody picked them up. These preliminary sketches – Swallowfield and Terrington – can lie where they have fallen. Our subject is neither local government nor village republics but the political culture of England at its centre and summit, in the age of Elizabeth I. Swallowfield has been invoked because its situation was that of all England in miniature, at this critical moment. As an enclave of Wiltshire isolated in Berkshire, the town was practically without magistrates and had to make arrangements for its own government: and this it did by means of a town meeting of the kind later set up in the vastly greater isolation of New England. And yet it was doubtless the case that a thousand other villages with a similar social structure, lacking a resident magistrate or gentleman, had the capacity to do something similar, in effect to constitute themselves republics, and a good many did, if with less formality. But the whole commonwealth – or republic – of Elizabethan England was potentially in a situation where the chief magistrate might be not merely 'far off' but totally absent, non-existent. This would have been the state of affairs (which many Elizabethans for much of their lifespan thought more likely than otherwise) if the queen had died suddenly and violently, leaving the vacuum of an uncertain succession behind her.

The sketches with which I shall end have to do with that scenario and with the political responses to it. They will not have the spontaneous originality of Picasso's idle scribblings on a Sheffield platform. We all know that Elizabeth I was a woman and that she died unmarried and without issue, the last of her immediate family line, dynastic ambitions unfulfilled because

---

[7] Smith, *County and Court*, pp. 98-9.
[8] Conrad Russell, *Parliaments and English Politics, 1621-1629* (Oxford, 1979), p. 189.

she had none. But the consequences of her singular endgame for the perceived political future of her people are not always squarely faced. The reason is not far to seek. Elizabeth's subjects professed to be so dazzled by their queen's regal splendour as to be incapable of looking beyond her or of contemplating any feature of their political culture other than her radiant presence. Peter Wentworth dared to say in the House of Commons that 'none is without fault, no not our noble queen', but he was not suffered to continue with his speech.[9] The lawyer and parliament man Thomas Norton, languishing under house arrest, reflected: 'Lord! how I wonder at my self that I shold offend my Queen Elizabeth! and therefore no marvel though all the world wonder at me, that wonder at my self.' Lawrence Humphrey had written in the opening moments of the reign: 'We advaunce not your might, not your arme, not your wisdom, but wonder at your weaknes and infirmity.'[10] Later he knew better. When we read John Aylmer's apology for Elizabeth's fitness to rule, composed in 1559, along the lines that the government of a woman was tolerable because in England it would not be so much her government as government in her name and on her behalf,[11] we feel sorry for the poor man, who in spite of having served as a tutor to royal and semi-royal personages had to wait another eighteen years for his bishopric. One might as well have justified the government of Mrs Thatcher on the grounds that her cabinet could be trusted to keep her in order.

Historians for the most part share in the general bedazzlement and Neale it must be said, was more uncritical than most. 'This woman', he wrote on one occasion, 'was as vital as Winston Churchill.'[12] Like the older, Victorian, historians J.A. Froude and Bishop Creighton, I am sometimes tempted to exclaim about 'this' or 'that woman' – and to leave it at that. Lest I offend, I hasten to explain that I have no motive to reduce Elizabeth in stature, or to diminish her vitality, if such a thing were possible. I know that her power to overawe, having first won the devotion of those personally and politically closest to her, has rarely been equalled.

Whether this power was predominantly personal, what Max Weber called 'charismatic', or was encased in the office itself and so more tradi-tional, we cannot say. Sir Thomas Smith observed that the prince (in principle, any prince) 'is the life, the head and the authoritie of all thinges that be doone in the realme of England'. The kings of England were 'farre more absolute then either the dukedome of Venice is, or the kingdome of

---

[9] J.E. Neale, *Elizabeth I and her Parliaments, 1559-1581* (1953) [henceforth Neale I], pp. 318-26.

[10] Thomas Norton to William Fleetwood. 8 January 1582, BL, MS Add. 48023, fol. 49 r; Laurence Humphrey, *The nobles, or of nobilitye* (1563), sig. Aii v.

[11] John Aylmer, *An harborowe for faithfull and trewe subiectes* ('at Strasborowe' but *recte* London, 1559), sigs. H3-4 r.

[12] J.E. Neale, *Essays in Elizabethan History* (1958), p. 124.

the Lacedemonians was'.[13] Constitutionally speaking, this was faultless. Everything which was done, publicly and by due legal authority, was in a sense done by the monarch. The legislation of Henry VIII admitted of no rival, no alternative government. If there had been doubt on that score in 1533 it was gone by 1536. But although personal monarchy under the Tudors was often literally personal, Smith was giving expression to what Kantorowicz called 'an abstract physiological fiction',[14] and it is a naive mistake to convert that fiction into a statement of simply literal fact, as if the queen really did attend personally to everything of any consequence which was done in her name. The Jesuit Philip Caraman published an anthology illustrating the experience of the Elizabethan Catholics under the title *The Other Face* (1960). My concern is with the 'other face' of Elizabethan public life, the Elizabethans without Elizabeth. For if Smith described the queen as 'the life, the head and the authoritie of all thinges that be doone in the realme of England', he also defined England, politically, as 'a society or common doing of a multitude of free men collected together and united by common accord and covenauntes among themselves for the conservation of themselves aswell in peace as in warre'.[15]

That sounds like a good description of a republic, and both statements appeared in a book to which Smith gave the title *De Republica Anglorum*. To be sure, *republica* in sixteenth-century parlance did not mean, as it has meant since the late eighteenth century, a type of constitution incompatible with monarchy. It was simply the common term for what we call the state. Smith's book was entitled in its English version *Of the Commonwealth of England* and that was a perfectly neutral term, albeit one which the Henrician Thomas Elyot in *The boke named the governour* (1531) found dangerously plebeian in its implications, preferring 'public weal'.[16] Nevertheless, that staunch republican Machiavelli – equally no democrat – would have recognised in Elizabethan England a species of republic, what the Englishman Thomas Starkey called 'living together in good and politic order',[17] not a kind of tyranny or despotism: a state which enjoyed that measure of self-direction which for him was the essence of liberty, but with a constitution which also provided for the rule of a single person by hereditary right. This needs to be said, since historians used to talk about a 'Tudor despotism' and an attempt was made a few years ago to revive this

---

[13] *De Republica Anglorum by Sir Thomas Smith*, ed. Mary Dewar (Cambridge, 1982), pp. 88, 85.

[14] Ernest H. Kantorowicz, *The King's Two Bodies: A Study in Medieval Political Theology* (Princeton, 1957), p. 4.

[15] *De Republica Anglorum*, p. 57.

[16] Michael Mendle, *Dangerous Positions: Mixed Government, the Estates of the Realm, and the Making of the Answer to the XIX Propositions* (University, AL, 1985), p. 43.

[17] Quoted, Quentin Skinner, *The Foundations of Modern Political Thought* (Cambridge, 1978), i, p. 229.

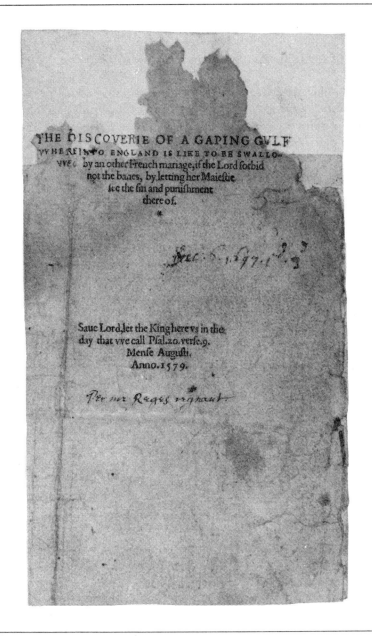

THE DISCOVERIE OF A GAPING GVLF
WHEREINTO ENGLAND IS LIKE TO BE SWALLO-
VVED by an other French mariage, if the Lord forbid
not the banes, by letting her Maieftie
fee the fin and punifhment
thereof.

Saue Lord,let the King here vs in the
day that vve call Pfal.20.verfe.9.
Menfe Augufti,
Anno.1579.

John Stubbs' *Gaping Gulf* is an excellent example of 'forwardness' leading to 'frowardness' (see 'Puritans, Men of Business and Elizabethan Parliaments'). Stubbs' outspoken attack on the Anjou marriage cost him his hand and William Page, who distributed the book, suffered the same fate. Both sat in the House of Commons minus their right hands. A reader has noted 'per me Reges regnant' a slogan for godly semi-republicanism. (*Cambridge University Library, sss.18.19*)

unpromising and unhelpful phrase.[18] It is a striking circumstance, recently underlined in a study of Charles I's *Answer to the xix propositions*, that in sixteenth- and seventeenth-century England it was possible to use the language of classical republicanism in order to deny that England was a republic.[19]

The very fact that 'republic' was an acceptable term for a variety of political systems in itself implies an important historical-etymological assumption about the origins of government, as well as the perseverance of the doctrine, to be found in Plato, that monarchy, aristocracy and democracy in their pure forms are all less desirable than a judicious blend of all three. So the Elizabethan Bishop Aylmer asserts that

> the regiment of England is not a mere monarchie, as some for lacke of consideration thinke, nor a meere oligarchie, nor democracie, but a rule mixte of all these ... thimage whereof, and not the image but the thinge in deede, is to be sene in the parliament house, wherin you shall find these three estates.[20]

None of this impresses John Pocock in his account of the origins of republicanism among the English-speaking peoples called *The Machiavellian Moment*. Pocock is satisfied that in sixteenth-century English thought the theory of corporate rationality served merely as an ideal and historical account of how political society had begun, and of how the single ruler emerged whose government subsequently excluded the intelligent participation of the subjects. In no way was Tudor England a *polis* or its inhabitants citizens.[21] Nor, according to Pocock, did conciliar government ever imply an acephalous republic. Every privy councillor took a separate oath to the monarch and gave counsel severally, each sitting in his place. To strengthen Pocock's point it may be noted that the death of the monarch, who in life had an absolute discretion and power to summon and dissolve parliament, led to an immediate dissolution of any parliament which might have been in session at that moment, which happened on 17 November 1558. Only a new monarch could renew and revive governmental and political activity, by appointing a new council and (only if he or she chose) summoning parliament. The implication is that the commonwealth of England had no existence, apart from its head. If so, then the origins of 'civic consciousness' must be sought outside the political economy of the sixteenth century, in exceptional modes of thought, mostly religious, which is where Pocock

---

[18] Joel Hurstfield, 'Was there a Tudor Despotism After All?', in *Freedom, Corruption and Government in Elizabethan England* (1973), pp. 23-49.

[19] Mendle, *Dangerous Positions*, p.15.

[20] Aylmer, *An harborowe*, sig. H3 r.

[21] J.G.A. Pocock, *The Machiavellian Moment: Florentine Political Thought and the Atlantic Republican Tradition* (Princeton, 1975). But see A.B. Ferguson, *The Articulate Citizen and the English Renaissance* (Durham, NC, 1965), esp. pp. 42-69.

looked for them. *Coriolanus* was written for an audience familiar with the notion of a balanced republic but not itself republican, nor experiencing republicanism. Nevertheless, we must take care not to underestimate both the political sophistication and the political capacity of high Elizabethan society, a society which had cut its political teeth in the acephalous conditions of Edward VI's minority. We should also not forget about Swallowfield.

IV

At this point, and before returning to the sketch pad, I shall offer a kind of manifesto on the subject of Elizabethan history and historiography, consisting of five points:

(1)   In the phrase 'the queen and her ministers', the copulative usually serves to weld the two elements indissolubly together, as if it scarcely matters how they interacted. Thus the Elizabethan religious settlement is attributed to 'the queen and her advisers', or to 'the queen and Cecil', as if they were the front and rear legs of a pantomime horse. Neale departed from this tradition when he attributed the shaping of the settlement (which, since it made England a Protestant state, is no trivial circumstance) to an independent political initiative taken against the queen by a strongly Protestant House of Commons.[22] Now that brilliant reconstruction of poorly documented transactions in the first Elizabethan parliament (which Neale never represented as anything more than a plausible hypothesis) has been demolished. The religious settlement looks like government policy after all.[23] But the question who, in the inner counsels of government, whether at court or council board, determined that policy remains not only unanswered (and probably it cannot be answered) but so far unasked.

(2)   Sir Geoffrey Elton, addressing himself to the Elizabethan parliaments in general, describes the more active elements in the Commons as cooperating and interacting with the privy council, or with particular councillors and courtiers. In the helpful perception of Elton and his pupils this means that they cease to be figures of opposition and become 'men of business'.[24] But it is not clear why that should make the true history of the Elizabethan parliaments any less political, and Elton has declared it to be a history which

[22]   J.E. Neale, 'The Elizabethan Acts of Supremacy and Uniformity', *English Historical Review*, 65 (1950), pp. 304-32; Neale I, pp. 51-84.

[23]   Norman L. Jones, *Faith by Statute: Parliament and the Settlement of Religion 1559* (1982); Winthrop S. Hudson, *The Cambridge Connection and the Elizabethan Settlement of 1559* (Durham NC, 1980).

[24]   M.A.R Graves, 'The Management of the Elizabethan House of Commons: The Council's "Men-of-Business"', *Parliamentary History*, 2 (1983), pp. 11-38; idem, 'Thomas Norton the Parliament Man: An Elizabethan M.P., 1559-1581', *Historical Journal*, 23 (1980), pp. 17-35. Cf. G.R. Elton, *The Parliament of England, 1559-1581* (Cambridge, 1986).

was not political at all.[25] Surely our new and more sophisticated understanding of these parliaments makes them more, not less political: although
the politics is now seen to have been one of differences and contentions
within a regime, not of 'government' versus 'opposition'.

(3) 'Regime' has proved a helpful expression, particularly as employed by
Professor Wallace MacCaffrey in his book *The Shaping of the Elizabethan
Regime*, which describes the coming together and settling down together of
a group of politicians to form a collective, quasi-organic and, for some
considerable time, stable governing group. A similar approach to Elizabethan public life, owing something to Washingtonian studies of the
making and unmaking of presidencies, is adopted by Professor Winthrop
Hudson in his book on the religious settlement. But these are (significantly)
the insights of American scholarship. English historians use 'regime' in a
different sense, as in Dr Penry William's admirable study *The Tudor
Regime*,[26] in which a chapter called 'The Servants of the Crown' discusses the
acquisition and enjoyment of office by individuals and the performance of
functions by individual office-holders, but not the workings of a regime in
MacCaffrey's sense.

(4)   The currently fashionable topic of court faction, the tendency of the
regime, of perhaps any regime, to divide against itself, is also helpful and
has been ever since Neale delivered his famous Raleigh Lecture on 'The
Elizabethan Political Scene'.[27] But too much attention has been paid to
factional in-fighting as the main principle of politics, too little to the
practical cooperation of leading members of the regime, its centripetal
rather than centrifugal tendencies.[28] In particular, Lord Burghley and the
earl of Leicester are supposed to have been mortal enemies and leaders of
mutually exclusive rival factions, anticipating the deadly struggle of
Elizabeth's declining years between Burghley's son Robert Cecil and
Leicester's step-son and legatee, Essex. Conyers Read believed that in the
1570s the Privy Council was effectively polarised.[29] Yet Leicester could
write to Burghley as he did in July 1584, apologising for an impromptu
descent made by himself and his countess on the lord treasurer's house at
Theobalds, at three o'clock in the afternoon, 'without any jote of warning
in the world': 'I have byn bold to make some of your stagges afrayd but

[25] G.R. Elton, 'Parliament in the Sixteenth Century: Functions and Fortunes', *Studies in Tudor and
Stuart Politics and Government*, iii (Cambridge, 1983), pp. 156-82.
[26] W.T. MacCaffrey, *The Shaping of the Elizabethan Regime* (Princeton, 1968); Hudson, *The
Cambridge Connection*; Penry Williams, *The Tudor Regime* (Oxford, 1979).
[27] J.E. Neale, 'The Elizabethan Political Scene', in *Essays in Elizabethan History*, pp. 59-84.
[28] Simon L. Adams, 'Faction, Clientage and Party: English Politics, 1550-1603', *History Today*, 32
(1982), pp. 33-9; S.L. Adams, 'Eliza Enthroned? The Court and its Politics', in *The Reign of Elizabeth
I*, ed. C. Haigh (1984), pp. 55-77.
[29] Conyers Read, 'Walsingham and Burghley in Queen Elizabeth's Privy Council', *English
Historical Review*, 28 (1913), pp. 34-58.

kylled none. Yf I had your lordship should have been presentyd with our good fortune'.[30] These are not the words of implacable enmity.

It should also be said that altogether too much deference is paid to the report of the Jacobean Sir Robert Naunton, made a quarter of a century after Elizabeth's death, that factions were devices by which the queen strengthened her own rule, making and unmaking them 'as her own great judgment advised'.[31]

(5) The subject of my fifth and final affirmation is policy. It is often said that Elizabethan policy was the queen's policy, in the sense that she alone determined what was to be done, or, as often as not, not done.[32] No doubt. But this directs attention away from policy discussion and policy making, and it buries in oblivion the interesting matter of policies which were constructed but never implemented. In 1577 the English ambassador in the Low Countries received welcome news that Robert Dudley, earl of Leicester, was to cross the North Sea with an expeditionary force. 'This is his full determination, but yet unknown unto her Highness, neither shall she be acquainted with it until she be fully resolved to send...'[33] And of course Elizabeth was *not* at that time 'fully resolved' to send a single soldier to the Netherlands. A few months later rumours still persisted that Leicester was about to embark with 10,000 men. But a ranking government official who gave currency to the report added: 'I would this were a true prognostication.'[34]

Another not untypical episode occurred in April 1580, when Sir Francis Walsingham wrote to the queen's viceroys in the north to advise them that the privy council had thought fit to despatch a thousand troops to the borders to shore up a crumbling Scottish policy. But 'when ytt came to hyr Majesties consent she wolde none of ytt' and proceeded to cut the force by half, to five hundred men. Later the same day she thought better of this – and decided to send no troops at all. Before news of this second decision had reached Walsingham, and when he still expected to have some force at his disposal, he had signed and sealed a letter which said this: 'I see that Scotland is clene lost and a great gate opened whereby for the losse of Ireland. My lords here have carefully and faithfully discharged their dueties in sekinge to staye this dangerous course, but God hath thought good to dispose other wyse of thinges, in whose handes the heartes of all princes are.'[35] On another occasion Walsingham wrote: 'I am sorrye to thincke of the dayngerouse inconveniences lykely to issue by thes straynge

[30] PRO, S.P. 12/172/37.

[31] Sir Robert Naunton, *Fragmenta Regalia*, ed. E. Arber, English Reprints (1870), pp. 16-17.

[32] W.T. MacCaffrey, *Queen Elizabeth and the Making of Policy, 1572-1588* (Princeton, 1981).

[33] PRO, S.P. 15/25/35.

[34] PRO, S.P. 15/25/74.

[35] Lord Hunsdon to the earl of Huntingdon, 14 April 1581; Sir Francis Walsingham to Huntingdon, 5 April 1581 (Huntington Library, MSS HA 1214; HA 13067).

courses: but I see no hope of redresse. God dyrect her Majesties harte to take an other waye of counsell...'[36]

'God open her Majesty's eyes' is consequently a recurring refrain in the state papers of the period, and it built up in the Victorian historian Froude a strong prejudice against the queen and an indignant sympathy for her ministers.

> Vain as she was of her own sagacity, she never modified a course recommended to her by Burghley without injury both to the realm and to herself. She never chose an opposite course without plunging into embarrassments from which his and Walsingham's were barely able to extricate her. The great results of her reign were the fruits of a policy which was not her own, and which she starved and mutilated when energy and completeness were most needed.[37]

That was unfair in its exaggeration, but anyone who has read the state papers knows why and how Froude arrived at such a verdict.

My manifesto concludes with two comments. If Leicester could complain, as he did in 1578, that 'our conference with her Majesty about affairs is both seldom and slender',[38] that implies a high-handed autocracy which councillors found unacceptable and which limited their capacity to be useful. Elizabethan government was often government without counsel, or with unorthodox or irregular counsel. But it also suggests that the privy council, with whatever futile consequences on some occasions, was in a position to contemplate the world and its affairs with some independent detachment, by means of its own collective wisdom and with the queen absent: headless conciliar government. Secondly, one does not have to share Froude's low estimation of the queen's effectiveness and decisiveness (and what we now know of the conduct of the Spanish War in the 1590s makes it impossible to agree with Froude unreservedly)[39] to perceive that at times there were two governments uneasily coexisting in Elizabethan England: the queen and her council, the copulative now serving to distance rather than unite two somewhat distinct poles of authority, as it were the magnetic pole and the true pole. This is not to say that for much and perhaps most of the time the queen and her sworn advisers did not participate harmoniously and constructively in the conduct of public business.

---

[36] PRO, S.P. 12/175/35.

[37] J.A. Froude, *History of England from the Fall of Wolsey to the Defeat of the Spanish Armada* (n.d.), xii, p. 508.

[38] Quoted, Williams, *Tudor Regime*, p. 32.

[39] R.B. Wernham, *After the Armada: Elizabethan England and the Struggle for Western Europe, 1588-1595* (Oxford, 1984). And now see Wallace T. MacCaffrey, *Elizabeth I, War and Politics, 1588-1603* (Princeton, 1992).

V

Elizabethan England was a republic which happened also to be a monarchy: or vice versa. The dichotomy is suggested by one of several 'devices' or memoranda proposing administrative reforms, drawn up at the start of the reign but apparently dating from the acephalous conditions of Edward's time. In this 'Ordre for Redresse of the State of the Realme',[40] one senses a political society taking stock and ordering itself with an attempt at efficiency and rationality. Totally new connections are proposed between court and council, and between both council and court and the country, thus on paper solving some of the most vexing problems of Tudor and Stuart government. But our concern is not so much with the details of this green paper, important though they are, but with the fact that it seems to have been an afterthought that the whole scheme would require royal approval if it were to take effect. For another hand has written in the margin: 'It would do well if it might please the prince to...', and so the memorandum is made to flow on from that essential precondition.

We return to the sketch pad and to two images of the other, non-adulatory face of Elizabethan politics, two moments in the sense that political scientists speak of convulsive episodes in history: 1572 and 1584. Students of Elizabethan history have been here before and the furniture and decorations are familiar: the queen's safety, the succession crisis, Mary, Queen of Scots. Yet what has sometimes been omitted from the story is the readiness of the political nation, including its leading statesman. William Cecil, Lord Burghley, to contemplate its own immediate political future, a future not only without Queen Elizabeth but without monarchy, at least for a season. This was the Elizabethan Exclusion Crisis.

To take the measure of our two moments something must first be said about what is vulgarly called 'resistance theory' but which is better described as the polemical critique of monarchy. No such critique is supposed to have survived the scorching sun of Elizabeth's benign rule except among certain marginalised Catholic elements.[41] The Protestant resistance theses of Knox, Goodman and Ponet were now as redundant as the Communist Manifesto at a Conservative Party Conference. By all her true Protestant subjects, Elizabeth was adored with unwavering devotion. Even if their

---

[40] Huntington Library, MS EL 2625. Another version of this essay, diverging substantially from it, bears the endorsement 'the xvith of Maii 1559. Toching the redresse of the comyn welth' (Huntington Library, MS EL 2580). I have benefited from discussing these documents with Dr Peter Roberts and Dr David Starkey.

[41] But see Gerald Bowler, 'English Protestant and Resistance Writings, 1553-1603' (unpublished London Ph.D. thesis, 1981) and his article '"An Axe or An Acte": The Parliament of 1572 and Resistance Theory in Early Elizabethan England', *Canadian Journal of History*, 19 (1984), pp. 349-59.

queen had not been a paragon of all conceivable virtue, resistance, criticism almost, would have been unthinkable. Churchgoers were taught by the Homily of Obedience that rebellion was worse than the worst government of the worst prince.[42] This was the outward face of Elizabethan political ideology. But there was another face, an anti-monarchical virus which was part of the legacy of early sixteenth-century humanism. Had not Erasmus preferred the 'lofty-minded beetle' to both eagle and lion, making the meaning of his imagery quite clear in a frankly mordant attack on 'people-devouring kings'? 'They must be called gods who are scarcely men, ... magnificent when they are midgets, most serene when they shake the world with the tumults of war and senseless political struggles'.[43]

Elizabeth was not actively resisted by her Protestant subjects but it does not follow that there was no ideological capacity for resistance, just as it would be a serious mistake to infer from the second Elizabethan peace that this country had no nuclear capability between 1951 and the 1980s. In fact, important weapons of resistance theory were still serviceable, like so many threatening missiles hidden in their siloes. These included the conviction that monarchy is a ministry exercised under God and on his behalf; that it is no more and no less than a public office; that as a public officer the monarch is accountable, certainly to God and perhaps to others exercising, under God, other public offices of magistracy or respecting an overriding and transcendent duty to God himself; and that there is a difference between monarchy and tyranny. Sir Francis Hastings noted these points of doctrine delivered at a Leicestershire sermon:

> The Magistrate is the minister of God and must submit him selfe to his worde as a rule to directe him in all his government... The Magistrate must commande in the Lorde. The subiecte must obey in the Lorde... Obedience, what it is: it is due unto the Lorde only.[44]

When the lawyer and parliamentarian Thomas Norton advised his son (writing under house arrest in December 1581): 'I have no dealing with the

---

[42] *Sermons or Homilies, Appointed to be Read in Churches* (1811 edn), pp. 124-38.

[43] The references are to the adage 'Scarabeus aquilam quaerit': Margaret Mann Phillips, *Erasmus on his Times: A Shortened Version of the 'Adages' of Erasmus* (Cambridge, 1967), pp. 47-72. To read this adage in connection with the allegorical passage in Spenser's *Shepheardes Calender,* in which the downfall of Archbishop Grindal is approximated to the classical legend of the eagle dropping a shellfish (or tortoise) on the bald head of Aeschylus in mistake for a stone, is to appreciate Spenser's barely suppressed republicanism. Erasmus uses this tale to demonstrate that the eagle, cruelly rapacious rather than truly courageous, is also myopic rather than 'eagle-eyed'. 'Anyone who considers all this will almost declare that the eagle is unworthy of being taken as an example of kingly rule.' On Grindal and Spenser, see Patrick Collinson, *Archbishop Grindal, 1519-1583: The Struggle for a Reformed Church* (1979), pp. 275-6; Paul E. McLane, *Spenser's Shepheardes Calender: A Study in Elizabethan Allegory* (Notre Dame, IN, 1961), pp. 140-57.

[44] Huntington Library, MS HA Religious Box 1 (9).

queen but as with the image of God'; and when he wrote to another correspondent ' it is the onely religion of God that knitteth true subiectes unto her',[45] his words would not have pleased Elizabeth entirely, if she had pondered their implications. In translating Calvin's *Institutes* the same Norton chose to speak of 'the outraging licentiousness of kings' as that fault which parliamentary estates existed to correct. Peter Martyr's *Commentary on Romans* (in English translation in 1568) spoke of inferior magistrates 'putting down' and 'constraining to do their duty' princes who transgressed 'the endes and limits of the power which they have received'.[46]

Quentin Skinner writes of 'a few wisps' of resistance theory lingering on in the marginalia of the most popular Elizabethan version of the Bible, the Geneva Bible. That is too dismissive. Geneva Bible readers were taught from sundry Old Testament examples that God takes vengeance on tyrants, even in this life. Queen Jezebel's example of 'monstrous cruelty' was delivered to us by the Holy Ghost that we should abhor all tyranny and (a telling point) especially in a woman. Her terrible death was a spectacle and example to all tyrants. When David refused to kill Saul on the grounds that he was the Lord's anointed, the Geneva Bible turned the apparent moral upside down. It would have been wrong for David to have slain the king in his own private cause, but as a public act it would have been lawful: 'for Jehu slew two kings at God's appointment, 2 Kings 9:24.'[47] It would be wrong to label, still less to dismiss such sentiments as 'Puritan' and therefore peripheral. The note on David's sparing of Saul was repeated without alteration in the Bishops Bible, the official version, as was a highly acerbic comment on King Asa who spared the life of his own wicked and usurping mother (2 Chronicles 15:16). The note reads: 'Herein he shewed that he lacked zeale: for she ought to have dyed both by the covenant and by the lawe of God, but he gave place to foolish pity.' This was the passage in the Geneva Bible which so offended James I, and for the most understandable of reasons. For was not his mother in the eyes of many a wicked usurper, and had he not consented unto her death ? But James could have found the same comment in the Bishops Bible and it survived without alteration in the Authorised (or King James) version of 1611.[48] According to Dr Bowler, its

---

[45] BL, MS Add. 48023, fol. 33.

[46] Bowler, 'English Protestant and Resistance Writings', pp. 305-7.

[47] Skinner, *Foundations of Modern Political Thought*, ii, pp. 221-2; Geneva Bible annotations to 1 Kings 21:15; 2 Kings 9:33; 1 Samuel 26:9. By contrast, the second part of the Homily of Obedience taught that David was absolutely inhibited from harming Saul. 'But holy David did know that he might in no wise withstand, hurt or kill his sovereign lord and king ... Therefore, though he were never so much provoked, yet he refused utterly to hurt the Lord's anointed', *Sermons or Homilies*, pp. 131-2.

[48] Bowler, 'English Protestant and Resistance Writings', pp. 291-9. See also Richard L. Greaves, 'Traditionalism and the Seeds of Revolution in the Social Principles of the Geneva Bible', *Sixteenth-Century Journal*, 7 (1976), pp. 94-109; Dan G. Danner, 'The Contribution of the Geneva Bible of 1560 to the English Protestant Tradition', *Sixteenth-Century Journal*, 12 (1981), pp. 5-18.

author was none other than Edwin Sandys, who ended his days as archbishop of York, no longer a radical in reputation or spirit but, as an old Marian exile, unreconstructed in his opinions.

This serves to usher us into the debates of the 1572 parliament when the issue was whether Mary Stuart should be executed or simply excluded from the succession: 'an axe or an act?' as one M.P. tersely put the question.[49] The mind of the political nation had been well prepared for this crucial debate by ten years of anxious indecision on the subject of the succession. The arrival in England of the deposed Scottish queen, with her pretensions to the English throne, had fanned the political temperature to white heat, especially after the exposure of the Ridolfi Plot, in which Mary was apparently implicated together with England's premier peer, the duke of Norfolk, already judicially condemned for his part in the affair. In the parliamentary oratory of the summer of 1572 both Queen Jezebel and King Asa's mother were never far from the speakers' thoughts. When one M.P. proposed that Mary's head should be cut off 'and make no more ado about her' (another version of the speech has him say 'her head cut off and noe more harme done to her'), this was an echo of a frequent comment on Jehu's execution of Jezebel 'without any ado made', that is, by lynch-law. But it was not so much the Commons as the bench of bishops who advanced these chilling precedents, M.P.s adding little to the episcopal argument beyond the violence of the language with which they referred to what one speaker called 'the monstrous and huge dragon and mass of the earth'.

In the lengthy episcopal indictment of the Scottish queen we find a kind of double-distilled resistance theory. The act of deposition which had removed Mary from her throne was enthusiastically endorsed. For the bishops she was 'the late queen of Scots'. But if the queen of England were to fail in her manifest duty to put the deposed Scottish queen to death, she herself would have cause to fear for her throne. Here the most telling precedent was that of King Saul, who allowed his enemy Agag to live. As the bishops put it, 'because Saul spared Agag, although he were a king, God took from the same his good Spirit and transferred the kingdom of Israel from him and from his heirs for ever'. The moral was spelt out in the New Testament in Romans chapter 13, a passage of Scripture normally cited in support of total obedience and non-resistance. For according to St Paul in that place, the magistrate is the minister of God and the avenger of wrath towards him that hath done evil. But 'yf the magistrate do not this, God threateneth heavie punishment... Her Majesty must needs offend in conscience before God if she do not punish the Scottish queen to the

---

[49] *Proceedings in the Parliaments of Elizabeth I*, i, *1558-1581*, ed. T.E. Hartley (Leicester, 1981), pp. 259-418. Particular references are to pp. 376, 324, 325, 312. The bishops' 'certeine argumentes collected out of the Scriptures ... againste the Queen of Scottes' are on pp. 274-90. I am much indebted to Dr Bowler's article '"An Axe or an Acte"'.

measure of her offence in the highest degree'. The only other Reformation preacher known to me who turned Romans 13 on its head in this fashion was Thomas Müntzer, the arch-Bolshevik of the age.[50]

For our purpose, the most telling implication of the memorials and debates of 1572 is that monarchy is taken to be not an indelible and sacred anointing but a public and localised office, like any other form of magistracy. Even if Mary had not been deposed, as queen of Scotland she had never been a queen in England, the lawyer Christopher Yelverton asserting 'but for certaine she is to be tryed as a subiect of another nation'.[51] Only two M.P.s took her part, the part of a queen of Scotland. Francis Alford insisted on the sacrosanctity of anointed kingship. Arthur Hall of Grantham thought that Mary's indelible regality would eventually embarrass her enemies: 'Yow will hasten the execucion of such whose feet hereafter yow would be glad to have againe to kisse.' It is no accident that Hall was openly and scandalously contemptuous of the pretensions of the House of Commons, in effect a complete absolutist.[52] The queen herself shared Hall's view, but it was the view of an isolated minority. Moreover the threatening implication of the debate was that Elizabeth was herself little more than the temporary custodian of her kingdom. The bishops insisted that 'being ... a publicke person', the prince ought to have a greater care of her own safety than a private person, 'if not for her selfe sake yet at the leaste for the furtherance of Gode's cause and stay of her countrye...'[53] As one speaker put it in the Commons: 'Since the Queene in respect of her owne safety is not to bee induced hereunto, let us make petition shee will doe it in respect of our safety.' And then he added, perhaps with sarcasm: 'I have heard shee delighteth to bee called our mother.' In a paper urging the execution of the duke of Norfolk, Thomas Digges (of whom more anon) observed that the queen's safety was 'not her private case', while Thomas Dannet warned that if she were to continue unmindful of 'our safetie' 'after her death', 'her true and faithfull subiectes despairing of safetie by her meanes shalbe forced to seke protection ellsewhere, to the end they be not altogether destitute of defense'. Dr Bowler rightly calls the implications of these remarks, which Elizabeth in all probability never saw, 'staggering'.[54]

In the event, M.P.s and bishops alike, privy councillors no less, were bitterly disappointed. At first they were told to expect an act rather than an axe. That was disturbing enough, if only because an act of parliament to remove Mary's title to the succession (and what would such an act be worth

---

[50] Müntzer's sermon is in G.H. Williams, ed., *Spiritual and Anabaptist Writers*, Library of Christian Classics, 25 (1957), pp. 47-70. See also E.G. Rupp, *Patterns of Reformation* (1969), pp. 201-2.

[51] Hartley, *Proceedings*, p. 391.

[52] Ibid., pp. 315-16, 328, 334-5, 273, 365-6. On Hall, see Neale, I, pp. 333-45; G.R. Elton, 'Arthur Hall, Lord Burghley and the Antiquity of Parliament', *Studies*, iii, pp. 254-73.

[53] Hartley, *Proceedings*, p. 281.

[54] Ibid., pp. 376, 294-8; Bowler, '"An Axe or an Acte"'.

in the future?) suggested that Mary had a title of which she could be deprived. 'This disabling shalbe an enabling.' Robert Snagge said that the bill ' were not to doe nothing but to doe starke nought ... He trusteth we were not called hyther for nought'.[55] And yet even this unsatisfactory second best was withdrawn by the queen's veto of the disabling bill at the close of the session.

VI

Twelve years later 'the late Scottish queen' was still bearing her head on her shoulders and breathing the bracing air of Sheffield. But in the Netherlands William of Orange was very dead and with the state papers as full of plots as today's newspapers are of terrorism the never-ending Elizabethan political crisis seemed more desperate than ever: sufficiently menacing to call for the extraordinary measure known as the Bond of Association.[56] This document engaged those who were sworn to its terms and who had applied to it their signatures and seals to pursue 'to the uttermost extermination' anybody attempting by any act, counsel or consent to bring harm to the queen's royal person, their comforters, aiders and abettors: and to resist the succession of any individual on whose behalf such acts might be attempted or committed. This was to hang a sword over Mary's head, to threaten this modern Jezebel with lynch-law in the event of an assassination attempt against Elizabeth, successful or not; and in such circumstances to disable not only Mary but her son, James VI.

To examine surviving copies of the Bond in the Public Record Office (they are huge parchments and a special table has to be cleared for the purpose) is to be given a vivid insight into both the autonomous political capacity of the Elizabethan republic and its extent and social depth, a carpet, as it were, with a generous pile. Not only the privy council was at Hampton Court on 19 October 1584 to sign and seal its own copy but much of the seniority of the clergy of the southern province. Bishops, archdeacons, deans and heads of houses had made their way to the court for this purpose, gathering in a kind of informal convocation. The Cornish bond bears 115 names, that for Hertfordshire 106. The Dorset bond was signed by the mayors of Blandford, Lyme, Weymouth and Melcombe, representing their fellow burgesses. More than 200 inhabitants of the town of Cardigan took the oath, signed or marked and applied their seals. The earl of Huntingdon forwarded to the council the names of 140 principal freeholders and farmers of Richmondshire who had committed themselves

[55] Ibid., pp. 374-5.

[56] Examples of the Bond are in PRO, S.P. 12/174; earlier drafts in S.P. 12/173/81-4. The most recent discussion of the Bond is in David Cressy, 'Binding the Nation: The Bonds of Association, 1584 and 1696', in *Tudor Rule and Revolution: Essays for G.R. Elton from his American Friends*, ed. Delloyd J. Guth and John W. McKenna (Cambridge, 1982), pp. 271-34.

to the 'Instrument of Association'.[57] Some sixty residents of Lincolns Inn, headed by Thomas Egerton, the future Lord Ellesmere, subscribed the Bond.[58] The circumstances in which the Bond was subscribed respected hierarchy. The gentlemen of Lancashire came to Wigan church to witness the earl of Derby taking the oath first of all, bare-headed and on his knees before the bishop of Chester, who in his turn administered it to the bishop, followed by the gentry, six at a time.[59]

Later it would be said that the Bond spoke for 'the moost parte of us, your lovinge subiectes'.[60] But 'the moost parte' consisted of Protestants, or of those who would gladly be mistaken for Protestants. In Kent it was thought inappropriate that any known Catholic Recusant should be admitted into 'this loyall societie'. Thomas Digges later proposed that all office holders should be obliged to take the oath of association 'for the defence and perpetuation of religion now publiquelie professed within the realme'.[62] Dr Diarmaid MacCulloch has demonstrated that in Suffolk the county government by this time (the critical date was 1578) had transferred into the hands of a group, not to say clique, of gentry whose outstanding quality was their reliability as Protestants, 'Godds flocke', to the exclusion of the East Anglian Catholics, many of whom might in other circumstances have ranked among the 'natural' leaders of their communities. This had happened not by accident but by a careful design in which the privy council played the leading part and the queen probably none, beyond allowing this provincial *coup d'état* to happen, under her very nose and in the course of a summer's stately progress.[63]

Now the Protestant state (for that is what it was, and in a partisan and prejudicial rather than consensual sense) was to be reinforced by the creation of what Burghley called a 'fellowship and societie'.[64] The Bond bore some resemblance to the Catholic leagues springing up in France at this same time, but with this difference: that whereas the League was a device to oppose the crown in the name of a higher religious loyalty, the

---

[57] PRO, S.P. 12/174/1, 2, 3, 5, 8, 7, 14, 13.

[58] Huntington Library, MS EL 1193; printed, *The Egerton Papers*, ed. J. Payne Collier, Camden Society (1840), pp. 108-11.

[59] Earl of Derby to the earl of Leicester, 7 November 1584 (PRO, S.P. 12/175/4).

[60] Huntington Library, MS EL 1191.

[61] Thomas Scott and Edward Boys to Sir Francis Walsingham, 20 November 1584 (PRO, S.P. 12/176/9).

[62] Thomas Digges, *Humble motives for association to maintaine religion established* (1601), p. 6. I have compared this printed text with the MS in the Folger Shakespeare Library, MS V.b.214.

[63] Diarmaid MacCulloch, 'Catholic and Puritan in Elizabethan Suffolk: A County Community Polarises', *Archiv für Reformationsgeschichte*, 72 (1981), pp. 232-89. See also MacCulloch, *Suffolk and the Tudors*.

[64] PRO, S.P. 12/173/87. My remark about partisan rather than consensual Protestantism is intended to conflict with Sir John Neale's suggestion that with the accession of Elizabeth 'the English Reformation ceases to be a partisan story: it became a national one' (*Essays in Elizabethan History*, p. 24).

English bond was the handiwork of the regime itself. However, the government found it politic to disguise its interventionist role with the appearance of spontaneity. Sir Francis Walsingham inserted these words into a form of letter which his colleague Burghley had drafted for circulation, probably to lords lieutenant in the counties:

> Your lordship shall not need to take knowledge that you receyved the coppye from me, but rather from some other frende of yours in thes parts; for that her Majesty would have the matter carryed in such sorte as this course held for her [safety] may seeme to [come more] from the pertyculer care of her well affected subiects then to growe from any publycke directyon.[65]

This revealing piece of evidence might seem to tell against the 'republican' argument of this essay. But I think that we can substitute for 'her Majesty would' 'we would'.[66]

In content, the Bond was paradoxical. Its ostensible purpose was to defend the life of the queen, which was said to be almost the only concern and function of her people. One is reminded of Edith Sitwell's metaphor of the bees and the hive. (So potent and persuasive was this implausible convention that it comes as rather a shock to find Lord Keeper Bacon frankly arguing in 1570 that if Elizabeth were to remain unmarried she would progessively forfeit the loyal duty of her subjects, whose first instinct was always, as we say today, to look out for number one: 'for that the naturall care in the moste parte of them that have possessions and families' was 'to see to the preservacion of them selves, their children and posteritie that must folowe her life'.[67]) Yet the Bond was also a quasi-republican statement. The circumstance it envisaged was the extinction of the queen and it provided for the sequel to that terrible event without reference to any laws or rights of succession. The inescapable consequence of its silence on this matter was to imply that the act of vengeance it provided for would be enforced by no other authority than that residing in the body politic. In form it was a covenant, constituted by the oaths and subscriptions of all those bound by it, and its sanctions were those of collective responsibility, investing none of its signatories with greater power or responsibility than any other, and not attributing any defined role to office holders, as public men. In this respect its republicanism was more advanced than that of Christopher Goodman or John Ponet. According to Goodman, it was only if and when magistrates and other officers failed in their duties that the people were 'as it were without officers' and obliged to take the law – and

---

[65] PRO, S.P. 12/173/88.

[66] See the exchange of letters between Burghley and Walsingham about tactical matters connected with the Bond, 19, 20 October 1584 (PRO, S.P. 12/173/85,86).

[67] Huntington Library, MS EL 1187.

the sword – into their own hands.[68] But the Bond of Association knew no officers, no magistrates.

Consequently a critic of the enterprise, probably the mathematician, engineer and M. P. Thomas Digges, pointed out its 'perils':

> Breefly me thought I did behowld a confuesed company of all partes of the Realme of all degrees and estates then risinge in Armes at such a tyme as there is no cowncell of estate in Lyfe, no Lawfull generall,... no presidente, no Judges, no sheriffes, no justices, breefly no officers...[69]

Yet the devisers and promoters of this putative exercise in total anarchy were not members of the sectarian political fringe but Lord Burghley and Sir Francis Walsingham, in effect the Prime Minister and Foreign Secretary of the day.

The extreme irregularity of the bond was soon remedied in a parliamentary Act for the Surety of the Queen's Most Royal Person,[70] which imposed by law a general obligation on loyal subjects to revenge the queen's violent death and by statute excluded from the succession those complicit in procuring her death; and further made the proceedings it envisaged conformable to due legal process. This was the process which duly took effect after the Babington Plot, when Mary was tried, sentenced and, in February 1587 and another parliament, executed. However, the 1584 Act was as silent as the Bond itself on the delicate subject of who, or what, in the scenario envisaged, would wield the sovereignty by which the tribunals allowed for were to sit and armed force be raised and deployed. Although the statute explicitly excluded and disabled any person pretending a title to the crown who might by armed force resist the implementation of the act, it did not presume to say who *should* succeed. Legally, sovereignty and all power to act, all offices and courts, would have lapsed with the queen, to be at once transferred to her lawful successor – whoever that was. But on that matter the act was as silent as the Bond, so appearing to condone an irregular, acephalous, quasi-republican state of emergency.

If this was to happen in any case, why not make it legal, or as legal as an English parliament could make anything? Why not a regularised interregnum? This, as a series of documents written or emended in his hand proves, was Burghley's preferred course of action.[71] Burghley was the political veteran of Edward VI's minority and had lived through more than one

---

[68] Christopher Goodman, *How superior powers ought to be obeyed of their subjects* (Geneva, 1558). See Skinner, *Foundations of Modern Political Thought*, ii, pp. 221-4.

[69] PRO, S.P. 12/176/26; further copies in Folger Shakespeare Library, MS V.b. 303, fos. 95-9; BL, MS Lansdowne 98, fos. 14-18; MS Add. 38823, fos. 14ff. See J.E. Neale, *Elizabeth I and her Parliaments, 1584-1601* (1957) [henceforth Neale II], p. 45.

[70] Ibid., pp. 50-3.

[71] PRO, S.P. 12/176/11, 22, 23, 25, 28, 30; Huntington Library, MS EL 1192.

irregular and potentially violent change of regime, first in 1549 and then in 1553.[72] It was understandable that he should take a very personal interest in the most rational means of handling the emergency in which he, of all people, would be exposed to the greatest risk. Besides, behind the deeply unoriginal mind of William Cecil, Lord Burghley, there often lurked a more inventive intelligence, in this case that of the instinctive analyst, Thomas Digges.[73]

Digges was an able, confident, not to say arrogant, man, one of those middling political and administrative animals, 'men of business' and brokers for the regime, whose importance Elizabethan historians are belatedly beginning to recognise.[74] Others were Thomas Norton 'the parliament man', William Fleetwood, recorder of the city of London, and the exceedingly perspicacious diplomat and clerk of the Privy Council, Robert Beale. Digges was at this time centrally and controversially involved in the Elizabethan equivalent of the Channel Tunnel project: the works to extend and improve the facilities of Dover Harbour, the details of which occupy whole volumes of State Papers Domestic. His reports to his masters of his 'proceedings' at Dover reverberate with such claims as 'I was the first that discovered the grosse errors...' or, 'I affirmed the contrary.'[75] The notion of a legalised interregnum was not new in 1584 but Digges made a new and original attack on the problem in a so-called 'Brief Discourse',[76] which saw the device as a tolerable compromise between the nomination of an heir apparent, which Digges conceded was not practical, and the no less dangerous vacuum of inactivity.

The root idea of several versions of the interregnum plan was that the privy council, or the parliament, or both, together with all officers and all courts for the administration of justice, institutions which would normally cease to exist or to have any power to act at the moment of the monarch's death, should on the contrary continue in being. Digges proposed that either the parliament then sitting (the 1584 parliament) should remain undissolved during the natural life of the queen (that would have been a 'long parliament' indeed – it would have sat for twenty years!) – or that upon its dissolution some other parliament should be immediately summoned: 'so that some parliament by your Majesty's summons may be in esse at your highness's decease'. Within thirty days such a parliament should hear and determine all challenges to the throne, having a special regard to candidates whom the late queen would by then be known to have preferred. That is to say, the parliament would, among other evidences, contemplate the

[72] On the events of 1553 see '*The Vita Mariae Angliae Reginae*'.

[73] For Digges, see *D.N.B.* and *The History of Parliament: The House of Commons, 1558-1601*, ed. P.W. Hasler (1981), ii, pp. 37-9; and PRO, S.P. 12/171/13, 13 I, 175/18.

[74] Graves in *Parliamentary History*, ii, pp. 11-38.

[75] PRO, S.P. 12/171/13, 13 I-V, 30, 301; S.P. 12/175/18.

[76] PRO, S.P. 12/176/32.

late queen's last will and testament, without, apparently, being bound by it. Pending this process, all officers of church and state were to remain at their posts and the helm of the ship of state was to be handled by five or seven magnates, temporal and spiritual.

Digges anticipated various objections to this scenario, amongst them the mere fact that it entailed an innovation, without precedent. He met head-on the point that innovations were a bad thing, and added that anyone who had been in Rome at the time of a papal conclave (had this happened to Digges?) would have some sense of 'the monstrous nature of an Interregnum': 'Hell it selfe, every man by force defending his owne, all kind of owtrage, ryot and villanye.' In England it would be worse, since there was, after all, no equivalent to the college of cardinals. But Digges seemed to think that the alternatives would be worse still. And if there were no precedents for filling the throne, Polish style, virtually by election, so much the more honour would accrue to the queen for inventing (in effect) a new constitution. That was truly radical, and not how most sixteenth-century political intelligences worked.

But that very unradical mind which belonged to Lord Burghley differed only in matters of detail, and in Burghley's single-minded, Reagan-like concentration on ensuring the successful pursuit, prosecution and execution of those guilty of terrorism. It was to achieve this end, primarily, that an interregnum would be necessary. Burghley's thinking is contained in a number of documents: two pages of notes in his own inimitable hand;[77] a draft of a bill in the solicitor general Popham's hand, extensively corrected by Burghley (this residing among the Ellesmere MSS in the Huntington Library in California);[78] and, thirdly, what appears to be the most advanced version of these devices: a parliamentary bill endorsed by Burghley 'January 1584[5]. A Bill for the Queen's Safety', and otherwise described as 'to be added to the Bill for the Queen's Safety' – thus indicating that what was in hand was an extension of the 1584 Act 'for Provision to be Made for the Surety of the Queen's Most Royal Person'.[79]

The commanding idea running through these drafts is that, in the event of the queen's untimely death, 'there remayn an ordinary power, to remedy all violence committed agaynst her'. 'The government of the realme shall still contynew in all respectes.' 'This', says Burghley in his rough notes, 'cannot be without an Interreyn.' 'Ther shall be decreed an Interreyn for some resonable tyme.' Government was to reside in a great council or grand council, acting 'in the name of the Imperiall Crown of England'. At first Burghley seems to have thought of a body consisting of the Privy Council with the addition of all the major offices of state. But in the Ellesmere

[77] PRO, S.P. 12/176/28, 29.
[78] Huntington Library, MS EL 1192.
[79] PRO, S.P. 12/176/11, 22, 23, 30.

document he (or Popham) conceives that this body should come into being by the privy council recruiting from the House of Lords (or as much of it as could be assembled within ten days) to make up a grand council of thirty persons, plus the four senior judges. Within thirty days (corrected by Burghley to twenty days) of the queen's assassination, the great council should recall the last parliament back to Westminster. Thereafter, the Great Council having actively promoted the apprehension and due punishment of all offenders against the queen's life, 'of what estate so ever they be', Parliament would give sentence against them. Anyone attempting during this period of time to lay claim to the throne by force would be *ipso facto* disabled from succeeding and would be actively resisted by the great council. The style to be employed in respect of this body in all writs, warrants, patents and the like would be thus, in Latin: *Magnum Consilium Coronae Angliae*, a phrase inserted in the documents in Burghley's own hand. One wonders whether such a device would have succeeded in defeating the *coup de théâtre* which brought that other Mary to the throne, against all the odds, in 1553.[80]

The Ellesmere document proposes that the Great Council 'with the said Parliament' shall continue 'above one year, but shall then cease', and sooner if due execution had by then been passed on the public enemy. But it is as uninformative as all previous papers of this kind, white, green or rainbow-coloured, on how the interregnum is to be terminated and England to find itself once again with a monarch in whose name writs would run. On this the parliamentary bill of January 1585 is more helpful. No one was to acknowledge any claimant as king or queen or affirm any one person to have more right than another. But the act of the great council in summoning a parliament – in composition the last parliament to have sat – was now seen as necessary 'because it is likely and very probable that the state of both the Realms [*sc*. England and Ireland] cannot long endure without a person that by justice ought to be the successor of the Crown shall be known'. 'Ought to be' referred to the law of succession. Accordingly, parliament would in peaceable manner consider and hear any pretensions to the throne and finally (in Burghley's inserted words 'in the name of God and as it were in his presence')

> accept and receive such a person to the Crown of the Realm as shall to them upon their peaceable deliberations *and trials had of them* [Burghley's interpolation] appear to have best right to the same in blood by the royal lawes of the Realm and such a person *so by the said Parliament allowed* [Burghley's hand again] they shall by a Proclamation warranted with the Great Seal of England in form of an Act of Parliament published to the people of the Realm to have the most right to the Crown.

[80] 'The *Vita Mariae Angliae Reginae*'.

In Burghley's telling interpolations, Poland was not far away.

It was known to Neale and therefore to us that Burghley's own ever-active pen inserted into this parliamentary draft the words 'uppon sure hope of the assent of our Soverayn Lady'. That is to say, Burghley expressed a hopeful presumption of the bill's successful passage and of the royal assent. It is equally well known that not only did the idea of an interregnum not commend itself to Elizabeth but that (so far as we know) there was, after Christmas 1584, no discussion of it on the floor of either house. Burghley had proposed; Elizabeth disposed. And that was that. What would have followed a successful attempt on the life of Elizabeth I we do not know, and Protestants may prefer to avert their imaginations: an interregnum possibly, but not one enjoying the legality, however constitutionally dubious, afforded by an act of parliament.

There has been no attempt on this occasion to suggest that that was not how the business of politics proceeded, so long as this remarkable woman lived. Two years later, in 1586, the political nation was back where it had been in 1572, beseeching the queen to carry out the sentence of death now passed against the Scottish queen. And it is remarkable that their petition, the petition of both houses of parliament, was buttressed with threats, the same biblical threats. And it is more striking still that this document too is extensively corrected and interpolated in Burghley's hand, in the copy which survives in San Marino, California.[81] We may note in particular this passage:

> The neglecting wherof [*sc.* the carrying out of the sentence] maye procure the heavy displeasure and punyshment of Almightie God as by sundry severe examples of his great Justice in that behalfe lefte us in the Sacred Scriptures doeth appere.

The drift of this essay has not been in the least 'whiggish', to employ the historical cant term. I have not argued for the incipience in Elizabethan England of a kind of constitutional monarchy, still less of a headless republic or even of a continuous, coherent republican movement. When Thomas Digges proposed that parliament should be always 'in esse' he was not writing in favour of parliamentary sovereignty. I do not see 1649 foreshadowed proleptically in 1572 or 1584. It is Neale, not I, who remarks of Burghley's interregnum plan: 'more congenial to the Commonwealth period of the next century than to the Tudor constitution'.[82] Nor have I set out to argue that late sixteenth-century England could, still less that it should, have been ruled more or less permanently by a rational regime composed of a team of political equals, experiencing effective collegiality. Early modern European history suggests that few such regimes ever

---

[81] Huntington Library, MS EL 1191; partly printed, Neale II, pp. 113-14.
[82] Ibid., p.45.

existed, or were likely to survive for very long. The rule of a single person under the crown, a Richelieu or an Olivares or a Buckingham, was to be almost the norm in the seventeenth century. And perhaps we have found something like that in these documents. The notion of a *regnum Cecilianum* was a canard invented by the enemies of the Cecils but it was not a total falsification of political realities. Cynics might find in the sketch-pad of papers examined in this essay, so many of them annotated or corrected in the spidery Cecilian italic hand, reflections not of the republican machiavellianism of the *Discourses* but of the individualistic *virtú* of *The Prince*: Burghley perpetuating his own kingdom, which he ruled in Elizabeth's name, using the likes of Thomas Digges as catspaws.

My argument has been less speculative, less ambitious. I suggest no more than that Burghley and his colleagues (and Cecil *did* have colleagues), like Swallowfield, were responding resourcefully and intelligently to a most unusual situation. The strangeness of the Elizabethan scenario, which so captivated Sir John Neale, was commented on soon after its passing by a more jaundiced observer, Francis Bacon. For Bacon, the whole episode of the later Tudors, contained within half a century, had been unique and bizarre: 'The strangest variety that in a like number of successions of any hereditary monarchy hath ever been known: the reign of a child, the offer of a usurpation, the reign of a lady married to a foreign prince, and the reign of a lady solitary and unmarried.'[83] Surely this was not what the inventor of the English monarchy had intended. For Bacon the Tudors were 'these barren princes', and, by contrast, he welcomed the advent of Scottish James and his fruitful progeny as a dynasty likely to endure 'for ever'. Bacon was not to know that the violent death of the second of these perpetual Stuarts would be followed by an interregnum – *the* Interregnum – and a shortlived English Republic. And nor, I think, do Elizabethan historians need to know that.

---

[83] Francis Bacon, 'A Letter to the Lord Chancellor, Touching the History of Britain' (1605), *Works of Francis Bacon*, ed. J. Spedding, R.L. Ellis and D.D. Heath, x (1868), pp. 249-50.

Appendix

On 30 July 1582 Sir Francis Walsingham sent the following advice to the earl of Shrewsbury, who had Mary queen of Scots in his custody:

For answer wherunto her Majestie doth thinke it meete that you shold lett her [*sc.* the Scottish Queen] understand that, first, shee doth find it straunge that shee shold directe her lettres unto her Counsell, as unto principall members of this Crowne (for so doth shee in her said letters terme them, a cowrse that hertofor hath not bene held), wherof her Majestie cannot otherwise conceave but that there shee doth not repute her to be so absolut as that without thassent of such whom she termeth 'principall members of the Crowne' she cannot direct her pollicie; or els, that uppon this charge given by her of delay used in satisfying of her requests, shee wer by them to be called to an accompt. Of which misconceipt of the said Queen and misunderstanding of the absolutenes of her Majesties government, shee thinketh meet shee shold by yor Lordship be better enfourmed: For althoughe her Highnes doth carry as great regard unto her Counsell as any of her progenitors have done, and hath just cause so to do in respecte of their wisdome and fidelity, yet is shee to be let understand that they are Councellors by choyce, and not by birth, whose services are no longer to be used in that publike function then it shall please her Majestie to dispose of the same; and therefore her Highnes cannot conceave to what ende a complainte shold be made unto them, unlesse ether shee repute her to be in her minoritye, or els doth meane to use her Counsell as witnesses against her.

Edmund Lodge, *Illustrations of British History* (1791), ii, pp. 276-7.

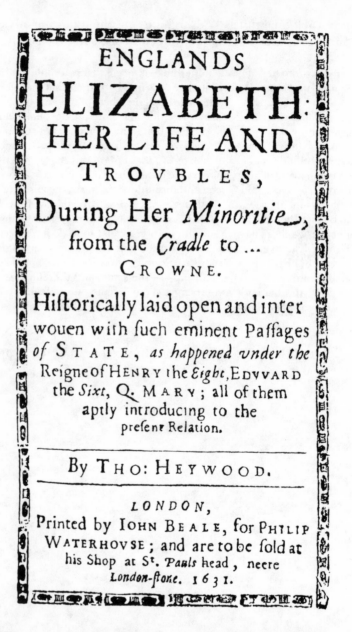

ENGLANDS ELIZABETH:

HER LIFE AND TROVBLES,

During Her *Minoritie*, from the *Cradle* to ... CROWNE.

Historically laid open and inter wouen with such eminent Passages of STATE, *as happened vnder the* Reigne of HENRY the *Eight*, EDVVARD the *Sixt*, Q. MARY; all of them aptly introducing to the present Relation.

By THO: HEYWOOD.

LONDON,
Printed by IOHN BEALE, for PHILIP WATERHOVSE; and are to be sold at his Shop at St. *Pauls* head, neere *London-stone*. 1 6 3 1.

Thomas Heywood's *Englands Elizabeth: her life and troubles during her minoritie, from the Cradle to the Crowne* (1631) fostered the post-Elizabethan myth of Elizabeth's martyr-like religious heroism by further embellishing the already partly fictive account in Foxe's 'Book of Martyrs'. (*Cambridge University Library*)

3

Puritans, Men of Business and Elizabethan Parliaments

'I like this college', Sir John Neale often said to me in the mid-'50s as we walked over from the History Department at lunchtime, usually in company with the late Joel Hurstfield. Sometimes Neale added that he had liked it even better when the college was smaller 'and the Senior Common Room was no larger than my office is now – and the chemists made the coffee'. I like University College too. It gave me my early opportunities, including the first class which I was ever allowed to teach. I also esteem the house of Jonathan Cape, my original publisher. But both these debts, to University College and Cape's, are as it were second mortgages on a career. The first charge is to the memory of Sir John Neale, whose name is inseparable from both Gower Street and Bedford Square, and who opened both these doors for me. The invitation to give the Neale Memorial Lecture, a great honour, took me back into the documentation of the Elizabethan Parliaments, which I had last penetrated more than thirty years ago, and to transcripts of my own in Tavistock Square which I had not set eyes on for half a lifetime.[1] And when I opened my own files I found that they also contained little notes saying 'tell Professor Neale' this, or 'show Professor Neale' that. And I noticed that even on the backs of envelopes, so to speak, it was never 'Neale', nor 'J.E.N', let alone anything more familiar still, but always 'Professor Neale'.

Interest in this subject has been rekindled by the appearance of Sir Geoffrey Elton's *The Parliament of England, 1559-1581*,[2] a study of the first seven of the thirteen parliaments of Elizabeth I which (unlike Neale's account of the same parliaments or, indeed, Professor Conrad Russell's *Parliaments and English Politics, 1621-1629*) treats parliamentary history not episodically but institutionally: the most authoritative account of parliament as a legislative arm of government so far published for any part of its history. Partly as a consequence of its approach and methodology, partly

[1] My thanks are due to the History of Parliament Trust and to its then Secretary, Mr P.W. Hasler, for providing access to these files. The transcripts for the parliaments of 1559-81 have been published by T.E. Hartley in *Proceedings in the Parliaments of Elizabeth 1*, i, *1558-1581* (Leicester, 1981). 1 am indebted to Dr Hartley for photocopies of many of the transcripts relating to the later parliaments which will be included in forthcoming volumes of his edition.

[2] G.R. Elton, *The Parliament of England, 1559-1581* (Cambridge, 1986). See also M.A.R. Graves, *The Tudor Parliaments: Crown, Lords and Commons, 1485-1603* (1985) and N.L. Jones, 'Parliament and the Governance of Elizabethan England: A Review', *Albion*, 19 (1987), pp. 327-46.

because it engages head-on with Neale's version of events, this book is inevitably cast as a piece of 'revisionism'. But this is a tired, over-worked term so let us rather call it a work of demythologising, since Elton sets out to expose the myth that these parliaments were altogether dominated, as a careless reading of Neale's two volumes on the subject might suggest,[3] by religion and related issues of great public and political moment, matters agitated by free-ranging and turbulent spirits in a House of Commons which was reaching for liberties which were already halfway to power. Elton's less mythological account of the matter establishes that the essential history of these as of other sixteenth-century parliaments consists of the many useful, mundane bills which were read, debated and committed, and of the minority which as acts succeeded in attaining the statute book. With a fine indifference, Simonds D'Ewes's digest of the Lords' Journal for the 1559 Parliament records that on 27 April the Bill Touching the Reviving of the Act for Killing of Rooks and Crows and the Bill for the Uniformity of Common Prayer were each given a second reading. From the Commons' Journal of the same Parliament we learn that two days earlier nine bills had been sent on their way to the upper House 'of which one was for the preservation of the Spawn of Fish etc. and the other was for the Uniformity of Common Prayer'. The clerk kept a due sense of proportion.[4]

However, myths, once exposed, are sometimes capable of rehabilitation through restatement in a modified, less mythological form. Often they contain important truths. Babies do not have to be thrown out with the bathwater. The historical Jesus has survived Schweitzer and Bultmann and with good reason, since he probably existed. And Puritans may yet prove to have been a significant force in the Elizabethan parliaments, even in the shape of that 'Puritan Movement' which Professor Elton tells us has 'turned out to be less a movement than a confusion'.[5]

For Elton, the myth of a coherent Puritan Movement has contributed to a greater myth: the story that Puritanism was an ideology of radical, undeferential political activism, motivating and uniting those who were unhappy about the crown's policies, or lack of policies, and who called in

---

[3] J.E.Neale, *Elizabeth I and her Parliaments, 1559-1581* (1953); idem, *Elizabeth I and her Parliaments, 1584-1601* (1957): hereafter 'Neale I' and 'Neale II'.

[4] Simonds D'Ewes, *The Journals of all the Parliaments during the Reign of Queen Elizabeth* (1682), pp. 27, 55. However D'Ewes's sense of proportion seems to have abandoned him when he reported of the Commons proceedings on 22 Feb. 1559 (ibid., p. 48) that 'two Bills of no great moment' were read 'of which the second being the Bill for Supremacy of the Church annexed to the Crown' was read the second time.

[5] P. Collinson, *The Elizabethan Puritan Movement* (1967). For Elton's comment, see *The Parliament of England*, p. 199. The role of the Marian exiles in the 1559 parliament, and by implication that of 'Puritans' in subsequent parliaments, is brought into doubt by N.L. Jones, *Faith by Statute: Parliament and the Settlement of Religion, 1559* (1982) and by N.M. Sutherland, 'The Marian Exiles and the Establishment of the Elizabethan Regime', *Archiv für Reformationsgeschichte*, 78 (1987), pp. 253-86.

question its prerogative, nominally in defence but in reality in aggressive assertion of the liberties of the House of Commons: a piece of the constitution which as Puritans they especially exalted. 'Under the warrant of Godes lawe', asked Job Throckmorton in a speech of 1586, 'what may not this House doe? [And then, as if in an afterthought] I mean the three estates of the land. To deny the power of this House ye knowe is treason.'[6] For Neale, such sturdy sentiments were the voice of manifest destiny and for him it was no accident that the man who uttered them also wrote (in all probability) the iconoclastic and almost seditious Marprelate Tracts.[7] But Elton now informs us that 'there was no concerted puritan programme moved in Parliament by a coherent party.'[8]

To be sure there were some religious enthusiasts inside and outside parliament whom Elton is happy to identify as Puritans. They included that 'grave and ancient man of great zeal' William Strickland who in 1571 introduced a bill to purge the Prayer Book of its supposed superstitious and erroneous elements; and Sir Anthony Cope who in 1586 moved a measure to replace the Prayer Book altogether and with it the entire hierarchical constitution of the Church of England with a Presbyterian form of worship and discipline.[9] 'Perhappes also they mean to dissolve the parisshes too' remarked Sir Walter Mildmay in evident exasperation at this excessively comprehensive engine of destruction and the antics of the loony left which had constructed it.[10] But Elton believes that such genuine militants were few and without influence, in Mildmay's words, 'men of small judgment and small experience'. Certainly they never came within sight of organising the House of Commons into an opposition, on these or any other issues.

Strickland and Cope were Puritans all right, if the word is to retain any substantial meaning at all. But we should not waste precious time debating whether or not some other Elizabethan Parliament-men are correctly identified as Puritans: and goodness knows much time was so spent, and perhaps misspent, in Professor Neale's postgraduate seminar in years gone by, the proceedings punctuated by the frequent question 'was he a Puritan? was he a radical?' 'Puritan' was a term of perception and of vicious stigmatisation, not of inherent quality and identity, and it tells as much or more about those who deployed it as about those to whom it was attached, or rather it informs us about both halves of a stressful relationship.[11] I think

---

[6] Pierpont Morgan Library, MA 276 (Phillipps MS 13891), p. 9.

[7] Proposed by Neale (on the evidence of Throckmorton's 1586 parliamentary speeches discovered in the Pierpont Morgan Library) in Neale II, p. 220; more extensively argued by L.H. Carlson, *Martin Marprelate, Gentleman: Master Job Throkmorton Laid Open in his Colors* (San Marino, CA, 1981).

[8] *Parl. of England*, p. 216.

[9] Neale I, pp. 193-203; Neale II, pp. 148-65.

[10] BL, MS Harley 7188, fol. 98 v.

[11] See my *English Puritanism* (1983); and my 'The Puritan Character: Polemics and Polarities in

continued

that it was probably not used in the context of parliamentary language before 1587, when Speaker Puckering (an anti-Puritan) warned the Commons not to give ear 'to the wearysome sollicitations of those that commonly be called Puritans': a provocation which seems to have prompted Job Throckmorton's complaint in a speech made in the same session that strong convictions on any of the great issues of the time were liable to be pilloried as Puritanism. 'I feare me we shall come shortly to this, that to doe God and her Majestie good service shalbe compted Puritanisme.' Two privy councillors had been called 'Puritanes' by the traitor Babington. 'The Lorde send her Majestie stoare of such Puritans.'[12] Similar complaints were voiced, the same polemics deployed, in the Long Parliament, more than fifty years later.

What does concern us is the contentious, insubordinate expression of deeply held convictions and its political reverberations, matters which can and perhaps should be investigated without once resorting to the category of Puritan. Lord Burghley suffered from a lifelong prejudice against the higher clergy and the use to which their power and jurisdiction were put which in anyone but the Lord Treasurer would be called 'radical'. But Burghley was careful not to expose his opinions on these matters in controversial circumstances and it would be absurd to call him a Puritan.

An important part of Professor Elton's argument depends upon the perception that many of the objectives pursued in the early Elizabethan Parliaments by Neale's so-called Puritans were shared by Elizabethans who are not helpfully so described, office-holders and other establishment figures, even bishops.[13] This means that the aspirations often associated with 'Puritanism' were almost consensual within the relatively broad-bottomed Protestant Political Nation. To desire the advancement of a learned preaching ministry, whether for political or theological reasons or both, was to be in favour of motherhood and apple pie. In the 1560s, privy councillors and bishops agreed with members of the House of Commons on the utility of a shopping list of further ecclesiastical measures, further that is to the religious settlement of 1559, bills called by Neale (from the method of identification used by the clerk of the House of Commons) 'alphabetical bills'. Only the queen thought that her first parliament had exhausted the need and opportunity for church legislation. In the 1570s the bishops shared with other public men a concern that England should be made a more nearly confessional state, by some such means as a statute requiring under penalty annual reception of the communion according to

continued

Early Seventeenth-Century English Culture', in *The Character of a Puritan*, a paper presented at a Clark Library Seminar, 25 April 1987 (University of California, Los Angeles).

[12] Queen's College, Oxford, MS 284, fol. 35; Pierpont Morgan Lib., MS MA 276 (Phillipps MS 13891), p. 18. The privy councillors so identified by Babington were, according to Throckmorton, the earl of Leicester and Sir Amyas Paulet.

[13] *Parl. of England*, pp. 199-216.

the Protestant rite, in effect a test act.[14] In 1584, the establishment, Lord Burghley included, supported a bill which would have left people with less freedom to spend Sundays as they chose, a measure which the queen vetoed.[15] Elizabeth so often rejected what almost everyone else wanted. But that did not make these Puritan measures or causes. In fact, Elton insists, none of them is properly so designated.

If we pierce through the permeable membrane thinly separating matters of religion from those of more secular concern, the 'great affairs' somewhat artifically distanced from the topic 'church and religion' by 130 pages in the organisation of *The Parliament of England,* we shall find the same loose coalition of privy councillors, bishops and more private men, inside and outside parliament, all urging the queen to marry, to limit the succession in the Protestant interest, to execute or otherwise exclude from their political future Mary queen of Scots: all aspects of the Protestant Ascendancy and of how it was to be perpetuated. It was the bishops (apparently the entire bench) who in a memorandum addressed to the queen in 1572 on the subject of the Scottish queen ventured the boldest and most coherent criticism of Elizabeth's alleged irresponsibility in the performance of her office, threatening her with the biblical example of the divine deposition of King Saul for failing to kill his enemy, King Agag. The queen was told that she 'must needs offend in conscience before God' if she left Mary Stuart alive.

> Every prince beinge the minister of God and a publicke person ought by Godes worde to have an especiall care of his owne safetie more then a private person... But so it is in the Queenes Majestie: therefore in conscience ought she to have a singuler care of her safetie, if not for her sake, yet at the leaste for the furtheraunce of Godes cause and stay of her countrye, to the maintenance whereof she is bounde before God.[16]

Neale knew that Protestantism, which was not necessarily the same thing as Puritanism, was capable of trenchant expression and concerted action. He believed that Protestants (it would be premature to call them Puritans) had so conducted themselves in Mary's parliaments. He knew that the bishops supported some of the so-called alphabetical bills and he remarked of these measures: 'they were Puritan reforms in the sense that Puritans desired them; but they were that part of the Puritan programme which might appeal to any earnest Churchman ...' Elton will not allow these pieces of defensible but abortive legislation to be called 'a Puritan programme', and in that he may be right.[17] Neale was less discriminating than more recent

---

[14] F.X. Walker, 'The Implementation of the Elizabethan Statutes against Recusants, 1581-1603' (unpublished University of London Ph.D. thesis, 1961), pp. 33-43.

[15] Neale II, pp. 58-60.

[16] Hartley, *Proceedings*, i, pp. 274-82.

[17] Neale I, p. 166; *Parl. of England*, pp. 205-7.

historians in his use of the labels 'Puritan' and 'radical'. And his logic was far from impregnable. He would have acknowledged the absurdity of calling the entire episcopal bench 'Puritan' on account of what it said to the queen in 1572. But he dodged the implications of the bishops' statement for our assessment of men who were not bishops but who said similar things, on the basis of which they were identified as 'Puritans'.

In short, the perspectives of Elizabethan parliamentary history have been altered by Sir Geoffrey Elton and his pupils for ever, and for the better. Dr David Dean writes of an atmosphere of cooperation and, while admitting that the later Elizabethan parliaments did not work very well in legislative terms, he suggests that their principal role was 'to provide the governing class of the realm with an opportunity to discuss problems and their solutions'.[18] In so far as there was a dividing line of contention present in these assemblies, it did not set a Puritan opposition over against the regime. On many interrelated public issues, ecclesiastical or political, the line very often ran between the backbone of the regime and the queen herself, with that minority of those admitted to the inner wheel of political life, be they courtiers or bishops or bishops' agents, who shared the queen's own eccentrically dispassionate outlook on these matters, or found it convenient to appear to share it. This shifting of the goalposts of Elizabethan parliamentary politics is a great gain. But it would be a gain at once lost to follow up that helpful redefinition of the terms of the game by limiting or even closing down the discussion of parliamentary politics, as if parliament was not political at all, since its business was not the ventilation of politically contentious issues but legislation: a point on which Professor Elton was insistent in his Neale Memorial Lecture of 1978.[19] Perhaps we can state it as a general rule that 'revisionism', if it is to be salutary, ought to open up areas of historical inquiry, not close them down.

II

What follows is a second look, in the manner of 'revisionism revised', at the religiously flavoured politics of some of the Elizabethan parliaments, engaging with the concept and category to which we have recently become accustomed in this context of 'men of business'.[20] 'Man of business', was not, I think, a term used in the sixteenth century. Presumably it has been

---

[18] D.M. Dean, 'Bills and Acts, 1584-1601' (unpublished University of Cambridge Ph.D. thesis, 1984), p. 255. I am grateful to Dr Dean for providing me with a copy of his dissertation.

[19] G.R. Elton, 'Parliament in the Sixteenth Century: Functions and Fortunes', *Historical Journal*, 22 (1979), pp. 255-78; repr. in G.R. Elton, *Studies in Tudor and Stuart Politics and Government*, 3 vols (Cambridge, 1974-83), iii, pp. 155-78.

[20] See especially M.A.R. Graves, 'The Management of the Elizabethan House of Commons: The Council's "Men-of-Business", *Parliamentary History* 2 (1983), pp. 11-38 and idem, 'Thomas Norton the Parliament Man: An Elizabethan M.P., 1559-1581', *Historical Journal*, 23 (1980), pp. 17-35.

continued

imported from a later age and from the culture of counting houses and lawyers' offices. We find it, for example, in the pages of Trollope, applied to those gentlemen who looked after the interests of, as it might be, the duke of Omnium or the Barchester ecclesiastical establishment. This is not to say that there have not always been men of business in the world of politics. Perhaps the ultimate in political men of business was Lord Hailsham's father, described by a Tory grandee of the day as an attorney called Pig who could be trusted to look after everything admirably. This is Professor Michael Graves's preferred term for many of those parliament-men whom Neale called Puritans, but who upon examination prove to have been noted as parliamentarians less for a religiously inspired habit of opposing and obstructing than for facilitating the interests and objectives of the privy council, or of individual privy councillors. They were secondary political figures whose identities were less important than the fact that they looked after everything admirably. They were not opponents of the regime but its functionaries, junior partners in a well adjusted and often fruitful legislative enterprise. Professor Elton, too, has made free and frequent use of the term.

The Members of the House of Commons so classified, or reclassified, include several Speakers, Onslow, Bell, Popham and Yelverton, lawyers all, and those outstanding men of the law, the Londoners William Fleetwood, the incurably garrulous and anecdotal recorder of the city, and Thomas Norton, the lord mayor's remembrancer, called by Professor Graves 'the most impressive of all the Council's men-of-business'. Graves's concept adheres especially to what the sixteenth century would have called 'private men', figures without public offices of profit but publicly engaged, from time to time. But we may extend it to office-holders like Robert Beale, clerk to the privy council and, later, to the Council in the North as well, and to James Morrice, attorney of the Court of Wards: as well to a number of diplomats and especially to the semi-permanent under-secretary of state for Dutch affairs, William Davison. None of these was a public servant in any exclusive all-defining sense, any more than Fleetwood and Norton were wholly private figures. In the House of Commons their relation to the regime was not noticeably different. So they too will be included among the men of business under scrutiny.

Who is right: Neale or Elton, following Graves? Was Thomas Norton a Puritan or was he a man of business? We shall find that these were not necessarily mutually exclusive categories. Men of business could be turned into Puritans, provoked by events and circumstances, especially by the circumstance of the episcopal leadership of the Church of England in the

---

continued

The earliest political use of the term 'man of business' cited by the *Oxford English Dictionary* occurs in a letter written by Bishop Gilbert Burnet in 1670: 'I am ... resolved never to have anything to do more with men of business, particularly with any in opposition to the Court.'

dangerous and ideologically highly charged 1580s. Sir Christopher Hatton, Elizabeth's unusual but perhaps inspired choice as lord chancellor, makes this point rather neatly. Addressing the 1589 parliament and staving off renewed attempts to debate matters of religion in the name of a queen who, he said, had 'placed hir Reformation as uppon a square stone to remayne constant', Hatton played with words and complained of 'some froward men, I should say forward men.'[21] We can assume that Puritans, men of business and many of those for whom they did business were all alike 'forward men', in that they favoured policies which were inspired by a more than formal Protestantism and were calculated to preserve the Protestant ascendancy actively rather than passively. In this sense such decidedly Protestant privy councillors as Sir Francis Walsingham and Sir Walter Mildmay were 'forward'. If, in any particular instance, they appeared to be backward, this would be a matter of remark. But Walsingham and Mildmay could not afford the luxury of being 'froward'. As Walsingham wrote on one occasion to Davison, the diplomat: 'If you knew with what difficulty we retain that we have, and that the seeking of more might hazard (according to man's understanding) that which we already have, ye would then, Mr Davison, deal warily in this time when policy carrieth more sway than zeal.'[22]

Froward men by definition preferred to be guided by zeal rather than by 'policy', a dirty word in their book. Men of business were betwixt and between in this muted but critically important debate. If the first and most significant dividing line in Elizabethan high politics distinguished between forwardness and the queen's own backwardness, there was a secondary dividing line running between the forward and the occasionally froward, separating from time to time and in particular circumstances politic pragmatists and impolitic dogmatists. If we are to distinguish between men of business and Puritans, then men of business remained for most of the time on the politic side of this line but occasionally, in or out of parliament, transgressed across it, for reasons which are able to take us far into the innernesses of Elizabethan political processes. In the ecclesiastical context, this is the difference between Archbishop Grindal, who stepped across the line only once, if with fatal consequences, and those Puritan clerics for whom nonconformity and some degree of habitual estrangement from the official church (of which Grindal was a pillar) was almost a way of life.[23]

Among Elizabethan Members of the Commons the two Wentworth brothers, Peter and Paul, can be taken as representative of those who took up more or less permanent residence on the far side of our critical line. They were almost professionally 'froward', or so it must have seemed after

[21] Washington, DC, Folger Shakespeare Library, MS V.b.303, pp. 183-6.

[22] Quoted in Collinson, *Elizabethan Puritan Movement*, p. 194.

[23] Ibid., *Archbishop Grindal, 1519-1583: The Struggle for a Reformed Church* (1979).

Peter Wentworth's remarkable speech of 1576 on the theme of liberty, which the House of Commons interrupted and for which the House, rather than the council or the queen, committed him to the Tower. The next session, of 1581, began with a motion by his brother Paul in favour of a 'public fast' and daily preaching, 'so that they beginning their proceedings with the service and worship of God, he might the better blesse them in their consultation and service'. There was a debate and, exceptionally, a division, with 115 for the fast and 100 against. Arrangements were accordingly made, only to be interrupted by the queen who refused to allow the fast to take place.[24] Although Professor Elton calls this a 'rather pointless skirmish',[25] there can be no doubt that Wentworth's well supported initiative was a significant, typical piece of Calvinist political methodology, with international as well as more local resonances. But Secretary Walsingham's comment was: 'Owre parlament hathe had a sowar begynnynge by reason of a motyon made by Mr Powle Wentworthe to have had a publyck fast: a matter not to be dyslowed of, in case the same had been orderly proceeded in.'[26] Some effort to handle the matter in an orderly fashion had in fact been made. The intention was that the preachers at the fast should be appointed by the privy councillors in the Commons, 'to the intent that they may be persons discreet to keep a convenient proportion of time, and to meddle with no matter of innovation or unquietness'. The place was to be the Temple church, a venue used by the Commons for committee meetings. Such religious occasions were to be non-controversial in the 1620s and were, of course, standard and regular practice from the early days of the Long Parliament. But there can be no doubt that one thing which had made the 1581 initiative inherently disorderly was that its prime sponsor was one of the Wentworth brothers. The queen herself said as much.[27]

In another episode our often elusive line between frowardness and forwardness can be seen, drawn across the floor of the chamber in Lincoln's Inn occupied by that notable man of business James Morrice, attorney of the Wards. On the eve of the 1593 parliament, Peter Wentworth, having held secret conferences with some other parliamentarians about the dangerous matter of the succession, had been advised to consult with 'some old discreete grave parliament men', living, in effect, on the safe side of the

---

[24] Neale I, pp. 378-82.

[25] *Parl. of England*, pp. 354-5.

[26] Huntington Library, MS HA 13055, Walsingham to the earl of Huntingdon, 24 Jan. 1580 [/1].

[27] PRO, S.P. 12/147/18. Fast sermons were often marathon performances lasting much of the day. Hence 'a convenient proportion of time'. See my *Elizabethan Puritan Movement*, pp. 214-19 and, for a fuller account of the Puritan fast and its significance, my unpublished University of London Ph.D. thesis (1957), 'The Puritan Classical Movement in the Reign of Elizabeth I', pp. 323-46. For a reference to a committee of the Commons meeting in the Temple Church (in 1584), see Thomas Cromwell's journal: Dublin, Trinity College, MS N.2.12, fol. 73.

tracks. Wentworth complained about occasions when he had been let down
by such wiseacres, so that, as he said, 'I have no great hope in the great
parliament men'. But he consented to visit Morrice, who later described his
shock at hearing the nature of Wentworth's business. 'Succession, said 1,
what is he that dare meddle with it?' Morrice went on to utter a warning
about private conferences. 'Mr Wentworth you should beware of conferences, for if you remember you and others were committed to the Tower
for your conference in matters of religion in the last parliament.'[28] Wentworth
was not likely to have forgotten! This was a reference to his second period
of imprisonment which had followed his involvement in the Presbyterian
venture of the 'Bill and Book', not in the last parliament (1589) but in 1586.
Soon Wentworth was back in the Tower, where he ended his days five years
later, a fate resembling that of Sir John Eliot in a later generation; and
reminding us that there was a Tudor Despotism after all, for there was no
more telling symbol of royal absolutism than the power to imprison without
cause shown.[29]

However, at the time that Morrice gave this testimony he himelf was in
custody (or 'durance') as the enforced house guest of the privy councillor
Sir John Fortescue; comfortably and courteously accommodated but, as the
summer came on, short of air, 'gasping for breath, like the taynted fyshe in
a corrupt water'. Morrice's offence had been to disregard the queen's oft-
repeated order that the House of Commons should not meddle with
matters of religion by proposing that parliament should seek to curb the
activities of the church courts, specifically in tendering to those brought
before them (Puritans) the *ex officio* oath which required a man to condemn
himself out of his own mouth and which conflicted with the spirit as well as
the letter of the laws of England, in Morrice's opinion. The courts spiritual
had few defenders in the House of Commons and on this occasion a
Member who spoke in their defence provoked much hawking and spitting,
the disgrace of which became a minor issue in itself. Morrice's offence, like
Paul Wentworth's in 1581, was *in modo* rather than *in re*. When he appeared
before the council Burghley several times remarked that his offence was
'onlie in form', although lord keeper Puckering, who thought better of
ecclesiastical lawyers and their ways than the lord treasurer, added 'and
somewhat in matter'.

When, after eight weeks, Morrice was released, Burghley, who was his
immediate superior at the Court of Wards and doubtless glad to see him
back, told him that as a servant of the crown he ought not to have voiced
his misgivings about the state of the church and the Commonwealth 'to the

---

[28] BL, MS Harley 7042, fos. 175-88.
[29] J.E. Neale, 'Peter Wentworth', *English Historical Review*, 39 (1924), repr. in *Historical Studies of
the English Parliament*, eds. E.B. Fryde and E. Miller, 2 vols. (Cambridge, 1970), ii, pp. 246-95.

common people' but privately, to the queen. 'And if it please hir to reforme it, it was well; if not, wee were to praie to God to move hir harte thereunto, and so to leave the matter to God and hir Majestie'. Burghley, never more like Polonius, reinforced this homily on the virtues of passive obedience with a topical reference to 'Mr Wentworths fonde dealing in that matter of succession'. Morrice knew that Wentworth's dealing had been 'fond' and had done all in his power to forestall it. But Sir Francis Knollys, himself a privy councillor and close kinsman of the queen, far from thinking Morrice's own initiative against the *ex officio* oath 'fond', thoroughly approved of it: although Knollys knew that his own strong convictions about the illegal conduct of the higher clergy (which the late James Cargill Thompson thought Protestant rather than Puritan – but the distinction is not very meaningful) were hard to reconcile with his status and function as a sworn councillor.[30]

Job Throckmorton, in one of his 1586 speeches, suggested that it would be much better if such 'grave and graye-headed' councillors as (presumably) Knollys would take it upon themselves to speak publicly and boldly about the great issues of the time. 'But alas ye see when gray heares grow sylent then younge headdes grow venterous ... When they that shoulde speake bee muette then burst out they that should bee stille It is wondred at above, that symple men of the countrey shoulde be so forwarde, and it doeth amaze us in the countrey that wise men of the Courte should be so backeward'.[31] In the 1560s grey heads, including those carried on episcopal shoulders, had raised themselves above the parapet. Now, with the queen more firmly in the saddle, they dared not do so. Hence the rise of Puritanism, or at least of frowardness.

Here was the crux and the essence of the politically contentious history of the Elizabethan parliaments. Our secondary line of demarcation traced no fundamental difference of principle, so far as salient issues were concerned, between men of business and the men whom they did business for, councillors and courtiers, unless it was a matter of principle whether these matters should be discussed at all. Throckmorton complained that freedom of speech in parliament meant liberty to utter, 'provided all wayes that ye medle neyther with the reformation of religion nor the establishment of succession'. Yet these were 'the verie pillers and grounde workes of all our blisse and happiness, and without the which ... dreadfull despayre will bee the end of our foolishe hope'.[32] Walsingham and Mildmay would not necessarily have disagreed. The world which they contemplated

---

[30] Cambridge University Library, MS Mm.i.51 (Baker 40), fos. 55-69. Neale's account of the Morrice affair is in the second volume of his *Elizabeth I and her Parliaments*, pp. 267-79. On Knollys, see J. Cargill Thompson, 'Sir Francis Knollys's Campaign against the *Jure Divino* Theory of Episcopacy', in his *Studies in the Reformation: Luther to Hooker*, ed. C.W. Dugmore (1980), pp. 94-130.

[31] Pierpont Morgan Lib., MS MA 276 (Phillipps MS 13891), p. 14.

[32] Ibid., p. 13.

was the same world as seen by Throckmorton, or Davison, or Norton, or Beale. But there were significant differences of a pragmatic order, differences of judgment. Beyond a certain line drawn across the affairs of the time, a line of prudence, reticence and self-preservation, men of business became something else. The pillars of the regime were careful never, or almost never, to cross it, but may have been content to see men with a lighter baggage of public responsibility live dangerously on their behalfs.

III

Men of business were learned and articulate, inhabiting the second tier of Elizabethan public life, as it were the political yeomanry. Professor Graves is right to see these figures as typically subordinate rather than insubordinate. Thomas Norton even applied to himself the somewhat pejorative adjective 'obsequious' to describe the services which he had rendered in the 1581 parliament, although his political value consisted in the fact that he was not so obviously obsequious as those who were notoriously known to speak for the court interest.[33] It is also correct to see such men of business as the key to top-down management of the Elizabethan House of Commons, rendering the physical presence of privy councillors if not redundant then less essential to efficient control of the House than Wallace Notestein supposed.[34] However, we must not allow the 'man of business' image to diminish those to whom it has been applied, diminish them that is to say as active politicians and strategists. For one thing they were for the most part experienced, informed men, esteemed as an important intellectual resource of government and looked to not only for information, historical, legal or diplomatic, but also for ideas, in the way that modern governments set up and operate more or less informal 'think tanks'.

So the relationship was upward as well as downward in direction, especially as reflected in the many white papers or 'devices' composed by Thomas Norton or Robert Beale or, to mention another name, the mathematician and engineer Thomas Digges, who was generous with his advice at the height of the Elizabethan Exclusion Crisis, in 1584.[35] Our men of business were also activists as well as intellectuals, freelances whose relatively loose and informal connexions with government enabled them to

[33] In one of his prison letters to Sir Francis Walsingham, Norton wrote: 'Such gracious persons to entreate for my relefe are your selfe, Mr Vicechamberlaine, Mr Chancellor and Sir Thomas Heaneage, that have knowne my obsequiousness and diligence in parliament' (BL, MS Add. 48023, fol. 42 v). On the importance of men of business avoiding a too obviously obsequious, courtly role in the Commons, see Graves, 'Management of the Elizabethan House of Commons', pp. 18-19.

[34] A significant contribution to our understanding of this important fact of parliamentary life was made by Nicholas Tyacke in 'Wroth, Cecil and the Parliamentary Session of 1604', *Bulletin of the Institute of Historical Research*, 50 (1977).

[35] See 'The Monarchical Republic of Queen Elizabeth I', above, pp. 51-3.

utter and act on issues more liberally and forcefully than their patrons. They also seem to have been workaholics, proud and confident of their industry and accomplishments. So it was that Norton boasted of the prodigious quantities of parliamentary bills which he had drafted and as a leading figure in the affairs of London listed the white papers he had written on such social topics as plague, overcrowding, the pressure on debtors' prisons and (Burghley's pet project) the promotion of fisheries.[36] After he was dead his old colleague Fleetwood complained in the next Parliament that he had never seen bills 'so illiterally drawne'.[37] In the early '80s Thomas Digges's advice on political matters was delivered from Dover where he was overseer of an ambitious project to improve the harbour which, or so he said, he alone understood. In parliament he was notorious for speaking last in debate, and decisively, remarking 'every matter must have an end.'[38] Beale's political and diplomatic experience had involved him in face to face negotiations with crowned heads, including Queen Elizabeth, whom he once encountered indisposed and told that headache or no headache she must attend to some exceptionally urgent business that very night. Such dealings reinforced Beale's contempt for his arch-enemy, Archbishop Whitgift. He had spoken with many at home and abroad 'far greater personages than his lordship is'. Taking his place at the council board, not as its servant but as an acting councillor in Walsingham's absence, Beale was immediately noted for being 'overbold in speaking', casting out heated words about 'papists, Gods and her Majesty's mortall enemies'.[39] George Carleton, another name and another author of position papers on the safety of the realm, was an active industrialist and a pioneer of fen drainage, 'one of the very first that inned any marsh in Holland' (Lincolnshire). Carleton told critics of his 'innovations': 'The term innovation is not understood of all that use it. For a thinge of experience is no innovation.' The same decisiveness was applied to religion and politics. A paper composed for Burghley's eye began: 'Eche man of us ought to be stirred carefully to weyghe the state wherein this realme of England nowe standeth.'[40]

[36] 'Further Particulars of Thomas Norton, and of State Proceedings in Matters of Religion, in the Years 1581 and 1582', ed. W.D. Cooper, *Archaeologia*, 36 (1855), pp. 109-15 (from PRO, S.P. 12/148/37, where the document is headed: 'Mr Nortons defence against Hamptons false report'); BL, MS Add. 48023, fos. 28-31. And see Graves, 'Thomas Norton the Parliament Man'.

[37] BL, MS Lansdowne 43, fol. 173 (anonymous journal).

[38] Collinson, 'Monarchical Republic of Queen Elizabeth I', and many items in the PRO, S.P. 12/152; P.W. Hasler, *The House of Commons, 1558-1603*, 3 vols. (1981) [hereafter cited as *HP 1558-1603*], ii, pp. 37-9; BL, MS Lansdowne 43, fol. 169.

[39] PRO, S.P. 12/164/34, Beale to Sir Francis Walsingham, 17 Dec. 1583; BL, MS Add. 48039, fos. 53 r, 55 v, 42-5; MS Lansdowne 42, no. 80, fos. 177-8.

[40] *HP 1558-1603*, i, pp. 552-4. Carleton's memorandum is endorsed by Burghley: 'Sent from Tho[mas] Cecill to me, wrytten by Mr Carleton concerning a power of M [a thousand] and iiM [two thousand] cullyvers; to suffer the precise sort to inhabit Ireland' (PRO, S.P. 15/21/121).

So these and other men of business have to be seen as part of the dynamic machinery of government, as decision makers and policy formers, not as passive tools or instruments. Many of them were in serious trouble at least once in their careers, and usually for reasons that had to do with religion and conscience. We have already had occasion to notice the temporary disgrace in 1593 of James Morrice, which he shared not only with Peter Wentworth and his fellow conspirators in the matter of the succession but with Beale who, as we shall see, was placed under house arrest in the course of this same session. Beale was in no doubt that his troubles had much to do with the part which he had played in bringing Mary queen of Scots to the block, a fate shared with William Davison who had obtained the signature on the warrant which Beale then took to Fotheringhay; 'sithe which time,' Beale wrote, 'I have neither had anie credit or countenance'.[41] Even William Fleetwood, the recorder of London, was subjected to the supreme indignity of imprisonment in one of his own lock-ups for the presumption of leading an over-enthusiastic raid on the Portuguese embassy, designed to secure the arrest of the Englishmen illegally attending mass in the ambassador's chapel. From the Fleet Prison he wrote: 'This is a place wherein a man may quietlie be acquainted with God.'[42]

IV

If we now look more closely at the difficulties experienced by two other men of business, Norton and Beale, we shall discover tensions, even contradictions, and much evidence that a kind of religious zeal not easily distinguishable from Puritanism, interacting with changing circumstances, was capable of turning such forward men into froward men, at least temporarily.

Thomas Norton was to London what Cecil was to all England, its principal secretary and the guarantor of administrative continuity. But he was also co-author of that daring early Elizabethan succession play *Gorboduc* (written and staged before such activities became too dangerous) and the translator of Calvin's *Institutes*. In Professor Graves's accounts of Norton so far published he is far from misrepresented but the intensity of his politico-religious passion as an aroused Protestant is understated.[43] However, Graves and Elton are justified in suggesting that it is not very appropriate to stick the Puritan label on Norton. Quite apart from his oft-

[41] 'Robert Beale's Apology Relating to Proceedings in Parliament', versions in BL, MS Lansdowne 73, fos. 4-13; MS Add. 48064, fos. 106-15.

[42] BL, MS Lansdowne 23, nos. 53-8, including no. 54, Fleetwood to Burghley, 'ex Fleta', 9 Nov. 1576.

[43] Graves, 'Thomas Norton the Parliament Man' and 'Management of the Elizabethan House of Commons'. Professor Graves is currently engaged on a fuller study of Norton.

repeated insistence that he was content with the existing religious settlement, if duly and rigorously enforced, and his criticism of the *Admonition to the Parliament* ('surely the book was fond'),[44] no Puritan could have commended Dr Andrew Perne of Peterhouse, that notorious turncoat, as Norton commended him, singling him out as easily the most competent head of house in either university.[45] Nevertheless Norton's instinct was to blame the troubles of the nonconforming clergy not on themselves but on the narrow rigour with which conformity had been imposed upon them, which is how we should read a remark about the 'maledicta questionis vestiaria' which Professor Elton thinks proves that Norton was 'not a puritan of any sort'.[46]

For much of the time, as Graves has demonstrated, Norton performed an invaluable semi-public role as middleman between the privy council and the government of the city. In parliament he was both an overworked draftsman of bills and an alert monitor of the progress of government business. As such he represents the model man of business and Professor Graves is entitled to call him 'an "establishment man" with friends in high places'. But a few months after the parliamentary session of 1581, as it happens his last, Norton transgressed in some respect, not clearly defined in the extant documents but evidently a matter of grave offence, which placed him where his friends were unable to help him: not only in the Tower of London but confined to that most discouraging of all addresses,

[44] Collinson, *Elizabethan Puritan Movement*, p. 121.

[45] In his 'Devices' (see n. 60 below for references), Norton wrote that there was 'not a better Master for the helping of his house, the avancement of learning, and the cherishing of toward studentes, and specially in divinitie and true religion than Dr Perne'. At the time of the queen's visit to the university, Edmund Grindal, then bishop of London, had begged Cecil that no public honour be paid to Perne, 'his apostacy being so notorious'. (Collinson, *Archbishop Grindal*, p. 117.) Among the 'toward students', cherished by Perne was the young John Whitgift, whom Norton had attempted to discourage from answering *An Admonition to the Parliament*.

[46] *Parl. of England*, p. 353. Professor Elton dates the 'Devices' in which these remarks occur from the early seventies, whereas they were in fact composed in the Tower in the winter of 1581-2. The context of Norton's comment on the Vestments Controversy, which immediately follows his commendation of Perne, was an equally fulsome tribute to Thomas Sampson, some time dean of Christ Church, as the most businesslike of all heads of houses, until his deprivation for nonconformity in 1566: 'I have heard that he found the house poore and in dett, he left it out of dett and riche in treasure aforehand, and he bountifully mainteined learning. As Bucer was wont to say of Germanie, *O maledictam questionem sacramentariam*, so say I of England, *O maledictam questionem vestiariam*.' The sentiment is very Bucerian (not to say Grindalian) and in the spirit of the German reformer's advice to Bishop John Hooper in the original vestiarian controversy of 1550; See Collinson, *Archbishop Grindal*, pp. 54-6, and my 'The Reformer and the Archbishop: Martin Bucer and an English Bucerian', in my *Godly People: Essays on English Protestantism and Puritanism* (1983), pp. 19-44. Cf. a comment of Robert Beale: 'This controversie of indifferent thinges of late yeres began in Germanye [Beale must mean Frankfort, in Mary's reign] and hathe ben occacion of muche harme', BL, MS Add. 48039, fol. 55 r. The positions here adopted by Norton and Beale were not 'Puritan'. But they were critical of those pertinacious conformists who opposed 'Puritans', and who (in their judgment) bore the major responsibility for the fact that 'Puritanism' existed.

the Bloody Tower.[47]

One cause of Norton's disgrace may have been certain caustic remarks made against the bishops at a dinner party held to celebrate the breaking up of the Parliament.[48] But although these words were exploited against him and had to be explained and defended they can hardly account for the severity of his treatment. It is not likely that John Whitgift, still only bishop of the minor see of Worcester, would have had the clout to do such a thing to a man with Norton's connexions, while Bishop Aylmer of London, whom Norton seems to have admired in some respects, could only have damaged him through Sir Christopher Hatton who, as Professor Elton has shown, was one of Norton's closest and most friendly patrons.[49] The mystery would remain unresolved but for a surviving letter from Roger Manners to his father, the earl of Rutland, reporting that the real reason for Norton's committal had been 'his overmuch and undutiful speaking touching this [Monsieur's] cause':[50] which is as much as to say that Norton had spoken out against the Anjou marriage which, at about the same time, cost John Stubbs his right hand for writing *The Gaping Gulf,* that most emotive symbol of the loyally outraged conscience of the Elizabethan Protestant, patriot and publicist.

Like other prisoners of conscience, Norton in the Tower was conscious of writing in the words of the Psalmist, *de profundis.* In one of many prison letters he refers,[51] perhaps, to both sets of rash speeches: 'Blind zeale, the mother of arrogance, is the destroyer of fooles.'[52] It was 'blind zeale' which had carried him beyond our critical line and had proved his undoing. In these writings Norton revolves endlessly like some fervent Flying Dutchman of the conscience within the three points of the painful triangle within which he is trapped, or like a moth between three candles. As a relentless opponent of papists, 'Norton the Rackmaster' who was involved in the examination under torture of those considered the most dangerous,[53] Norton's fervently expressed allegiance to the queen was the sheet-anchor

----

[47] A version of Norton's 'Devices' was sent to Walsingham and dated 'in the bloody toure of the toure this 13 of Jan[uary] [1582]' BL, MS Add. 48023, fol. 57 v.

[48] Cooper, ed., 'Further Particulars of Thomas Norton', pp. 109-15.

[49] G.R. Elton, 'Arthur Hall, Lord Burghley and the Antiquity of Parliament', in *Studies,* iii, p. 262. Norton commented favourably in his 'Devices' on the religious state of London and on his own representations to Aylmer to increase the preaching ministry in the city: 'But here is the least lack where is the most labor. London is a true knott of true subiectes.' (BL, MS Add. 48023, fol. 43 r.)

[50] HMC., *Rutland MSS,* i, p. 130.

[51] BL, MS Add. 48023 (Yelverton 26), fos. 26 v-58 r.

[52] Ibid., fol. 33 v.

[53] In a letter to Walsingham dated by Walsingham's secretary 27 Mar. 1582 and written from his 'home prison' in the Guildhall, to which he had been released from the Tower, Norton defended himself against the stigma of 'Mr Norton the Rackmaster': 'For my part I was never the Rackmaister but the meanest of all that were in commission and as it were clerk unto them, and the doing was by the handes only of the quenes servauntes, and by Mr Lieutenant [of the Tower] only direction for muche or litle' (PRO, S.P. 12/152/72).

of his existence: 'Lord, how I wonder at my selfe that I shold offend my Queen Elizabeth! and therefore no marvel though all the world wonder at me, that wonder at my self.' 'Whatsoever myne overboldnesse hath ben used in other cases and toward other persones, yet now when God and iustice hath made her Majestie my adverse partie, I neither have nor seeke to have other course than to lye downe under her foote and to crepe into the lowest depths of deiection, hell only excepted.'[54] As this implies, the second point of the triangle was in tension with the first. It was the higher loyalty owed to God and his cause, and to the lodestar of his own conscience, which conditioned his allegiance and had impelled him into 'overmuch and undutifully speaking', like Beale at the council board. That higher loyalty is inferred in these words written to his thirteen-year-old son: 'I have no dealing with the queen but as with the image of God'.[55] At first glance that sentiment looks absolutist, but on second thought is seen to be anything but. Norton was perhaps haunted by a possibility too fearful to commit to paper, a ghost well known to a later generation, the subjects of Charles I. This was the prospect of a divorce between that pair whom Norton calls 'my soverayne lord and ladye, God and the Queen'.[56]

The third point of Norton's triangle provides an elusive clue to some of the more covert roles performed from time to time by the council's men of business. From the partly encoded messages of the prison letters it appears possible that Norton found himself where he was less as the penalty of his own zeal and folly than as the consequence of shouldering burdens for men more powerful than himself but less free to utter, and to whom he now looked for rescue. His hopes were placed ultimately in the lord treasurer, Burghley, 'the only man in whome I have and do lay the course of my relefe',[57] and who alone seems to have had the power to get him out of the Tower. But, as he told his wife, if Sir Walter Mildmay could be told of his situation through Mildmay's daughter Fitzwilliam, who happened to be Mrs Norton's gossip, doubtless he would help. For Mildmay knew 'how there were layed upon me a number of burdens the last parlament in service'. Mildmay might also recall how Norton had tried to avoid some of these commissions, fearing precisely what had since happened, 'a note of too busy a witt … encreased against me'. To Burghley he wrote: 'Mr

[54] BL, MS Add. 48023, fos. 49, 26 v.

[55] Ibid., fol. 33 r. To William Fleetwood, Norton wrote: 'When all is sayd and done, this is true, that God sent us our Quene with his blessing, it is the onely religion of God that knitteth true subiectes unto her. She hath no iust feare but the feare of God' (ibid., fol. 33 v). This looks like a conditional obedience but it was less obviously conditional (in Norton's perception) than that of the papists, 'false subiectes', who yielded 'a temporarie obedience, dissoluble at the pope's pleasure' (ibid., fol. 43 r).

[56] BL, MS Add. 15891, fos. 81 v-2 v. Cf. Norton to Walsingham, n.d.: 'London is a strong knott of true subiectes to their soveraines bothe, lord and ladie, God and her Majestie' (BL, MS Add. 48023, fol. 43 r).

[57] S.P. 12/152/72, Norton to Walsingham, 27 Mar. 1582.

Chauncellor [Mildmay] knoweth what burdens of labor in the last parlament I did beare at his and Mr Vicechamberlain's [Hatton's] commandment, in hope and zele to please her Majestie.' And to his London colleague, Recorder Fleetwood: 'And yet you knowe I toke a course in policie, but not plainly, to advance that which the queen's most noble counsellors advised.'[58]

While Norton waited for release to the easier conditions of house arrest in his office behind the Guildhall, Secretary Walsingham continued to use him, and surely to abuse him, as a one-man think tank, asking him to prepare white papers on such subjects as 'the stay of the present corruption in religion',[59] which meant the more effective repression of popery in educational and other public institutions: out of which came the small treatise known as 'Mr Norton's Devices' which was held by both Walsingham and Burghley.[60] That was scarcely finished when Walsingham asked him to make a digest of all the more salient points of English political history since the Conquest, while not responding to requests for the books without which such a daunting task could not even be attempted. No wonder Norton compared himself to 'an old blinde iade fast tyed and still going round in a horsemill'.[61]

What those 'burdens' were in the 1581 parliament is not specified, and it is not clear that they contributed directly to Norton's subsequent disgrace. They may have concerned the anti-Catholic legislation of that session, which the queen intervened to moderate, or Bishop Whitgift's unsatisfactory response to the demand for further church reform, which prompted Norton's supper party tirade; or, just conceivably, 'Monsieur', which might explain Burghley's inability, or even reluctance, to help. But whichever of these particular but related causes may have been uppermost, it is possible that Norton's vigilant Protestant conscience had been used by Mildmay, and perhaps by Hatton, Sir Thomas Heneage and Walsingham himself (and, in the background, the earl of Leicester?) to extract certain hot chestnuts from the fire at a critically dangerous time when the future of the Protestant ascendancy seemed desperately insecure. For such purposes Norton was indispensable: but later he was dispensable, for 'all the world foloweth the preiudice of her Majesties displeasure'.[62] Hence his wounded agony of spirit. 'My eyes be so dymmed with weping that I can ill see by a tallow light.'[63] Poor Norton! While he was in prison his wife fell into

[58]   BL, MS Add. 48023, fos. 27 v, 43 v, 33 r.

[59]   Ibid., fol. 41.

[60]   Drafts of the 'Devices', sent to Walsingham piecemeal, as they were completed, are in BL, MS Add. 48023, fos. 45-8, 49 v-51, 51 v-2 v, 53 v-6 v, 57 r. Copies of the finished article are in PRO, S.P. 12/177/59, fos. 143-70 and BL, MS Lansdowne 155, fos. 87ff.

[61]   BL, MS Add. 48023, fos. 44 v, 48, 56 v.

[62]   PRO., S.P. 12/153/6, Norton to Walsingham, 6 Apr. 1582.

[63]   BL, MS Add. 48023, fol. 27 v.

an incurable melancholy connected with the menopause from which even that notable spiritual physician John Foxe was unable to release her. [64] And within two years of his release he himself was dead. But before the end there was a coda to his career in which he was once again busy with a hundred things on behalf of the government and the city, examining Catholic suspects, discoursing on policy, making arrangements for the Russian ambassador. [65]

V

Norton's Tower correspondence is preserved, I think significantly, among the papers of that other man of business with an overactive conscience, Robert Beale (British Library, Yelverton Manuscripts). And since Beale outlived Norton by more than twenty years his conscience became more thickly entangled with the changing ecclesiastical politics of the 1580s, of which Norton at the supper table had only an inkling. These were the politics of Whitgift who, in the six years of Archbishop Grindal's disgrace from 1577 to 1583, began to emerge as the hand-picked general in a merciless war against the forward but often froward preaching ministry. [66] The timing of this onslaught, to which the queen was personally committed, could not have been more unfortunate, in the perception of the Protestant political nation. For it coincided with ever-growing threats to the safety of the queen and the realm, threats connected not with the little local difficulty of Puritanism but with the global menace of international popery, and so provoking the penal anti-Catholic legislation of 1581, the Bond of Association and the Act for the Queen's Safety of 1584. Religion was consequently an issue which enjoyed a cumulative momentum through the parliaments of 1576, 1581 and 1584, although this is necessarily obscured in Professor Elton's book by his choice of 1581 as a terminal date.

1576 represented a change of strategy on the part of those who wanted to improve the Elizabethan settlement of religion. In place of the abortive bills of earlier sessions there was now to be an orderly process of polite petitioning, asking the queen to secure action by the bishops to remedy sundry abuses in the ministry and to improve church discipline, matters which were not wholly contentious. Elton suggests that this more sensible course proved successful. 'She conferred with the bishops and secured the passage of reforming canons in Convocation.'[67] These were the hopeful years of Archbishop Grindal when many hoped that 'civil wars of the

---

[64] PRO, S.P. 12/152/72, 153/6, Norton to Walsingham, 27 Mar., 6 Apr. 1582.
[65] PRO, S.P. 12/158/20, 37; 164/32, 45.
[66] The fullest account is in my *Elizabethan Puritan Movement*, pp. 243-88.
[67] *Parl. of England*, p. 216.

Church of God' were a thing of the past.[68] The parliamentary implications of this truce were that the initiative of 1576 was mounted by the two Members who had supported Strickland's manifestly Puritan attempt to proceed by bill in 1571 and the further attempt to alter the terms of the Act of Uniformity made in 1572: Tristram Pistor and Robert Snagge. But now both the tone and the mode were studiously moderate and all the privy councillors in the House were appointed to the committee which drafted the petition to the Queen, while six councillors drawn from the House presented it. But the sequel in the form of the Canons of 1576 was a grave disappointment. Even Mildmay described the Canons as 'little or nothing to the purpose'.[69]

So the Commons had another go in 1581, in a comprehensive petition of many articles, with the privy councillors in the lower House, including Walsingham and Mildmay, again actively involved. But by now Grindal was in limbo and the Church of England was in commission to the archbishop of York, Sandys, the bishop of London, Aylmer, and Whitgift, bishop of Worcester. At least two of these three prelates were unsympathetic and one, Whitgift, proved downright hostile. He worried some of the Commons by the stateliness of his arrival at Westminster and soon by the evident contempt with which he responded to their great petition, dealing with Members of Parliament as he would soon deal, as archbishop, with nonconformist preachers, as if they were 'malaperts'. Robert Beale later reminded Burghley:

> No man can better remember what requests have been from time to time made by the Commons, which represent many millions of her Majesty's subjects. Her Majesty once promised her poor Commons that such abuses should be reformed, and commanded the bishops to see it done. But your lordships can I think remember what angry words the then bishop of Worcester used to your lordship and Sir Walter Mildmay. I have not forgotten what that honourable councillor then reported.

Addressing Whitgift himself, Beale wrote: 'Your lordship … chardged the whole House with such malapertness as though it became them not to deale with their betters, when as indeed nothing was spoken undecentlie or uncomely as was then answered by some honourable persons of the House.' Norton testified to the same effect: 'The whole House … did impute the default to the bishops.'[70] Norton, who was married first to a daughter and then to a niece of Archbishop Cranmer, was no Presbyterian enemy of bishops as such. But who can doubt that if he had lived another ten years he would have found it impossible to remain their friend? As for Mildmay, his main concern was now to prevent the harm which the queen and the

[68] Collinson, *Archbishop Grindal*, pp. 219-32.
[69] Neale I, pp. 349-52; Collinson, *Elizabethan Puritan Movement*, p. 163.
[70] Ibid., pp. 205-6; BL, MS Add. 48039, fol. 42; Neale I, pp. 398-405.

Commons were capable of doing to each other and if this meant throwing the bishops to the wolves, too bad for the bishops. The earl of Leicester was evidently of the same mind and would soon take sides with the Commons against Whitgift as archbishop in open debate in the House of Lords.[71] This was emphatically not an issue which divided the Houses, any more than Mary queen of Scots had separated the lords spiritual and temporal from the Commons in 1572.

Such was the background to 1584. The queen's promise to instruct the bishops to reform the church still stood, had not been forgotten. But equally it had yet to be honoured. Politically it was impossible to reproach the queen. But in his first year as metropolitan, Whitgift proceeded to silence and suspend hundreds of preachers for refusing subscription to articles which in the opinion of some lawyers, Beale included, were of dubious legality. What kind of response was that to the promises of 1576 and 1581? As information accumulated from the country of pastoral neglect, now compounded by the wholesale suspension of godly preachers, the Commons, again with Mildmay's prominent participation, pursued their concern, 'the grief of the whole realm', as they had done in 1581, through a grand petition of sixteen articles and an attempt at conference with the Lords: only to encounter inexplicable delays, and two months later, another disparaging brush-off from Whitgift, who pulled seniority as well as rank and spoke of Parliament-men who were still in their swaddling clothes when he was already a preacher. One insulted committee man spoke of 'the cardnall and metropoliticall answer' and Beale complained that there was 'nether law of God nor man, learning nor wit in the answer'. These remarks were carefully noted by Whitgift. In later years Beale recalled that 'in all the histories and records of time past, never any prince or subject gave such an insufficient and opprobious answer'. When Mildmay and others of the committee reported back 'the House was nothinge satisfyed'. It was a committee which included Mildmay and Knollys which responded by calling the legality of the bishops' recent actions in question, while not forgetting to remind them that their particular identities as individuals were not relevant. They were representatives, speaking on behalf of 'all the Commons of the realm in general'.[72]

But at this point a scenario soon to be all too familiar was enacted. The Speaker was summoned to court and the next day transmitted a peremptory royal command to meddle no further with these matters. A special reprimand was served for those privy councillors (Mildmay must have been meant especially) who had failed to restrain the House. Some of them had been present in the privy chamber a day or two before when Elizabeth had remarked, in the hearing of the bishops and for their benefit, that if her

[71] Neale II, p. 81.
[72] Ibid., pp. 58-66, 71-3; BL, MS Add. 40629, fol. 36; PRO, S.P. 12/175/51.

councillors continued to support the insubordination of the Commons she would 'uncounsel some of them'.[73] The Fitzwilliam diary tells how the House by this message found itself 'so greatlie moved and so deeplye wounded' that it fell into private meetings 'to devise how they might salve this sore'.[74] The sequel was a new attempt to proceed by legislation, including some pointedly anti-episcopal legislation, a procedure which only one member of the House openly opposed. His speech was not 'particularlie confuted' but it met with 'a generall voyce thorowe the House' to have one of these bills read: not with any expectation that it would reach the statute book but in order to strike a defiant posture. In this there was some of the awesome magnificence of the Charge of the Light Brigade.[75]

All this has been told before, by Neale.[76] However, it proves to be necessary to remind ourselves that these things happened. How can one disagree with Neale's judgment that in these later stages of the 1584 parliament the Commons were 'out of control'? Privy councillors could only exercise a measure of control at the cost of being more than half out of control themselves. Even the earl of Leicester was less concerned for the dignity of his colleague in the Lords, the archbishop, than with the danger that Whitgift could poison the reputation of the Commons in the estimation of the Queen, and vice versa. This mood of 1584 carried over into the next session of 1586-7, not yet satisfied, not yet defused, a powerful enough beast to carry on its back the almost unbelievably fond and froward Bill and Book.[77] 'Yf I were asked' said Job Throckmorton in a speech ostensibly addressed to the Bill and Book, 'what is the bane of the church and common wealth, awnswere make, *The dombe ministerie, The dombe ministerye:* yea, yf I were asked a thowsande times, I must say, *The dombe ministerye.*'[78]

Throckmorton was an extreme Puritan, a Presbyterian: no doubt about that. But to ask whether others in the House who were content to hear him out, perhaps even to cheer him on, were Puritans or merely outraged and frustrated Protestants is to ask a fairly meaningless question. Yet in the person of Robert Beale it is possible to trace in voluminous detail a process of progressive radicalisation, as he engaged in noisy wrangles with Whitgift, face to face in his gallery at Lambeth, on paper, in parliament.[79] His papers, in the Yelverton collection in the British Library,[80] show that he collected and annotated petitions and accounts of the troubles of individual Puritans

[73] PRO, S.P. 12/176/88.

[74] Northamptonshire R.O., Fitzwilliam of Milton Papers 2, fol. 33 v.

[75] Ibid., fos. 33 v-5 r.

[76] Neale II, pp. 72-83.

[77] Ibid., pp. 148-65; Collinson, *Elizabethan Puritan Movement*, pp. 303-16.

[78] Pierpont Morgan Lib., MS MA 276 (Phillipps MS 13891), p. 20.

[79] Collinson, *Elizabethan Puritan Movement*, pp. 255-6, 258, 259, 270-1.

[80] Of particular interest in this connexion are many of the items in Yelverton 44 (BL, MS Add. 48039) and Yelverton 70 (MS Add. 48064).

not casually but with the intention of causing embarrassment to particularly unpopular bishops such as Cooper of Winchester or Aylmer of London. The contents of BL MS Add. 48064 (Yelverton 70), in their somewhat chaotic integrity, tell their own story, particularly the headings and endorsements in Beale's thick, vigorous hand: 'offred to the Parlament 27 Eliz.', on a petition from someone complaining of hard dealings by bishop Overton of Coventry and Lichfield; '1588 in Parlament'; 'Norff[olk]'; 'Farneham' (allegations of appalling neglect by Bishop Cooper whose stately castle overshadowed the town); 'Deprivation of Mr Hopkins chaplen to the E[arl] of Essex', 'Mr Hubbock' – this written on a paper describing the sequel to a provocative sermon preached in Oxford, 'wherefore the author is still in trouble'.[81]

Like some Captain Ahab in pursuit of his own great white whale, Beale's purpose, indeed obsession, sustained with massive if perverse learning, was to prove that the ecclesiastical establishment was proceeding in causes ecclesiastical contrary to the Act for the Submission of the Clergy and in general defiance of the 'charters, lawes and liberties of this realme'. He intended his major contribution to the 1584 parliament to be a speech to this effect 40,000 words long, which, if uttered, would have run for four or five hours. There is no evidence that this oration of heroically Soviet proportions was in fact delivered and Neale calls it a 'treatise'. [82] Yet in form it is a speech and at its foot Beale has written in his own inimitable handwriting words from Psalm 40: 'I have declared thy righteousness in the great congregation. Lo I will not restraine my lipps, O lord thou knoweth yt.'[83]

When his enemies caught up with him in the midst of the 1593 parliament and secured his exclusion from both court and Commons and a period of house arrest,[84] there were a number of offences which they were able to exploit, including Beale's apparent unhelpfulness in transactions over the subsidy bill of that session. Yet Beale himself was in no doubt that the prime cause of his restraint was the image he enjoyed of a 'plotter of a new ecclesiastical government'. He strenuously denied that he was any such thing. If it could be shown that he had ever assented to any 'newe plott of reformacion' he would be gladly strung up at the gates of the court.[85] Well,

[81] BL, MS Add. 48064, fos. 42 v-3 v, 48, 212-14 r, 72-4, 90, 148.

[82] Neale II, pp. 66-8.

[83] BL, MS Add. 48116 (Yelverton 131), fos. 154-211.

[84] Neale reported 'a mystery' surrounding Beale and his troubles in the 1593 parliament. The mystery is dispelled by a letter from Richard West to William Pitt, dated 16 Mar. 1592[/3]: 'Newes we have none, for I talked with Thomas, and whatsoever you perchance may here beleve yt not for they are but fables unles yt be the comytting of some of parliament house to durance [=house arrest]. Sir H[enry] Bromley and his fellow knight of the shire of Worcester, Mr Morys of the Wardes and Mr Beale clarke of the Councell' (BL, MS Add. 22924, fol. 69. I owe this reference to Mrs Sybil Jack).

[85] Robert Beale's Apology, copies in BL, MS Lansdowne 73, fos. 4-13 (original) and MS Add. 48064, fos. 106-15 (draft), both emended in Beale's hand.

perhaps. But Beale's detestation of the bishops was now an unbreakable habit ('I would to God her Majestie understoode all their doinges') and he had busied himself with the legal defence of Thomas Cartwright and other ministers tried in the Star Chamber for experimenting with the shadow of a Presbyterian constitution for the Church of England.[86]

Yet for Burghley this same Beale was still above all an invaluable man of business and for him too there was the horsemill. Two years after his disgrace the lord treasurer put to him a string of historical and contemporary questions, writing in his own hand as 'your assured lovyng frend': 'Mr Beale I am bold because I know that yow can satisfye in sondry thyngys ......' 'Mr Beale I hartely thank you for your tardy answers to my questions, perswading with my self that few or non others cold so amply answer the same.'[87]

So far the plan has been to engage with the concept and argument of serviceable men of business with which Neale's critics have proposed to replace the category of Puritan troublemakers in the annals of the Elizabethan parliaments. A rather different approach would have come more directly at Neale's demythologisers by reasserting the evidence from the high Elizabethan parliaments for a coherent and even concerted attack on religion and its concomitant issues, an attack which was nothing if not political. The evidence is not so much in the so-called 'choir' described in the satire of 1566 known as the 'Lewd Pasquil'. I do not think that Neale ever intended to invest this curious lampoon with great evidential rather than illustrative value: and what it seems to have illustrated for him was a certain significant self-consciousness on the part of the House of Commons and in respect of some of its more notorious worthies: as it were a set of Elizabethan 'Spy' caricatures. Nor did he suppose it to be an exclusive list of the card-carrying faithful. It sang, he remarked, not in unison but only with a 'predominantly' Puritan voice. Neale can be censured for making excessive and rhetorically reiterative use of this somewhat marginal document. On the other hand his critics never cease to ram it down our throats.[88]

The real evidence for a concerted attempt to protect and advance the godly cause and to protect it by advancing it, if necessary by froward means, is to be found in the role played by Tristram Pistor and Robert Snagge, in

---

[86] Collinson, *Elizabethan Puritan Movement*, pp. 414-15, 421-3, 427.

[87] BL, MS Add. 48101 (Yelverton 110), fos. 303, 328. Beale's answers, of prodigious legal, historical and political learning, intervene, fos. 304-26.

[88] 'A lewd pasquil set forth by certain of the parliament men' is preserved in Cambridge University Library, MS Ff. v.14. See Neale I, pp. 91-2 and critical remarks of Elton, *Parl. of England*, pp. 350-4 and in 'Parliament in the Sixteenth Century', in *Studies*, iii, pp. 175-6. Elton has ingeniously suggested that the names on the list constituted the membership of the committee appointed on 19 Oct. 1566 to deal with the Lords over the succession. Apart from the privy councillors in the House, the committee had forty-four members. Although the identities of the forty-four are unknown, it may be significant that the 'Lewd Pasquil' contains forty-three names and implies a forty-fourth: the author of the libel.

1571, 1572 and 1576;[89] in the precious testimony of Peter Wentworth towards the end of his stormy petrel of a career that he had been 'first stirred up to deal' in the succession question as early as 1562 'by sundry grave and wise menn unknowne unto mee, and allso by lamentable messages sent unto mee by men likewise unknowne unto mee' (the reiterated 'men unknown unto mee' sounds like the opening bars of a modern style of politics); and also in Wentworth's own electoral activities thirty years later, travelling into 'divers places ... to procure such burgesses as might further the same cause'.[90] The evidence is in 'Observacions for the tyme', a paper, probably dating from 1584, and filed by that exemplary godly magistrate Edward Lewkenor of Denham, Suffolk, which opens: 'Men must endevor to know one another, that in matters of waight which have apparance of daunger many men show the like forwardnes and courage, that so some few be not singled out for the terror of the rest. And this will keape the honor and dignity of the House.'[91] This was perhaps the hidden agenda behind the motion of a fast on the first day of the 1581 parliament, that men might 'endevor to know one another'.[92]

The evidence is to be found in some of the elections and returns of the 1580s such as that for Christchurch, Hampshire, in 1584, when the electors having chosen one of the two nominees of their lord, the earl of Huntingdon (Professor Cross's 'Puritan Earl'), proceeded to reject Secretary Walsingham's choice for the second seat in favour of another of Huntingdon's clients, 'a gentleman zealous in religion';[93] and for Buckinghamshire in 1586, when Francis Goodwin's godliness ('wise, honest and sound in religion') and the fact that he was the son-in-law of that godly if somewhat violent peer Lord Grey, compensated for his extreme youth.[94] Warwick in that same year was

[89] Neale I, pp. 199-200, 299, 349-50. Pistor and Snagge supported Strickland's motion in 1571 and the Puritan-inspired bill concerning rites and ceremonies in 1572. In 1576 they were in the forefront of the altered tactic, to proceed towards religious reform by petition rather than by bill. Their names were always linked, with each other and with other would-be religious reformers in the House such as Peter Wentworth, George Carleton and Edward Lewkenor. Elton makes no mention of either in these connexions and merely remarks that in 1571 'two members offered Strickland some very hesitant support' (*Parl. of England*, p. 209).

[90] Neale, 'Peter Wentworth', in Fryde and Miller, ed., *Historical Studies*, ii, p. 247; BL, MS Harley 7042, fol. 189.

[91] BL, MS Add. 38492, fol. 42. For Lewkenor, see my 'Magistracy and Ministry: A Suffolk Miniature', in Collinson, *Godly People*, pp. 445-66.

[92] Bishop Godfrey Goodman reported on the parliamentary tactics of a later generation: 'Always the first bill that was proposed was either against papists or the Church, or for the keeping of the Sabbath, only to feel men's pulses, to see how they stood affected', *The Court of King James the First, by Godfrey Goodman*, ed. J.S. Brewer, 2 vols (1839), i, p. 86.

[93] *HP 1558-1603*, i, pp. 168-9; PRO, S.P. 12/173/89, mayor of Christchurch to Walsingham, 21 Oct. 1584.

[94] Huntington Library, Stowe MSS, Temple corresp., STT 1651. Goodwin was twenty-two when elected to the 1586 Parliament. See *HP 1558-1603*, i, pp. 204-5 and Linda Levy Peck, '*Goodwin* v. *Fortescue*: The Local Context of Parliamentary Controversy', *Parliamentary History*, 3 (1984), pp. 33-56.

constrained against its better judgment by a combination of popular and aristocratic pressures to return a Member with three hot speeches in his belly, Job Throckmorton. The shrewd oligarchs of the town correctly judged their man when they accused him of not so much wanting to be their burgess as to be elected 'for the Parliament where peradventure some freends of yours may have some causes in handeling'.[95]

More evidence exists in the connexions of a member of the Commons so far hardly mentioned, certainly a Puritan, George Carleton, of new North-amptonshire gentry stock (but a great nephew of Queen Catherine Howard's mother), soldier, fenland adventurer, Irish planter, and gaoler to the Jesuits at Wisbech. Anthony Cope of Bill and Book fame was Carleton's stepson and business partner. Another partner was Sir Richard Knightley of Fawsley, under whose Northamptonshire roof some of the Marprelate Tracts which Job Throckmorton probably wrote were printed, after the press had been moved out of the Thames-side house of the widow Elizabeth Crane, whom Carleton at about the time of the Marprelate affair married: and that was not necessarily the full extent of Carleton's connexion with the Marprelate conspiracy. Carleton was the most incorrigible supporter of Paul Wentworth in his fast motion of 1581, defying the Speaker's rebuke and twice offering to move formally on 'the liberty of the House'. His will refers to Peter Wentworth as 'my beloved in the Lord'. Perhaps Carleton was one of those who, thirty years before and then 'unknown' to Wentworth, had first established contact with him across the twenty miles of the enclosed fields of south Northamptonshire which separated his Overston from Wentworth's Lillingston Lovell. For some reason not yet fully ex-plored, still less explained, the clannish gentry of the neighbouring pasture lands of south Northamptonshire, east Warwickshire and north Oxford-shire were marked by a radically political Puritanism, from the days of the Elizabethan prophesyings when Carleton's Overston was notorious for preaching and psalm-singing conducted by unlicensed, running preachers to the ship money decade of the 1630s when John Pym and his friends held a kind of political 'classis' at Fawsley and there was a more overt and political resistance to the king's service than in any other part of England.[96]

Above all the evidence for a Puritan Movement, rather than a 'confusion', is contained in its grassroots documentation: those impressive 'surveys of the ministry' preserved in the manuscript collections known as 'The Seconde Parte of a Register' and the many petitions (one alone, from

95 *The Black Book of Warwick*, ed. T. Kemp (Warwick, 1898), pp. 389-97.

96 *HP 1558-1603*, i, pp. 552-4; W.J. Sheils, *The Puritans in the Diocese of Peterborough, 1558-1610*, Northamptonshire Record Society, 30 (Northampton, 1979), chapter 7; information on Northamp-tonshire and ship money communicated by Dr Alison Gill. See also Ann Hughes, 'Thomas Dugard and his Circle in the 1630s: A "Parliamentary-Puritan" Connexion?', *Historical Journal*, 29 (1986), pp. 771-93; and eadem, *Politics, Society and Civil War in Warwickshire, 1620-1660* (Cambridge, 1987), pp. 64-87.

Dunmow in Essex, bearing no less than 236 names) which are no phantas-
magoria and which deserve more attention than they have received from
historians of emergent populist politics like Professor Derek Hirst.'[97] In
1584 Edward Lewkenor M.P. opened his mail from rural Suffolk and read
this: 'We cease not here in our smale measure to lift up our unworthie eies
and handes toward the god of heaven ... for all necessarie blessing upon
you and the rest of yor worthie yokefellowes.'[98] If this was not some kind
of movement, what was it?

As all serious students of this subject will have noticed, there is little
enough in this essay which cannot be found in print, mainly in Sir John
Neale's books but to a lesser extent what I have written, in *The Elizabethan
Puritan Movement* and elsewhere. Only two of its sources, to the best of my
knowledge, have not previously been cited: Walsingham's comment on
Paul Wentworth's fast motion (Huntington Library) and Hatton's speech
to the 1589 parliament (Folger Shakespeare Library). The furniture is
otherwise perhaps all too familiar. Sir Geoffrey Elton and Professor Graves
have moved it about the room and have removed some of the fancier pieces,
replacing them with plainer, more utilitarian articles. Many of the new
arrangements are acceptable and represent a great improvement. But
some of the original and ornate items of furniture deserve to be dusted
down and restored to positions of honour. But everything must have an
end, as Thomas Digges would have reminded us. The last word will be left
to James Morrice of the Court of Wards who in the midst of his troubles said
to Burghley:

> Billes of assize of bread, shippinge of fyshe, and such like maie be offred and receayved
> into the House and no offence to hir Majesties Royal Commaundement, being but as
> the tithing of mint. But the greate thinges of the lawe and publique Justice maie not be
> tollerated without offence. Well, my good lord, be it so.

I hope that it is not yet the case that historians of these parliaments are to

---

[97] The greatest concentration of this material is in the 'Register' compiled by the London
preacher John Field and others, preserved in Dr Williams's Library, London, and calendared by
Albert Peel in *The Seconde Parte of a Register*, 2 vols. (Cambridge, 1915). (See 'John Field and
Elizabethan Puritanism', in my *Godly People*, pp. 335-70.) The presence of many surveys, petitions
and narratives of 'troubles' in the files of the Suffolk M.P. Edward Lewkenor (BL, MS Add. 38492)
and, as already noted, of the clerk of the council, Robert Beale, BL, MS Add. 48064 (Yelverton 70)
is also most significant. Professor Hirst seems to me to underestimate this evidence in his remarks
in *The Representative of the People? Voters and Voting in England under the Early Stuarts* (Cambridge,
1975), esp. pp. 139-53. The early seventeenth-century scope of Hirst's study may explain the
relatively scant attention paid to popular (or orchestrated) 'religious' politicking. But this in itself
calls in question the 'Whiggishness' of Hirst's evident assumptions about a progressive rise in
political awareness, since it is altogether possible that public awareness of these issues was more
effectively and politically harnessed in the 1580s than at any subsequent time, short of 1640. That
was in the nature of the decade.

[98] BL, MS Add. 38492, fos. 68-9.

be subject to the same sort of inhibitions as those assemblies themselves, forbidden to mention great things but only permitted to speak of the shipping of fish. And let us not be so afraid of the appellation 'Whiggish' as to cease to be strangely moved, as Neale was, by the vigorous rhetoric of the great Elizabethan parliament-men, allowing Morrice to speak for all: 'And by God's grace whilst lif doth last ... I will not be ashamed in good and lawfull sorte to stryve for the freedom of conscience, publique Justice, and the liberties of my country.'[99]

[99] Cambridge University Library, MS Mm.i.5. (Baker 40), fol. 63 v.

4

Windows in a Woman's Soul:
Questions about the Religion of Queen Elizabeth I

Dr Samuel Johnson claimed to have read a book about Iceland which included a chapter on snakes consisting of a single sentence: 'There are no snakes to be found anywhere in the island.' Some historians have treated this subject with almost equal brevity. Surely there *are* no questions; there is no religion to be found in the lady. A.F. Pollard's verdict on Queen Elizabeth's religion was that 'it can hardly be doubted that she was sceptical or indifferent'. Moreover, she was 'almost as devoid of a moral sense as she was of religious temperament'.[1] Among historians in the Protestant-Secularist-Whiggish tradition, to acknowledge the *politique* in Elizabeth was intended as a compliment. Pollard's pupil, Sir John Neale, suspicious as he was of most of the more or less apocryphal 'sayings' attributed to her, nevertheless liked to quote with admiration the rhetorical question she was supposed on one occasion to have put: why couldn't the king of Spain allow his subjects to go to the Devil in their own way?[2] One could do business with such a woman. Catholic writers, well into our own century, have indicted Elizabeth of actual atheism. Christopher Hollis boldly asserted in the year that I was born that while 'possessed of a certain talent in the production of conventional religious phraseology', she was 'certainly an atheist in practice. Religion did not at all influence her conduct.'[3]

Yet in 1550 the Protestant Bishop John Hooper had assured the Swiss reformer Bullinger that the young Edward VI's sister, 'the daughter of the late King by queen Ann', was 'inflamed with the same zeal for the religion of Christ', that is, a zeal equal to that of her royal brother. 'She not only knows what the true religion is, but has acquired such proficiency in Greek and Latin that she is able to defend it...'[4]

---

[1]   A.F. Pollard, *The History of England from the Accession of Edward VI to the Death of Elizabeth (1547-1603)*, The Political History of England, vi (1910), pp. 179-80.

[2]   J.E. Neale, 'The Sayings of Queen Elizabeth', reviewing Frederick Chamberlin's book of that title (1923), in his *Essays in Elizabethan History* (1958), pp. 85-112. I have forgotten where, and indeed whether, Sir John Neale published his endorsement of the alleged remark about the king of Spain and the Devil. But I often heard him quote it in conversation.

[3]   Christopher Hollis, *The Monstrous Regiment* (1929), pp. 28-30.

[4]   Bishop John Hooper to Bullinger, 5 February 1550, *Original Letters Relative to the English Reformation*, ed. H. Robinson, i, Parker Society (Cambridge, 1846), p. 76.

Later, when in the tenth year of her reign the great English pulpit Bible known as the Bishops' Bible was published, its title page bore a fetching but regal engraved portrait, the work of Franciscus Hogenberg, embellished with the motto: 'Non me pudet Evangelii Christi. Virtus enim Dei est ad salutem Omni credenti Rom.1°', rendered on the title-page of the New Testament for non-Latinists as 'I am not ashamed of the Gospel of Christ, because it is the power of God unto salvation to all that beleve': a text with deeply emotional resonances for anyone brought up in the modern evangelical tradition and hard to relate to a Tudor monarch, certainly a sentiment antithetical to the *politique* position. (But the same text had been made an emblem by or on behalf of Henry VIII.)[5] In 1585, Elizabeth told parliament:

> I am supposed to have many studies ... And yet, amidst my many volumes, I hope God's book hath not been my seldomest lectures; in which we find that which by reason (for my part) we ought to believe – that, seeing so great wickedness and griefs in the world, in which we live but as wayfaring pilgrims, we must suppose that God would never have made us but for a better place and of more comfort than we find here.[6]

In a tiny sextodecimo New Testament preserved in the Bodleian Library, Elizabeth has inscribed with her own hand in the flyleaf: 'I walke many times in the pleasaunt fieldes of the holye scriptures, Where I plucke up the goodlie greene herbes of sentences by pruning: Eate the[m] by reading: Chawe the[m] by musing': a conceit attributed to St Augustine.[7]

So suddenly the whole island appears to be alive with snakes. But were they real snakes? Was Elizabeth really religious? Dealing as we are with a woman of such accomplished and rarely relaxed artifice, not to say prevarication, the question cannot be answered. And what did it mean, in the circumstances of Elizabethan England, indeed in any circumstances, to be 'really religious'? We may assume (and the assumption will not be further discussed) that Elizabeth was conventionally religious in the sense that she attended with regularity to her religious duties and heard in her

---

[5]   It occurs in Holbein's engraved title-page for Coverdale's Bible. The engraved portraits of Elizabeth in the 1568 Bishops' Bible are attributed to Franciscus Hogenberg by A.M. Hind in *Engraving in England in the Sixteenth and Seventeenth Centuries*, i (Cambridge, 1952), p. 65. However, Margaret Aston notes that Remigius Hogenberg, brother of Franciscus, was in Archbishop Parker's employ. Dr Aston also notes that the portraits are absent from the 1574 and all subsequent editions of the Bishops' Bible. She attributes their suppression to 'the conviction of some contemporary purists that portraiture was an inherently idolatrous act': Margaret Aston, 'The *Bishops' Bible* Illustrations', in *The Church and the Arts*, Studies in Church History, 28, ed. Diana Wood (Oxford, 1992), pp. 267-85.

[6]   J.E. Neale, *Elizabeth I and her Parliaments, 1584-1601* (1957), p. 100,

[7]   Quoted by John N. King, *Tudor Royal Iconography: Literature and Art in an Age of Religious Crisis* (Princeton, 1989), p. 109.

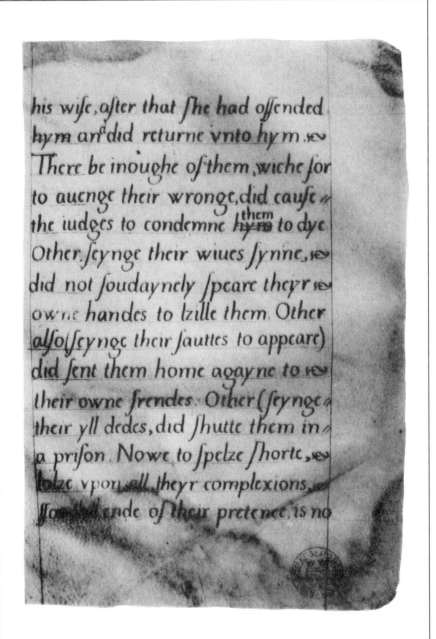

his wife, after that she had offended
hym an did returne vnto hym.
There be inoughe of them, wiche for
to auenge their wronge, did cause
the iudges to condemne hym them to dye.
Other, seynge their wiues synne,
did not soudaynely speare theyr
owne handes to kille them. Other
also seynge their fauttes to appeare)
did sent them home agayne to
their owne frendes. Other (seynge
their yll dedes, did shutte them in
a prison. Nowe, to spelke shorte,
kelke vpon all theyr complexions,
so the ende of their pretence, is no

Princess Elizabeth's 'Freudian' error in translating the *Miroir de l'âme pechereuse* of
Marguerite d'Angoulême, *The glasse of the synnefull soule* (see p. 97). Elizabeth's
'Englishing' of the *Miroir* was executed in 1545, when she was eleven years of age.
(*Cambridge University Library*)

time many hundreds of sermons.[8] We can say no less, and no more, of the vast majority of her subjects, which is a grave embarrassment to the Elizabethan religious historian. Religious conformity has, if not no history, a most elusive history.

However, the question put by the late Neville Williams was legitimately as well as neatly posed: was there no window into her own soul?[9] Williams has supplied our title, with a little help from the nineteenth-century historian J.A. Froude, talking about Erasmus. You will best see the sixteenth century as it really was, said Froude, if you look at it through the eyes of Erasmus (meaning his letters).[10] But what do you see if you look back through the eyes of Erasmus into his mind and inner being, in any of the famous portraits? Elizabeth, said Francis Bacon, was reluctant to look into her subjects' souls. If we dared to make spiritual eye contact, scrutinising her own soul, what might we see?

II

One tiny window exists in the form of an exquisite little book of private devotions in five languages (English, French, Italian, Latin, Greek) measuring exactly three inches by two, enriched by Hilliard miniatures of the queen and her suitor François duc d'Anjou and so fabricated (one assumes) in about 1578 or 1579: a precious little thing now sadly lost (or at least misplaced), but fortunately not before a limited number of facsimiles had been published.[11] At first, among modern writers, these prayers attracted the attention only of two high Anglican clerics, Adam Fox of Westminster and Canon J.P. Hodges.[12] But presently they excited the interest and admiration of the great Reformation historian Roland Bainton, who quoted these among other passages, remarking: 'If there be any who doubt the sincerity of her religious sentiment let them ponder this her private prayer.'

---

[8]   Her reactions to some of these were reported by Sir John Harington in the little book known (from its mid seventeenth-century title) as *A briefe view of the state of the Church of England*. See Patrick Collinson, 'If Constantine, Then Also Theodosius: St Ambrose and the Integrity of the Elizabethan *Ecclesia Anglicana*', in my *Godly People: Essays on English Protestantism and Puritanism* (1983), pp. 119-20.

[9]   Neville Williams, *Elizabeth Queen of England* (1967), p. 79.

[10]   J.A. Froude, *Life and Letters of Erasmus* (1900), p. 431.

[11]   BL, MS FACS 218. J.W. Whitehead exhibited the MS at the Fine Art Society in 1902, after which it was 'lost to sight'. Forty copies of the facsimile were printed in 1893, with notes by Whitehead on its saleroom history.

[12]   *A Book of Devotions Composed by Her Majesty Elizabeth R with Translations by the Reverend Adam Fox D.D. and a Foreword by the Reverend Canon J.P. Hodges* (Gerrards Cross, 1970). See also J.P. Hodges, *The Nature of the Lion: Elizabeth I and our Anglican Heritage* (1962), pp. 131-41.

This God of my life and life of my soul, the King of all comfort, is my only refuge. For his sake therefore, to whom thou hast given all power, and wilt deny no petition, hear my prayers. Turn thy face from my sins (O Lord) and thine eyes to thy handiwork. Create a clean heart, and renew a right spirit within me. Order my steps in thy word, that no wickedness have dominion over me, make me obedient to thy will, and delight in thy law. Grant me grace to live godly and to govern justly: that so living to please thee, and reigning to serve thee I may even glorify thee, the Father of all goodness and mercy.[13]

More recently, another American church historian, W.P. Haugaard, has written an article of 7000 words on this tiny object, while Dr Christopher Haigh has endorsed the firm evidence it appears to provide of Elizabeth's religious sincerity, and equally of her essential and unwavering Protestantism.[14] Dr Haigh concedes that the prayers were a piece of image-making, perhaps even for the queen's own private purposes, Elizabeth as she would have liked God to have seen her, rather than as she actually was. 'But her self-image was as patroness of the Gospel and she took her religious duties seriously.' 'There can be little doubt of Elizabeth's Protestantism.'

One does not have to be a radical deconstructionist to have one's doubts about these readings of this text, or to consider other possibilities. The little collection of prayers with their Hilliard miniatures evidently had some connection with the Anjou marriage negotiations which, if they had come to fruition, would have struck a damaging if not fatal blow at the Protestant cause in the perception of very many of the queen's Protestant subjects.[15] Moreover we cannot be sure that this book of devotions contains a *self-image* of Elizabeth. It has been widely assumed that the queen wrote the prayers herself and there has even been speculation about the hands in which they are written, whether any or all of them were her own. They are certainly very royal and in the first person – 'drawing my blood from kings ... placing me a Sovereign Princess over thy people of England' – but so are other prayers which we can be confident she did *not* compose herself but which were placed in her hand and mouth, whole collections of 'right godlie Psalmes, fruitfull Praiers, and comfortable Meditations to be said of our most vertuous and deere Soveraigne Ladie Elizabeth'.[16] But let us by all

[13] R.H. Bainton, *Women of the Reformation in France and England* (Minneapolis, 1973), pp. 248-50.

[14] William P. Haugaard, 'Elizabeth Tudor's *Book of Devotions*: A Neglected Clue to the Queen's Life and Character', *Sixteenth-Century Journal*, 12 (1981), pp. 79-105; Christopher Haigh, *Elizabeth I* (1988), pp. 27-8.

[15] *John Stubbs's 'Gaping Gulf'*, ed. L.E. Berry (Charlottesville, VA, 1968); W.T. MacCaffrey, 'The Anjou Match and the Making of Elizabethan Foreign Policy', in *The English Commonwealth, 1547-1640: Essays on Politics and Society Presented to Joel Hurstfield*, ed. Peter Clark et al. (Leicester, 1979), pp. 59-75.

[16] Thomas Bentley, *The Monument of Matrones* (1582), p. 253. For detailed discussion of Bentley's *Monument*, see pp. 104-8 below.

means allow that the dignity and restraint of that tiny book of private devotions places it in a different class and makes it very probable that these were Queen Elizabeth's own prayers.

We may at this point consider one or two other small devotional books which we can assume to have been presented to Elizabeth and to have been in her possession and use, on the evidence not only of the wording of the prayers themselves but of the red velvet bindings which were standard in the queen's personal library, in at least one case embellished with the embroidered royal monogram.[17] British Library, Stowe MS 30 is a tiny set of prayers and meditations in Italian, Spanish, German, French, Dutch, Hebrew and English, 'appropriate', says Professor John King, 'to a royal or aristocratic lady broadly learned in languages'. Elizabeth's piety is further connected, by a strong and in itself plausible tradition, with two printed collections of private prayers, both familiarly referred to as 'Queen Elizabeth's Prayer Book'. *Christian Prayers and meditations in English French Italian Spanish Greeke and Latine* was an anonymous compilation published by the doughty Protestant printer John Day in 1569. Day prepared a special tailor-made, coloured-in copy of this book for the queen's own use, with certain imprecations transposed into the first person. This was preserved in the royal Wardrobe at Whitehall until the Interregnum and survives at Lambeth Palace Library as MS 1049. Later, Day appropriated the woodcut portrait of the queen at prayer and other decorative details from *Christian prayers* and used them in his son Richard Day's *A booke of Christian prayers* (1578), leading to understandable confusion.[18]

It may be as relevant, perhaps more relevant, to take account of these devotional books as *objects* as to analyse the theology and religious sentiments of their contents. They evidently connect with the late Henrician fashion (the fashion of Elizabeth's formative years) of ladies wearing diminutive and richly decorated prayer books on ornamental chains, the precious little items known to connoisseurs and art historians as girdle books. A Protestant development out of this fashion was to substitute the

---

[17] Elizabeth's aversion from other, more utilitarian bindings can be documented from two Cambridge episodes. In 1564 she visited the university and was presented with a large collection of gratulatory verses, somewhat crudely bound in unadorned vellum. This precious memento is currently (August, 1992) being purchased for the Cambridge University Library. Its preservation is due to the queen's rejection of the gift, passing it over to Sir William Cecil, with whose descendants it remained. When Elizabeth returned to the vicinity of Cambridge in 1578 and prepared to receive the vice-chancellor and heads of houses at Audley End, Cecil advised that the book they proposed to present should on no account be bound by country bookbinders, who tended to drench the strong natural odour of the vellum (which Elizabeth is otherwise known to have detested) with 'spike' (lavender) which she could not abide. See below, pp. 211-12.

[18] King, *Tudor Royal Iconography*, pp. 108-14, The confusing history of these imprints is concisely clarified in the revised *Short-Title Catalogue of Books Printed in England, 1475-1640*, STC nos. 6428 and 6429, noting a further connection with Henry Bull, *Christian prayers and holy meditations* (1568 and many subsequent editions, STC nos. 4028-4032.3).

New Testament for these little 'portuises', a practice made popular by Queen Ann Boleyn, Elizabeth's mother, but denounced by conservatives. This was to subordinate image to word and even to eliminate imagery altogether in favour of calligraphy, coloured titles and capitals. In this way 'Queen Elizabeth's Prayer Book' in its various guises derives from the Catholic *Pomander of prayer*, printed up to the end of Mary's reign.[19] We may conclude that these precious Elizabethan relics may be evidence of piety but are equally indicative of fashion and taste.

Referring, as we may at this point, to the doctrine of the monarch's two bodies, as explored by Ernst Kantorowicz and applied to the Elizabethan monarchy by Marie Axton, it is not clear that any of this material derives from or sheds much light on the queen's natural body (still less her natural mind and soul), what one Elizabethan writer called her 'self's self', as distinct from her body politic, public *persona* and image.[20] However it is evident that various presentations of the queen as a body politic were shaped in their particulars by perceptions of what were taken to be her natural qualities, or what were thought to be appropriate natural qualities. Only the principle of the queen's two bodies preserved the Elizabethan panegyrist from blatant blasphemy. To compare the queen as a body politic to the sinless Virgin, Mother and Bride of Christ, was one thing; to have claimed that the woman, Elizabeth Tudor, was perfectly sinless would have been quite another.

III

At first glance, another precious relic of Elizabeth's religiosity may appear to open wider that elusive window on her emergent soul. A second glance may suggest conventions so stilted as to tell us very little. Whereas a third proves surprisingly and intriguingly informative. I refer to Elizabeth's translation into English prose of the *Miroir de l'âme pechereuse*, a mystical religious poem composed by Marguerite d'Angoulême, queen of Navarre, the 'Pearl of the Valois', sister of one king of France and grandmother of another. The *Miroir* was printed several times between its composition in 1530-1 and Princess Elizabeth's prose rendering, which was executed in

---

[19] The authority on Henrician girdle books is Hugh Tait. See David Starkey, ed., *Henry VIII: A European Court in England* (Greenwich, 1991), pp. 112-14. For examples of the critical attention paid by religious conservatives to testaments carried in the hand or used as girdle books, see Thomas Elyot, *Pasquil the Playne*, by Sir Thomas Elyot, ed. Lillian Gottesaman (Gainesville, FL, 1967), pp. 46-7 (a thinly disguised attack on Thomas Cranmer) and the Canterbury material calendared as 'Thomas Cranmer and the Heretics of Kent', *Letters and Papers of the Reign of Henry VIII*, xviii (2).

[20] Ernst Kantorowicz, *The Kings Two Bodies: A Study in Medieval Political Theology* (Princeton, 1957); Marie Axton, *The Queen's Two Bodies: Drama and the Elizabethan Succession* (1977); John Stubbs's '*Gaping Gulf*', p. 68.

1545 at the age of eleven and presented to her step-mother, Queen Catherine Parr, as a New Year's gift. The original copy survives in the Bodleian Library, bound and embroidered by the princess herself, in a rather over-worked version of what was already her favourite style in the crafting of books.[21]

The backcloth to Elizabeth's translation of Marguerite d'Angoulême concerns the Renaissance chapter in the perennial *querelle des femmes* which Ruth Kelso has investigated in the 891 titles on noblewomen written between 1400 and 1600 which fed into her *Doctrine for the Lady of the Renaissance*.[22] This 'lady' exemplified such gender-specific virtues as modesty, humility, constancy, temperance, pity. This was as much as to say that such women were more naturally religious than men, or at least had a higher quality of religiosity attributed to them. These qualities were non-assertive, but were compatible with the acquisition of an advanced philological and rhetorical education, expressing itself, typically, in literary works of translation rather than in original composition. The Tudor educators, Grindall, Aylmer, Ascham, seem to have found aristocratic girls perfect recipients for their pedagogical programmes of double translation, in and out of the ancient languages. Such were the female Greys, especially Lady Jane, Cookes, especially Lady Ann (Bacon), and Tudors, especially Elizabeth.[23]

The cultivated, pious Renaissance lady also related, with increasing frequency and consistency, to an entourage or coterie of similar ladies,

---

[21] *Le miroir de l'âme pechereuse* was printed at Alençon in 1531, Paris in 1533, Geneva in 1539 and Toulouse in 1552. There is a critical edition of the 1531 text, ed. Joseph L. Allaire (Munich, 1972). Princess Elizabeth's translation, to which she gave the title *The glasse of the synnefull soule*, was printed in facsimile from the original MS by Percy W. Ames in 1897. A more recent edition from Oxford, Bodleian Library, MS Cherry 36, is in *Annales Academica Scientiarum Fennicae Dissertationes Litterarum*, 22 (Helsinki, 1979). On this entire subject I have been helped immeasurably by the work of the late Dr Heather Vose of Perth, Western Australia, in her unpublished University of Western Australia Ph.D. thesis 'Marguerite d'Angoulême: A Study in Sixteenth-Century Spirituality Based on her 1521-1524 Correspondence with Guillaume Briçonnet' (1985); and her article, 'Marguerite of Navarre: that "Righte English Woman"', *Sixteenth-Century Journal*, 16 (1985), pp. 315-33. Ames (*The Mirror*, pp. 30-1) suggests that Elizabeth received the text from her mother, who he thought might have been in Marguerite' s service as duchesse d'Alençon. Hugh Richmond, *Shakespeare Studies*, 12 (1979), 49-63, thought it possible that Ann Boleyn carried the *Miroir* to the scaffold. Retha Warnicke, *Women of the English Renaissance and Reformation* (1983), p. 95, preferred the theory that it was Queen Catherine Parr who made the original available to Elizabeth. However Dr Vose ('Marguerite d'Angoulême', p. 114) believes that Elizabeth had access to it through her father, who is known to have received a copy. Anne Lake Prescott (see n. 26 below) is 'fairly confident' that Elizabeth worked from the Geneva edition of 1539.

[22] Ruth Kelso, *Doctrine for the Lady of the Renaissance* (Urbana, IL, 1956).

[23] See several of the studies collected in Margaret P. Hannay, ed., *Silent but for the Word: Tudor Women as Patrons, Translators and Writers of Religious Works* (Kent, OH, 1985), with extensive references supplied to other literature. See also John N. King, 'The Godly Woman in Elizabethan Iconography', *Renaissance Quarterly*, 38 (1985), pp. 41-84, and 'The "Godly" Queens', in his *Tudor Royal Iconography*, pp. 182-266.

The Conclusyon.

At all tymes God.is with the iust/
Bycause they put,in hym their trust.
Who shall therfor, from Syon geue,
That helthe whych hāgeth,in our beleue?
Whan God shall take,frō hys the smart,
Than wyll Jacob,reioyce in hart.
Prayse to God.

Imprented in the yeare of our lords
1548. in Apryll.

Princess Elizabeth is depicted as Mary Magdalene on the final page of John Bale's edition of her translation from Marguerite d'Angoulême, *A godly medytacyon of the Christen sowle* (see p. 98). In Thomas Bentley's *The Monument of Matrones*, Elizabeth is made to address God as 'Rabboni'. (*Cambridge University Library*)

some of them grouping themselves around a great and suitably talented patroness. This is the stuff of those many studies by Christopher Hare (not his, or rather her, real name) with titles like *Ladies of the Reformation in Italy*.[24] Princess Elizabeth was connected with such an entourage through her semi-filial dependence upon her step-mother, Catherine Parr; but which included, sometimes in uneasy sorority, such other notable ladies of the late Henrician courtly scene as Anne Seymour, duchess of Somerset, Catherine Brandon, duchess of Suffolk, and that stylish, skittish noblewoman, Mary Fitzroy, duchess of Richmond.[25]

Marguerite d'Angoulême's *Miroir* might seem a suitable text for a young woman reared in this tradition to concern herself with, but this would be on a very superficial reading. The opening words (in Elizabeth's translation) 'Is there any hell so profounde that is sufficient to punish the tenth parte of my synnes?' sets the scene for a sombre mood of self-accusation from which the soul emerges only through a series of passionate encounters with the Trinitarian Godhead, conceived according to the metaphors of familial relationship. God is addressed as father by the soul as daughter; but also by the soul employing the holy title of Mother of God – with due apologies to the Virgin for usurping her title. God then calls the soul 'sister' and speaks of 'the fraternitie that thou hast towards me'. 'And likewise thou dost call me wife'. 'Rise up my spouse ' (Canticles, chapter 2). 'Therefore shall i say with loving faith, thou art mijn and i am thine. Thou doest call me love and faire spouse, if so it be, suche hast thou made me.' 'O my father, brother, childe and spouse.' Here, in the context of a religion anchored to the words 'Our Father', are reasons more compelling than many often given for the so often observed religious propensity of women, whose lives within our culture are structured by family relationships to a greater extent than those of men, or are commonly supposed to be so structured. Such gender-related and generational confusions and elisions were standard to the repertoire, especially of Marian piety.

Nevertheless, these were deep waters into which to plunge a pre-pubescent eleven-year old: a psychological shark pool. According to Anne Lake Prescott's reading of the text, the young Elizabeth knew what she was doing, to the extent of indulging in wilful mistranslations which perhaps uniquely reveal the psyche of a child whose mother had been executed for adultery in her infancy, and whose father was remote and uncaring.[26] It was

---

[24] Christopher Hare, *The Most Illustrious Ladies of the Italian Renaissance* (1904); *A Princess of the Italian Reformation: Giulia Gonzaga (1513-1566)* (1912); *Men and Women of the Italian Reformation* (1914),

[25] My dependence upon Professor John King here and in what follows is considerable. See in addition to the citations already made his 'Patronage and Piety: The Influence of Catherine Parr', in *Silent but for the Word*, pp. 43-59.

[26] Anne Lake Prescott, 'The Pearl of the Valois and Elizabeth I: Marguerite de Navarre's *Miroir* and Tudor England', in Hannay, ed., *Silent but for the Word*, pp. 61-91.

odd to put such a text into her hands. But there were good bread and butter reasons. Marguerite d'Angoulême had always been on good terms with Henry VIII and at this very time was playing a constructive part in the diplomacy designed to end the last of his wars. The late Dr Heather Vose writes of 'the wide and worldly setting for her lively Christian faith'. (One is reminded of Elizabeth's great grandmother, the Lady Margaret Beaufort.) If Wolsey had had his way, or so according to Shakespeare, Marguerite might have been Elizabeth's mother, or, indeed, her step grandmother, since there had been plans to marry her to Henry VII.[27] Of course the princess's teacher, Roger Ascham, would have regarded her work on the *Miroir* as a simple exercise in translation, as with the scriptural passages in four languages (Latin, Greek, French, Italian) which she later added to it, or, her other labour of love (or duty), the prayers and meditations translated from the English of Catherine Parr into Latin, French and Italian and dedicated to her father, another New Year's gift.[28]

But the *Miroir* in the hands of its translator was explosive material to which she reacted in curious ways. Where Marguerite had written 'père, fille, o bieneureux lignaige', speaking of the father's love for the daughter, Elizabeth translated *père* as 'mother': further gender confusion and surely a Freudian if not a deliberate mistake. Where Marguerite compares divine mercy to a father's forgiveness of his child – 'si père a eu de son enfant mercy' – Elizabeth omits the line altogether. And then, most curiously of all, where Marguerite writes of husbands who put adulterous wives to death (that was near the bone), Elizabeth reverses the genders and makes the husband die the death: 'Assez en est, qui pour venger leur tort,/Par les juges les on faict mettre à mort.' Elizabeth rendered this: 'There be inoughe of them, wiche for to avenge their wronge, did cause the judges to condemne hym to dye.' She then crossed out 'hym' and wrote 'them' above it. So 'hym' may have been intended as 'hem', which is to say, them. This is all splendidly speculative, but Miss Prescott believes that Elizabeth is (perhaps subliminally?) turning Marguerite's poem into an 'impassioned evocation of God as a great king and judge who is kind to daughters and does not execute adulterous wives'.[29] In her 1579 prayers (if they were hers), Elizabeth asks Christ the Son to let her love him 'for thy promises as my father'.[30]

Presently English Protestants, in particular that brilliantly opportunistic

[27] Vose, 'Marguerite d'Angoulême', pp. i, 96, 103.
[28] BL, MS Royal 7.D.X. The MS is bound in an embroidered cover, doubtless Elizabeth's own handiwork, with the title beginning 'precationes seu meditationes'. It is dated from Hertford 30 December 1545 and dedicated to Henry VIII by 'Elizabeta Maiest. s. humillissime filia'.
[29] Prescott, 'Pearl of the Valois and Elizabeth I', pp. 69-71.
[30] Haugaard, 'Elizabeth Tudor's *Book of Devotions*', p. 86.

propagandist John Bale,[31] were turning Elizabeth's translation of the *Miroir* into something else: a godly Protestant manifesto. The original doctrine of the *Miroir* appears to have been composed of that subtle blend of the traditional and the novel, typical of the 'pre-Reform', which historical theologians have found it difficult to classify or define, except as something somewhat inchoate called Evangelism, and which caused the Sorbonne to look at it critically. The printer of the Paris edition of 1553 would soon be executed (in another connection) for 'scandalous blasphemy'.[32] But the *Miroir* is Pauline-Augustinian, not Protestant, as in Elizabeth's translation of this passage: 'Now as far fourth as i can see i ought to have no hope of succoure, but through the grace of God, wiche i can not deserve, the wiche maye rayse everyone from death.' For all that we know to the contrary, Elizabeth's soteriology would never move beyond or outside these quasi-Lutheran, proto-Protestant, Augustinian limits.

But in 1548, shortly before his return from his first period of exile, Bale published at Wesel the first printed edition of Elizabeth's *Miroir*, now called *A godly medytacyon of the christen sowle*.[33] This publication in effect hi-jacked Elizabeth's juvenile exercise for the Protestant cause; and with it Elizabeth herself, who was made to collude in a typically vituperative attack on the 'Romyshe clergye ymagenynge to exalte themselves above the lewde layte [i.e., laity]', and on the images themselves. How curious that the British Library copy of this tract should once have belonged to the mid seventeenth-century East Anglian iconoclast, William Dowsing![34] But this is also ironical given the views of the mature Elizabeth on the subject of religious images.[35] It is instructive to note how Bale has subtly converted into the key of godly, Protestant edification the tone of Elizabeth's discourse. Where Elizabeth, addressing the reader, wrote 'if thou doest rede thys whole worke', Bale has: 'If thu [sic] do throughly reade thys worke (dere frynde in the lorde).'

So little relating to this subject is certain. It is possible, as Bale implies, that Elizabeth herself had a copy of her translation sent to him overseas, together with some additional matter, scriptural texts rendered in Latin, Greek, French and Italian, 'whyche she wrote first with her owne hande'.[36]

---

[31]   On Bale, see Honor McCusker, *John Bale: Dramatist and Antiquary* (Bryn Mawr, PA, 1942); Leslie P. Fairfield, *John Bale: Mythmaker for the English Reformation* (West Lafayette, IN, 1976).

[32]   Prescott, 'Pearl of the Valois and Elizabeth I', p. 62.

[33]   The full title of this text (*STC* no. 17320) is *A godly medytacyon of the Christen sowle concerninge a love towardes God and hys Christe, compiled in Frenche by Lady Margaret queene of Navere and aptely translated into Englysh by the ryght vertuous lady Elyzabeth doughter to Kynge Henri the viii*. A substantially different edition also appeared in 1548 (not included in the *Short-Title Catalogue*, but see British Library, C.38.c.57), *A godly meditacion of the inwarde love of the soule*. Yet another version would later appear in Bentley's *Monument of matrones*. (See p. 105 below.)

[34]   BL, C.12.d.1. The title-page bears Dowsing's signature.

[35]   See pp. 110-14 below.

[36]   *A godly medytacyon*, epistle, fol. 41.

But it is more likely that Bale's copy reached him from other ladies in the super-aristocratic, crypto-Protestant entourage of the late 1540s: perhaps from the duchess of Richmond whose patronage Bale enjoyed as soon as he set foot back in England, who was also the patron of the martyrologist John Foxe.[37]

Bale included in his preface to *A godly medytacyon* a catalogue of queens and princesses, some mythical or semi-mythical, who had served as rulers in their own right or as queens regent, which suggests that his motive in this publication may have been to favour and advance the claims of Queen Catherine Parr to a kind of regency in the early months of Edward VI's reign, in which case events overtook him, for Catherine would soon be dead. But his flattery of Princess Elizabeth for her extraordinary philological prowess and model piety was significant, and especially in that he almost approximated her to the recent Protestant martyr, Anne Askew, herself a kind of hanger-on to the evangelical-aristocratic-female connection, a sprat intended to catch the mackerel of the queen, no less. After extolling Askew as 'Christes myghty member' who had 'strongly troden downe the head of the serpent', Bale spoke of what 'other noble women' had achieved and would achieve. 'Marke thys present boke for one, whose translacyon was the worke of her whyche was but a babe at the doynge therof.'[38]

In publishing the first and second examinations of Anne Askew in 1546 and 1547 (narratives composed by Anne herself), Bale had, in effect, reinvented the genre of martyrology with which John Foxe would presently do so much, making Askew in a sense the proto-martyr and a figure of almost cosmic significance, since for page after page he compared her to the primitive martyr of second-century Lyons, Blandina, who had been treated in the pages of the church historian Eusebius as a type of the church itself, the spouse of Christ.[39] The identification is further established by an emblematic woodcut on the title-page, depicting Anne Askew according to an old iconographical convention, treading down the dragon (but now equipped with papal tiara), while she holds in one hand the martyr's palm but in the other, instead of the usual cross, a book, *Biblia*. There is an implied reference to an earlier woodcut, used to introduce Bale's major work in the apocalyptic vein *The Image of Both Churches*, in which the figure of the Woman Clothed With the Sun (Revelation, 12) confronts that demonic parody of the faithful woman, the Whore of Babylon. And we are carried forwards to the woodcut adorning Bale's edition of Elizabeth's *Miroir*, where the princess is seen, Bible in hand, kneeling at Christ's feet in the posture of a Magdalene.

[37] King, 'Patronage and Piety', in *Silent but for the Word*, pp. 51-2.

[38] *A godly medytacyon*, fos. 46-7 r.

[39] *The first examinacyon of Anne Askew lately martyred in Smythfelde, by the Romesh popes upholders, with the Elucydacyon of Johan Bale* (Marburg, 1546) (*STC* no. 848); *The lattre examinacyon of Anne Askewe, with the elucydacyon of J. Bale* (Marburg, 1547) (*STC* no. 850).

The lattre examinacyon

on of Anne Askewe, latelye mar
tyred in Smythfelde, by the wyc‑
ked Synagoge of Antichrist,
with the Elucydacyon of
Johan Bale.

The veryte of the lorde endureth for euer.

Psalme 116.

BIB LIA

Anne Askewe stode fast by thys veryte of God to the ende.

I wyll poure out my sprete vpõ all flesh
(sayth God) your sonnes and your dough‑
ters shall prophecye. And who so euer call
on the name of the lorde/shall be saued.
Johel. ij.

Title-page of John Bale's edition of *The lattre examinacyon of Anne Askewe*. John Bale's
representation of Anne Askewe, whom he used to launch a new genre of Protestant
martyrology, is a parody of the conventional Catholic image of St Margaret of
Antioch. The traditional cross is replaced by the Bible and the dragon is made to wear
a papal tiara. (*Cambridge University Library*)

This was to tap a rich vein of scriptural and especially of apocalyptic imagery and metaphor, all destined in the dimensions of gender and generational inversion very like those explored by Marguerite d'Angoulême to be united with Christ as spouse, but also as the fruit of their wombs. These were the emblems of the Bride of Canticles, the Woman Who Feareth the Lord of Proverbs 13, and, most significantly and prophetically, the Woman Who Flees into the Wilderness who becomes the Woman Clothed With the Sun, the Woman of Revelation 12. Such emblems had both a general and a more particular application. Generally, and in the spirit both of the Protestant emphasis on the priesthood (or ministry) of all believers and of Erasmian educational aspirations, they appropriated to godly womankind in general, and as an emblem of the status and experience of all Christians, the exemplary qualities hitherto attributed only to special women, saints, above all to the Virgin Mary. The point is made by the women who are prominent among the throng of faithful and obedient subjects at the foot of the prodigious woodcut which forms the title-page of Henry VIII's Great Bible of 1539; and equally by the centrally positioned, essentially emblematic women who sits, Bible open on her lap, at the preacher's feet in John Foxe's picture of Bishop Hugh Latimer preaching before Edward VI. More particularly, first Mary Tudor, and then, more famously and enduringly, Elizabeth Tudor would be credited with the traditional *persona* and roles of the Virgin.[40]

Given the emphasis often and justifiably placed on the mysoginistic chauvinism of the Protestant reformers, it is necessary to insist on the gynophilia which, at one level, characterises these texts and evidently motivated John Bale in his handling of Anne Askew, and equally John Foxe in his celebration of a whole parade of female martyrs, something which greatly impressed Roland Bainton.[41] There is a concealed element of parodic and even paradoxical inversion in the female martyrologies of the Reformation. Presumably Bale and Foxe would not have disagreed with the conventional wisdom of the domestic courtesy books. Wives should obey their husbands. This, after all, was the teaching of Ephesians. They should be circumspect, reticent, humble, submissive. But Mrs Askew was none of these things. Scolds were a scourge.[42] But many of Foxe's martyrs were quick-witted, sharp-tongued scolds in the cause of the Gospel. The Gospel, and martyrdom, made it all right. Foxe's handling of the threat to Queen Catherine Parr from the conservative faction at court makes an

[40] John Bale, *The image of both churches* (Antwerp, ?1545) (*STC* no. 1296.5); *A godly medytacyon*; King, 'The Godly Woman'.

[41] Bainton, 'John Foxe and the Women Martyrs', in *Women of the Reformation*, pp. 211-29.

[42] Susan Amussen, *An Ordered Society: Gender and Class in Early Modern England* (Oxford, 1988); D.E. Underdown, 'The Taming of the Scold', in Anthony Fletcher and John Stevenson, ed., *Order and Disorder in Early Modern England* (Cambridge, 1985), pp. 116-36.

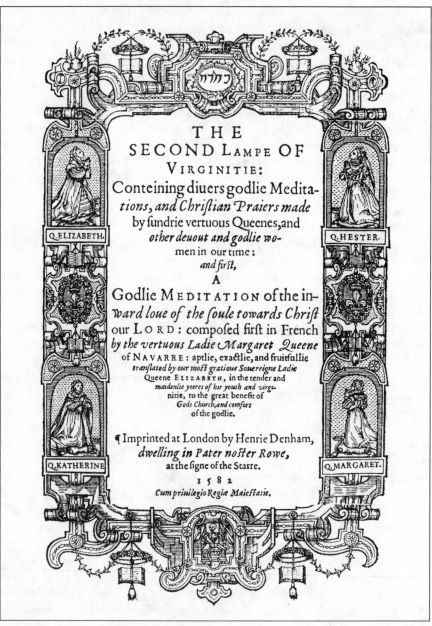

THE
SECOND LAMPE OF
VIRGINITIE:
Conteining diuers godlie Meditations, and Chriſtian Praiers made
by ſundrie vertuous Queenes, and
other deuout and godlie wo-
men in our time:
and firſt,
A
Godlie MEDITATION of the in-
ward loue of the ſoule towards Chriſt
our LORD: compoſed firſt in French
by the vertuous Ladie Margaret Queene
of NAVARRE: aptlie, exactlie, and fruitfullie
tranſlated by our moſt gratious Souereigne Ladie
Queene ELIZABETH, in the tender and
maidenlie yeeres of hir youth and virgi-
nitie, to the great benefit of
Gods Church, and comfort
of the godlie.

¶ Imprinted at London by Henrie Denham,
dwelling in Pater noſter Rowe,
at the ſigne of the Starre.
1582
Cum priuilegio Regiæ Maieſtatis.

Q. ELIZABETH.
Q. HESTER.
Q. KATHERINE
Q. MARGARET.

The engraved title-page of *The Seconde Lampe of Virginitie*, the second part of
Thomas Bentley, *The Monument of Matrones*, places Queen Elizabeth in a tradition
of queen intercessors whose prototype was the Old Testament Queen Esther.
'Q. Katherine' is presumably her step-mother, Catherine Parr. 'Q. Margaret'
is Marguerite d'Angoulême. The object of worship is God represented by the
non-representational tetragrammaton, flanked by other Old Testament symbols.
(*Cambridge University Library*)

especially piquant parody. Catherine wittily outwitted her adversaries by obediently submitting to her lord and master; perhaps with fingers crossed, tongue in cheek and winking eye.[43] It is possible, of course, and a suspicious feminist historian might well make this point, that the apparent gynophilia was patriarchally motivated, a device for subordinating women by emphasising the submissive qualities characteristic of their piety.

Princess Elizabeth was never depicted as a scold. And yet she was the principal inheritor (both beneficiary and victim) of this well-established tradition of apotheotic gynophilia. This is especially apparent in the narrative inserted by Foxe as a kind of appendix to the 1563 of his Book of Martyrs, or *Acts and Monuments*, a narrative which I believe to be in form a sort of fiction, even an early form of the novel: 'The Miraculous Preservation of the Lady Elizabeth, now Queen of England, From Extreme Calamity and Danger of Life; in the Time of Queen Mary, Her Sister'. As a kind of preface to this romantic tale, 'we all Englishmen' are exhorted to give thanks for 'so good, godly and virtuous a queen; such a chosen instrument of [God's] clemency, so virtuosly natured, so godly disposed, ... as amends and recompense, now to be made to England, for the cruel days that were before.'[44]

The account of Elizabeth's tribulations which follows, in the Tower and at Woodstock, was later embellished in such secondary and derivative works as Thomas Heywood's *Englands Elizabeth* and in his play *If You Know Not Me You Know Nobody*. In *Englands Elizabeth*, the trivial episode of an accidental fire at Woodstock is enlarged until it becomes all one with the fires of Smithfield: 'the whole Kingdom was then enflamed with *Bonfires* of Gods Saints'. A humble, prostrate prayer is put into the princess's mouth: 'Lady Elizabeths prayer in the midst of her sorrow'. 'Thus did shee both devoutly and religiously make use of all afflictions imposed upon her ... ' In the play, Elizabeth awakens from sleep to find a Bible miraculously placed in her hand by an angel and open at the text: 'Whoso putteth his trust in the Lord shall not be confounded.'

> My saviour thankes, on thee my hope I build,
> Thou lov'st poore Innocents, and art their shield.[45]

In Protestant England, Elizabeth's Stuart successors were at a considerable disadvantage in not being able to claim to have undergone such experiences. What Foxe and these poets and dramatists do not tell us about

---

[43] *The Acts and Monuments of John Foxe*, ed. S.R. Cattley, v (1838), pp. 553-61.

[44] Ibid., viii (1839), 600-25; this passage at p. 601.

[45] Thomas Heywood, *Englands Elizabeth: her life and troubles during her minoritie, from the Cradle to the Crowne* (1631), pp. 166-7, 169, 175; idem, *If You Know Not Me You Know Nobody*, part I, Malone Society Reprint (Oxford, 1934), scene xiv, lines 1047-67.

Elizabeth 'in the time of Queen Mary her sister' was that she conformed outwardly to her sister's religion and regularly heard mass. Mary would not have done the opposite thing and have heard Protestant prayers. In later years it would not be proposed that Elizabeth's various Catholic suitors should abandon the practice of their own religion. So what Elizabeth was in religion, in 1559, was not as transparent as her apologists and myth-makers would have us believe.

IV

With Elizabeth on the throne, as Deborah, some adjustment was necessary to convert the godly woman as sinful, dependent, meek and ripe for martyrdom, if active active only in prayer and meditation, into the histori-cally, even biblically, less familiar figure of the female ruler in her own right, something the Scottish reformer John Knox regarded as simply unnatural, a 'monstrous regiment'. But remarkably little was done by publicists to alter the fundamental image of the female as penitent, ever aware of her sins and infirmities, hanging upon God as her strength and redemption. The apotheosis of this tradition arrived with the publication in 1582 of an extraordinarily ambitious literary undertaking, a vast compilation of prayers, meditations, role models, all written by or for or relating to women. This was Thomas Bentley's *The Monument of Matrones*, 'to remaine unto women as one entire and godlie monument of praier, precepts and examples'.[46] Bentley styled himself 'of Graies Inne student', otherwise 'T.B. gentleman', but little seems to be known about him and still less about his motivation or connections with the Court and other interested patrons. (Bentley must be the only sixteenth-century author to have put together a work of more than 1600 closely printed pages who has so far failed to make it into the *Dictionary of National Biography*.)

Bentley's large if not great work was planned in seven volumes, called seven 'Lamps of Virginitie'. This image is hard to reconcile with the 'matrons' of the main title until we decode the implied emblems, spelt out in the engraved title pages. The lamps of the Wise and Foolish Virgins (Matthew 25) conflate with the seven-branched candlestick of the Temple, translated in sixteenth-century versions of Revelation as 'seven golden candlesticks', a symbol for the Woman Clothed with the Sun, offsetting the parodic antitype of the seven-headed dragon, and fused with the five Wise Virgins; in Professor John King's words, 'in a complex skein of apocalyptic imagery descending from the union of the Bridegroom and Spouse celebrated in Canticles'.[47]

[46] Thomas Bentley, *The Monument of Matrones: contening seven severall lamps of virginitie, or distinct treatises: whereof the first five concerne praier and meditation: the other two last, preceptes and examples* (1582) (*STC* nos. 1892-4).

[47] King, *Tudor Royal Iconogaphy*, pp. 243-56.

Bentley's *Monument* resembles the 'albums' children used to receive at Christmas. It contains a catalogue of famous, godly and 'notablie learned' women, the prayers hymns and songs made by holy women in scripture (the bulk of the first 'lamp'), 'certaine prayers made by godlie women martyrs' (pp. 214ff), a catechism for the instruction and examination of young persons before receiving communion, conducted exceptionally and perhaps uniquely by the mother (pp. 232ff); and, in the seventh 'lamp', a kind of biographical concordance of every woman mentioned in the Bible, good and bad, this section alone running to 211 pages. (One notes a certain consistency in what has purported to be 'feminist' literature. It has never occurred to anyone to produce a biographical concordance of all the *men* who figure in the Bible, which seems to indicate a certain double standard, which ever way we take it.) Bentley collects a great quantity of prayers for every category of woman, and these are not exactly a compendium of liberation theology. A 'praier for silence, shamefastnes and charitie' runs: 'There is nothing that be commeth a maid better than soberne, silence, shamefastnes and chastitie, both of bodie and minde. For these things being once lost, she is no more a maid, but a strumpet in the sight of God.'[48] One has to remember that Elizabeth, too, was a 'maid'.

One wonders whether this huge tome was really intended for women readers, or whether that was simply a monstrous literary conceit, working with the commonplace of a differentially more intense female religiosity, but tending towards the subordination of women by religious means. The title-page announces that the collection was 'compiled for the necessarie use of both sexes'. But, on the face of it, the enterprise was primarily intended to both flatter and admonish the queen, who dominates under every conceivable literary device and pretext. Besides sundry extensive collections of prayers which the queen either allegedly used or should use, Bentley reprints her translation of Marguerite d'Angoulême, called here *The Queenes meditation*, invents spiritual acrostics from the letters of her name, and composes 'The King's Heast or Gods familiar speech to the Queene',[49] addressed as 'Daughter'; with the queen's ecstatic 'selfe-talke with God' in response, beginning 'Rabboni'.[50] There is a special liturgy for November 17th, 'commonlie called The Queenes daie', to be celebrated by 'Mother and Daughter'.[51]

It was only a year since the French marriage negotiations had been finally broken off, and this was perhaps the earliest unrestrained celebration of Elizabeth's perpetual virginity. One of the prayers put into the queen's

[48] Bentley, *Monument*, p. 1 of the fifth 'lamp', which otherwise consists of prayers and meditations for 'Virgins, Wives, Women with Child, Midwives, Mothers, Daughters, Mistresses, Maids, Widowes and old women ... compiled to the glorie of God and comfort of al godlie wemen'.

[49] Ibid., pp. 306ff.

[50] Ibid., pp. 320ff.

[51] Ibid., pp. 686ff.

THE
THIRD LAMPE OF VIR-
GINITIE;
Conteining sundrie formes of diuine
meditations & Christian praiers; penned by
the godlie learned, to be properlie vsed of the
QVEENES most excellent Maiestie, as especiallie
vpon the 17.daie of Nouember, being the daie of
the gladnesse of hir hart, and memorable feast of
hir coronation : so on all other daies
and times at hir Graces
pleasure.

Wherevnto also is added a most heauenlie
HEAST spoken as it were in the person of GOD
vnto hir Maiestie, conteining his diuine will and com-
mandement concerning gouernement : and a right godlie and
Christian Vow vttered againe by hir Grace vnto God, com-
prehending the heroicall office and dutie of a Prince : faithfullie compiled out of the holie Psalmes of that Princelie Prophet King
DAVID, as they are learnedlie explaned by Theodore Beza : verie profitable to be often read and meditated vpon of hir
Maiestie, and all other Christian Rulers and Gouer-
nours, to the glorie of God ; the benefit of
his Church, and their owne euerla-
sting ioie and comfort in the
holie GHOST.

PSALME. 45.
Audi filia, & vide, & inclina aurem tuam, obliuiscere populi
tui, & domus patru tui.
Et concupiscet Rex formam tuam, quia ipse est Dominus tu-
us, ipsum adorabis.
Omnis gloria filiæ Regis intùs est.

1582

ELIZABETH.

BETHSABE

DEBORA.

IVDITH

The engraved title-page of *The Third Lampe of Virginitie*, the third part of Thomas Bentley, *The Monument of Matrones*, associates Queen Elizabeth with the three heroic women of the Old Testament, Deborah, Bathsheba and Judith. The object of devotion is now the IHS of Christian tradition. (*Cambridge University Library*)

In this illustration from Thomas Bentley, *The Monument of Matrones*, the iconographical restraint of Bentley's title-pages is exuberantly abandoned. Elizabeth was represented by Bentley as singing 'the sugred songs of my wedding-daie' to her 'heavenlie Bridegroom and spirituall spouse'. The reason for the prominence accorded to the recumbent tomb effigy of Queen Catherine Parr (?) is not clear. (*Cambridge University Library*)

mouth by Bentley ends by asking that she may

> in the purenesse of my virginitie, and holinesse of mine innocencie, be presented to the
> Lambe my sovereigne Lord and onlie God, my heavenlie Bridegroom and spirituall
> spouse, my everlasting King deere Christ, and onlie sweet saviour Jesus, there to see the
> Saincts, and to be a Sainct, and with all the holie Patriarches, Judges, Kings and Queens,
> yea with all Archangells, Angels, saints, martyrs, confessors, Virgins, and the whole
> companie of thy celestiall and blessed spirits, to reyne with him over spirituall powers
> and principalities for ever, and to sing the sugred songs of my wedding-daie to my
> perpetuall ioie, and thine eternall praise.[52]

The late Frances Yates (especially) has shown how Elizabeth, from about
this point in her reign, was identified with the Virgin and consequently with
the virginal figure of Astraea who appears in the Fourth Eclogue of Virgil,
the restorer of peace and justice, a theme soon to be richly embroidered
around the figure of Una in Spenser's *Faerie Queene*.[53] Professor John King
has more recently suggested that the potent historical myth of the Virgin
Queen belongs properly to the later Elizabethan years, but was projected
backwards by Camden, her first historian, particularly in his unwarranted
version of the speech in which she responded to a petition by her first
parliament that she should marry.[54]

It is not clear whether Bentley composed his own material or whether
he employed several desk-fulls of hacks at so much a thousand words. But
the title-page of the third 'lamp' claims that the queen's prayers were
'penned by the godlie learned'. It is not known whether the queen or
anyone close to the queen authorised publication, or even inspired it, which
is possible. The title page of the second 'lamp', which contains Elizabeth's
own compositions, including the *Miroir*, bears the formal sanction '*cum
privilegio regiae Maiestatis*', the other volumes not. Much has been written
about the Elizabethan propaganda machine. Almost nothing is known
about how it worked.

V

The essential point is that in Bentley's monstrous text Elizabeth was being
fashioned (to use a term made fashionable by Professor Stephen Greenblatt)
and almost marketed as a commodity.[55] The product was doubtless consistent with the queen's perception and presentation of herself and was
consequently a piece of what Greenblatt calls *self*-fashioning, but it does

---

[52]   Ibid., p. 272.

[53]   Frances Yates, 'Queen Elizabeth I as Astraea', in her *Astraea: The Imperial Theme in the Sixteenth
Century* (1975), pp. 29-87; King, *Tudor Royal Iconography*, pp. 241-2, 261-4.

[54]   Idem, 'Queen Elizabeth I: Representations of the Virgin Queen', *Renaissance Quarterly*, 43
(1990), pp. 30-74. See also Roy Strong, *Gloriana: The Portraits of Queen Elizabeth I* (revised edn, 1987).

[55]   Stephen Greenblatt, *Renaissance Self-Fashioning: From More to Shakespeare* (Chicago, 1980).

little to lift the blinds on those opaque windows into her soul; and takes us not very far in determining whether the queen in her natural self was a convinced and devoutly Protestant Christian (and what kind of a Protestant), and whether that impinged perceptibly upon her public self, and policy.

As reported at the outset, the view has recently prevailed that Elizabeth was indeed a sincere and committed Protestant. Dr Haigh has already been quoted.[56] Professor Norman Jones, whose deconstructive work on Sir John Neale's interpretation of the parliamentary settlement of religion will probably stand, concludes that Elizabeth in 1559 knew what kind of religious settlement she wanted and got it, after overcoming objections and resistance, which were confined to conservative, Catholic objections and resistance, mainly in the House of Lords. That may well be in substance correct. But to go further, as Jones does, and suggest that the queen was 'as Protestant as Jewel, Grindal or Cox' is to go too far, and to exclude the distinct possibility (however hard to establish from evidence) that the queen who made the settlement was manipulated and constrained, if not inside the parliament then outside it, in her own court and household.[57] Winthrop Hudson seems to be of the same doubtful persuasion. His book on the Elizabethan Settlement dismisses as evidentially unfounded suggestions that Elizabeth favoured the late Henrician position, or Lutheranism, or, as vaguely consistent with Lutheranism, the 1549 Prayer Book. He concludes that she was a Protestant leaning, like most of her first bishops, towards the Swiss confessions and the Zwinglian model of 'pure' religion, her own position on the confessional spectrum accurately indicated by the 1559 Prayer Book.[58]

It is necessary to consider evidence to the contrary. Evidence of Elizabeth's religious conservatism and of the consequent strains in her relations with her more unreservedly Protestant bishops hardly constitutes news. Much of it has provided the most familiar themes of Elizabethan ecclesiastical history. But its interpretation leaves room for significant differences. Some historians may choose to interpret the evidence in its entirety as examples of rational public policy. The queen could not afford to alienate the religious sensibilities of a nation which was still widely and deeply addicted to the old ways, not least in its aristocratic and politically powerful upper levels, still less to offend gratuitously foreign Catholic powers. Dr Haigh writes: 'Elizabeth's liturgical conservatism, her enforcement of clerical conformity, her reluctance to support Protestant rebels

[56] Haigh, *Elizabeth I*, pp. 27-46.
[57] Norman L. Jones, *Faith By Statute: Parliament and the Settlement of Religion 1559* (1982). The quoted remark is at p. 9.
[58] Winthrop S. Hudson, *The Cambridge Connection and the Elizabethan Settlement of 1559* (Durham, NC, 1980), esp. pp. 90-9, 131-7. A forthcoming study by Dr Roger Bowens of the music of the Chapel Royal in 1559 calls in question the Jones-Hudson interpretation of the religious settlement.

abroad, her restraint of Protestant preaching, and her moderation of the persecution of Catholics, all suggest a determination not to drive the Catholics into outright opposition.'[59] This may well be what her policies and actions most plausibly suggest. Her personal preferences (it must again be said) are all but inaccessible. And yet her religious conservatism was so consistently manifested, applied with such apparent conviction, that it is hard to believe that it went against the grain of her own beliefs and tastes. To take the opposite view is a little like suspecting Lady Thatcher as Prime Minister of harbouring a secret sympathy for socialism or European federalism which she dared not disclose for fear of upsetting the markets or destabilising the currency. It remains possible that the Elizabethan compromise of Protestantism was a concession not only to the conservative prejudices of Elizabeth's subjects but to her own feelings.

Most of the episodes which found Elizabeth more or less publicly at odds with more advanced Protestant opinion are well known: a story central to any discussion of the Elizabethan Injunctions, Articles and Homilies, as well as to the particular matter of the ornaments rubric of the Prayer Book, that tiny Trojan horse out of which, in a sense, all the subsequent contention between conformists and nonconformist Puritans presently poured.[60] It makes sense to regard as concessions to the old religion the rules about surplices and square caps and even more the injunction which required the use at communion not of plain baker's bread (as the Prayer Book pre-scribed) but wafers somewhat resembling the old hosts or 'singing cakes'. It would matter to an unreconstructed Catholic that he should receive his maker in a still familiar form from a celebrant vested like some kind of priest. The absence from the Injunctions of any specific order to remove stone altars and replace them with plain wooden tables can be explained in the same way. The case only has to be turned upside down to account for the insistence of Grindal and other bishops that altars must indeed be eradicated: Bishop Ridley, Bishop Latimer, Bishop Hooper and Mr Bradford had all gone to the stake as witnesses against the doctrine of which the stone altar was a symbol. 'So that by re-edifying of altars we shall also seem to join with the adversaries that burned those good men in condemning some part of their doctrine.' On this issue Elizabeth appears to have climbed down.[61]

[59] Haigh, *Elizabeth I*, p. 36.

[60] R.W. Dixon, *History of the Church of England from the Abolition of the Roman Jurisdiction* (1902), v and vi; Patrick Collinson, *The Elizabethan Puritan Movement* (1967); idem, *Archbishop Grindal, 1519-1583: The Struggle for a Reformed Church* (1979); W.P. Haugaard, *Elizabeth and the English Reformation: The Struggle for a Stable Settlement of Religion* (Cambridge, 1968); John H. Primus, *The Vestments Controversy: An Historical Study of the Earliest Tensions within the Church of England in the Reigns of Edward VI and Elizabeth* (Kampen, 1960).

[61] Collinson, *Grindal*, pp. 100-1. The Injunctions can be found in H. Gee and W. Hardy, ed., *Documents Illustrative of English Church History* (1896), pp. 417-67.

The related issue of the cross as an emotive Christian symbol and focal point of vision in worship brings us closer to the queen's own convictions and is harder to square with a purely *politique* explanation for her conservatism. The 1559 Injunctions had called for the removal from all churches of 'things superstitious', specifying monuments of feigned miracles, pilgrimages, idolatry and superstition. Apparently it had not occurred to Elizabeth that crosses were included in that catalogue. Indeed, if Bishop Sandys is to be believed, writing to Peter Martyr on 1 April 1560, 'the queen's majesty considered it not contrary to the word of God, nay, rather for the advantage of the church, that the image of Christ crucified, together with Mary and John, should be placed as heretofore, in some conspicuous part of the church, where they might more readily be seen by all the people'.[62] As Margaret Aston has recently remarked: 'This passage speaks volumes for Elizabeth's religious position.'[63] Protestants – the Protestants' sort of Protestants – felt very differently about the cross, whether used as a bodily gesture (for example, after sneezing) or as personal adornment or as street furniture, and above all in the form of the great 'rood' with its flanking imagery in a commanding position above the heads of the worshipping congregation. To a considerable extent these 'idols' were understood to be included among the 'monuments of superstition' condemned in the Injunctions and were removed from many, perhaps most parish churches in or soon after the Royal Visitation of the summer of 1559. When, some years later, the suffragan bishop of Dover and future dean of Canterbury Richard Rogers found the rood still standing in a Kentish church of which he was rector, he was so indignant that in expostulating with a leading parishioner he swore 'by God's soul!' – a scandalous story which immediately went the round of Kentish hostelries, forcing the bishop to take action for slanderous defamation.[64]

But that oath would not have troubled Elizabeth Tudor in the least. An old friend of her youth later remonstrated with her for her habit of using oaths a great deal stronger than 'by God's soul'. 'Your gratious M[ajesty] in your anger hath used to sweare, sometime by that abhominable Idoll the Masse, and often and grievouslie by God, and by Christ, and by manie parts of his glorified bodie, and by Saints, faith, troth, and other forbidden things.'[65] Trivial it may seem, but this (by no means the only evidence of Elizabeth's use of the old catholic oaths) opens not a mere window but a whole wall on the queen's soul. There were no Protestant oaths. The

[62] Sandys to Peter Martyr, 1 April 1560, *Zurich Letters*, ed. Hastings Robinson, i, Parker Society (Cambridge, 1842), pp. 73-4.

[63] Margaret Aston, *England's Iconoclasts*, i, *Laws against Images* (Oxford, 1988), p. 303.

[64] Patrick Collinson, *The Birthpangs of Protestant England: Religious and Cultural Change in the Sixteenth and Seventeenth Centuries* (1988), p. 52.

[65] *The Seconde Parte of a Register*, ed. Albert Peel (Cambridge, 1915), ii, pp. 53-4.

Puritan who dared to rebuke the queen for her swearing and accused her of wholesale backsliding from true religion ('but halflie by your Majesty hath God been honoured, his Church reformed and established') had known her in early days, when she had lived with Catherine Parr. He had found his wife in that household, and his reminiscences about those good old days have the stamp of authenticity. He recalled how Elizabeth had said that she would one day walk down by the river and visit his old and ailing mother, who 'joyed then not a little to hear of your godly study and virtuous inclination'. But later he had heard that she was 'so marvellously altered in mind, manners and manie things, that there was no hope of any such reformation ... as was before hoped for'.[66]

We must return to the issue of the cross. There seems little doubt that the reinstatement of a cross and candlesticks in the royal chapel in the autumn of 1559 was a calculated retort to the unauthorised holocaust of roods and rood imagery in the Visitation of the previous summer; little doubt either, given the alarmed reaction of the newly elected bishops, that she also intended to signal in this way that the crosses should be restored, throughout the country. That was how her action was interpreted in the precincts of Canterbury Cathedral. In the event that retrograde measure, which would have been utterly damaging to the credit of the newly appointed bishops, was headed off by spirited acts of protest which included an episcopal letter accompanying a short treatise, 'Reasons Against Images in Churches': 'We beseech your Highness most humbly not to strain us any further ... We pray your Majesty also not to be offended with this our plainness and liberty, which all good and Christian princes have ever taken in good part at the hands of godly bishops.'[67]

But in the Chapel Royal the cross remained, to provoke a whole series of teacup storms for years to come, including a verbal attack from the pulpit in the queen's presence, a major literary engagement with the Catholic writer John Martial who (no doubt embarrassingly) came to the queen's defence on the issue, and a whole succession of temerarious iconoclastic attacks on the offensive idol, smashing it, burning it, treading it under foot. One of these incidents involved the queen's fool, apparently instigated by Protestant courtiers. Elizabeth fought back, shouting down the dean of St Paul's in the pulpit and regularly repairing the work of the inonoclasts. A similar battle was fought in the public thoroughfares of London where the great cross of Cheapside was more than once saved from destruction by the queen's personal intervention.[68] The biblical precedent and *topos* for the

[66] Ibid.

[67] Collinson, *Grindal*, pp. 97-9; Collinson, *Birthpangs* p. 52; Haugaard, *Elizabeth and the English Reformation*, pp. 185-200.

[68] Aston, *England's Iconoclasts*, i, pp. 310-14; Patrick Collinson, 'If Constantine, Then Also Theodosius', in *Godly People*, pp. 130-1. For the literary exchanges, see *An Answer to John Martial's Treatise of the Cross by James Calfhill*, ed. R. Gibbings, Parker Society (Cambridge, 1846).

strongly negative feelings entertained towards the image of the cross among 'godly' Protestants was the act of King Hezekiah who in his general purge of idolatry broke in pieces the brazen serpent which Moses had lifted up in the wilderness. Like that serpent, the cross in its original erection was a living, saving force, but preserved as a kind of museum piece and idol, dead and corrupting. It appears that Queen Elizabeth did not like to be compared to King Hezekiah.[69]

So while the symbolism of the royal chapel furnishings may have served a diplomatic purpose, in the perception of foreign Catholic governments, it is hard not to believe that Elizabeth was personally addicted to her little cross, impossible to accept the contrary: that she tolerated it with barely concealed distaste for thirty years, as a mere political necessity. The cross still stood on her altar in 1586.

Not just 'Puritans' but the early Elizabethan bishops, like the Swiss reformers and Calvin, their role models, accorded the second commandment (as most of us know it) independent and free-standing status, implying that the inhibition on the making and use of religious images was of equal and distinct validity, even apart from the first commandment prohibiting other gods. In their 'Treatise Against Images', the bishops told Elizabeth plainly: 'If by vertue of the second commaundement, Images were not lawful in the temple of the Jewes, then by the same commaundement they are not lawful in the churches of the Christians.[70]

This does not seem to have been the queen's position, which was evidently in the Augustinian-Catholic-Lutheran tradition which, by fusing together the first and second commandments, made the matter of images dependent upon the worship of the one true God.[71] This was to equate images with idols only insofar as they attracted that worship, *latria*, due to God only. Margaret Aston, reviving the Victorian scholarship of John Griffiths, editor of the official Homilies of the reformed Church of England, has shown that this critical difference is transparently revealed in the process by which the second, Elizabethan edition of the Homilies emerged from the 1563 Convocation into and out of the Court and, in all

---

[69] This will be brilliantly expounded in a monograph by Margaret Aston, *The King's Bed-Post* (Cambridge University Press, forthcoming).

[70] Corpus Christi College Cambridge, MS 115, pp. 201-15; printed in *Correspondence of Matthew Parker*, ed. J. Bruce and T.T. Perowne, Parker Society (Cambridge, 1853), pp. 79-95. However, apart from its provenance there is no reason to connect this 'open letter' to the queen specifically with Parker and rather more to attribute it to Grindal. (See Collinson, *Grindal*, p. 98.)

[71] On the status and force of the second commandment, see Aston, *England's Iconoclasts*, i, 'Hermeneutical Differences', chapter 7, 'The Sin of Idolatry: The Teaching of the Decalogue', pp. 343-479. A weakness of Carlos M.N. Eire's otherwise useful survey *War against Idols: The Reformation of Worship from Erasmus to Calvin* (Cambridge, 1986) is that it fails to engage with the fundamental significance of alternative readings, divisions and punctuation of the Decalogue. Neither 'Decalogue' nor 'Commandments' will be found in the index.

probability, the queen's own hands.[72] The copy placed in those hands survives in the royal collection in the British Library. Griffiths found that it differed in a number of significant respects from all other copies subsequently printed and promulgated, indeed from the Homilies as they would be published and read in parish churches for many generations to come.

In the first part of the Homily against Peril of Idolatry, as it came from convocation, Elizabeth read: 'Which place both enforceth that neither the material Church or temple ought to have any images in it, ... neither that any true Christian ought to have any ado with filthy and dead images.' When Elizabeth had finished with it (and that it was Elizabeth who made or called for these changes cannot be absolutely proven), others would read and hear: 'Which place enforceth, both that we should not have images in the temple, for fear and occasion of worshipping them, though they be of themselves things indifferent.' Where the same homily had originally referred to the Word of God speaking against not only idolatry and the worshipping of images but against idols and images themselves, the emended version remarked 'not as though they were simply forbidden by the New Testament without such occasion and danger', that is, of rendering idolatrous worship.[73]

Elizabeth's unusually deep prejudice against clerical marriage is notorious. It was an odd and eclectic kind of Protestantism which was consistent with such views. When they were first shared with Matthew Parker, himself a married man (but destined to be the last married archbishop of Canterbury for well over a century), the primate's reaction was one of utter consternation: 'I was in an horror to hear such words to come from her mild nature and Christianly learned conscience.' 'We have cause all to be utterly discomforted and discouraged.'[74]

It was equally an odd sort of Protestant who nursed a negative prejudice against the preaching ministry and wished it to be reduced to a bare, skeletal, ancillary service, like some draconian Minister of Health determined to confine kidney dialysis and hip replacements to a very few select

[72] Aston, *England's Iconoclasts*, i, pp. 320-4.

[73] John Griffiths's Preface to the Oxford, 1859 edition of *The Two Books of Homilies Appointed to be Read in Churches*. The unique presentation copy on which Griffiths's argument rests, according to him the Homilies as they left the 1563 Convocation, is British Library, C.25.h.3. The alterations in the Homilies as promulgated extend beyond the matters of interest to Dr Aston and include the number of the sacraments, Christology, and the communication of the elements of the sacrament to the unbelievers and faithless. So far as the latter issue is concerned, it is well known that the 29th Article of Religion 'Of the wicked which do not eate the body of Christe in the use of the Lord's Supper' was included in the Articles as approved synodally but omitted in their subsequent public authorisation, by the council and, later, parliament. There are implications here of theological disagreements of substance between the queen and leading churchmen: *Synodalia*, i, ed. E. Cardwell (Oxford, 1842), pp. 34-41, 101; Haugaard, *Elizabeth and the English Reformation*, p. 253.

[74] Parker to Cecil, 1561, *Parker Correspondence*, pp. 156-7.

hospitals. There may have been good reasons why Elizabeth thought that three or four preachers were sufficient for a shire.[75] But it is hard to reconcile that opinion with the reputation otherwise attributed to her of a godly evangelical Protestant, not ashamed of that Gospel of Christ which is the power of God unto salvation. Archbishop Grindal, no less dismayed than his predecessor had been when confronting the queen on clerical marriage, found this hard to stomach: 'Alas, Madam! is the scripture more plain in any one thing, than that the Gospel of Christ should be plentifully preached; and that plenty of labourers should be sent into the Lord's harvest; which, being great and large, standeth in need, not of a few, but many workmen.' 'But God forbid, Madam, that you should ... any way go about to diminish the preaching of Christ's gospel: for that would ruinate all together at the length.'[76] Grindal knew that the queen preferred the authorised Homilies to the unpredictability of preaching, That was why she had taken some trouble with the text presented to her in 1563. But he told her that if every parish could be provided with a preaching pastor, 'which is rather to be wished then hoped for', there would be no need to read homilies. But, until then, 'better half a loaf than no bread'. Elizabeth was not persuaded. Eight years later she told a number of bishops that there was more learning in one of those homilies than in twenty of some of their sermons.[77]

VI

It was rare and unusual for Elizabeth's conservative religious prejudices to be attacked with such vehement directness as Archbishop Grindal used in his famous but fatal letter; or William Fuller in his 'Book to the Queen' which contained those strictures against swearing already quoted; or Dean Alexander Nowell when he preached against the cross in the royal chapel; and for understandable reasons. Grindal's effective career was abruptly terminated. After his unfortunate sermon, Archbishop Parker took Nowell home to dinner 'for pure pity'. 'He was utterly dismayed.'[78]

More often, covert and tactful ways and means were found to instruct the queen's conscience. This returns us to the prayers and pious ejaculations put into her mouth which it is tempting but not always safe to read as first-

[75] A view attributed to the queen by Archbishop Grindal in his famous letter of 20 December 1576; presumably uttered in one of the interviews known to have preceded its composition. See *Remains of Edmund Grindal*, ed. W. Nicholson, Parker Society (Cambridge, 1843), p. 379. Elizabeth's negative attitude to preaching comes through strongly in the conversation recorded on the occasion of the presentation of the clerical subsidy in February 1585, Neale, *Elizabeth I and her Parliaments, 1584-1601*, pp. 69-71.

[76] *Remains of Grindal*, pp. 378, 382; Collinson, *Grindal*, pp. 239-45.

[77] *Remains of Grindal*, pp. 382-3; Neale, *Elizabeth I and her Parliaments, 1584-1601*, p. 70.

[78] *Parker Correspondence*, p. 235.

hand evidence not only of Elizabeth's religious beliefs and opinions but of the depth and quality of her spirituality. When Alexander Nowell was accused of flattery in his court sermons (the attack on the cross was not in his usual style), he replied that 'he had no other way to instruct the queen what she should be but by commending her'.[79]

Bentley's *Monument of Matrones* represented a variant of this strategy, although it cut closer to the bone by making Elizabeth confess, profusely, indeed with prolixity, her many sins. This she may not have been in the least reluctant to do, but surely not in the full public light of day, for all her female subjects to read. Bentley's texts also underline in the very words placed in the queen's mouth, or in the mouth of God as he addresses her, that her office is a public office and a solemn trust, held in subordination to God and for the sole purpose of advancing his kingdom and conserving the souls and bodies of the people committed to her charge. In a prayer which in Bentley's third 'lamp' immediately follows Theodore Beza's paraphrase of Psalm 18 ('The Lord is my rock and my fortress') Elizabeth is made to call herself God's handmaid, 'a subject and servant to thy most high and sacred Maiestie, and a child depending alone and wholie upon thy divine and fatherlie providence for all things.'

> And that I remembering whose minister I am may first above all things in a perfect zeale of thy house, and love of thy people, ever seeke thy honour and glorie, and studie continuallie to preserve thy people committed to my charge, in wealth, peace or godlinesse.

> Lastlie, O most mightie God, looke what remaineth yet of the happie building, enlarging and finishing of thy Church, and to the establishing and planting of thy Religion perfectlie therein, according to the prescript rule of thy blessed word and full discharge of my dutie ...[80]

This last passage is redolent of the evangelical ecclesiology of 'edification', the very hallmark of the puritan reading of St Paul.[81]

There is no 'or else' in these petitions; no suggestion of 'if not, remove me from this place'. So there is less of the politics of Old Testament prophecy, less menace, than we find, for example, in a memorandum drawn up by the bishops at the time of the 1572 parliament, which threatened the queen with divine displeasure and even divine deposition if she failed to execute Mary queen of Scots, citing the precedent of King Saul who lost his throne for the sin of sparing the life of Agag.[82] But trained sniffer dogs ought

---

[79] Ralph Churton, *The Life of Alexander Nowell* (Oxford, 1809), p. 92.

[80] Bentley, *Monument*, pp. 253-71.

[81] John S. Coolidge, *The Pauline Renaissance in England: Puritanism and the Bible* (Oxford, 1970).

[82] *Proceedings in the Parliament of Elizabeth I*, i, *1558-1581*, ed. T.E. Hartley (Leicester, 1981), pp. 274-82.

nevertheless to be able to pick up the scent of a kind of resistance doctrine in Bentley's prayers and meditations. In the section called 'The Kings Heast or Gods familiar speech to the Queene', God tells her: 'Beware therefore that yee abuse not this authoritie given unto you by me, under certaine lawes and conditions ... For be you sure that I have placed you in this seate upon this condition.'[83] I am reminded of the great parliament man Thomas Norton who wrote to his son (from his imprisonment in the Tower): 'I have no dealing with the queen but as with the image of God', which at first sight looks like a piece of divine-right absolutism but in fact is anything but; and of the earl of Huntingdon's brother, Sir Francis Hastings, who made this note at a sermon: 'Obedience, what it is, it is due unto the Lorde only.'[84]

There was a note of conditionality, an implied threat, in Bentley's ostensibly flattering text, as none would have known better than Elizabeth herself. It was not difficult in the sixteenth century for any woman, royal or not, to pass, in one or two false moves on the chauvinistic snakes and ladders board, from the shining emblem of the Woman Clothed with the Sun to its antitype, the Whore of Babylon, those contrasted images pictured side by side in Bale's *Image of both churches*, the whore seductive and curvaceous, sexy and sexist. Patterns of godly and faithful womanhood were always balanced and opposed by their opposites, seductresses, harlots, female tyrants, according to the all-pervading rhetorical repertoire of binary opposition.[85] Any royal lady was liable, by putting a moral, religious or political foot wrong, to find herself newly type-cast as Jezebel, as in their times were Mary Tudor, Mary of Guise, Catherine de Médicis and Mary queen of Scots; and eventually Elizabeth herself, on the catholic continent, after the execution of Mary Stuart, in the polemical poem published at Antwerp, *De Jezebelis*.[86]

So, since Elizabeth understood such matters perfectly well, it is likely that she was as conscious of this protestant factor as of the need to conciliate Catholicism. If the one factor helps to account for her religious

[83] Bentley, *Monument*, p. 309.
[84] BL, MS Add. 48023, fol. 33 r; Huntington Library, MS HA Religious Box 1 (9).
[85] King, *Tudor Royal Iconography*, p. 183.
[86] The Antwerp text attacked Elizabeth in the following extreme terms:

> Batarde incestueuse, et paillard publique
> Perfide, deloyale, et fille de ta soeur.

Bentley might have been glad to use such language with respect to other 'Jezebels'. Readers of his *Monument* (p. 35) read: 'There is not a more wicked head than the head of a serpent: and there is no wrath above the wrath of a woman .... It were better to dwell with a Lion and a Dragon, then to keep house with a wicked woman.' But nothing is quite what it seems. These were texts from the book of Ecclesiastes and the young Princess Elizabeth had copied them out 'with her owne hande', or so according to John Bale who incorporated her scriptural texts into his edition of *A godly medytacyon of the christen sowle*, which Bentley reprinted.

conservatism, the other may explain the fulsomeness of her widely acclaimed evangelical piety. If Paris was worth a mass to Henry of Navarre, a secure place in the hearts of Elizabeth's protestant subjects was worth Bentley's *Monument of Matrones*.

But if we were able to strip off both these layers, open all the Chinese boxes and Russian dolls, what should we find inside? Are there, after all, any snakes in Iceland?

5

'Not Sexual in the Ordinary Sense':
Women, Men and Religious Transactions

'It was a curious relationship: not at all a sexual relationship in the ordinary sense. And yet it was a relationship which could only have existed between persons of different sexes.'[1] What was this 'curious relationship? It concerned John Knox, the Scottish reformer of the sixteenth century, and a number of women with whom he was acquainted and, we might say, more or less intimate, including two wives, a mother-in-law and a Very Dear Friend. This essay has a somewhat wider scope than Knox and his extended family. But Knox provides us with a clearing in the forest where, having landed as it were by helicopter, we can commence exploration of that dense jungle which is women, men and religious transactions.

Knox is the first Scot whom we can claim to know as a person, and also the first whose relations with women are well-documented.[2] It is a remarkable fact that some of the secrets of Knox's personality should have been disclosed in his correspondence with women.[3] Remarkable because, as everyone knows, Knox was the author of the diatribe called *A First Blast of the Trumpet Against the Monstrous Regiment of Women* (which is to say, the 'Unnatural Government' of women). Knox was himself a victim of 'the odious empire' (as he called it) of two women: Mary Tudor, queen of England, and Mary of Guise, regent of Scotland, rulers from whom he was estranged on religious grounds and from whose threats against his person he was constrained to flee, like Elijah from Jezebel, with whom he and other Protestants freely identified those female tyrants. But Knox's tirade was less than flattering on the general topic of women, who are dismissed as 'weake, fraile, impacient, feble, and foolishe, ... unconstant, variable, cruell, and lacking the spirit of counsel and regiment'. 'And these notable faultes have men in all ages espied in that kinde ...'[4]

Yet this mysogonistical prophet was also, as Robert Louis Stevenson observed, a 'man of many women friends; a man of some expansion toward

---

[1] Majorie Bowen, *Life of John Knox* (1949), p. 48.

[2] Among Knox's many biographers, one may compare the differing tones, interests and values of Thomas McCrie, *Life of John Knox*, 2 vols (Edinburgh, 1814), Lord Eustace Percy, *John Knox* (1937), and Jasper Ridley, *John Knox* (Oxford, 1968).

[3] Contained in vols 3 and 6 of *The Works of John Knox*, ed. David Laing (Edinburgh, 1844-).

[4] *Works of Knox*, iv, pp. 365-420: this passage occurring on p. 374.

the other sex; a man ever ready to comfort weeping women, and to weep along with them'.[5] The author of *The First Blast of the Trumpet* could write to Mrs Elizabeth Bowes, a gentlewoman living in the north east of England: 'Since the first day that it pleasit the providence of God to bring yow and me in familiaritie, I have alwayis delytit in your company.' And to another woman friend he wrote: 'Of nature I am churlish ... Yet one thinge I ashame not to affirme, that familiaritie once throughlie contracted was never yet brocken on my default.'[6]

Knox was in his mid forties when his 'familiarity' began with Mrs Bowes, who was born Elizabeth Aske of Richmondshire, the wife of Richard Bowes, son of Sir Ralph Bowes, and the mother of his fifteen children. These included Margery, her fifth daughter, whom Knox was to marry, against the strenuous opposition of the father and perhaps more for the sake of the mother than for any qualities of her own.[7] He addressed his mother-in-law, who was of his own age, as 'deirlie belovit Mother', 'deir mother and spous', her daughter, his wife, as 'dear sister'. He assured the mother that there was no one on earth to whom he felt closer, with the exception of his wife, 'whome God hath offrit unto me, and commandit me to lufe as my awn flesche'.[8] Yet Knox's marriage was evidently a satisfactory one: and useful, since Margery became her husband's secretary as well as the mother of his two sons. But her mother would survive her, looking after her son-in-law and grandsons in her old age.

When Mary Tudor had come to the throne, Knox had withdrawn to the Continent as a religious refugee. Elizabeth Bowes's husband had assumed that that would be the end of the absurd plan for his daughter to marry a man who was both a priest and a Scot, and so doubly objectionable. But the marriage duly took place and not only Knox's bride but his mother-in-law, who was already fifty and elderly according to sixteenth-century standards, followed him to Geneva, abandoning her husband and forfeiting the comfortable life of a country gentlewoman for an uncertain future. And presently Knox had the company in Geneva of another woman friend, Mrs Anne Locke, a young, well-educated London housewife, born and married

---

[5]   R.L. Stevenson, 'John Knox and his Relations to Women' in his *Familiar Studies of Men and Books* (1901 edn), p. 255.

[6]   *Works of Knox*, iii, pp. 337-8; vi, p.11.

[7]   There are two recent studies of the Knox-Bowes correspondence and relationship: Christine M. Newman, 'The Reformation and Elizabeth Bowes: A Study of a Sixteenth-Century Northern Gentlewoman', in *Women in the Church*, Studies in Church History, 27, ed. W.J. Sheils and Diana Wood (Oxford, 1990), pp. 325-33; and A. Daniel Frankforter, 'Elizabeth Bowes and John Knox: A Woman and Reformation Theology', *Church History*, 56 (1987), pp. 333-47.

[8]   *Works of Knox*, iii, p. 370. The implied reference is to Ephesians 5:25 ('husbands, love your wives'), which is perhaps significantly indicative of a constrained rather than purely voluntary emotion.

IOANNES CNOXVS.

The Scottish reformer John Knox as presented to a European audience in the
Protestant emblem book, Theodore Beza's *Icones* (1580).

into the merchant aristocracy.[9] Knox had been surrounded in both Edin-burgh and London by circles of dependent and admiring women – 'sisters' – for whom (as he sometimes explained without excessive gallantry) he felt more or less equal responsibility: 'To me ye ar all equall in Chryst.'[10]

But Anne Locke was rather more equal than most. Knox wrote: 'Ye wryt that your desyre is ernist to sie me. Deir Sister, yf I suld expres the thrist and langoure whilk I haif had for your presence, I suld appeir to pass measure.'[11] And soon Mrs Locke joined him in exile, leaving her husband in London and travelling with two small children, one of whom she buried within four days of arriving in Geneva. It is important to understand the circumstances. Although Knox might seem to have been guilty of double enticement, both Mrs Bowes and Mrs Locke had decamped for a religious purpose, to preserve their safety and the integrity of their Protestant consciences.[12] If they had remained in England they could have been confronted with a choice between conforming to a religion which they equated with idolatry and being roasted alive. Henry Locke must have approved, for he later appointed his wife sole executrix of his considerable estate. (Bowes, on the other hand, made no mention of his wife in his will, and was dead before she returned from Geneva.) So the relations between Knox and these 'sisters' was 'not sexual in the ordinary sense' but spiritual and ideological. Knox later explained that so far as his mother-in-law was concerned, 'the caus of our great familiaritie and long acquentance ... was nether fleshe nor bloode, but a troubled conscience upon hir part'.[13] Nevertheless, when Knox as a widower in his fifties made a second marriage and chose a girl of scarcely seventeen and of vaguely royal blood (she was a Stuart) there was more occasion for malicious gossip.

---

[9]   Patrick Collinson, 'The Role of Women in the English Reformation Illustrated by the Life and Friendships of Anne Locke', in *Studies in Church History*, 2, ed. G. J. Cuming (1965), pp. 258-72; reprinted in Patrick Collinson, *Godly People: Essays on English Protestantism and Puritanism* (1983), pp. 273-87.

[10]   Knox 'to his loving sisters in Edinburgh, Janet Adamsone and Janet Henderson', *c.* 1557, *Works of Knox*, iv, pp. 244-5.

[11]   Knox 'to his loving sister, Mistres Anne Locke, wife to Mr Harie Locke, Marchand, nygh to Bowe Kirk, in Chaipside in London', 19 November 1556, *Works of Knox*, iv, pp. 238-9.

[12]   See Knox's letter 'to Mistress Locke and Mistress Hickman, merchandis wyffis in London', also 1556, admonishing and beseeching them 'evin in Chrystis bowellis' to 'flie the present idolatrie', but also referring to 'the consall and discretioun of thois that God hath apoyntit to your heidis (your husbandis I meane).' (*Works of Knox*, v, p. 219.) Rose Hickman was Anne Locke's sister-in-law. See Maria Dowling and Joy Shakespeare, 'Religion and Politics in Mid-Tudor England through the Eyes of an English Protestant Woman: The Recollections of Rose Hickman', *Bulletin of the Institute of Historical Research*, 55 (1982), pp. 94-102.

[13]   The words occur in Knox's defence of his dealings with Elizabeth Bowes attached to his book against the Jesuit James Tyrie (1572); *Works of Knox*, vi, pp. 513-14.

II

If we look for a path out of our clearing in the jungle which will lead to some of the wider implications of this subject, one trail is signposted The Role of Women in Religious Movements. Elizabeth Bowes and even more Anne Locke are notable examples of the signal contribution made by women in the cause of the Protestant Reformation. The very fact that Mrs Bowes was probably the first committed Protestant of her sex and class in the entire north east of England makes her sufficiently remarkable: quite apart from her willingness to abandon the all-enveloping circles of neighbourhood and kindred to live with her unusual son-in-law in strange surroundings, first in Switzerland and later in Scotland. As for Mrs Locke, she represents a generation of women who were highly educated in classical and modern languages and other intellectual skills thought proper to their sex by Vives, Erasmus and other Renaissance educators. Her time in Geneva was spent not in housekeeping or embroidery but in translating John Calvin's sermons. (The translation was published and the copy now in the British Library is inscribed by her husband in an elegant Italic hand: 'Liber Henrici Lock ex dono uxoris suae', doubtless the first such inscription in English history.) When Knox returned to Scotland to fling himself into a revolution, it was to Anne Locke that he sent regular reports of the developing religious and political situation, with the intention that she should pass these on to the English government.[14] After the death of her husband, Anne Locke married Edward Dering, the most popular London preacher of the day, who perhaps reminded her of Knox. His letter of proposal survives, the earliest, I think, from a minister of religion in English history. Finally, after Dering's premature death from consumption, she made a third marriage to a merchant and mayor of Exeter. In her sixties she was still translating and publishing foreign theology.[15]

On the whole, Anne Vaughan/Locke/Dering/Prowse seems to had a more satisfying life than her exact contemporary and fellow-translator, Lady Ann Bacon, Francis Bacon's mother, a brilliant scholar (she read Latin and Greek, French and Italian, 'as her native tongue'), an able theologian and a religious enthusiast who seems to have found the conditions of her marriage to Queen Elizabeth's lord keeper, Sir Nicholas Bacon, so vexing

---

[14] Knox's distinctly uneasy relations with the English government, the cost of *The First Blast*, made Mrs Locke a necessary as well as convenient intermediary. His most dramatic despatch is dated 18 November 1559 (the first anniversary of Queen Elizabeth's accession): 'I cannot weill write to anie other, becaus the actioun may seeme to appertaine to my countrie onlie. But becaus I trust yee suspect me not of avarice, I am bold to say to you, that if we perishe in this our interprise, the limits of Londoun will be straiter than they are now, within few yeeres.' (*Works of Knox*, vi, pp. 100-1).

[15] Patrick Collinson, 'The Role of Women', in *Godly People*, pp. 273-87; idem, *A Mirror of Elizabethan Puritanism: The Life and Letters of 'Godly Master Dering'*, Friends of Dr William's Library Annual Lecture (1965), reprinted in *Godly People*, pp. 288-324.

(yet it was an ideal, Stoic match) that, as was said, 'she was but little better than frantic in her age'.[16]

Anne Locke was in many respects exceptional, but also representative of a generation of women whose lives were bissected by the religious revolution of the sixteenth century. In France, it has been said, it was mainly through the evangelism of mothers, wives and daughters that Protestantism spread with such rapidity through the landed aristocracy, in such regions as Normandy and Languedoc.[17] For great numbers of these Calvinist gentlewomen (and citizens' wives too) religion became the dominant interest of their lives. Like Mrs Locke, they were serious students of divinity and bosom friends and patrons of the Calvinist preachers. And in the wars of religion, they played an active political and even military role. In England, where the Reformation matured in the secondary movement of exacting religious seriousness known as Puritanism, women were equally to the forefront.[18] And when some Puritan sects broke away from the church in the mid seventeenth century, the decisive leadership was sometimes provided by women: women like Mrs Dorothy Hazard of Bristol, the effective founder of a Baptist church which, more than three hundred years later, still flourishes. In the annals of this society, Mrs Hazard is described as 'like a hee-goat before the flock ... like a Deborah she arose, with strength of holy Resolution in her soul from God, even a Mother in Israell'.[19]

'Hee-goat before the flock' and 'Mother in Israel' were expressions not necessarily meant ironically and pejoratively, but they could be and sometimes were. There is a continuity of chauvinistic comment on female ascendancy in religious affairs which seems to have had a long ancestry.

[16]   Patrick Collinson, 'Sir Nicholas Bacon and the Elizabethan *Via Media*', Historical Journal, 23 (1980), reprinted in *Godly People*, pp. 149-51.

[17]   Lucien Romier, *Le royaume de Catherine de Médicis: la France à la veille des guerres de réligion* (Paris, 1922), iii, pp. 234-40. See the more recent scholarship of Nancy L. Roelker, 'The Appeal of Calvinism to French Noblewomen in the Sixteenth Century', *Journal of Interdisciplinary History*, 2 (1972), pp. 391-418; idem, 'The Role of Noblewomen in the French Reformation', *Archiv für Reformationsgeschichte*, 63 (1972), pp. 168-95; and Natalie Zemon Davis, 'City Women and Religious Change', in her *Society and Culture in Early Modern France* (1975), pp. 65-95. Roelker's 'The Role of Noblewomen' appeared in *Archiv für Reformationsgeschichte* as one of three articles on women in the Reformation, which also included Miriam U. Chrisman, 'Women and the Reformation in Strasbourg, 1490-1530' (pp. 143-68), with an introduction by Roland H. Bainton who was currently writing his three volumes (Minneapolis, 1971-7) on *Women of the Reformation*. See also S.M. Wyntjes, 'Women and Religious Choices in the Sixteenth-Century Netherlands', *Archiv für Reformationsgechichte*, 75 (1984), pp. 276-89.

[18]   See Jacqueline Eales's account of Lady Brilliana Harley, *Puritans and Roundheads: The Harleys of Brampton Bryan and the Outbreak of the English Civil War* (Cambridge, 1990).

[19]   Patrick Collinson, 'The English Conventicle', in *Voluntary Religion*, Studies in Church History, 23, ed. W.J. Sheils and Diana Wood (Oxford, 1986), pp. 223-59. See also Claire Cross, ' "He-Goats before the Flock": A Note on the Part Played by Women in the Founding of Some Civil War Churches', in *Popular Belief and Culture*, Studies in Church History, 8, ed. G.J. Cuming and D. Baker (Cambridge, 1972), pp. 195-210; Keith Thomas, 'Women and the Civil War Sects', in T. Aston, ed., *Crisis in Europe, 1560-1660* (1965), pp. 317-40.

ON SLEDGE AND HORSEBACK

TO OUTCAST SIBERIAN LEPERS.

Illustrated from Photographs and Drawings.

BY

KATE MARSDEN.

MEMBER (SPECIAL BADGE) OF THE ROYAL BRITISH NURSES' ASSOCIATION;
MEMBER AND MEDALLIST OF THE RUSSIAN IMPERIAL RED CROSS SOCIETY, etc., etc.;
FELLOW OF THE ROYAL GEOGRAPHICAL SOCIETY.

———

LONDON:
THE RECORD PRESS, LIMITED,
376, STRAND, W.C.

Title-page of Kate Marsden, *On Sledge and Horseback to Outcast Siberian Lepers* (1893). Kate Marsden's one-woman mission to the neglected lepers of Siberia is representative of many other remarkable missionaries and travellers of her sex. She became a controversial figure who in 1921 had to defend herself in *My Mission to Siberia: A Vindication*. (*Cambridge University Library*)

Everyone knows about Anthony Trollope's contribution to this theme:
'The bishop shook in his shoes. When Mrs Proudie began to talk of the souls
of the people he always shook in his shoes. She had an eloquent way of
raising her voice over the word soul that was qualified to make any ordinary
man shake in his shoes.' But here is a seventeenth century letter out of
Northamptonshire: 'Besse Alleyn who is my grand Mistress of that Parish
... and the sole Judge of Sermons there.' And here is some gossip about the
wife of the bishop of Norwich in 1575, a man whose name was Freke and
who had much in common with poor Bishop Proudie: 'This is *vox populi*, a
principle well known throughout all Norfolk, spread by his household, that
whatsoever Mrs Freke will have done, the Bishop must and will accom-
plish.'[20]

The preponderance of women in these religious movements may
indicate the greater natural religiosity of women. Whether this proposition
requires proof, or, if true, explanation is a question which may divide the
sexes. Richard Hooker, writing in the 1590s about the popularity of Puritan
religion among women, put it down to four factors. Women were more
'propense and inclinable to holines' than men; they made zealous partisans
and evangelists, 'diligent in drawing their husbands, children, servants,
friends and allies the same waie'; they were pitiful and bountiful to needy
preachers; and they were what in Scotland is called 'postit', 'giving verie
large and particular intelligence how all neere about them stand affected
as concerning the same cause'.[21]

Such mildly 'sexist' reflections should be balanced by the often over-
looked gynophilia of the Protestantism of the sixteenth century which
attributed (in principle) to all women qualities traditionally ascribed to a
few remarkable women, remarkable that is in rank, learning and piety. The
devout woman even became (as a type of the church) a kind of emblem for
the representative and ideal Christian, as in the case of the early protestant
martyr Anne Askew, who was treated as a reincarnation of the early
Christian martyr Blandina, herself a symbolic *ecclesia* figure.[22] But to discover that even this apparent pro-feminism had a double edge and was by no
means wholly favourable to women's interests and rights, we may read Dr
Lyndal Roper's book on sixteenth-century Augsburg, *The Holy Household* .[23]

[20] Anthony Trollope, *The Last Chronicle of Barset*, World Classics (Oxford, 1980), p. 104; Robert
Sybthorpe to Sir John Lambe, 20 May 1639, Huntington Library, MS STT 1886; PRO, S.P. 15/25/
119, fol. 278 v.

[21] Richard Hooker, *Of the Laws of Ecclesiastical Polity*, Folger Library Edition of the Works of
Richard Hooker, i, ed. W. Speed Hill (Cambridge, MA, 1977), pp. 18-19.

[22] See the evidence assembled elsewhere in this volume in 'Windows in a Woman's Soul', pp. 99-
103 above. See also John N. King, *Tudor Royal Iconography* (Princeton, 1989), pp. 201-2; idem 'The
Godly Woman in Elizabethan Iconography', *Renaissance Quarterly*, 38 (1985), pp. 41-84; idem,
English Reformation Literature: The Tudor Origins of the Protestant Tradition (Princeton, 1982), pp. 71-
5.

[23] Lyndal Roper, *The Holy Household: Women and Morals in Reformation Augsburg* (Oxford, 1989).

A small detail of cultural history can be prised out of the funeral sermons preached over the corpses of dead and notably godly women, together with the reflections of grieving husbands, committed to their letters and diaries. 'My beloved, the ioye of all my travayles departed about sixe of the clocke at night ... This my beloved was full of vertewes, devout in her secret prayers. I will leave this for trewthe, her knees were harde with kneeling, she being a tender woman.' So wrote a desolate Somerset clothier at the end of the sixteenth century. The professional moralist Philip Stubbes committed similar thoughts to print upon the death of his partner: *A christal glasse for christian women, contayninge an excellent discourse of the life and death of Katherine Stubbes* (1591). 'She was by nature very humble and lowly, not disdaining any: very loving and kind, shewing courtesie to all: very meeke and milde in forbearing every one ... For matters of religion, few went before her.' Such was the character of the youthful matron Mistress Katherine Brettargh, according to the Lancashire preacher who delivered her funeral sermon. As Stubbes's title indicates, such effusions, ostensibly laudatory, were in fact vehicles for patriarchal prescriptions about acceptable and exemplary female conduct.[24]

The role of women in the affairs of the continuing English Catholic community was, if anything, even more striking, so that the modern historian of that community, Professor John Bossy, can describe post-Reformation Catholicism as a matriarchy. In spite of the active participation of women in Protestant and Puritan religious life and experience, which we have already noted, Professor Bossy believes that the patriarchal conditions of family life, which Protestantism tended to reinforce and for which it provided no alternative, suggested to the average woman of the Elizabethan and Jacobean upper classes that the Reformation had not been designed with her in mind.[25] The Catholic community may have owed its very existence to the particular dissatisfaction of gentlewomen with the Protestant establishment, not least in its domestic manifestation. We are talking about the origins of a culture observed at the moment of its dissolution in Waugh's *Brideshead Revisited*.

Among the remarkable catholic women of the late sixteenth and early seventeenth centuries, 'imperious dames of high stomach and stirring humour', we may single out for special mention Dorothy Lawson, as the archetypal religious matriarch, and Mary Ward as the unattached, roving,

---

[24] The first writer is William Leonard, Sir Simonds D'Ewes's grandfather, BL, MS Harley 70, fol. 2 v; *Deaths advantage little regarded and the sowles solace against sorrow: Preached in two funeral sermons at Childwal in Lancashire at the buriall of Mistris Katherine Brettargh* (1602) (*STC* no. 12866), p. 79. Dr Susan Wabuda detects the same strategy in a ballad composed for the godly Mary Glover by her second husband, Richard Bott, preserved in BL, MS Stowe 958. (Susan Wabuda, 'Shunamites of the English Reformation: The Activities of Mary Glover, Niece of Hugh Latimer', in *Women in the Church*, pp. 335-44).

[25] John Bossy, *The English Catholic Community, 1570-1850* (1975), pp. 150-8.

adventurous feminist. Mrs Lawson was the mother of fifteen children, but saw so little of her husband, a busy London lawyer and not a Catholic, until Dorothy converted him on his deathbed, that Bossy reflects that in this kind of family the father had few functions beyond the begetting of children. Mrs Lawson saw to it that her children were educated as Catholics in Flemish convents, and she converted hundreds of her neighbours to the faith, or so according to the hagiographers. At St Anthony's, on the Tyne near Newcastle, she built a house which became known as the headquarters of the Jesuits in the north of England, and which, in an age of supposedly draconic persecution, had the name JESUS prominently displayed on the gable end, so that mariners passing by along the Tyne should know that this was a religious house. After her husband's death, she adopted a religious habit. It was said that 'everyone loved her with fear and feared her with love'. Everyone, from the mayor of Newcastle upwards and downwards, Protestant as well as Catholic, attended her funeral.[26]

Mary Ward belonged to a not dissimilar social background and to Yorkshire, but as a single woman she defied every social convention of the time as well as the strategies of her own Church by organising an incipient religious order of thirty or forty young women, an Institute of the Blessed Virgin Mary. The members experimented with an unstructured, free-ranging apostolate to women in this world of men: a kind of female Society of Jesus.[27]

Needless to say, the heroic capacities of religious women, real or attributed, is not a topic confined to the age of Reformation and Counter-Reformation. We could travel back in time to the famous *mulieres sacrae* of the twelfth and thirteenth centuries, and forward to much more recent times. Film-goers once learned about the Chinese exploits in this century of the ex-London housemaid, Gladys Aylward, who in real life managed very well without Gregory Peck.[28] But not everyone will have heard of the intrepid Kate Marsden, author of *On Sledge and Horseback to Outcast Siberian Lepers*;[29] or of Dr Mary Wakefield who, not content with having qualified as one of the first medical practitioners of her sex, proceeded to spend a lifetime in Tamanrasset, where she 'went native'. Besides dispensing some medicine to the Tuareg tribesmen of the Hoggar Mountains, Dr Wakefield translated the Bible into their language, Tamahak, only to find, thirty years

[26] J.D. Hanlon, 'These Be But Women', in C.H. Carter, ed., *From the Renaissance to the Counter-Reformation: Essays in Honour of Garrett Mattingly* (1966), pp. 371-400, following William Palmes, *The life of Mrs Dorothy Lawson, of St Antony's near Newcastle-on-Tyne* (1646), modern edn by G. Bouchier Richardson (1855).

[27] Bossy, *English Catholic Community*, p. 160, and further references supplied by Bossy.

[28] Alan Burgess, *The Small Woman* (1957); P. Thompson, *A London Sparrow* (1971).

[29] Kate Marsden, *On Sledge and Horseback to Outcast Siberian Lepers* (1893); Kate Marsden, *My Mission to Siberia; A Vindication* (1921). See also Henry Johnson, *The Life of Kate Marsden* (2nd edn, 1985). I am grateful to Mrs Ursula Aylmer for introducing me to Kate Marsden.

later, when her translation was published, that it was utterly rejected by the people for whom it was intended.[30] These were worthy successors in our own century of the two Quaker women who set out in the seventeenth century to convert the Turks, only to languish in a Maltese prison.[31]

In his once famous book *Enthusiasm*, Monsignor Ronald Knox pronounced that 'from the Montanist movement onwards, the history of enthusiasm is largely a history of female emancipation.'[32] Perhaps. But what is emancipation? Whether the Protestant and Catholic women of the sixteenth and seventeenth centuries were overtly or consciously feminist is a nice question. When I lived some years ago in a conservative Islamic society and observed how the personal and social frustrations of women were apparently fed into radical political movements, it occurred to me that the part played by women in early modern European religion offered some sort of parallel to what could be observed in the streets and milkbars of Khartoum. (A common form of protest for Sudanese women was to enter milkbars from which, at least by convention, they were excluded.) The patriarchal, male-dominant system was not directly challenged in or by means of the religious and politico-religious movements of the sixteenth and seventeenth centuries. In the years of the English Civil War, women demonstrated in London in their thousands in support of peace, or on behalf of the Levellers. But they never demanded the vote for themselves and, whatever Clarendon may have thought and insinuated, were not in open revolt against their husbands.[33]

But was there an indirect challenge, a covert revolt? Sometimes women who behaved in what looks like a rebellious fashion were performing roles which the community acknowledged and, within the terms of its unwritten, even unspoken moral economy, allowed for. Since they enjoyed a relative degree of legal immunity, women might be licensed, in effect, to vent feelings which their menfolk shared, to take direct action which it would have been inconvenient and even perilous for their husbands to undertake.

[30] Information on Dr Wakefield communicated orally by my parents, who knew her.

[31] C.V. Wedgewood, 'The Conversion of Malta', in her *Velvet Studies* (1946), pp. 129-37. The year was 1659, the Quaker women Katherine Evans and Sarah Chever. See also M.R. Brailsford, *Quaker Women, 1650-1690* (1915), pp. 206-10, and W.C. Braithwaite, *The Beginnings of Quakerism* (1923), pp. 428-32. A much fuller account will be found in William Sewel, *History of the Rise, Increase and Progress of the Christian People Called Quakers* (successive editions).

[32] Ronald Knox, *Enthusiasm* (Oxford, 1950), p. 20. Knox traced the continuities apparently linking such notable female enthusiasts as Lucilla, the Donatist, the women who greeted the seventeenth-century Quaker James Nayler with hosannas as he made his parodically triumphant entry into Bristol, Madame Guyon, the high priestess of Quietism, and Selina, countess of Huntingdon.

[33] Patricia Higgins, 'The Reactions of Women, with Special Reference to Women Petitioners', in Brian Manning, ed., *Politics, Religion and the English Civil War* (1973), pp. 177-222. Ms Amanda Whiting of Melbourne University is currently at work on tumultuous petitioning by women in the English Civil War.

They may have been sent out to riot, or to commit acts of iconoclasm. Such an arrangement is perhaps implicit in the words used by Bishop Grindal of London to some sixty housewives who in 1566 made a 'womanish brabble' outside his house in favour of the suspended Puritan preachers of the city. They should send 'half a dozen of their husbands and with them I would talk'.[34]

Consequently such acts of ritual protest have been called 'collusive'. But the notion of collusion underpins a holistic concept of 'society' as expressing a single will through its component parts, and this entails an element of nostalgic wish-fulfilment about 'worlds we have lost', so that social and cultural historians are entitled to be suspicious of it; or at least to preserve a certain openness of mind. The idea that overtly insubordinate and even lawless acts, inverting the natural order of things, were nevertheless intended subliminally to maintain the status quo has to be balanced by Bakhtin's sense that a potential for actual uncontrolled subversion and revolution was often present on these occasions.[35]

In any case, Natalie Zemon Davis tells us, it may be a mistake to interpret an active, assertive female role in progressive and dissident religious movements in terms of feminism or suppressed and displaced rebellion. Such women (she had in mind French city women) were naturally capable and competent and it was only to be expected that they would play as capable and competent a role in religion as in their domestic and business affairs.[36] Social and cultural historians are obliged to engage in deconstruction. The kind of evidence they handle rarely bears a single, obvious meaning. Blessed Margaret Clitherow, the Elizabethan housewife of York who harboured Catholic priests and was crushed to death by the rare mode of execution known as the *peine forte et dure*, must have been a deeply alienated person. Her relations with her husband, a respectable alderman and not a Catholic, were perhaps not very satisfactory. But she never said a word against him. Shortly before her martyrdom, she sent him her hat 'in sign of her loving duty to him as to her head'. What are we to make of that? The signal intended is no less inscrutable than Oliver Cromwell's words written to his wife: 'Thou art dearer to me than any

[34] Patrick Collinson, *Archbishop Grindal, 1519-1583: The Struggle for a Reformed Church* (1979), p. 177.

[35] Classic studies of the meaning of sectional but in some respects collusive rituals in early modern society are contained in Natalie Davis's *Society and Culture in Early Modern France* and in Sir Keith Thomas's *Rule and Misrule in the Schools of Early Modern England* (Reading, 1976). Mikhail Bakhtin's ideas are contained in *Rabelais and his World*, tr. H. Iswolsky (Cambridge, MA, 1968). A particular historical episode implicitly supportive of those ideas is dealt with in Emmanuel le Roy Ladurie, *Carnival in Romans: A People's Rising at Romans, 1579-1580* (1980). See also Natalie Davis, 'Women on Top', in *Society and Culture in Early Modern France*, pp. 124-51.

[36] Eadem, 'City Women and Religious Change', ibid., pp. 65-95.

creature; let that suffice.'[37]

The calamitous or triumphant story of Margaret Clitherow (depending upon your point of view) can be offset by the more obviously successful and prudent pragmatism of the Puritan housewife of Chester, Mrs Jane Ratcliffe, as recorded by her favourite preacher, John Ley. It is significant that we observe Mrs Ratcliffe and her relations with her aldermanic husband through the eyes of this second man in her life. What we see is the small but precious independent space which religion opened up in Mrs Ratcliffe's life, a chink in the otherwise all-encompassing authority of her husband and head, even some room for assertion. Dr Peter Lake, the male historian who becomes the third man to be involved with Mrs Ratcliffe, writes of 'the formally patriarchal content of puritan ideology', but also of 'the subtle ways in which the personal godliness of individual women could be invoked to subvert that patriarchalism'.[38]

It is time to return to our forest clearing and to take stock. In the long term, it cannot be said that either the Reformation or the Counter-Reformation were vehicles of emancipation for the generations of women which followed. In Protestant societies, the fast bands of patriarchal authority were tightened, leaving few alternatives to the roles of submissive wives and daughters. In Catholic communities, the religious energies of women were acknowledged and engaged, but for the most part they were contained and canalised within the innumerable orders for women which were such conspicuous cultural artefacts of the church of the Counter-Reformation, above all in seventeenth-century France, and this was liberating to a strictly limited extent. It was not vouchsafed to Mary Ward to break the mould. Nevertheless both Protestantism/Puritanism and Catholicism offered ways and means of ameliorating the condition of women. According to Helene Deutsch, espousal of a cause, religious or otherwise, enables some women to find what she calls a 'circuitous route' to the solution of their problems. Nancy Roelker adds that the Calvinist ethic offered a way to cope with the passivity imposed by physiology and society without resort to 'masculine' aggressiveness.[39]

[37] Mary Claridge, *Margaret Clitherow (1556?-1586)* (1966), p. 171; Cromwell to Elizabeth Cromwell, 4 September 1650; *Oliver Cromwell's Letters and Speeches*, ed. T. Carlyle, 2nd rev. edn (n.d.), p. 391. It must be admitted that Cromwell wrote these terse words on the morning after the battle of Dunbar.

[38] Peter Lake, 'Feminine Piety and Personal Potency: The "Emancipation" of Mrs Jane Ratcliffe', *The Seventeenth Century*, 2, (1987), pp. 143-65. The source is John Ley, *A pattern of piety or the religious life and death of that gracious matron Mrs Jane Ratcliffe, widow and citizen of Chester* (1640). An abridged version, 'The Life and Death of Mrs Jane Ratcliffe', was included by Samuel Clarke in *A Collection of the Lives of Ten Eminent Divines* (1662), pp. 415-48.

[39] Roelker, 'The Role of Noblewomen', pp. 193-4. I am reliant upon Professor Roelker for my reference to Helene Deutsch, being unable to find the ideas to which she refers in the pages cited of Deutsch's *The Psychology of Women: A Psychoanalytic Interpretation* (New York, 1944).

III

The celebration, and equally the investigation, of female roles and achievements is a modern variant on an old theme, 'in praise of famous women', the ancient *querelle des femmes*. Women's history now likes to speak of women's 'agency', even 'empowerment', rather than endlessly harping on passivity and exploitation. But a more radical proposition must now be confronted: that our time is not well spent in constructing a one-sided, single-sex women's history of religious participation. Natalie Davis has written critically of 'the tradition of Women Worthies' and of treating women in isolation from men. The agenda which she proposes concerns the history of both women and men, if our purpose is to understand the place and significance of gender in the past.[40] That advice might seem to mean that we should concentrate on the institution of marriage, and of domestic relations more generally, which, to be sure, social historians are in no danger of neglecting, the institution of divorce included.[41] However, the subject of the present enquiry is not so much marriage as a series of affairs, spiritual affairs involving men and women who, for the most part, were not married to each other.

Only the surface of this subject can be scratched in an essay of modest and conventional proportions. The French Catholic sociologist Gabriel le Bras envisaged an institute of many storeys devoted to the historical and sociological investigation of religion, most of which would necessarily be given over to the study of non-European, non-Christian religion.[42] If such an appalling edifice were ever to be erected, it would be necessary to allocate two or three floors to the subject which the Germans call the *Frauenfrage*, which is not so much the woman question as the question of woman from the male perspective and therefore of male and female religious interaction.

Somewhere on these floors a whole room would be needed for the study of the mixed monasteries which were the main centres of religious life in the early middle ages. The antechamber to this room would belong to St Jerome and his female confidantes and dependents on the Aventine and at

[40] N.Z. Davis '"Women's History" in Transition: The European Case', *Feminist Studies*, 3 (1976), pp. 83-103. Titles beginning 'The Role of ...' appear to be indicative of the epoch before the transition of which Professor Davis writes. A late example of pre-transition women's historiography is *Triumph over Silence: Women in Protestant History*, ed. Richard L . Greaves (Westport, CT, 1985), which has such article titles as 'Women in the Lutheran and Calvinist Movements' and 'The Role of Women in Early English Nonconformity'.

[41] Lawrence Stone, *The Road to Divorce: England, 1530-1987* (Oxford, 1990).

[42] Gabriel le Bras, *Études de sociologie religieuses*, 2 vols in 1 (Paris, 1955-6), preface. Les Bras writes (p. ix): 'Les vastes perspectives que nous ouvrons et qui dépassent infiniment la vue d'un homme, requièrent le concours de beaucoup de savants: historiens et géographes, ethnologues et psychologues, qui eclaireront nos recherches. Pourquoi douter? ... de vastes espoirs sont permis.'

Bethlehem.[43] Much more space would have to be found for work on the many forms and versions of the reformed religious life, the *vita apostolica*, which were pursued in tandem by both women and men in the late twelfth and early thirteenth centuries. There was Robert of Abrissel, roaming around the French countryside with a mixed bag of groupies who included widows and virgins, rich and poor, prostitutes and man-haters.[44] The lives of notable religious women were written by Jacques de Vitry and others, not only to extol the saintly virtues of these *mulieres sacrae*, but because it was believed that these spiritual mothers had the capacity to enrich the entire life of the church.[45]

Most religious initiatives in this most fertile period of initiatives began as movements of both sexes. In his early days, when he encouraged St Clare and her companions to embark on an apostolic life in the church of St Damian, St Francis of Assisi seems to have envisaged a mixed society of men and women. Those at work on that floor of our institute will have to discover why St Francis later changed his mind and attitudes, and why most Franciscan brothers later tried to have as little to do with the sisters as possible.[46] And some of their colleagues will have to determine why, in spite (or because?) of the demographic preponderance of women in this society, and the strength of their religious feelings, so little was done in the thirteenth century (in contrast to the seventeenth century, or the nineteenth century) to provide religious orders and other acceptable institutions for women; so that the women were obliged to fend for themselves, pooling their inheritances and by other means securing property which could support the unofficial communal life of so-called *béguines*. (And perhaps it is a piece of unconscious male chauvinism to speak of women 'fending for themselves'. Why not so 'fend'?) But these same researchers, especially if they are German and thorough, will draw detailed maps, showing how the *béguinages* in, for example Cologne, and there were 169 of them in 1400, were clustered in close proximity to the Dominican and

---

[43] *The Letters of St Jerome*, tr. C.C. Mierow, Ancient Christian Writers, i (1963); *Early Latin Theology*, ed. S.L. Greenslade, Library of Christian Classics, 5 (1956), pp. 281-385; Hans van Campenhausen, *The Fathers of the Latin Church* (1964), pp. 129-82. Van Campenhausen describes (p.159) how Jerome's thirty-four years at Bethlehem were accompanied by 'the interest and sympathy of his devout women friends who clung to him and cared for him with ever constant devotion'.

[44] Jacqueline Smith, 'Robert of Abrissel: Procurator Mulierum', in *Medieval Women*, ed. D. Baker, Studies in Church History, subsidia 1 (Oxford, 1978), pp. 175-84. However, Dr Smith is properly critical of the romanticisation of Robert and his dealings with women at the hands of Michelet and other nineteenth-century historians.

[45] For discussion of De Vitry's Life of Mary of Oignies (d. 1213) *Vita B. Mariae Oigiacensis* and other texts, see three articles by Brenda Bolton: '*Mulieres Sanctae*', in *Sanctity and Secularity: The Church and the World*, Studies in Church History, 10, ed. D. Baker (Oxford, 1973), pp. 77-96; '*Vitae Matrum*: A Further Aspect of the *Frauenfrage*', in *Medieval Women*, pp. 253-73; 'Daughters of Rome: All One in Christ Jesus', in *Women in the Church*, pp. 101-15.

[46] Rosalind B. Brooke and Christopher N.L. Brooke, 'St Clare', in *Medieval Women*, pp. 275-87.

Franciscan friaries. Out of that propinquity and consequential traffic came the distinctive vein of spirituality which we know as the *theologia germanica*, German mysticism. This was the milieu to which Meister Eckhart belonged.[47]

Members of the institute with interests in later centuries would contribute studies of some of the famous double acts in subsequent religious history: St Catherine of Siena and William Flete; St Teresa of Avila and St Peter of Alcantara; Ste Jeanne de Chantal and St Francis de Sales; Mme de Guyon and Father Lacombe; E.B. Pusey and Miss Lydia Sellon.

So, to return to our clearing in the jungle for fresh supplies, there was nothing unprecedented about the little circles of female piety which had John Knox at their centre, in mid sixteenth-century Edinburgh, Newcastle and London. 'Love maketh me fervent', wrote Knox to his 'sisters in Edinburgh'. And from London he told Mrs Elizabeth Bowes about 'thrie honest pure [i.e., 'poor'] women' (materially they were rather rich) who had been so moved by Mrs Bowes's account of her religious difficulties that 'all oure eis wypit at anis.'[48] (The film rights to this essay would have to be sold under the title 'Carry On Weeping'.) It appears that priests and pastors have found it easier to penetrate to these spiritual and emotional levels with the help of women rather than by themselves or simply among men.

Why was (and perhaps is) this so? To refer to some general theory of the greater natural religiosity of women, as Hooker did, is no answer. What was the ground of the relationship enjoyed between Knox and his 'sisters', and what was the character, typically, of such bonds? Much evidence suggests that it was a relationship of gender dominance, based on a certain female vulnerability: what Knox would have frankly called the 'imbecility' of that sex.

This relationship had been, and in a sense still was, dictated in its terms by the sacrament of penance. Knox, as a Protestant, no longer heard confessions and pronounced absolution, but his dealings with Mrs Bowes or Mrs Locke were indebted to established Catholic sacramental procedures, at least to the extent that Knox conducted himself as a spiritual director of life and conscience. In the western Christian tradition, with its

---

[47]   R.W Southern, *Western Society and the Church in the Middle Ages*, Pelican History of the Church, ii (1970), pp. 309-31. With reference to Eckhart's dealings with women, see 'Appendix, The Sister Catherine Treatise', in Elvira Borgstadt, *Meister Eckhart* (New York, 1986), pp. 349-87.

[48]   Knox 'to his sisters in Edinburgh', n.d., *Works of Knox*, iv, p. 236; Knox to Elizabeth Bowes, 1 March 1553, ibid., iii, pp. 379-80. Loving and fervent or not, the letter to the Edinburgh 'sisters' was as judgmental in respect of womankind as any that Knox wrote. It took the form of a casuistical essay on the subject of womens' attire and contained such advice as this: 'The garmentis of wemen do declair thair weaknes and unabilitie to execute the office of men.' Within the limits of the Pauline doctrine of Christian liberty, which made such things not actually unlawful, Knox condemned as inconvenient ' the common superfluite whilk now is usit amang wemen in thair apparell', 'the imbrodering and wresting of the hair', 'verdingallis, and sic other fond fantassies', which 'can not be justifeit'. (Ibid., iv, pp. 226-8).

distinctive and perhaps excessive emphasis on sin, personal guilt and the conditions of personal salvation, the root of female religiosity may have been an extreme anxiety about the subject's religious state and destiny. This the sacrament of penance could foster and exacerbate, more especially as it dwelt progressively on the details and scruples of an interior spiritual life.[49]

A seventeenth-century English pastor committed to his diary a little sketch of one of his parishioners: 'a good woman, she is ill, a woman of much selfe-judging and feares concerning her condition'.[50] This runs counter to what is sometimes said about the natural religious genius of women as consisting in a serene enjoyment of the love of God, the kind of experience recorded by the great English mystic, Julian of Norwich. But this is not what we often find in the godly women of the sixteenth and seventeenth centuries.

Within the particular form of western religious culture which was Calvinism, especially in the developed, fully internalised variant current in the early seventeenth century and sometimes referred to as 'experimental' Calvinism, a particular concern, even neurosis, manifested itself about the subject's religious status, whether elect or reprobate. It was, said the famous and influential English divine William Perkins in the title of one of his works, *A case of conscience, the greatest that ever was: how a man may know whether he be a childe of God or no* (1592). The remedy was prescribed in the New Testament, 2 Peter 1:10: 'Give all diligence to make your calling and election sure: for if ye do these things ye shall never fail' – the so-called 'practical syllogism'.[51] We cannot tell whether such a strenuously anxious state of mind was so widespread as to be typical of the Calvinist experience, as Max Weber evidently thought, identifying the tap-root of what he called the Protestant Ethic. The absence of anxiety, like conventional conformity, has little or no history. Nor is it proposed that only women were deeply and chronically troubled about their eternal state and destiny. Perkins wrote of how 'a man' might know, and some of the more painful accounts of the practical syllogism running dysfunctionally out of control were written by men; for example, the autobiography and journal of the New England divine Thomas Shepard.[52] However it is proposed that a set of conventions

---

[49] T.N. Tentler, *Sin and Confession on the Eve of the Reformation* (Princeton, 1977); L.G. Duggan, 'Fear and Confession on the Eve of the Reformation', *Archiv für Reformationsgeschichte*, 75 (1984), pp. 153-75.

[50] *The Diary of Ralph Josselin, 1616-1683*, ed. Alan Macfarlane (1976), p. 140.

[51] Ian Breward, ed., *The Work of William Perkins*, Courtenay Library of Reformation Classics, iii (Appleford, 1970); R.T. Kendall, *Calvin and English Calvinism to 1649* (Oxford, 1979); Dewey Wallace, *Puritans and Predestination: Grace in English Protestant Theology* (Chapel Hill, NC, 1982); C.L. Cohen, *God's Caress: The Psychology of Puritan Religious Experience* (Oxford, 1986).

[52] Michael McGiffert, ed., *God's Plot: The Paradoxes of Puritan Piety* (University of Massachusetts, 1972).

operated within which it was appropriate for a godly woman of the upper or middle classes to share her religious symptoms with a learned and godly preacher, a spiritual physician whose role was not greatly dissimilar from that of the Catholic confessor with a specialist interest in women.

It is not grossly reductionist to account for female religious melancholia and hysteria (terms which early seventeenth-century medical science and eclectic opinion would have employed) with reference to physiological and social-psychological intrusion, injury and deprivation.[53] Many of these women were the victims of more or less enforced marriage and of all too frequent and punitive child-bearing. As Dorothy Stenton once remarked: 'No farm labourer's wife can ever have felt well.'[54] And why only, or especially, labourers' wives? Women from the upper ranks of society bore far more, indeed far too many children. Mrs Joan Drake of Esher in Surrey was a young Jacobean married lady who (according to the title of a book written about her) *suffered the power and severe discipline of Satan for the space of ten years until she was redeemed from his tyranny. instrumentally, by the extraordinary pains of four reverend divines.* Mrs Drake, we are told, was accidentally rather than naturally melancholy. In herself she was 'of a lovely browne complexion, having a full nimble quick sparrow-hawk eye, of a naturall joviall constitution.' But after her first and difficult experience of childbirth she was never free of headaches. It was then that Satan struck. Mrs Drake began to tell the world that 'shee was undone, undone, shee was damned, and a cast away, and so of necessity must need goe to Hell... That now shee was a forlorne creature, being assuredly damned ... with shrieks and loud Cryes, the bed shaking, yea, the whole chamber seeming to rock and reele.' Famous divines spent years on this interesting case. Thomas Hooker, the future founder of Connecticut, cut his pastoral teeth on it.[55]

---

[53] Michael MacDonald, *Mystical Bedlam: Madness, Anxiety, and Healing in Seventeenth-Century England* (Cambridge, 1981), esp. chapter 5, 'Psychological Healing'; *Witchcraft and Hysteria in Elizabethan London: Edward Jorden and the Mary Glover Case*, ed. Michael MacDonald (1991); John Stachniewski, *The Persecutory Imagination: English Puritanism and the Literature of Religious Despair* (Oxford, 1991). (I owe the latter two references to Miss Alex Walsham.) Stachniewski believes that Calvinism and Puritanism were of their proper nature conducive to despair. He writes (p. 46) of 'the dark shadow of puritanism' and quotes Dr Blair Worden (p. 1): 'The volume of depair engendered by Puritan teaching on predestination is incalculable.' See also forthcoming work by Michael MacDonald on the long-running *locus classicus* of Calvinist 'desperation', the case of the Protestant Italian lawyer Francis Spira, with which Elizabeth Bowes was already familiar in Northumberland in the early 1550s. See also much relevant material in Michael MacDonald and Terence R. Murphy, *Sleepless Souls: Suicide in Early Modern England* (Oxford, 1990).

[54] Dorothy Stenton, *The English Woman in History* (1957), p. 118.

[55] The story of Mrs Drake is told in an anonymous account first published in 1647 as *Troden down strength* and reprinted in 1654 as *The firebrand taken out of the fire, or, the wonderfull history, case and cure of Mrs Drake*. Wing's *Short-Title Catalogue*, while apparently regarding these as distinct works, attributes both (nos. 960, 949) to John Hart. G.H. Williams identifies the author as Jasper Heartwell (or Hartwell). See 'Called by Thy Name, Leave Us Not: The Case of Mrs Joan Drake, a Formative Episode in the Pastoral Career of Thomas Hooker in England', *Harvard Library Bulletin*, 16 (1968),

continued

Elizabeth Bowes was the mother of fifteen children, So was the Catholic matriarch, Dorothy Lawson, not that anyone ever called Mrs Lawson a melancholic. Margery Kempe, the would-be religious virtuoso of late medieval Kings Lynn, who has left behind that remarkable testimony of her experiences and adventures, *The Book of Margery Kempe*, was another mother who had a difficult and dangerous time with her first-born. She wrote of 'the labowr sche had in chyldyng & for sekenesse goyng beforn', and of how 'sche dyspered of hyr lyfe, wenyng sche myght not levyn.' After this, 'for dred sche had of dampnacyon' and fear of an unsympathetic father confessor, 'this creatur went owt of hir mende, & was wondyrlye vexid & labowryd wyth spyritys'. In spite of a certain distaste for sexual intercourse, at least with her husband, Mrs Kempe bore thirteen more children. Like Dorothy Lawson in a later generation, she hankered for the nun's habit.[56]

Mrs Mary Honeywood, an Elizabethan Kentish worthy, was famous both as the matriarch who gave birth to sixteen children, lived for ever and so became great-grandmother to half the gentry of Kent, and as a chronic religious melancholic. 'I am as sure to be damned as this glass is to be broken', she said to one of many ministers who attended upon her in a professional capacity (John Foxe the martyrologist, no less), throwing the Venice glass in her hand to the ground. But then happened a wonder. The glass rebounded entire, which somewhat helped Mrs Honeywood. There are letters to this lady 'in her heaviness' from Edward Dering, the preacher who became the second husband of Knox's friend, Mrs Locke: 'Hath your husband beene unkind to you, beare it, and you shal winne him at the last: If not, thank God that you can continue loving and obedient, even unto an unkind husband ...' 'And therefore (good Mistres Honeywood) give not your selfe to any inordinate affections to offende God, and hurt yourselfe...'[57]

Knox's letters to his mother-in-law Mrs Bowes are concerned to the exclusion of all other topics with similar symptoms of spiritual malaise. As Knox later explained to his critics: 'For her tentation was not in the fleshe, ... but it was in spirite: For Sathan did continually buffette her, that remission of sinnes in Christ Jesus apperteyned nothing unto her, by reason of her former idolatrie and other iniquities.'[58] In one of his letters,

continued

pp. 111-28, 278-300; see also Frank Shuffleton, *Thomas Hooker, 1586-1647* (Princeton, 1977), pp. 28-68; and Amanda Porterfield, *Female Piety in Puritan New England: The Emergence of Religious Humanism* (Oxford, 1992), pp. 46-8, 90-1.

[56] *The Book of Margery Kempe*, ed. S.B. Meech, Early English Text Society, o.s. 212 (1940), pp. 6-7.

[57] Collinson, *Godly People*, p. 318; Edward Dering, *Godly and comfortable letters*, in *M. Derings Workes* (1597), sigs. C1 v-3 r, A6-B3 v. The letters in their published form address 'Mistress H.' (who was still living at the time of publication and for long afterwards). The name appears as Mrs Honeywood in the MS in the Kent Archives Offices, MS Dering U 350 C1/1.

[58] *Works of Knox*, vi, pp. 513-14.

Knox had to contend with a morbid conviction that Mrs Bowes had committed all the sins of Sodom and Gomorrah. 'Deir Mother, my dewtie compellis me to adverteis yow, that in comparing your synnis with the synnis of Sodom and Gomorhe ye do not weill ... Ye knaw not what wer the synnis of Sodome and Gomore': and then he proceeds to conduct a tutorial on this interesting subject.[59] Such opportunities enabled the reformer to rise to his highest powers in exposition of the evangelical doctrine of saving grace: 'Dispair not Mother, your synnis (albeit ye had committit thousands ma) ar remissabill. What! think ye that Godis gudnes, mercie and grace, is abill to be overcum with your iniquitie? Will God, wha can not dissave, be a lier, and lose his awn glorie, because that ye ar a synner?'[60]

The thirty letters from Knox to Mrs Bowes were preserved, numbered and published out of true chronological order. 'The firste letter' proves to be nothing of the kind, whereas Knox remarks in concluding what purports to be the twenty-fourth: 'I think this be the first Letter that ever I wrait to you.'[61] The impression left by this incoherent material is that Mrs Bowes's spiritual problems circulated in a hopeless spiral, never to be resolved. But Daniel Frankforter has proposed an alternative ordering of the letters which suggests that with Knox's help she made progress and eventually emerged from her state of 'desperation' (in Calvinist parlance) to enjoy some measure of spiritual confidence and protestant conviction. It was, Dr Frankforter believes, the reimposition of Catholicism under Mary which removed from the wavering conscience of Elizabeth Bowes any lingering temptation to revert to the spiritual panaceas of the old faith.[62]

Comparing the spiritual letters of the godly puritan divines with those of the great spiritual directors of the seventeenth-century French schools of devotion, the theological differences between Calvinism and, as it might be, Molinism or Quietism, while formally significant appear superficial in relation to the consistency of the underlying pastoral structures and of the symptoms to which the spiritual physicians addressed themselves. It is the same ground bass which runs through the famous letters to women of Bishop Fénelon: 'Do not indulge your scruples so much and you will be at rest.' 'The matters which you speak of with such horror are mere trivialities of talk, devoid of all malice, and perfectly harmless to your neighbours.'[63]

This points to an equally consistent pattern in the alleviation of the spiritual symptoms so often encountered among women of the leisured

---

[59] Knox to Elizabeth Bowes, 'this Saturday at Newcastell', n.d., *Works of Knox*, iii, pp. 382-5.

[60] Knox to Elizabeth Bowes, 'London 1553', ibid., pp. 380-2.

[61] Ibid., pp. 337, 395.

[62] Frankforter, 'Elizabeth Bowes and John Knox'. We may note that Mrs Bowes's problems were not so much those of a 'typically' anxious Calvinist as of a Catholic converted (in some social isolation) to the new religion and while still uncertain about the wisdom and safety of her choice, stricken with guilt about her past 'idolatory'.

[63] *Spiritual Letters of Archbishop Fénelon: Letters to Women* (1877), pp. 84, 93.

classes. Within the Catholic economy of spiritual direction, liberation was often found to consist in the substitution of an understanding, encouraging adviser for a harsh, legalistic, insensitive confessor. Elizabeth Adamson, one of Knox's Edinburgh 'sisters', 'delyted much' in his companie 'becaus that he ... opened more fullie the fontane of Goddis mercyes, then did the commoun sorte of teachearies that sche had hard befoir'.[64] One classical example of this kind of happy exchange was the beginning of the sublime love affair between the young bishop of Geneva and the widow, St Francis de Sales and Ste Jeanne de Chantal. Ste Chantal remembered: 'The manner and speech of this blessed one were most majestic and grave, yet he was always the humblest, sweetest and simplest one has ever seen ... He spoke low, gravely, sedately, sweetly and wisely.'[65] For the nineteenth century this kind of quasi-erotic relationship was the very essence of insidious, poisonous Jesuitry. Michelet wrote a whole book on the subject.[66]

But the extreme example of liberation theology (in this sense) was seventeenth-century Quietism, a spiritual school much opposed to the Jesuits, which discouraged extreme spiritual and moral effort and excessive concern for personal salvation. When the Spanish Quietist Miguel de Molinos was arrested by the papal police in 1685, he was found to have 12,000 letters from pious women in his possession (or was it 20,000 – reports vary), letters which the Inquisition spent years toothcombing for scandalous and incriminating evidence, with a certain amount of success. Some of the letters must have been written by the high priestess of this religious tendency, Madame de Guyon; and it is only Mme de Guyon, with her complete ascendancy over her own director, Father Lacombe, who prevents us calling Quietism a religious panacea dispensed to women by men.[67]

It may be that we are here touching on something a great deal more primitive and archetypal than any of the systems of spiritual advancement explored in the precious salons of the France of Louis XIII and XIV; as primitive as Emmanuel Ladurie's *Montaillou*, where we learn that Pyrenean village women of the fourteenth century were not unwilling to include the parish priest among their lovers because priests were relatively gentle and used no violence. 'But it wasn't rape at all', testified Grazide Rives in describing her first carnal encounter at the age of fourteen with the parish priest of Montaillou, the ambiguous Pierre Clergue. 'With Pierre Clergue,

---

[64] John Knox, *History of the Reformation in Scotland*, in *Works of Knox*, i, p. 246.

[65] Henri Brémond, *A Literary History of Religious Thought in France*, tr. K.L. Montgomery, ii, *The Coming of Mysticism (1590-1620)* (1930), p. 403.

[66] Jules Michelet, *Du prêtre, de la femme, de la famille* (Paris, 1845), tr. by C. Cocks in the same year as *Priests, Women and Families*.

[67] These remarks draw upon Ronald Knox, whose four chapters on Quietism constitute the core of his *Enthusiasm*, pp. 231-355.

I liked it.'[68] This (as it were) Montaillou level of experience was perhaps only lightly submerged in the search of the Kings Lynn housewife, business woman and religious superstar Margery Kempe for an acceptable father confessor, a priest capable of matching her vision of the Lord Jesus Christ, with whom she experienced mystical 'dalliance'. Christ appeared to Margery 'in the lyknesse of a man most semly, most bewtyows, & most amyable'. He asked her: 'Dowtyr, whom wylt thow han felaw wyth the?'; and when Margery asked for an especially favoured priest: 'Why askyst [thow] mor hym than thyn owyn fadyr er thin husbond?' 'A, blysful Lord' she told Jesus in another of her meditations: 'I wolde I wer as worthy to ben sekyr [i.e., "secure"] of thy lofe as Mary Mawdelyn was.' 'Than seyd Owr Lord "Trewly, dowghtyr, I love the as wel ..."' '"I bydde the & commawnd the, boldly clepe me Ihesus, thi love, for I am thi love, & schal be thi love wyth-owtyn ende."'[69]

Phenomenonologically, this resembles the case of Benedetta Carlini, the seventeenth-century Italian abbess, to whom Jesus appeared in visionary form to take her heart and replace it with his own: 'I have given you my love, now return my love.' In due course, Jesus plighted his troth to the abbess in a mystical ceremony; the effect of these ecstatic experiences being somewhat sullied and compromised by the fact, uncovered by an ecclesiastical tribunal, that in her waking moments Carlini enjoyed an active lesbian relationship with one of her nuns.[70]

In other cases, the comforting, reassuring voice might share the subject's own sex. For Margery Kempe's contemporary, Mother Julian, an anchoress living not far away in Norwich and exploring what most conoisseurs find to have been a richer and more authentic vein of spirituality, the femininity and motherhood of God was a source of deep comfort. Addressing Jesus as mother, Julian rhapsodised: 'This fair lovely word Mother, it is so sweet and kind itself that it may not verily be said of none but of him.' 'As truly

---

[68] Emmanuel le Roy Ladurie, *Montaillou: Cathars and Catholics in a French Village, 1294-1324* (1978), pp. 158-9. I am aware that Ladurie's critics believe that many of these Montaillou stories were made up, with a certain amount of help from the Inquisition. But that hardly affects the argument.

[69] *Book of Margery Kempe*, pp. 8, 20, 176, 17. Amanda Porterfield provides a similar interpretation of the case of Mrs Joan Drake, the young Surrey gentlewoman whose religious hysteria was treated by Thomas Hooker, among other early seventeenth-century divines. Mrs Drake had been forced into an unwelcome marriage. Hooker spoke to her of Christ's 'husbandly love' and by enabling her to regard God as Father and God's Son as Husband, sanctified her human relationships, whilst himself basking in some of the resultant glow. 'By deifying paternal authority, by making that authority sexually attractive, and by presenting himself as its ambassador, Hooker persuaded Joanna Drake to accept the government of male authority in her life.' (Porterfield, *Female Piety*, pp. 48-9). Compare the case of the young Elizabeth Tudor, as reflected in her translation of the *Miroir de l'âme pechereuse* of Marguerite d'Angoulême, see above, pp. 96-8.

[70] Judith Brown, *Immodest Acts: The Life of a Lesbian Nun in Renaissance Italy* (New York, 1986). Some reviewers of Dr Brown's book have been as sceptical about the reality of what may have been fantasies as some readers of le Roy Ladurie's *Montaillou*.

as God is our Father, so truly is God our Mother.' 'We know that all our mothers beare us to pain and to dying: a strange thing that! But our true Mother, Jesus, he alone beareth us to joy and to endless living; blessed may he be.' It is an interesting theological and historical question how and why this concept of the bisexuality of God and of God's's motherhood became displaced towards the analogy of the Virgin. Mary had her place in Julian's devotions but it was not the highest place, no more than 'her that is the very Mother of [Jesus] and of all'.[71]

Bisexual religious imagery and gender confusion were not confined to the discourse of women, or of Catholics. The Protestant martyr John Careless, a weaver by trade from Coventry, referred to his own soul in the female gender: 'For verely Sathan hath made a sore ruffelyng wyth her of late, that he myghte have bereft her of her vyrginytie, wyth the fornication of mistruste and infidelitye.'[72]

IV

So far the case material may suggest the religious passivity of women and their vulnerability and exploitability in the transactions of religion, which were perhaps also wars of the sexes. A Marxist feminist might represent these transactions as the manipulation of a range of illusions for a sexist purpose: even a kind of spiritual rape, or at least spiritual seduction. As for the relationship between John Knox and Elizabeth Bowes, it appears to provide a perfect illustration for Milton's profoundly sexist lines:

> He for God only, she for God in him;
> His fair large front and eye sublime declared
> Absolute rule.

In most of the transactions we have observed, the man stands between the woman and God, interprets, explains, exhorts, sustains, the only source of theodicy available to the female subject. Robert Louis Stevenson observed of Knox: 'Many women came to learn from him, but he never condescended to become a learner in his turn.'[73]

But that is neither fair nor the whole truth. Stevenson, who never encountered the myth or theory of the androgyne, misses the point that Knox found in his mother-in-law a perfect reflection of his own spiritual problems and, in effect, an image of his own soul. 'The expositioun of your trubillis, and acknawledging of your infirmitie, was first unto me a verie

---

[71] Julian of Norwich, *Revelations* ('Long Text', 1901), pp. 149-51. See David Knowles, *The English Mystical Tradition* (1961), pp. 128-9; R.H. Thouless, *The Lady Julian: A Psychological Study* (1924).

[72] (Miles Coverdale), *Certain most godly, fruitful and comfortable letters [of the Martyrs]* (1564), p. 581.

[73] Stevenson, 'John Knox and his Relations to Women', p. 275.

mirrour and glass whairin I beheld my self sa rychtlie payntit furth, that nathing culd be mair evident to my awn eis.'[74] Only to Elizabeth Bowes did Knox the thunderer confess that he shared the very sins which he was obliged to denounce in others, the same remorse, the same doubts. 'Call to your mynd what I did standing at the copburd in Anwik: in verie deid I thought that na creature had bene temptit as I wes.' No one knows or will ever know what Knox did beside that cupboard in Alnwick. But this has not hindered speculation. Probably he means that he burst into tears. Knox goes on: 'And when that I heard proceid fra your mouth the verie same wordis that [God] trubillis me with, I did wonder, and fra my hart lament your sair trubill, knawing in my selfe the dolour thairof.'[75] Knox's 'wonder' was in itself genuine and heart-felt, not some polite convention. He was truly surprised to find a spiritual depth he could recognise in one of the 'imbecile' sex.

So although Knox later complained of 'trouble and fasherie of body' sustained on her behalf,[76] it appears that without Elizabeth Bowes his own religious experience would have been relatively impoverished, his knowledge of himself less than complete. In very few of the cases so far touched upon was the relationship one-sidedly exploitative. The *Vitae Matrum* which recorded the lives of the holy women who flourished in northern France and what is now the Benelux in the twelfth century were written by men, but their purpose was to testify to what these men owed, as Christians and as priests, to the inspiration of members of the opposite sex. Jacques de Vitry, in his account of Mary of Oignies, calls her his *mater spiritualis*, and it was at her instigation that this future cardinal and prince of the church offered himself for ordination.[77] The Life of St Catherine of Siena by her confessor, Blessed Raymond of Capua, has much of the same character. To be confessor to a religious genius of the calibre of St Catherine was to be also a kind of manager.[78] The spiritual power of such women gave shape and structure and purpose to the careers of priests who were drawn into their orbit and formed, often, a kind of family centred upon the spiritual mother.

So very often in Christian history the primary religious inspiration and energy has come from a female source. The role of men has been the secondary, if often dominant, one of channeling, direction, protection. In east Kent, towards 1530, half the clergy of the county had to decide what they ought to do about the religious original who had suddenly and unpredictably appeared in their midst, in the person of Elizabeth Barton, the young woman known to history as the Maid (and later the Nun) of

[74] Knox to Elizabeth Bowes, 23 June 1553, *Works of Knox*, iii, p. 338.

[75] Knox to Elizabeth Bowes, 26 February 1553, ibid., p. 350.

[76] *Works of Knox*, vi, p. 514.

[77] See Brenda Bolton's essays '*Mulieres Sacrae*' and '*Vitae Matrum*'.

[78] Raymundus de Vineis (Blessed Raymond of Capua), *The Life of St Catherine of Siena*, tr. G. Lamb (1960).

Kent.[79] But if Elizabeth Barton was an original, she and those who were drawn into her orbit at once fitted into a familiar pattern, prescribed by the literature of holy women. The Nun established an ascendancy over a number of priests and monks. A kind of family was formed in which Elizabeth was addressed as 'mother' by learned clergy twice her age. One of them, as Dom David Knowles puts it, became her 'impresario'.[80]

So it was, at a more exalted level, between St Francis de Sales and Ste Jeanne de Chantal. Henri Brémond describes 'these two souls together as they scale the heights of mysticism, each assisting the other in the ascent.'[81]

I conclude with some more recent case studies. The story of the Mariavite Church in twentieth-century Poland, as told by Jerzy Peterkiewicz in his book *The Third Adam*, exemplifies the sexual element (whether or not 'in the ordinary sense') which is often part of the chemistry of religious transactions, and it poses in an acute and intriguing form questions of sexual ascendancy and dominance, over and against possibilities of reciprocity and mutual benefit.[82]

The Mariawita (the name comes from *Mariae Vita*, underlining the Marian devotion fundamental to the movement) have not been mentioned in recent despatches from Poland. But twenty years ago there were still estimated to be 30,000 Mariavites and in about 1930, ten times as many. The 'third Adam', leader and eventually archbishop of this schismatic splinter from Polish Catholicism, was Jan Kowalski, born in 1871 and dead in Dachau in 1942, a man who in his prime, says Peterkiewicz, became a personified religious fantasy for thousands of Polish women, grown to preposterous dimensions.[83]

Kowalski belonged to a generation of Polish clergy who were demoralised, then as more recently, by the conflicting claims of national sentiment, foreign domination and their obligations towards an international ecclesiastical organisation. He was one of several such priests who experienced a kind of redemption as they came under the spell of a woman called Feliksa

[79] Alan Neame, *The Holy Maid of Kent: The Life of Elizabeth Barton, 1506-1534* (1971).

[80] Dom David Knowles, *The Religious Orders in England*, iii, *The Tudor Age* (Cambrige, 1961), pp. 182-91. See p. 184: 'Dr Edward Bocking was her adviser and impresario'. Knowles compares Bocking's role to that of William Flete in the *famiglia* of St Catherine of Siena, almost two centuries earlier. The version of the *Life of the Blessed Virgin, Saint Catherine of Siena* translated by John Fen, confessor to the English nuns at Louvain and printed at Louvain in 1609, continually refers to the saint as 'the holy maid'.

[81] Brémond, *Literary History*, ii, p. 394.

[82] It goes against the grain, and may even call for an apology, to include in this essay such a substantial amount of material derived from a single, secondary source, Jerzy Peterkiewicz, *The Third Adam* (1975). But I shall only offer a mild apology, since I have yet to meet anyone, within or without the guild of the religious historians, who has read this book or heard of its subject, the Mariavites. All recent public discussions of the ordination of women betray, in their points of historical reference and precedent, a comparable ignorance.

[83] Peterkiewicz, *The Third Adam*, p. 2.

Kozlowska, who had established a vaguely Franciscan sisterhood devoted to prayer and needlework in a private house in the sleepy provincial city of Plock. Kozlowska was the recipient of divine revelations and 'understandings' which instructed her to found a congregation of priests dedicated to the Virgin as Our Lady of Perpetual Succour. The priests whom she recruited experienced an opening or laying bare of the soul, waves of radiating strength and peace, and a spiritual and moral transformation. (They gave up vodka and cigarettes.) They called Kozlowska *Matezka*, the Little Mother, and they all but identified her with the Virgin.

Jan Kowalski's own conversion was a kind of mystical rebirth. 'The Little Mother saw me as a small baby, given to her by the Lord Jesus.' It was as if he had 'torn off all his skin.' His emotional dependence upon Kozlowska became total. 'She was his mediatrix, his hope and comfort.'[84] It was a quasi-erotic, quasi-incestuous relationship in which Kowalski was both child and lover: a mystical marriage modelled on the Song of Songs, on which Kowalski later wrote an immense commentary. And probably it was a physical union as well and so sexual 'in the ordinary sense'. [85]

To summarise a great deal of history: the Mariavites having been refused recognition in Rome broke away to form a schismatic church which came into communion with the Old Catholics of Germany and Holland. This became a vigorous and highly successful religious organisation with its own churches, schools, orphanages, brass bands and many money-making enterprises, even three fire engines, all crowned by a monstrous gothic temple at Plock, where the Little Mother presided with her mystical son and lover Kowalski: a mixed monastery of Mariavite fathers and sisters.

In 1921 the Little Mother died after a long ordeal which served to complete the myth of her *Vita* and to contribute the important and hitherto missing element of martyrdom, Her illness was a cancer which was accompanied by acute ascites, an immense accumulation of fluid in the peritoneal cavity. After she was dead a photograph was taken of her grossly distended corpse, washed, robed and serene, presenting the illusion of prodigious pregnancy. To this day this image of the little Mother (or rather the Great Mother, or Earth Mother, one might suppose) is displayed on Mariavite altars.

But with Kozlowska's death, there was a shift of archetypal image from Great Mother to Great Father, who was of course Kowalski. Kowalski was constructing a new and eclectic theology in which the Trinity was seen as a marriage and the Little Mother was identified as a female manifestation of the Holy Spirit, who as the third person of the Trinity effected the marriage. She was made to say (in words which occur in the breviary of the Mariavite Church): 'Because of my Passion you will be joined to my Divine

[84] Ibid., pp. 28-9.
[85] Ibid., pp. 30-1.

Beloved and Husband with the bond of married love, a love similar to that which exists between myself and my Divine Husband.'[86] The practical implications of this startling heresy was a series of mystical but also physical marriages between the leading Mariavite fathers and the sisters, which in Kowalski's own case were polygamous marriages. The meaning of this was that the children of these unions (and presently, children began to appear, and were brought up in a communal nursery and, as it were, laboratory) were supposed to be born in the likeness of the Trinity, a new kind of human being without original sin. It was, as Peterkiewicz remarks, a major sexual revolution and experiment in social engineering, achieved in the 1920s in a sanctimonious provincial town on the outskirts of Europe. But while the experiment was a not illogical outgrowth from the original vision, it appeared deviant to the Mariavites as a whole who, after Kowalski's fall, put it behind them under a new and more conventional leadership.

For Kowalski's erotic fantasies had led him into increasingly bizarre and scandalous patterns of behaviour. There were rumours of offences committed against some of the younger members of the cloister and of strange goings on with a band of pretty young mandolinists. In 1928 the affair came to a sensational climax in a trial in Warsaw in which Kowalski was given a prison sentence which, some years later and after a series of appeals, he duly served.

The reaction of Kowalski to his conviction was extraordinary. It was to explore a further dimension of the Mariavite theme of salvation through the Eternal Feminine by ordaining the Mariavite sisters to the priesthood. Presently there were bishopesses as well as priestesses, splendidly arrayed in chasubles and diadems. These were, from a strictly canonical point of view, the first validly ordained women priests. For Kowalski and his fellow Mariavite bishops had received their episcopal consecration from the Old Catholics, within the apostolic succession.

And what did it all mean? In 1934 Bishopess Isabel (the first of Kowalski's women and regarded by the law as his wife) greeted a visitor to Plock with these words: 'In the past it was the time of the male. Now it is the age of the women. We have been slaves until now.'[87] In the parishes, the women priests were popular and in demand. There was a real prospect that the Mariavite priesthood would become predominantly female, something we may yet live to see in other churches. Yet Bishopess Isabel was in truth Kowalski's totally submissive slave, entirely at his disposal and obliged to tolerate the competition for his favours of other wives and the younger, prettier sisters. One reason for the preference which he himself expressed for the women priests was that they were more loyal and submissive than the men. However, when Kowalski went a step further and instituted a

[86]   Ibid., p. 215.
[87]   Ibid., p. 148.

people's mass, which allowed any Mariavite to celebrate the eucharist, he sanctioned a form of popular religion which still exists and in which women play the active, priestly role. For Mariavites still have their mass, simply, on the kitchen table, and it is often the wife and mother who presides. Peterkiewicz described and photographed such a mass in 1974, in a working-class home:

> Visibly nervous, the peasant priestess knelt and read out the opening prayers from the Mariavite breviary. But as she spoke on in a trembling voice she forgot our presence, her face altered, became almost beautiful, and at the moment of consecration I saw tears pouring down her face. Her whole being seemed to be lifted up in another dimension ... How could this Mass be anything else but valid?[88]

If Feliksa Kazlowska could have performed that office, back at the beginning, perhaps she would have been satisfied.

In these same middle years of the twentieth century, there were other, more private religious transactions in the London suburb of Ealing: private, yet for the participants, no less transcendent. At a couple of earlier points in this essay we have drawn upon the scholarship of the late Dom David Knowles, who here and there in his writings commented on Julian of Norwich, Margery Kempe and Elizabeth Barton and her impresario, always with sensitive discrimination. But now he enters the story in his own right. For Knowles himself knew what it was to live in a special relationship of mutual spiritual and psychological dependence with a remarkable woman, in his case the Swedish psychiatrist and Catholic convert, Dr Elizabeth Kornerup. In a close replication of a number of historical episodes which he must have known so well, Knowles both ministered to and depended emotionally and in other respects on this 'perfect soul', as he came to regard her, in spite of ecclesiastical disapproval and formal censure. Dom Adrian Morey has written: 'It would seem that the normal role of spiritual director and penitent became reversed and that she assumed the dominant role.' Dom Aelred Sillem adds: 'It sometimes looked as though Father David and his group was to be animated by her influence rather as St Catherine of Siena inspired her *famiglia*.'[89]

We have disturbed a few stray cards in one drawer of one filing cabinet in one room of one floor of Gabriel le Bras's Institute of Religious Phenomena. We have not looked so much as once towards America. We have not reached as far as Sister Briege McKenna, an Irish-American nun

[88] Ibid., p. 220.
[89] Dom Adrian Morey, *David Knowles: A Memoir* (1979), pp. 88-92; Christopher Brooke et al., *David Knowles Remembered* (Cambridge, 1991), pp. 38-40. Was Dom Adrian conscious of repeating a very old topos? Bishop St John Fisher, hearing the confessions of Lady Margaret Beaufort, mother of King Henry VII, felt himself to be as much pupil as teacher; Michael K. Jones and Malcolm G. Underwood, *The King's Mother: Lady Margaret Beaufort, Countess of Richmond and Derby* (Cambridge, 1992), p. 257.

of the 1980s who is credited with saving the priesthood of hundreds if not thousands of priests and other religious in the Roman Catholic Church in five continents in this age of confusion over ministry, the means an extraordinary and so far unexplained charisma, perhaps resembling that manifested by the Little Mother in late nineteenth-century Poland.[90] Not far away in the files, but a little yellowed (we are back in the 1920s), is another index card with details of a Protestant missionary society deployed in early twentieth-century North Africa: the Algiers Mission Band, a society composed exclusively of English ladies, living in what had been the palace of a Barbary corsair in a muslim city (known as Dar Naama), a society whose affairs were looked after in England by a home committee consisting entirely of men. In the 1920s the distance from London to Algiers alone would have discouraged any of the irregularities which were occurring simultaneously in Plock. But they did not prevent my father (who was a member of the home committee and greatly esteemed among the *mulieres sacrae* with whom he was conversant) from marrying my mother, who was one of the mission band in Algiers.[91]

V

We may end with a dash of theory and a few drops of controversy. Implicit in the cases which have been presented are a number of themes from the psychology of Jung which, for reasons that Dr Johnson might have equated with pure ignorance, this essay neither endorses nor opposes. Among these themes we may identify the bisexual, androgynous character of human being, and, by projection and analogy, of divine being; the androgynous source of human yearning and striving to find completion, fulfilment and perfection in and through another human being of the opposite sex; the part played in that process by contra-sexual nostalgia, the female principle or *anima* in the male, the *animus* in the female, both buried within the archetypal images, dreams and memories of the collective unconscious; the difference between paternal and maternal love. Knox and Elizabeth Bowes, Kowalski and Kazlowska, Knowles and Kornerup: all appear to be suitable subjects for Dr Jung's case-book.[92]

---

[90] Sister Briege McKenna, O.S.C., *Miracles Do Happen* (Dublin, 1987.)

[91] Again, I plead oral evidence, for the most part. But the story of the Algiers Mission Band and its foundress, Miss Lilias Trotter, a favourite pupil of Ruskin (who is said to have said 'what a waste') and my mother's employer, is briefly mentioned by Stephen Neill, *Christian Missions*, Pelican History of the Church, vi (1964), p. 369.

[92] *The Essential Jung*, ed. Anthony Storr (Princeton, 1983), part 4, 'Archetypes: Shadow; Anima; Animus; the Persona; the Old Wise Man', pp. 87-127; Carl Gustav Jung, *Memories, Dreams, Reflections* (New York, 1961). See also Suzanne Lilar, 'The Androgyne: A Myth of the Couple', in her *Aspects of Love in Western Society*, tr. J. Griffin (1965), pp. 117-54; and John P. Downley, *The Goddess, Mother of the Trinity: A Jungian Implication*, Studies in the Physchology of Religion, iv (Lampeter, 1990).

These Jungian notions have been attacked as fundamentally sexist and as supportive of an actual and social discrimination against women.[93] The concealed *anima* in the male unconscious, it is said, mattered more to Jung than the submerged animus in the female, since his primary purpose was to achieve the integration of the feminine, the Eros, into the male pscyhe: which was what Lady Bowes did for Knox, the Little Mother for Kowalski. The male element concealed in woman was, by comparison, a mere embarrassment, in no way proper to woman and called by Jung 'a regrettable accident': so that a woman who moves into a role proper to the male psyche is performing a somewhat unnatural act. In any case, the characterisation of the *anima/animus* polarity is said to derive from simple prejudice, the purpose of which is to perpetuate the subjugation of women. According to this argument, an unprejudiced psychology ought to abandon sexual stereotypes altogether and acknowledge the common human *libido*, almost regardless of gender, which survives as a merely social construct.

To propose, as some of the material included in this essay implicitly proposes, that women have a distinctive and other contribution to bring to religious experience which ought not to be confused with the male contribution is also suspect as a subtle chauvinism, ammunition for those who oppose the ordination of women. For 'other' may mean lesser and subordinate. In the hierarchies of status, management and reward, it is a means of keeping women down. Why, asks a a writer in the journal *Signs* (the *Journal of Women in Culture and Society*), why in the thirteenth century were religious women forced out of an active ministry and into a primarily contemplative life?[94] The underlying assumption seems to be that the contemplative life is not worth very much, when the chips are down.

There is no necessity why Jungian thinking should become so patently a sexist ideology. It could equally favour a division of roles which acknowledges the difference but equally the complementarity of the sexes on a basis of formal and actual parity. The argument runs: The priest needs to develop both feminine and masculine qualities and this may best be brought about by a mixed priesthood in which complementary influence and an interchange of qualities would be possible. Parental love is a sacrament in both kinds. So it could be with the sacrament of orders. There are benefits in the sense found in Mother Julian, and also in St Anselm, of

[93] Naomi Goldenberg, 'A Feminist Critique of Jung', *Signs: A Journal of Women in Culture and Society*, ii (1976), pp. 443-9; Carol Christ, 'Some Comments on Jung, Jungians and the Study of Women', *Anima*, 3 (1977), pp. 66-9; Denmaris S. Wehr, 'Jung and Feminism: Opposition or Dialogue', in her *Jung and Feminism: Liberating Archetypes* (1988), pp. 1-11.

[94] A.B. Driver, 'Religion', *Signs*, 2 (1976), 434-42. Apart from a number devoted to non-European, non-Christian religious faiths, this rather negative article is the only item on the subject of religion to have appeared in *Signs*.

the motherhood of God, and these may best be enjoyed with the aid of a female priesthood.

The only lesson of history is that there are no lessons from history: and little predictive power either. History cannot prove either Jung or his feminist critics right or wrong. Jung may well have been talking through his hat. Far from the human psyche being influenced at the level of collective unconsciousness by ancient myths and archetypes, its undertows may be socially and culturally determined. Knox and Mrs Bowes, Kowalski and the Little Mother are perhaps fully explicable within the particular contexts to which they belonged which were in no way universal, not the contexts of our present, still less of the future. It is possible to stand Jung on his head and to make the public *persona*, the socially prescribed role, more determinative of behaviour than any subconscious element. That may dispose of sexual archetypes. And more radically it may dispose of religion as well: or at least of religion as Jung understood and encouraged it, since it points in the direction of a general secularisation of persons and personality.

We may presently find ourselves in a set of social circumstances where it becomes practically irrelevant for a human organisation and for those who work within it that some of them are men and others women, or that all of them may carry at a certain level below consciousness attributes of the other sex, with certain dynamic consequences. Perhaps we are already in such a situation in industry, or some industries, in the media, in some university departments. But perhaps, given the nature of religion and its quasi-erotic experience and discourse, gender is rather less likely to fade away from the churches. But that is a matter of opinion, and of experience, and we do not all share the same opinions, or identical experiences.

As to all this, history offers uncertain guidance. A psychologist, a sociologist, or a bishop, or a woman, might resent the intervention of a male historian into these sensitive and highly contemporary issues. But if this essay has had any point, it is that historically the record of religious transactions indicates the importance of gender and suggests that the question of male and female places and roles in religious societies and organisations cannot be a simple issue of rights and equal opportunities, to be resolved by legislating for parity. A church in which men and women enjoyed total parity in appointments and roles, to such an extent that they ceased for all practical purposes to be women and men, becoming simply church persons, might find at the end of the day that it had almost ceased to be religious. If the historian is allowed to pronounce on these matters, he (or she) must report that without the sex-specific contribution of women and men to religious transactions there would have been many less religious transactions: less mysticism, less dissent and pressure for change, less exploration of the inner and psychological implications of schemes of salvation. In short, there would have been less religion. Some, looking into the future, might regard the absence of religion as gain. But historians, religious or not, looking back on the past which is their livelihood, could only regard it as loss.

6

Truth and Legend: The Veracity of John Foxe's Book of Martyrs

John Foxe's 'Book of Martyrs' or, more properly, *Acts and Monuments of the Church* needs no elaborate introduction. Even for a Dutch audience it would not be appropriate to call Foxe the English van Haemstede. [1] Adriaan van Haemstede is a figure who deserves both admiration and sympathy, but Foxe was a more considerable martyrologist and historian, whose work exercised a critical and enduring influence on the civilisation of the English-speaking peoples. For a certain class of seventeenth-century reader, Foxe was much more than a popular and, indeed, standard author. He was read formally, systematically and, in the language of the time, 'throughly', as men read Scripture. Nicholas Ferrar of Little Gidding had a chapter read in his model household every Sunday evening, [2] and so perhaps did most of his contemporaries of a strongly religious disposition. Ignatius Jordan, mayor and M.P. of Exeter in the 1620s, was said to have read the Bible 'above twenty times over' and *Acts and Monuments* 'seven times over'.[3] That implies a daily and nightly reading from these two sacred books. Those who follow Jordans's example may well find that after perhaps twenty-five years they will have matched his performance, having read through the Bible a score of times but Foxe only seven times. For *Acts and Monuments* is a longer book, containing perhaps two and a half million words to the Bible's mere million and occupying eight volumes of 700 pages each in the nineteenth-century editions:[4] in its time, the longest book ever conceived and published in English.

The reference in my title to veracity may call for rather more in the way of explanation. It is an echo of 'old unhappy far-off things and battles long ago': as long ago as the 1560s, when Foxe's book was first called by Catholics

---

[1] A.J. Jelsma, *Adriaan van Haemstede en zijn Martelaarsboek* (The Hague, 1970). The title echoes, perhaps intentionally, a book to which much reference will be made in this essay, J.F. Mozley, *John Foxe and his Book* (1940). See also J.-F. Gilmont, 'La génèse du martyrologe d'Adrien van Haemstede (1559)', *Revue d'histoire ecclésiastique*, 63 (1968), pp. 379–414. This essay was originally read to an Anglo-Dutch conference of historians.

[2] Mozley, *John Foxe and his Book*, p. 180.

[3] Samuel Clarke, *A Collection of the Lives of Ten Eminent Divines ... and of Some Other Eminent Christians* (1662), p. 453.

[4] *The Acts and Monuments of John Foxe* 'with a preliminary dissertation' by the Rev. George Townsend and ed. by the Rev. Stephen Reed Cattley (1837-41): hereafter *A. & M.*

a dunghill of lies,[5] and when, according to one of his correspondents, detractors called daily: 'Lies! lies; so many lines, so many lies!'[6] Presently the Jesuit Robert Parsons claimed to have detected more than 120 lies in less than three pages.[7] The battle was renewed in the early nineteenth century, when the Catholic journalist William Eusebius Andrews devoted 1300 pages to what he called *A Critical and Historical Review of Foxe's Book of Martyrs, Showing the Inaccuracies, Falsehoods and Misrepresentations in that Work of Deception,*[8] while the Anglican S.R. Maitland, with more up-to-date and sophisticated weapons, entered the fray with a long series of attacks on Foxe and the Foxeian tradition, some of them published under the running headline 'Puritan Veracity'.[9] For Maitland believed that among the members of the Puritan sect (who on his terms included Foxe) it was considered not only allowable but positively meritorious to tell lies for the sake of the cause.[10]

But unlike little Wilhelmina and Peterkin in Robert Southey's poem, not all modern students of history will be crying:

> Now tell us all about the war,
> And what they fought each other for ...

For the veracity of Foxe's Book of Martyrs is a question which may be thought retrogressive and almost redundant, in the perspective of current philosophies of history. According to a modern writer on the subject, Foxe was notable not for his veracity but as a maker of mighty myths. Another commentator has dubbed him the 'prince of English historical myth-makers'.[11] In current literature, and especially in the late Professor William Haller's attractively written and influential study *Foxe's Book of Martyrs and the Elect Nation,*[12] the myths, and especially the grand, apocalyptic myth of the divine blueprint for human history and the lesser myth of the place within that plan assigned to the English church and nation, has largely

---

[5]   Mozley, *John Foxe and his Book*, p. 138.

[6]   John Loude (Lowth) to John Foxe, n.y. (1579), BL, MS Harley 425, fol. 134; printed, *Narratives of the Days of the Reformation, Chiefly from the Manuscripts of John Foxe the Martyrologist* (ed. J.G. Nichols, Camden Series, o.s., 77, 1859), pp. 15–16. Cf. Thomas Purye to Foxe, 6 May n.y.: 'The God of truth defend you and all other that maintain his truth from the venomous poison of liars!' (BL, MS Harley. 416, fol. 100; printed, *Narratives of the Days of the Reformation*, 87–8.)

[7]   James Gairdner, *Lollardy and the Reformation in England: An Historical Survey* (4 vols., 1908–13), i, p. 340.

[8]   2 vols. (1853).

[9]   J.F. Mozley has a bibliographical note on Maitland's extensive writings on Foxeian topics, most of which appeared originally in the *British Magazine* between 1837 and 1847; Mozley, *John Foxe and his Book*, p. x. See also *Narratives of the Days of the Reformation*, pp. xxii–xxiii.

[10]   S.R. Maitland, *Essays on Subjects Connected with the Reformation in England* (1849), p. 1.

[11]   Leslie P. Fairfield, *John Bale: Mythmaker for the English Reformation* (West Lafayette, IN, 1976), p. 119; Glanmor Williams, *Reformation Views of Church History* (1970), p. 62.

[12]   (1963).

displaced the old-fashioned question of Foxe's reliability as a recorder of historical fact. More recently, the most notable development in Foxe studies has been the correction of Haller's exaggerated account of the ethnocentricity and imperialism of *Acts and Monuments* in several acute studies of Reformation and post-Reformation apocalyptic by William Lamont, Leslie Fairfield, Richard Bauckham and Katharine Firth, who all come closer than Haller to a faithful rendering of elements of the Foxeian philosophy of history. But all these scholars share a common concern with Foxe's mentality rather than with his facts, or the merits of the great book as history.[13] For Haller, the question was not, did Foxe tell the truth as we would have it told, but what did he take the truth to be and induce so many of his countrymen in so critical a moment to accept as such. 'Whether the facts and the meaning of the facts were in every respect what he made them out to be, we need not inquire.'[14]

That is all very well, and myths are by no means the same things as lies. However, historians of the English Reformation and especially of the pre-Reformation Lollard heresy and of the Marian persecution, for whom Foxe is often a prime and indispensable source, cannot afford to be so cavalier. For us it is a matter of some importance whether Foxe reported these events and circumstances in any sense truthfully and reliably. Professor Geoffrey Elton, who thinks that he did, has remarked that Foxe did not create a myth: he commemorated a truth. 'He did not have to invent the persecution.'[15]

Whether Foxe invented, even lied, or on the contrary witnessed to the simple truth, was a matter of even greater concern to his first readers, who found their friends and relations and sometimes even themseleves depicted in his pages. On the facts of relatively minor episodes, extensive quasi-judicial enquiries were mounted, either on behalf of Foxe or of those whom he was held to have defamed, and evidence was taken in a formal way from numerous witnesses.[16] There was even a real legal action which acquired a certain notoriety and importance when a man indicted by Foxe as a perjurer sued a clergyman who had read out the offending passage in church. The question for the lawyers was whether such a reading, in good

---

[13] William Lamont, *Godly Rule: Politics and Religion, 1603–60* (1969); and cf. his *Marginal Prynne* (1963); Fairfield, *John Bale*; Richard Bauckham, *Tudor Apocalypse*, Courtenay Library of Reformation Classics (Appleford, 1978); Katharine R. Firth, *The Apocalyptic Tradition in Reformation Britain, 1530-1645* (Oxford, 1979).

[14] Haller, *Foxe's Book of Martyrs*, pp. 15, 187.

[15] G.R. Elton, *Reform and Reformation: England, 1509-1547*, The New History of England (1977), p. 386.

[16] A mere fragment of the dossier compiled against the Reading schoolmaster Thomas Thackham, who had protested against his implication in the betrayal of the martyr Julins Palmer, occupies forty-six folios of Foxe's papers. (BL, MS Harley 425, fos. 18–64; printed, *Narratives of the Days of the Reformation*, pp. 85–131.) See *A. & M.*, viii, pp. 210, 721–2.

faith, constituted a criminal slander.[17] Foxe's *dramatis personae* were capable
of storming into his publishers demanding 'Is Foxe here?', and on being
told that the great man was not at home but that they might speak to the
printer: 'Marry, you have printed me false in your book.' This worthy was
the Kentish gentleman John Drainer who, as Foxe had reported, earned
the nickname 'Justice Nine-Holes' because in Mary's reign he had bored
nine holes in the roodloft of his parish church so that he could conceal his
person and spy out any of his fellow-parishioners who failed to behave as
good Catholics should when the holy sacrament was elevated in their
presence. Drainer was anxious to establish that he had bored but fives holes,
not nine, and with the more excusable purpose of looking upon fair
wenches.[18] Such episodes remind us that the historian of contemporary
events works under a liability which is more than a rule of conscience, and
from which those of us who are distanced by three or four centuries from
our material are immune. We are not likely to be visited by the ghosts of the
historical personages to whom we are sometimes unkind or unfair.

When the dust had settled, English Protestants were convinced, more as
a matter of faith than as something factually verified, that Foxe was virtually
beyond criticism in the fidelity of his record. Readers whose local knowledge detected minor errors were anxious to bring these to light, not in any
hostile spirit but because their general confidence in the accuracy of the
history was so secure. Fifty years after Foxe's death, an elderly man in
Gloucestershire wrote to the martyrologist's son to correct an error of
identity in the account of a certain Marian episode: 'I wish for the reverence
I bear to the memory of Mr Fox, whose person and place of dwelling I knew,
and the honour and love I bear to his works, that this small error, which is
none of his, were amended.'[19] Sir John Harington, referring familiarly to
a certain passage in the Book of Martyrs as 'so full' and therefore perhaps
tedious, adds 'though I doubt not, very faithful'.[20] Another early Jacobean
writer reports: 'Men read the Book of Martyrs as a book of credit, next to
the book of God.'[21] This was to claim more than Foxe ever claimed for
himself. In a notable disclaimer, he declared: 'I profess no such title to write
of Martyrs, but, in general, to write of Acts and Monuments passed in the

[17] Gairdner spent a disproportionate fourteen pages on the case of the alleged perjury of John
Grimwood of Hitcham, Suffolk. (*Lollardy and the Reformation*, i, pp.343-56.) The offending passage
occurs in *A. & M.*, viii, pp. 630-1.

[18] *A. & M.*, viii, pp. 663-4.

[19] Letter of John Deighton, occurring in BL, MS Harley 425, fol. 121; printed, *Narratives of the
Days of the Reformation*, pp. 69-70. The letter was written (doubtless to the martyrologist's son Simeon
Foxe) in about 1636. (Mozley, *John Foxe and his Book*, pp. 186-7, 194.)

[20] Sir John Harington, *A Supplie or Addicion to the Catalogue of Bishops to the Yeare 1608*, ed. R.H.
Miller (Potomac, 1979), pp. 64-5.

[21] Peter Fairlambe, *The recantation of a Brownist* (1606), sig. E.

church and realm of England; wherein, why should I be restrained from the free walk of a story writer, more than others that have gone before me?'[22]

II

In this essay the question whether Foxe told stories will not be confined to matters of factual accuracy and scholarly integrity but will extend to those rhetorical and stylistic features which are the key to the martyrologist's remarkable success as a myth-maker. But it will be as well to begin with the bedrock of facts and documents. For his original readers, Foxe established his credentials not only or even principally as an accurate narrative historian but as a kind of registrar of original documents, the 'monuments' of his title. In the Little Gidding circle in the 1620s it was noted that a certain passage from St Cyprian had been 'registered' by Foxe.[23] We may compare the documents recording the Elizabethan Puritan controversies which were collected by one of Foxe's collaborators, the radical London preacher John Field, and published as *A parte of a register*.[24] For Foxe's Elizabethan and Jacobean public almost as much as for us, original sources were a guarantee of authenticity.

It is no longer necessary to spend time in the defence of these sources. No one would now argue, as a certain Fellow of the Society of Antiquaries once did, that the vanished register of Bishop Longland of Lincoln on which Foxe drew for his account of the Lollards of the Chiltern Hills of Buckinghamshire and their trials (the fullest and mot valuable of all records of early Tudor Lollardy) never existed but was forged by Foxe to give his narrative a spurious 'appearance of veracity'.[25] A.G. Dickens has observed that Foxe lacked the intent, the incentive and the diabolical erudition to forget his voluminous and highly specific mass of evidence.[26] The missing Lincoln act book is not now likely to be rediscovered. Foxe seems to have used a transcript of it together with other Lollard trial records at Lambeth Palace, where it no longer exists.[27] But other 'registers' in similar form have been found by modern research (notably the record of the Coventry trials of

[22] *A & M.*, iii, p. 705.

[23] *Conversations at Little Gidding* ed. A.M. Williams (Cambridge, 1970), p. 182.

[24] Edinburgh or Middelburg?, 1593? See also much further material from the same collection preserved in MS and calendared by Albert Peel as *A Seconde Parte of a Register*, 2 vols. (Cambridge, 1915).

[25] This arch-sceptic was the Rev. A.R. Maddison, F.S.A. See W.H. Summers, *The Lollards of the Chiltern Hills: Glimpses of English Dissent in the Middle Ages* (1906), pp. 103-8.

[26] A.G. Dickens, 'Heresy and the Origins of English Protestantism', *Britain and the Netherlands*, 2, ed. J.S. Bromley and E.H. Kossmann (Groningen, 1964), p. 49.

[27] J.A.F. Thomson, 'John Foxe and Some Sources for Lollard History: Notes for a Critical Appraisal', *Studies in Church History*, 2, ed. G.J. Cuming (1965), p. 253.

1511)[28] and comparison of these sources with the passages in Foxe which are based on them suggest that the martyrologist worked only a little more carelessly and a few shades more partially than would be tolerable in a modern doctoral thesis, but with essentially the same methods.[29] Many of his working papers, now preserved among the Harleian collection of manuscripts in the British Library, resemble the material which we may leave behind at our deaths, to the embarrassment of our heirs and executors; reams of unused transcripts and notes from two or three centuries of royal and ecclesiastical records.[30]

As late as 1929 the *Encyclopedia Britannica*, that useful repository of past erudition, indicted Foxe of 'wilful falsification of evidence'. But the more intelligent of his critics had always recognised that his alleged crimes lay in the presentation and interpretation of evidence, not in its fabrication. In a hostile essay in the *Dictionary of National Biography*, Sir Sidney Lee called Foxe 'neither scrupulous nor scholarly' but admitted that he was 'appallingly industrious' and 'a compiler on a gigantic scale'; while the severest of all Foxe's censors, James Gairdner, called him 'a very careful editor'. 'It is not to be supposed that he connived at forgery.'[31] Nor is it any longer profitable to debate whether certain episodes in the Book of Martyrs were Foxe's own invention, or accepted by him as factual in such a casual fashion as to bring his credibility into general question. It was natural that readers should have doubted the facts of the bizarre episode in Guernsey, when a woman reportedly gave birth in the fire and the newly born infant was tossed back into the flames to share the mother's grisly fate. The circumstances stretch credulity. But it appears from other documents that this obscenity indeed happened, very much as Foxe reported it.[32] If there were any remaining doubts about Foxe's fundamental honesty in such respects, they were removed by J.F. Mozley's scholarly albeit overly defensive study published in 1940, *John Foxe and his Book*. *Acts and Monuments* is stuffed with as many detailed and minor errors as we should expect of a history written on this scale and in great haste, in Foxe's words 'so hastily raked up ... in such shortness of time'.[33] There are mistakes of both person and place, mistakes of dating in plenty, faults of transcription and in proof-reading. But the only elements of pure invention (and not primarily Foxe's own invention) occur in the recounting of sundry extraordinary 'providences' and other

[28] 'Heresy Trials in the Diocese of Coventry and Lichfield', *Journal of Ecclesiastical History*, 14 (1963), pp. 160-74.

[29] 'The words of the register' sometimes appears as a marginal comment by Foxe. See, for example, *A. & M.*, iii, pp. 585.

[30] BL, MSS Harley 416-26, with other fugitive materials in MSS Lansdowne 335, 388, 389, 819, 1045. For an example of a regular magpie's nest, see MS Harley 420.

[31] Gairdner, *Lollardy and the Reformation*, i, p. 364.

[32] Mozley, *John Foxe and his Book*, pp. 223-35.

[33] *A. & M.*, iii, p. 704.

acts of divine judgment visited upon those responsible for the deaths of the martyrs: fragments in the manner of the *De mortibus persecutorum* of Lactantius. But here Foxe was following in a tradition which was in a literal and strict sense fabulous. For example, the story that an escaped bull running through the streets of a Gloucestershire town made straight for the ecclesiastical official who had just presided over a burning and gored him to death was too good to be true. Foxe had it at third hand as a piece of dubious oral tradition which was already sixty years old and we now know that the official in question lived for many years after his allegedly fatal accident.[34]

In the past, an essay on this subject would have devoted many pages to such test cases of Foxe's veracity, in order to establish whether or not he is entitled to the accolade of historian. Today we can short-circuit such altercations. assuming that Foxe was indeed a historian and a great one, whose veracity is to be judged by the manner in which he composed his history, a matter not of invention, still less of forgery, but of discrimination, interpretation, and most of all of omission and deliberate exclusion. Since not even a writer of Foxe's supreme prolixity could include everything which could conceivably be said on such a universal subject as the history of the church, it is the exercise of paring, shaping and discarding which ought to concern us. And here it must be frankly admitted that the task of establishing Foxe's method with respect to the total scheme of the work is at present beyond us, and likely to remain so. We are dealing with a book which grew progressively: from the 112 octavo leaves of the earliest, Strasbourg edition of 1554, through the 732 folio pages of the 1559 Basle edition, to the massive tome published in English (for the first time) in 1563 as *Acts and Monuments of these latter and periolous dayes touching the matters of the Church* (now not far short of 2000 folio pages); and on to the nearly definitive version of 1570, two volumes and well over 2000 pages in double columns; and beyond, for further matter was introduced in 1576, 1583 and even in 1596, nine years after Foxe's death.

If each of these successive editions had simply added new material our task would be relatively simple. A reliable edition would simply print the latest text. But even Foxe, who was under some pressure to limit the size and cost of his formidable work,[35] felt constrained to cut out some his matter in order to accommodate more recent and exciting accessions to his knowledge. And as we know from his papers, which fill twelve volumes of the Harleian MSS, many of the sources and eye-witness accounts which

[34] Ibid., iv, 128. See Mozley, *John Foxe and his Book*, p. 164. The Grimwood case comes into this same category. The allegation that the perjured Grimwood's bowels 'suddenly fell out of his body' adheres to the *topos* of the death of Arius, from which it was presumably derived.

[35] In 1563, William Turner, dean of Wells, urged Foxe to shorten his book. (Mozley, *John Foxe and his Book*, pp. 137-8.) As we know, the reverse happened, But in 1589 the physician Timothy Bright published *An abridgement of the Actes and Monumentes*.

reached him were simply filed away and never used, for reasons which may sometimes be worth consideration. One would suppose that a basic necessity for Foxeian studies would be a critical edition of *Acts and Monuments* which at the very least would indicate the point of entry, or of departure, of every episode, passage or document, with source references and cross references to the unpublished material in the author's papers. The Victorian editor of some of this discarded matter called for such an edition as long ago as 1859,[36] but we are no closer to it now than we were then. So no collated edition of Foxe exists or, given the exigencies of modern publishing, is ever likely to exist. Instead we all use, a little shamefacedly perhaps, the eight-volume, nineteenth-century edition associated with the names of Stephen Reed Cattley and George Townsend, which is not a work of scholarship at all and makes little attempt to analyse or even convey a sense of process of progressive accretion by which the book grew.

Foxe by grace of Cattley and Townsend has suffered a sad sea-change which Reformation historians ought to find a real handicap to an imaginative grasp of their subject. For example, in the great Elizabethan editions the celebrated account of the Buckinghamshire heresy trials of 1520 – 1 (which appeared for the first time in 1570, something which Cattley never tells us) is laid out with stunning compositorial brilliance (a fine piece of the printer John Day's virtuosity) with two differing type-faces and the devices of headed columns and brackets employed to reveal at a glance who among the victims accused whom of what. This is not so clear in Cattley-Townsend,[37] where the original medium has been lost, leaving only the verbal message. In other words, the nineteenth-century editions bear the same relation to the authentic Foxe as the print of a painting to the painting itself, or the sadly degenerate Victorian versions of Foxe's illustrations to the original wood-cuts, used for all editions before that of 1641.

Sometimes the failure of Foxe's editors to date the supplements to his history obscures problems which cry out for investigation. In June 1555, the first of sixty-one Kentish Marian martyrs was burned in a gravel pit near Dartford, on the Thames estuary. He was a young linen-draper of that town called Christopher Wade. As late as 1576, Foxe knew nothing about this incident beyond Wade's name and the date of his execution, and about this he was mistaken. But by the time the next edition went to press, in 1583, he had been supplied with one of the most circumstantially vivid of all his eye-witness accounts. We learn that Wade's burning attracted 'the people of the country' in such numbers that fruiterers came with horse-loads of cherries to sell to the crowd; that Wade's wife prepared a long white shirt for the burning; that the stake was sunk in a pitch-barrel; and, what was most to the point, that Wade died exhorting the people to embrace and

[36] John Gough Nichols in his preface to *Narratives of the Days of the Reformation*. However, since this paragraph was written, Professor David Loades has proposed just such a scholarly edition, which has been adopted (1993) by the British Academy.

[37] *A & M.*, iv, pp. 217-46.

adhere to the doctrine of the Gospel proclaimed in the days of King Edward, and witnessing to the truth of this doctrine by holding his hands above his head 'even when he was dead and altogether roasted'. These things were witnessed and recorded by Richard Fletcher, a prominent Kentish cleric in Elizabethan days, and by his nine-year-old son who finished his days as bishop of London and fathered the famous dramatist, John Fletcher. I think that I now know why the Fletchers sent this account to the martyrologist more than twenty years after the event and not before. It is an interesting story which I have told elsewhere. But only by comparing the 1576 and 1583 editions, an exercise which the presence of Cattley and Townsend on one's shelves tends to discourage, was the fact itself established.[38] It would be a formidable task to collate the various Elizabethan editions with respect to all their contents. The late William Haller told me in 1954 that he supposed that he was the only person to have inspected every page of every edition of Foxe. I cannot say whether he did anything more than scan them. Certainly there is no evidence in Haller's published work of any serious onslaught on the comparative textual history of *Acts and Monuments*.

III

Nor can I pretend to make good the omission in a single essay. But in order to probe a little more deeply into Foxe's method, an inch or two deeper than the point reached in J.F. Mozley's over-apologetic study, I propose that we remain in the county of Kent and examine the account given by Foxe of some of Christopher Wade's fellow martyrs. This will have the advantage of bringing us face to face with the most serious and still active charge which Foxe must be forced to answer, but which Mozley failed to press: that in dealing, to an extent faithfully, with the record of the repression and persecution of convicted heretics, both before and after the onset of the official Reformation, Foxe represented as true Protestants and co-religionists men and women who were nothing of the kind but rather rank heretics of a more extreme and eclectic kind, whose opinions Foxe and all other orthodox reformers should have found a deplorable embarrassment.

Since Foxe and his readers were familiar with the Augustinian dictum that not the death but the cause is the ground and matter of martyrdom, he was inevitably challenged on the ground that his heroes may have died violent and unpleasant deaths but were not true martyrs by virtue of that fact. While the Marian persecution was still in progress, the Catholic Miles

---

[38] Patrick Collinson, 'Cranbrook and the Fletchers: Popular and Unpopular Religion in the Kentish Weald', in *Reformation Principle and Practice: Essays in Honour of A.G. Dickens*, ed. P.N. Brooks, (1980), pp. 178–9, 196. The account of Wade's burning, which first appeared in the 1583 edition of Foxe at pp. 1679-80, will be found in *A. & M.*, vii, pp. 319-21.

Huggarde (the only anti-Protestant writer of his period to match Foxe's own polemical and journalistic verve) published his *Displaying of the protestantes* which alleged that 'the punishments are not so diverse in Hell ... as the sundry opinions of these Protestants' and presented a gallery of the more idiosyncratic specimens as so many ideal types of the spirit of anarchy to which Luther, 'the father of many monstrous births', had given rise. Huggarde was able to quote from a sermon of the most celebrated of English Protestant preachers (and martyrs) in which Bishop Latimer reminded his Edwardian hearers that it was not the death but the cause which made the martyr: 'This is a deceivable argument, he went to death boldly, ergo he standeth in a just quarrel. The Anabaptists that were burnt here in England in divers towns ... went to their death even *intrepide, as* ye will say, without any fear in the world, cheerfully. Well, let them go.'[39]

How many of Foxe's small army of intrepid, cheerful confessors were in a sense 'anabaptists', holding a variety of sectarian opinions and totally lacking in the coherence and firmness of orthodox belief which both Catholics and Protestants agreed to be an indispensable mark of the true church, and which would have earned their recognition as Christian martyrs? A major objective of *Acts and Monuments* was to give the lie to the charge that Protestantism was a principle of novelty and variance: a purpose which it shared with Bishop John Jewel's officially sponsored *Apology of the Church of England*, where the shoe was placed on the other foot and Catholicism was represented as a religious system incurably plagued by partisan division, 'so very uncertain and full of doubts'.[40] Jewel's opponent Thomas Harding had called the heresiarch Michael Servetus, executed by the Geneva Protestants, 'a brother of yours' and the rank English heretic Joan Boucher, burned by the Edwardian government, 'a sister of yours'. Jewel protested. 'We detected their heresies and not you. We arraigned them. We condemned them ... It seemeth very much to call them our brothers, because we burnt them. It is known to children, it is not the death but the cause of the death, that maketh a martyr.'[41]

Unlike Jewel, Foxe would never have boasted of the burning of a Servetus or a Joan Boucher. On the contrary, he had pleaded for Joan's life as he would later vainly beg mercy for two Dutch anabaptists executed in London in 1575.[42] Because Foxe was unusually tolerant and opposed to the death penalty in all cases concerning heresy, the charge that many of his

[39] Miles Huggarde, *The displaying of the protestantes* (London, 1556), fos. 14, 44 v-5. Huggarde quotes accurately a passage which will be found in Latimer's fourth sermon preached before Edward VI, 29 March 1549: *Sermons by Hugh Latimer*, ed. G.E. Corrie, Parker Society (Cambridge, 1854), p.160.

[40] John Jewel, *An Apology of the Church of England*, ed. J.E. Booty, Folger Documents of Tudor and Stuart Civilization (Ithaca, NY, 1963), p. 47.

[41] *The Works of John Jewel*, ed. J. Ayre, 4 vols., Parker Society (Cambridge, 1845-50), iii, pp. 187-8.

[42] Mozley, *John Foxe*, pp. 86-9.

Bishop Bonner beating his prisoners in his orchard (*Acts and Monuments*, 1563). The bishop, according to Sir John Harington in *A Brief View of the State of the Church of England*, is alleged to have remarked when he saw this woodcut: 'A vengeance on the fool! How could he get my picture drawn so right?' Reproduced from Mozley, *John Foxe and his Book* (1940), p. 174.

martyrs were not true martyrs inflicts only a glancing blow upon him. In a sense, Foxe's subject, and that of all martyrology, was not so much the martyr as the persecuting force which victimised him, and the overweening fault of the Catholic Church was not, as it may have been for Jewel, confusion and division, but malevolent cruelty. This was the sheet anchor of Foxe's ecclesiology, for a cruel church would never be a true church. In his biblical drama *Christus triumphans*, Foxe put these words into the mouth of Ecclesia: 'Dismiss all force: let us exchange threats for patience and turn violence into prayers.'[43] And in a remarkable preface addressed to 'all the professed friends and followers of the pope's proceedings' he asked the papists whether in Scripture Mount Sion were not a type of the spiritual church of Christ, and whether Isaiah had not prophesied that they should not hurt nor kill in all his holy mountain: 'Upon these premises now followeth my question: "How the church of Rome can be answerable to this hill of Sion, seeing in the said church of Rome is, and hath been, now so many years, such killing and slaying, such cruelty and tyranny shewed, such burning and spilling of christian blood, such malice and mischief wrought …?'[44] So if some of the victims of popish malice were deluded or intellectually confused simpletons, something which Foxe from time to time conceded, the church which responded by burning such people alive still put itself out of court. Of one such 'half foolish' victim Foxe observes: 'But what he was we know not; but this we are sure, he died a good man, and in a good cause, whatsoever they judge of him. And the more simplicity and feebleness of wit appeared in him, the more beastly and wretched doth it declare their cruel and tyrannical act therein.' In his account of an Ipswich martyr of 1546, Foxe reports the supporting shouts of the people who admired his constancy, 'being so simple and unlettered'.[45] Gairdner made a polemical but almost valid point when he observed that it was sufficient to have been condemned by the bishop of Rome to win Foxe's respect. Opposition to Rome was in itself virtual proof of sanctity.[46]

Nevertheless, it would be damaging to Foxe's credibility as a Protestant apologist if it could be shown that a significant proportion of the victims of popish cruelty whose pious ends he extolled fell into the category of even honestly mistaken and deluded sectaries and fanatics. After all, he arranged even the most obscure of them, including Rawlins White, an illiterate Welsh fisherman, a nameless blind boy, 'an old man of Buckinghamshire', in his new Kalendar, which if it was not intended to replace the Kalendar of ecclesiastical saints was meant as a kind of challenge to the traditional

[43] Printed by Oporinus at Basle, 1556; and in English translation in 1579, 1607 and 1672.

[44] *A. & M.*, i, pp. 523-4. On Foxe's tolerant disposition, see V.N. Olsen, *John Foxe and the Elizabethan Church* (Berkeley, 1973).

[45] *A. & M.*, viii, p. 462; v, p. 532.

[46] Gairdner, *Lollardy and the Reformation*, i, pp. 337-8.

Kalendar. And what Gairdner called this 'strange medley' of human types is represented in Foxe's rhetoric monochromatically as a 'a secret multitude of true professors', without nuances or shades of colouring so many faithful representatives of Christ's true church.

Unlike some other questions concerning Foxe's veracity, which are effectively dead and buried, it remains an important and still partly open question whether the victims of the Henrician and Marian persecutions are fairly represented by Foxe as orthodox Protestants who, like Wade the Dartford linen draper, witnessed by their deaths not to some eclectic opinions learned and imparted in holes and corners but to the truths asserted in the Edwardian Book of Common Prayer and other statements of the official Reformation. And the question remains alive because of the continuing desire of historians to understand the character of early English Protestantism, especially at a popular level; and to relate it appropriately both to the older, diffuse tradition of dissent known as Lollardy and to the more coherent and authoritative religious influences entering society from the Continent and from the English universities and expressed in the public formularies of belief and worship.

Kent is a suitable area in which to pursue these enquiries, partly because of the survival of relevant documents, partly because of the likelihood that the heresy anciently endemic in some parts of this county, both in the Medway valley and in the Weald with its teeming but scattered population, large and demographically unstable parishes and partially industrialised economy, was of an extreme variety, strongly negative in its rejection of orthodox Catholic belief and practice and virulent in its anticlericalism. [47] The record of heresy trials conducted in this region by Archbishop Warham in 1511, which was seen by Foxe, still survives in Warham's Register,[48] and seems to indicate a deeply ingrained, obstinately individualistic strain of heresy characterised by unbelief rather than the positive, evangelical belief and piety which can be traced in the nearly contemporaneous Buckinghamshire and Coventry trials: although this impression may depend upon the line of investigation pursued by Archbishop Warham's staff and must be entertained with considerable caution. Later, in the reign of Edward VI, 'anabaptists' (often a loose and unspecific label for sectaries of any kind) were said to 'swarm' in Kent. Some of those who frequented the conventicles acknowledged the leadership of one Henry Hart, apparently an old Wealden Lollard and an embittered opponent of all 'learned men', 'for all errors were brought in by learned men'. Hart persistently

---

[47] This is persuasively argued and extensively justified in the unpublished Oxford D. Phil. thesis by J.F. Davis, 'Heresy and the Reformation in the South-East of England, 1520-1559' (1966) and his *Heresy and Reformation in the South-East of England, 1520-1559* (1983). See also C.J. Clement., 'The English Radicals and their Theology, 1535-65' (unpublished Cambridge Ph.D. thesis, 1980).

[48] Lambeth Palace Library, Archbishop Warham's Register, fos. 159 r–75 v. See J.A.F. Thomson, *The Later Lollards, 1414-1520* (Oxford, 1965), pp. 186-91.

attacked the error most characteristic of learned Protestantism: predestination. Special commissions were sent into Kent to detect the beliefs and activities of his followers, the 'free will men', and Archbishop Cranmer himself was actively involved.[49] Beliefs more deviant still, including the Melchiorite doctrine of Christ's celestial flesh, took to a Protestant stake Joan Boucher, latterly a resident of Canterbury. Joan claimed that there were a thousand of her opinion in London and doubtless there were others of her persuasion in Kent.[50] In a published attack on Joan's errors, *An apology for spitting upon an Arian*, Archdeacon John Philpot, himself fated to burn under Mary, complained of 'these late sprung heresies' which 'go about to pervert you from the true faith in corners and dens'.[51] Historians who know their Kent will be tempted to identify some of these 'dens': Tenterden, Biddenden, Benenden, Smarden.

This well-tended seedbed of heresy presently yielded more victims to the Marian persecution than any other region of England, London not excepted: an astonishing total of sixty-one (forty-three men and eighteen women), of whom no less than forty-one perished at Canterbury in seven separate holocausts.[52] About one in five of the Marian martyrs was Kentish, and one in seven died in Cardinal Pole's metropolitan city. Foxe has the bare facts of almost all these cases, including the names, but often nothing more. Some of the victims who can be identified are known to have taken part in the 'free will' conventicles of the recent past. With an irony which may have been lost on the ecclesiastical authorities, for whom one heretic was much like another, two leading freewillers were burned in the same fire as their most formidable clerical opponent, the north countryman John

[49] J.W. Martin, 'English Protestant Separatism at its Beginnings: Henry Hart and the Free-Will Men', *Sixteenth-Century Journal*, 7 (1976), pp. 55-74; Clement, 'The English Radicals', pp. 125-99.

[50] John Davis, 'Joan of Kent, Lollardy and the English Reformation', *Journal of Ecclesiastical History*, 33 (1982), pp. 225-33.

[51] *The Examinations and Writings of John Philpot* ed. R. Eden, Parker Society (Cambridge, 1842), p. 314.

[52] This calculation is based on a comparison of the relevant passages in *A. & M.* with the tally in Lord Burghley's papers (Lansdowne MSS) 'An account of such as were burned for religion in this reign; printed, John Strype, *Ecclesiastical Memorials*, 3 vols. (Oxford 1820-40), iii, pt. ii, pp. 554-6) which appears to be accurate for Kent, except for the omission of a group of three martyrs who were burned at Canterbury on 30 November 1555 (*A. & M.*, vii, p. 604); and two further victims, not otherwise recorded, whose names are supplied by significavits of relaxation to the secular arm (PRO, C 85/44). My tally includes two men of Kent burned outside the county, but not the five persons who died in Canterbury Castle, 'famished', according to Foxe, who were 'buried by the highway' about November 1556, and another man who died in Maidstone gaol (*A. & M.*, viii, pp. 253-5, 300.) This corrects A.G. Dickens, who estimates fifty-eight Kentish victims, 'all except six of them executed at Canterbury', *The English Reformation* (1964), p. 266; G.R. Elton, who reports forty-nine in Canterbury (sc. Canterbury diocese, where there were in fact fifty-four burnings), *Reform and Reformation*, p. 386; and Philip Hughes *The Reformation in England*, 3 vols. (1950-54), ii, pp. 262-3, who in three places on two pages gives the Kent total variously as fifty-six, fifty-eight and fifty-nine.

Bland.[53] Bland was one of only two clerics out of the grand Kentish total of
sixty-one martyrs. All the remainder were lay men and women, the great
majority apparently artisans and husbandmen. These were formally un-
educated but often well-informed and highly opinionated 'scripture men'.
The freewiller Nicholas Shetterden wrote from prison to say that he knew
the craftiness of those who would ask: 'Where went he to school?' 'For
though I be not learned (as the vain men of the world call learning) yet I
thank my Lord God I have learned out of God's book ...'[54] 'Why are we
called christians', asked Edmund Allin the miller of Frittenden (perhaps
the only godly miller known to the sixteenth century!) 'if we do not follow
Christ, if we do not read his law, if we do not interpret it to others that have
not so much understanding?'[55]

These lay evangelists were Foxe's folk heroes, his indispensable cast of
hundreds. But were they soundly instructed Protestants, disciples of
learned preachers like Bland? Or had they learned their religion from each
other, in conventicles which owed more to endemic heretical tradition than
to prayer books, articles and homilies? Two celebrated historians of the
English Reformation, the Anglican C.H. Smyth and the Roman Catholic
Philip Hughes, agreed that a majority of such victims were heretics in a
more radical sense, and would have been at risk under any sixteenth-
century regime, Protestant no less than Catholic. Indeed, according to
Smyth, if Edward VI had lived two-thirds of those destined to die under
Mary would have been burned 'in the normal course' by the Church of
England.[56] Leaving aside the question whether it was ever likely to have
been a normal course for the reformed Church of England to burn heretics
in any quantity (the tally appears to be two in each of the reigns of Edward
VI, Elizabeth I and James I) we may well ask whether a high proportion of
the Marian martyrs were radically heretical sectaries, and whether Foxe
wilfully concealed this embarrassing fact. These matters are best investigated in Kentish evidence which was preserved and utilised by Foxe. There
is not very much of it, and not quite enough to settle the matter, unless we
adopt Father Hughes's dubiously negative argument that the fact that Foxe
tells us so little about most of his vernacular martyrs is itself a telling piece

[53] The 'History of Master John Bland', with its ironical conclusion in the fire which Bland and
the vicar of Rolvenden, John Frankesh, shared with the freewillers Nicholas Sheterden and
Humfrey Middleton, is in *A. & M.*, vii, pp. 287-318. Bland, a native of Sedbergh, had taught two
archbishops of Cumbrian origin, Edmund Grindal of York and Canterbury and Edwin Sandys of
York, probably at Cambridge; Patrick Collinson, *Archbishop Grindal, 1519-1583: The Struggle for a
Reformed Church* (1979), p.34, an account kindly corrected by Dr Richard Rex.
[54] *A. & M.*, viii, p. 322.
[55] Ibid. Compare Allin with his basically orthodox, scriptural learning with Domenico Scandella
(called Menocchio), the eclectic Friuli miller of Carlo Ginzburg's *The Cheese and the Worms: The Cosmos
of a Sixteenth-Century Miller* (1980).
[56] C.H. Smyth, *Cranmer and the Reformation under Edward VI* (Cambridge, 1926), p. 3; Hughes,
The Reformation in England, ii, pp. 261-2.

of evidence against their orthodoxy and his integrity. But, as Hughes suspected would be the case, there is enough evidence to test the veracity of Foxe in one important respect, and to lend some support to the proposition that he was, on occasion, 'a wilful falsifier of evidence'.

Among the Foxe papers in the Harleian collection in the British Library there are certain folios (to be specific, folios 92 to 103 of MS Harley 421) which are original documents, having been extracted from the trial register of the special Marian commission which investigated heresy in the diocese of Canterbury and particularly, it would seem, in the Wealden parishes. This commission was headed by Archdeacon Nicholas Harpsfield who would later launch the first public attack on Foxe's 'pseudomartyrs' and on Foxe himself as the most notorious of 'pseudomartyrologists'.[57] It was an unusual, and perhaps suspicious course for Foxe to dismember original evidence rather than transcribe it and it may be that he was concerned that no one else should read these particular folios. Moreover, to pursue a Hughesian line of speculation, since the folios which Foxe impounded are not in continuous sequence it may be that other missing sheets contained even more damning evidence, which Foxe destroyed.

However, the material which Foxe preserved is telling enough, establishing as it does that several of the Kentish martyrs denied orthodox Trinitarian and Christological doctrines. William Prowtyng, a sawyer of Thornham, insisted at his trial that

> it is no article of our faith that there is one God and three Persons, but ever God Almighty ... and saith that Christ is not almighty of himself but received all power from his father ... And saith that [he] was not God of the said substance of God from the beginning. And as for the Holy Ghost, he saith that he believeth he is not God, but believeth he is the spirit of God the Father only, given to the Son, and not God of himself.

John Symes of Brenchley denied that Christ was consubstantial, that is to say, God from the beginning and of one substance with the Father, while Robert King of (East?) Peckham said that if anyone could show him the word consubstantial in Scripture he would believe it, and that if anyone could show him the word 'person' in Scripture he would believe that there are three persons and one God. 'Or else not.' 'Item, he saith that he doubteth whether it can be proved by Scripture that the Holy Ghost is God or no.'[58]

---

[57] Nicholas Harpsfield, *Dialogi sex* (Antwerp, 1566). Harpsfield's attack on Foxe recalls the *bon mot*: 'Cet animal est très méchant. Quand on l'attaque il se defend.' Foxe had written of Harpsfield that as 'among all the bishops, Bonner bishop of London principally excelled in persecuting the poor members and saints of Christ: so of all archdeacons, Nicholas Harpsfield archdeacon of Canterbury ... was the sorest and of least compassion (only Dunning of Norwich excepted), by whose unmerciful nature and agrest disposition, very many were put to death in that diocese of Canterbury ...' *A & M.*, viii, p. 253.

[58] BL, MS Harley 421, fos. 94-5 r.

And what did Foxe do with this embarrassing evidence? He suppressed it, pleading that it would be 'too tedious exactly and particularly to prosecute the several story of every one of these godly martyrs', or covering their eclectic errors with bland blanket statements, such as: 'To these articles what their answers were likewise needeth here no great rehearsal, seeing they all agreed together, though not in the same form of words, yet in much like effect of purposes.' Or again:

> And although certain of these upon ignorant simplicity, swerved a little in the number of the sacraments, some granting one sacrament … some more, some less; yet in the principal matter touching the doctrine of salvation for faith to stay upon, and in disagreeing from the dreaming determinations of the popish church, they most agreed.[59]

These evasions and equivocations are consistent with similar touches of cosmetic surgery which can be detected in Foxe's rendering of certain Lollard trials, where the accounts in *Acts and Monuments* can be compared with original sources.[60] In dealing with the Kentish inquisition of 1511, Foxe chose to overlook the fact that several of the accused denied the efficacy of baptism.[61] And when a group of Norfolk heretics of the 1420s were found to be even more sceptical about the value of this primary Christian sacrament, Foxe suppressed the relevant article in one case and while reporting it in another, poured scorn upon it. Such views were so manifestly unscriptural that it was beyond belief that anyone could be so ignorant of the Gospel as to entertain them. Foxe also avoided all mention of the pacifism of some of these East Anglians, and in general glossed over the teeming variety of an exceptionally copious collection of trials with the statement: 'First, this is to be considered, as I find it in the registers, such society and agreement of doctrine to be amongst them, that in their assertions and articles there was almost no difference. The doctrine of one was the doctrine of all the others.'[62] In yet another case, Foxe omitted from the list of charges brought against one of the victims of Bishop Fitzjames's drive against heresy in early sixteenth-century London denial of the Resurrection. But here we should note that in reporting these London trials, Foxe admitted that not all these 'faithful martyrs and professors of Christ' displayed 'the like perfection of knowledge and constancy in all'.[63]

[59] *A. & M.*, viii, pp. 326, 300, 254.

[60] Thomson, 'John Foxe and Some Sources for Lollard History', pp. 251-7.

[61] *A. & M.*, v, pp. 647-52, compared with Lambeth Palace Library, Archbishop Warham's Register, fos. 159 r-75 v.

[62] *A. & M.*, iii, pp. 585-600, compared with Dr Norman Tanner's edition of the original trial register, Westminster Archives, MS B 2: *Heresy Trials in the Diocese of Norwich, 1428-31*, ed. Norman P. Tanner, Camden 4th ser., 20 (1977).

[63] Thomson, 'John Foxe and Some Sources for Lollard History', p. 255.

The pattern is now reasonably clear. Foxe was sometimes prepared to falsify his evidence to the extent of misrepresenting heretics (in a proper and classical sense which was common to both Protestant and Catholic perceptions) as orthodox and conformable if often confused and poorly-informed Christians of his own persuasion. It would be wrong to suggest that he did this on a massive scale, and risky to conclude from these cases that most of the dissidence against which the Marian authorities proceeded was of such a character. Many of the victims appear as impeccable Protestants on the first-hand evidence of the articles objected against them. Others professed curiously hybrid beliefs, suggesting the mixed influence of 'learned men' and preachers in 'dens and corners'. John Fishcock of Headcorn in the Kentish Weald seems to have had a background in the conventicles and as an adolescent he had shown signs of violent alienation from the pious traditions of the parish community.[64] But he told his Marian judges that he had a good judgment of the Trinity and deplored the evil and ungodly opinions of those who believed otherwise. He also endorsed the royal supremacy and condemned unauthorised preaching by laymen.[65] We may recall the death of the Kentish protomartyr, Wade the linen draper, who witnessed dramatically to the truth of official Edwardian doctrine.[66] As Professor David Loades has insisted, the evidence for the continued use of the second Edwardian Prayer Book in the teeth of the Marian hurricane is very impressive.[67] So Foxe was not necessarily deceiving us when he conveyed the impression that 'magisterial' Protestantism was the dominant tendency, even at a popular level, among those mid sixteenth-century Englishmen who defied Catholicism. It was perhaps a valid emphasis to conclude that when all was said and done the important thing was that the Marian martyrs were at one in rejecting what Foxe called 'the dreaming determinations of the papists'. And we should note that nowhere does the martyrologist suggest that death at the stake conferred infallibility on the mental capacities of poorly educated people. Their deaths were edifying, their opinions not always correct. Foxe allowed for the category of non-culpable ignorance in the 'silly sheep and simple lambs of Christ's flock', but held that by their very simplicity the wisdom and power of God were more clearly manifested.[68] We may compare an exchange between the Coventry weaver John Careless and Dr Martin, as

---

[64] In 1543 it was reported of 'John Fishcock the younger' of Headcorn that he 'will not receive the pax but is ready to strike the children that bring it'. *Letters and Papers Foreign and Domestic of the Reign of Henry VIII*, ed. J.S. Brewer et al., 22 vols. (1862-1932), xviii, part ii, no. 546, p. 311.

[65] BL, MS Harley 421, fol. 101.

[66] See pp. 158-9 above.

[67] David Loades, 'Anabaptism and English Sectarianism in the Mid-Sixteenth Century', in *Reform and Reformation: England and the Continent, 1500-1750*, Studies in Church History, subsidia 2, ed. Derek Baker (Oxford, 1979), pp. 59-70.

[68] *A. & M.*, viii, pp. 310-11.

recorded by Foxe under the year 1556: 'Martin: "How say you to the two brethren that are in the King's Bench which deny the divinity of Christ? How say you to their opinions?' Careless: "O Lord! I perceive your mastership knoweth that which of all other things I wish to have been kept from you. Verily he was to blame that told you of that. Truly sir, these be but two simple poor men.""[69]

IV

Careless's interrogator, Dr Martin, proved to be all too well-informed about the divisions between predestinarians and free-willers which persisted in the very prisons where members of both parties awaited their deaths: 'You are one against the other, and both against the Catholic Church.' When asked whether he knew the arch-freewiller, Henry Hart, Careless stoutly denied it. 'But yet I lied falsely, for I knew him indeed and his qualities too well.' Further denials that there were any contentions among the prisoners in King's Bench were followed by a confidential aside: 'This I spake to make the best of the matter; for I was sorry that the papists should hear of our variance.'[70]

In all editions after 1563, Foxe abridged Careless's examination to exclude all incriminating reference to the differences between predestinarians and freewillers and to suppress altogether Careless's lies and prevarications. In place of one expunged passage we read: 'And so after other bytalk then spent about much needless matter ... '[71] It underlines the complaints expressed earlier about Cattley and Townsend to note that they chose to collate the fuller, 1563 version of this interview with the post-1563 text, without any explanation of the significance of what they were doing. But for further light on the counsels which seem to have prevailed between the 1563 and 1570 editions, we may refer to a letter from one of Foxe's correspondents, written even while the 1563 text was in preparation, and begging him not to meddle with a celebrated quarrel of King Edward's days between the soon-to-be-martyred Bishop Ferrar of St David's and the legal establishment of his diocese.

> I think you may well either leave it out altogether either else touch it in such sort that no man may be slandered. The controversy was for prophane matters and therefore unmeet for your History. We must be circumspect in our doings, that we give the papists no occasion to accuse us for persecutors, which we lay so much to their charge.[72]

---

[69] Ibid., viii, p. 169.
[70] Ibid., viii, pp. 164-6.
[71] In the 1570 edition, p. 2101; in the 1631 edition, iii, p. 713.
[72] Richard Prat to Foxe, 20 Jan. 1560(/1), BL, MS Harley 116, fol. 176.

Foxe and his collaborators seem to have taken their own version of the Hippocratic oath. If possible they must not lie. But it was not necessary in all circumstances to strive officiously to tell the whole truth.

Foxe's reluctance to believe the evidence of his own eyes contained in documents which were in his own possession suggests that it may have been a kind of self-deception with which we are dealing. This pardonable handicap he seems to have shared with two of his informants, the Hall brothers of Maidstone, prominent townsmen and one of them a surgeon and poet of some local renown. The Halls wrote to Foxe (and this was a letter for which he failed to find a use) in order to expose and denounce their curate, John Day. In June 1557, in one of the most sensational episodes of the entire persecution, seven victims had perished in one fire in the King's Meadow at Maidstone. Among the seven was our godly miller, Edmund Allin. Day had preached the sermon, struggling with the dense smoke driven by a strong wind to indict those at the stake as 'heretics most damnable', doctrine which he repeated in church on the following Sunday. When the Halls returned from exile to find Day still curate of Maidstone, they demanded that he make a public retraction, acknowledging that the men and women whom he had defamed were godly martyrs who had refuted the gross heresies attributed to them. At first Day stood his ground, insisting that some of the Maidstone seven had denied the humanity of Christ and the equality of the Trinity, 'and no man doubteth that such are heretics'. But after some intimidation, he later admitted that this was a lie. 'Are you men, and did you never lie in your lives?'[73] As we have seen, poor Mr Day may have been perfectly correct in his assessment of some of the Maidstone martyrs as full-blooded heretics in the classical sense. Yet the indignation of the Hall brothers is equally understandable. On the day after the Maidstone holocaust, their sister had burned in Canterbury, after suffering appalling privations in prison. Her last act was to unwind some lace from her middle and to desire that it be given to her brother Roger as a keepsake.[74] As a child of the Second World War I have only to recall my stereotyped attitudes to the then enemy, and to the resistance in occupied Europe, to understand why the Halls, and Foxe, had difficulty in apportioning approval and disapproval among the victims of what they saw as popish cruelty and repression.

---

[73] BL, MS Harley 116, fos. 123–4. John Hall was the author of *The proverbs of Salomon, three chapters of Ecclesiastes etc.* (?1549); *Certayn chapters of the Proverbes etc. translated into metre* (1550); and *The courte of vertu: comtayninge many holy songes, psalmes and ballates* (1565). See John W. Bridge, 'John Hall of Maidstone: A Famous Surgeon of the Sixteenth Century', *Archaeologia Cantiana*, 63 (1951), pp.119-21.

[74] *A. & M.*, viii, pp. 326–8.

V

Finally, I propose to move forward from matters of documented fact and to look briefly, and sufficiently inexpertly, at Foxe as rhetorician and polemicist. To do so will be to discover that his distorting but subtle persuasiveness operated on a far grander scale than in minor improvements here and there to the written record. Foxe's rhetorical sleight of hand in refashioning his human material into models of exemplary Christian perfection, so many clones of Elizabethan godliness, is most apparent in his treatment of the Lollards and other pre- and proto-reformers. When a certain Gloucestershire gentleman living in 1531 is described as 'a great maintainer of the godly',[75] we are alert to the need to ask who, in 1531, were 'the godly', and whether they resembled in all essential respects those so described fifty and a hundred years later. In Foxe's handling of these 'glorious and sweet societies of faithful favourers'[76] there may have been a quite deliberate suppression of the sense of anachronism which he was perfectly capable of entertaining, when it suited his purpose. After all, he admitted in discussing Thomas Bilney, the 'little Bilney' who was depicted as the founder of an evangelical movement in Tudor Cambridge, that his opinion of the mass never differed from that of 'the most gross Catholics', which is as much as to say that whatever Bilney was, he was not a Protestant.[77]

But in respect of Bilney's Lollard contemporaries, the only difference in religious culture which Foxe allowed his Elizabethan readers to observe lay in the superior piety and fidelity of their spiritual grandparents. The Lollards were more religious, but not differently religious. 'Certes, the fervent zeal of those christian days seems much superior to these our days and times ... To see their travails, their earnest seekings, their burning zeal, their readings, their watchings, their secret assemblies, their love and concord, their godly living, their faithful demeaning with the faithful, may make us now, in these our days of free profession, to blush for shame.'[78] The language is distracting, not merely imposing Foxe's own values on the inhabitants of the Chiltern Hills in about 1520 but, for the modern reader, provoking resonances of evangelical experience in later centuries which appropriated words like 'zeal', 'earnest', 'sweet' and 'faithful' for their own needs.[79] Sometimes the alchemy of changing one form of religion into another has been effected by minor adjustments in the language of the

---

[75] Ibid., iv, p. 697.
[76] Said of a Newbury group of the early sixteenth century (ibid. iv, p. 213).
[77] Ibid., iv, p. 649.
[78] Ibid., iv, p. 218.
[79] In his pioneering study *The Lollards of the Chiltern Hills*, W.H. Summers noted (p. 128) significant differences in the vocabulary of the Buckinghamshire Lollards and later Protestants: 'In all the remains we have of them the word "gospel" scarcely ever occurs, though it was so constantly on the lips of the first Protestants a few years later.'

IOHANNES FOXVS

Colligit vt FOXVS Sanctorum gesta Virorum
Digna facit Sanctis plurima martijribus.

The engraved portrait of John Foxe which appeared in Holland's *Heroologia* (1620) recalls the withdrawn, abstracted figure of the later years whose friends, according to his son Simeon, were hardly able to recognise him in the street.

sources. Some East Anglian Lollards of the 1420s paradoxically regarded their teacher William White as a saint, 'sanctissimus et doctissimus doctor legis divinae', and one of them declared that after his death White was become 'magnus sanctus in celo'.[80] This suggests that the religious mentality of these Norfolk farmers was in some respects closer to the popular forms of Catholicism than to a refined and fully internalised Protestantism. Foxe defuses these irksome phrases, rendering the first as 'a true preacher of the law of God' and the second as 'a good and godly man'.[81]

In these cases it is not difficult to see what the martyrologist is up to. Nearer to his own time, and with respect to the Marian events which were the prolonged climax of his story, we may be less dismissive, more trusting of Foxe as our guide, swayed perhaps by a certain awe in the face of the almost imcomprehensible heroism of the martyrs. For all that we know (the historian may say to himself) that extraordinary behaviour was accurately observed and reported, whether we seek to explain it in terms of Christian fortitude or, as a recent psycho-historian has done, as something achieved through the practice of obsessive personal rituals.[82] But of course in our perception of these circumstances, no less than of the history of early Tudor Lollardy, we are at the mercy of Foxe's persuasive rhetoric, indeed never more so. Compare two accounts of the behaviour of the London crowds at the Smithfield burnings, the first Foxe's own, the second from the pen of the Catholic controversialist Miles Huggarde:

> *Foxe*   It was appointed before, of the godly there standing together, which was a great multitude, that so soon as the prisoners should be brought, they should go to them to embrace them and to comfort them; and so they did. For as the said martyrs were coming towards the place in the people's sight, being brought with bills and glaves (as the custom is) the godly multitude and congregation with a general sway made towards the prisoners ... So the godly people, meeting and embracing and kissing them brought them in their arms (which might as easily have conveyed them clean away) unto the place where they should suffer.[83]

> *Huggarde*   At the deaths of [these 'brainsick fools'] ye shall see more people in Smithfield flocking together on heaps in one day than you shall see at a good sermon or exhortation made by some learned man in a whole week. Their glory is such upon these glorious martyrs. And why is this? Because their minds are given wholly to vain things, much like the *Athenians* ... If there be any vain sights to be seen, or any foolish matters to be heard, Lord how they run and sweat in their business![84]

---

[80]   *Heresy Trials*, pp. 45, 47.

[81]   *A. & M.*, iii, p. 595.

[82]   Seymour Byman, 'Ritualistic Acts and Compulsive Behavior: The Pattern of Tudor Martyrdom', *American Historical Review*, 83 (1978), pp. 625-43.

[83]   *A. & M.*, viii, p. 559.

[84]   Huggarde, *The displaying of the Protestantes*, fol. 49, Cf. Foxe's description of a crowd in a very different temper, at Exeter in 1533, when, at the burning of Thomas Benet, 'such was the devilish rage of the blind people that well was he or she that could catch a stick or furze to cast into the fire.' (*A. & M.*, v, p. 26.)

Note how 'the godly multitude and congregation' with its almost super-human courage and responsible adherence to the principle of non-resistance has become in Huggarde a mindless, sensation-seeking mob. But when we learn that the godly Protestant matron Mary Honeywood lost her shoes in the mêlée which surrounded John Bradford's burning and had to walk home barefoot, we cannot be sure that Huggarde's description is any more fanciful than Foxe's.[85]

Elsewhere I have suggested how insidiously Foxe's prose style is infil-trated, or rather saturated, with the ethical values of the classical tradition, often expressed through the conventions of Plutarchan biography.[86] Char-acter was rendered in perhaps the only manner available, in terms of the desirable mean between two extremes. Even Julins Palmer, the Angry Young Man of the Book of Martyrs, a fanatical papist under Edward and an equally ardent gospeller under Mary, is depicted as 'of manners courteous without curiosity, of countenance cheerful without high looks, of speech pleasant without affectation'. The martyrs enjoy perfect control of both emotions and bodily functions. It is their tormentors who fall into uncontrollable passions and often in their ends die 'desperately', 'miser-ably' or 'horribly'. The formal reasons for which the martyrs are content to die are theological. But what their deaths tend to demonstrate is only secondarily the truth of doctrine. Primarily it witnesses to the strength of inherent virtue, which is Aristotelian as much as Christian virtue. And the supreme virtue which the martyrs are called upon to exemplify is *apatheia*, the true courage which is a mean between foolish temerity and despicable cowardice. The martyrs neither seek their destruction, as suicides, nor shrink from it, as apostates. They demonstrate true courage by standing motionless at the stake, often with arms elevated or extended. Bishop Ferrar tells the onlookers that if he should be seen to stir but once in the flames, they should never more trust his doctrine. Or they clap their hands, as an agreed signal to indicate that the pain is tolerable. Bishop Hooper washed his hands in the fire as if it were cold water. At Canterbury, a young man called Roper, 'of a fresh colour, courage and complexion', 'fetched a great leap' as he approached the stake and then stood in the fire with arms making a cross, not plucking them in until the flames had consumed them. Some proved their *apatheia* by cracking jokes: no prerogative of Protestant

---

[85] P.F. Johnston, 'The Life of John Bradford, the Manchester Martyr, 1510–1555' (unpublished B.Litt. thesis, University of Oxford, 1963), p. 138. And see Foxe himself, decribing one of the last burnings, at Ipswich in November 1558: 'With that a great number ran to the stake.' (*A. & M.*, viii, p. 496.)

[86] Patrick Collinson, " 'A Magazine of Religious Patterns": An Erasmian Topic Transposed in English Protestantism', in *Renaissance and Renewal in Christian History*, Studies in Church History, 14, ed. Derek Baker (Oxford, 1977), pp. 223-49.

martyrs, as witness the famous 'mocks' with which Sir Thomas More had earlier mounted the scaffold.[87] Whether it was really in any way like that we cannot tell and may think it naïve even to ask. Foxe processed reality through the alembic of a profoundly classical education (it was with some reluctance that he was persuaded to turn from the medium of Latin to his native language) and like so many other children of the northern Renaissance, there was stoicism as well as Christianity in his philosophy. His prose style elevated and dignified his heroes, reserving the sharp edge of satire and the blunt instrument of abuse for the villains of the piece. Consequently, an analysis of Foxe's rhetorical and polemical art, such as no literary scholar has yet seen fit to undertake, might depict a style in transition from the racy vulgarity of many of his sources and of his more polemical passages to the decorousness of a text designed for the edification of the pious world of what Louis B. Wright called Elizabethan 'middle class culture'.[88] In 1859, J.G. Nichols published a selection of vivid narratives from Foxe's papers.[89] The copy in my university library once belonged to the notable Elizabethan bibliophile John Crow, himself a delightfully rumbustious character, and Crow has made many manuscript notes of the biting language which seethes in these sharply-etched novelettes. Indeed, Nichols himself, as befitted the scion of a famous literary family, listed the more striking words and phrases in a special glossarial index. When a Winchester scholar designed a device for pulling down the images in his college chapel they fell 'heyho Rumbelow'. A certain papist had a 'mighty pouch hanging by his mighty Bonner paunch'. (Bishop Bonner was notoriously fat.) His 'Croydon complexion' (a reference to the charcoal burners of that Surrey village) would not suffer him to blush 'more than the black dog of Bungay' (a topical reference to a recent apparition of the Devil in Norfolk). A slanderer accused others of lying 'as if the cat had licked you clean'. We read of 'desperate Dicks', 'ruffeling roisters', of a payment 'worth as many pence as there be shillings in a groat', of 'the clean-fingered clergy'.[90]

This uninhibited repartee had its literary succession and fulfilment in Nashe and Greene, and it continued to teem in the coarse vernacular of the streets, whence it has been retrieved in thousands of legal actions for

[87] References in *A. & M.*, viii, pp. 202, 629, 633, 635, 637; vii, pp. 26, 115, 367; vi, p. 611; vii, p. 604; vi, pp. 700, 696. See R.W. Chambers on 'the humorous side of martyrdom', *Thomas More* (1938), p. 347.

[88] Louis B. Wright, *Middle-Class Culture in Elizabethan England* (Chapel Hill, NC, 1935). Foxe's Victorian editors continued the process of bowdlerisation. Dr Susan Brigden points out that it is they who have substituted 'offend' for 'piss' in the articles of 1531 against Thomas Arthur who had compared the multitude of ecclesiastical laws, which invited contempt, to the great number of crosses set in the walls, of London, upon which men 'of necessity' were compelled to 'offend' ('piss'). (*A. & M.*, iv, p. 623.)

[89] *Narratives of the Days of the Reformation*.

[90] Ibid., pp. 29, 51, 89, 127, 346, 174, 90, 37. Crow's copy of Nichols is in the library of the University of Kent at Canterbury.

slander, the greatest untapped reservoir of evidence for the history of our language. But we do not find such verbal inventiveness in subsequent religious discourse, which was increasingly conditioned by its own conventional and pious decorum. When Foxe quotes this pungent language he is recording, almost fossilising, the discourse of an age when Protestantism was not yet fully internalised, not yet decorous; just as the vigorous woodcuts which continued to adorn each successive edition of *Acts and Monuments* carried into the profoundly iconophobic seventeenth-century a Protestant aesthetic which was not yet puritan. The Protestant movement which Foxe discloses to us, almost in spite of himself, was not part of the social establishment but a current of protest, expressing itself not in passive iconophobia but in active, even violent iconoclasm; and in so so-called psalms and 'scripture songs', which were in fact protest songs, sung to popular tunes by professional musicians, something not to be looked for in the godly circles of the seventeenth century. Marian Protestants held their meetings in drinking houses over many pots of beer, whereas their spiritual grand-children scrupulously avoided the alehouse as if it were 'a little hell'. It was a riotous time, when Mary Honeywood lost her shoes at Bradford's burning. When the Protestant cook George Tankerfield was arrested in 1555, his wife, 'like a tall women', picked up a spit and offered to run it through the Judas who had betrayed him. Forcibly restrained, she still managed to heave a brickbat after the traitor which struck him in the back.[91]

Against this background, which if it was godly was godly in a tumultuous fashion, Foxe arranged his meek lambs, whose discourse, written or spoken, was nothing but a pastiche of edifying biblical phrases, providing some early models for the puritan way of life of the future, practised or aspired to by Foxe's seventeenth-century readers. To be sure, the proto-puritanism was not Foxe's fabrication. Its voice sounds incessantly in the interminable prison letters of the martyrs, where the biblical topoi are embellished, as in Bradford's epistles, by fervent exhortations to his dear hearts and darlings in the Lord, and by more particular messages to 'hearty Hooper', 'sincere Saunders', 'trusty Taylor'.[92] Foxe had no more need to forge these documents than the Buckinghamshire Lollard trials. But whether outside their correspondence Bradford's 'darlings' carried themselves like meek lambs of Christ or like Mrs Tankerfield we cannot now tell. But we may compare the heavenly language of the lambs with this complaint of a female Kentish heretic in about 1530: 'A vengeance and a

---

[91] The Tankerfield story is in *A. & M.*, vii, p. 344. See now, 'Protestant Culture and the Cultural Revolution' in my *The Birthpangs of Protestant England: Religious and Cultural Change in the Sixteenth and Seventeenth Centuries* (London, 1988).

[92] *A. & M.*, vii, p. 217. See *The Writings of Bradford … Letters Treatises, Remains*, ed. A. Townsend, Parker Society (Cambridge, 1853). And see also Johnston, 'The Life of John Bradford'.

mischief on him, whoreson hook-nosed Scot!'[93]

The conclusion cannot be anything but discouraging to historical positivists. We can no more rewrite Foxe than the Gospels in the New Testament and Foxe is no less indispensable. We cannot and never shall be able to see the events he describes except through his spectacles. It would be absurd to write of the deaths of Bishops Ridley and Latimer as if Foxe had not written first. We can never forget Latimer, stumbling on after Ridley in his 'poor Bristol frieze frock, all worn', Ridley calling 'O, be ye there?', Latimer calling back, 'Yea, have after, as fast as I can follow'. These touches were not trivial but desperately important. According to Foxe, a man who saw 'that knave' Latimer on that occasion and later recalled (in an alehouse) that he had 'teeth like a horse' was at once visited with a terrible judgment. In the very same hour his son hanged himself, not far away.[94]

So we must live with Foxe, who will correct any arrogant notion we may have that we can presume to see the past 'wie es eigentlich war'. Professor Elton has rightly insisted that Foxe did not have to invent the Marian persecution. But invention is but one part, and almost the least part, of the rhetorical repertoire, just as the question of Foxe's strict veracity, though by no means unimportant, is perhaps the smallest of the problems with which this great writer confronts historians of the sixteenth century.

---

[93] J.F. Davis, *Heresy and the Reformation in the South-East of England*, p. 128.
[94] *A. & M.*, vii, pp. 547-8; Collinson, 'A Magazine of Religious Patterns', p. 236.

7

Perne the Turncoat: An Elizabethan Reputation

Andrew Perne died at Lambeth Palace in his seventieth year in 1589, apparently in the very presence of his old friend of more than thirty years' standing, first his client and later his patron, the archbishop of Canterbury, John Whitgift. Perne had been master of Peterhouse for thirty-five years, the senior academic statesman of Elizabethan Cambridge and perhaps its most learned luminary, since he left behind him one of the greatest of sixteenth-century libraries, a larger collection than the University Library itself. However, but for the Whitgift connection and the unfortunate timing of his demise, Perne might have remained respectably obscure, whereas the fates were to determine that like Captain Boycott or Mrs Malaprop his name would become a byword, in Perne's case a byword for a religious turncoat.

In the months before Perne's death, Archbishop Whitgift and his episcopal colleagues had been mercilessly and hilariously lampooned in the brilliant satires known as the Marprelate Tracts. And Perne had come in for his own small share of the abuse, not only as Whitgift's old colleague but as something less respectable, indeed scarcely mentionable. Such was the power of Martin Marprelate's satire that a series of jokes about the patter of an Essex preacher and comedian manqué called William Glibery appears to have given us the useful word 'glib'.[1] Similarly, 'Perne' was close enough to the Latin *pernere*, to turn, to make the master of Peterhouse for all time to come a kind of vicar of Bray of the ivory towers. In the eighteenth century a weathercock on Peterhouse roof bearing Perne's initials, A.P., would be read as 'A Papist, a Protestant, A Puritan'.[2]

Yet, as we shall see, the character assassination of Andrew Perne, if that is what it was, began a little earlier than Martin Marprelate, with the *odium academicum* entertained for him by another ornament of Elizabethan Cambridge, hardly less learned if much less successful, Gabriel Harvey. Harvey too was a pamphleteer with a sharply satirical gift, and presently, perhaps encouraged by Martin, he launched an impassioned attack on the recently deceased Perne which included an ironically emblematic epitaph. Recalling that Archimedes wished to have the figure of a cylinder erected

---

[1] See my forthcoming essay 'Ecclesiastical Vitriol: Religous Satire in the 1590s and the Invention of Puritanism', in John Guy, ed., *The Reign of Elizabeth I* (Cambridge, 1993).

[2] J.C.T Oates, *Cambridge University Library: A History*, i (Cambridge, 1986), pp. 90-1.

on his tomb, Harvey proposed for Perne the device of an equilateral
triangle and composed on this triangular theme three verses, each of three
lines, of which this was the third:

> Three-headed Cerberus, wo be unto thee:
> Here lyes the Onely Trey, and Rule of Three:
> Of all Triplicities the A.B.C.

As with that Oxford worthy of a later generation, Dr Fell, Gabriel Harvey,
to whom we shall return, did not like Dr Perne. But what were the three
sides of that triangle? Not Papist-Protestant-Puritan (for no-one ever
accused Perne of Puritanism) but Catholic-Protestant-of No Religion, or
Neutral. 'What an Ambidexterity, or rather Omnidexterity had the man,
that at one and the same meeting, had a pleasing Tongue for a Protestant,
a flattering Eye for a Papist, and a familiar nodd for a good fellow.'[3]

Such was the telling if mostly posthumous damage inflicted by Harvey
and Martin Marprelate that I temporarily mistook the intention of the
genuine emblem designed for Perne in all good faith by Geffrey Whitney
in his *A choice of emblemes*, published in Leyden two years before his death,
in 1586. A scholar stands at a lectern, surrounded by such weighty tomes
as made up the already famous Perne Library, while another scholar lifts
an admonitory finger. The motto and the verses which accompany this
picture are a warning against book learning for book learning's sake: 'First
reade, then marke, then practise that is good/ For without use, we drinke
but LETHE flood.' A text from Seneca follows: 'Lectio multorum voluminum,
& omnis generis auctorum, habet aliquid vagum et instabile.' I found that
ambiguous. Was it, I wondered, a lesson which Perne needed to learn or
one which he, the profound student, was best fitted to impart? However,
discovery of the original, the emblem which Whitney appropriated as a
compliment to Perne from the *Emblemata* of Sambucus (1564), makes it
unlikely that Whitney's purpose was ironical or in any way critical of the
learned master of Peterhouse.[4] Nor does it appear that such criticism would
have been deserved. Ideologically, Perne was condemned by posterity and,
among his contemporaries, by Gabriel Harvey, for what the twentieth
century might call a lack of commitment. Yet we shall find that his career
was by no means deficient in commitment of a different kind, to the
institutions and corporate bodies which he served and (to persist with
modern jargon) to academic values and standards, which is to say, to good
learning.

---

[3]   *The Works of Gabriel Harvey*, ed. A.B. Grosart (1884), ii, pp. 299, 316.
[4]   I am much indebted to Mr Arnold Hunt who discovered the source of Whitney's emblem
'Usus, non lectio prudentes facit', dedicated to Perne, in Sambucus, *Emblemata* (1564), where it was
dedicated 'Ad Fuluium Ursinum sum'.

II

Like his early patron Archbishop Matthew Parker, Perne came up to Cambridge from the depths of rural Norfolk, one of a family of minor gentry with property in and around Pudding Norton. A draft of his will refers to lands which had belonged to his father in East Bilney (where he was born), Gressenhall, Beetley, Bittering Parva and Stanfield.[5] These were parishes in the very epicentre of Norfolk, midway between the Waveney and the north coast, King's Lynn and Norwich. Family connections may explain how Perne's career got off to a good start, with two fat Norfolk livings and fellowships in two colleges (but not in Parker's Corpus), all secured before his thirtieth birthday.[6]

Unlike Parker, reluctantly elevated in 1559, Perne never subsequently left the university, except to attend to such duties at Ely as required his occasional presence. He was dean of Ely for thirty-two years, from 1557 until his death in 1589, but master of Peterhouse for thirty-five, having begun his academic career as a fellow of St John's, his undergraduate college, followed by a fellowship at Queens', where he was successively bursar, dean and vice-president. Why did Perne not become a bishop? That was perhaps the question lurking behind Geoffrey Whitney's emblem. Gabriel Harvey would have it that 'he long yawned to be an Archbishop, or Byshop, in the one, or the other Church.'[7] Historians tell us that Queen Elizabeth was more or less obliged to commit her church to an advanced Protestant leadership since more moderate churchmen, Catholics without the pope, were no longer available. But Perne was available. To be a successful head of house in Oxford or Cambridge was the normal road to a bishopric in the Elizabethan and Jacobean Church.[8] Perne was arguably the most successful of all the heads of his time. It could only have worked to his advantage that he never married. But so far as we know, Perne was considered for a bishopric only once, and that five years before his death, when his old protégé Archbishop Whitgift shortlisted him for two sees, Bath

---

[5]   Augustus Jessop, *One Generation of a Norfolk House: A Contribution to Norfolk History* (1878), p. 74; *Andrew Perne: Quatercentenary Studies*, ed. David McKitterick, Cambridge Bibliographical Society Monograph, 11 (Cambridge, 1991), p. 87.

[6]   T.A. Walker, *A Biographical Register of Peterhouse Men*, i, *1283-1574* (Cambridge, 1927), pp. 177-8. Perne retained a lifelong attachment to his kindred, devoting whole pages of his will to brothers, brothers-in-law, nephews and kin as remote as 'Robert Harward my cosens sone' and John Rayner 'my wellbelovyd and trustie servant and kynesman', *Andrew Perne*, pp. 90-1. Perne's continuing interest in his native county is inferred by further bequests, a sermon preached in Norwich Cathedral in August 1573 which provoked a hostile response from John More, the famous 'apostle' of Norwich, and a letter written a year or so later which referred to 'that great disordered diocess'. *The Letter Book of John Parkhurst Bishop of Norwich, Compiled during the Years 1571-5*, ed. R.A. Houlbroooke (Norfolk Record Society, 43, 1974 and 1975) p. 208; Inner Temple Library, MS Petyt 538/47, fol. 494.

[7]   Grosart, *Works of Harvey*, ii, p. 299.

[8]   Patrick Collinson, *The Religion of Protestants: The Church in English Society, 1559-1625* (Oxford, 1982), pp. 60-1.

Vsus libri, non lectio prudentes facit.

Ad D. A. P.

T H E volumes great, who ſo doth ſtill peruſe,
  And dailie turnes, and gazeth on the ſame,
If that the fruicte thereof, he do not vſe,
He reapes but toile, and neuer gaineth fame:
  Firſte reade, then marke, then practiſe that is good,
  For without vſe, we drinke but L E T H E flood.

Of practiſe longe, experience doth proceede;
And wiſedome then, doth euermore enſue:
Then printe in minde, what wee in printe do reade,
Els looſe wee time, and bookes in vaine do vewe:
  Wee maie not haſte, our taleht to beſtowe,
  Nor hide it vp, whereby no good ſhall growe.

The motto, picture and verses which make up this emblem dedicated to Andrew Perne in Geffrey Whitney, *A choice of emblemes* (1586) may appear to leave it in doubt whether Perne is giving or receiving the advice that mere learning without useful application is vain. (*Cambridge University Library*)

Vsus, non lectio prudentes facit.
Ad Fuluium Vrsinum suum.

NON *doceo semper, non est cur sæpè reuisas,*
  Lectorum memorem pagina nostra facit.
Possidet ingentem numerum qui vendit auarus,
  Doctior at nunquam bibliopola fuit.
Perpetuò si nos verses, relegasque seuerus,
  Si non vtaris, contineas ue memor:
Nunquam proficies, periit labor, atque lucerna.
  Officij hoc nostri vt te moneamus erat.
Id quoniam rectè noras doctissime Fului,
  Imprimis veteres te erudiere libri.
Horum tu numerum insignem, rarumque tueris,
  Ingenio multos restituisque libros.
Id quoque delectat Sambucum, & tota vetustas:
  Prosimus quibus est copia nulla, vale.

The discovery that Whitney's emblem for Perne was not original but lifted from the *Emblemata* of Johannes Sambucus (Antwerp, 1564), where it was dedicated to Fulvius Ursinus, makes it unlikely that Whitney intended to admonish Perne. I owe this discovery to Mr Arnold Hunt. (*Cambridge University Library*)

and Wells and Chichester.[9] This was Whitgift's first opportunity to promote his old patron and perhaps it was a mere act of courtesy. Who, apart from Whitgift, was ever taken with the thought of Dr Perne in a rochet?

Fifty years earlier, Perne had arrived in a university which, according to J.B. Mullinger, was about to step out of the middle ages into the modern world. Perne may have matriculated in the very month in which Thomas Cromwell's reforming injunctions for the university were received, which Mullinger saw as constituting that watershed. The Royal Injunctions of 1535 imposed on Cambridge an altered relationship with the state and a new and progressive curriculum which abolished the study of canon law and intended to outlaw scholastic theology.[10] That was to make the Reformation official, but the Injunctions by speaking opaquely of instruction on the basis of the 'true sense' of the Bible left ample scope for confusion. For what was the 'true sense'? Perne would later argue that that was something which only the church, as anterior to Scripture and so more authoritative, could determine.[11] The legendary annals of the Cambridge reformers in a Protestant sense, Bilney, Barnes, Latimer, the White Horse circle, have obscured the persistence and predominance of these more conservative tendencies, which however were also reforming tendencies, taking their title-deeds from the Christian humanism of John Fisher, and from Erasmus.[12] These men too read the Bible but in a different sense; and not only the Bible. An awkward text for those advancing to academic seniority in the unpredictable forties and fifties of the sixteenth century were those biblical words: 'How long halt ye between two opinions?' Perne was to acquire a uniquely sinister reputation as (we might say) the Husak or Kadar of Tudor Cambridge. Yet his confessional fluctuations were typical of the times, by no means exceptional.

There were political as well as intellectual reasons for halting between opinions. John Young, master of Pembroke Hall, was a notable conservative. At least, that was where he began and where he was to end. For under Elizabeth he would spend twenty years in various prisons, as an incorrigible Catholic Recusant. But in November 1551, with radical Protestantism in the political saddle, Young seems to have wavered. He was present at the deathbed of another critic of Protestant positions, Bishop Cuthbert Tunstal's nephew John Redman, who was twice Lady Margaret professor, the last warden of the King's Hall and the first master of Trinity, in reality

---

[9]   John Strype, *Life of Whitgift* (Oxford, 1822), i, p. 337.

[10]   J.B. Mullinger, *The University of Cambridge from the Earliest Times to the Royal Injunctions of 1535* (Cambridge, 1873), p. 631; D.R. Leader, *A History of the University of Cambridge*, i, *The University to 1546* (Cambridge, 1988), pp. 332-41.

[11]   In the disputation before Queen Elizabeth in 1564. See pp. 191-5 below.

[12]   *Humanism, Reform and the Reformation: The Career of Bishop John Fisher*, ed. Brendan Bradshaw and Eamon Duffy (Cambridge, 1989). I have benefited from discussing the Cambridge conservatives with Dr Richard Rex and with Mr Colin Armstrong.

Subtracting Larger Numbers

A. 8,583 people were in Davis Hall.
4,973 people were in Lincoln Hall.
How many fewer people were in Lincoln Hall?

Subtract.

Ones	Tens	Hundreds	Thousands
		7 15	7 15
8,583	8,583	8,583	8,583
−4,973	−4,973	−4,973	−4,973
0	10	610	3,610

There were 3,610 fewer people in Lincoln Hall.

B. Subtract.

Ones	Tens	Hundreds	Thousands	Ten-Thousands
	13	1013	1013	1013
3 15	0 3 15	6 0 3 15	6 0 3 15	6 0 3 15
57,145	57,145	57,145	57,145	57,145
−35,698	−35,6 8	−35,698	−35,698	−35,698
7	47	,447	1,447	21,447

TRY THESE

Find each difference.

1. 6,632
    −5,430

2. 4,521
    − 799

3. $99.45
    − 39.86

4. 28,274
    −16,417

5. 80,391
    −62,283

6. 5,074 − 469 = ▨   7. 18,372 − 3,745 = ▨   8. $786.19 − $512.78 = ▨

Reviewing One-Step Division

A. Pam has 19 candles.
She puts 6 candles in each holder.
How many holders can she fill?
How many candles are left over?

You can use division to solve this problem.

Divide: 6)‾19‾

Think: ▧ × 6 = 19
    2 × 6 = 12
    3 × 6 = 18
    4 × 6 = 24   Too big!

Use 3.

```
   3 R1
6)19
  18  ← | 3 × 6 = 18 | ← number used
   1  ← | 19 − 18 = 1 | ← number left over
```

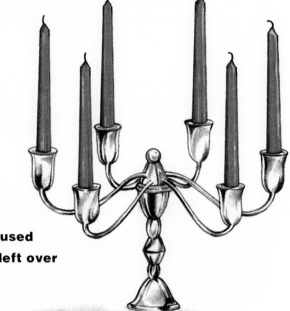

Pam fills 3 holders. 1 candle is left over.

B. Check your division.

Multiply the divisor (6)
and the quotient (3).

Then add the remainder (1).
The sum should equal the dividend (19).

```
    6
  ×3
   18
 + 1
   19 ✓
```

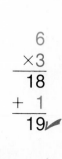

TRY THESE

Find the quotients and remainders. Check your answers.

1. $2\overline{)7}$ 2. $3\overline{)19}$ 3. $5\overline{)38}$ 4. $7\overline{)19}$ 5. $8\overline{)24}$ 6. $6\overline{)28}$

7. $9\overline{)20}$ 8. $3\overline{)15}$ 9. $9\overline{)60}$ 10. $9\overline{)29}$ 11. $4\overline{)22}$ 12. $6\overline{)17}$

13. $42 \div 7 =$ ▨   14. $32 \div 4 =$ ▨   15. $45 \div 9 =$ ▨

SKILLS PRACTICE

Divide.

1. $8\overline{)19}$ 2. $9\overline{)70}$ 3. $2\overline{)8}$ 4. $5\overline{)16}$ 5. $8\overline{)54}$ 6. $3\overline{)17}$

7. $8\overline{)42}$ 8. $2\overline{)15}$ 9. $5\overline{)37}$ 10. $4\overline{)13}$ 11. $8\overline{)29}$ 12. $6\overline{)36}$

13. $5\overline{)49}$ 14. $7\overline{)28}$ 15. $9\overline{)75}$ 16. $3\overline{)10}$ 17. $2\overline{)15}$ 18. $4\overline{)23}$

19. $6\overline{)59}$ 20. $8\overline{)49}$ 21. $4\overline{)17}$ 22. $9\overline{)39}$ 23. $7\overline{)58}$ 24. $5\overline{)9}$

25. $9\overline{)76}$ 26. $4\overline{)35}$ 27. $5\overline{)29}$ 28. $7\overline{)51}$ 29. $9\overline{)72}$ 30. $6\overline{)56}$

31. $27 \div 9 =$ ▨   32. $48 \div 6 =$ ▨   33. $72 \div 8 =$ ▨

PROBLEM SOLVING

34. Dan had 25 candles. He put 8 candles in each box. How many boxes did he fill? How many candles were left over?

★ 35. Miguel had $20. He used $5 to buy candles. He has $15 left to buy candleholders. Each candleholder cost $6. How many candleholders can he buy? How much money will he have left?

197

Two-Step Division

There are 27 socks in all.
2 socks fill each package.
How many packages are there?
How many socks are left over?

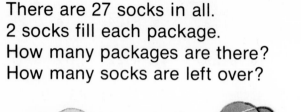

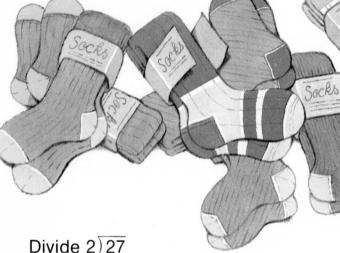

Divide 2)27

First divide the tens. Then divide the ones.

Divide the 2 tens.

Think: ■ × 2 = 2
     0 × 2 = 0
     1 × 2 = 2   Just right!
     Use **1**.

$$\begin{array}{r} 1 \\ 2\overline{)27} \\ 2 \\ \hline 0 \end{array}$$ ← 1 × 2 = 2

Divide the 7 ones.

Think: ■ × 2 = 7
     3 × 2 = 6
     4 × 2 = 8   Too big!
     Use **3**.

$$\begin{array}{r} 13 \text{ R}1 \\ 2\overline{)27} \\ 2 \\ \hline 07 \\ 6 \\ \hline 1 \end{array}$$ ← 3 × 2 = 6

There are 13 packages with 1 sock left over.

TRY THESE

Copy and complete. Check your answers.

1.
```
    1 □ R
  4)46
    4
   ──
    06
    4
   ──
```

2.
```
    1 □
  3)36
    3
   ──
    06
    6
   ──
```

3.
```
        □ □ R
  5)32
   30
   ──
```

4.
```
        □ □ R
  7)78
    7
   ──
    08
    7
   ──
```

5. 2)64   6. 3)38   7. 4)48   8. 5)47   9. 2)45   10. 3)68

11. 69 ÷ 3 = □   12. 66 ÷ 6 = □   13. 81 ÷ 9 = □

SKILLS PRACTICE

Divide.

1. 3)94   2. 5)55   3. 3)65   4. 6)68   5. 4)39   6. 2)28

7. 6)69   8. 2)17   9. 4)44   10. 3)34   11. 2)86   12. 8)88

13. 4)85   14. 3)97   15. 5)56   16. 2)24   17. 6)32   18. 2)88

19. 3)39   20. 2)43   21. 3)22   22. 2)66   23. 2)89   24. 3)66

25. 2)49   26. 4)49   27. 8)50   28. 2)65   29. 3)93   30. 5)59

31. 42 ÷ 2 = □   32. 96 ÷ 3 = □   33. 77 ÷ 7 = □

34. 88 ÷ 4 = □   35. 63 ÷ 7 = □   36. 82 ÷ 2 = □

PROBLEM SOLVING

37. There are 33 T-shirts. 3 are in each box. How many full boxes are there? How many T-shirts are left over?

★ 38. Mrs. Johnson bought 4 boxes of T-shirts to share among her 6 children. There are 3 T-shirts in each box. How many T-shirts did she buy?

More Two-Step Division

Divide: $3\overline{)58}$

Divide the 5 tens.

Think: ▨ × 3 = 5
   1 × 3 = 3
   2 × 3 = 6 Too big!
   Use **1**.

$$\begin{array}{r} 1 \\ 3\overline{)58} \\ 3 \\ \hline 2 \end{array}$$ ← $\boxed{1 \times 3 = 3}$

You have 2 tens left over.
You also have 8 ones.

$$\begin{array}{r} 1 \\ 3\overline{)58} \\ 3 \\ \hline 28 \end{array}$$ ← Write the 8 with the 2 to show 28 ones.

Divide the 28 ones.

Think: ▨ × 3 = 28
   9 × 3 = 27
   9 is the largest
   number to try.
   Use **9**.

$$\begin{array}{r} 19 \text{ R}1 \\ 3\overline{)58} \\ 3 \\ \hline 28 \\ 27 \\ \hline 1 \end{array}$$ ← $\boxed{9 \times 3 = 27}$

The quotient is 19. The remainder is 1.

TRY THESE

Divide. Check your answers.

1. 7)‾90   2. 4)‾64   3. 6)‾53   4. 3)‾94   5. 3)‾22   6. 8)‾64

7. 24 ÷ 2 = ▓   8. 72 ÷ 9 = ▓   9. 52 ÷ 4 = ▓

SKILLS PRACTICE

Divide.

1. 6)‾78   2. 5)‾75   3. 4)‾39   4. 8)‾91   5. 3)‾67   6. 7)‾19

7. 7)‾56   8. 4)‾86   9. 5)‾88   10. 4)‾58   11. 8)‾24   12. 5)‾68

13. 3)‾17   14. 4)‾84   15. 4)‾79   16. 3)‾95   17. 7)‾77   18. 3)‾40

19. 5)‾57   20. 6)‾49   21. 5)‾32   22. 3)‾75   23. 7)‾89   24. 2)‾50

25. 8)‾99   26. 3)‾39   27. 8)‾31   28. 6)‾92   29. 4)‾56   30. 8)‾98

31. 96 ÷ 2 = ▓   32. 63 ÷ 3 = ▓   33. 96 ÷ 8 = ▓

34. 42 ÷ 7 = ▓   35. 88 ÷ 4 = ▓   36. 84 ÷ 6 = ▓

Find the missing numbers.

37.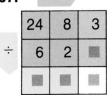

38.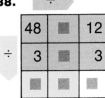

★ 39.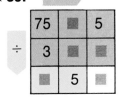

PROBLEM SOLVING

40. 5 players are on each basketball team. How many teams can be made with 80 players? How many players will be left over?

41. 7 people can sit on each bench. There are 99 people. How many benches can be filled? How many people will be left over?

Zero in the Quotient

A. Joe bought 3 shirts for $60.
Each shirt costs the same amount of money.
How much did he spend for each shirt?

Divide: 3)60

Divide the 6 tens.

Think: ■ × 3 = 6
  Use 2.

$$
\begin{array}{r}
2 \\
3\overline{)60} \\
6 \\
0
\end{array}
$$
← 2 × 3 = 6

Divide the 0 ones.

Think: ■ × 3 = 0
  Use 0.

$$
\begin{array}{r}
20 \\
3\overline{)60} \\
6 \\
00 \\
0 \\
\hline
0
\end{array}
$$
← 0 × 3 = 0

Joe spent $20 for each shirt.

B. Divide: 4)41

Divide the 4 tens.

Think: ■ × 4 = 4
  Use 1.

$$
\begin{array}{r}
1 \\
4\overline{)41} \\
4 \\
0
\end{array}
$$
← 1 × 4 = 4

Divide the 1 one.

Think: ■ × 4 = 1
  Use 0.

$$
\begin{array}{r}
10 \text{ R1} \\
4\overline{)41} \\
4 \\
01 \\
0 \\
\hline
1
\end{array}
$$
← 0 × 4 = 0

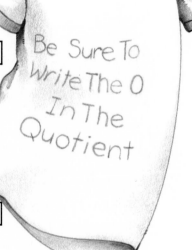

The quotient is 10 with remainder 1.

TRY THESE

Divide. Check your answers.

1. $5\overline{)54}$
2. $3\overline{)62}$
3. $2\overline{)46}$
4. $7\overline{)89}$
5. $3\overline{)30}$

6. $52 \div 2 =$
7. $42 \div 7 =$
8. $90 \div 3 =$

SKILLS PRACTICE

Divide.

1. $2\overline{)60}$
2. $2\overline{)81}$
3. $6\overline{)84}$
4. $3\overline{)63}$
5. $5\overline{)56}$
6. $4\overline{)82}$

7. $3\overline{)67}$
8. $4\overline{)83}$
9. $9\overline{)75}$
10. $4\overline{)42}$
11. $2\overline{)30}$
12. $6\overline{)68}$

13. $4\overline{)86}$
14. $4\overline{)80}$
15. $5\overline{)43}$
16. $4\overline{)40}$
17. $2\overline{)61}$
18. $3\overline{)32}$

19. $2\overline{)19}$
20. $8\overline{)83}$
21. $7\overline{)92}$
22. $6\overline{)64}$
23. $2\overline{)20}$
24. $3\overline{)18}$

25. $6\overline{)49}$
26. $4\overline{)81}$
27. $8\overline{)97}$
28. $5\overline{)50}$
29. $9\overline{)93}$
30. $4\overline{)90}$

31. $80 \div 2 =$
32. $96 \div 3 =$
33. $55 \div 5 =$

34. $36 \div 6 =$
35. $60 \div 2 =$
36. $70 \div 7 =$

PROBLEM SOLVING

37. Mrs. Lee bought 18 yards of material to make dresses. She needs 2 yards of material to make each dress. How many dresses can she make?

38. Mr. Rella has 32 yards of material. He wants to make 8 drapes. If all the drapes are the same size, how much material can he use for each drape?

39. Mrs. Jones bought 4 blouses for $48. Each blouse cost the same amount of money. How much did each blouse cost?

★ 40. Maria and her 2 sisters want to share 21 hair ribbons. How many ribbons should each girl get?

Workbook   page 426

Maintaining Skills

How much money?

1.

2.

3.

4.

Multiply.

5. 263 × 7	**6.** 412 × 5	**7.** 904 × 6	**8.** 287 × 4	**9.** 791 × 8
10. 3,729 × 9	**11.** 8,063 × 2	**12.** 4,199 × 5	**13.** 6,934 × 3	**14.** 8,888 × 7
15. 846 × 6	**16.** 392 × 4	**17.** 7,902 × 8	**18.** 859 × 5	**19.** 9,185 × 3

Add, subtract, or multiply.

20. 36 +54	**21.** 47 × 5	**22.** 642 − 75	**23.** 943 +658	**24.** 1,432 × 7
25. 3,607 +4,595	**26.** 20,000 − 7,642	**27.** 349 × 4	**28.** 83,409 −76,842	**29.** 44,865 +64,135

Solve the problems.

30. Mr. Jones paid $59.95 for a table. The tax was $4.80. How much did he spend?

31. A large bottle of apple juice costs $1.09. Karen bought 3 bottles. How much did she spend?

Project: Time Zones

This map shows the *time zones* of the United States. The clocks show you what time it will be in each zone, when it is noon, Mountain Time.

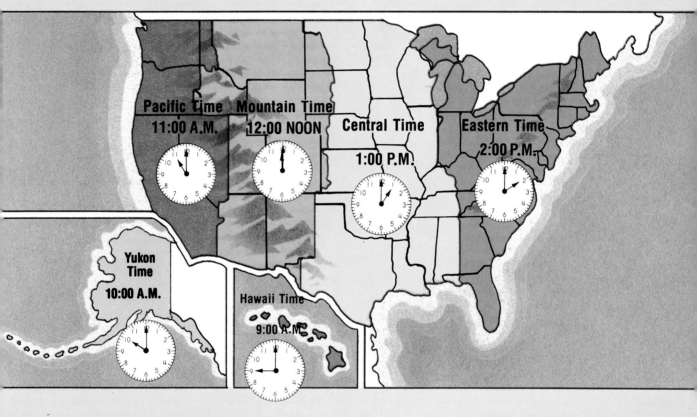

How many hours difference is there between:

1. Mountain Time and Eastern Time?   **2.** Central Time and Hawaii Time?

What time is it in California when it is:

3. 2:00 P.M. in Maine?   **4.** 11:00 A.M. in Hawaii?

5. 9:00 A.M. in Iowa?   **6.** Midnight in Wyoming?

The entire earth is divided into time zones. Find a map that shows time zones for the world. How many time zones are there in all? What time zone is London in?

Pretend you want to call friends in Paris so that you reach them at 6:00 P.M. At what time should you call? Pick other places and decide what time to call to reach a person at 6:00 P.M.

Dividing 3-digit Numbers

Kennedy School has 785 students. There are 5 grades with the same number of students in each grade. How many students are in each grade?

Divide: 5)785

Divide the 7 hundreds.

Think: ▦ × 5 = 7
    Use 1.

$$\begin{array}{r} 1 \\ 5\overline{)785} \\ \underline{5} \\ 2 \end{array}$$

Write the 8 with the 2.

$$\begin{array}{r} 1 \\ 5\overline{)785} \\ \underline{5\downarrow} \\ 28 \end{array}$$

| 2 hundreds 8 tens is 28 tens |

Divide the 28 tens.

Think: ▦ × 5 = 28
    Use 5.

$$\begin{array}{r} 15 \\ 5\overline{)785} \\ \underline{5} \\ 28 \\ \underline{25} \\ 3 \end{array}$$

Write the 5 with the 3.

$$\begin{array}{r} 15 \\ 5\overline{)785} \\ \underline{5} \\ 28 \\ \underline{25\downarrow} \\ 35 \end{array}$$

| 3 tens 5 ones
is 35 ones |

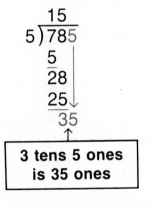

Divide the 35 ones.

Think: ▦ × 5 = 35
    Use 7.

$$\begin{array}{r} 157 \\ 5\overline{)785} \\ \underline{5} \\ 28 \\ \underline{25} \\ 35 \\ \underline{35} \\ 0 \end{array}$$

157 students are in each grade.

TRY THESE

Divide. Check your answers.

1. $5\overline{)920}$ 2. $2\overline{)779}$ 3. $4\overline{)85}$ 4. $8\overline{)986}$ 5. $3\overline{)957}$

6. $585 \div 5 = $ ▨   7. $64 \div 4 = $ ▨   8. $588 \div 4 = $ ▨

SKILLS PRACTICE

Divide.

1. $6\overline{)768}$ 2. $9\overline{)99}$ 3. $4\overline{)895}$ 4. $3\overline{)937}$ 5. $5\overline{)690}$

6. $3\overline{)637}$ 7. $2\overline{)91}$ 8. $3\overline{)664}$ 9. $7\overline{)847}$ 10. $3\overline{)92}$

11. $8\overline{)899}$ 12. $5\overline{)709}$ 13. $7\overline{)898}$ 14. $6\overline{)68}$ 15. $4\overline{)593}$

16. $4\overline{)967}$ 17. $7\overline{)882}$ 18. $7\overline{)60}$ 19. $3\overline{)578}$ 20. $2\overline{)807}$

21. $5\overline{)44}$ 22. $6\overline{)774}$ 23. $4\overline{)589}$ 24. $7\overline{)801}$ 25. $3\overline{)689}$

26. $405 \div 3 = $ ▨   27. $596 \div 4 = $ ▨   28. $952 \div 8 = $ ▨

29. $830 \div 5 = $ ▨   30. $76 \div 4 = $ ▨   31. $474 \div 3 = $ ▨

Find the missing numbers.

32.

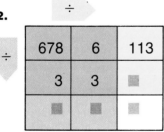

÷		
678	6	113
3	3	▨
▨	▨	▨

★ 33.

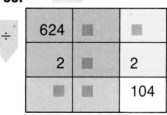

÷		
624	▨	▨
2	▨	2
▨	▨	104

★ 34.

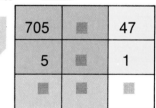

÷		
705	▨	47
5	▨	1
▨	▨	▨

PROBLEM SOLVING

35. The school spent $560 on paper. Each package of paper costs $2. How many packages did the school buy?

36. There are 575 boxes of pencils in the supply room. Each box has 8 pencils. How many pencils are in the supply room?

2-digit Quotients

Juan has 378 photos.
4 photos will fit on each
page of his album.
How many pages can he fill?
How many photos will be
left over?

Find $4\overline{)378}$.

There are not enough hundreds.
Start by dividing the **37 tens.**

Divide the 37 tens.

$$
\begin{array}{r}
9 \\
4\overline{)378} \\
\underline{36} \\
1
\end{array}
$$

Write the 8 with the 1.

$$
\begin{array}{r}
9 \\
4\overline{)378} \\
\underline{36\downarrow} \\
18
\end{array}
$$

Divide the 18 ones.

$$
\begin{array}{r}
94 \text{ R2} \\
4\overline{)378} \\
\underline{36} \\
18 \\
\underline{16} \\
2
\end{array}
$$

Juan can fill 94 pages.
There will be 2 photos left over.

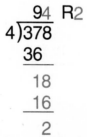

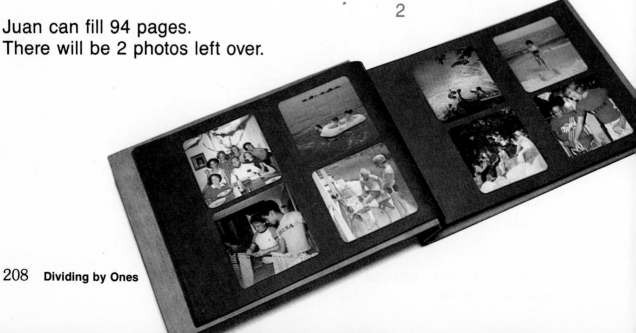

TRY THESE

Divide. Check your answers.

1. $8\overline{)745}$
2. $5\overline{)406}$
3. $6\overline{)45}$
4. $3\overline{)338}$
5. $7\overline{)665}$

6. $285 \div 3 = $ ▦
7. $48 \div 8 = $ ▦
8. $152 \div 4 = $ ▦

SKILLS PRACTICE

Divide.

1. $6\overline{)496}$
2. $4\overline{)300}$
3. $9\overline{)894}$
4. $2\overline{)60}$
5. $4\overline{)886}$

6. $3\overline{)47}$
7. $5\overline{)325}$
8. $6\overline{)933}$
9. $7\overline{)476}$
10. $3\overline{)149}$

11. $5\overline{)440}$
12. $8\overline{)74}$
13. $9\overline{)90}$
14. $3\overline{)200}$
15. $4\overline{)284}$

16. $7\overline{)397}$
17. $2\overline{)129}$
18. $4\overline{)372}$
19. $6\overline{)687}$
20. $8\overline{)96}$

21. $2\overline{)19}$
22. $9\overline{)95}$
23. $7\overline{)987}$
24. $3\overline{)524}$
25. $6\overline{)209}$

26. $297 \div 9 = $ ▦
27. $658 \div 7 = $ ▦
28. $252 \div 4 = $ ▦

29. $386 \div 2 = $ ▦
30. $492 \div 6 = $ ▦
31. $744 \div 8 = $ ▦

PROBLEM SOLVING

32. Eric has 102 photos. He puts the same number of photos in each of 4 albums. How many photos can he put in each album? How many photos are left over?

★ 33. Sally went on a vacation for 7 days. She used 3 rolls of film and took 108 pictures. How many pictures were on each roll of film?

Zeros in the Quotient

Don't forget to record zeros in the quotient. You may
get 12 as an answer when the right answer is 102 or 120.

A.
$$
\begin{array}{r}
102\ \text{R5} \\
7\,\overline{)719} \\
\underline{7} \\
01 \\
\underline{0} \leftarrow \boxed{0 \times 7 = 0} \\
19 \\
\underline{14} \\
5
\end{array}
$$

Write 0 in the quotient!

B.
$$
\begin{array}{r}
120\ \text{R3} \\
8\,\overline{)963} \\
\underline{8} \\
16 \\
\underline{16} \\
03 \\
\underline{0} \leftarrow \boxed{0 \times 8 = 0} \\
3
\end{array}
$$

Be sure to write 0 in the quotient!

C.
$$
\begin{array}{r}
200 \\
4\,\overline{)800} \\
\underline{8} \\
00 \\
\underline{0} \leftarrow \boxed{0 \times 4 = 0} \\
00 \\
\underline{0} \leftarrow \boxed{0 \times 4 = 0} \\
0
\end{array}
$$

Write 0 in the quotient in both the tens step and the ones step!

Divide. Check your answers.

1. $3\overline{)904}$
2. $6\overline{)840}$
3. $4\overline{)364}$
4. $3\overline{)60}$
5. $9\overline{)903}$

6. $624 \div 3 = $ ▨
7. $980 \div 5 = $ ▨
8. $960 \div 8 = $ ▨

SKILLS PRACTICE

Divide.

1. $2\overline{)619}$
2. $7\overline{)910}$
3. $4\overline{)834}$
4. $2\overline{)801}$
5. $9\overline{)72}$

6. $3\overline{)90}$
7. $5\overline{)452}$
8. $2\overline{)353}$
9. $7\overline{)56}$
10. $3\overline{)863}$

11. $6\overline{)628}$
12. $9\overline{)90}$
13. $5\overline{)80}$
14. $4\overline{)802}$
15. $9\overline{)813}$

16. $4\overline{)420}$
17. $8\overline{)324}$
18. $7\overline{)819}$
19. $5\overline{)543}$
20. $3\overline{)662}$

Find the quotients. Look for the pattern.

21. $9 \div 3 = $ ▨ $90 \div 3 = $ ▨ $900 \div 3 = $ ▨

22. $8 \div 4 = $ ▨ $80 \div 4 = $ ▨ $800 \div 4 = $ ▨

PROBLEM SOLVING

23. A used-car dealer had 275 cars. He sold 5 cars in one day. How many cars were left?

24. The used-car dealer spent $320 for tires. He bought 8 tires. How much did each tire cost?

EXTRA! Making Logical Choices

To go from A to B in each figure you can travel *only* to the *right* or *down* along the streets that are shown. For each figure, find the length of the shortest path *and* the number of paths of this length.

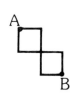
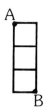
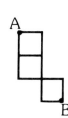
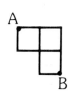
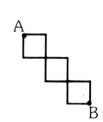

Length: 2
2 paths

Dividing 4-digit Numbers

A. A store received 8,395 blankets. 3 blankets were in each box. How many full boxes did the store receive? How many extra blankets were there?

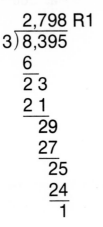

```
      2,798 R1
  3) 8,395
     6
     2 3
     2 1
       29
       27
       25
       24
        1
```

The store received 2,798 full boxes.
There was 1 extra blanket.

B. Sometimes there are not enough thousands. Start by dividing the hundreds.

```
      604 R2
  9) 5,438
     5 4
       03
        0
       38
       36
        2
```

> **Don't forget to write 0 in the quotient.**

TRY THESE

Divide. Check your answers.

1. $6\overline{)9,709}$
2. $8\overline{)722}$
3. $4\overline{)8,721}$
4. $7\overline{)92}$
5. $2\overline{)1,642}$

6. $1,449 \div 7 = \blacksquare$
7. $3,860 \div 2 = \blacksquare$
8. $5,464 \div 8 = \blacksquare$

SKILLS PRACTICE

Divide.

1. $9\overline{)1,732}$
2. $4\overline{)82}$
3. $3\overline{)9,024}$
4. $2\overline{)9,540}$
5. $8\overline{)5,638}$

6. $4\overline{)48}$
7. $9\overline{)2,713}$
8. $7\overline{)8,063}$
9. $9\overline{)1,534}$
10. $6\overline{)684}$

11. $5\overline{)4,545}$
12. $3\overline{)870}$
13. $1\overline{)904}$
14. $5\overline{)2,367}$
15. $8\overline{)8,083}$

16. $4\overline{)3,616}$
17. $5\overline{)89}$
18. $3\overline{)7,291}$
19. $6\overline{)543}$
20. $9\overline{)6,485}$

21. $9,056 \div 8 = \blacksquare$
22. $1,845 \div 9 = \blacksquare$
23. $3,150 \div 5 = \blacksquare$

24. $476 \div 2 = \blacksquare$
25. $2,756 \div 4 = \blacksquare$
26. $5,648 \div 8 = \blacksquare$

PROBLEM SOLVING

★ 27. A factory wants to deliver 1,029 stoves. 9 stoves fit on a truck. How many trucks can be filled? How many trucks must be used in order to deliver all the stoves?

★ 28. A factory shipped 1,275 boxes of radios on one day and 2,850 boxes on another day. How many boxes were shipped in all? There were 4 radios in each box. How many radios were shipped in all?

EXTRA! **Making a List**
How many digits are used to number the pages of a 200-page book? How many page numbers contain the digit 5?

Problem Solving: Finding Averages

A. A *bar graph* can show information. This bar graph shows the number of points scored by a football team in each of 5 games.

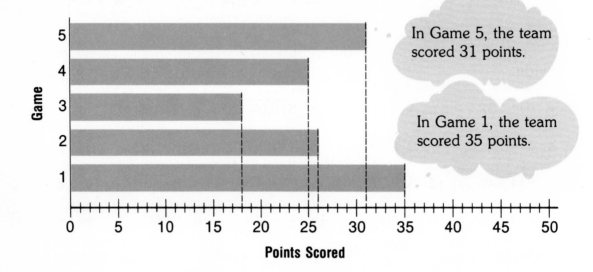

In Game 5, the team scored 31 points.

In Game 1, the team scored 35 points.

To find the team's *average* score for these 5 games, use **two steps**.

Step 1 Add to find the total score for the 5 games.

35	Game 1
26	Game 2
18	Game 3
25	Game 4
+31	Game 5
135	

Step 2 Divide the total score by the number of games played.

$$\begin{array}{r} 27 \\ 5\overline{)135} \end{array}$$

The team's average score was 27 points.

B. Susan bowled 3 games. Her total score for the 3 games was 372. What was her average score?

Total score ÷ Number of games = Average score

372 ÷ 3 = 124

$$\begin{array}{r} 124 \\ 3\overline{)372} \end{array}$$

Susan's average score was 124.

214 **Dividing by Ones**

Find the average score.

1. Points scored in 6 games: 35, 21, 47, 27, 31, 25

2. Points scored in 4 games: 196, 173, 185, 178

3. Total points scored: 776
   Games played: 8

4. Total points scored: 1,771
   Games played: 7

PROBLEM SOLVING PRACTICE

Use this bar graph.
Find the average score for:

1. Games 1, 2, and 3.

2. Games 4, 5, and 6.

3. Games 1, 2, 5, and 6.

4. Games 3 and 4.

5. Games 1 to 6.

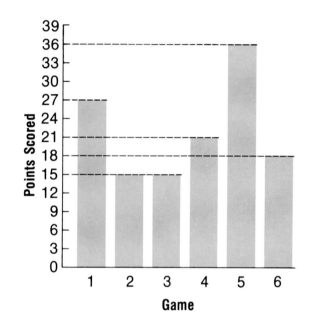

Find the average score.

6. Joel scored 156, 129, 140, and 171 points in 4 games of bowling. What was his average score?

7. The Yale Bulldogs scored 3, 1, 7, 6, and 3 runs in 5 baseball games. What was their average score?

8. The Columbia Lions scored 67, 83, 72, 63, 78, 61, 85 and 75 points in 8 basketball games. What was their average score?

9. In 7 hockey games, the Clark Cougars scored a total of 35 goals. What was their average score?

★10. Earl scored 14, 13, 8, 18, 15 and 22 points in basketball games during March. What was his scoring average?

★11. The average score for a golfer's 6 rounds in a tournament was 72. What was his total score for the 6 rounds?

Problem Solving: Dividing Dollars and Cents

Jan spent $4.36 for 4 pens. Each pen cost the same amount. How much did each pen cost?

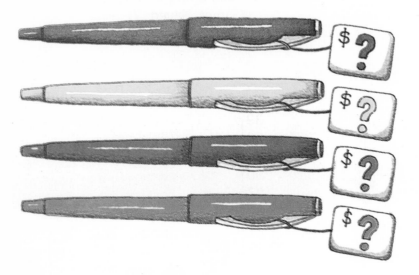

$4.36 in all.
Same amount in each of 4 sets

Divide 4)$4.36

To divide dollars and cents, think of the number of cents.

$$4)\overline{\$4.36} \quad \$4.36 = 436¢$$
$$4)\overline{436¢}$$

$$
\begin{array}{r}
\$1.09 \\
4)\overline{\$4.36} \\
\underline{4} \\
0\,3 \\
\underline{0} \\
36 \\
\underline{36} \\
0
\end{array}
$$

Remember to record the dollar sign and the point in the right place in the quotient.

Each pen cost $1.09.

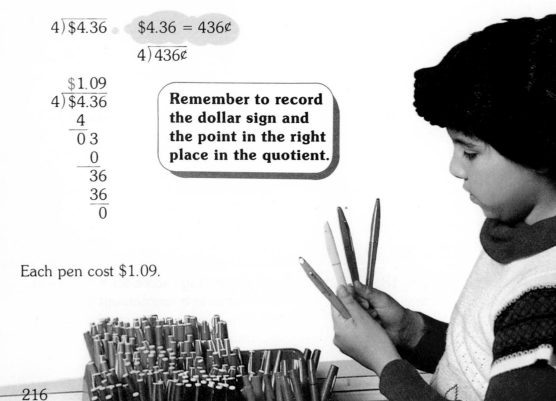

216

TRY THESE

Would you add, subtract, multiply, or divide?

1. A store sells ties at 2 for $4.88. What is the cost of each tie?

2. One shirt costs $5.95. How much would 12 shirts cost?

3. José had $12.75. He spent some of this money for a belt. He had $6.76 left. How much had he spent?

4. Julia spent $18.00 for shoes and $45.00 for a coat. How much did she spend in all?

PROBLEM SOLVING PRACTICE

Use the five steps to solve each problem.

1. Alice spent $3.56 for socks. She bought 4 pairs. How much did each pair cost?

2. A store sold dresses at 3 for $33.33. What was the cost of each dress?

3. Each hat costs $4.79. Alice bought 6 hats. How much did she spend?

4. Ellen paid $39.92 for 4 blouses. What was the cost of each blouse?

5. Mr. Norton bought 3 pairs of pants. Each pair cost $16.49. How much did he spend in all?

6. Sue spent $11.89 for sneakers and $7.99 for a new shirt. How much did she spend in all?

7. Alice spent $3.45. She bought 3 bracelets. Each bracelet cost the same amount. How much did each bracelet cost?

8. Joe wanted to buy a pair of roller skates for $15.98. He had $9.55. How much more money did he need?

★9. Carl had $15.00. He spent $7.00 for gloves and $6.98 for a scarf. How much money did he spend? How much money did he have left?

★10. Bob spent $18.60 on shirts. He bought 3 shirts. How much did each shirt cost? He also spent $12.75 on a pair of pants. How much did he spend in all?

✓ Unit Checkup

Divide. *(pages 196–197)*

1. $7\overline{)54}$ 2. $4\overline{)38}$ 3. $6\overline{)34}$ 4. $9\overline{)72}$ 5. $7\overline{)50}$ 6. $8\overline{)47}$

7. $5\overline{)27}$ 8. $8\overline{)64}$ 9. $7\overline{)62}$ 10. $3\overline{)26}$ 11. $3\overline{)26}$ 12. $2\overline{)7}$

13. $56 \div 7 = $ ▦   14. $36 \div 4 = $ ▦   15. $72 \div 9 = $ ▦

Divide. *(pages 198–201)*

16. $2\overline{)65}$ 17. $6\overline{)78}$ 18. $4\overline{)84}$ 19. $7\overline{)78}$ 20. $9\overline{)99}$ 21. $8\overline{)83}$

22. $7\overline{)85}$ 23. $6\overline{)98}$ 24. $3\overline{)39}$ 25. $4\overline{)59}$ 26. $7\overline{)78}$ 27. $2\overline{)47}$

28. $3\overline{)40}$ 29. $5\overline{)77}$ 30. $8\overline{)92}$ 31. $2\overline{)33}$ 32. $4\overline{)64}$ 33. $3\overline{)73}$

34. $96 \div 3 = $ ▦   35. $88 \div 8 = $ ▦   36. $72 \div 2 = $ ▦

Divide. *(pages 206–209)*

37. $3\overline{)715}$ 38. $5\overline{)467}$ 39. $3\overline{)849}$ 40. $4\overline{)342}$ 41. $7\overline{)810}$

42. $2\overline{)728}$ 43. $8\overline{)543}$ 44. $4\overline{)710}$ 45. $6\overline{)858}$ 46. $3\overline{)116}$

47. $5\overline{)359}$ 48. $7\overline{)931}$ 49. $6\overline{)676}$ 50. $8\overline{)124}$ 51. $2\overline{)832}$

52. $798 \div 7 = $ ▦   53. $248 \div 4 = $ ▦   54. $565 \div 5 = $ ▦

Divide. *(pages 212–213)*

55. $7\overline{)8,621}$ 56. $5\overline{)2,865}$ 57. $3\overline{)9,193}$ 58. $9\overline{)5,499}$ 59. $6\overline{)9,649}$

60. $3\overline{)2,588}$ 61. $6\overline{)8,578}$ 62. $4\overline{)9,215}$ 63. $7\overline{)7,930}$ 64. $9\overline{)5,362}$

65. $2\overline{)6,428}$ 66. $8\overline{)8,934}$ 67. $3\overline{)1,597}$ 68. $4\overline{)5,522}$ 69. $5\overline{)4,395}$

70. $2,808 \div 9 = $ ▦   71. $8,478 \div 6 = $ ▦   72. $3,208 \div 8 = $ ▦

Divide. *(pages 206–213)*

73. $7\overline{)73}$ **74.** $6\overline{)618}$ **75.** $3\overline{)312}$ **76.** $5\overline{)5,049}$ **77.** $4\overline{)41}$

78. $7\overline{)4,268}$ **79.** $8\overline{)325}$ **80.** $6\overline{)720}$ **81.** $9\overline{)4,800}$ **82.** $2\overline{)80}$

83. $4\overline{)7,642}$ **84.** $3\overline{)615}$ **85.** $8\overline{)8,076}$ **86.** $9\overline{)276}$ **87.** $7\overline{)3,220}$

88. $5,200 \div 4 = \blacksquare$ **89.** $540 \div 3 = \blacksquare$ **90.** $6,472 \div 8 = \blacksquare$

Solve the problems. *(pages 196–203, 206–217)*

91. 80 boxes of shoes arrived at the store. There were 5 cartons with the same number of boxes in each carton. How many boxes were in each carton?

92. Dan put 84 baseball caps in boxes. He put 3 baseball caps in each box. How many boxes did he use?

93. One pair of boots costs $19.95. How much do 7 pairs of boots cost?

94. Lee paid $29.70 for 6 scarfs. What was the cost of each scarf?

95. Mrs. West had $202.00. She spent $63.74 for a coat and hat. How much money does she have left?

96. A store sells socks for $3 a pair. How many pairs would $525 buy? How many dollars would be left over?

97. A baseball team had a total score of 35 runs for 5 games. What was the average score for the 5 games?

98. A basketball team had a total score of 462 points for 7 games. What was the average score for the 7 games?

Use this table to solve the following problems. *(pages 214–215)*

99. What was Tina's average score?

100. What was Terry's average score?

101. What was Tom's average score?

	Tina	Terry	Tom
Game 1	100	72	80
Game 2	95	66	85
Game 3	87	99	90

102. What was the average score for Game 1?

103. What was the average score for Game 2?

219

Reinforcement

More Help with Division

Divide.

```
  14 R1
4)57
  4   ←[ 1 × 4 = 4 ]
 17
 16   ←[ 4 × 4 = 16 ]
  1
```

1. 3)63
2. 4)84
3. 3)34
4. 2)86

5. 4)49
6. 2)65
7. 4)88
8. 3)97

9. 2)56
10. 3)75
11. 2)57
12. 4)92

13. 8)96
14. 7)85
15. 9)82
16. 8)92

17. 3)25
18. 6)75
19. 6)84
20. 7)81

```
   1,159 R1
8)9,273
  8    ←[ 1 × 8 = 8 ]
  12
   8   ←[ 1 × 8 = 8 ]
  47
  40   ←[ 5 × 8 = 40 ]
  73
  72   ←[ 9 × 8 = 72 ]
   1
```

21. 3)663
22. 4)848
23. 2)487
24. 5)556

25. 3)847
26. 7)994
27. 3)246
28. 5)255

29. 2)124
30. 2)107
31. 5)359
32. 8)169

33. 7)498
34. 4)897
35. 3)651
36. 6)187

37. 3)5,621
38. 4)3,702
39. 8)9,712
40. 7)2,642

```
   307 R1
2)615
  6    ←[ 3 × 2 = 6 ]
  01
   0   ←[ 0 × 2 = 0 ]
  15
  14   ←[ 7 × 2 = 14 ]
   1
```

41. 5)503
42. 2)404
43. 4)201
44. 2)60

45. 4)823
46. 7)140
47. 5)516
48. 4)81

49. 6)63
50. 2)800
51. 5)450
52. 9)910

53. 8)4,009
54. 5)5,025
55. 6)3,904
56. 2)6,121

57. 5)6,450
58. 6)4,200
59. 6)5,407
60. 4)4,327

Prime Numbers

You can draw rows of dots to show the factors of a number.

First factor = Number of rows
Second factor = Number in each row

Number	Factors	Number of Factors	Dot Pictures	
1	1	1	.	1 × 1
2	1, 2	2	. .	1 × 2
3	1, 3	2	. . .	1 × 3
4	1, 2, 4	3	. . . .	1 × 4
			. . . .	2 × 2
5	1, 5	2	. . . . .	1 × 5
6	1, 2, 3, 6	4	. . . . . .	1 × 6
			. . . . . .	2 × 3

You could also draw

.
. 2 × 1

but the factors would be the same.

Any number with only two factors is a **prime number.** The table shows that 2, 3, and 5 are prime numbers.

There are 3 different dot pictures that show the factors of 12.

12	1, 2, 3 4, 6, 12	. . . .	1 × 12
		. . . .	2 × 6
		. . . .	3 × 4

12 has more than two factors, so 12 is not a prime number.

1. Make a table like the one above to show the factors of 7 to 30.

2. What prime numbers did you find?

Choose the correct answer. Mark NG if the correct answer is NOT GIVEN.

1. $\begin{array}{r} 8 \\ \times 7 \\ \hline \end{array}$	**2.** $\begin{array}{r} 4 \\ \times 6 \\ \hline \end{array}$	**3.** $9 \times 9 = \blacksquare$	**4.** $7 \times 5 = \blacksquare$
a. 48 b. 56 c. 15 d. NG	a. 25 b. 10 c. 24 d. NG	a. 18 b. 81 c. 72 d. NG	a. 35 b. 28 c. 42 d. NG
5. $49 \div 7 = \blacksquare$	**6.** $72 \div 8 = \blacksquare$	**7.** $4\overline{)36}$	**8.** $6\overline{)55}$
a. 7 b. 42 c. 56 d. NG	a. 56 b. 8 c. 80 d. NG	a. 8 R3 b. 8 c. 9 d. NG	a. 8 b. 9 R1 c. 9 d. NG
9. $2\overline{)68}$	**10.** $8\overline{)249}$	**11.** $5\overline{)512}$	**12.** $3\overline{)3,729}$
a. 33 R1 b. 43 c. 34 d. NG	a. 301 b. 31 R1 c. 32 R3 d. NG	a. 12 R2 b. 102 c. 10 R2 d. NG	a. 1,243 b. 124 R3 c. 1,240 d. NG

13. There are 5 people. Each person buys 3 pens. How many pens do they buy?

a. 8 pens   b. 15 pens
c. 2 pens   d. NG

14. Ms. Wong paid $10.20 for 4 notebooks. How much did each notebook cost?

a. $2.55   b. $25.50
c. $40.80   d. NG

Fractions 8

Fractions

A. You can write *fractions* for parts of objects.

This flag has 2 equal pieces.
1 of the 2 pieces is red.

$\frac{1}{2}$ of the flag is red.

one-half

This flag has 3 equal pieces.
2 of the 3 pieces are green.

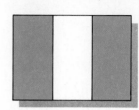

$\frac{2}{3}$ of the flag is green.

two-thirds

B. You can write fractions for parts of sets.

2 of the 5 lights are blue.

$\frac{2}{5}$ of the set is blue.

4 of the 6 lights are yellow.

$\frac{4}{6}$ of the set is yellow.

C. A fraction has a *numerator* and a *denominator.*

numerator ⟶ 4
denominator ⟶ 6

TRY THESE

Write a fraction for the red part of each object or set.

1.

2.

3.

4.

5.

6.

SKILLS PRACTICE _____

Write a fraction for the blue part of each object.

1.
2.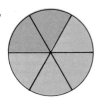
3.
4.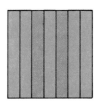

5.
6.
7.
8.

Write a fraction for the green part of each set.

9.
10.
11.
12.

13.
14.
15.
16.

★ 17. A sandwich was divided like this. Could 3 people get equal or fair shares?

EXTRA! Drawing a Picture
Show at least three ways to divide this pan of cornbread so that 4 people can get equal shares.

225

Mixed Numerals

A. You can write a fraction or a standard numeral for these shaded strips.

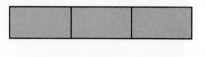 $\frac{3}{3}$ or 1 strip

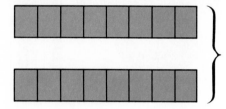 $\frac{16}{8}$ or 2 strips

B. You can write a fraction or a **mixed numeral** for these shaded strips.

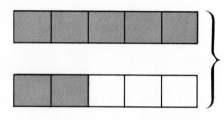 $\frac{7}{5}$ or $1\frac{2}{5}$ strips

Read the mixed numeral $1\frac{2}{5}$ as one and two-fifths.

TRY THESE

Give a fraction for the number of boxes filled. For 1 or greater, also give a mixed numeral or standard numeral.

1.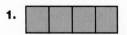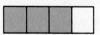

2.

3.

4.

SKILLS PRACTICE

Give a fraction for the number of boxes filled. For 1 or greater, also give a mixed numeral or standard numeral.

1.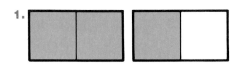

2.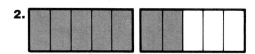

3.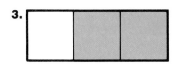

4.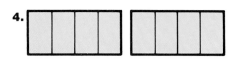

5.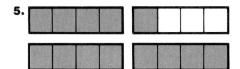

6.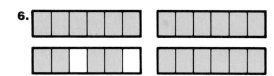

7.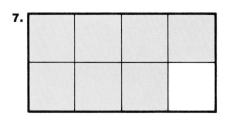

★8.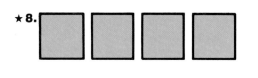

9.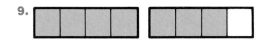

10.

11.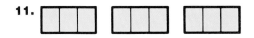

12.

13.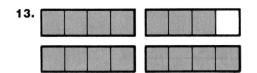

14.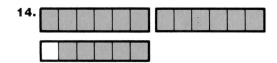

15.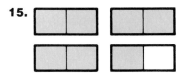

★16.

Finding Mixed Numerals

A. Karen picked 23 apples.
4 apples fill each box.
How many boxes of
apples did Karen pick?

The picture shows that Karen picked $5\frac{3}{4}$ boxes of apples.

You can also divide to solve this problem.

$$\begin{array}{r} 5\frac{3}{4} \\ 4\overline{)23} \\ 20 \\ \hline 3 \end{array}$$

Number in each $\longrightarrow$

3 left-over apples fill $\frac{3}{4}$ of a box of 4.

$\longleftarrow$ **Number left over**

B. You can divide to find a mixed numeral for $\frac{20}{3}$.

$$\begin{array}{r} 6\frac{2}{3} \\ 3\overline{)20} \\ 18 \\ \hline 2 \end{array}$$

2 is $\frac{2}{3}$ of a set of 3.

$\frac{20}{3} = 6\frac{2}{3}$

C. Now you can give the answer for a division in two ways.

Quotient and Remainder

$$\begin{array}{r} 38\,\text{R}4 \\ 9\overline{)346} \\ 27 \\ \hline 76 \\ 72 \\ \hline 4 \end{array}$$

or

Mixed Numeral

$$\begin{array}{r} 38\frac{4}{9} \\ 9\overline{)346} \\ 27 \\ \hline 76 \\ 72 \\ \hline 4 \end{array}$$

4 is $\frac{4}{9}$ of a set of 9.

TRY THESE

Give a mixed numeral or standard numeral for each.

1. $\frac{9}{4}$ 2. $\frac{18}{3}$ 3. $\frac{3}{1}$ 4. $\frac{26}{3}$ 5. $\frac{4}{4}$ 6. $\frac{35}{8}$

Give each division answer as a mixed numeral or standard numeral.

7. $5\overline{)38}$ 8. $3\overline{)64}$ 9. $6\overline{)42}$ 10. $8\overline{)509}$

SKILLS PRACTICE

Give a mixed numeral or standard numeral for each.

1. $\frac{29}{4}$ 2. $\frac{15}{5}$ 3. $\frac{19}{2}$ 4. $\frac{31}{6}$ 5. $\frac{22}{5}$ 6. $\frac{3}{3}$

7. $\frac{22}{7}$ 8. $\frac{13}{4}$ 9. $\frac{19}{8}$ 10. $\frac{5}{1}$ 11. $\frac{20}{9}$ 12. $\frac{45}{8}$

13. $\frac{17}{3}$ 14. $\frac{8}{8}$ 15. $\frac{33}{7}$ 16. $\frac{40}{3}$ 17. $\frac{37}{5}$ 18. $\frac{35}{2}$

19. $\frac{50}{9}$ 20. $\frac{61}{4}$ 21. $\frac{8}{1}$ 22. $\frac{60}{5}$ 23. $\frac{47}{6}$ 24. $\frac{64}{9}$

Give each division answer as a mixed numeral or standard numeral.

25. $3\overline{)20}$ 26. $6\overline{)48}$ 27. $5\overline{)32}$ 28. $8\overline{)75}$

29. $5\overline{)84}$ 30. $3\overline{)40}$ 31. $2\overline{)85}$ 32. $4\overline{)99}$

33. $8\overline{)943}$ 34. $5\overline{)364}$ ★35. $3\overline{)2,403}$ ★36. $6\overline{)7,311}$

Equivalent Fractions

A. You can use strips of paper to make fraction rulers. Each fraction tells the length of the part of the ruler to its left.

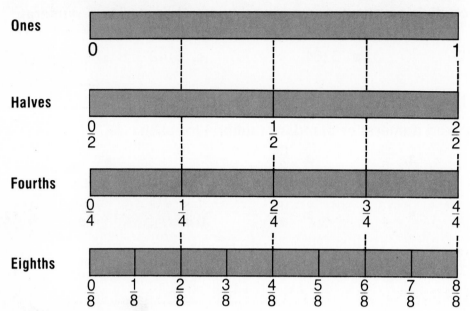

Follow the dotted line from the fourths ruler to the eighths ruler.

$\frac{2}{8}$ names the same part as $\frac{1}{4}$.

$\frac{1}{4}$ and $\frac{2}{8}$ are *equivalent fractions.* $\frac{1}{4} = \frac{2}{8}$

Equivalent fractions name the same part.

Also: $\frac{1}{2} = \frac{2}{4} = \frac{4}{8}$ $\frac{6}{8} = \frac{3}{4}$ $1 = \frac{2}{2} = \frac{4}{4} = \frac{8}{8}$

B. Give two equivalent fractions for the blue part.

Counting small squares: $\frac{4}{6}$ is blue.

Counting stacks of 2 squares: $\frac{2}{3}$ is blue.

TRY THESE

Use the fraction rulers.

1. Write the missing numerators for the fifths ruler and the tenths ruler.

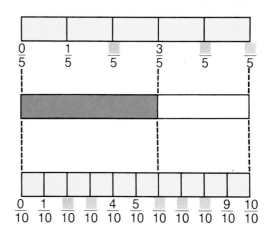

2. Write two equivalent fractions for the green part.

3. Write a fraction equivalent to $\frac{2}{10}$, to $\frac{4}{5}$.

4. Give two fractions for 1.

5. Write two equivalent fractions for the red part.

SKILLS PRACTICE

1. Give the missing labels for the sixths ruler and the twelfths ruler.

Use the fraction rulers to complete.

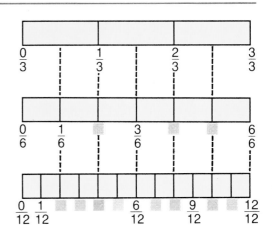

2. $\frac{1}{6} = \frac{\blacksquare}{12}$ 3. $\frac{4}{12} = \frac{\blacksquare}{3}$

4. $\frac{10}{12} = \frac{\blacksquare}{6}$ 5. $\frac{2}{6} = \frac{\blacksquare}{3}$

6. $\frac{2}{3} = \frac{\blacksquare}{6} = \frac{\blacksquare}{12}$ 7. $1 = \frac{\blacksquare}{3} = \frac{\blacksquare}{6} = \frac{\blacksquare}{12}$

Write two equivalent fractions for the green part.

8.

9.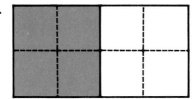

10.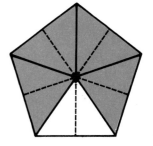

231

Dividing to Find Equivalent Fractions

A.

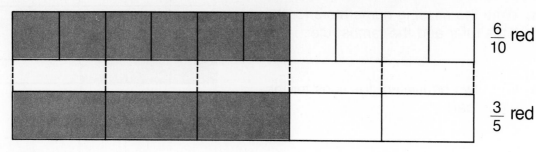

$\frac{6}{10}$ red

$\frac{3}{5}$ red

$6 \div 2 = 3$

$\frac{6}{10}$ = $\frac{3}{5}$

$10 \div 2 = 5$

$6 = 3 \times 2$ 2 is a **common factor**
$10 = 5 \times 2$ of 6 and 10.

> To get an equivalent fraction, divide the numerator and the denominator of the fraction by a common factor.

B. Divide to find a fraction equivalent to $\frac{12}{16}$.

2 is a common factor
of 12 and 16. $\frac{12}{16} = \frac{12 \div 2}{16 \div 2} = \frac{6}{8}$

But 12 and 16 have another common factor.

4 is a common factor
of 12 and 16. $\frac{12}{16} = \frac{12 \div 4}{16 \div 4} = \frac{3}{4}$

Both $\frac{6}{8}$ and $\frac{3}{4}$ are equivalent to $\frac{12}{16}$.

TRY THESE

Copy and complete.

1. $\dfrac{4}{6} = \dfrac{4 \div 2}{6 \div 2} = \dfrac{\blacksquare}{\blacksquare}$

2. $\dfrac{10}{15} = \dfrac{10 \div \blacksquare}{15 \div 5} = \dfrac{\blacksquare}{3}$

3. $\dfrac{3}{9} = \dfrac{3 \div 3}{9 \div \blacksquare} = \dfrac{\blacksquare}{\blacksquare}$

Divide to find an equivalent fraction.

4. $\dfrac{6}{8}$

5. $\dfrac{4}{12}$

6. $\dfrac{5}{10}$

7. $\dfrac{8}{12}$

8. $\dfrac{6}{12}$

SKILLS PRACTICE

Copy and complete.

1. $\dfrac{4}{8} = \dfrac{4 \div 4}{8 \div 4} = \dfrac{\blacksquare}{\blacksquare}$

2. $\dfrac{6}{15} = \dfrac{6 \div 3}{15 \div 3} = \dfrac{\blacksquare}{\blacksquare}$

3. $\dfrac{10}{14} = \dfrac{10 \div 2}{14 \div 2} = \dfrac{\blacksquare}{\blacksquare}$

4. $\dfrac{9}{12} = \dfrac{9 \div \blacksquare}{12 \div 3} = \dfrac{\blacksquare}{4}$

5. $\dfrac{4}{10} = \dfrac{4 \div 2}{10 \div \blacksquare} = \dfrac{2}{\blacksquare}$

6. $\dfrac{4}{16} = \dfrac{4 \div \blacksquare}{16 \div 4} = \dfrac{\blacksquare}{4}$

7. $\dfrac{2}{8} = \dfrac{2 \div 2}{8 \div \blacksquare} = \dfrac{\blacksquare}{\blacksquare}$

8. $\dfrac{9}{15} = \dfrac{9 \div 3}{15 \div \blacksquare} = \dfrac{\blacksquare}{\blacksquare}$

9. $\dfrac{12}{18} = \dfrac{12 \div 6}{18 \div \blacksquare} = \dfrac{\blacksquare}{\blacksquare}$

10. $\dfrac{2}{6} = \dfrac{2 \div \blacksquare}{6 \div 2} = \dfrac{\blacksquare}{\blacksquare}$

11. $\dfrac{12}{15} = \dfrac{12 \div \blacksquare}{15 \div 3} = \dfrac{\blacksquare}{\blacksquare}$

12. $\dfrac{9}{21} = \dfrac{9 \div \blacksquare}{21 \div \blacksquare} = \dfrac{\blacksquare}{7}$

Divide to find an equivalent fraction.

13. $\dfrac{7}{14}$

14. $\dfrac{6}{9}$

15. $\dfrac{15}{20}$

16. $\dfrac{8}{10}$

17. $\dfrac{2}{4}$

18. $\dfrac{4}{8}$

19. $\dfrac{16}{20}$

20. $\dfrac{4}{20}$

21. $\dfrac{9}{18}$

22. $\dfrac{6}{18}$

23. $\dfrac{6}{36}$

24. $\dfrac{9}{27}$

25. $\dfrac{2}{10}$

26. $\dfrac{8}{16}$

27. $\dfrac{6}{24}$

Lowest Terms Fractions

A. Divide to find a fraction equivalent to $\frac{2}{8}$.

2 is a common factor of 2 and 8.

$$\frac{2}{8} = \frac{2 \div 2}{8 \div 2} = \frac{1}{4}$$

1 and 4 have no common factor greater than 1.

$\frac{1}{4}$ is a **lowest terms fraction.**

B. Find a lowest terms fraction equivalent to $\frac{30}{45}$.

5 is a common factor of 30 and 45.

$$\frac{30}{45} = \frac{30 \div 5}{45 \div 5} = \frac{6}{9}$$

Since 3 is a common factor of 6 and 9, $\frac{6}{9}$ is not a lowest terms fraction.

Divide again: $\frac{6}{9} = \frac{6 \div 3}{9 \div 3} = \frac{2}{3}$

no common factor greater than 1

$\frac{2}{3}$ is a lowest terms fraction.

> **In a lowest terms fraction the numerator and the denominator have no common factor greater than 1.**

Give the lowest terms fraction for each.

1. $\frac{2}{4}$ 2. $\frac{9}{15}$ 3. $\frac{4}{10}$ 4. $\frac{2}{3}$ 5. $\frac{15}{20}$

Give the lowest terms fraction for each. Then give the mixed numeral or standard numeral.

6. $\frac{12}{10}$ 7. $\frac{16}{6}$ 8. $\frac{12}{9}$ 9. $\frac{13}{5}$ 10. $\frac{12}{4}$

SKILLS PRACTICE

Give the lowest terms fraction for each. For 1 or greater, also give a mixed numeral or standard numeral.

1. $\frac{3}{6}$ 2. $\frac{6}{8}$ 3. $\frac{5}{15}$ 4. $\frac{8}{20}$ 5. $\frac{4}{6}$

6. $\frac{12}{8}$ 7. $\frac{4}{12}$ 8. $\frac{8}{6}$ 9. $\frac{3}{4}$ 10. $\frac{10}{5}$

11. $\frac{6}{10}$ 12. $\frac{11}{5}$ 13. $\frac{6}{2}$ 14. $\frac{16}{12}$ 15. $\frac{3}{13}$

16. $\frac{9}{12}$ 17. $\frac{7}{21}$ 18. $\frac{18}{10}$ 19. $\frac{15}{25}$ 20. $\frac{8}{8}$

21. $\frac{12}{18}$ 22. $\frac{2}{5}$ 23. $\frac{15}{4}$ 24. $\frac{6}{18}$ 25. $\frac{14}{8}$

EXTRA! Making Logical Choices

Use the clues to tell what numeral is on the hidden face of each card *and* the color of each numeral.

There is a 1 next to and to the right of a 2, and a 1 next to and to the left of a 1.

There is a red numeral next to and to the left of a black numeral and a red numeral next to and to the right of a red numeral.

Addition: Common Denominators

A. Tony painted $\frac{2}{5}$ of his poster red. He painted $\frac{1}{5}$ of it green. What part of his poster has he painted?

The picture shows that Tony has painted $\frac{3}{5}$ of his poster.

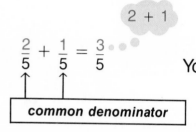

$$\frac{2}{5} + \frac{1}{5} = \frac{3}{5}$$

common denominator

You can also write:

$$\begin{array}{r} \frac{2}{5} \\ + \frac{1}{5} \\ \hline \frac{3}{5} \end{array}$$

> **To add with fractions that have a common denominator, add the numerators and use the same denominator.**

B. $\frac{3}{7} + \frac{2}{7} = \blacksquare$

Add numerators.

$$\frac{3}{7} + \frac{2}{7} = \frac{5}{7}$$

same denominator

C. You can write a standard numeral or a mixed numeral for sums 1 or greater.

$\frac{1}{6} + \frac{5}{6} = \frac{6}{6}$ or 1   standard numeral

$\frac{3}{5} + \frac{4}{5} = \frac{7}{5}$ $\frac{7}{5} \rightarrow 5\overline{)7}\ 1\frac{2}{5}$ mixed numeral

$\frac{5}{2}$

TRY THESE

Add.

1. $\frac{2}{7} + \frac{1}{7} = \blacksquare$

2. $\frac{1}{4} + \frac{3}{4} = \blacksquare$

3. $\frac{2}{9} + \frac{5}{9} = \blacksquare$

4. $\begin{array}{r} \frac{2}{3} \\ +\frac{2}{3} \\ \hline \end{array}$

5. $\begin{array}{r} \frac{3}{10} \\ +\frac{4}{10} \\ \hline \end{array}$

6. $\begin{array}{r} \frac{4}{8} \\ +\frac{7}{8} \\ \hline \end{array}$

7. $\begin{array}{r} \frac{3}{5} \\ +\frac{0}{5} \\ \hline \end{array}$

8. $\begin{array}{r} \frac{1}{2} \\ +\frac{1}{2} \\ \hline \end{array}$

9. $\begin{array}{r} \frac{7}{6} \\ +\frac{4}{6} \\ \hline \end{array}$

SKILLS PRACTICE

Add.

1. $\frac{1}{3} + \frac{1}{3} = \blacksquare$

2. $\frac{1}{6} + \frac{4}{6} = \blacksquare$

3. $\frac{1}{4} + \frac{2}{4} = \blacksquare$

4. $\frac{4}{5} + \frac{2}{5} = \blacksquare$

5. $\frac{4}{7} + \frac{5}{7} = \blacksquare$

6. $\frac{2}{8} + \frac{5}{8} = \blacksquare$

7. $\frac{5}{10} + \frac{4}{10} = \blacksquare$

8. $\frac{2}{5} + \frac{3}{5} = \blacksquare$

9. $\frac{2}{4} + \frac{5}{4} = \blacksquare$

10. $\begin{array}{r} \frac{3}{6} \\ +\frac{2}{6} \\ \hline \end{array}$

11. $\begin{array}{r} \frac{1}{3} \\ +\frac{2}{3} \\ \hline \end{array}$

12. $\begin{array}{r} \frac{6}{10} \\ +\frac{1}{10} \\ \hline \end{array}$

13. $\begin{array}{r} \frac{2}{8} \\ +\frac{7}{8} \\ \hline \end{array}$

14. $\begin{array}{r} \frac{2}{9} \\ +\frac{8}{9} \\ \hline \end{array}$

15. $\begin{array}{r} \frac{0}{7} \\ +\frac{5}{7} \\ \hline \end{array}$

16. $\begin{array}{r} \frac{3}{12} \\ +\frac{4}{12} \\ \hline \end{array}$

17. $\begin{array}{r} \frac{7}{10} \\ +\frac{3}{10} \\ \hline \end{array}$

18. $\begin{array}{r} \frac{5}{6} \\ +\frac{2}{6} \\ \hline \end{array}$

19. $\begin{array}{r} \frac{4}{9} \\ +\frac{3}{9} \\ \hline \end{array}$

20. $\begin{array}{r} \frac{7}{4} \\ +\frac{2}{4} \\ \hline \end{array}$

★21. $\begin{array}{r} \frac{5}{8} \\ +\frac{7}{8} \\ \hline \end{array}$

PROBLEM SOLVING

22. Jill painted $\frac{2}{9}$ of a picture red and $\frac{5}{9}$ of the picture yellow. What part of the picture did Jill paint?

23. Joe had $\frac{3}{7}$ of a can of paint. Carla had $\frac{6}{7}$ of a can of paint. How much paint did they have in all?

Subtraction: Common Denominators

A. Mr. Mora had $\frac{3}{4}$ of a box of flour. He used $\frac{2}{4}$ of the box of flour. What part of the box of flour was left?

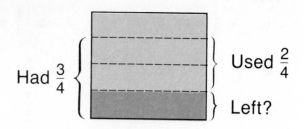

Had $\frac{3}{4}$ { Used $\frac{2}{4}$

} Left?

The picture shows that $\frac{1}{4}$ of the box of flour was left.

$3 - 2$

$$\frac{3}{4} - \frac{2}{4} = \frac{1}{4}$$

You can also write:

$$\begin{array}{r} \frac{3}{4} \\ - \frac{2}{4} \\ \hline \frac{1}{4} \end{array}$$

> **To subtract with fractions that have a common denominator, subtract the numerators and use the same denominator.**

B. $\frac{5}{7} - \frac{3}{7} = \blacksquare$

Subtract numerators.

$$\frac{5}{7} - \frac{3}{7} = \frac{2}{7}$$

same denominator

C. $\frac{7}{8} - \frac{3}{8} = \blacksquare$ Give a lowest terms fraction for the difference.

$$\frac{7}{8} - \frac{3}{8} = \frac{4}{8}$$

$$\frac{4}{8} = \frac{4 \div 4}{8 \div 4} = \frac{1}{2}$$

not lowest terms fraction

lowest terms fraction

TRY THESE

Subtract.

1. $\dfrac{2}{3} - \dfrac{1}{3} = $ ▦

2. $\dfrac{6}{7} - \dfrac{2}{7} = $ ▦

3. $\dfrac{5}{6} - \dfrac{4}{6} = $ ▦

4. $\begin{array}{r} \frac{7}{9} \\ -\frac{5}{9} \\ \hline \end{array}$

5. $\begin{array}{r} \frac{4}{5} \\ -\frac{1}{5} \\ \hline \end{array}$

6. $\begin{array}{r} \frac{7}{10} \\ -\frac{2}{10} \\ \hline \end{array}$

7. $\begin{array}{r} \frac{1}{2} \\ -\frac{0}{2} \\ \hline \end{array}$

8. $\begin{array}{r} \frac{7}{8} \\ -\frac{5}{8} \\ \hline \end{array}$

9. $\begin{array}{r} \frac{7}{8} \\ -\frac{1}{8} \\ \hline \end{array}$

SKILLS PRACTICE

Subtract.

1. $\dfrac{3}{5} - \dfrac{2}{5} = $ ▦

2. $\dfrac{5}{8} - \dfrac{2}{8} = $ ▦

3. $\dfrac{6}{7} - \dfrac{1}{7} = $ ▦

4. $\dfrac{9}{10} - \dfrac{7}{10} = $ ▦

5. $\dfrac{8}{9} - \dfrac{5}{9} = $ ▦

6. $\dfrac{5}{6} - \dfrac{2}{6} = $ ▦

7. $\dfrac{5}{7} - \dfrac{4}{7} = $ ▦

8. $\dfrac{7}{12} - \dfrac{2}{12} = $ ▦

9. $\dfrac{7}{10} - \dfrac{3}{10} = $ ▦

10. $\begin{array}{r} \frac{4}{5} \\ -\frac{2}{5} \\ \hline \end{array}$

11. $\begin{array}{r} \frac{7}{8} \\ -\frac{4}{8} \\ \hline \end{array}$

12. $\begin{array}{r} \frac{3}{4} \\ -\frac{1}{4} \\ \hline \end{array}$

13. $\begin{array}{r} \frac{9}{10} \\ -\frac{2}{10} \\ \hline \end{array}$

14. $\begin{array}{r} \frac{5}{9} \\ -\frac{1}{9} \\ \hline \end{array}$

15. $\begin{array}{r} \frac{4}{5} \\ -\frac{0}{5} \\ \hline \end{array}$

16. $\begin{array}{r} \frac{7}{8} \\ -\frac{1}{8} \\ \hline \end{array}$

17. $\begin{array}{r} \frac{10}{11} \\ -\frac{7}{11} \\ \hline \end{array}$

18. $\begin{array}{r} \frac{11}{12} \\ -\frac{2}{12} \\ \hline \end{array}$

19. $\begin{array}{r} \frac{9}{14} \\ -\frac{4}{14} \\ \hline \end{array}$

20. $\begin{array}{r} \frac{9}{10} \\ -\frac{3}{10} \\ \hline \end{array}$

★ 21. $\begin{array}{r} \frac{11}{8} \\ -\frac{1}{8} \\ \hline \end{array}$

PROBLEM SOLVING

22. Lois had $\dfrac{5}{8}$ of a box of apples. She sold $\dfrac{1}{8}$ of the box. What part of the box of apples did she have then?

23. Joel mowed $\dfrac{7}{10}$ of the lawn. Rob mowed $\dfrac{3}{10}$ of the lawn. How much more of the lawn did Joel mow?

Workbook   page 432

More Addition and Subtraction

Remember that your sum or difference may not be a lowest terms fraction. Your sum or difference may also be 1 or greater.

A. Find the sum of $\frac{3}{4}$ and $\frac{3}{4}$.

lowest terms fraction

$$\frac{3}{4} + \frac{3}{4} = \frac{6}{4} \qquad \frac{6}{4} = \frac{6 \div 2}{4 \div 2} = \frac{3}{2}$$

mixed numeral

$$\frac{3}{2} \longrightarrow 2\overline{)3}^{\,1\frac{1}{2}}$$
$$\frac{2}{1}$$

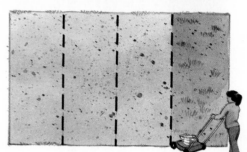

The sum is $\frac{6}{4}$, $\frac{3}{2}$, or $1\frac{1}{2}$.

B. Find the difference of $\frac{8}{3}$ and $\frac{2}{3}$.

$$\frac{8}{3} - \frac{2}{3} = \frac{6}{3} \qquad \frac{6}{3} = \frac{6 \div 3}{3 \div 3} = \frac{2}{1} \text{ or } 2$$

The difference is $\frac{6}{3}$, $\frac{2}{1}$, or 2.

TRY THESE

Add or subtract.

1. $\frac{3}{8} + \frac{1}{8} = $ ▨

2. $\frac{7}{4} - \frac{3}{4} = $ ▨

3. $\frac{3}{8} + \frac{7}{8} = $ ▨

4. $\frac{12}{9}$
   $-\frac{2}{9}$

5. $\frac{1}{2}$
   $+\frac{3}{2}$

6. $\frac{10}{6}$
   $-\frac{1}{6}$

7. $\frac{2}{9}$
   $+\frac{3}{9}$

8. $\frac{12}{8}$
   $-\frac{1}{8}$

9. $\frac{1}{4}$
   $+\frac{1}{4}$

SKILLS PRACTICE

Add or subtract.

1. $\frac{2}{6} + \frac{1}{6} =$ ▨

2. $\frac{3}{2} - \frac{0}{2} =$ ▨

3. $\frac{1}{6} + \frac{3}{6} =$ ▨

4. $\frac{12}{8} - \frac{2}{8} =$ ▨

5. $\frac{3}{4} + \frac{5}{4} =$ ▨

6. $\frac{4}{5} - \frac{2}{5} =$ ▨

7. $\frac{6}{2} + \frac{1}{2} =$ ▨

8. $\frac{6}{3} - \frac{2}{3} =$ ▨

9. $\frac{7}{9} + \frac{5}{9} =$ ▨

10. $\begin{array}{r} \frac{7}{4} \\ -\frac{2}{4} \\ \hline \end{array}$

11. $\begin{array}{r} \frac{1}{8} \\ +\frac{5}{8} \\ \hline \end{array}$

12. $\begin{array}{r} \frac{6}{7} \\ -\frac{4}{7} \\ \hline \end{array}$

13. $\begin{array}{r} \frac{3}{4} \\ +\frac{5}{4} \\ \hline \end{array}$

14. $\begin{array}{r} \frac{7}{10} \\ -\frac{2}{10} \\ \hline \end{array}$

15. $\begin{array}{r} \frac{5}{8} \\ +\frac{2}{8} \\ \hline \end{array}$

16. $\begin{array}{r} \frac{7}{4} \\ +\frac{3}{4} \\ \hline \end{array}$

17. $\begin{array}{r} \frac{7}{9} \\ -\frac{2}{9} \\ \hline \end{array}$

18. $\begin{array}{r} \frac{13}{10} \\ -\frac{1}{10} \\ \hline \end{array}$

19. $\begin{array}{r} \frac{7}{10} \\ +\frac{1}{10} \\ \hline \end{array}$

20. $\begin{array}{r} \frac{9}{5} \\ -\frac{2}{5} \\ \hline \end{array}$

21. $\begin{array}{r} \frac{5}{2} \\ +\frac{1}{2} \\ \hline \end{array}$

22. $\begin{array}{r} \frac{9}{7} \\ -\frac{2}{7} \\ \hline \end{array}$

23. $\begin{array}{r} \frac{5}{6} \\ +\frac{4}{6} \\ \hline \end{array}$

24. $\begin{array}{r} \frac{6}{15} \\ +\frac{4}{15} \\ \hline \end{array}$

25. $\begin{array}{r} \frac{12}{6} \\ -\frac{5}{6} \\ \hline \end{array}$

26. $\begin{array}{r} \frac{5}{12} \\ +\frac{3}{12} \\ \hline \end{array}$

27. $\begin{array}{r} \frac{5}{6} \\ +\frac{4}{6} \\ \hline \end{array}$

PROBLEM SOLVING

28. Karen had to paper $\frac{7}{8}$ of a wall. After papering all morning, she still had $\frac{3}{8}$ of the wall to paper. What part of the wall did Karen paper in the morning?

29. Carlos used $\frac{7}{10}$ of a bag of grass seed on the front lawn and $\frac{8}{10}$ of a bag of seed on the back lawn. How many bags of seed did Carlos use in all?

30. Ed had a bottle $\frac{4}{6}$ full. He poured out $\frac{1}{6}$ of the bottle. What part was left?

★ 31. Ann wanted to fill a bag with papers. She filled only $\frac{6}{10}$ of the bag. What part of the bag did she still have to fill? (*Hint:* 1 bag $= \frac{10}{10}$ bag)

Upside-down answers 1. $\frac{3}{6}$ or $\frac{1}{2}$ 4. $\frac{10}{8}$, $\frac{5}{4}$, or $1\frac{1}{4}$ 10. $\frac{5}{4}$ or $1\frac{1}{4}$

Workbook page 433

241

Problem Solving: Using Circle Graphs

Circle graphs can be used to show information.

Jamie made this circle graph to show what part of her day she spends doing each thing.

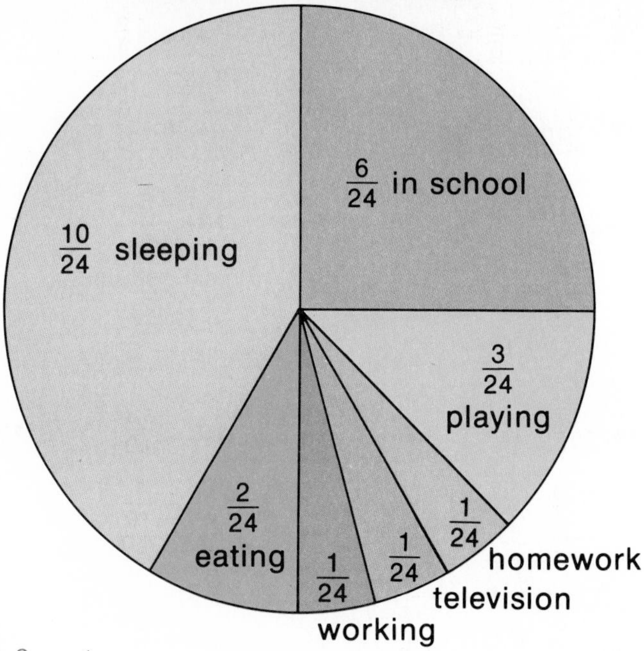

Parts of Jamie's Day

$\frac{6}{24}$ in school

$\frac{10}{24}$ sleeping

$\frac{3}{24}$ playing

$\frac{2}{24}$ eating

$\frac{1}{24}$ homework

$\frac{1}{24}$ television

$\frac{1}{24}$ working

A. What part of her day does Jamie spend working or eating?

Working: $\frac{1}{24}$ of her day

Eating: $\frac{2}{24}$ of her day

Add to find what part in all.

$$\frac{1}{24} + \frac{2}{24} = \frac{3}{24} \longrightarrow \frac{3}{24} = \frac{3 \div 3}{24 \div 3} = \frac{1}{8}$$

Jamie spends $\frac{1}{8}$ of her day working or eating.

B. How much more of her day does Jamie spend sleeping than she spends in school?

Sleeping: $\frac{10}{24}$ of her day

In school: $\frac{6}{24}$ of her day

Subtract to find what part more.

$$\frac{10}{24} - \frac{6}{24} = \frac{4}{24} \longrightarrow \frac{4}{24} = \frac{4 \div 4}{24 \div 4} = \frac{1}{6}$$

Jamie spends $\frac{1}{6}$ more of her day sleeping than she spends in school.

READ   PLAN   DO   ANSWER   CHECK

TRY THESE

Use the circle graph on page 242 to solve these problems.

1. What part of her day does Jamie spend sleeping or eating?

2. How much more of her day does Jamie spend in school than she spends doing homework?

PROBLEM SOLVING PRACTICE

This circle graph shows parts of Mark's school day.

1. What part of his school day does Mark spend on spelling or on mathematics?

2. How much more of his day does Mark spend on reading than on science?

3. How much more of his day does Mark spend on mathematics than on science?

4. What part of his school day in all does he spend at lunch and recess or on reading?

5. What does Mark spend as much of his day doing as on spelling? What part of his day does he spend on these two things?

★**6.** What part of his school day does Mark spend on science, on mathematics, or on spelling?

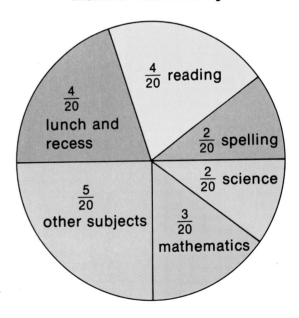

Parts of Mark's School Day

$\frac{4}{20}$ reading

$\frac{2}{20}$ spelling

$\frac{2}{20}$ science

$\frac{3}{20}$ mathematics

$\frac{5}{20}$ other subjects

$\frac{4}{20}$ lunch and recess

★**7.** How much of his school day does Mark spend doing all six things?

ⓐ Maintaining Skills

Read each clock.

1.

▓:▓

▓ minutes past ▓

2.

▓:▓

▓ minutes to ▓

3.

▓:▓

▓ minutes to ▓

4.

▓:▓

▓ minutes past ▓

5.

▓:▓

▓ minutes to ▓

6.

▓:▓

▓ minutes past ▓

Multiply.

7. 5 ×9	**8.** 6 ×7	**9.** 4 ×5	**10.** 18 × 2	**11.** 26 × 6
12. 15 × 3	**13.** 325 × 5	**14.** 307 × 7	**15.** 2,368 × 4	**16.** 3,762 × 5

Divide.

17. $2\overline{)18}$ **18.** $3\overline{)28}$ **19.** $6\overline{)79}$ **20.** $4\overline{)58}$ **21.** $5\overline{)88}$

22. $7\overline{)824}$ **23.** $4\overline{)632}$ **24.** $8\overline{)177}$ **25.** $5\overline{)685}$ **26.** $3\overline{)129}$

27. $2\overline{)4,137}$ **28.** $9\overline{)1,895}$ **29.** $4\overline{)9,571}$ **30.** $8\overline{)1,880}$ **31.** $6\overline{)7,667}$

Solve the problems.

32. Julia paid $9.45 for 5 blank tapes. How much did she pay for 1 tape?

33. Joe bought records for $4 each. He spent $24. How many records did he buy?

Project: Using Pictographs

A *pictograph* can be used to show information. This pictograph tells how many people each state has in the U.S. House of Representatives. Each ♠ stands for 4 representatives.

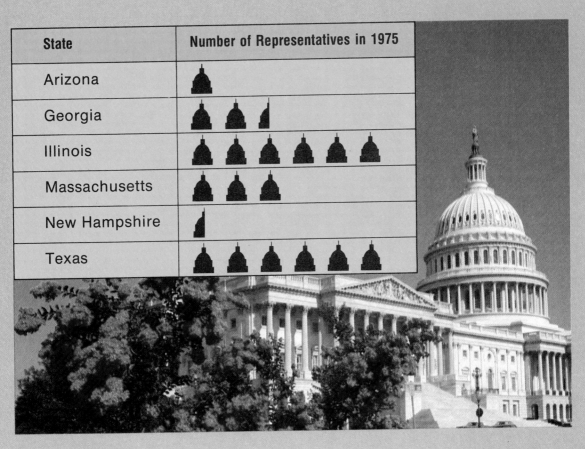

State	Number of Representatives in 1975
Arizona	♠
Georgia	♠ ♠ ♠
Illinois	♠ ♠ ♠ ♠ ♠ ♠
Massachusetts	♠ ♠ ♠
New Hampshire	♦
Texas	♠ ♠ ♠ ♠ ♠ ♠

1. How many representatives does ♠ stand for?

2. How many representatives does ♦ stand for?

3. How many representatives did each of the states shown above have?

4. Which two states had the same number of representatives?

How is the number of representatives for each state decided? How many representatives does your state have?

Copy the pictograph above. Find the number of representatives for some other states. Draw ⊞ to show the number of representatives. Remember that each ⊞ stands for 4 representatives.

Multiplying to Find Equivalent Fractions

A.

$\dfrac{3}{5}$

$\dfrac{6}{10}$

$$3 \times 2 = 6$$

$$\dfrac{3}{5} = \dfrac{6}{10}$$

$$5 \times 2 = 10$$

> **To get an equivalent fraction, you can multiply the numerator and denominator of the fraction by the same number.**

B. Here are some lists of equivalent fractions.

$$\dfrac{2}{3} = \dfrac{2 \times 2}{3 \times 2} = \dfrac{4}{6}$$

$$\dfrac{2}{3} = \dfrac{2 \times 3}{3 \times 3} = \dfrac{6}{9}$$

$$\dfrac{2}{3} = \dfrac{2 \times 4}{3 \times 4} = \dfrac{8}{12}$$

$$\dfrac{2}{3} = \dfrac{2 \times 5}{3 \times 5} = \dfrac{10}{15}$$

$$\dfrac{2}{3} = \dfrac{2 \times 6}{3 \times 6} = \dfrac{12}{18}$$

$$\dfrac{1}{4} = \dfrac{1 \times 2}{4 \times 2} = \dfrac{2}{8}$$

$$\dfrac{1}{4} = \dfrac{1 \times 3}{4 \times 3} = \dfrac{3}{12}$$

$$\dfrac{1}{4} = \dfrac{1 \times 4}{4 \times 4} = \dfrac{4}{16}$$

$$\dfrac{1}{4} = \dfrac{1 \times 5}{4 \times 5} = \dfrac{5}{20}$$

$$\dfrac{1}{4} = \dfrac{1 \times 6}{4 \times 6} = \dfrac{6}{24}$$

$$\dfrac{6}{5} = \dfrac{6 \times 2}{5 \times 2} = \dfrac{12}{10}$$

$$\dfrac{6}{5} = \dfrac{6 \times 3}{5 \times 3} = \dfrac{18}{15}$$

$$\dfrac{6}{5} = \dfrac{6 \times 4}{5 \times 4} = \dfrac{24}{20}$$

$$\dfrac{6}{5} = \dfrac{6 \times 5}{5 \times 5} = \dfrac{30}{25}$$

$$\dfrac{6}{5} = \dfrac{6 \times 6}{5 \times 6} = \dfrac{36}{30}$$

You can continue the lists by multiplying by other numbers.

TRY THESE

Copy and complete.

1. $\dfrac{2}{5} = \dfrac{2 \times 3}{5 \times 3} = \dfrac{\blacksquare}{\blacksquare}$

2. $\dfrac{5}{8} = \dfrac{5 \times \blacksquare}{8 \times 2} = \dfrac{\blacksquare}{16}$

3. $\dfrac{9}{10} = \dfrac{9 \times 5}{10 \times \blacksquare} = \dfrac{\blacksquare}{\blacksquare}$

Multiply each numerator and denominator by 2, 3, 4, and 5 to find equivalent fractions.

4. $\dfrac{1}{9}$

5. $\dfrac{5}{6}$

6. $\dfrac{2}{1}$

7. $\dfrac{4}{3}$

8. $\dfrac{3}{4}$

SKILLS PRACTICE

Copy and complete.

1. $\dfrac{1}{3} = \dfrac{1 \times 4}{3 \times 4} = \dfrac{\blacksquare}{\blacksquare}$

2. $\dfrac{5}{7} = \dfrac{5 \times 2}{7 \times 2} = \dfrac{\blacksquare}{\blacksquare}$

3. $\dfrac{3}{4} = \dfrac{3 \times 2}{4 \times \blacksquare} = \dfrac{6}{\blacksquare}$

4. $\dfrac{1}{10} = \dfrac{1 \times \blacksquare}{10 \times 3} = \dfrac{\blacksquare}{30}$

5. $\dfrac{3}{2} = \dfrac{3 \times 4}{2 \times \blacksquare} = \dfrac{\blacksquare}{\blacksquare}$

6. $\dfrac{5}{1} = \dfrac{5 \times 3}{1 \times \blacksquare} = \dfrac{\blacksquare}{\blacksquare}$

7. $\dfrac{3}{8} = \dfrac{3 \times \blacksquare}{8 \times 5} = \dfrac{\blacksquare}{\blacksquare}$

8. $\dfrac{4}{5} = \dfrac{4 \times \blacksquare}{5 \times 6} = \dfrac{\blacksquare}{\blacksquare}$

★9. $\dfrac{9}{10} = \dfrac{9 \times \blacksquare}{10 \times \blacksquare} = \dfrac{63}{\blacksquare}$

Multiply each numerator and denominator by 2, 3, 4, 5, and 6 to find equivalent fractions.

10. $\dfrac{3}{7}$

11. $\dfrac{1}{6}$

12. $\dfrac{4}{5}$

13. $\dfrac{3}{10}$

14. $\dfrac{4}{1}$

15. $\dfrac{5}{2}$

16. $\dfrac{2}{9}$

17. $\dfrac{4}{9}$

18. $\dfrac{3}{2}$

★19. 3

EXTRA! Finding Parts of Sets

What part of the set of wallpaper samples is green? red? blue? brown? Find four equivalent fractions for each part.

Upside-down answers
Workbook Page 434

Upside-down answers:
1. $\dfrac{1}{3} = \dfrac{1 \times 4}{3 \times 4} = \dfrac{4}{12}$
10. $\dfrac{3}{7} = \dfrac{6}{14} = \dfrac{9}{21} = \dfrac{12}{28} = \dfrac{15}{35} = \dfrac{18}{42}$

247

Comparison: Using Equivalent Fractions

A.

$\frac{7}{10}$ of the strip is red.

$\frac{4}{10}$ of the strip is blue.

$\frac{7}{10}$ is greater than $\frac{4}{10}$. $\frac{4}{10}$ is less than $\frac{7}{10}$.

$$7 > 4$$
$$\frac{7}{10} > \frac{4}{10}$$

$$4 < 7$$
$$\frac{4}{10} < \frac{7}{10}$$

> **Common** denominator.
> **Compare numerators.**

B. When fractions have **unlike** denominators, find equivalent fractions with a common denominator.

Compare $\frac{1}{6}$ and $\frac{2}{9}$.

$$\times 2 \quad \times 3 \quad \times 4$$
$$\frac{1}{6} = \frac{2}{12} = \boxed{\frac{3}{18}} = \frac{4}{24}$$

$$\frac{3}{18} < \frac{4}{18} \quad so \quad \frac{1}{6} < \frac{2}{9}$$

$$\times 2 \quad \times 3 \quad \times 4$$
$$\frac{2}{9} = \boxed{\frac{4}{18}} = \frac{6}{27} = \frac{8}{36}$$

$$\frac{4}{18} > \frac{3}{18} \quad so \quad \frac{2}{9} > \frac{1}{6}$$

C. Write $>$, $<$, or $=$ for ●. $\frac{2}{3}$ ● $\frac{4}{5}$

From the lists: $\frac{2}{3} = \frac{10}{15}$ *and* $\frac{4}{5} = \frac{12}{15}$

$$\frac{10}{15} < \frac{12}{15} \quad so \quad \frac{2}{3} < \frac{4}{5}$$

Lists of Equivalent Fractions

	×2	×3	×4	×5	×6		×2	×3	×4	×5	×6
$\frac{1}{2}$ =	$\frac{2}{4}$ =	$\frac{3}{6}$ =	$\frac{4}{8}$ =	$\frac{5}{10}$ =	$\frac{6}{12}$	$\frac{4}{5}$ =	$\frac{8}{10}$ =	$\frac{12}{15}$ =	$\frac{16}{20}$ =	$\frac{20}{25}$ =	$\frac{24}{30}$
$\frac{2}{3}$ =	$\frac{4}{6}$ =	$\frac{6}{9}$ =	$\frac{8}{12}$ =	$\frac{10}{15}$ =	$\frac{12}{18}$	$\frac{5}{6}$ =	$\frac{10}{12}$ =	$\frac{15}{18}$ =	$\frac{20}{24}$ =	$\frac{25}{30}$ =	$\frac{30}{36}$
$\frac{3}{4}$ =	$\frac{6}{8}$ =	$\frac{9}{12}$ =	$\frac{12}{16}$ =	$\frac{15}{20}$ =	$\frac{18}{24}$	$\frac{5}{8}$ =	$\frac{10}{16}$ =	$\frac{15}{24}$ =	$\frac{20}{32}$ =	$\frac{25}{40}$ =	$\frac{30}{48}$

TRY THESE

Write >, <, or = for ●. Use the lists of equivalent fractions on page 248 if you need to.

1. $\frac{2}{3}$ ● $\frac{1}{3}$

2. $\frac{2}{3}$ ● $\frac{3}{4}$

3. $\frac{3}{4}$ ● $\frac{9}{12}$

4. $\frac{5}{6}$ ● $\frac{5}{8}$

Use your own lists of equivalent fractions.

5. $\frac{3}{7}$ ● $\frac{4}{7}$

6. $\frac{1}{4}$ ● $\frac{4}{16}$

7. $\frac{4}{9}$ ● $\frac{9}{9}$

8. $\frac{1}{3}$ ● $\frac{2}{5}$

SKILLS PRACTICE

Write >, <, or = for ●. Use the lists of equivalent fractions on page 248 if you need to.

1. $\frac{1}{2}$ ● $\frac{2}{3}$

2. $\frac{3}{5}$ ● $\frac{2}{5}$

3. $\frac{5}{6}$ ● $\frac{3}{4}$

4. $\frac{4}{5}$ ● $\frac{1}{2}$

5. $\frac{3}{4}$ ● $\frac{5}{8}$

6. $\frac{2}{7}$ ● $\frac{5}{7}$

7. $\frac{3}{4}$ ● $\frac{1}{2}$

8. $\frac{5}{2}$ ● $\frac{4}{2}$

9. $\frac{7}{8}$ ● $\frac{5}{8}$

10. $\frac{5}{6}$ ● $\frac{10}{12}$

11. $\frac{2}{3}$ ● $\frac{5}{6}$

12. $\frac{4}{5}$ ● $\frac{5}{6}$

Use your own lists of equivalent fractions.

13. $\frac{5}{9}$ ● $\frac{7}{9}$

14. $\frac{3}{5}$ ● $\frac{9}{15}$

15. $\frac{3}{8}$ ● $\frac{5}{8}$

16. $\frac{5}{6}$ ● $\frac{7}{9}$

17. $\frac{1}{3}$ ● $\frac{3}{1}$

18. $\frac{3}{7}$ ● $\frac{3}{4}$

19. $\frac{5}{1}$ ● $\frac{4}{1}$

★ 20. $\frac{0}{3}$ ● $\frac{0}{7}$

PROBLEM SOLVING

21. Tom worked $\frac{5}{10}$ of a day. Barry worked $\frac{7}{10}$ of a day. Who worked longer?

★ 22. Jan painted $\frac{5}{12}$ of a fence. Jean painted $\frac{8}{15}$ of the fence. Who painted less?

Addition: Unlike Denominators

Find the sum of $\frac{3}{10}$ and $\frac{1}{6}$.

Step 1 The fractions have unlike denominators. Find equivalent fractions with a common denominator.

From the lists below: $\frac{3}{10} = \frac{9}{30}$ $\quad$ $\frac{1}{6} = \frac{5}{30}$

Step 2 Add. $\quad \frac{3}{10} + \frac{1}{6} = \blacksquare$

$$\frac{9}{30} + \frac{5}{30} = \frac{14}{30}$$

Lowest Terms

$$\frac{14}{30} = \frac{14 \div 2}{30 \div 2} = \frac{7}{15}$$

The sum is $\frac{14}{30}$ or $\frac{7}{15}$.

Lists of Equivalent Fractions

$\frac{1}{2} = \frac{2}{4} = \frac{3}{6} = \frac{4}{8} = \frac{5}{10}$ $\qquad$ $\frac{1}{6} = \frac{2}{12} = \frac{3}{18} = \frac{4}{24} = \frac{5}{30}$

$\frac{2}{3} = \frac{4}{6} = \frac{6}{9} = \frac{8}{12} = \frac{10}{15}$ $\qquad$ $\frac{5}{8} = \frac{10}{16} = \frac{15}{24} = \frac{20}{32} = \frac{25}{40}$

$\frac{1}{4} = \frac{2}{8} = \frac{3}{12} = \frac{4}{16} = \frac{5}{20}$ $\qquad$ $\frac{3}{10} = \frac{6}{20} = \frac{9}{30} = \frac{12}{40} = \frac{15}{50}$

$\frac{3}{4} = \frac{6}{8} = \frac{9}{12} = \frac{12}{16} = \frac{15}{20}$ $\qquad$ $\frac{1}{12} = \frac{2}{24} = \frac{3}{36} = \frac{4}{48} = \frac{5}{60}$

TRY THESE

Add. Use the lists of equivalent fractions above.

1. $\frac{2}{3} + \frac{1}{6} = \blacksquare$ $\qquad$ **2.** $\frac{1}{4} + \frac{1}{12} = \blacksquare$ $\qquad$ **3.** $\frac{5}{8} + \frac{3}{10} = \blacksquare$

Use your own lists of equivalent fractions.

4. $\frac{1}{4} + \frac{7}{10} = \blacksquare$ $\qquad$ **5.** $\frac{2}{3} + \frac{5}{9} = \blacksquare$ $\qquad$ **6.** $\frac{1}{6} + \frac{8}{15} = \blacksquare$

SKILLS PRACTICE

Add. Use the lists of equivalent fractions on page 250.

1. $\dfrac{1}{2} + \dfrac{2}{3} =$

2. $\dfrac{1}{4} + \dfrac{1}{6} =$

3. $\dfrac{3}{4} + \dfrac{1}{12} =$

4. $\dfrac{5}{8} + \dfrac{1}{12} =$

5. $\dfrac{5}{8} + \dfrac{1}{2} =$

6. $\dfrac{2}{3} + \dfrac{1}{4} =$

7. $\begin{aligned}\dfrac{1}{4}\\+\dfrac{5}{8}\end{aligned}$

8. $\begin{aligned}\dfrac{1}{2}\\+\dfrac{1}{6}\end{aligned}$

9. $\begin{aligned}\dfrac{2}{3}\\+\dfrac{1}{12}\end{aligned}$

10. $\begin{aligned}\dfrac{1}{4}\\+\dfrac{3}{10}\end{aligned}$

11. $\begin{aligned}\dfrac{3}{4}\\+\dfrac{5}{8}\end{aligned}$

12. $\begin{aligned}\dfrac{1}{6}\\+\dfrac{5}{8}\end{aligned}$

Use your own lists of equivalent fractions.

13. $\dfrac{2}{3} + \dfrac{5}{6} =$

14. $\dfrac{3}{10} + \dfrac{3}{5} =$

15. $\dfrac{1}{2} + \dfrac{7}{10} =$

16. $\dfrac{7}{9} + \dfrac{1}{6} =$

17. $\dfrac{7}{9} + \dfrac{5}{6} =$

18. $\dfrac{7}{10} + \dfrac{1}{5} =$

19. $\begin{aligned}\dfrac{2}{3}\\+\dfrac{8}{15}\end{aligned}$

20. $\begin{aligned}\dfrac{1}{6}\\+\dfrac{5}{9}\end{aligned}$

21. $\begin{aligned}\dfrac{2}{3}\\+\dfrac{3}{12}\end{aligned}$

22. $\begin{aligned}\dfrac{3}{4}\\+\dfrac{5}{12}\end{aligned}$

23. $\begin{aligned}\dfrac{7}{10}\\+\dfrac{1}{6}\end{aligned}$

24. $\begin{aligned}\dfrac{5}{9}\\+\dfrac{5}{12}\end{aligned}$

PROBLEM SOLVING

25. The hardware store sold $\dfrac{1}{2}$ of a box of tacks one day and $\dfrac{3}{4}$ of a box the next day. How many boxes of tacks were sold in all?

26. One screwdriver weighs $\dfrac{1}{6}$ lb. Another screwdriver weighs $\dfrac{1}{12}$ lb. How much do the two screwdrivers weigh all together?

★ 27. A customer bought $\dfrac{3}{4}$ yd of pine molding and $\dfrac{5}{12}$ yd of walnut molding. How much molding did the customer buy in all?

★ 28. The store sold $\dfrac{1}{2}$ of a roll of twine to one customer and $\dfrac{5}{6}$ of a roll to another. How many rolls of twine were sold in all?

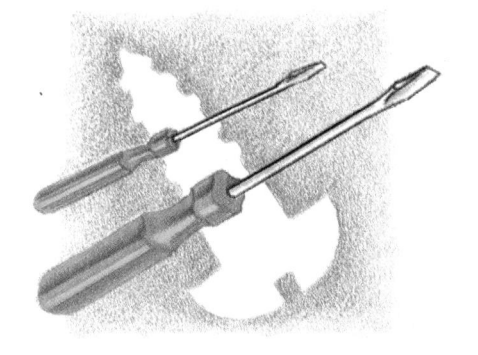

Subtraction: Unlike Denominators

Find the difference of $\frac{5}{3}$ and $\frac{4}{15}$.

Step 1 Find equivalent fractions with a common denominator.

From the lists below: $\frac{5}{3} = \frac{25}{15}$ $\frac{4}{15} = \frac{4}{15}$

Step 2 Subtract. $\frac{5}{3} - \frac{4}{15} = \blacksquare$

$$\frac{25}{15} - \frac{4}{15} = \frac{21}{15}$$

Lowest Terms

$$\frac{21}{15} = \frac{21 \div 3}{15 \div 3} = \frac{7}{5} = 1\frac{2}{5}$$

The difference is $\frac{21}{15}$, $\frac{7}{5}$, or $1\frac{2}{5}$.

Lists of Equivalent Fractions

$$\frac{3}{2} = \frac{6}{4} = \frac{9}{6} = \frac{12}{8} = \frac{15}{10} \qquad \frac{7}{9} = \frac{14}{18} = \frac{21}{27} = \frac{28}{36} = \frac{35}{45}$$

$$\frac{5}{3} = \frac{10}{6} = \frac{15}{9} = \frac{20}{12} = \frac{25}{15} \qquad \frac{9}{10} = \frac{18}{20} = \frac{27}{30} = \frac{36}{40} = \frac{45}{50}$$

$$\frac{3}{5} = \frac{6}{10} = \frac{9}{15} = \frac{12}{20} = \frac{15}{25} \qquad \frac{11}{12} = \frac{22}{24} = \frac{33}{36} = \frac{44}{48} = \frac{55}{60}$$

$$\frac{1}{6} = \frac{2}{12} = \frac{3}{18} = \frac{4}{24} = \frac{5}{30} \qquad \frac{4}{15} = \frac{8}{30} = \frac{12}{45} = \frac{16}{60} = \frac{20}{75}$$

TRY THESE

Subtract. Use the lists of equivalent fractions above.

1. $\frac{11}{12} - \frac{7}{9} = \blacksquare$ 2. $\frac{9}{10} - \frac{1}{6} = \blacksquare$ 3. $\frac{5}{3} - \frac{1}{6} = \blacksquare$

Use your own lists of equivalent fractions.

4. $\frac{5}{6} - \frac{8}{15} = \blacksquare$ 5. $\frac{2}{3} - \frac{5}{12} = \blacksquare$ 6. $\frac{9}{10} - \frac{1}{6} = \blacksquare$

252

SKILLS PRACTICE

Subtract. Use the lists of equivalent fractions on page 252.

1. $\dfrac{7}{9} - \dfrac{1}{6} = $ ▨

2. $\dfrac{5}{8} - \dfrac{3}{16} = $ ▨

3. $\dfrac{11}{12} - \dfrac{1}{6} = $ ▨

4. $\dfrac{5}{3} - \dfrac{3}{2} = $ ▨

5. $\dfrac{5}{3} - \dfrac{7}{9} = $ ▨

6. $\dfrac{9}{10} - \dfrac{1}{6} = $ ▨

7. $\dfrac{3}{2}$ $-\dfrac{1}{6}$

8. $\dfrac{9}{10}$ $-\dfrac{3}{5}$

9. $\dfrac{4}{15}$ $-\dfrac{1}{6}$

10. $\dfrac{7}{9}$ $-\dfrac{4}{15}$

11. $\dfrac{5}{3}$ $-\dfrac{11}{12}$

12. $\dfrac{3}{2}$ $-\dfrac{3}{5}$

Use your own lists of equivalent fractions.

13. $\dfrac{1}{2} - \dfrac{3}{10} = $ ▨

14. $\dfrac{5}{8} - \dfrac{5}{12} = $ ▨

15. $\dfrac{5}{3} - \dfrac{1}{6} = $ ▨

16. $\dfrac{4}{5} - \dfrac{6}{15} = $ ▨

17. $\dfrac{5}{3} - \dfrac{5}{9} = $ ▨

18. $\dfrac{7}{10} - \dfrac{1}{2} = $ ▨

19. $\dfrac{7}{9}$ $-\dfrac{5}{12}$

20. $\dfrac{3}{10}$ $-\dfrac{1}{6}$

21. $\dfrac{1}{4}$ $-\dfrac{1}{12}$

22. $\dfrac{11}{12}$ $-\dfrac{2}{3}$

23. $\dfrac{3}{4}$ $-\dfrac{7}{10}$

24. $\dfrac{7}{10}$ $-\dfrac{8}{15}$

PROBLEM SOLVING

25. Martha had $\dfrac{3}{5}$ of a box of pins. She used $\dfrac{4}{15}$ of the box to pin a suit pattern. What part of a box of pins was left?

26. Klaus had $\dfrac{1}{2}$ yd of red felt and $\dfrac{9}{10}$ yd of green felt. How much felt did he have in all?

★ 27. Jackie had $\dfrac{5}{3}$ ft of ribbon. She used $\dfrac{5}{12}$ ft to trim a jeans pocket. How much ribbon was left?

★ 28. Connie had to hem $\dfrac{5}{6}$ of her skirt. After sewing for 2 hours she still had to hem $\dfrac{3}{10}$ of the skirt. How much of the skirt did she hem?

Finding Parts of Numbers

A. Mrs. Jensen gathered 24 eggs.

$\frac{1}{4}$ of the eggs are brown.

How many brown eggs does she have?

$\frac{1}{4}$ of 24 is ▨   1 of 4 equal parts of 24

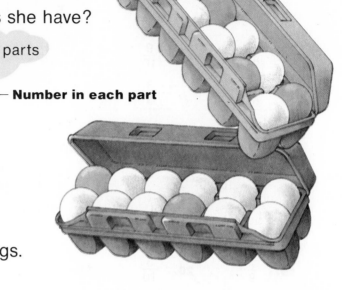

$$\begin{array}{r} 6 \leftarrow \textbf{Number in each part} \\ \textbf{Number of parts} \longrightarrow 4\overline{)24} \\ \underline{24} \\ 0 \end{array}$$

$\frac{1}{4}$ of 24 is 6.

Mrs. Jensen has 6 brown eggs.

B. Mrs. Jensen picked 21 pears.

$\frac{2}{3}$ of the pears were ripe.

How many ripe pears did she pick?

$\frac{2}{3}$ of 21 is ▨   2 of 3 equal parts of 21

Step 1. Divide by 3.

$$\begin{array}{r} 7 \\ 3\overline{)21} \\ \underline{21} \\ 0 \end{array}$$

in 1 of 3 equal parts

Step 2. Multiply by 2.

$$\begin{array}{r} 7 \\ \times 2 \\ \hline 14 \end{array}$$

in 2 of these parts

$\frac{2}{3}$ of 21 is 14.

She picked 14 ripe pears.

TRY THESE

Find:

1. $\frac{1}{2}$ of 16 **2.** $\frac{1}{4}$ of 12 **3.** $\frac{1}{5}$ of 30 **4.** $\frac{1}{8}$ of 40

5. $\frac{3}{5}$ of 15 **6.** $\frac{2}{3}$ of 27 **7.** $\frac{3}{4}$ of 36 **8.** $\frac{3}{8}$ of 32

SKILLS PRACTICE

Find:

1. $\frac{1}{3}$ of 18 **2.** $\frac{1}{2}$ of 40 **3.** $\frac{1}{4}$ of 28 **4.** $\frac{1}{8}$ of 32

5. $\frac{1}{5}$ of 20 **6.** $\frac{1}{6}$ of 42 **7.** $\frac{5}{9}$ of 27 **8.** $\frac{4}{7}$ of 21

9. $\frac{2}{5}$ of 25 **10.** $\frac{3}{8}$ of 32 **11.** $\frac{5}{6}$ of 42 **12.** $\frac{8}{9}$ of 45

PROBLEM SOLVING

13. Mr. Jensen has 16 horses. $\frac{1}{4}$ of them are brown. How many horses are brown?

14. There are 15 cats on the farm. $\frac{1}{3}$ of them are white. How many cats are white?

15. Mrs. Jensen sold some eggs and some milk for a total of $54. $\frac{2}{3}$ of the total was paid for the milk. How much was paid for the milk?

16. Mr. Jensen had 40 meters of fencing. He used $\frac{3}{4}$ of it to put a fence around a pen. How many meters of fencing did he use?

★17. Kathy Jensen travels 24 kilometers to school each day. She walks $\frac{1}{12}$ of the distance and rides the bus the rest of the way. How far does she walk? How far does she ride the bus?

★18. It took Mr. Jensen a total of 20 days to pick his corn and harvest his wheat. $\frac{3}{5}$ of this time was spent picking corn. For how many days did he pick corn? For how many days did he harvest wheat?

✓ Unit Checkup

Write a fraction for the red part of each object or set. *(pages 224–225)*

1.   2.   3.    4.

Give a mixed numeral or standard numeral for each. *(pages 226–229)*

5.

6. $\dfrac{22}{7}$

7. $\dfrac{8}{4}$

8. $5\overline{)33}$

9. $8\overline{)427}$

Complete to find a fraction equivalent to each. *(pages 230–233)*

10. $\dfrac{6}{8} = \dfrac{6 \div \blacksquare}{8 \div 2} = \dfrac{\blacksquare}{4}$

11. $\dfrac{25}{30} = \dfrac{25 \div 5}{30 \div \blacksquare} = \dfrac{\blacksquare}{\blacksquare}$

12. $\dfrac{16}{12} = \dfrac{16 \div \blacksquare}{12 \div 4} = \dfrac{\blacksquare}{\blacksquare}$

Give the lowest terms fraction for each. For 1 or greater, also give a mixed numeral or standard numeral. *(pages 234–235)*

13. $\dfrac{8}{12}$ 14. $\dfrac{5}{10}$ 15. $\dfrac{9}{6}$ 16. $\dfrac{45}{35}$ 17. $\dfrac{10}{2}$ 18. $\dfrac{9}{15}$

Add or subtract. *(pages 236–241)*

19. $\dfrac{3}{5} + \dfrac{1}{5} = \blacksquare$

20. $\dfrac{5}{2} - \dfrac{3}{2} = \blacksquare$

21. $\dfrac{5}{8} + \dfrac{6}{8} = \blacksquare$

22. $\dfrac{4}{9} + \dfrac{2}{9} = \blacksquare$

23. $\dfrac{7}{5} - \dfrac{4}{5} = \blacksquare$

24. $\dfrac{11}{4} - \dfrac{3}{4} = \blacksquare$

25. $\dfrac{2}{7}$ $+\dfrac{3}{7}$

26. $\dfrac{9}{15}$ $-\dfrac{3}{15}$

27. $\dfrac{8}{10}$ $-\dfrac{3}{10}$

28. $\dfrac{1}{3}$ $+\dfrac{4}{3}$

29. $\dfrac{7}{6}$ $-\dfrac{2}{6}$

30. $\dfrac{11}{8}$ $-\dfrac{1}{8}$

Multiply each numerator and denominator by 2, 3, 4, and 5 to find equivalent fractions. *(pages 246–247)*

31. $\dfrac{2}{3}$ 32. $\dfrac{1}{4}$ 33. $\dfrac{5}{3}$ 34. $\dfrac{3}{8}$ 35. $\dfrac{4}{5}$

$$\frac{5}{2} = \frac{10}{4} = \frac{15}{6} = \frac{20}{8} = \frac{25}{10}$$

$$\frac{1}{9} = \frac{2}{18} = \frac{3}{27} = \frac{4}{36} = \frac{5}{45}$$

$$\frac{4}{3} = \frac{8}{6} = \frac{12}{9} = \frac{16}{12} = \frac{20}{15}$$

$$\frac{7}{12} = \frac{14}{24} = \frac{21}{36} = \frac{28}{48} = \frac{35}{60}$$

$$\frac{5}{6} = \frac{10}{12} = \frac{15}{18} = \frac{20}{24} = \frac{25}{30}$$

$$\frac{8}{15} = \frac{16}{30} = \frac{24}{45} = \frac{32}{60} = \frac{40}{75}$$

In Exercises 36 to 51, use the lists of equivalent fractions above, or use your own lists.

Write >, <, or = for ●. *(pages 248–249)*

36. $\frac{5}{8}$ ● $\frac{3}{8}$ **37.** $\frac{5}{2}$ ● $\frac{4}{3}$ **38.** $\frac{7}{12}$ ● $\frac{5}{6}$ **39.** $\frac{2}{3}$ ● $\frac{7}{9}$

Add or subtract. *(pages 250–253)*

40. $\frac{1}{9} + \frac{4}{3} = $ ▨   **41.** $\frac{5}{6} - \frac{7}{12} = $ ▨   **42.** $\frac{4}{3} - \frac{5}{6} = $ ▨

43. $\frac{5}{6} + \frac{1}{9} = $ ▨   **44.** $\frac{5}{6} - \frac{8}{15} = $ ▨   **45.** $\frac{1}{9} + \frac{7}{12} = $ ▨

46. $\begin{array}{r} \frac{1}{2} \\ + \frac{3}{10} \\ \hline \end{array}$ **47.** $\begin{array}{r} \frac{7}{9} \\ - \frac{2}{3} \\ \hline \end{array}$ **48.** $\begin{array}{r} \frac{5}{6} \\ - \frac{3}{4} \\ \hline \end{array}$ **49.** $\begin{array}{r} \frac{1}{4} \\ + \frac{5}{12} \\ \hline \end{array}$ **50.** $\begin{array}{r} \frac{4}{9} \\ + \frac{1}{6} \\ \hline \end{array}$ **51.** $\begin{array}{r} \frac{2}{3} \\ - \frac{4}{15} \\ \hline \end{array}$

Find the parts. *(pages 254–255)*

52. $\frac{1}{5}$ of 15   **53.** $\frac{2}{3}$ of 21   **54.** $\frac{3}{8}$ of 40   **55.** $\frac{7}{9}$ of 54

Solve. Use the circle graph. *(pages 242–243)*

56. How much more of her allowance does Kim spend on entertainment than on clothing?

57. What part of her allowance in all does Kim spend on clothing or lunches?

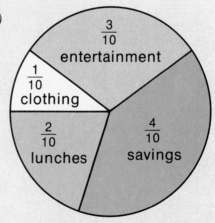

Reinforcement

More Help with Fractions

$\frac{1}{3}$ red part / parts in object

$\frac{3}{4}$ red objects / objects in set

Write a fraction for the red part of each.

1.
2.
3.
4.
5.
6.

$\frac{3}{2}$ or $1\frac{1}{2}$

$\frac{13}{5} \longrightarrow$ $5)\overline{13}$ $2\frac{3}{5}$ $\frac{10}{3}$

Give a mixed numeral or standard numeral for each.

7.
8.

9. $\frac{9}{5}$ 10. $\frac{13}{4}$ 11. $\frac{6}{3}$ 12. $\frac{16}{7}$

$\frac{2}{4}$

$+\frac{1}{4}$

$\overline{\frac{3}{4}}$

$7 - 2 = 5$

$\frac{7}{8} - \frac{2}{8} = \frac{5}{8}$

$2 + 1 = 3$

Add or subtract.

13. $\frac{4}{10} + \frac{5}{10} = $ ▦   14. $\frac{7}{6} - \frac{2}{6} = $ ▦

15. $\frac{8}{4} - \frac{3}{4} = $ ▦   16. $\frac{2}{7} + \frac{4}{7} = $ ▦

17. $\frac{8}{9}$ 18. $\frac{11}{3}$ 19. $\frac{8}{5}$ 20. $\frac{7}{11}$

    $+\frac{5}{9}$ $-\frac{4}{3}$ $-\frac{1}{5}$ $+\frac{2}{11}$

$\frac{3}{8} = \frac{3 \times 3}{8 \times 3} = \frac{9}{24}$

$\frac{14}{21} = \frac{14 \div 7}{21 \div 7} = \frac{2}{3}$

Multiply or divide to find a fraction equivalent to each.

21. $\frac{1}{6} = \frac{1 \times 4}{6 \times 4} = \frac{▦}{▦}$ 22. $\frac{3}{2} = \frac{3 \times 5}{2 \times ▦} = \frac{▦}{▦}$

23. $\frac{10}{12} = \frac{10 \div 2}{12 \div 2} = \frac{▦}{▦}$ 24. $\frac{6}{18} = \frac{6 \div 6}{18 \div ▦} = \frac{▦}{▦}$

Mental Arithmetic

Sometimes it is easy to add or subtract in your head. You may use methods that are different from those you learned for paper-and-pencil arithmetic.

A. Add. $39 + 63 =$ ▦

Think of 63 as $1 + 62$.

To add 63 to 39, add 1 and then add 62.

$$39 + 1 = 40 \rightarrow 40 + 62 = 102$$
$$39 + 63 = 102$$

Use mental arithmetic to add. Use the method above or one of your own.

1. $23 + 49 =$ ▦   2. $45 + 68 =$ ▦   3. $61 + 17 =$ ▦

4. $77 + 56 =$ ▦   5. $39 + 46 =$ ▦   6. $98 + 53 =$ ▦

7. $19 + 67 =$ ▦   8. $85 + 77 =$ ▦   9. $54 + 38 =$ ▦

B. Subtract. $96 - 29 =$ ▦

Think of 29 as near 30.

To subtract 29 from 96, subtract 30 and then add 1.

$$96 - 30 = 66 \rightarrow 66 + 1 = 67$$
$$96 - 29 = 67$$

Use mental arithmetic to subtract. Use the method above or one of your own.

10. $87 - 39 =$ ▦   11. $63 - 28 =$ ▦   12. $77 - 48 =$ ▦

13. $51 - 18 =$ ▦   14. $96 - 17 =$ ▦   15. $81 - 57 =$ ▦

16. $102 - 66 =$ ▦   17. $82 - 49 =$ ▦   18. $70 - 28 =$ ▦

Ask other students to show you the methods they used to answer **1–18**.

b Maintaining Skills

Choose the correct answer.

1.

a. 2:25

b. 2:05

c. 1:25

d. 2:27

2.

a. 5:08

b. 6:38

c. 5:40

d. 5:20

3.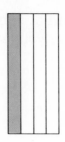

a. $\frac{3}{4}$ shaded

b. $\frac{1}{2}$ shaded

c. $\frac{1}{3}$ shaded

d. $\frac{1}{4}$ shaded

4.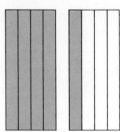

a. $\frac{5}{4}$ shaded

b. $\frac{3}{5}$ shaded

c. $\frac{5}{3}$ shaded

d. $\frac{5}{8}$ shaded

---

5. $\frac{3}{5} + \frac{1}{5} = $ ▨

a. $\frac{4}{10}$ b. $\frac{2}{5}$

c. $\frac{4}{5}$ d. 4

6. $\frac{5}{4} - \frac{2}{4} = $ ▨

a. $\frac{7}{4}$ b. 3

c. $\frac{3}{0}$ d. $\frac{3}{4}$

7. $\frac{3}{8} + \frac{4}{8} = $ ▨

a. $\frac{7}{8}$ b. $\frac{1}{8}$

c. $\frac{7}{16}$ d. 7

8. $\frac{5}{9} - \frac{1}{9} = $ ▨

a. 4   b. $\frac{5}{9}$

c. $\frac{4}{18}$ d. $\frac{4}{9}$

---

9.   7,362
      +5,279

a. 2,083
b. 12,541
c. 12,641
d. 13,641

10.   18,642
      − 7,956

a. 11,686
b. 10,686
c. 11,696
d. 26,598

11.   9,000
      −6,284

a. 3,826
b. 3,716
c. 3,284
d. 2,716

12. $75.62
      + 38.99

a. $113.62
b. $114.61
c. $ 36.63
d. $104.51

---

13. Jason just missed the 7:15 A.M. train. The next train was at 7:45 A.M. How long did Jason have to wait?

a. 30 minutes   b. 45 minutes

c. 60 minutes   d. 15 minutes

14. Kimberly swam $\frac{3}{6}$ mile and rested. Then she swam $\frac{4}{6}$ mile. How far did she swim all together?

a. $\frac{7}{12}$ mile   b. $\frac{6}{6}$ mile

c. $1\frac{1}{6}$ miles   d. $\frac{1}{6}$ mile

Multiplying by Tens and Ones **9**

Reviewing Multiplying by 1-digit Numbers

There are 4 apartment buildings.
Each building can hold 1,396 people.
How many people in all
can the buildings hold?

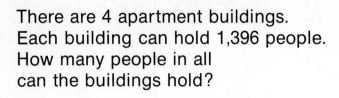

4 sets
1,396 in each set
Multiply to find how many in all.

Multiply ones.	Multiply tens.	Multiply hundreds.	Multiply thousands.
②	③②	①③②	①③②
1,39**6**	1,3**9**6	1,**3**96	**1**,396
× 4	× 4	× 4	× 4
4	84	584	5,584

The buildings can hold
5,584 people.

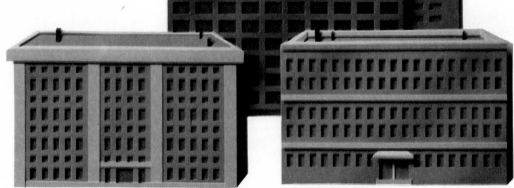

TRY THESE

Multiply.

1. 23
    × 4

2. 38
    × 7

3. 249
    × 3

4. 581
    × 6

5. 4,139
    × 2

6. 8,398
    × 9

7. 6 × 56 = ▨

8. 4 × 932 = ▨

9. 8 × 2,758 = ▨

SKILLS PRACTICE

Multiply.

1. 305
   × 6

2. 78
   × 3

3. 2,742
   × 4

4. 3,057
   × 8

5. 39
   × 5

6. 803
   × 2

7. 517
   × 7

8. 6,935
   × 0

9. 1,200
   × 5

10. 253
    × 7

11. 16
    × 8

12. 25
    × 6

13. 2,868
    × 4

14. 390
    × 1

15. 72
    × 7

16. 7,392
    × 9

17. 3,802
    × 3

18. 898
    × 2

19. 4,471
    × 6

20. 713
    × 3

21. 7,940
    × 8

22. 65
    × 7

23. 488
    × 5

24. 52
    × 9

25. 6,125
    × 3

26. 9,726
    × 6

27. 192
    × 4

28. 3,002
    × 7

29. 8
    ×94

30. 729
    × 9

31. $4 \times 6{,}114 = \blacksquare$

32. $7 \times 408 = \blacksquare$

33. $8 \times 62 = \blacksquare$

34. $9 \times 4{,}300 = \blacksquare$

35. $394 \times 5 = \blacksquare$

36. $9{,}285 \times 6 = \blacksquare$

PROBLEM SOLVING

37. The Stately Manor has 274 apartments. Each apartment has 4 rooms. How many rooms are there?

38. Another building has 352 apartments. Each apartment has 5 windows. How many windows are there in all the apartments?

39. 1,010 people live in the Astor. A family of 7 people moved out. How many people were left?

★ 40. 233 families live in the Winslow. 3 families moved out. Each of the families had 5 people. How many people moved out? How many families were left in the Winslow?

Multiplying by 10

A. Find 10 × 9.

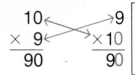

$$\begin{array}{r} 10 \\ \times\ 9 \\ \hline 90 \end{array} \qquad \begin{array}{r} 9 \\ \times 10 \\ \hline 90 \end{array}$$

When you change the order of the factors, you do not change the product.

B. Find 10 × 12.

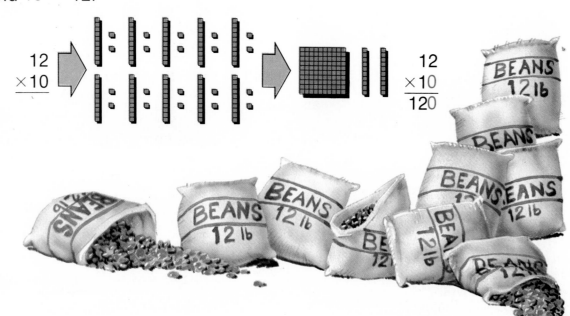

$$\begin{array}{r} 12 \\ \times 10 \end{array} \qquad \begin{array}{r} 12 \\ \times 10 \\ \hline 120 \end{array}$$

C. You can use this pattern to multiply *any number* by 10.

Write a 0. Write the other digits to the left.

$$\begin{array}{r} 6 \\ \times 10 \\ \hline 60 \end{array} \qquad \begin{array}{r} 24 \\ \times 10 \\ \hline 240 \end{array} \qquad \begin{array}{r} 475 \\ \times\ \ 10 \\ \hline 4{,}750 \end{array}$$

TRY THESE

Multiply. Use the pattern.

1. $\begin{array}{r} 6 \\ \times 10 \end{array}$ 2. $\begin{array}{r} 3 \\ \times 10 \end{array}$ 3. $\begin{array}{r} 95 \\ \times 10 \end{array}$ 4. $\begin{array}{r} 80 \\ \times 10 \end{array}$ 5. $\begin{array}{r} 235 \\ \times\ 10 \end{array}$ 6. $\begin{array}{r} 937 \\ \times\ 10 \end{array}$

7. 10 × 5 = ▨   8. 10 × 63 = ▨   9. 10 × 907 = ▨

SKILLS PRACTICE

Multiply. Use the pattern.

1. 151
   × 10

2. 70
   × 10

3. 516
   × 10

4. 289
   × 10

5. 810
   × 10

6. 971
   × 10

7. 805
   × 10

8. 17
   × 10

9. 620
   × 10

10. 43
    × 10

11. 682
    × 10

12. 743
    × 10

13. 81
    × 10

14. 100
    × 10

15. 1
    × 10

16. 29
    × 10

17. 10
    × 10

18. 427
    × 10

19. 73
    × 10

20. 546
    × 10

21. 302
    × 10

22. 49
    × 10

23. 243
    × 10

24. 56
    × 10

25. 79
    × 10

26. 450
    × 10

27. 983
    × 10

28. 63
    × 10

29. 347
    × 10

30. 90
    × 10

31. $10 \times 618 = $ ▧

32. $10 \times 37 = $ ▧

33. $10 \times 271 = $ ▧

34. $10 \times 75 = $ ▧

35. $10 \times 111 = $ ▧

36. $10 \times 909 = $ ▧

PROBLEM SOLVING

37. Mrs. Layton is opening a restaurant. She bought 10 bags of beans. The mass of each bag was 940 grams. How many grams of beans did she buy?

38. Each bag of beans cost $3. She bought 10 bags. How much money did she spend?

★ 39. Mrs. Layton bought 10 dozen eggs. How many eggs did she buy?

★ 40. Mrs. Layton used 2 bags of beans to cook 3 pots of bean soup. She could fill 10 bowls from each pot. How many bowls could she fill?

Multiplying by Multiples of 10

A. The supply clerk ordered 20 boxes of pens. There were 64 pens in each box. How many pens did he order?

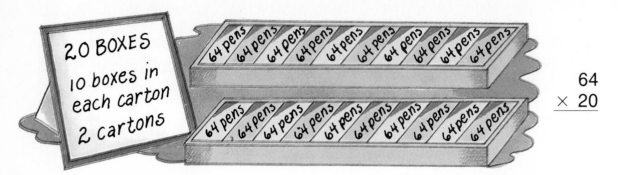

$$\begin{array}{r} 64 \\ \times\ 20 \end{array}$$

To find 20 × 64:

Pens in one carton of 10 boxes

$$\begin{array}{r} 64 \\ \times\ 10 \\ \hline 640 \end{array}$$ pens in 10 boxes

Pens in two cartons of 10 boxes

$$\begin{array}{r} 640 \\ \times\ \ \ 2 \\ \hline 1{,}280 \end{array}$$ pens in 20 boxes

He ordered 1,280 pens.

B. You can use this shortcut to find 20 × 64.

First, write **0** to show you are multiplying by 10.   **then**   **Multiply 64 by 2.**

$$\begin{array}{r} 64 \\ \times\ 20 \\ \hline 0 \end{array} \qquad \begin{array}{r} 64 \\ \times\ 20 \\ \hline 1{,}280 \end{array}$$

TRY THESE _____

Multiply.

1. $\begin{array}{r} 79 \\ \times\ 10 \\ \hline \end{array}$

2. $\begin{array}{r} 360 \\ \times\ \ 20 \\ \hline \end{array}$

3. $\begin{array}{r} 48 \\ \times\ 50 \\ \hline \end{array}$

4. $\begin{array}{r} 201 \\ \times\ \ 30 \\ \hline \end{array}$

5. $40 \times 120 = $ ▢

6. $50 \times 82 = $ ▢

Multiply.

1. $\begin{array}{r} 92 \\ \times\ 50 \\ \hline \end{array}$	2. $\begin{array}{r} 210 \\ \times\ 10 \\ \hline \end{array}$	3. $\begin{array}{r} 600 \\ \times\ 80 \\ \hline \end{array}$	4. $\begin{array}{r} 400 \\ \times\ 50 \\ \hline \end{array}$	5. $\begin{array}{r} 55 \\ \times\ 20 \\ \hline \end{array}$	6. $\begin{array}{r} 398 \\ \times\ 10 \\ \hline \end{array}$
7. $\begin{array}{r} 33 \\ \times 30 \\ \hline \end{array}$	8. $\begin{array}{r} 212 \\ \times\ 40 \\ \hline \end{array}$	9. $\begin{array}{r} 13 \\ \times 20 \\ \hline \end{array}$	10. $\begin{array}{r} 10 \\ \times 30 \\ \hline \end{array}$	11. $\begin{array}{r} 312 \\ \times\ 90 \\ \hline \end{array}$	12. $\begin{array}{r} 41 \\ \times 80 \\ \hline \end{array}$
13. $\begin{array}{r} 221 \\ \times\ 60 \\ \hline \end{array}$	14. $\begin{array}{r} 84 \\ \times 20 \\ \hline \end{array}$	15. $\begin{array}{r} 721 \\ \times\ 60 \\ \hline \end{array}$	16. $\begin{array}{r} 200 \\ \times\ 90 \\ \hline \end{array}$	17. $\begin{array}{r} 806 \\ \times\ 30 \\ \hline \end{array}$	18. $\begin{array}{r} 57 \\ \times 40 \\ \hline \end{array}$
19. $\begin{array}{r} 587 \\ \times\ 70 \\ \hline \end{array}$	20. $\begin{array}{r} 111 \\ \times\ 50 \\ \hline \end{array}$	21. $\begin{array}{r} 593 \\ \times\ 80 \\ \hline \end{array}$	22. $\begin{array}{r} 119 \\ \times\ 70 \\ \hline \end{array}$	23. $\begin{array}{r} 343 \\ \times\ 20 \\ \hline \end{array}$	24. $\begin{array}{r} 668 \\ \times\ 10 \\ \hline \end{array}$
25. $\begin{array}{r} 60 \\ \times 60 \\ \hline \end{array}$	26. $\begin{array}{r} 289 \\ \times\ 90 \\ \hline \end{array}$	27. $\begin{array}{r} 484 \\ \times\ 10 \\ \hline \end{array}$	28. $\begin{array}{r} 720 \\ \times\ 50 \\ \hline \end{array}$	29. $\begin{array}{r} 46 \\ \times 70 \\ \hline \end{array}$	30. $\begin{array}{r} 327 \\ \times\ 30 \\ \hline \end{array}$

31. $50 \times 500 =$ ▧

32. $80 \times 49 =$ ▧

33. $30 \times 88 =$ ▧

34. $60 \times 935 =$ ▧

35. $10 \times 779 =$ ▧

36. $80 \times 264 =$ ▧

PROBLEM SOLVING

37. The supply clerk ordered 40 boxes of paper clips. There were 128 paper clips in each box. How many paper clips did he order?

38. There were 125 boxes of staples. One of the secretaries took 10 boxes of staples. How many boxes were left?

39. The Super Supply Company sent 50 boxes of thumbtacks. Each box contained 675 thumbtacks. How many thumbtacks did it send?

★40. The Super Supply Company also sent 3 cartons of tape. Each carton contained 40 rolls of masking tape and 60 rolls of clear tape. How many rolls were in each carton?

Multiplying by 2-digit Numbers

A. 21 boxes of oranges were sold at the farmer's market. There were 43 oranges in each box. How many oranges were sold?

In 1 box:
1 × 43

```
  43
 ×21
  43  ← 1 × 43
```

In 20 boxes:
20 × 43

```
  43
 ×21
  43  ← 1 × 43
 860  ← 20 × 43
```

In 21 boxes:
43 + 860

```
  43
 ×21
  43  ← 1 × 43
 860  ← 20 × 43
 903  ← 21 × 43
```

903 oranges were sold.

B. Find the product of 34 and 52.

Step 1
Multiply by 4.

```
  52
 ×34
 208  ← 4 × 52
```

Step 2
Multiply by 30.

```
  52
 ×34
 208  ← 4 × 52
1560  ← 30 × 52
```

Step 3
Add.

```
   52
  ×34
  208  ← 4 × 52
1 560  ← 30 × 52
1,768  ← 34 × 52
```

TRY THESE _____

Find the missing numbers.

1.
```
  33
 ×23
  99  ← ▦ × 33
 660  ← ▦ × 33
 759  ← ▦ × 33
```

2.
```
   82
  ×42
  164  ← ▦ × ▦
3 280  ← ▦ × ▦
3,444  ← ▦ × ▦
```

SKILLS PRACTICE

Multiply.

1. 52
   ×24

2. 94
   ×12

3. 81
   ×18

4. 73
   ×13

5. 71
   ×78

6. 93
   ×13

7. 84
   ×22

8. 71
   ×43

9. 11
   ×23

10. 21
    ×52

11. 83
    ×30

12. 92
    ×12

13. 44
    ×22

14. 63
    ×33

15. 51
    ×87

16. 61
    ×46

17. 73
    ×33

18. 62
    ×14

19. 60
    ×25

20. 42
    ×33

21. 52
    ×42

22. 92
    ×43

23. 31
    ×76

24. 82
    ×34

25. 10
    ×37

26. 81
    ×45

27. 32
    ×23

28. 41
    ×88

29. 93
    ×31

30. 91
    ×91

31. 41 × 72 = ▦

32. 14 × 72 = ▦

33. 24 × 22 = ▦

34. 31 × 21 = ▦

35. 11 × 69 = ▦

36. 44 × 52 = ▦

PROBLEM SOLVING

Follow the instructions.

	Record
Start with 14.	14
Multiply by 12.	168
37. Subtract 147.	▦
38. Multiply by 35.	▦
39. Add 162.	▦

	Record
Start with 28.	28
40. Multiply by 40.	▦
41. Subtract 672.	▦
42. Divide by 8.	▦
43. Multiply by 11.	▦

Upside-down answers 1. 1,248 31. 2,952

Workbook page 437

269

Saving in One Step

A. Eli collects science magazines.
He has 13 piles of magazines.
25 science magazines are in each pile.
How many magazines does he have?

Mark out your saves before you multiply again.

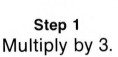

Step 1
Multiply by 3.

①
25
×13
75

Step 2
Multiply by 10.

⊗
25
×13
75
250

Step 3
Add.

⊗
25
×13
75
250
325

He has 325 science magazines.

B. Find the product of 82 and 74.

Step 1

74
×82
148

Step 2

③
74
×82
148
5920

Step 3

③
74
×82
148
5 920
6,068

TRY THESE

Multiply.

1. 22
×48

2. 54
×29

3. 11
×75

4. 87
×31

5. 68
×17

6. 92
×84

7. 61 × 85 = ▧

8. 19 × 54 = ▧

9. 38 × 63 = ▧

Multiply.

1. 24 ×28	**2.** 13 ×63	**3.** 79 ×16	**4.** 68 ×71	**5.** 84 ×82	**6.** 69 ×18
7. 53 ×53	**8.** 12 ×36	**9.** 79 ×91	**10.** 27 ×10	**11.** 34 ×31	**12.** 88 ×18
13. 64 ×62	**14.** 92 ×23	**15.** 59 ×17	**16.** 14 ×29	**17.** 98 ×40	**18.** 60 ×56
19. 32 ×64	**20.** 83 ×83	**21.** 22 ×38	**22.** 14 ×92	**23.** 42 ×46	**24.** 41 ×77
25. 74 ×26	**26.** 31 ×35	**27.** 78 ×19	**28.** 63 ×52	**29.** 60 ×99	**30.** 40 ×90

31. $11 \times 57 =$ ▨

32. $19 \times 76 =$ ▨

33. $74 \times 92 =$ ▨

34. $32 \times 61 =$ ▨

35. $12 \times 88 =$ ▨

36. $81 \times 87 =$ ▨

PROBLEM SOLVING

37. Each student collected 75 old newspapers. There were 18 students in the class. How many newspapers did the class collect?

★ **38.** Each class collected 45 cans and 25 bottles. There were 16 classes in the school. How many cans did the whole school collect?

EXTRA! Using a Pattern

$11 \times 1 = 11$ $11 \times 11 = 121$ $11 \times 111 = 1,221$

What do you think these products will be?

$11 \times 1,111 =$ ▨ $11 \times 11,111 =$ ▨

Workbook   page 437

Saving in Two Steps

A. There are 54 classrooms in the school.
There are 27 students in each classroom.
How many students are in the school?

Step 1
Multiply by 4.

②
27
×54
‾‾‾‾
108

Mark out
your saves
before you
multiply again.

Step 2
Multiply by 50.

③
⊗
27
×54
‾‾‾‾
108
1350

Step 3
Add.

③
⊗
27
×54
‾‾‾‾
108
1 350
‾‾‾‾‾
1,458

There are 1,458 students in the school.

B. Each package of paper costs $.86.
What is the total cost of 72 packages?

72 sets of $.86

Step 1
Multiply by 2.

①
$ .86
× 72
‾‾‾‾‾
172

Step 2
Multiply by 70.

④
⊗
$ .86
× 72
‾‾‾‾‾
172
6020

Step 3
Add.

④
⊗
$ .86
× 72
‾‾‾‾‾
172
6020
‾‾‾‾‾
$ 61.92
↑ ↑

Remember the dollar sign
and point.

72 packages cost $61.92.

Find each product. Then estimate to check your product.

1. 79
   ×52

2. 16 × 83 = ▦

3. $ 62
   ×98

4. 34
   ×64

5. $ .55
   × 45

SKILLS PRACTICE

Multiply.

1. 46
   ×68

2. 16
   ×23

3. 54
   ×75

4. 45
   ×32

5. 62
   ×57

6. 24
   ×98

7. $51
   ×91

8. 83
   ×14

9. 35
   ×26

10. 19
    ×41

11. $76
    ×10

12. 25
    ×95

13. $ .79
    × 47

14. 53
    ×90

15. 82
    ×70

16. 80
    ×34

17. 42
    ×67

18. $ .31
    × 89

19. 97
    ×12

20. 61
    ×36

21. 55
    ×84

22. $77
    ×33

23. 20
    ×80

24. $ .15
    × 96

25. 56 × 55 = ▦

26. 85 × $63 = ▦

27. 44 × $ .76 = ▦

PROBLEM SOLVING

28. The school bought 50 chairs for $23 each. How much was spent for chairs?

29. Each pad has 64 sheets of paper. How many sheets of paper in 72 pads?

ⓐ Maintaining Skills

Write a fraction for the red part of each.

1.

2.

3.

4.

5.

6.

Add or subtract.

7. $\begin{array}{r} 39 \\ +58 \\ \hline \end{array}$

8. $\begin{array}{r} 61 \\ -43 \\ \hline \end{array}$

9. $\begin{array}{r} 537 \\ +684 \\ \hline \end{array}$

10. $\begin{array}{r} 3{,}478 \\ +5{,}329 \\ \hline \end{array}$

11. $\begin{array}{r} 7{,}352 \\ -6{,}298 \\ \hline \end{array}$

Add.

12. $\frac{2}{8} + \frac{3}{8} =$ ▦

13. $\frac{1}{5} + \frac{2}{5} =$ ▦

14. $\frac{3}{7} + \frac{5}{7} =$ ▦

15. $\begin{array}{r} \frac{6}{10} \\ +\frac{7}{10} \\ \hline \end{array}$

16. $\begin{array}{r} \frac{2}{13} \\ +\frac{22}{13} \\ \hline \end{array}$

17. $\begin{array}{r} \frac{18}{4} \\ +\frac{3}{4} \\ \hline \end{array}$

18. $\begin{array}{r} \frac{3}{6} \\ +\frac{0}{6} \\ \hline \end{array}$

19. $\begin{array}{r} \frac{5}{15} \\ +\frac{13}{15} \\ \hline \end{array}$

20. $\begin{array}{r} \frac{16}{12} \\ +\frac{8}{12} \\ \hline \end{array}$

Subtract.

21. $\frac{3}{4} - \frac{1}{4} =$ ▦

22. $\frac{7}{6} - \frac{3}{6} =$ ▦

23. $\frac{13}{10} - \frac{10}{10} =$ ▦

24. $\begin{array}{r} \frac{8}{16} \\ -\frac{4}{16} \\ \hline \end{array}$

25. $\begin{array}{r} \frac{9}{12} \\ -\frac{4}{12} \\ \hline \end{array}$

26. $\begin{array}{r} \frac{8}{6} \\ -\frac{1}{6} \\ \hline \end{array}$

27. $\begin{array}{r} \frac{5}{4} \\ -\frac{5}{4} \\ \hline \end{array}$

28. $\begin{array}{r} \frac{21}{11} \\ -\frac{12}{11} \\ \hline \end{array}$

29. $\begin{array}{r} \frac{16}{9} \\ -\frac{2}{9} \\ \hline \end{array}$

Solve the problems.

30. Sara had $\frac{5}{4}$ of a box of oranges. She gave away $\frac{1}{4}$ of a box. How many boxes were left?

31. Sam had $\frac{3}{7}$ of a roll of stamps. Jim had $\frac{6}{7}$ of a roll. How many rolls of stamps did they have in all?

Project: Calling Long Distance

The amount you will be charged for a long-distance telephone call depends on when you make the call. It is most expensive to call during the **day**. It costs less to call during the **evening**. It costs even less if you call late at **night**.

This table shows the cost of some calls made from New York. Notice that you are charged more for the first minute of your call.

Call from New York to:	day 8:00 A.M. to 5:00 P.M.		evening 5:00 P.M. to 11:00 P.M.		night 11:00 P.M. to 8:00 A.M.	
	first minute	each minute more	first minute	each minute more	first minute	each minute more
Chicago	$.50	$.34	$.32	$.22	$.20	$.13
Houston	.52	.36	.33	.23	.20	.14
Los Angeles	.54	.38	.35	.24	.21	.15

Tina called from New York to Houston at 7:00 P.M. She talked for 8 minutes. How much will she be charged?

Cost for first minute	Cost for next 7 minutes	Total Cost
$.33	$ .23 $\times$ 7 $1.61	$ .33 + 1.61 $1.94

Tina will be charged $1.94.

Each of the following calls was made from New York. Find the cost of each call.

1. An 8 minute call to Chicago made at 9:00 A.M.
2. An 8 minute call to Chicago made at 7:00 P.M.
3. An 11 minute call to Los Angeles made at midnight.

Use your telephone book. Pick a city and find the cost of a 7-minute call at 8:00 P.M. Find the cost of this 7-minute call at 2:00 P.M.

A telephone **operator** is the person who can help you make your calls. How do you dial to get the operator? What will the operator do if you want to make a person-to-person call?

275

Multiplying Larger Numbers

46 postal workers work in the post office.
Each worker sorted 534 letters.
How many letters did they sort in all?

Step 1	**Step 2**	**Step 3**
Multiply by 6.	Multiply by 40.	Add.

Step 1
```
  ②②
  534
×  46
 3204
```

Mark out your saves before you multiply again.

Step 2
```
  ①①
  ⊗⊗
  534
×  46
 3204
21360
```

Step 3
```
  ①①
  ⊗⊗
   534
×   46
  3204
 21360
 24,564
```

They sorted 24,564 letters in all.

TRY THESE

Multiply.

1. 959
    × 54

2. 706
    × 65

3. 363
    × 74

4. 640
    × 84

5. 33 × 158 = ▨

6. 75 × 824 = ▨

SKILLS PRACTICE

1. 188
   × 25

2. 543
   × 57

3. 369
   × 94

4. 375
   × 42

5. 802
   × 95

6. 833
   × 49

7. 422
   × 68

8. 909
   × 46

9. 340
   × 56

10. 913
    × 79

11. 188
    × 66

12. 470
    × 44

13. 289
    × 82

14. 113
    × 37

15. 427
    × 61

16. 809
    × 59

17. 741
    × 23

18. 904
    × 75

19. 333
    × 85

20. 800
    × 31

21. 713
    × 45

22. 289
    × 72

23. 914
    × 55

24. 340
    × 46

25. 959
    × 29

26. 740
    × 62

27. 960
    × 21

28. 400
    × 30

29. 843
    × 76

30. 320
    × 49

31. 75 × 500 = ▨

32. 87 × 605 = ▨

33. 49 × 421 = ▨

34. 35 × 524 = ▨

35. 40 × 739 = ▨

36. 58 × 685 = ▨

PROBLEM SOLVING

37. One postal worker sent 45 books. Stamps for each cost 85¢. How much money should the postal worker have collected?

38. 983 letters arrived at the post office. 57 of them did not have stamps. The rest of the letters had stamps. How many letters had stamps?

39. 16 mail trucks left the post office. Each truck carried 25 bags of mail. How many bags of mail did the trucks carry?

★40. Mrs. Lorell bought 15 books of stamps. Each book had 24 stamps. She used 200 of the stamps to mail invitations. How many stamps did she buy?

Workbook   page 438

Upside-down answers   1. 4,700   31. 37,500

Estimating Products

You can use estimation to find a number that is near the exact product of two numbers.

A. Use three steps to estimate a product.

   1. Circle the first digit of each factor.

$$\begin{array}{r} ④56 \\ \times \ ⑦2 \end{array}$$

   2. Round each factor to the circled place.

$$\begin{array}{r} ④56 \longrightarrow 500 \\ \times \ ⑦2 \longrightarrow 70 \end{array}$$

   3. Multiply the rounded factors to get the estimate.

$$\begin{array}{r} 500 \\ \times \quad 70 \\ \hline 35{,}000 \end{array}$$

35,000 is an estimate of 72 × 456.

B. Estimate the products.

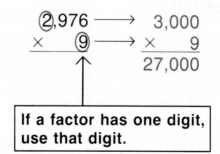

$$\begin{array}{r} \$⑧2 \longrightarrow \$.80 \\ \times \ ②8 \longrightarrow \times \ 30 \\ \hline \$24.00 \end{array}$$

$$\begin{array}{r} ②,976 \longrightarrow 3{,}000 \\ \times \quad ⑨ \longrightarrow \times \quad 9 \\ \hline 27{,}000 \end{array}$$

If a factor has one digit, use that digit.

C. Estimation can be used to check exact products. If your product is near the estimate your answer is reasonable.

Exact product	Estimate

$$\begin{array}{r} ⑧43 \\ \times \ ⑥8 \\ \hline 57{,}324 \end{array} \qquad \begin{array}{r} 800 \\ \times \quad 70 \\ \hline 56{,}000 \end{array}$$

57,324 is near 56,000. The answer is reasonable.

TRY THESE

Find each product. Then estimate to check your product.

1. 621
   × 8

2. 78
   ×42

3. 380
   × 26

4. 1,289
   × 3

5. $2.16
   × 4

SKILLS PRACTICE

Find each product. Then estimate to check your product.

1. 75
  × 3

2. 909
  × 5

3. 750
  × 3

4. 34
  × 7

5. 560
  × 2

6. 2,820
  × 9

7. 822
  × 56

8. 129
  × 28

9. 32
  ×57

10. 549
  × 39

11. 607
  × 14

12. 179
  × 20

13. $2.35
  × 4

14. $1.43
  × 2

15. $2.05
  × 17

16. $5.84
  × 23

17. $6.61
  × 24

18. $1.84
  × 66

Estimate. Watch the signs.

19. 86
  ×11

20. 582
  +914

21. 3,532
  − 444

22. 30
  ×36

23. 747
  ×6,294

24. 5,643
  −1,651

25. 954
  × 53

26. 862
  − 94

27. 3,581
  +3,482

28. 2,680
  × 16

29. 1,840
  + 275

30. 76,674
  −22,700

31. $29.32
  + 8.96

32. $6.14
  × 8

33. $582.07
  − 271.79

EXTRA! Looking for a Pattern

Mrs. Katz offered Marty a job for 20 days. She would pay him 1¢ for the first day, 2¢ for the second day, 4¢ for the third day, 8¢ for the fourth day, and so on. How much would Marty get on the twentieth day?

Upside-down answers   **1.** 225; 3 × 80 = 270   **13.** $9.40   **19.** 900

Workbook   page 439

279

Problem Solving: Order Forms

To complete an **order form,** fill in one line at a time. Make sure you fill in all the information asked for.

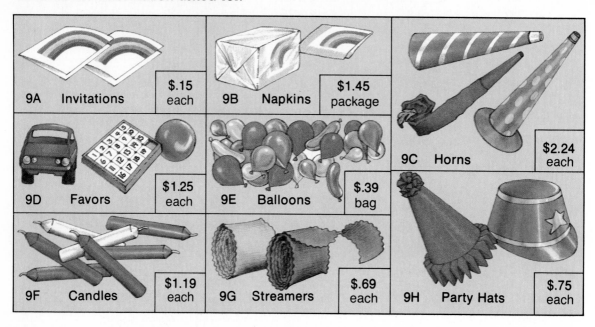

9A Invitations	$.15 each	9B Napkins	$1.45 package	9C Horns	$2.24 each
9D Favors	$1.25 each	9E Balloons	$.39 bag		
9F Candles	$1.19 each	9G Streamers	$.69 each	9H Party Hats	$.75 each

Item No. The number shown by the item.

Description The name of the item.

Quantity The number of items being ordered.

Price The price of the item.

Total Price = Quantity × Price

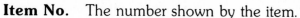

ITEM NO.	DESCRIPTION	QUANTITY	PRICE	TOTAL PRICE
9A	Invitations	12	$ .15	$ 1.80
9B	Napkins	1	1.45	1.45
9E	Balloons	3	.39	1.17
9G	Streamers	8	.69	5.52
9H	Party Hats	12	.75	9.00
			TOTAL PRICE OF ORDER ⟹	$ 18.94

Total Price of Order The sum of the amounts in the Total Price column.

Copy and complete this order form.

	ITEM NO.	DESCRIPTION	QUANTITY	PRICE		TOTAL PRICE	
1.	9B	Napkins	2	$ 1.	45	$	
2.	9C	Horns	10	2.	24		
3.	9D	Favors	2				
4.	9F	Candles	16				
5.	9G	Streamers	5				
6.			TOTAL PRICE OF ORDER ⇨			$	

PROBLEM SOLVING PRACTICE

Copy and complete each order form.

	ITEM NO.	DESCRIPTION	QUANTITY	PRICE		TOTAL PRICE	
1.	9A	Invitations	8	$	15	$	
2.	9E	Balloons	2				
3.	9F	Candles	25				
4.	9H	Party Hats	8				
5.			TOTAL PRICE OF ORDER ⇨			$	

	ITEM NO.	DESCRIPTION	QUANTITY	PRICE		TOTAL PRICE	
6.	9C	Horns	6	$		$	
7.	9D	Favors	5				
8.	9E	Balloons	1				
9.	9G		4				
10.	9H		9				
11.			TOTAL PRICE OF ORDER ⇨			$	

★ **12.** What other information might be asked for in an order form?

✓ Unit Checkup

Multiply. *(pages 264–267)*

1. 38
×10

2. 56
×10

3. 481
× 10

4. 718
× 10

5. 30
×10

6. 902
× 10

7. 560
× 20

8. 252
× 50

9. 73
×40

10. 674
× 70

11. 150
× 10

12. 86
×60

13. $90 \times 500 = $ ▦

14. $80 \times 409 = $ ▦

15. $10 \times 49 = $ ▦

16. $60 \times 36 = $ ▦

17. $60 \times 360 = $ ▦

18. $40 \times 617 = $ ▦

Multiply. *(pages 268–273)*

19. 22
×31

20. 52
×41

21. 13
×33

22. 83
×21

23. 64
×72

24. 49
×17

25. 34
×41

26. 79
×19

27. 63
×63

28. 47
×52

29. 84
×56

30. 75
×25

31. $74 \times 18 = $ ▦

32. $90 \times 63 = $ ▦

33. $27 \times 27 = $ ▦

34. $96 \times 80 = $ ▦

35. $14 \times 56 = $ ▦

36. $69 \times 53 = $ ▦

Multiply. *(pages 276–279)*

37. 418
× 31

38. 304
× 62

39. 730
× 43

40. 865
× 91

41. 482
× 51

42. 786
× 25

43. 223
× 47

44. 693
× 78

45. 536
× 36

46. 879
× 38

47. 157
× 59

48. 210
× 63

49. $29 \times 712 = $ ▦

50. $907 \times 11 = $ ▦

51. $375 \times 22 = $ ▦

52. $623 \times 99 = $ ▦

53. $101 \times 34 = $ ▦

54. $955 \times 45 = $ ▦

Estimate each product. *(pages 278–279)*

55. 32
×27

56. 85
×49

57. 38
×52

58. 69
×19

59. 73
×85

60. 51
×53

61. 732
× 91

62. 403
× 86

63. 192
× 14

64. 287
× 26

65. 501
× 33

66. 647
× 50

67. 93 × 48 = ▨

68. 84 × 52 = ▨

69. 89 × 695 = ▨

70. 29 × 730 = ▨

71. 55 × 71 = ▨

72. 60 × 800 = ▨

Solve the problems. *(pages 262–273, 276–281)*

73. The hardware store had 73 boxes of nails. 150 nails were in each box. How many nails were in the store?

74. The hardware store sold 45 packages of screwdrivers. 13 screwdrivers were in each package. How many screwdrivers were sold?

75. Amy bought a box of 125 bolts. She already had 28 bolts at home. How many bolts did she have all together?

76. 132 boxes of fuses were on the shelf. Each box contained 12 fuses. How many fuses were on the shelf?

Use the catalog page. Copy and complete this order form. *(pages 280–281)*

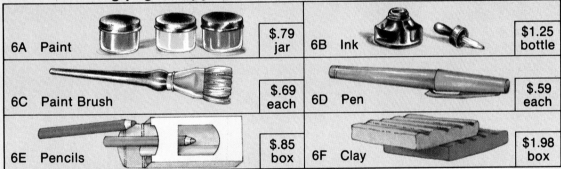

6A	Paint		$.79 jar	6B	Ink		$1.25 bottle
6C	Paint Brush		$.69 each	6D	Pen		$.59 each
6E	Pencils		$.85 box	6F	Clay		$1.98 box

	ITEM NO.	DESCRIPTION	QUANTITY	PRICE	TOTAL PRICE
77.	6A		8	$.	$.
78.	6C		5	.	.
79.		Pen	10	.	.
80.		Clay	6	.	.
81.				TOTAL PRICE OF ORDER	$.

Reinforcement

More Help with Multiplication

Multiply.

$$
\begin{array}{r}
① \\
251 \\
\times\ 30 \\
\hline
7{,}530
\end{array}
$$

1. $\begin{array}{r} 45 \\ \times 10 \\ \hline \end{array}$
2. $\begin{array}{r} 69 \\ \times 10 \\ \hline \end{array}$
3. $\begin{array}{r} 232 \\ \times\ 10 \\ \hline \end{array}$
4. $\begin{array}{r} 856 \\ \times\ 10 \\ \hline \end{array}$

5. $\begin{array}{r} 13 \\ \times 20 \\ \hline \end{array}$
6. $\begin{array}{r} 74 \\ \times 50 \\ \hline \end{array}$
7. $\begin{array}{r} 539 \\ \times\ 80 \\ \hline \end{array}$
8. $\begin{array}{r} 611 \\ \times\ 40 \\ \hline \end{array}$

9. $70 \times 25 =$ ▧
10. $90 \times 408 =$ ▧

$$
\begin{array}{r}
432 \\
\times\ 33 \\
\hline
1296 \\
12960 \\
\hline
14{,}256
\end{array}
\quad
\begin{array}{l}
\leftarrow \boxed{3 \times 432} \\
\leftarrow \boxed{30 \times 432} \\
\leftarrow \boxed{33 \times 432}
\end{array}
$$

11. $\begin{array}{r} 31 \\ \times 14 \\ \hline \end{array}$
12. $\begin{array}{r} 62 \\ \times 24 \\ \hline \end{array}$
13. $\begin{array}{r} 96 \\ \times 11 \\ \hline \end{array}$
14. $\begin{array}{r} 73 \\ \times 83 \\ \hline \end{array}$

15. $\begin{array}{r} 230 \\ \times\ 32 \\ \hline \end{array}$
16. $\begin{array}{r} 801 \\ \times\ 59 \\ \hline \end{array}$
17. $\begin{array}{r} 623 \\ \times\ 13 \\ \hline \end{array}$
18. $\begin{array}{r} 904 \\ \times\ 21 \\ \hline \end{array}$

19. $31 \times 18 =$ ▧
20. $43 \times 710 =$ ▧

$$
\begin{array}{r}
②① \\
143 \\
\times\ 52 \\
\hline
286 \\
7150 \\
\hline
7{,}436
\end{array}
\quad
\begin{array}{l}
\leftarrow \boxed{2 \times 143} \\
\leftarrow \boxed{50 \times 143} \\
\leftarrow \boxed{52 \times 143}
\end{array}
$$

21. $\begin{array}{r} 67 \\ \times 41 \\ \hline \end{array}$
22. $\begin{array}{r} 18 \\ \times 17 \\ \hline \end{array}$
23. $\begin{array}{r} 53 \\ \times 43 \\ \hline \end{array}$
24. $\begin{array}{r} 702 \\ \times\ 64 \\ \hline \end{array}$

25. $\begin{array}{r} 358 \\ \times\ 61 \\ \hline \end{array}$
26. $\begin{array}{r} 613 \\ \times\ 34 \\ \hline \end{array}$
27. $\begin{array}{r} 273 \\ \times\ 51 \\ \hline \end{array}$
28. $\begin{array}{r} 607 \\ \times\ 19 \\ \hline \end{array}$

29. $12 \times 39 =$ ▧
30. $52 \times 94 =$ ▧

$$
\begin{array}{r}
②① \\
⊛⊠ \\
563 \\
\times\ 47 \\
\hline
3941 \\
22520 \\
\hline
26{,}461
\end{array}
\quad
\begin{array}{l}
\leftarrow \boxed{7 \times 563} \\
\leftarrow \boxed{40 \times 563} \\
\leftarrow \boxed{47 \times 563}
\end{array}
$$

31. $\begin{array}{r} 62 \\ \times 53 \\ \hline \end{array}$
32. $\begin{array}{r} 78 \\ \times 95 \\ \hline \end{array}$
33. $\begin{array}{r} 38 \\ \times 22 \\ \hline \end{array}$
34. $\begin{array}{r} 46 \\ \times 24 \\ \hline \end{array}$

35. $\begin{array}{r} 382 \\ \times\ 25 \\ \hline \end{array}$
36. $\begin{array}{r} 694 \\ \times\ 57 \\ \hline \end{array}$
37. $\begin{array}{r} 286 \\ \times\ 49 \\ \hline \end{array}$
38. $\begin{array}{r} 815 \\ \times\ 66 \\ \hline \end{array}$

39. $32 \times 87 =$ ▧
40. $98 \times 145 =$ ▧

More Mental Arithmetic

Sometimes you can solve problems without writing them down.
You can do them in your head.

A. To find the cost of 4 records at $5.98 each,
think $5.98 = $6.00 − $.02

If the records had cost $6.00 each,

$$4 \times \$6.00 = \$24.00$$

But you save $.02 on each record,

$$4 \times \$.02 = \$.08$$

$$\$24.00 - \$.08 = \$23.92$$

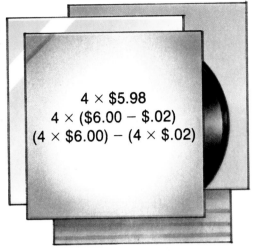

$4 \times \$5.98$
$4 \times (\$6.00 - \$.02)$
$(4 \times \$6.00) - (4 \times \$.02)$

B. To find the cost of 8 tapes at $7.09 each,
think $7.09 = $7.00 + $.09

If the tapes had cost $7.00 each,

$$8 \times \$7.00 = \$56.00$$

But you spend $.09 more on each record,

$$8 \times \$.09 = \$.72$$

$$\$56.00 + \$.72 = \$56.72$$

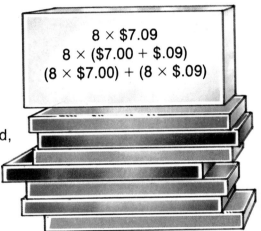

$8 \times \$7.09$
$8 \times (\$7.00 + \$.09)$
$(8 \times \$7.00) + (8 \times \$.09)$

Use the easy way to find these products.

1. $8 \times 42 = $ ▨

2. $7 \times 29 = $ ▨

3. $6 \times 98 = $ ▨

4. $9 \times 204 = $ ▨

5. $5 \times 488 = $ ▨

6. $4 \times 310 = $ ▨

7. $11 \times 71 = $ ▨

8. $12 \times 103 = $ ▨

9. $7 \times \$9.99 = $ ▨

10. $8 \times \$2.05 = $ ▨

11. $6 \times \$1.90 = $ ▨

12. $9 \times \$7.80 = $ ▨

b Maintaining Skills

Choose the correct answer.

1. 42
  −28

  a. 24
  b. 14
  c. 16
  d. not above

2. 769
  −384

  a. 385
  b. 425
  c. 479
  d. not above

3. 308
  − 74

  a. 224
  b. 238
  c. 334
  d. not above

4. 5,000
  −2,602

  a. 3,398
  b. 2,398
  c. 2,499
  d. not above

5. 3)68

  a. 24 R3
  b. 13
  c. 22 R2
  d. not above

6. 6)84

  a. 14 R2
  b. 24
  c. 15
  d. not above

7. 4)328

  a. 107
  b. 87 R5
  c. 82
  d. not above

8. 7)765

  a. 790 R2
  b. 109 R2
  c. 190 R3
  d. not above

9. 98
  ×61

  a. 5,978
  b. 686
  c. 4,592
  d. not above

10. 85
  ×48

  a. 1,020
  b. 4,080
  c. 4,045
  d. not above

11. 405
  × 23

  a. 2,025
  b. 9,310
  c. 9,205
  d. not above

12. 659
  × 78

  a. 51,402
  b. 49,302
  c. 9,885
  d. not above

13. The factory shipped 38 boxes of paper cups. 480 cups were in each box. How many cups did they ship?

  a. 4,280 cups
  b. 184,840 cups
  c. 18,240 cups
  d. not above

14. The machine put 375 spoons into 5 bags. It put the same number in each bag. How many spoons did it put in each bag?

  a. 75 spoons
  b. 60 spoons
  c. 125 spoons
  d. not above

Dividing by Tens and Ones 10

Reviewing 1-Digit Divisors

A. The Basic Book Company shipped 416 books in 8 boxes. The same number of books were in each box. How many books were in each box?

8)416   8 > 4   Not enough hundreds. Start by dividing the 41 tens.

Step 1
Divide the 41 tens.

Think: ▩ × 8 = 41
Use **5**.

```
    5
8)416
  40
   1
```

Step 2
Divide the 16 ones.

Think: ▩ × 8 = 16
Use **2**.

```
   52
8)416
  40
  16
  16
   0
```

There were 52 books in each box.

B. Find 6)6,045.

```
  1,007 R3
6)6,045
  6
  0 0
    0
    04
     0
     45
     42
      3
```

Be sure to write 0's in the quotient for these steps.

Check
```
      ④
    1,007
  ×     6
    6 042
  +     3
    6,045 ✓
```

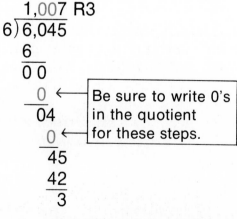

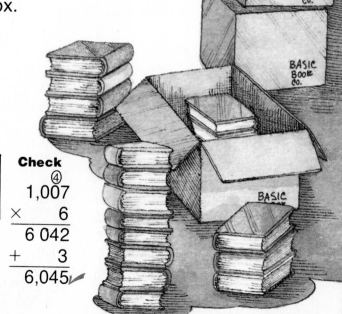

288   **Dividing by Tens and Ones**

TRY THESE

Divide. Check your answers.

1. $3\overline{)85}$
2. $5\overline{)892}$
3. $4\overline{)360}$
4. $6\overline{)2,355}$
5. $4\overline{)7,973}$

6. $600 \div 8 = $ ▨
7. $198 \div 6 = $ ▨
8. $2,612 \div 4 = $ ▨

SKILLS PRACTICE

Divide.

1. $8\overline{)93}$
2. $2\overline{)81}$
3. $5\overline{)860}$
4. $9\overline{)3,512}$
5. $4\overline{)50}$

6. $1\overline{)70}$
7. $4\overline{)5,404}$
8. $4\overline{)432}$
9. $3\overline{)53}$
10. $8\overline{)8,751}$

11. $3\overline{)622}$
12. $6\overline{)92}$
13. $8\overline{)2,440}$
14. $9\overline{)607}$
15. $3\overline{)84}$

16. $7\overline{)5,001}$
17. $4\overline{)313}$
18. $9\overline{)4,305}$
19. $6\overline{)50}$
20. $3\overline{)200}$

21. $567 \div 9 = $ ▨
22. $612 \div 3 = $ ▨
23. $6,588 \div 9 = $ ▨

24. $8,382 \div 2 = $ ▨
25. $108 \div 6 = $ ▨
26. $3,812 \div 4 = $ ▨

PROBLEM SOLVING

27. A company printed 8,000 magazines. They loaded the same number of magazines on each of 3 trucks. How many magazines could they load on each truck? How many magazines would be left over?

28. A stock clerk had to pack 162 books. He could put 8 books in each box. How many boxes could he fill? How many books would be left over?

29. The bookstore had 108 racks on the wall. 9 comic books were in each rack. How many comic books were on the wall?

★ 30. On June 7, 110 copies of the fourth-grade newspaper were printed. Each of 3 classes received the same number of copies. What is the greatest number of copies each class could receive? How many copies would be left over?

Dividing by Multiples of 10

A. Find $30\overline{)628}$.

Not enough hundreds.
Start by dividing the 62 tens.

Step 1
Divide the 62 tens.

Think: ▓ × 30 = 62
     2 × 30 = 60
     3 × 30 = 90 Too big!
Use **2**.

$$\begin{array}{r} 2 \\ 30\overline{)628} \\ \underline{60} \\ 2 \end{array}$$

Step 2
Divide the 28 ones.

Think: ▓ × 30 = 28
     1 × 30 = 30 Too big!
Use **0**.

$$\begin{array}{r} 20\ \text{R}28 \\ 30\overline{)628} \\ \underline{60} \\ 28 \\ \underline{0} \\ 28 \end{array}$$

B. Find $60\overline{)271}$.

60 > 2   Not enough hundreds.
60 > 27   Not enough tens.

Divide the 271 ones.

Think: ▓ × 60 = 271
Use **4**.

$$\begin{array}{r} 4\ \text{R}31 \\ 60\overline{)271} \\ \underline{240} \\ 31 \end{array}$$

TRY THESE

Divide. Check your answers.

1. $40\overline{)90}$ 2. $70\overline{)890}$ 3. $10\overline{)806}$ 4. $60\overline{)408}$ 5. $30\overline{)600}$

6. 480 ÷ 80 = ▓   7. 180 ÷ 30 = ▓   8. 840 ÷ 70 = ▓

SKILLS PRACTICE

Divide.

1. $10\overline{)72}$ 2. $40\overline{)200}$ 3. $50\overline{)96}$ 4. $80\overline{)952}$ 5. $60\overline{)685}$

6. $20\overline{)112}$ 7. $30\overline{)289}$ 8. $40\overline{)300}$ 9. $90\overline{)350}$ 10. $10\overline{)302}$

11. $40\overline{)92}$ 12. $30\overline{)85}$ 13. $20\overline{)484}$ 14. $50\overline{)627}$ 15. $70\overline{)463}$

16. $90\overline{)323}$ 17. $50\overline{)401}$ 18. $20\overline{)600}$ 19. $30\overline{)990}$ 20. $80\overline{)80}$

21. $40\overline{)591}$ 22. $10\overline{)25}$ 23. $60\overline{)151}$ 24. $70\overline{)565}$ 25. $90\overline{)729}$

26. $960 \div 80 = $ ▧   27. $240 \div 60 = $ ▧   28. $620 \div 10 = $ ▧

29. $960 \div 60 = $ ▧   30. $600 \div 40 = $ ▧   31. $450 \div 50 = $ ▧

PROBLEM SOLVING

32. Mike had a rope 93 meters long. He cut it into pieces which were 20 meters long. How many 20-meter pieces did he have? How much rope was left over?

33. Stan is tying up the tomato plants in his garden. It takes 30 centimeters of string to tie up each plant. He has 27 plants. How much string does he need?

34. Betty has 450 centimeters of string. She wants to use the same amount of string to tie up 10 bean plants. What is the most string she can use to tie each plant?

★ 35. At the farmer's market there are 6 fruit stands. Each stand has 25 bins. How many bins are there? Each bin can hold 4 baskets of fruit. How many baskets of fruit can all the bins hold?

Using Tables of Multiples

This table shows some multiples of 13. It will help you divide by 13.

In each step, use the largest multiple of 13 that you can.

$13 \times 0 = 0$	$13 \times 1 = 13$	$13 \times 2 = 26$	$13 \times 3 = 39$	$13 \times 4 = 52$
$13 \times 5 = 65$	$13 \times 6 = 78$	$13 \times 7 = 91$	$13 \times 8 = 104$	$13 \times 9 = 117$

A. Find $13\overline{)585}$.

Step 1

Divide the 58 tens.

Think:

■ × 13 = 58
5 × 13 is too big.
Use **4**.

$$\begin{array}{r} 4 \\ 13\overline{)585} \\ 52 \\ \hline 6 \end{array}$$

Step 2

Divide the 65 ones.

Think:

■ × 13 = 65
5 × 13 is just right.
Use **5**.

$$\begin{array}{r} 45 \\ 13\overline{)585} \\ 52 \\ \hline 65 \\ 65 \\ \hline 0 \end{array}$$

B. Find $13\overline{)107}$.

Divide the 107 ones.

Think:

■ × 13 = 107
Use **8**.

$$\begin{array}{r} 8\ R3 \\ 13\overline{)107} \\ 104 \\ \hline 3 \end{array}$$

1. Make a table that shows the products 0×21 to 9×21.

Use the table you have just made to help you divide.

2. $21\overline{)420}$ **3.** $21\overline{)548}$ **4.** $21\overline{)385}$ **5.** $21\overline{)409}$ **6.** $21\overline{)75}$

7. $735 \div 21 = $ ▨   **8.** $882 \div 21 = $ ▨   **9.** $966 \div 21 = $ ▨

SKILLS PRACTICE

Use the tables of multiples for 13 and 21 to help you divide.

1. $13\overline{)715}$ **2.** $21\overline{)210}$ **3.** $13\overline{)42}$ **4.** $21\overline{)812}$ **5.** $13\overline{)960}$

6. $21\overline{)96}$ **7.** $13\overline{)70}$ **8.** $21\overline{)756}$ **9.** $13\overline{)140}$ **10.** $13\overline{)450}$

11. $21\overline{)300}$ **12.** $13\overline{)533}$ **13.** $21\overline{)666}$ **14.** $13\overline{)700}$ **15.** $21\overline{)903}$

16. $21\overline{)600}$ **17.** $13\overline{)125}$ **18.** $21\overline{)99}$ **19.** $21\overline{)680}$ **20.** $13\overline{)50}$

21. $13\overline{)884}$ **22.** $13\overline{)157}$ **23.** $21\overline{)342}$ **24.** $21\overline{)702}$ **25.** $13\overline{)993}$

26. $231 \div 21 = $ ▨   **27.** $234 \div 13 = $ ▨   **28.** $357 \div 21 = $ ▨

29. $988 \div 13 = $ ▨   **30.** $624 \div 13 = $ ▨   **31.** $84 \div 21 = $ ▨

PROBLEM SOLVING

32. Jefferson Elementary School had 338 fourth graders. The principal wanted to form 13 fourth-grade classes of the same size. How many students would be in each class?

★ **33.** Jackson Elementary School has 21 classrooms, 590 desks, and 697 chairs. The same number of desks are put in each classroom. How many desks can be put in each classroom? How many desks will be left over?

a Maintaining Skills

Multiply.

1. 5
    ×7

2. 8
    ×4

3. 9
    ×9

4. 7
    ×5

5. 6
    ×6

6. 47
    × 5

7. 50
    × 8

8. 93
    × 7

9. 20
    × 5

10. 35
     × 4

11. 155
     × 3

12. 452
     × 4

13. 265
     × 8

14. 117
     × 6

15. 338
     × 9

16. 2,148
     × 2

17. 3,165
     × 4

18. 1,397
     × 7

19. 4,032
     × 5

20. 5,184
     × 6

21. 34
     ×10

22. 49
     ×30

23. 62
     ×43

24. 395
     × 17

25. 648
     × 25

Round to the nearest ten.

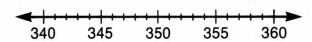

26. 341   27. 358   28. 345   29. 353   30. 355

Add, subtract, or multiply.

31. 6,842
     +4,179

32. 43
     ×27

33. 68
     +95

34. 873
     − 95

35. 11,642
     − 3,955

36. 45
     ×10

37. 5,832
     +7,609

38. 86,279
     − 5,899

39. 175
     × 28

40. 76,841
     +23,795

Solve the problems.

41. A DC-6 carries 58 passengers. A DC-7 carries 95. How many passengers can the two airplanes carry?

42. 56 people are traveling by plane. Each person has 20 kilograms of baggage. What is the total mass of the baggage?

294   **Dividing by Tens and Ones**

Project: Using Line Graphs

A *line graph* is used to show information. This line graph shows the average temperature for each month in Philadelphia, Pennsylvania.

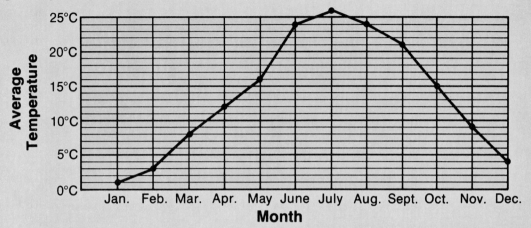

1. What month has the highest average temperature?

2. What month has the lowest average temperature?

3. What is the average temperature in May?

4. What is the average temperature in November?

5. Is the average temperature higher in April or October?

6. In which month is the average temperature 4°C?

Keep a record for a week of the highest temperature each day for your city or town. A newspaper or weather report can help you. Draw a line graph to show your results.

Use a different color and keep a record of the lowest temperature each day for your city or town.

295

Rounding the Divisor

Rounding 2-digit divisors to the nearest ten can help you find quotients.

A. Find $17\overline{)65}$.

> **Round 17 up to 20.**

Divide the 65 ones.

Think:
$\blacksquare \times 20 = 65$
$2 \times 20 = 40$
$3 \times 20 = 60$
$4 \times 20 = 80$ Too big!
  Try 3.

Do:

$$\begin{array}{r} 17 \\ \times\ 3 \\ \hline 51 \end{array} \rightarrow \begin{array}{r} 17 \\ \times\ 4 \\ \hline 68 \end{array}$$

$68 > 65$
Use 3.

$$\begin{array}{r} 3\ \text{R}14 \\ 17\overline{)65} \\ \underline{51} \\ 14 \end{array}$$

B. Find $34\overline{)857}$.

> **Round 34 down to 30.**

Step 1 Divide the 85 tens.

Think:
$\blacksquare \times 30 = 85$
$2 \times 30 = 60$
$3 \times 30 = 90$ Too big!
  Try 2.

Step 2 Divide the 177 ones.

Do:

$$\begin{array}{r} 34 \\ \times\ 2 \\ \hline 68 \end{array}$$

$68 < 85$
Use 2.

$$\begin{array}{r} 2\ \ \\ 34\overline{)857} \\ \underline{68} \\ 17 \end{array}$$

Think:
$\blacksquare \times 30 = 177$
$5 \times 30 = 150$
$6 \times 30 = 180$ Too big!
      Try 5.

Do:

$$\begin{array}{r} 34 \\ \times\ 5 \\ \hline 170 \end{array}$$

$170 < 177$
Use 5.

$$\begin{array}{r} 25\ \text{R}7 \\ 34\overline{)857} \\ \underline{68}\ \ \\ 177 \\ \underline{170} \\ 7 \end{array}$$

TRY THESE

Divide. Check your answers.

1. $36\overline{)825}$ 2. $47\overline{)687}$ 3. $52\overline{)763}$ 4. $24\overline{)480}$ 5. $38\overline{)81}$

6. $88 \div 11 = \blacksquare$ 7. $434 \div 62 = \blacksquare$ 8. $575 \div 23 = \blacksquare$

SKILLS PRACTICE

Divide.

1. $16\overline{)64}$ 2. $39\overline{)698}$ 3. $41\overline{)987}$ 4. $37\overline{)989}$ 5. $54\overline{)630}$

6. $44\overline{)908}$ 7. $28\overline{)498}$ 8. $42\overline{)84}$ 9. $34\overline{)785}$ 10. $59\overline{)789}$

11. $43\overline{)870}$ 12. $31\overline{)954}$ 13. $18\overline{)628}$ 14. $11\overline{)89}$ 15. $78\overline{)957}$

16. $61\overline{)978}$ 17. $22\overline{)444}$ 18. $46\overline{)866}$ 19. $23\overline{)578}$ 20. $56\overline{)800}$

21. $24\overline{)555}$ 22. $14\overline{)294}$ 23. $22\overline{)222}$ 24. $83\overline{)997}$ 25. $35\overline{)84}$

26. $990 \div 33 = \blacksquare$ 27. $816 \div 34 = \blacksquare$ 28. $588 \div 21 = \blacksquare$

29. $984 \div 41 = \blacksquare$ 30. $273 \div 13 = \blacksquare$ 31. $901 \div 53 = \blacksquare$

PROBLEM SOLVING

32. A collector paid $800 for 32 coins. He paid the same amount for each coin. What was the price of each coin?

33. A ship sank carrying 147 bags of old coins. A diver found 44 bags. How many bags have not been found?

34. Ricardo has 289 rare stamps. He can put 22 stamps on each page of his album. How many pages can he fill? How many stamps will be left over?

★35. Mrs. Stevens can pack 6 plates in each box. There are 92 plates in her collection. How many boxes can she fill? How many boxes does she need to pack all of her plates?

EXTRA! Drawing Figures

A building set contains 72 rods and 40 connectors.

rod ——— connector ○

How many of each figure can be made from the set?

a.   b.

Trial Quotients: Rounding Up

When rounding up, the first number
you try may be too small.

PARTS

Steering Wheels
Head Lights
Motor Oil

Eastern Auto Store has 992 spark plugs.
There are 16 spark plugs in each box.
How many boxes of spark plugs does the
store have?

Find 16)992. **Round 16 up to 20.**

Step 1
Divide the 99 tens.

Think:	*Do:*	16	16	16	16	6
▦ × 20 = 99		× 4 →	× 5 →	× 6 →	× 7	16)992
Try 4.		64	80	96	112	96
						3

112 > 99
Use 6.

Step 2
Divide the 32 ones.

Think:	*Do:*	16	16	62
▦ × 20 = 32		× 1 →	× 2	16)992
Try 1.		16	32	96
				32
				32
				0

32 = 32
Use 2.

The store has 62 boxes of spark plugs.

Divide. Check your answers.

1. $18\overline{)94}$
2. $35\overline{)762}$
3. $57\overline{)500}$
4. $16\overline{)984}$
5. $49\overline{)348}$

6. $90 \div 15 = $ ▨
7. $780 \div 65 = $ ▨
8. $688 \div 86 = $ ▨

SKILLS PRACTICE

Divide.

1. $56\overline{)478}$
2. $25\overline{)80}$
3. $26\overline{)910}$
4. $47\overline{)240}$
5. $26\overline{)184}$

6. $67\overline{)938}$
7. $45\overline{)328}$
8. $26\overline{)364}$
9. $28\overline{)84}$
10. $15\overline{)654}$

11. $76\overline{)555}$
12. $8\overline{)196}$
13. $36\overline{)76}$
14. $65\overline{)276}$
15. $87\overline{)509}$

16. $35\overline{)291}$
17. $86\overline{)360}$
18. $16\overline{)583}$
19. $37\overline{)690}$
20. $45\overline{)96}$

21. $56\overline{)359}$
22. $26\overline{)891}$
23. $26\overline{)209}$
24. $15\overline{)138}$
25. $27\overline{)531}$

26. $984 \div 8 = $ ▨
27. $352 \div 88 = $ ▨
28. $912 \div 38 = $ ▨

PROBLEM SOLVING

29. Mr. Williams owns a garage. He wants to buy 96 headlights. There are 12 headlights in a box. How many boxes should he buy?

30. Mr. Williams has $125. Each case of oil costs $26. How many cases can he buy? How much money will he have left?

31. Levine's Auto Parts has 62 boxes of spark plugs. 16 spark plugs are in each box. How many spark plugs do they have?

★32. Levine's Auto Parts had 130 steering wheels in 13 different colors. They sold 46 wheels. How many did they have left?

Trial Quotients: Rounding Down

When rounding down, the first number you try may be too big.

Mr. Russo has 896 silver links.
He wants to make 14 necklaces with the same number of links in each.
How many links can be in each necklace?

Find 14)896.

Round 14 down to 10.

Step 1
Divide the 89 tens.

Think:
▓ × 10 = 89
Try 8.

Do: 14 → 14 → 14
       × 8   × 7   × 6
      ───   ───   ───
      112   98   84

84 < 89
Use 6.

$$
\begin{array}{r}
6 \\
14\overline{)896} \\
84 \\
\hline
5
\end{array}
$$

Step 2
Divide the 56 ones.

Think:
▓ × 10 = 56
Try 5.

Do: 14 → 14
       × 5   × 4
      ───   ───
       70   56

56 = 56
Use 4.

$$
\begin{array}{r}
64 \\
14\overline{)896} \\
84 \\
\hline
56 \\
56 \\
\hline
0
\end{array}
$$

There can be 64 silver links in each necklace.

TRY THESE

Divide. Check your answers.

1. 14)45   2. 24)165   3. 32)891   4. 53)880   5. 41)800

6. 81 ÷ 27 = ▓   7. 828 ÷ 23 = ▓   8. 918 ÷ 34 = ▓

SKILLS PRACTICE

Divide

1. 34)925
2. 12)97
3. 22)583
4. 24)930
5. 42)331

6. 23)666
7. 84)700
8. 64)307
9. 14)86
10. 30)600

11. 82)735
12. 12)720
13. 31)96
14. 13)90
15. 23)206

16. 14)810
17. 43)375
18. 86)909
19. 74)928
20. 51)756

21. 91)368
22. 24)852
23. 72)960
24. 33)625
25. 44)361

26. $968 \div 11 =$ ■
27. $882 \div 9 =$ ■
28. $780 \div 30 =$ ■

PROBLEM SOLVING

29. Mr. Russo has 153 pairs of earrings in his jewelry store. He can fit 24 pairs of earrings on each stand. How many stands can he fill? How many pairs will be left over?

30. Mr. Russo had a sale on one type of gold necklace. He sold 34 necklaces for a total of $748. What was the sale price of each necklace?

31. Mr. Russo gave each of 32 employees a bracelet as a holiday gift. He now has 168 bracelets left. How many bracelets did he have before he gave out the gifts?

★32. Mr. Russo received 2 boxes of watches, with 192 watches in each box. How many watches did he receive? He wants to put 64 watches in each display case. How many cases can he fill?

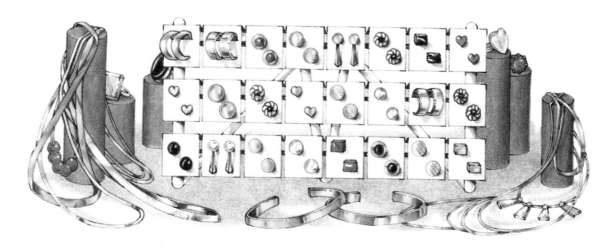

Changing Customary Units

Sometimes you need to change the unit used in the report of a measure. The facts shown in this table will help you.

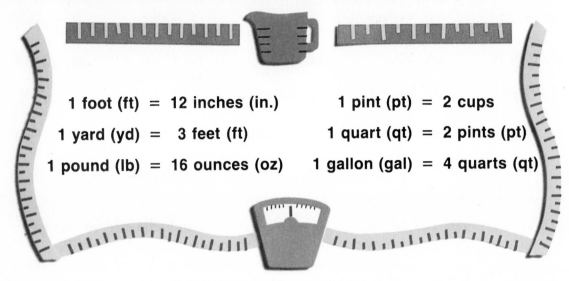

1 foot (ft) = 12 inches (in.)   1 pint (pt) = 2 cups

1 yard (yd) = 3 feet (ft)   1 quart (qt) = 2 pints (pt)

1 pound (lb) = 16 ounces (oz)   1 gallon (gal) = 4 quarts (qt)

To replace a larger unit by a smaller unit, you can multiply.

A. 5 ft is how many inches?

| 1 ft = 12 in. |

5 ft ←→ 5 sets of 12 in.

5 × 12 = 60
5 ft = 60 in.

B. 7 gal is how many quarts?

| 1 gal = 4 qt |

7 gal ←→ 7 sets of 4 qt

7 × 4 = 28
7 gal = 28 qt

To replace a smaller unit by a larger unit, you can divide.

C. 10 cups is how many pints?

| 1 pt = 2 cups |

How many sets of 2 cups in 10 cups?

10 ÷ 2 = 5
10 cups = 5 pt

D. 64 oz is how many pounds?

| 1 lb = 16 oz |

How many sets of 16 oz in 64 oz?

64 ÷ 16 = 4
64 oz = 4 lb

TRY THESE

Multiply to find the missing numbers.

1. 5 lb = ▓ oz   **2.** 9 pt = ▓ cups   **3.** 3 gal = ▓ qt

Divide to find the missing numbers.

4. 10 pt = ▓ qt   **5.** 156 in. = ▓ ft   **6.** 30 ft = ▓ yd

SKILLS PRACTICE

Find the missing numbers.

1. 5 yd = ▓ ft   **2.** 8 cups = ▓ pt   **3.** 3 lb = ▓ oz

4. 44 qt = ▓ gal   **5.** 40 pt = ▓ qt   **6.** 7 ft = ▓ in.

7. 9 yd = ▓ ft   **8.** 16 gal = ▓ qt   **9.** 24 cups = ▓ pt

10. 18 pt = ▓ qt   **★11.** 8 ft 9 in. = ▓ in.   **★12.** 100 oz = ▓ lb ▓ oz

PROBLEM SOLVING

13. 144 oz is how many pounds?

14. 6 qt is how many pints?

15. 7 pt is how many cups?

16. 180 in. is how many feet?

17. The rug in Shawna's room is 6 ft long. How many inches long is the rug?

18. Cam's family used 20 qt of milk last week. How many gallons of milk did they use?

★19. A turkey weighed 14 lb 5 oz. What was its weight in ounces?

★20. Jack rode his bicycle 4 miles on Saturday. How many feet did he ride? (Hint: 1 mile = 1,760 yards)

EXTRA! Making Logical Choices

Three people wanted to cross the river from St. Paul to Minneapolis. They had only one boat that would carry 300 lb. One person weighed 190 lb, another weighed 160 lb, and the third weighed 140 lb. How could they use the boat to cross the river?

Workbook   page 442

Problem Solving: Comparison Shopping

A. Frozen orange juice costs 42¢ per can or 3 cans for $1.23.
Find the cost per can for the 3 cans.
Which is the better buy?

To find the cost per
can for the 3 cans,
divide.

$.41 is the cost per can.

$$
\begin{array}{r}
\$\,.41 \\
3)\overline{\$1.23} \\
\underline{12} \\
03 \\
\underline{3} \\
0
\end{array}
$$

To find the better buy, compare.

$.41 is less than $.42

3 cans for $1.23 is the better buy.

Per means for each.

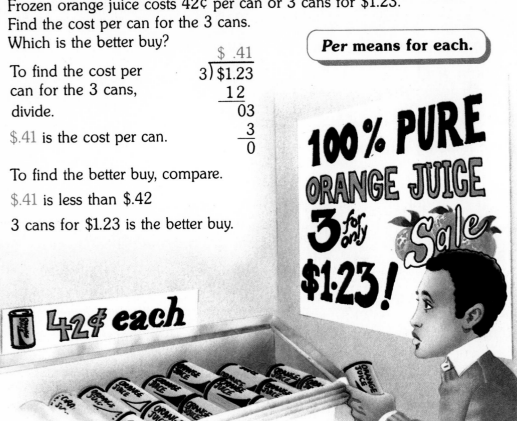

100% PURE ORANGE JUICE 3 for only $1·23! Sale

42¢ each

B. Boxes of cereal cost $1.04 for 8 oz, $1.32 for 12 oz, and $1.92 for
16 oz. Find the cost per ounce for each. Which is the best buy?

To find the cost per ounce
of each, divide.

8 oz	**12 oz**	**16 oz**

$$
\begin{array}{r}
\$\,.13 \\
8)\overline{\$1.04} \\
\underline{8} \\
24 \\
\underline{24} \\
0
\end{array}
\qquad
\begin{array}{r}
\$\,.11 \\
12)\overline{\$1.32} \\
\underline{12} \\
12 \\
\underline{12} \\
0
\end{array}
\qquad
\begin{array}{r}
\$\,.12 \\
16)\overline{\$1.92} \\
\underline{16} \\
32 \\
\underline{32} \\
0
\end{array}
$$

The costs per ounce are $.13, $.11, and $.12.

To find the best buy, compare.

$.11 per ounce is the lowest price. The 12-oz size is the best buy.

TRY THESE

Find the prices per box. Which is the better buy?

1. 29¢ per box
or 5 boxes for $1.55

2. 78¢ per box
or 4 boxes for $3.04

3. 2 boxes for $1.62
or 3 boxes for $2.46

Find the prices per pound. Which is the best buy?

4. 6 lb for $1.44,
10 lb for $2.60,
or 14 lb for $3.50

5. 3 lb for $3.51
4 lb for $4.60
or 5 lb for $5.80

6. 5 lb for 60¢,
10 lb for $1.10,
or 25 lb for $2.50

PROBLEM SOLVING PRACTICE

Find the prices per jar. Which is the better buy?

1. 35¢ per jar
or 6 jars for $2.04

2. 23¢ per jar
or 2 jars for 42¢

3. 19¢ per jar
or 8 jars for $1.68

4. 5 jars for $2.30
or 7 jars for $3.01

5. 28¢ per jar
or 10 jars for $2.70

6. 4 jars for $1.52
or 9 jars for $3.51

Find the prices per ounce. Which is the best buy?

7. 7 oz for $1.54,
13 oz for $2.60,
or 18 oz for $3.24

8. 2 oz for $1.34,
4 oz for $2.64,
or 10 oz for $6.70

9. 20 oz for $7.40,
24 oz for $8.64,
or 28 oz for $9.80

10. 6 oz for $4.20,
10 oz for $6.90,
or 14 oz for $9.38

11. 16 oz for $2.08,
32 oz for $4.80,
or 48 oz for $6.72

★**12.** 9 oz for $2.70,
25 oz for $8.00,
or 33 oz for $9.90

Solve the problems.

13. The grocery store sells cheddar cheese at 8 oz for $1.36, or 16 oz for $2.56. Find the prices per ounce. Which is the better buy?

14. The grocery sells nuts at 2 lb for $1.98, 5 lb for $4.85, or 10 lb for $9.80. Find the prices per pound. Which is the better buy?

✓ Unit Checkup

Divide. *(pages 290–291)*

1. $10\overline{)36}$ 2. $30\overline{)478}$ 3. $60\overline{)292}$ 4. $40\overline{)96}$ 5. $50\overline{)186}$

6. $60\overline{)850}$ 7. $80\overline{)746}$ 8. $30\overline{)80}$ 9. $20\overline{)180}$ 10. $10\overline{)70}$

11. $90\overline{)665}$ 12. $70\overline{)520}$ 13. $40\overline{)719}$ 14. $60\overline{)780}$ 15. $90\overline{)493}$

16. $30\overline{)480}$ 17. $50\overline{)683}$ 18. $70\overline{)600}$ 19. $20\overline{)534}$ 20. $90\overline{)910}$

21. $940 \div 20 = $ ▦   22. $800 \div 50 = $ ▦   23. $560 \div 70 = $ ▦

24. $420 \div 30 = $ ▦   25. $360 \div 90 = $ ▦   26. $900 \div 60 = $ ▦

Divide. *(pages 296–301)*

27. $35\overline{)782}$ 28. $48\overline{)578}$ 29. $43\overline{)704}$ 30. $24\overline{)74}$ 31. $37\overline{)855}$

32. $56\overline{)904}$ 33. $25\overline{)75}$ 34. $23\overline{)466}$ 35. $12\overline{)386}$ 36. $27\overline{)597}$

37. $33\overline{)84}$ 38. $48\overline{)975}$ 39. $57\overline{)744}$ 40. $11\overline{)78}$ 41. $44\overline{)892}$

42. $38\overline{)812}$ 43. $22\overline{)98}$ 44. $66\overline{)866}$ 45. $69\overline{)750}$ 46. $26\overline{)599}$

47. $851 \div 37 = $ ▦   48. $882 \div 63 = $ ▦   49. $72 \div 24 = $ ▦

50. $675 \div 45 = $ ▦   51. $28 \div 14 = $ ▦   52. $812 \div 58 = $ ▦

53. $36\overline{)254}$ 54. $24\overline{)848}$ 55. $19\overline{)782}$ 56. $26\overline{)48}$ 57. $33\overline{)698}$

58. $14\overline{)74}$ 59. $37\overline{)653}$ 60. $28\overline{)490}$ 61. $31\overline{)692}$ 62. $26\overline{)64}$

63. $54\overline{)418}$ **64.** $47\overline{)836}$ **65.** $29\overline{)844}$ **66.** $16\overline{)87}$ **67.** $34\overline{)722}$

68. $39\overline{)932}$ **69.** $55\overline{)330}$ **70.** $24\overline{)66}$ **71.** $36\overline{)583}$ **72.** $38\overline{)680}$

73. $945 \div 63 = $ ▨   **74.** $486 \div 18 = $ ▨   **75.** $81 \div 27 = $ ▨

76. $992 \div 31 = $ ▨   **77.** $92 \div 23 = $ ▨   **78.** $925 \div 37 = $ ▨

Solve the problems.   *(pages 288–293, 296–305)*

79. There were 720 seats in the gym. They were arranged in 40 rows, with the same number of seats in each row. How many seats were in each row?

80. 208 campers are divided into football teams. 15 players are on each team. How many teams are formed? How many campers are left over?

81. 26 children were in a gym class. They each did 15 sit-ups. How many sit-ups did they do all together?

82. 112 bats are divided equally among 36 players. How many bats can each player receive? How many bats are left over?

83. 76 qt is how many gallons?

84. 144 in. is how many feet?

85. 12 pt is how many cups?

86. 64 lb is how many ounces?

87. Jimmy drank 2 pints of juice during the tennis match. How many cups did he drink?

88. Eddie climbed a rope that was 15 feet long. How many yards did he climb?

89. The coach bought apples for the baseball team. The 3 lb bag cost $1.17. The 5 lb bag cost $1.75. Find the price per pound. Which bag was the better buy?

90. The sports store sells 3 tennis balls for $2.19, or 4 tennis balls for $2.80. Find the prices per ball. Which is the better buy?

91. The sports store sells 4 golf balls for $2.60, 8 balls for $6.00, or 12 balls for $8.88. Find the prices per golf ball. Which is the best buy?

92. The coach could buy 10 feet of rope for $1.70, 20 feet of rope for $3.20, or 30 feet of rope for $4.50. Find the prices per foot. Which is the best buy?

Reinforcement

More Help with Division

Divide.

31 R26
30)956
90 ← $3 \times 30 = 90$
56
30 ← $1 \times 30 = 30$
26

1. 10)82
2. 30)45
3. 20)80
4. 70)612

5. 40)562
6. 20)840
7. 60)900
8. 90)410

9. 20)106
10. 40)734
11. 60)386
12. 80)950

13. $480 \div 80 = $ ■
14. $840 \div 40 = $ ■

Round 25 up to 30.

2 R12
25)62
50
12

15. 22)90
16. 13)27
17. 33)74
18. 45)602

19. 42)868
20. 22)308
21. 56)803
22. 27)303

23. 34)480
24. 48)593
25. 13)289
26. 75)483

27. $572 \div 22 = $ ■
28. $884 \div 52 = $ ■

Round 32 down to 30.

8 R2
32)258
256
2

29. 23)139
30. 43)396
31. 34)109
32. 21)110

33. 63)275
34. 74)132
35. 38)817
36. 34)146

37. 62)256
38. 73)539
39. 46)156
40. 67)283

41. $330 \div 33 = $ ■
42. $602 \div 43 = $ ■

You may need to correct your quotient.

41 R11
16)667
64
27
16
11

43. 16)89
44. 42)281
45. 13)72
46. 16)982

47. 54)404
48. 19)324
49. 35)642
50. 62)903

51. 16)277
52. 28)820
53. 34)940
54. 14)273

55. $816 \div 24 = $ ■
56. $624 \div 78 = $ ■

Base Eight

The manager of a soup factory made these rules.

1. If there are 8 cans of soup, put them in a box.
2. If there are 8 boxes of soup, put them in a carton.

1 can

1 box = 8 cans

1 carton = 8 boxes = 64 cans

This table shows how many cartons and boxes will be needed
to package different numbers of cans.

Number of Cans	50	100	150
Cartons [64 cans]	0	1 $1 \times 64 = 64$	2 $2 \times 64 = 128$
Cans not in Cartons	50	$100 - 64 = 36$	$150 - 128 = 22$
Boxes [8 cans]	6 $6 \times 8 = 48$	4 $4 \times 8 = 32$	2 $2 \times 8 = 16$
Cans not in Boxes	$50 - 48 = 2$	$36 - 32 = 4$	$22 - 16 = 6$
Cans left over	2	4	6

The manager wanted to give each number of cans a
"packaging number." He used these rules to find each
"packaging number."

1. The first digit tells the number of **cartons** needed.
2. The second digit tells the number of **boxes** needed.
3. The third digit tells the number of **cans** left over.

Cartons	Boxes	Cans left over
50 → 0	6	2
100 → 1	4	4
150 → 2	2	6

Find the "packaging number" for each of the following numbers of cans.

1. 10   **2.** 20   **3.** 25   **4.** 40   **5.** 60   **6.** 75

7. 95   **8.** 115   **9.** 175   **10.** 200   **11.** 300   **12.** 400

b Maintaining Skills

Choose the correct answer.

1. 24
$\times$ 6

a. 124
b. 118
c. 144
d. not given

2. 586
$\times$ 5

a. 2,930
b. 2,925
c. 2,900
d. not given

3. 3,408
$\times$ 7

a. 23,806
b. 24,664
c. 23,856
d. not given

4. 7,586
$\times$ 4

a. 28,324
b. 30,344
c. 30,044
d. not given

5. 49
$\times$70

a. 3,430
b. 343
c. 2,830
d. not given

6. 689
$\times$ 61

a. 36,029
b. 4,813
c. 41,360
d. not given

7. 752
$\times$ 58

a. 9,776
b. 43,616
c. 36,606
d. not given

8. 928
$\times$ 83

a. 77,008
b. 10,208
c. 77,024
d. not given

9. 80$\overline{)93}$

a. 11 R5
b. 1 R13
c. 1
d. not given

10. 23$\overline{)91}$

a. 45 R1
b. 4
c. 3 R22
d. not given

11. 65$\overline{)392}$

a. 6 R2
b. 60 R2
c. 62
d. not given

12. 76$\overline{)857}$

a. 12 R11
b. 11 R19
c. 11 R21
d. not given

13. A clothes store received 16 boxes of shirts. There were 224 shirts in all. Each box had the same number of shirts. How many shirts were in each box?

a. 10 shirts   b. 13 shirts
c. 14 shirts   d. not given

14. A hat store received 14 boxes of hats. 14 hats were in each box. How many hats did the store receive?

a. 70 hats   b. 1 hat
c. 196 hats   d. not given

Solids and Their Parts

A. Here are six different kinds of **solids.**

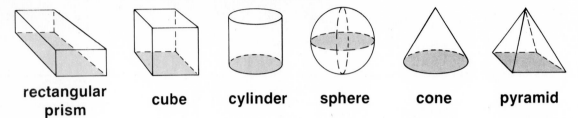

| rectangular prism | cube | cylinder | sphere | cone | pyramid |

B. All solids have **faces** and **edges.**

flat face

straight edge

curved edge

flat face

curved face

Figure	Number of flat faces	Number of curved faces	Number of straight edges	Number of curved edges
rectangular prism	6	0	12	0
cube	6	0	12	0
cylinder	2	1	0	2
sphere	0	−1	0	0
cone	1	1	0	1
pyramid	5	0	8	0

C. A **plane** is a flat surface, like a table top. If you trace the flat faces of each of the solids above, you will get these four **plane figures.**

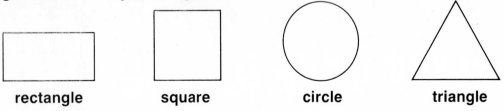

| rectangle | square | circle | triangle |

TRY THESE

Name some things that remind you of a:

1. rectangular prism　　　**2.** cube　　　**3.** cylinder

4. sphere　　　**5.** cone　　　**6.** pyramid

SKILLS PRACTICE

Tell whether each object is a rectangular prism, cube, cylinder, sphere, cone, or pyramid.

1.

2.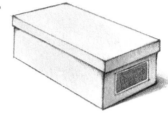

3.

4.

5.

6.

What plane figures would you get by tracing the flat faces of a:

7. rectangular prism　　　**8.** cube　　　**9.** cylinder　　　★**10.** pyramid

EXTRA! Looking Carefully
How many different triangles
can you find?

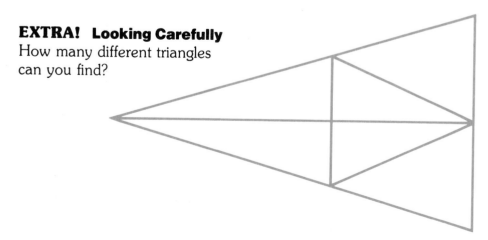

Polygons

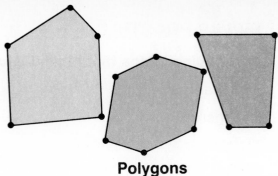

Polygons

A. A *polygon* is a plane figure. It has straight *sides.* Each pair of sides meet at a *vertex.*

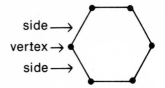

6 sides
6 vertices (the plural of vertex is vertices)

B. Some polygons have special names.

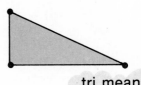
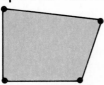
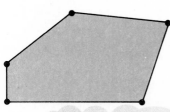

tri means 3   quad means 4   penta means 5

triangle
3 sides
3 vertices

quadrilateral
4 sides
4 vertices

pentagon
5 sides
5 vertices

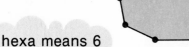

hexa means 6   octa means 8

hexagon
6 sides
6 vertices

octagon
8 sides
8 vertices

TRY THESE

1. Which of the plane figures below are polygons?

2. Which are pentagons?   **3.** Which are hexagons?

a   b   c   d   e

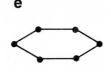

SKILLS PRACTICE

1. Which of the plane figures below are polygons?

2. Which are triangles?

3. Which are quadrilaterals?

4. Which are pentagons?

5. Which are hexagons?

6. Which are octagons?

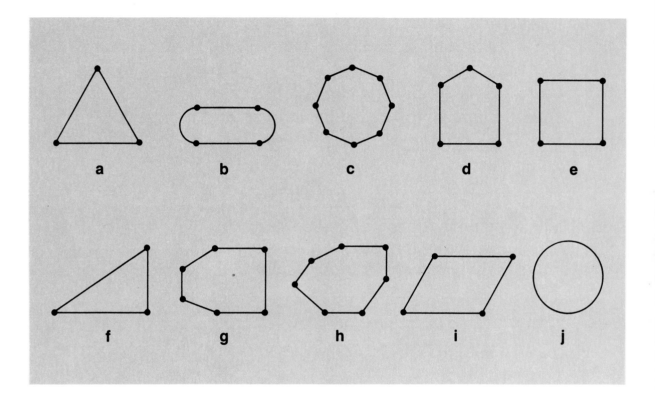

7. How many sides does a pentagon have?
   How many vertices does a pentagon have?

8. How many sides does an octagon have?
   How many vertices does an octagon have?

9. What can you say about the number of sides
   and the number of vertices in a polygon?

★ 10. Copy this pentagon. Two of the vertices
   have been joined. Join all the vertices that
   are not already joined by sides. What
   figure do you get?

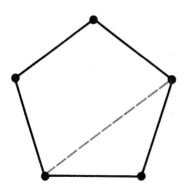

Line Segments and Lines

A. Each side of a polygon is a *line segment.*

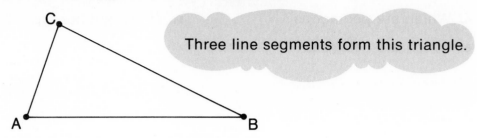

Three line segments form this triangle.

Each line segment has two **endpoints.**
To name a line segment, use its endpoints.

Write $\overline{XY}$ or $\overline{YX}$

B. If a line segment "goes on forever" in both
directions, a *line* is formed. A line has no endpoints.
To name a line, use any two points on it.

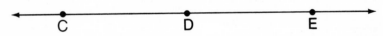

Write $\overleftrightarrow{CD}$, $\overleftrightarrow{DC}$, $\overleftrightarrow{CE}$, $\overleftrightarrow{EC}$, $\overleftrightarrow{DE}$, or $\overleftrightarrow{ED}$

The arrows mean
that the line "goes
on forever."

C. $\overleftrightarrow{FG}$ and $\overleftrightarrow{HI}$ are *intersecting lines.*
They meet, or intersect, at point P.

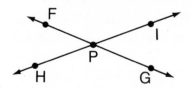

D. $\overleftrightarrow{JK}$ and $\overleftrightarrow{LM}$ are *parallel lines.*
Parallel lines are lines in a
plane that will never intersect.

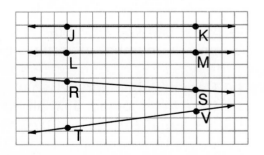

$\overleftrightarrow{RS}$ and $\overleftrightarrow{TV}$ will intersect.
They are intersecting lines.

TRY THESE

1. Which are line segments?

   a.    b. ·———·   c.    d.

2. Give 6 names for this line.

3. Name 3 different line segments that are part of this line.

SKILLS PRACTICE

1. Give 2 names for each line segment in this figure.

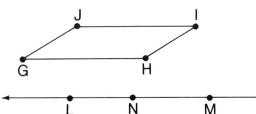

2. Give 6 names for this line.

   ←——·——·——·——→
        L   N   M

Write *intersecting* or *parallel* to describe each pair of lines.

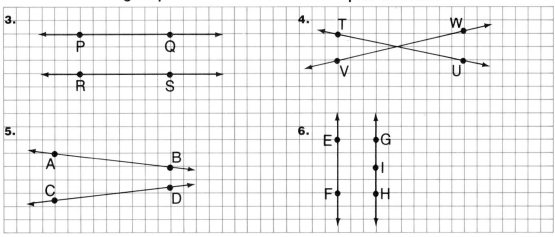

★ 7. Can you find the length of a line segment?
   Can you find the length of a line?

EXTRA! Finding a Pattern
Copy and complete the table.

Number of points (no 3 points are on a line)	2	3	4	5	6	7	8
Number of line segments you can draw			6			21	

Rays and Angles

A. If a line segment "goes on forever" in only one
direction, a **ray** is formed. A ray has one endpoint.

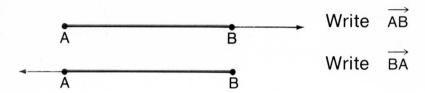

Write $\overrightarrow{AB}$

Write $\overrightarrow{BA}$

B. Two rays with the same endpoint form an **angle.**
The rays are **sides** of the angle.
Their common endpoint is the **vertex** of the angle.

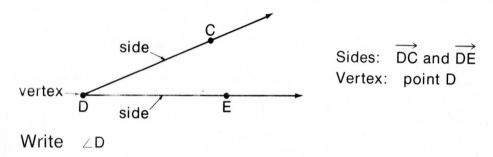

Sides: $\overrightarrow{DC}$ and $\overrightarrow{DE}$
Vertex: point D

Write $\angle D$

C. An angle that forms a square corner is a
right angle.

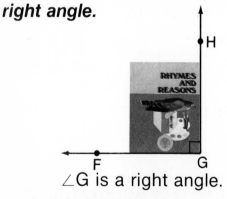

$\angle G$ is a right angle.

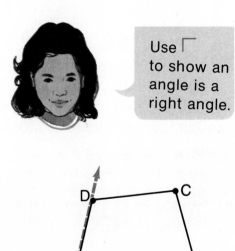

Use ⌐
to show an
angle is a
right angle.

D. $\angle A$ (sides $\overrightarrow{AD}$, $\overrightarrow{AB}$) is an
angle of this quadrilateral.
The quadrilateral has four angles.

318 **Geometry**

TRY THESE

Name each ray.

1.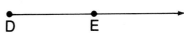
D   E

2.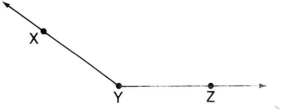
G   E

3. Name the angle shown.

4. Name the sides of the angle.

5. Name the vertex of the angle.

6. Which look like right angles?

a.   **b.**   **c.**   **d.**

SKILLS PRACTICE

1. Name 2 rays with endpoint K.

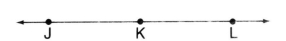
J   K   L

Draw each of these.

2. Point P   **3.** $\overline{CD}$ **4.** $\overrightarrow{JK}$ **5.** $\overleftrightarrow{ST}$

How many endpoints does each figure have?

6. line   **7.** ray   **8.** line segment

**Use a corner of a ruler or a card to draw right angles.
Can you draw a triangle with:**

9. one right angle?   ★ **10.** two right angles?

How many angles do you see?

11. 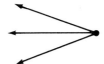   **12.**

Special Quadrilaterals

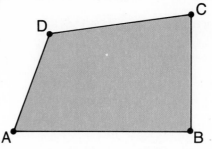

A. Sides of a quadrilateral that intersect are **adjacent sides.** Sides that do not intersect are **opposite sides.**

Pairs of adjacent sides: $\overline{AB}$ and $\overline{BC}$ $\overline{BC}$ and $\overline{CD}$
                               $\overline{CD}$ and $\overline{DA}$ $\overline{DA}$ and $\overline{AB}$

Pairs of opposite sides: $\overline{AB}$ and $\overline{DC}$ $\overline{AD}$ and $\overline{BC}$

B. Some quadrilaterals have special names. A quadrilateral in which both pairs of opposite sides are parallel is a **parallelogram.**

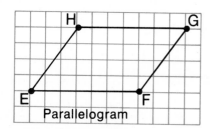

$\overline{EF}$ and $\overline{HG}$ are parallel.

$\overline{FG}$ and $\overline{EH}$ are parallel.

> **Opposite sides of a parallelogram have equal lengths.**

A **rectangle** is a parallelogram with four right angles.

A **square** is a rectangle with all four sides of equal lengths.

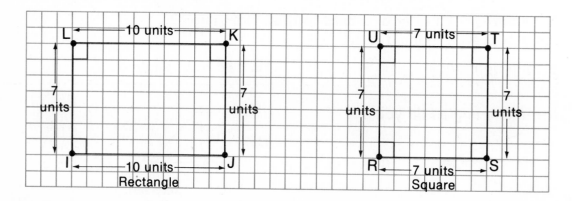

TRY THESE

1. Name all pairs of adjacent sides of this quadrilateral.

2. Name all pairs of opposite sides of this quadrilateral.

3. This is a parallelogram. What is the length of $\overline{PS}$? What is the length of $\overline{PQ}$?

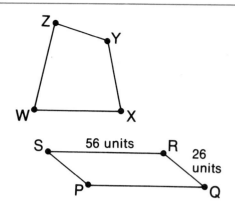

SKILLS PRACTICE

1. Which of the figures below are quadrilaterals?

2. Which of the figures below are parallelograms?

3. Which are rectangles?

4. Which are squares?

5. Which are parallelograms but not rectangles or squares?

6. Which are rectangles but not squares?

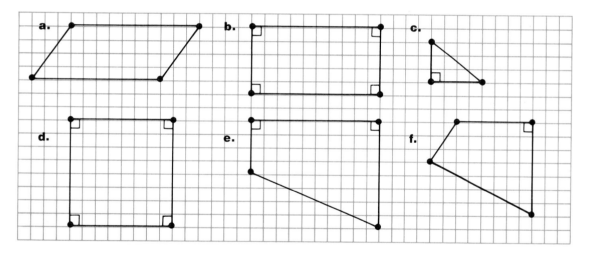

PROBLEM SOLVING

7. Ms. Zayre's garden is shaped like a rectangle. The lengths of two of its sides are 10 units and 22 units. What are the lengths of the other two sides?

★ 8. The top of Mr. Riccardo's table is shaped like a square. One side of the top is 95 units long. What is the total distance around the top of this table?

Lines of Symmetry

A. If you fold this figure along the red line, one part of the figure will fit exactly on the other.

The red line is a *line of symmetry* for the figure.

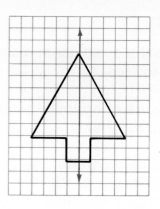

B. Some figures have more than one line of symmetry. Some figures have no line of symmetry.

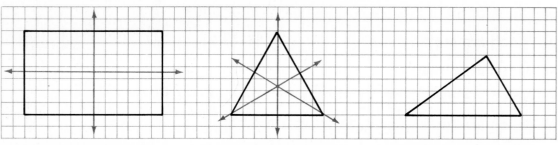

2 lines of symmetry   **3 lines of symmetry**   **no line of symmetry**

C. Complete this figure so that the red line is a line of symmetry.

Think about folding along the red line. Mark the points where A, B, and C would "hit." Join these points to complete the figure.

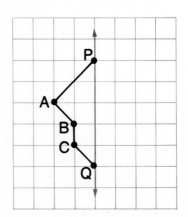

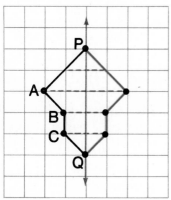

Is the red line a line of symmetry?

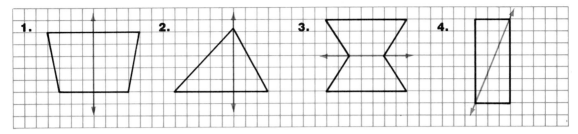

1.   2.   3.   4.

SKILLS PRACTICE

How many lines of symmetry does each figure have?

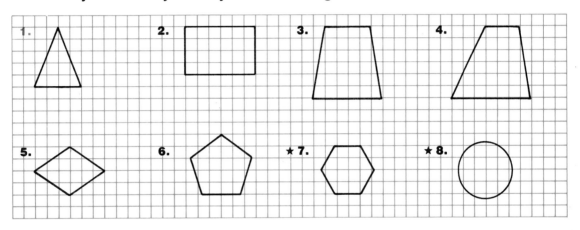

1.   2.   3.   4.

5.   6.   ★ 7.   ★ 8.

Copy each figure on graph paper. Complete so that the red line is a line of symmetry.

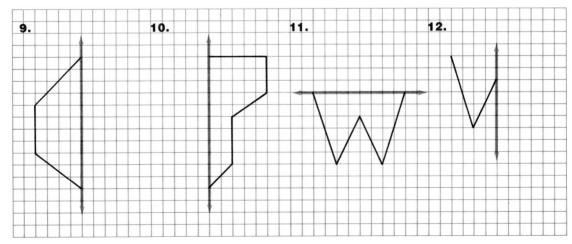

9.   10.   11.   12.

Divide.

1. $7\overline{)65}$ 2. $6\overline{)57}$ 3. $4\overline{)33}$ 4. $9\overline{)88}$ 5. $3\overline{)20}$

6. $2\overline{)396}$ 7. $5\overline{)683}$ 8. $7\overline{)479}$ 9. $4\overline{)858}$ 10. $6\overline{)629}$

11. $7\overline{)7,632}$ 12. $9\overline{)9,062}$ 13. $5\overline{)3,296}$ 14. $6\overline{)8,649}$ 15. $8\overline{)4,732}$

16. $10\overline{)75}$ 17. $30\overline{)90}$ 18. $34\overline{)70}$ 19. $48\overline{)97}$ 20. $16\overline{)99}$

21. $80\overline{)726}$ 22. $97\overline{)987}$ 23. $17\overline{)527}$ 24. $34\overline{)680}$ 25. $89\overline{)379}$

Multiply.

26. $\begin{array}{r} 65 \\ \times\ 4 \\ \hline \end{array}$ 27. $\begin{array}{r} 97 \\ \times\ 8 \\ \hline \end{array}$ 28. $\begin{array}{r} 149 \\ \times\ 5 \\ \hline \end{array}$ 29. $\begin{array}{r} 648 \\ \times\ 3 \\ \hline \end{array}$ 30. $\begin{array}{r} 291 \\ \times\ 9 \\ \hline \end{array}$

31. $\begin{array}{r} 1,763 \\ \times\ 7 \\ \hline \end{array}$ 32. $\begin{array}{r} 1,492 \\ \times\ 4 \\ \hline \end{array}$ 33. $\begin{array}{r} 7,320 \\ \times\ 6 \\ \hline \end{array}$ 34. $\begin{array}{r} 9,034 \\ \times\ 2 \\ \hline \end{array}$ 35. $\begin{array}{r} 6,104 \\ \times\ 8 \\ \hline \end{array}$

36. $\begin{array}{r} 47 \\ \times 30 \\ \hline \end{array}$ 37. $\begin{array}{r} 94 \\ \times 20 \\ \hline \end{array}$ 38. $\begin{array}{r} 53 \\ \times 18 \\ \hline \end{array}$ 39. $\begin{array}{r} 64 \\ \times 25 \\ \hline \end{array}$ 40. $\begin{array}{r} 73 \\ \times 37 \\ \hline \end{array}$

41. $\begin{array}{r} 213 \\ \times\ 14 \\ \hline \end{array}$ 42. $\begin{array}{r} 608 \\ \times\ 27 \\ \hline \end{array}$ 43. $\begin{array}{r} 924 \\ \times\ 33 \\ \hline \end{array}$ 44. $\begin{array}{r} 725 \\ \times\ 49 \\ \hline \end{array}$ 45. $\begin{array}{r} 314 \\ \times\ 95 \\ \hline \end{array}$

Solve the problems.

46. The Helpful Hardware Store sold 220 lightbulbs. They shipped the lightbulbs in boxes that held 20 bulbs each. How many boxes did they use?

47. The Helpful Hardware Store received 38 boxes of tacks. If there were 250 tacks in each box, how many tacks did the store receive in all?

48. The store received 48 hammers. The total cost of the hammers was $576. How much did one hammer cost?

49. There are 48 boxes of fuses in a carton. There are 4 fuses in a box. How many fuses are there in a carton?

Project: Patterns from Congruent and Similar Figures

Figures that are the same shape and the same size are **congruent figures**. Congruent figures are often used to make patterns for wallpaper or fabric. Here are 3 ways to start with a figure and make a pattern using figures that are congruent to it.

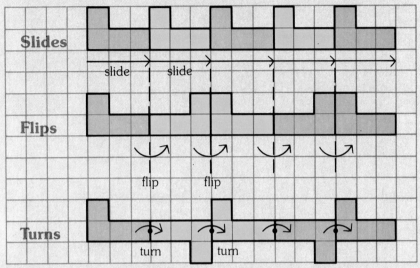

1. Draw the figure used to make the patterns above on graph paper. Use different slides, flips, or turns to make other patterns using congruent figures. Use combinations of slides, flips, and turns to make other patterns.

Figures that are the same shape but not the same size are **similar figures**. The pattern below was made using one of the green figures above and figures similar to it.

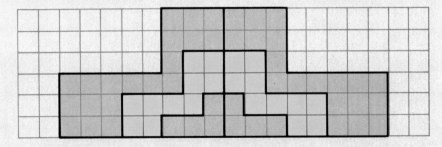

2. Use the same three similar figures to make patterns on your own graph paper. Use slides, flips, or turns to make other patterns with the similar figures.

3. Look for patterns at home or school that use congruent or similar figures. Are slides, flips, or turns used to form the patterns?

Perimeter

A. The distance around a polygon is the **_perimeter_** of the polygon. To find the perimeter of a polygon, add the lengths of its sides.

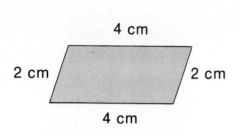

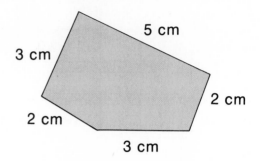

Perimeter = 4 + 2 + 4 + 2
= 12 cm

Perimeter = 3 + 2 + 5 + 3 + 2
= 15 cm

B. Mr. Rella wants to put a fence around his field. The field is in the shape of a rectangle. It is 900 m long and 500 m wide. How much fencing does he need?

Find the perimeter of the field.

Opposite sides of rectangles have equal lengths.

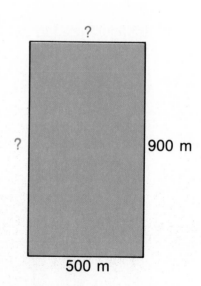

Perimeter = 500 + 900 + ? + ?
= 500 + 900 + 500 + 900
= 2,800 m

Mr. Rella needs 2,800 m of fencing.

TRY THESE

Find the perimeter of each polygon.

1.

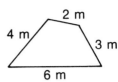

2.

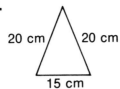

3. a rectangle with
length: 12 cm
width: 5 cm

SKILLS PRACTICE

Find the perimeter of each polygon.

1.

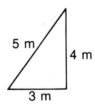

2.

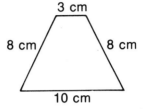

3. a rectangle with
length: 14 m
width: 27 m

4.

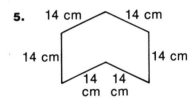

5. 14 cm   14 cm
14 cm   14 cm
14   14
cm   cm

6. a rectangle with
length: 420 cm
width: 380 cm

PROBLEM SOLVING

7. A woman walked from her home to
to the post office, then to the library,
then back home. How far did the
woman walk?

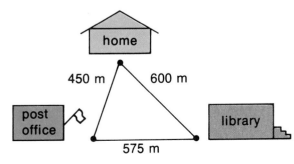

8. A jogger ran once around the
park. How far did the jogger run?

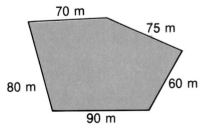

9. A napkin is shaped like a square.
The length of one side is 38 cm.
What is the perimeter of the napkin?

Area

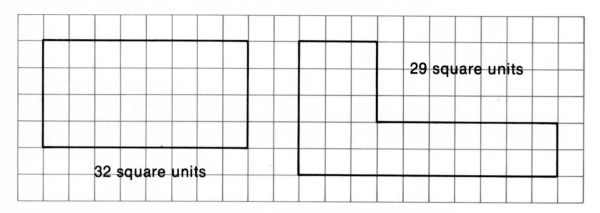

A. The *area* of a figure tells the
size of the inside of the figure.
Square units are used to measure area.

1 unit

Area
1 square unit

1 unit

To find the area of a figure, count the
square units that fill the inside of the figure.

32 square units

29 square units

B. Some metric units used to measure area are the
square centimeter (cm²) and the *square meter* (m²).

Length of each side of a square	1 centimeter (1 cm)	1 meter (1 m)
Area of the square	1 square centimeter (1 cm²)	1 square meter (1 m²)

The area of this page is about 500 cm².
The area of the floor of a large room is about 70 m².

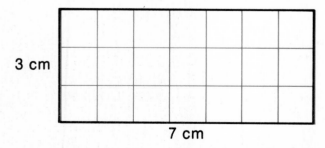

3 cm

7 cm

The area of this rectangle is 21 cm².

TRY THESE

Use the grid squares as square units. Find the area of each figure.

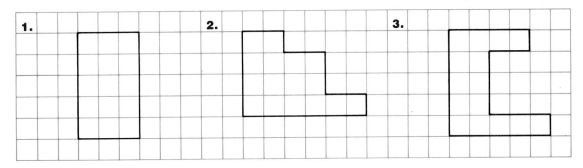

1. **2.** **3.**

SKILLS PRACTICE

Use the grid squares as square units. Find the area of each figure.

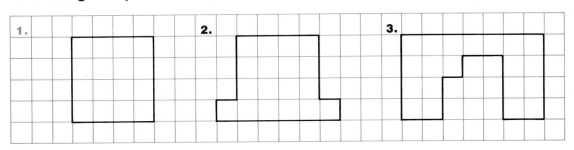

1. **2.** **3.**

Use cm² or m² to complete each sentence.

4. The area of a dollar bill is about 90 ____.

5. The area of a library card is about 30 ____.

6. The area of a rug is about 12 ____.

Select the answer that seems reasonable.

7. The area of a table top is about ____.
   a. 2 m²   **b.** 20 m²   **c.** 200 m²

8. The area of a parking lot is about ____.
   a. 6 m²   **b.** 60 m²   **c.** 600 m²

9. The area of a postage stamp is about ____.
   a. 5 cm²   **b.** 50 cm²   **c.** 500 cm²

Upside-down answer   **1.** 16 square units

329

Workbook   page 446

Multiplying to Find Area

A. You can multiply to find the area of a rectangle.
Use the grid squares as square units.

In each row:
    8 square units

In 4 rows:
    4 × 8 = 32 square units

Area = 32 square units

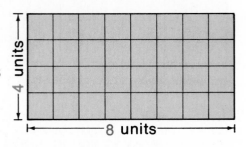

B. Find the area of a rectangle with length 10 cm and width 3 cm.

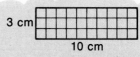

3 rows with 10 cm² in each row.
Multiply to find how many in all.

$$\begin{array}{r} 10 \\ \times\ 3 \\ \hline 30 \end{array}$$

Area = 30 cm²

C. Tammy's yard is shaped like a rectangle. It is 49 m long and 18 m wide. What is the area of her yard?

Multiply to find the area.

$$\begin{array}{r} \overset{7}{4}9 \\ \times 18 \\ \hline 392 \\ 490 \\ \hline 882 \end{array}$$

> **Don't forget to report the unit with your answer.**

The area of Tammy's yard is 882 m².

TRY THESE

Find the area of each rectangle.

1.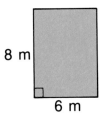

8 m

6 m

2. length: 18 cm
width: 8 cm

3. a square with length
of one side: 10 cm

SKILLS PRACTICE

Find the area of each rectangle.

1.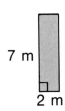

7 m

2 m

2.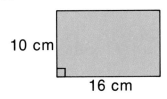

10 cm

16 cm

3.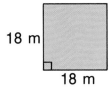

18 m

18 m

Complete this table. Each figure is a rectangle.

		4.	**5.**	**6.**	**7.**	**8.**
length	4 cm	8 m	24 cm	12 m	50 cm	64 m
width	2 cm	5 m	10 cm	15 m	50 cm	75 m
area	8 cm²		240 cm²			
perimeter	12 cm	26 m				

PROBLEM SOLVING

9. The lid of a rectangular sewing box is 45 cm long and 40 cm wide. What is its area? What is its perimeter?

10. A playground is shaped like a rectangle. It is 86 m long and 55 m wide. Find its area. Find its perimeter.

11. A sheet of paper is 22 cm wide and 35 cm long. What is its area? What is its perimeter?

★12. A floor is 12 m long and 8 m wide. What is the area of the floor? What is the area of $\frac{1}{2}$ of the floor?

Volume

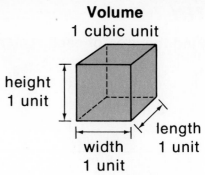

Volume
1 cubic unit

A. The *volume,* or *capacity,* of a container tells the size of the inside of the container. *Cubic units* are used to measure volume.

height
1 unit

width
1 unit

length
1 unit

B. You can multiply to find the volume of a rectangular prism.

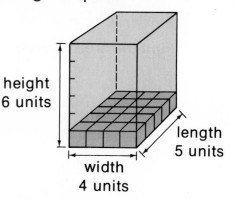

In the bottom layer:
　4 rows with 5 cubic units in each.
　4 × 5 = 20 cubic units

In the prism:
　6 layers with 20 cubic units in each.
　6 × 20 = 120 cubic units

Volume = 120 cubic units

height
6 units

width
4 units

length
5 units

C. Some metric units used to measure volume are the *cubic centimeter* (cm³) and the *cubic meter* (m³).

Length of each edge of a cube	1 centimeter (1 cm)	1 meter (1 m)
Volume of the cube	1 cubic centimeter (1 cm³)	1 cubic meter (1 m³)

The volume of an ice cube is about 30 cm³.
The volume of the air in a classroom is about 250 m³.

D. Find the volume of a rectangular prism with length 12 cm, width 8 cm, and height 6 cm.

$$\begin{array}{r} \overset{①}{12} \\ \times\ 8 \\ \hline 96 \end{array} \longrightarrow \begin{array}{r} \overset{③}{96} \\ \times\ 6 \\ \hline 576 \end{array}$$

Volume = 576 cm³

TRY THESE

Find the volume of each rectangular prism.

1.

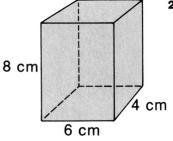

8 cm
6 cm
4 cm

2. length: 7 cm
width: 5 cm
height: 3 cm

3. length: 10 m
width: 10 m
height: 10 m

SKILLS PRACTICE

Find the volume of each rectangular prism.

1.

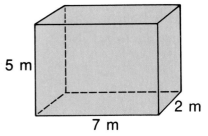

5 m
7 m
2 m

2.

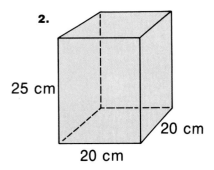

25 cm
20 cm
20 cm

Complete this table. Each figure is a rectangular prism.

		3.	**4.**	**5.**	**6.**
length	4 m	8 cm	5 m	12 cm	30 m
width	3 m	5 cm	4 m	12 cm	20 m
height	2 m	4 cm	3 m	12 cm	10 m
volume	24 m³				

PROBLEM SOLVING

7. Jennie bought a tool box that was 34 cm long, 12 cm wide, and 21 cm high. What was the volume of this tool box?

★ 8. A room is 7 m long, 5 m wide, and 3 m high. What is the area of the floor of this room?

Using Customary Units

A. Some customary units used to measure area are the
square inch (in.²), the **square foot** (ft²), and the **square yard** (yd²).

Length of each side of a square	1 inch (1 in.)	1 foot (1 ft)	1 yard (1 yd)
Area of the square	1 square inch (1 in.²)	1 square foot (1 ft²)	1 square yard (1 yd²)

The area of this page is about 78 in.²
The area of the floor of a large room is about 630 ft²
or 70 yd².

B. Some customary units used to measure volume are the
cubic inch (in.³), **cubic foot** (ft³), and the **cubic yard** (yd³).

Length of each side of a square	1 inch (1 in.)	1 foot (1 ft)	1 yard (1 yd)
Volume of the cube	1 cubic inch (1 in.³)	1 cubic foot (1 ft³)	1 cubic yard (1 yd³)

The volume of an ice cube is about 2 in.³
The volume of the inside of a refrigerator is about 10 ft³.
The volume of the air in a classroom is about 250 yd³.

C. Find the area of a rectangle with length 18 ft and width 9 ft.

$$
\begin{array}{r}
18 \\
\times \ 9 \\
\hline
162
\end{array}
$$

Area = 162 ft²

D. Find the volume of a rectangular prism with length 12 in., width 4 in., and height 8 in.

$$
\begin{array}{r}
12 \\
\times \ 4 \\
\hline
48
\end{array}
\longrightarrow
\begin{array}{r}
48 \\
\times \ 8 \\
\hline
384
\end{array}
$$

Volume = 384 in.³

TRY THESE

Find the area of each bottom and the volume of each box.

1.

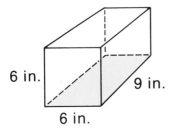

6 in.   6 in.   9 in.

2.

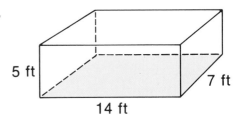

5 ft   14 ft   7 ft

SKILLS PRACTICE

Find the area of each rectangle.

1.

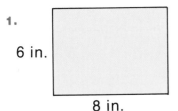

6 in.   8 in.

2.

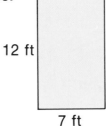

12 ft   7 ft

3.

15 in.   32 in.

Complete this table. Each figure is a rectangular prism.

		4.	5.	6.	7.	8.
length	5 yd	6 in.	8 ft	12 in.	14 ft	30 yd
width	3 yd	4 in.	2 ft	6 in.	14 ft	20 yd
height	4 yd	6 in.	5 ft	3 in.	14 ft	10 yd
volume	60 yd³					

PROBLEM SOLVING PRACTICE

9. The lid of a rectangular sewing box is 18 in. long and 16 in. wide. What is its area? What is its perimeter?

10. A tool box is 20 in. long, 6 in. wide, and 8 in. high. What is the volume of this tool box?

11. A playground is rectangular in shape. It is 86 yd long and 55 yd wide. Find its area. Find its perimeter.

12. A grain bin is shaped like a rectangular prism. It is 35 ft long, 24 ft wide, and 20 ft high. Find its volume.

13. A sheet of paper is 9 in. wide and 14 in. long. What is its area?

14. A room is 18 ft long, 12 ft wide, and 10 ft high. What is the floor area?

✔ Unit Checkup

Match each word with the picture it describes. *(pages 312–327)*

1. ray
2. cone
3. angle
4. parallelogram
5. line segment
6. pyramid
7. pentagon
8. line

A.

B.

C.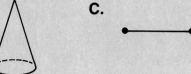

D.

E.

F.

G.

H.

Find the perimeter of each polygon. *(pages 326–327)*

9.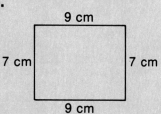

10.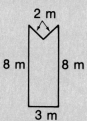

11.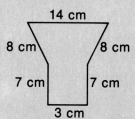

12. a square with one side of length 6 m

13. a rectangle with length: 32 m width: 45 m

14. a triangle with each side of length 13 cm

Find the area of each rectangle. *(pages 328–331)*

15.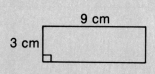

16.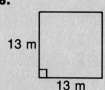

17.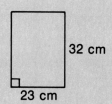

18. length: 8 m width: 8 m

19. length: 7 cm width: 3 cm

20. length: 52 m width: 50 m

Find the volume of each rectangular prism. *(pages 332–333)*

21.

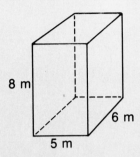

8 m
6 m
5 m

22.

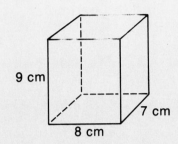

9 cm
7 cm
8 cm

23.

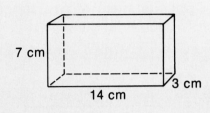

7 cm
14 cm
3 cm

24. length: 5 cm
width: 4 cm
height: 3 cm

25. length: 12 m
width: 10 m
height: 6 m

26. length: 8 cm
width: 8 cm
height: 8 cm

Solve the problems using metric units. *(pages 326–333)*

27. A football field has the shape of a rectangle. It is 108 m long and 48 m wide. What is its area? What is its perimeter?

28. A swimming pool has the shape of a rectangular prism. It is 50 m long, 20 m wide, and 2 m deep. What is its volume?

29. Janet's kite is shaped like a rectangle. It is 95 cm long and 60 cm wide. Find its area. Find its perimeter.

30. Serena received a chemistry set in a box. The box was 80 cm long, 25 cm wide, and 14 cm high. What was the volume of the box?

Solve the problems using customary units. *(pages 334–335)*

31. A football field has the shape of a rectangle. It is 120 yd long and 53 yd wide. What is its area? What is its perimeter?

32. A swimming pool has the shape of a rectangular prism. It is 55 yd long, 22 yd wide, and 2 yd deep. What is its volume?

33. Seth's kite is shaped like a rectangle. It is 3 ft long and 2 ft wide. Find its area. Find its perimeter.

34. Tony received a chemistry set in a box. The box was 32 in. long, 10 in. wide, and 6 in. high. What was the volume of the box?

337

Reinforcement

More Help with Perimeter, Area, and Volume

Opposite sides of a rectangle have equal lengths.

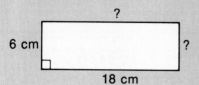

Perimeter = 6 + 18 + ? + ?
= 6 + 18 + 6 + 18
= 48 cm

Find the perimeter.

1.
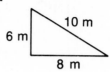

2.
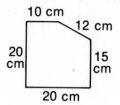

3. a rectangle with
length: 8 m
width: 6 m

4. a rectangle with
length: 46 cm
width: 28 cm

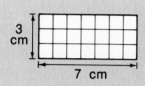

In each row: 7
In 3 rows: 3 × 7 = 21
Area = 21 cm²

Find the area of each rectangle.

5.

6.
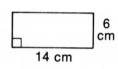

7. length: 14 m
width: 10 m

8. a square with
one side of length
12 cm

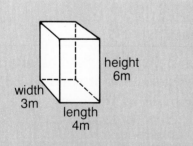

In one layer: 3 × 4 = 12
In the prism: 6 × 12 = 72
Volume = 72 m³

Find the volume of each rectangular prism.

9.
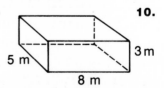

10.
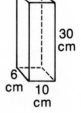

11. length: 15 cm
width: 10 cm
height: 5 cm

12. length: 40 m
width: 20 m
height: 30 m

Enrichment

Coordinate Geometry

You can use a **number pair** to name a point on a grid. The first number tells the number of units to the *right* of the **origin**. The second number tells the number of units *up* from the origin.

Point A is 6 units to the right and 2 units up. The number pair (6, 2) names point A.

Point B is 2 units to the right and 6 units up. The number pair (2, 6) names point B.

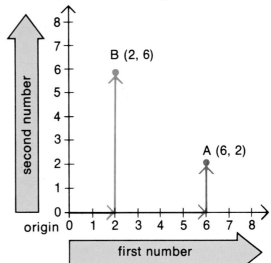

Give the point for each number pair.

1. (1, 1)   **2.** (5, 2)   **3.** (0, 7)

4. (6, 0)   **5.** (3, 5)   **6.** (4, 4)

Give the number pair for each point.

7. point L   **8.** point Q

9. point T   **10.** point R

11. point W   **12.** point Y

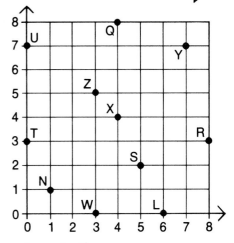

Draw a grid like the one above on graph paper. Locate the following points on the grid. Then draw line segments to join the points in order.

13. (3, 2); (0, 2); (1, 0); (5, 0); (7, 2); (3, 2)

14. (3, 2); (3, 7); (1, 3); (3, 4)

15. (3, 4); (5, 4); (3, 6)

339

Maintaining Skills

Choose the correct answer.

1.

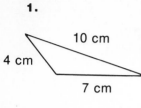

10 cm
4 cm
7 cm

Perimeter = ▓

a. 17 cm
b. 38 cm
c. 21 cm
d. 22 cm

2.

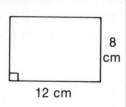

8 cm
12 cm

Area = ▓

a. 20 cm²
b. 40 cm²
c. 88 cm²
d. 96 cm²

3.

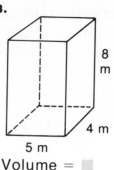

8 m
4 m
5 m

Volume = ▓

a. 160 m³
b. 40 m³
c. 150 m³
d. 20 m²

4. A square with one side of length 8 m

Area = ▓

a. 16 m²
b. 64 m²
c. 32 m
d. 56 m²

5.
```
   36
 ×  9
```
a. 324
b. 315
c. 288
d. 314

6.
```
   298
 ×   7
```
a. 1,788
b. 2,036
c. 2,096
d. 2,086

7.
```
    27
 × 18
```
a. 243
b. 475
c. 486
d. 222

8.
```
   365
 ×  32
```
a. 10,680
b. 11,680
c. 1,825
d. 11,780

---

9. 4)87

a. 2 R7
b. 11 R3
c. 22 R1
d. 21 R3

10. 7)379

a. 54 R1
b. 111 R2
c. 5 R9
d. 55 R4

11. 16)375

a. 18 R15
b. 187 R1
c. 23 R7
d. 37 R5

12. 35)293

a. 73 R1
b. 7 R13
c. 8 R13
d. 97 R2

---

13. A room is 16 ft long, 12 ft wide, and 10 ft high. What is the volume of the room?

a. 38 ft³   b. 1,920 ft³
c. 1,760 ft³   d. 1,800 ft³

14. The rectangular playground is 45 m long and 28 m wide. Find its perimeter.

a. 101 m   b. 118 m
c. 73 m   d. 146 m

Decimals **12**

Tenths

A.

1   1 $\frac{4}{10}$

$2\frac{4}{10}$ squares are shaded.

You can write a **decimal** to show how much is shaded.

Ones	Tenths
2.	4

↑
Decimal point

10 tenths = 1

4 in the **tenths place** means 4 tenths.

2.4 squares are shaded.

Read 2.4 as two *and* four tenths
or two *point* four.

B. Write a decimal to tell how much is shaded.

Ones	Tenths
.	7

seven tenths or *point* seven

7 of 10 pieces

.7 square is shaded.

You can also write 0.7 for the shaded part.

C. You can use decimals to name whole numbers.

| 3 ones | 3 ones 0 tenths |

└→ 3 = 3.0 ←┘   48 = 48.0   126 = 126.0

TRY THESE

Write a decimal to tell how much is shaded. Then name the place of each digit.

1.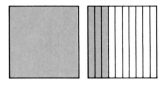

2.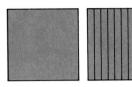

3.

Show how to read each decimal two ways.

4. 2.9   **5.** .4   **6.** 38.4   **7.** 400.3   **8.** 20.0

Write decimals that mean:

9. 2 ones 4 tenths   **10.** 6 ones 9 tenths   **11.** 4 tens 5 ones 0 tenths

SKILLS PRACTICE

Write a decimal to tell how much is shaded. Then name the place of each digit.

1.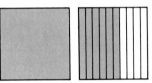

2.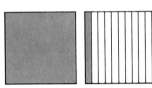

3.

Show how to read each decimal two ways.

4. 3.5   **5.** .9   **6.** 10.1   **7.** 8.0   **8.** 20.2

Write decimals that mean:

9. 6 ones 2 tenths   **10.** 9 tenths   **11.** 2 tens 6 ones

Write a decimal for each.

12. 4 in the ones place, 5 in the tenths place

13. 0 in the ones place, 6 in the tenths place

14. fifty and four tenths   **15.** eight point four

16. seventy point three   **17.** zero point six

★18. six thousand and six tenths   **★19.** ninety point zero

Hundredths

A. Write a decimal to tell how much is shaded.

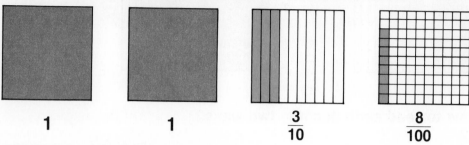

Ones	Tenths	Hundredths
2.	3	8

10 hundredths = 1 tenth

8 in the **hundredths place** means 8 hundredths.

2.38 squares are shaded.

> 3 tenths 8 hundredths is 38 hundredths

Read 2.38 as two *and* thirty-eight hundredths
or two *point* three eight.

B. You can use decimals to name whole numbers and tenths or hundredths.

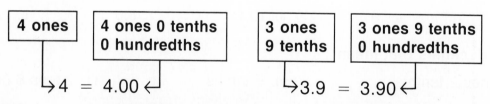

You must **be careful** when you write 0's in decimals.

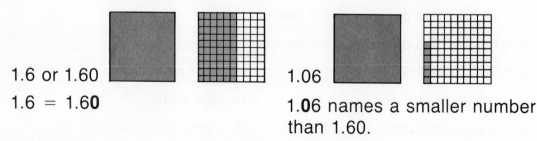

1.6 or 1.60
1.6 = 1.60

1.06

1.06 names a smaller number than 1.60.

TRY THESE

Write a decimal to tell how much is shaded. Then name the place of each digit.

1.
2.
3.

Show how to read each decimal two ways.

4. 2.46   **5.** 6.30   **6.** 16.03   **7.** 5.02   **8.** .28

Which name the same number?

9. 1.09, 1.90, 1.9   **10.** .4, .04, .40   **11.** 2.50, 2.5, 2.05

SKILLS PRACTICE

Write a decimal to tell how much is shaded. Then name the place of each digit.

1.
2.
3.

Show how to read each decimal two ways.

4. 9.25   **5.** 6.02   **6.** 20.1   **7.** 1.01   **8.** 50.50

Write decimals that mean:

9. 6 ones 4 tenths 3 hundredths   **10.** 1 ten 8 ones 3 tenths 7 hundredths

11. 8 hundredths   **12.** 2 ones 0 tenths 2 hundredths

★13. seven tenths one hundredth   **★14.** one tenth two hundredths

Which name the same number?

15. 13.00, 13, 13.0   **16.** 1.05, 1.50, 1.5   **17.** .60, .06, .6

Write a decimal for each.

18. four and thirty-seven hundredths   **19.** eight hundredths

20. sixty and four hundredths   **21.** ninety and nine hundredths

Comparing with Decimals

A. Compare 27.18 and 27.3.

Use two steps.

Step 1 Write the decimals **with the decimal points lined up.**

27.3
27.18

Step 2 Read from left to right until you find **different digits** in the **same place.** The decimal with the **greater digit** is **greater.**

27.③
27.①8

3 > 1 so
27.3 > 27.18 and 27.18 < 27.3

B. Write >, <, or = for ●:   6.95 ● 14

Step 1

Write 14.0 for 14.

6.95
14.0

Step 2

6.95
①4.0

0 tens in 6.95
0 < 1

6.95 < 14

C. Write in order from greatest to least: .7; .59; 1

Find the greatest.

.7
.59
①.0

Find the next greatest.

.⑦
.⑤9
1. 0

1 is the greatest.

.7 is the next greatest.

Greatest to least: 1; .7; .59

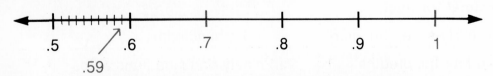

.5   .6   .7   .8   .9   1

.59

TRY THESE

Write >, <, or = for ⬤.

1. .9 ⬤ .10   **2.** 11 ⬤ 10.5   **3.** 1.00 ⬤ .99   **4.** 9.75 ⬤ 12.3

SKILLS PRACTICE

Write >, <, or = for ⬤.

1. .56 ⬤ .73   **2.** 105.7 ⬤ 150.7   **3.** 100 ⬤ .99   **4.** 86 ⬤ 9.5

5. .46 ⬤ .6   **6.** 76.25 ⬤ 72.68   **7.** 10 ⬤ 10.00   **8.** 17.00 ⬤ 170.00

9. 3.05 ⬤ 19.6   **10.** 8.6 ⬤ 8.56   **11.** 1.4 ⬤ 4   **12.** .57 ⬤ 5.70

13. 856 ⬤ 85.6   **14.** 18.00 ⬤ 18.0   **15.** 42.3 ⬤ 4.32   **16.** 12.11 ⬤ 111.2

17. 9.90 ⬤ 10   **18.** .76 ⬤ 18   **19.** 52 ⬤ 43.6   **20.** 37.52 ⬤ 41.1

21. 1.01 ⬤ 1.00   **22.** 2.01 ⬤ 2.10   **23.** .90 ⬤ .9   **24.** .81 ⬤ .79

25. .40 ⬤ .04   **26.** 8.1 ⬤ 79   **27.** 5 ⬤ 4.0   **28.** 7.9 ⬤ .86

Write in order from greatest to least.

29. .07; 3; 1.2   **30.** 2.08; 4; 3.7   **31.** .50; .05; 5.0; .55

EXTRA! Pairing Decimals with Letters

Write each letter in the blank above the decimal
that names that letter's point on the number line
to find what you call a sleeping farm animal.

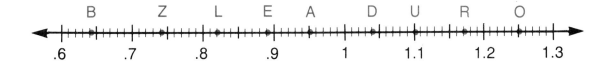

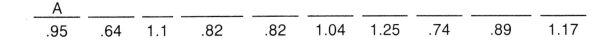

A									
.95	.64	1.1	.82	.82	1.04	1.25	.74	.89	1.17

Maintaining Skills

Find the perimeter of each polygon.

1.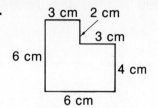
   3 cm 2 cm
   3 cm
   6 cm
   4 cm
   6 cm

2.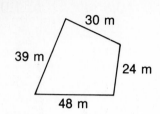
   30 m
   39 m
   24 m
   48 m

3. a rectangle with
   length: 214 m
   width: 37 m

Find the area of each rectangle.

4.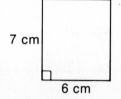
   7 cm
   6 cm

5.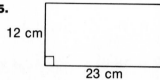
   12 cm
   23 cm

6. length: 75 m
   width: 30 m

Find the volume of each rectangular prism.

7.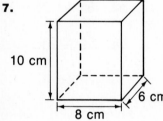
   10 cm
   6 cm
   8 cm

8.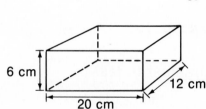
   6 cm
   20 cm
   12 cm

9. length: 8 m
   width: 5 m
   height: 6 m

Divide.

10. $7\overline{)65}$

11. $6\overline{)57}$

12. $5\overline{)375}$

13. $48\overline{)97}$

14. $17\overline{)527}$

15. $30\overline{)90}$

16. $10\overline{)75}$

17. $34\overline{)70}$

18. $77\overline{)203}$

19. $34\overline{)680}$

20. $80\overline{)726}$

21. $97\overline{)987}$

22. $60\overline{)567}$

23. $49\overline{)506}$

24. $89\overline{)379}$

25. $7\overline{)7,632}$

26. $9\overline{)9,062}$

27. $5\overline{)3,296}$

28. $6\overline{)8,649}$

29. $8\overline{)4,732}$

Solve the problems.

30. A rectangular parking lot is
    94 m long and 65 m wide. Find
    its perimeter. Find its area.

31. A room is 7 m long, 5 m wide,
    and 4 m high. What is the
    volume of the room?

Project: Sales Tax

When you buy something, you may have to pay **sales tax.** The sales tax is added to the price of what you buy.

Stores often have a tax table to help salespeople find the amount of sales tax. This tax table could be used in many states.

Price	Tax	Price	Tax
$.00–$.16	$.00	$1.50–$1.83	$.05
$.17–$.49	$.01	$1.84–$2.16	$.06
$.50–$.83	$.02	$2.17–$2.49	$.07
$.84–$1.16	$.03	$2.50–$2.83	$.08
$1.17–$1.49	$.04	$2.84–$3.16	$.09

The price of a roll of film is $1.44. How much is the tax? How much is the total price?

    $1.44 is between $1.17 and $1.49.

The tax is $.04.

Add the price and the tax to find the total price.
    Price + Tax = Total Price
    $1.44 + $.04 = $1.48

The total price for the film is $1.48.

For each amount, find the sales tax and the total price.

1. $.75
2. $.14
3. $.90
4. $1.65
5. $3.08
6. $2.99
7. $2.12
8. $2.62

Find a sales tax table for your state or another state. What would be the total price of an item with a price tag of $5.00? $7.50? $10.00?

CAREER

A **salesperson** must know how much sales tax to charge. Some states do not charge tax on food and clothes. Does your state have a sales tax? What things are taxed in your state?

349

Adding with Decimals

A. You can think of adding with decimals as adding dollars and cents.

Add hundredths.

$$
\begin{array}{r}
\$5.26 \\
+ \ 2.31 \\
\hline
7
\end{array}
$$

Add tenths.

$$
\begin{array}{r}
\$5.26 \\
+ \ 2.31 \\
\hline
.57
\end{array}
$$

Don't forget the decimal point.

Add ones.

$$
\begin{array}{r}
\$5.26 \\
+ \ 2.31 \\
\hline
\$7.57
\end{array}
$$

B. You may have to regroup.

Add hundredths. Regroup.

$$
\begin{array}{r}
\overset{1}{4}.9\ 6 \\
+2.1\ 7 \\
\hline
3
\end{array}
$$

13 hundredths is 1 tenth 3 hundredths

Add tenths. Regroup.

$$
\begin{array}{r}
\overset{1}{4}.\overset{1}{9}\ 6 \\
+2.1\ 7 \\
\hline
1\ 3
\end{array}
$$

11 tenths is 1 one 1 tenth

Add ones.

$$
\begin{array}{r}
\overset{1}{4}\ \overset{1}{9}\ 6 \\
+2\ 1\ 7 \\
\hline
7.1\ 3
\end{array}
$$

Decimal point

C. 1.8 + 5 = ▨

Write **5.0** for **5**. Then line up the decimal points.

Line up the decimal points.

$$
\begin{array}{r}
1.\ 8 \\
+5.\ 0 \\
\hline
\end{array}
$$

Add tenths.

$$
\begin{array}{r}
1.\ 8 \\
+5.\ 0 \\
\hline
8
\end{array}
$$

Add ones.

$$
\begin{array}{r}
1.\ 8 \\
+5.\ 0 \\
\hline
6.\ 8
\end{array}
$$

TRY THESE

Add.

1. 14.6
+ 3.4

2. 15.0
+ 9.3

3. 10.5
+ 5.02

4. $15.84
+ 10.16

5. 461.7
+138.3

6. 3.3 + 11 = ▨

7. 8.5 + 14.68 + 83 = ▨

8. 3.7 + 8 + 19 + .6 = ▨

SKILLS PRACTICE

Add.

1. 82.5
+76.5

2. 180.9
+793.3

3. 14.19
+ 5.83

4. 88.6
+106.5

5. 8.99
+1.01

6. 5.1
+7.0

7. .7
+.4

8. 54
+39.61

9. 3.98
+82.52

10. 2.6
+8.0

11. 92.7
+10.6

12. 62.6
+ 5.4

13. .37
+.68

14. 5.23
+ .86

15. 82.99
+ 8.1

16. .8
+5.2

17. 665.9
+142.1

18. 24.6
+59.4

19. 195.5
+ 89.3

20. 9.1
+9.7

21. 4.60
+6.00

22. 108.5
+ 25.7

23. $.90
+ .40

24. $3.07
+ .96

25. $ 7.30
+ 10.86

26. 1.8 + 2.7 = ▨

27. .12 + .04 = ▨

28. 160.8 + 40.2 = ▨

29. 81 + 26.48 = ▨

30. 4.2 + 9.3 = ▨

31. 119.7 + 3.32 = ▨

32. 10.7 + 5 = ▨

33. $.07 + $1.08 = ▨

★ **34.** $.08 + $.94 + $.59 = ▨

PROBLEM SOLVING

Find the total number of hours a musician practiced each day.

		Morning	Afternoon	In All
35.	**Mon.**	4 hours	3 hours	▨
36.	**Tues.**	3.6 hours	4.2 hours	▨
37.	**Wed.**	2.75 hours	3.67 hours	▨
38.	**Thurs.**	4.17 hours	.33 hours	▨

351

Subtracting with Decimals

A. You can think of subtracting with decimals as subtracting dollars and cents.

Subtract hundredths.	Subtract tenths.	Subtract ones.
$8.96 − 4.72 4	$8.96 − 4.72 .24	$8.96 − 4.72 $4.24

B. You may have to regroup.

Regroup. Subtract hundredths.	Regroup. Subtract tenths.	Subtract ones.
0 16 7.16 −2.38 8	10 6 0 7.16 −2.38 .78	10 6 0 16 7.16 −2.38 4.78

C. 8 − 7.96 = ▓

Write **8.00** for **8**. Then line up the decimal points.

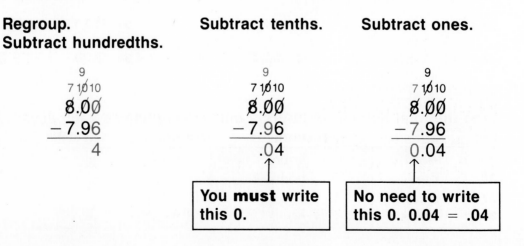

Regroup. Subtract hundredths.	Subtract tenths.	Subtract ones.
9 7 10 10 8.00 −7.96 4	9 7 10 10 8.00 −7.96 .04	9 7 10 10 8.00 −7.96 0.04

You **must** write this 0.

No need to write this 0. 0.04 = .04

TRY THESE

Subtract.

1. 10.0
     − .1

2. 82.5
    −76.6

3. 135.7
    −135.6

4. 18.7
    − 8.82

5. .57
    −.48

6. 200 − 70.81 = ■

7. .85 − .85 = ■

8. 14 − .9 = ■

SKILLS PRACTICE

Subtract.

1. 5.3
    − .8

2. 7.1
    −5.9

3. 70
    − 18.9

4. 5.1
    −4.5

5. .94
    −.53

6. 1.59
    − .61

7. 12.0
    − 6.8

8. 67.04
    −20.85

9. 70.14
    −69.25

10. 11.3
     − .91

11. 2.7
     −2.5

12. 6.0
     − .6

13. 23.1
     − 9.4

14. 80.5
     − 7.6

15. 74.67
     − 7.94

16. 29.17
     − 9.82

17. 13.7
     − 6.9

18. .56
     −.49

19. 8.80
     −5.30

20. 10.01
     − 1.1

21. 11.62
     − 2.99

22. 100.00
     − 1.00

23. 20.3
     − 7.5

24. $6.00
     − .73

25. $10.00
     − 5.05

26. 4.8 − 3 = ■

27. 13.4 − 5.1 = ■

28. 30 − 4.7 = ■

29. 8.7 − 2.2 = ■

30. 1.7 − .3 = ■

31. 18 − .61 = ■

32. 23.3 − 2.9 = ■

33. $9.00 − $.32 = ■

34. $10 − $9.03 = ■

PROBLEM SOLVING

Follow the instructions.

35. Start with 8.25. Add 1.22. → ■ → Subtract 4.95. → ■

36. Start with 12.55. Subtract 1.89. → ■ → Add 20.5. → ■

Rounding and Estimating

A. To **round to the tenths place,** circle the **tenths digit.** Look at the digit to its right.

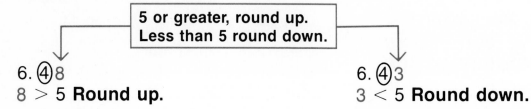

6. ④8	6. ④3
8 > 5 **Round up.**	3 < 5 **Round down.**

To round up:
Add 1 to the tenths digit.
Do not write anything
to its right.

To round down:
Keep the tenths digit.
Do not write anything
to its right.

$$\begin{array}{r} 6.\,④\,8 \\ +\quad 1 \\ \hline 6.\,5 \end{array}$$

$$\begin{array}{r} 6.\,④\,3 \\ \downarrow \\ \hline 6.\,4 \end{array}$$

B. You can round to any place in the same way.
Round 2.97 to the **nearest tenth.** To the **nearest one.**

Nearest tenth

$$\begin{array}{r} 2.\,⑨\,7 \\ +\quad 1 \\ \hline 3.\,0 \end{array}$$ 7 > 5 Add 1.

Nearest one

$$\begin{array}{r} ②.\,9\,7 \\ +\,1 \\ \hline 3 \end{array}$$ 9 > 5 Add 1.

C. To **estimate sums or differences** find the smallest number. Circle the first digit of this number that is not zero. Round all numbers to that place. Then add or subtract the rounded numbers.

Estimate the sum.

$$\begin{array}{r} 4.⑦6 \longrightarrow \quad 4.8 \\ +\ .⑥1 \longrightarrow +\ .6 \\ \hline 5.4 \end{array}$$

Estimate the difference.

$$\begin{array}{r} ⑧.21 \longrightarrow \quad 8 \\ -①96 \longrightarrow -2 \\ \hline 6 \end{array}$$

TRY THESE

Round to the nearest tenth. To the nearest one.

1. 5.61   **2.** 2.45   **3.** 6.03   **4.** 1.96   **5.** 3.05

Find the sum or difference. Use estimation to check.

6. 12.32
    $+$ .86

7.   1.21
    $-$ .07

8. 18.07
    $+$ 9.6

9. $17 - 3.61 = $ ▨

10. $6.74 + .98 = $ ▨

SKILLS PRACTICE

Round to the nearest tenth. To the nearest one.

1. 1.47   **2.** .75   **3.** 12.03   **4.** 5.59   **5.** 6.17

6. 7.92   **7.** 4.27   **8.** 19.06   **9.** 9.51   **10.** 9.99

Find the sum or difference. Use estimation to check.

11.   2.79
    $+$ .8

12.   8.18
    $-$ .55

13.   1.08
    $+$ 3.93

14.   4.2
    $-$ 1.8

15.   15.07
    $+$ 4.03

16.   .73
    $-$ .34

17.   3.09
    $+$ .91

18.   .82
    $-$ .3

19.   .17
    $+$ .95

20.   2.39
    $-$ .64

21. $14 + 5.6 = $ ▨   **22.** $40 - 7.8 = $ ▨   **23.** $\$7 - \$1.64 = $ ▨

PROBLEM SOLVING

Follow the instructions.

24. a) Start with 100.
    b) Subtract 2.98.
    c) Then add 6.81.
    d) Round to the nearest tenth.
    e) Give the result.

25. a) Start with 56.8.
    b) Round to the nearest one.
    c) Add 7.2.
    d) Then subtract 4.16.
    e) Give the result.

EXTRA! Completing a Magic Square

sum 1.5

Complete the magic squares. The sum for each straight line must be the same.

sum .75

Problem Solving: Using Decimals

A. This chart lists the times for the first three runners on a relay team. What was the total time for these three runners?

RUNNERS	TIME
1. Maria	13.59
2. Jason	15.24
3. Sarah	14.09

Draw a picture to plan what to do.

Maria	Jason	Sarah
13.59 seconds	15.24 seconds	14.09 seconds

total time

Must find: total time   Add!

$$13.59 + 15.24 + 14.09 = 42.92$$

The total time was 42.92 seconds.

B. The school record for this relay race is 56.31 seconds. With the total time of 42.92 seconds for the first three runners, what must be the fourth runner's time to tie the record?

Draw a picture to plan what to do.

Record: 56.31 seconds

Fourth runner

Three runners: 42.92 seconds

Must find: time for fourth runner to tie the record   Subtract!

$$56.31 - 42.92 = 13.39$$

The fourth runner's time must be 13.39 seconds.

TRY THESE

1. The first jumper jumped 4.27 meters. The second jumper jumped 3.25 meters. Which jumper jumped farther? How much farther?

2. Ian used 1.65 liters of paint from a full 3.5 liter can to paint the track team's bench. How much paint was left in the can?

3. The track team's coach spent $34.56 for a jacket and $12.96 for a shirt. What was the total she spent for the jacket and shirt?

4. John needed 39 meters of string. He already had 6.19 meters. How much more string did he need?

PROBLEM SOLVING PRACTICE

Use this table to solve the following problems.

Day	M	T	W	Th	F
Hours Joan Worked	7.5	8.25	7	7.75	6.5

1. Find the total time Joan worked on the five days.

2. How long in all did Joan work on Monday and Thursday?

3. How much longer did Joan work on Thursday than on Friday?

4. How long in all did Joan work on Tuesday and Wednesday?

5. Joan worked 4.5 hours Thursday morning. How long did she work Thursday afternoon?

6. How much longer did Joan work on Tuesday than on Friday?

7. How long in all did Joan work on Wednesday, Thursday, and Friday?

★8. List the numbers of hours worked in order from least to greatest.

✓ Unit Checkup

Write a decimal to tell how much is shaded. Then name the place of each digit. *(pages 342–345)*

1.    2. 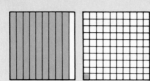   3.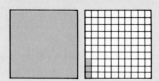

Show how to read each decimal in two ways. *(pages 342–343)*

4. 6.1   **5.** 9.0   **6.** 30.7

7. .4   **8.** 17.6   **9.** 53.2

Write decimals that mean: *(pages 344–345)*

10. 0 tenths 3 hundredths   **11.** 8 hundredths

12. 3 ones 0 tenths 7 hundredths   **13.** 1 tenths 5 hundredths

Write >, <, or = for ●. *(pages 346–347)*

14. .2 ● .02   **15.** .96 ● 20   **16.** 1.001 ● 1.010   **17.** 30.91 ● 17.8

18. .09 ● .134   **19.** 76.8 ● 7.78   **20.** 3.30 ● 3.3   **21.** .7 ● 7.0

22. 1.02 ● 10.2   **23.** 8.80 ● 9   **24.** 746 ● 74.6   **25.** 11.9 ● 2.31

Add. *(pages 350–351)*

26. 97.6
 +82.4

27. 6.73
 + .65

28. 549.5
 +327.6

29. .7
 +9.2

30. 7.96
 +1.05

31. 456.8
 + 26.3

32. .64
 +3.97

33. 659.3
 + 74.8

34. 5.62
 +3.58

35. 8.06
 +9.49

36. 73.94
 + 5.00

37. 94.8
 +106.3

38. 321.4
 + 87.3

39. $.62
 + .75

40. $86.14
 + 62.92

41. 10.9 + 73.1 + .63 = ▨   **42.** 306.3 + 29.3 = ▨   **43.** $3.25 + $2.50 + $.75 = ▨

Subtract. *(pages 352–353)*

44. 6.2
− .7

45. 8.3
−4.8

46. 50.0
−22.3

47. 9.07
−6.48

48. 47.23
−26.39

49. 29.4
−17.6

50. 11.13
− 9.87

51. 6.91
− .47

52. 80.9
−71.3

53. 43.97
−29.76

54. 8.84
−3.25

55. 17.93
− 8.34

56. 700.00
− 9.00

57. $4.30
− .81

58. $20.00
− 18.97

59. 30.0 − 18.3 = ▩   **60.** $1.29 − .79 = ▩   **61.** $90.00 − 87.29 = ▩

Add or subtract. *(pages 354–355)*

62. 5.7
− .29

63. 1.0
− .07

64. 17.06
+ 7.9

65. 41.3
− 6.11

66. 8.0
+4.65

67. 7.12
+ .36

68. 3.09
− .7

69. 43.21
− 1.68

70. 9.3
+ .83

71. 6.74
−5.89

72. 5.34
+ .67

73. 8.02
− .45

74. 7.86
+6.79

75. $10.00
− 8.35

76. $99.59
+ 76.84

77. 1.7 − .83 = ▩   **78.** $1.86 + $3.29 + $.72 = ▩   **79.** $100 − $.96 = ▩

Solve the problems. *(pages 342–347, 350–357)*

80. Judy ran the race in 19.2 seconds. Joan ran the race in 17.9 seconds. How much faster did Joan run the race?

81. One swimmer drank 1.05 liters of juice. Another swimmer drank 1.5 liters of juice. How much juice did they drink in all?

82. Jim threw the discus 41.95 meters on his first throw. He threw it 39.8 meters on his second throw. How much longer was his first throw?

83. Willie jumped 5.32 meters on his first try. He jumped 5.6 meters on his second try. How far did he jump all together?

359

Reinforcement

More Help with Reading Decimals

5.76 is read as

**five and
seventy-six hundredths
or
five point seven six**

Show how to read each decimal two ways.

1. 7.5   2. .42

3. 6.08   4. 9.01

5. 400.1   6. 20.25

7. 37.0   8. 100.01

5 ones 8 tenths → 5.8

**4 ones 1 tenth}
6 hundredths}** → 4.16

Write decimals that mean:

9. 7 ones 2 tenths

10. 3 tenths 4 hundredths

11. 10 ones 0 tenths 1 hundredth

12. 9 tenths 9 hundredths

More Help with Adding and Subtracting with Decimals

4.8 + .57 = ▓

4.8   4.80
+ .57 ⟹ + .57
          5.37

Add.

13.	.48	14.	.67	15.	9.7	16.	24
	+.57		+.98		+6.3		+ 8.3

17.	9.7	18.	86.7	19.	173.7	20.	$2.77
	+8		+ 8.9		+726.4		+ 1.68

60 − 19.23 = ▓

          9 9
          5 10 10 10
60   ⟹ 60.00
−19.23   −19.23
          40.77

Subtract.

21.	.65	22.	8	23.	.73	24.	50.7
	−.48		−3.8		−.64		− 8.9

25.	6.2	26.	93.1	27.	20	28.	$40
	− .56		−58.7		−19.8		− 39.86

Squares and Boxes

You can use squares to make patterns. Select the number of squares you will use. Follow these rules.

RULE 1 — At least one *full side* of every square must touch one *full side* of another square.

RULE 2 — Any pattern that can be flipped or turned to fit exactly on another pattern is *the same* as that other pattern.

When you use 4 squares, there are only 5 different patterns.

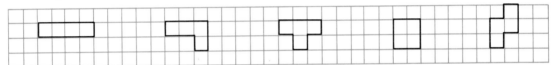

1. Use 5 squares. Follow the rules. Use graph paper to draw as many patterns as you can.

 Here is one 5-square pattern.

Hint: There are 12 different patterns in all.

2. Cut out the 5-square patterns you drew in Exercise 1. Which patterns can you fold to make an open box?

This pattern makes an open box.

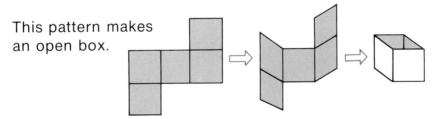

3. Use 6 squares. Follow the rules. Draw at least 10 different patterns. (There are *many* more.)

4. Which of your 6-square patterns can you fold to make a closed box?

 Maintaining Skills

Choose the correct answer. Mark NG if the correct answer is NOT GIVEN.

1.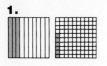

a. 36
b. 3.6
c. .36
d. NG

2.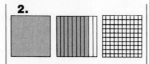

a. .18
b. 1.8
c. 1.08
d. NG

3. Which means 5 ones 3 tenths?

a. 53
b. 5.3
c. 5.03
d. NG

4. Write the decimal that means nine hundredths.

a. .09
b. .9
c. .90
d. NG

---

5. 101.01 ● 101.10

a. >
b. <
c. =
d. NG

6. 17.8 ● 2.03

a. >
b. <
c. =
d. NG

7.   87.2
       +38.9

a. 25.1
b. 2.61
c. 26.1
d. NG

8.   83.0
       −67.9

a. 16.1
b. 15.1
c. 13.1
d. NG

---

9.   8.9
       +4.35

a. 4.55
b. 13.35
c. 13.25
d. NG

10.   24.2
        − 9.86

a. 1.434
b. 14.34
c. 34.06
d. NG

11. $79.54
        + 67.96

a. $147.50
b. $146.50
c. $147.60
d. NG

12. $90.00
        − 73.21

a. $17.79
b. $16.79
c. $16.89
d. NG

---

13. William had $100 in his savings account. If he withdrew $43.94, how much would he have left in his account?

a. $56.16   b. $56.06
c. $57.06   d. NG

14. Susan saved $38.98 in January and $59.99 in February. How much money did she save in all during January and February?

a. $98.87   b. $97.87
c. $98.97   d. NG

END-YEAR REVIEW: Skills

Show how to read each standard numeral.

1. 7,500 **2.** 103,070 **3.** 296,004

Write each standard numeral.

4. forty-two thousand three hundred eighty **5.** ten thousand eight

Add or subtract.

$$
\begin{array}{r}
{}^{1\,1} \\
\$65.69 \\
+\ 47.80 \\
\hline
\$113.49
\end{array}
$$

6.
$$
\begin{array}{r} 4 \\ +9 \\ \hline \end{array}
$$
7.
$$
\begin{array}{r} 12 \\ -\ 7 \\ \hline \end{array}
$$
8.
$$
\begin{array}{r} 8 \\ +6 \\ \hline \end{array}
$$
9.
$$
\begin{array}{r} 13 \\ -\ 5 \\ \hline \end{array}
$$
10.
$$
\begin{array}{r} 9 \\ +8 \\ \hline \end{array}
$$
11.
$$
\begin{array}{r} 18 \\ -\ 9 \\ \hline \end{array}
$$

12.
$$
\begin{array}{r} 32 \\ -25 \\ \hline \end{array}
$$
13.
$$
\begin{array}{r} 85 \\ +97 \\ \hline \end{array}
$$
14.
$$
\begin{array}{r} 806 \\ +856 \\ \hline \end{array}
$$
15.
$$
\begin{array}{r} 235 \\ -\ 99 \\ \hline \end{array}
$$

$$
\begin{array}{r}
{}^{1\,1}\;\;{}^{9} \\
4\ \not{2}\ \not{0}\ 13 \\
5\,2{,}0\,3\,4 \\
-4\,2{,}0\,8\,2 \\
\hline
9{,}952
\end{array}
$$

16.
$$
\begin{array}{r} \$1.58 \\ +\ 6.75 \\ \hline \end{array}
$$
17.
$$
\begin{array}{r} \$8.00 \\ -\ 7.17 \\ \hline \end{array}
$$
18.
$$
\begin{array}{r} 5{,}314 \\ +2{,}594 \\ \hline \end{array}
$$
19.
$$
\begin{array}{r} 4{,}009 \\ -3{,}424 \\ \hline \end{array}
$$

20. $478 + 9{,}824 + 89 = $ ■ **21.** $\$100.00 - \$90.62 = $ ■

Find the total value.

							Total Value
22.		2	1	3	4	1	■
23.	1		6	5	3		■

Read each clock.

24.

■:■

■ minutes past ■

25.

■:■

■ minutes to ■

26.

■:■

■ minutes past ■

363

Multiply.

$$
\begin{array}{c}
\textcircled{7}\textcircled{3} \\
7{,}094 \\
\times \quad 8 \\
\hline
56{,}752
\end{array}
$$

27. $\begin{array}{r} 6 \\ \times 3 \\ \hline \end{array}$ **28.** $\begin{array}{r} 4 \\ \times 9 \\ \hline \end{array}$ **29.** $\begin{array}{r} 7 \\ \times 5 \\ \hline \end{array}$ **30.** $\begin{array}{r} 9 \\ \times 6 \\ \hline \end{array}$ **31.** $\begin{array}{r} 5 \\ \times 8 \\ \hline \end{array}$ **32.** $\begin{array}{r} 8 \\ \times 9 \\ \hline \end{array}$

33. $\begin{array}{r} 93 \\ \times 3 \\ \hline \end{array}$ **34.** $\begin{array}{r} 2 \\ \times 57 \\ \hline \end{array}$ **35.** $\begin{array}{r} 85 \\ \times 4 \\ \hline \end{array}$ **36.** $\begin{array}{r} 810 \\ \times 6 \\ \hline \end{array}$ **37.** $\begin{array}{r} 4 \\ \times 204 \\ \hline \end{array}$

38. $\begin{array}{r} 118 \\ \times 8 \\ \hline \end{array}$ **39.** $\begin{array}{r} 613 \\ \times 7 \\ \hline \end{array}$ **40.** $\begin{array}{r} 390 \\ \times 5 \\ \hline \end{array}$ **41.** $\begin{array}{r} 500 \\ \times 6 \\ \hline \end{array}$ **42.** $\begin{array}{r} 419 \\ \times 9 \\ \hline \end{array}$

43. $4 \times 2{,}300 = $ ▦ **44.** $5 \times 1{,}714 = $ ▦ **45.** $7 \times 1{,}290 = $ ▦

46. $3{,}976 \times 8 = $ ▦ **47.** $6 \times 2{,}540 = $ ▦ **48.** $9 \times 2{,}615 = $ ▦

Divide.

$$
\begin{array}{r}
906 \; R6 \\
8\overline{)7{,}254} \\
72 \\
\hline
05 \\
0 \\
\hline
54 \\
48 \\
\hline
6
\end{array}
$$

49. $8\overline{)48}$ **50.** $3\overline{)23}$ **51.** $7\overline{)63}$ **52.** $9\overline{)36}$

53. $6\overline{)86}$ **54.** $3\overline{)70}$ **55.** $5\overline{)78}$ **56.** $7\overline{)91}$

57. $8\overline{)967}$ **58.** $3\overline{)900}$ **59.** $9\overline{)634}$ **60.** $5\overline{)702}$

61. $4\overline{)260}$ **62.** $6\overline{)654}$ **63.** $9\overline{)2{,}549}$ **64.** $4\overline{)4{,}163}$

65. $5{,}720 \div 8 = $ ▦ **66.** $8{,}014 \div 2 = $ ▦

Write a fraction for the red part of each.

67.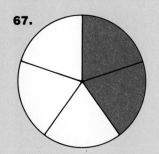

68.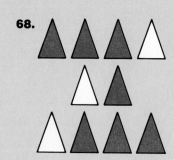

69.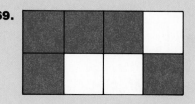

Find:

70. $\frac{1}{3}$ of 24 **71.** $\frac{1}{5}$ of 20 **72.** $\frac{3}{8}$ of 16 **73.** $\frac{7}{9}$ of 45

Add or subtract.

$$\begin{array}{r} \frac{4}{7} \\ + \frac{5}{7} \\ \hline \frac{9}{7}, \text{ or } 1\frac{2}{7} \end{array}$$

$$\begin{array}{r} \frac{11}{12} \\ - \frac{5}{12} \\ \hline \frac{6}{12}, \text{ or } \frac{1}{2} \end{array}$$

74. $\frac{2}{5} + \frac{1}{5} = $ ▨

75. $\frac{3}{10} + \frac{5}{10} = $ ▨

76. $\frac{1}{4} + \frac{3}{4} = $ ▨

77. $\frac{5}{8} - \frac{3}{8} = $ ▨

78. $\frac{7}{9} - \frac{5}{9} = $ ▨

79. $\frac{13}{10} - \frac{8}{10} = $ ▨

80. $\frac{5}{6} - \frac{3}{6} = $ ▨

81. $\frac{2}{3} + \frac{2}{3} = $ ▨

82. $\frac{5}{4} - \frac{3}{4} = $ ▨

83. $\begin{array}{r} \frac{3}{7} \\ + \frac{2}{7} \\ \hline \end{array}$
84. $\begin{array}{r} \frac{4}{3} \\ - \frac{2}{3} \\ \hline \end{array}$
85. $\begin{array}{r} \frac{5}{8} \\ + \frac{7}{8} \\ \hline \end{array}$
86. $\begin{array}{r} \frac{1}{2} \\ + \frac{5}{2} \\ \hline \end{array}$
87. $\begin{array}{r} \frac{7}{8} \\ - \frac{1}{8} \\ \hline \end{array}$

Multiply each numerator and denominator by 2, 3, 4, and 5 to find equivalent fractions.

88. $\frac{1}{2}$ **89.** $\frac{4}{5}$ **90.** $\frac{3}{4}$ **91.** $\frac{3}{8}$ **92.** $\frac{2}{3}$ **93.** $\frac{1}{6}$ **94.** $\frac{7}{9}$

Multiply.

$$\begin{array}{r} ①② \\ ③④ \\ 245 \\ \times\ 48 \\ \hline 1960 \\ 9800 \\ \hline 11,760 \end{array}$$

95. $\begin{array}{r} 63 \\ \times 10 \\ \hline \end{array}$
96. $\begin{array}{r} 407 \\ \times 10 \\ \hline \end{array}$
97. $\begin{array}{r} 79 \\ \times 20 \\ \hline \end{array}$
98. $\begin{array}{r} 52 \\ \times 70 \\ \hline \end{array}$
99. $\begin{array}{r} 23 \\ \times 32 \\ \hline \end{array}$

100. $\begin{array}{r} 81 \\ \times 75 \\ \hline \end{array}$
101. $\begin{array}{r} 90 \\ \times 45 \\ \hline \end{array}$
102. $\begin{array}{r} 47 \\ \times 16 \\ \hline \end{array}$
103. $\begin{array}{r} 92 \\ \times 92 \\ \hline \end{array}$
104. $\begin{array}{r} 54 \\ \times 83 \\ \hline \end{array}$

105. $\begin{array}{r} 84 \\ \times 56 \\ \hline \end{array}$
106. $\begin{array}{r} 73 \\ \times 35 \\ \hline \end{array}$
107. $\begin{array}{r} 256 \\ \times\ 24 \\ \hline \end{array}$
108. $\begin{array}{r} 506 \\ \times\ 36 \\ \hline \end{array}$
109. $\begin{array}{r} 851 \\ \times\ 62 \\ \hline \end{array}$

110. $42 \times 703 = $ ▨   **111.** $248 \times 19 = $ ▨   **112.** $37 \times 560 = $ ▨

Divide.

$$\begin{array}{r} 20 \text{ R28} \\ 42\overline{)868} \\ \underline{84} \\ 28 \\ \underline{0} \\ 28 \end{array}$$

113. $40\overline{)640}$ **114.** $70\overline{)490}$ **115.** $23\overline{)978}$ **116.** $26\overline{)962}$

117. $36\overline{)864}$ **118.** $72\overline{)590}$ **119.** $67\overline{)370}$ **120.** $47\overline{)280}$

121. $35\overline{)900}$ **122.** $32\overline{)276}$ **123.** $13\overline{)786}$ **124.** $24\overline{)190}$

125. $336 \div 12 = $ ▨   **126.** $392 \div 56 = $ ▨

Find the perimeter and area of each rectangle.

length: 24 m
width: 18 m

Perimeter = 24 + 18 + 24 + 18
= 84 m
Area = 24 × 18
= 432 m²

127. length: 13 cm
width: 8 cm

128. length: 25 m
width: 7 m

129. length: 30 cm
width: 16 cm

130. length: 400 m
width: 50 m

Find the volume of each rectangular prism.

131. length: 8 m
width: 6 m
height: 5 m

132. length: 30 cm
width: 20 cm
height: 20 cm

133. length: 43 m
width: 20 m
height: 9 m

Show how to read each decimal two ways. Then tell what the digit 7 means.

134. 4.7   **135.** 1.67   **136.** 72.05   **137.** 9.07

Write a decimal for each.

138. 6 in the ones place, 8 in the tenths place

139. 1 in the ones place, 0 in the tenths place, 1 in the hundredths place

140. nine point six   **141.** two and three tenths

142. five and forty-seven hundredths   **143.** zero point eight

Add or subtract.

¹.9
+6.7
‾‾‾‾
7.6

7 − 3.2 = ▨

⁶ ¹⁰
7.Ø
−3.2
‾‾‾‾
3.8

144.   13.67
+ 8.19
‾‾‾‾‾

145.   31.6
− 8.9
‾‾‾‾‾

146.   17.6
+23.8
‾‾‾‾‾

147.   .45
+.75
‾‾‾‾‾

148.   2.93
−1.4
‾‾‾‾‾

149.   26.7
+ 9.47
‾‾‾‾‾

150.   12.5
− 8.16
‾‾‾‾‾

151.   1.2
− .83
‾‾‾‾‾

152. 20 − 6.3 = ▨

153. 4 + 1.6 + .7 = ▨

154. 12.4 + 5.63 + .97 = ▨

155. 1.6 + .48 + 2 = ▨

END-YEAR REVIEW: Problem Solving

A. A store advertises 6 shirts for $58.68. What is the price of each shirt?

6 shirts ⟷ $58.68

1 shirt ⟷ ■

Divide to find the price of each shirt.

$$6\overline{)58.68} = \$9.78$$

$$\begin{array}{r} \$9.78 \\ 6\overline{)\$58.68} \\ \underline{54} \\ 4\,6 \\ \underline{4\,2} \\ 48 \\ \underline{48} \\ 0 \end{array}$$

The price of each shirt is $9.78.

B. Karen has $\frac{8}{9}$ of a basket of red apples and $\frac{6}{9}$ of a basket of yellow apples. How many baskets of apples does she have in all?

Add to find how many baskets in all.

$$\begin{array}{r} \frac{8}{9} \\ +\frac{6}{9} \\ \hline \frac{14}{9} \text{ or } 1\frac{5}{9} \end{array}$$

Karen has $\frac{14}{9}$ or $1\frac{5}{9}$ baskets in all.

C. Mr. Hastings bought a lot that is rectangular in shape. It is 29 m long and 14 m wide. What is its area?

14 m

29 m

Area=length x width

Multiply to find the area.

$$\begin{array}{r} 14 \\ \times 29 \\ \hline 126 \\ 280 \\ \hline 406 \end{array}$$

Its area is 406 m².

D. Ms. Aaron has 796 kg of sand to put into sacks. Each sack will hold 24 kg of sand. How many sacks can she fill? How much sand will be left over?

Divide to find how many sacks.

$$\begin{array}{r} 33\ R4 \\ 24\overline{)796} \\ \underline{72} \\ 76 \\ \underline{72} \\ 4 \end{array}$$

She can fill 33 sacks. 4 kg of sand will be left over.

E. Mrs. Brown drove 796.43 km. Mr. Carrey drove 900 km. How much farther than Mrs. Brown did Mr. Carrey drive?

Subtract to find how much farther.

$$\begin{array}{r} 900.00 \\ -796.43 \\ \hline 103.57 \end{array}$$

Mr. Carrey drove 103.57 km farther.

367

1. An auditorium had 1,200 seats. 916 people were seated. How many empty seats were there?

2. There were 25 boxes. Each box contained 4 cups. How many cups were there all together?

3. Mr. George had 65 folders in one file and 78 folders in another file. How many folders did he have in all?

4. Mr. Han had $60 to spend for campaign posters. How many posters could he buy, if each cost $2?

5. The Horn family wants to buy a car which costs $6,700. They have $1,550. How much more money do they need?

6. Anna has 36 books. She puts the same number on each of 4 shelves. How many books does she put on each shelf?

7. 750 people attended a banquet. 6 people sat at each table. How many tables were filled?

8. Tickets to the movies cost $6 for adults and $4 for children. How much do 9 adult tickets cost?

9. On her birthday Jenny was 122 cm tall. A year ago on her birthday her height had been 118 cm. How much had she grown during the year?

10. It took John 16 minutes to walk from his home to the store. It took him 19 minutes to walk back home. How much time did it take John in all?

11. A clerk started the day with $16.50. In the morning the clerk took in $87.68 and in the afternoon he took in $109.47. How much did the clerk have at the end of the afternoon?

12. Ms. Morgan talks on a radio program for 15 minutes each day. The program is on 5 days each week. How long does she talk on the radio each week?

13. There are 26 students in Mary's class. One day 5 students were ill. How many students were not ill?

14. A library received 4,030 books. 8 books were in each box. How many full boxes did the library receive? How many extra books were there?

15. Each day Mr. Lowe rides a bus a distance of 45 km. How far does he ride in 10 days?

16. A cycle shop paid $300 for 4 bicycles. Each cost the same. How much did each cost?

17. There are 24 students in Joe's class. $\frac{1}{3}$ of them are older than Joe. How many are older than Joe?

18. At the beginning of the day a supermarket had 840 loaves of bread. At the end of the day 79 were left. How many loaves were sold?

19. Mrs. Crown wanted to buy a new sofa for $300.00. She had $216.80. How much more money did she need?

20. There were 30 packages of paper in the cabinet. Each package had 500 sheets. How many sheets of paper were in the cabinet?

21. Ms. Harris paid $38.25 for 5 theater tickets. How much did each ticket cost?

22. A carpenter had a strip of wood 180 cm long. How many pieces, each 30 cm long, could the carpenter cut from this strip?

23. A car dealer had 40 cars on sale. $\frac{3}{8}$ of the cars were new. How many new cars were on sale?

24. An auditorium had 24 rows of seats. Each row had 32 seats. How many seats were there in the auditorium?

25. Mr. Herman has $500 to spend for plants. Each plant costs $74. How many plants can he buy? How much money will he have left over?

26. A jar of paste was $\frac{5}{8}$ full before Joan made her poster. When she finished, the jar was $\frac{3}{8}$ full. How much of the jar of paste did Joan use?

27. During one week the squirrels ate $\frac{7}{10}$ of a box of peanuts. The next week the squirrels ate $\frac{9}{10}$ of a box of peanuts. How many boxes of peanuts did they eat all together?

28. 65 people attended a dinner meeting. Each paid $8.75 for the meal. How much did they pay all together?

29. A company bought 45 packages of typing paper for $315. How much did each package cost?

30. A sewing box is 30 cm long, 14 cm wide, and 16 cm high. What is the volume of the box?

31. Ms. Mann has 144 small tomato plants for her garden. She puts 24 in each row. How many rows of tomato plants will there be in her garden?

32. A grocery store sells grapefruit at 8 for $2.08, or 12 for $2.88. Find the prices per grapefruit. Which is the better buy?

33. A garden in the park is rectangular in shape. It is 50 m long and 30 m wide. What is its area? What is its perimeter?

34. Harry bought 12 packages of paper cups. Each package had 48 cups. How many cups did Harry buy?

35. How much in all was Mr. Kole's heating bill for February, March, and April?

36. How much less was Mr. Kole's bill for April than for February?

Month	February	March	April
Mr. Kole's heating bill	$95.06	$73.65	$51.82

37. A bank clerk kept a record of the money taken in and the money given out. Complete the clerk's record.

38. Mr. Good bought four kinds of canned food. Complete the table.

Time	Money in	Money out	Has
9:00 A.M.	$200		$200
9:10 A.M.	$450		▩
9:15 A.M.		$176	▩
9:18 A.M.	$765		▩
9:25 A.M.		$309	▩

Number of cans	Cost of each can	Total cost
5	$.41	$2.05
10	$.75	▩
24	$.58	▩
18	$1.03	▩

Computers in Our World

A. Computers are used in many places. They are used in some homes, schools, stores, offices, and factories. You probably already know about many of these uses of computers.

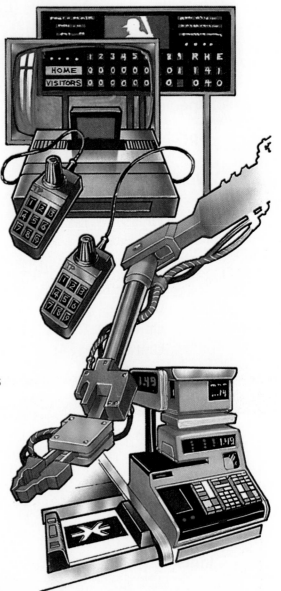

Home video games are small computers.

Large scoreboards at baseball or football games are run by computers.

In some libraries a computer may help you find a book.

Your telephone calls are timed by computers. The computer also prepares the monthly bill!

Some supermarket cash registers are computers.

Many schools now use computers to keep student records.

Computers are built into some cars to check that they are working properly.

Some factories use robots on assembly lines. These are special kinds of computers.

1. Which of the computer uses described above have you seen?

2. Do you know about any other uses of computers?

B. Computers cannot do anything until someone tells them exactly what to do and how to do it. With these instructions, computers can do some tasks very well.

A small computer can remember or **store** and **recall** about 30 pages of information.

Computers can **calculate, compare numbers,** and **sort** information much faster than people can. In just 1 second a small computer can do hundreds of thousands of 2-digit additions.

Because they never get tired or bored the way people do, computers can do the same things many times—and make very few mistakes.

There are some things a computer cannot do. They cannot feel happy or sad. Also, computers cannot make decisions that depend on judgment or common sense.

3. What would you ask a computer to do?

HISTORY OF COMPUTERS

The first modern computer was built in 1946. It was called ENIAC. It could do in 2 hours the calculations that would have taken 100 engineers an entire year to complete. ENIAC took up a space about half the size of a classroom.

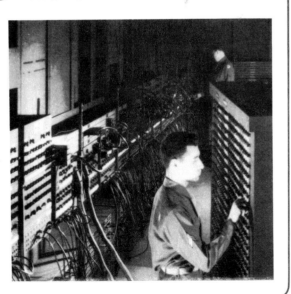

How Computers Work

A. When you add 2 numbers, how do you do it?

First you use your eyes to read the exercise. The exercise is the **input**—the information you are given. Your eyes are the **input device**.

Next your mind or mental **processor** decides what other information you need.

Find: Addition facts
Rules for adding

3	3	3	5	5	5
+3	+4	+5	+5	+6	+7
6	7	8	10	11	12

Then you recall from your **memory** the addition facts and the rules of adding that you need.

Then your processor does the calculations.

```
  53
+ 64
-----
 117
```

Finally you use your pencil as an **output device** to write the sum. The sum is the **output.**

B. The 4 parts of your **thinking system**—input device, processor, memory, output device—are also found in a **computer system.**

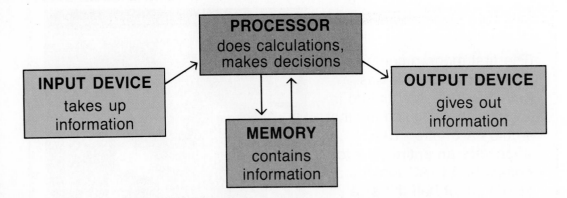

PROCESSOR
does calculations, makes decisions

INPUT DEVICE
takes up information

MEMORY
contains information

OUTPUT DEVICE
gives out information

A computer finds the sum of 2 numbers very much as you do. It also uses an input device, a processor, a memory, and an output device.

1. Suppose you wanted to solve the problem:

   There are 8 apples in a bag. How many are in 3 bags? What part of your thinking system would you use for each of these steps?
   a. read the problem
   b. decide what information you need
   c. recall problem-solving steps and multiplication facts
   d. follow the problem-solving steps
   e. write the answer

2. What is the name for information that:
   a. we give a computer?   b. a computer gives us?

3. What input device do you use when your teacher reads an addition exercise to you? What output device do you use when you say the sum?

C. A large computer can **store** a lot of information in its memory. A small computer can store less. The amount of information a computer can store is measured in **bytes.** A byte is a single letter, digit, space, or punctuation mark. A larger unit, the **kilobyte,** is also used. A kilobyte, or 1 KB, is 1,024 bytes or characters.

4. Estimate the number of bytes, or characters, in exercise **3.** Are there fewer than 1 kilobyte?

HISTORY OF COMPUTERS

Computers belong to different **generations** if they have different processors.

First generation. 1946–1960: Used vacuum tubes: ENIAC and EDVAC.

Second generation. 1960–1964: Transistors replaced vacuum tubes, giving smaller, more dependable computers at much less cost.

Third generation. 1964–late 1960's: Integrated circuits allowed computers to "talk" to many other computers at the same time.

Fourth generation. late 1960's–now: Silicon chips led to small computers like those used in homes and classrooms.

Writing Instructions

Computers work very quickly, but they are not smart. People have to tell computers *exactly* what to do. Before you can write instructions for a computer you must be able to write, in order, step-by-step instructions that people can understand. Such a set of instructions is called an **algorithm.**

A. This is a teacher's record of student test scores. At the end of the term this teacher gives grades based on these scores.

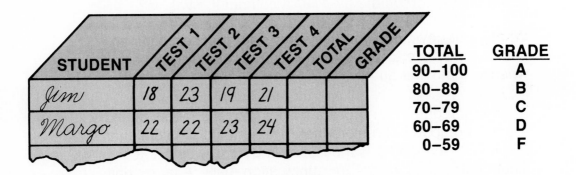

STUDENT	TEST 1	TEST 2	TEST 3	TEST 4	TOTAL	GRADE
Jim	18	23	19	21		
Margo	22	22	23	24		

TOTAL	GRADE
90–100	A
80–89	B
70–79	C
60–69	D
0–59	F

To find whether a student has earned an A, the teacher could follow the steps of this algorithm:

Step 1. Find the sum of the 4 test scores.

Step 2. Write the sum in the column marked TOTAL.

Step 3. If TOTAL > 89, write A in the column marked GRADE.

1. Use the algorithm to see if either Jim or Margo earned an A.

2. To find whether a student has earned a B, add this step:

    Step 4. If TOTAL > 79 *and* TOTAL < 90, write B in the column marked GRADE.

    Did either Jim or Margo earn a B?

3. Use the patterns of **Steps 3** and **4** to write 3 more steps for grades C, D, and F.

B. Sometimes you don't use every step of an algorithm. This algorithm is for comparing 2 different numbers.

Step 1. Write the numerals one above the other, lining up the ones digits.

Step 2. If one numeral has more digits than the other, write: longer numeral > shorter numeral, and stop.

Step 3. Read the digits in the leftmost place.

Step 4. If the digits are the same, go to **Step 7.**

Step 5. If the top digit is greater, write: top numeral > bottom numeral, and stop.

Step 6. If the bottom digit is greater, write: top numeral < bottom numeral, and stop.

Step 7. Read the digits one place farther right, and go to **Step 4.**

To compare 36 and 34, you would read **Steps 1, 2, 3, 4, 7, 4,** and **5** of the algorithm, in that order. Your output would be: 36 > 34. (Try it!)

4. Use the algorithm to compare 256 and 258. What steps did you have to read? What was your output?

5. What steps in the algorithm would you read if you compared:
   a. two 3-digit numbers with the same first digit and different second digits?
   b. a 3-digit number and a 2-digit number?

PEOPLE IN COMPUTING

John von Neumann (1903–1957) was born in Budapest, Hungary. He moved to the United States and designed the first computer with a memory, the EDVAC, in 1947.

377

Communicating with a Computer

In order to "talk" to a computer you must know how to give and receive information from the computer. You must also use a computer **language.**

A. You use an input device to give information to a computer and an output device to receive information from a computer.

Computers in schools usually have a **keyboard** for an input device and a **TV set** for an output device.

You use the keyboard to give instructions to the computer and to answer its questions. With some computers you press the RETURN key after *every* instruction and answer.

The computer shows the input it "hears" on the TV screen. It also shows the output on the TV screen.

A box, or **cursor** (■), appears on the TV screen to show where you are working. If you make a typing mistake, press the backup key ⟵ to move the cursor back to the incorrect letter. Type the correct letter, then retype the rest of the line.

You use the SHIFT key together with another key to type the character shown at the top of that key.

1. Look at a computer keyboard. Find:

   a. RETURN b. ⟵ c. % / 5 d. SHIFT e. SPACE

2. What character would appear if you pressed these keys?

   a. SHIFT and $ / 4 b. SHIFT and < / , c. SHIFT and + / ;

3. Suppose you wanted to type SQUARE, but the TV screen shows SQUAFE ■. What keys would you use to correct the mistake?

B. There are many computer languages that you can use to talk with a computer. Each language has its own words and rules.

LOGO is a computer language that can be used to tell a turtle how to draw shapes. Here are some of the words and rules in the LOGO language:

DRAW means: Erase the TV screen. Put the turtle in the middle of the screen and facing the top of the screen.

FORWARD 100 means: Move forward 100 turtle steps.

RIGHT 90 means: Turn right to make a square corner or **right angle.**

4. On a piece of graph paper outline an area that is 28 squares wide and 24 squares high. Find where the 2 middle grid lines cross. Draw a turtle facing the top of the paper at this place.

5. The distance from one grid to another is 10 turtle steps. Draw the output that the turtle would give by following these instructions *in order:*

   a. FORWARD 50   **b.** RIGHT 90   **c.** FORWARD 80

CAREERS IN COMPUTING

Data-entry clerks enter information into a computer's memory. They use input devices such as keyboards. To learn to be a data-entry clerk you would study at a high school or business school.

Programming with LOGO

An algorithm written in a language that a computer can understand is called a **program.** LOGO is called a **programming language** because you can use it to write programs.

A. Pretend that you are the turtle. Suppose you want to walk along the sides of a **square.** You could tell someone how you would move by writing this algorithm:

Step 1. Walk forward 100 steps.
Step 2. Turn right.
Step 3. Walk forward 100 steps.
Step 4. Turn right.
Step 5. Walk forward 100 steps.
Step 6. Turn right.
Step 7. Walk forward 100 steps.
Step 8. Turn right.

Now you can translate the algorithm into LOGO so that the computer will understand. This program uses the LOGO instructions on page 379 and some new ones:

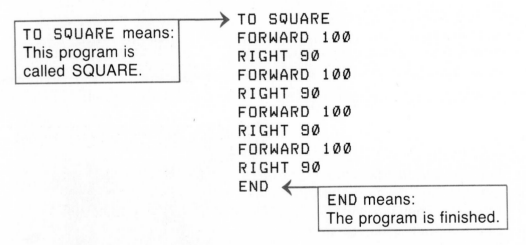

```
TO SQUARE
FORWARD 100
RIGHT 90
FORWARD 100
RIGHT 90
FORWARD 100
RIGHT 90
FORWARD 100
RIGHT 90
END
```

TO SQUARE means:
This program is
called SQUARE.

END means:
The program is finished.

As soon as you type END the computer will print: SQUARE DEFINED. This means that the computer "knows" the program. To see the shape again just type SQUARE, the program's name.

1. Draw the output on graph paper: DRAW
SQUARE

B. You can create new programs by making very simple changes in SQUARE. For example, to make squares of different sizes change the number of turtle steps along the side. This program is called SMALLSQUARE:

```
TO SMALLSQUARE
FORWARD 50    RIGHT 90  ←
FORWARD 50    RIGHT 90
FORWARD 50    RIGHT 90
FORWARD 50    RIGHT 90
END
```

> Notice that you can put more than 1 instruction on a line.

2. Draw the output: DRAW
   SMALLSQUARE

3. Write a new program that tells the turtle to turn left when making a square corner (LEFT 90). Use 40 turtle steps along the sides. Call the program SQUARELEFT.

4. PENUP tells the turtle *not* to draw a line as it moves, PENDOWN tells the turtle to begin drawing again.
   Draw the output: DRAW
   ```
   SQUARE
   PENUP    FORWARD 20    RIGHT 90
   FORWARD 20    LEFT 90    PENDOWN
   SMALLSQUARE
   ```

READY-MADE PROGRAMS

You can use programs that someone else has written. They may be stored on a **floppy disk.** A floppy disk looks like a small, flexible record in a black envelope. Never touch the brown surface of a disk!

To use a ready-made program put the disk into the **disk drive,** close its door, and turn on the computer. The disk drive light will come on, and the drive will whirr. Soon you will see a **menu** on the TV screen telling you what you can choose. Press the key for the number of the item you want from the menu.

Calculators: Multiple Operations

A. When using a hand-held calculator, if you enter

different calculators will all display **7** as a result.

If you enter

different calculators will display different results.

1. Make this entry in your calculator. What result do you get?

The result you get tells you what type of calculator you have.

Type I does
first: 3 + 4 = 7
then: 7 × 5 = **35**

Type I reads 3 + 4 × 5
  as: (3 + 4) × 5

Type II does
first: 4 × 5 = 20
then: 3 + 20 = **23**

Type II reads 3 + 4 × 5
  as: 3 + (4 × 5)

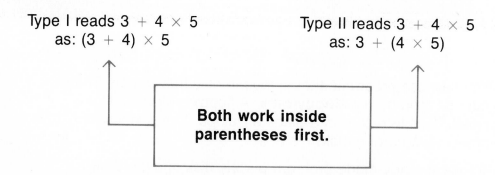

Both work inside parentheses first.

2. If your calculator works as Type I does, find how to enter the numbers so that it does 4 × 5 = 20 first, then 20 + 3 = **23**. If your calculator works as Type II does, find how to enter the numbers so that it does 3 + 4 = 7 first, then 7 × 5 = **35**.

3. The correct result to $5 \times (3 + 4)$ is **35.** Try to find it by entering

| 5 | × | 3 | + | 4 | = |

What result do you get?

To get **35** with a Type I calculator enter

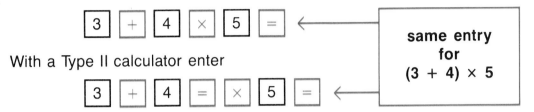

| 3 | + | 4 | × | 5 | = | ←

With a Type II calculator enter

| 3 | + | 4 | = | × | 5 | = | ←

> **same entry for (3 + 4) × 5**

B. Some calculators have parentheses buttons. You can use these buttons to find the correct result to $(3 + 4) \times 5$ which is **35.**

| (| 3 | + | 4 |) | × | 5 | = |

The correct result to $5 \times (3 + 4)$ is **35.** To find this result using the parentheses buttons enter

| 5 | × | (| 3 | + | 4 |) | = |

Find how to enter each exercise in the type of calculator you have to get the correct result that is shown at the right.

4. $(2 + 3) \times 4$ **20**   **5.** $2 + (3 \times 4)$ **14**   **6.** $(6 + 4) \div 2$ **5**

7. $6 + (4 \div 2)$ **8**   **8.** $(8 - 2) \times 3$ **18**   **9.** $8 - (2 \times 3)$ **2**

10. $(10 - 4) + 3$ **9**   **11.** $(10 - 4) - 3$ **3**   **12.** $10 - (4 + 3)$ **3**

13. $10 - (4 - 3)$ **9**   **14.** $12 \div (3 \times 2)$ **2**   **15.** $(12 \div 3) \times 2$ **8**

16. $(12 \div 3) \div 2$ **2**   **17.** $(12 \div 4) + 2$ **5**   **18.** $12 \div (4 + 2)$ **2**

Probability: Making Random Selections

A. This box contains 10 counters. They are the same size and shape but have different colors.

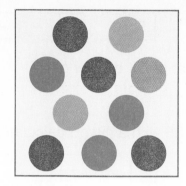

1. How many counters are red? Green? Orange? Blue?

To select one counter **at random** means you select a counter without looking in the box so that each counter is equally likely to be selected.

2. If one counter is selected at random which color is most likely to be selected? Least likely?

3. Is a blue counter or a green counter more likely to be selected?

4. Is it more likely that the counter selected will be red or that it will be either blue or green?

5. What counter is *exactly* as likely to be selected as either a green or an orange counter?

6. Make 10 counters colored as shown above. Place them in a box. Select one counter at random. Record its color in a table. Replace the counter and stir the counters in the box. Then select again. Make a total of 100 selections in this same way. Use a tally system to show your results in the table. This table shows 20 results: 10 red, 6 blue, 3 green, 1 orange.

Red	卌 卌
Blue	卌 l
Green	lll
Orange	l

7. Write a fraction for the part of your selections that were red. Blue. Green. Orange.

8. $\overset{\times 10}{\dfrac{4}{10}} = \dfrac{40}{100}$ of the counters in the box are red.

$\overset{\times 10}{\dfrac{\blacksquare}{10}} = \dfrac{\blacksquare}{100}$ of the counters in the box are blue.

$\dfrac{\blacksquare}{10} = \dfrac{\blacksquare}{100}$ of the counters in the box are green.

$\dfrac{\blacksquare}{10} = \dfrac{\blacksquare}{100}$ of the counters in the box are orange.

9. Compare the part of the counters that are red with the part of your selections that were red. Do the same for blue, green, and orange. What do you find?

10. Combine the results of your selections with those of several other students. Write fractions for the parts of the total number of selections that were red, blue, green, or orange. Compare with your results in exercise **8**.

B. Use the set of counters shown here.

11. Which of the following is the most likely outcome of a random selection: red, blue, odd number, or even number?

12. Is a blue *and* an even number or a blue *and* an odd number more likely to be selected?

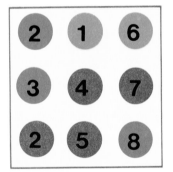

13. Make a table with these labels: red; blue; green; odd; even; red and odd; red and even; blue and odd; blue and even; green and odd; green and even. Use colored and numbered counters to make 90 random selections. Be sure to record each result in 3 places in your table. Write a fraction for each part of your selections.

Probability: Finding Probabilities

A. In this set of counters $\frac{3}{8}$ of the counters are blue. Write a fraction for the part that is:

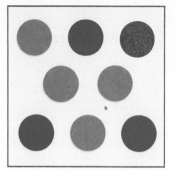

1. Red   **2.** Green

3 chances out of 8, or $\frac{3}{8}$, tells how likely it is that a blue counter will be selected in one random selection. Another way of saying this is:

The **probability** that a random selection will give a blue counter is $\frac{3}{8}$.

Write: Probability of getting a blue counter $= \frac{3}{8}$

or P(blue) $= \frac{3}{8}$

3. Probability of getting a red counter $= \dfrac{\blacksquare}{8}$

or P(red) $= \blacksquare$

4. P(green) $= \blacksquare$

5. $\frac{7}{8}$ of the counters are either blue or green.

P(blue or green) $= \blacksquare$

6. $\dfrac{\blacksquare}{8}$ of the counters are either green or red.

P(green or red) $= \blacksquare$

7. P(blue or red) $= \blacksquare$

B. $\frac{8}{8}$ or all of the box of counters are either blue, or green, or red. If you select a counter at random it is *sure* to be either blue, or green, or red.

P(blue or green or red) = $\frac{8}{8}$ or 1

> **If something is *sure* to happen as the result of a random selection, the probability that it will happen is 1.**
>
> **P(something sure) = 1**

$\frac{0}{8}$ of the box of counters are yellow.

P(yellow) = $\frac{0}{8}$ or 0

> **If something is *impossible* as the result of a random selection, the probability that it will happen is 0.**
>
> **P(something impossible) = 0**

C. Use the box of counters shown here to find the probabilities.

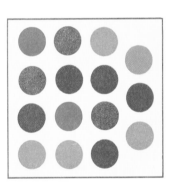

8. P(blue) = ▨

9. P(orange) = ▨

10. P(red) = ▨

11. P(brown) = ▨

12. P(green) = ▨

13. P(black) = ▨

14. P(orange or green) = ▨

15. P(blue or red) = ▨

16. P(not orange) = ▨

17. P(not purple) = ▨

Probability: Listing Possible Outcomes

A. When one counter is selected from a box of counters the **possible outcome** of the selection is any one of the counters in the box. For this box there are 8 possible outcomes of selecting one counter.

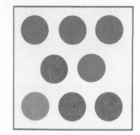

Sometimes it is not easy to find the set of possible outcomes. If 1 nickel and 1 dime are tossed, there are 4 possible outcomes.

N	D
Head	Head
Head	Tail
Tail	Head
Tail	Tail

If the coins are fair coins and they are fairly tossed the four outcomes in the table are equally likely. After the set of possible outcomes has been found you can find probabilities just as for random selections from a box of counters.

$\frac{1}{4}$ of the set of outcomes gives two heads.

Probability of 2 heads = $P(2H) = \frac{1}{4}$

1. $\frac{\blacksquare}{4}$ of the set of outcomes gives one head and one tail.

Probability of one head and 1 tail = P(1H and 1T) = ▨

2. $P(2T)$ = ▨

3. P(at least 1H) = ▨

4. P(at least 1T) = ▨

5. P(no H) = ▨

6. Why are the results in exercises **2.** and **5.** the same?

7. Copy and complete the table at the right to list the 8 possible outcomes of tossing 1 penny, 1 nickel, and 1 dime.

P	N	D
H	H	H
H	H	T
H	T	H
H	T	T
T		
T		
T		
T		

8. $P(3H) =$ ▨

9. $(2H \text{ and } 1T) =$ ▨

10. $P(1H \text{ and } 2T) =$ ▨

11. $P(3T) =$ ▨

12. P(Penny is heads) = ▨

13. P(Penny and dime are both heads) = ▨

14. P(Penny and nickel are both heads) = ▨

15. Make a table like the one in exercise 7. Use it to record the results for 1 penny, 1 nickel, 1 dime, and 1 quarter. Find P(4H); P(3H and 1T); P(2H and 2T); P(1H and 3T); P(4T).

B. A number cube has the numbers 1, 2, 3, 4, 5, 6 on its six faces. Copy and complete the table shown below to list all possible outcomes of tossing one blue and one green number cube.

16.

B	1	1	1	1	1	1	2	⋯	6	6	6
G	1	2	3	4	5	6	1	⋯	4	5	6

If the number cubes are fair and are tossed fairly these 36 possible outcomes are equally likely. Find the probabilities.

17. Probability (sum is 3) = P(3) = ▨   18. P (sum is 5) = P(5) = ▨

19. $P(2) =$ ▨   20. $P(7) =$ ▨   21. $P(10) =$ ▨   22. $P(8) =$ ▨

Statistics: Some Important Statistics

Statisticians have invented special numbers that give information about sets of numbers. These special numbers are called **statistics.**

A. The scores of 15 students on a 50-point test are listed below. You can use statistics to give information about the scores.

35	38	46	36	39
36	41	34	43	45
41	50	37	41	38

The **mean** is the average of the scores.

Mean = Sum of the scores ÷ Number of scores

= (35 + 36 + ... + 45 + 38) ÷ 15

= 600 ÷ 15

= 40

1. Find the mean of these 5 numbers: 86, 58, 75, 91, 70

2. Replace 58 by 63 in exercise **1.** and find the mean of the new set of numbers.

To find other statistics first list the scores in order from largest to smallest.

50, 46, 45, 43, 41, 41, 41, 39, 38, 38, 37, 36, 36, 35, **34**

↑

The **median** is the middle score.
7 scores are above 39. 7 scores are below 39.

median = 39

3. Replace one score of 38 by 42 in the set of scores in exercise **2.** Find the median of this new set of scores.

In a set with an even number of numbers, there are two middle numbers. In this case the median is the mean of these two numbers.

$$165, \ 159, \ 148, \ 144, \ 140, \ 135$$
$$\downarrow \qquad \downarrow$$
$$\text{median} = (148 + 144) \div 2$$
$$= 146$$

The mode is the score that is listed the most times.

50, 46, 45, 43, 41, 41, 41, 39, 38, 38, 37, 36, 36, **34**

$$\text{mode} = 41$$

4. In the list above replace one 41 by 38. Find the mode of this new set of scores.

If two or more numbers are listed the same number of times and more often than the other numbers all of these numbers are modes. The set of scores below has 2 modes.

98, 96, 95, 95, 95, 94, 89, 89, 89, 86, 84

89 and 95 are modes.

5. Replace 45 by 36 in the set of scores in exercise **2**. Find the mode of the new set of scores.

> **The mean, median, and mode describe the center, or middle, of a set of scores.**

B. The **range** tells the difference between the largest and smallest scores. To find the range subtract the smallest score from the largest score.

50, 46, 45, 43, 41, 41, 41, 39, 38, 38, 37, 36, 36, 35, **34**

$$\text{range} = 50 - 34$$
$$= 16$$

Find the range of each set of scores.

6. 86, 58, 75, 91, 70   7. 65, 59, 48, 44, 40, 35

Statistics: Picturing Information

A. Twenty people rated two television shows from 1 (very bad) to 10 (very good!). This table shows the results.

Person	1	2	3	4	5	6	7	8	9	10
Show 1	7	8	6	3	5	8	10	2	4	2
Show 2	4	6	4	5	7	7	8	5	3	3

Person	11	12	13	14	15	16	17	18	19	20
Show 1	8	7	6	9	7	2	4	7	8	7
Show 2	4	2	5	3	7	1	4	8	8	6

A **coordinate plane** can be used to show the two ratings given by each person as a dot of a **scattergram**.

Person 1

Ratings: 7 for Show 1
6 for Show 2

Dot: Directly above 7
Directly to the right of 4

Person 2

Ratings: 8 for Show 1
6 for Show 2

Dot: Directly above 8
Directly to the right of 6

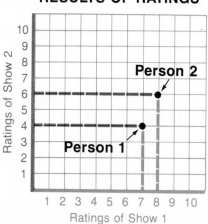

RESULTS OF RATINGS

1. Copy the picture shown on graph paper. Draw dots for **person 3** through **20** to complete the scattergram for these pairs of ratings.

Your completed scattergram should look like the one shown below. You can use this scattergram to find the median, mode, and range of the ratings for Show 1 or Show 2.

RESULTS OF RATINGS

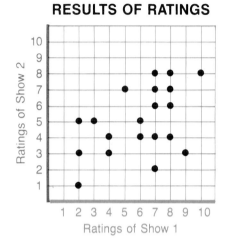

To find the median you must find the two dots in the middle of the 20 dots. These are the tenth and eleventh dots.

For Show 1 start at the left. Count the dots above 1, above 2, and so on. The tenth and eleventh dots are both above the rating 7. 7 is the median of the ratings for Show 1.

2. Start at the bottom and count across for each rating to find the median of the ratings for Show 2.

There are 5 dots above the rating 7 for Show 1. This is the greatest number of dots above any rating for Show 1. 7 is the mode of ratings for Show 1.

3. Find the mode of the ratings for Show 2.

The greatest rating for Show 1 is 10. The least rating for Show 1 is 2.

4. Find the range of the ratings for Show 1.

5. Find the greatest rating for Show 2. Find the least rating for Show 2.

6. Find the range of the ratings for Show 2.

7. Which show has the greater range of ratings?

A scattergram does not help you find the mean of the ratings for each show. To find each mean you must add the ratings for each show and divide by 20.

8. Use the table on page 392 to find the mean of the ratings for Show 1. For Show 2.

B. The line shown goes through three points of the scattergram. The pairs of ratings these points show are:

4 and 4
7 and 7
8 and 8

Each of these people liked the shows equally well.

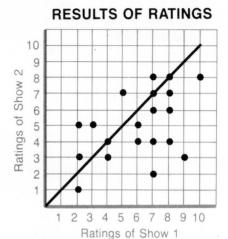

RESULTS OF RATINGS

Ratings of Show 2

Ratings of Show 1

9. How many dots are above the line? Which show has the higher rating for these dots?

10. How many dots are below the line? Which show has the higher rating for these dots?

11. Use the scattergram to find how many persons rated Show 1 higher than Show 2.

12. Describe the general shape of the scattergram.

13. Make up 20 pairs of ratings. Most of the 20 persons should like one show very much and the other show very little. Draw dots for the 20 persons on another piece of graph paper. Describe the shape of the scattergram.

14. Find the range of the new ratings for each show.

UNIT 1: Reviewing Addition and Subtraction Facts

Addition Facts *(pages 2–3)*

Add.

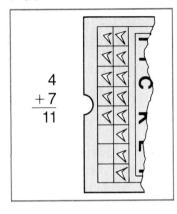

$$\begin{array}{r} 4 \\ +7 \\ \hline 11 \end{array}$$

1. $\begin{array}{r} 4 \\ +5 \\ \hline \end{array}$	**2.** $\begin{array}{r} 8 \\ +4 \\ \hline \end{array}$	**3.** $\begin{array}{r} 6 \\ +3 \\ \hline \end{array}$	**4.** $\begin{array}{r} 9 \\ +6 \\ \hline \end{array}$	**5.** $\begin{array}{r} 1 \\ +8 \\ \hline \end{array}$
6. $\begin{array}{r} 3 \\ +7 \\ \hline \end{array}$	**7.** $\begin{array}{r} 5 \\ +5 \\ \hline \end{array}$	**8.** $\begin{array}{r} 8 \\ +9 \\ \hline \end{array}$	**9.** $\begin{array}{r} 0 \\ +4 \\ \hline \end{array}$	**10.** $\begin{array}{r} 2 \\ +7 \\ \hline \end{array}$
11. $\begin{array}{r} 9 \\ +2 \\ \hline \end{array}$	**12.** $\begin{array}{r} 6 \\ +6 \\ \hline \end{array}$	**13.** $\begin{array}{r} 7 \\ +3 \\ \hline \end{array}$	**14.** $\begin{array}{r} 8 \\ +1 \\ \hline \end{array}$	**15.** $\begin{array}{r} 3 \\ +8 \\ \hline \end{array}$

16. $8 + 7 = $ ▨   **17.** $5 + 9 = $ ▨   **18.** $2 + 5 = $ ▨

19. $4 + 6 = $ ▨   **20.** $4 + 8 = $ ▨   **21.** $9 + 9 = $ ▨

Addition Properties *(pages 4–5)*

Add.

$$\begin{array}{r} 3 \\ +7 \\ \hline 10 \end{array} \bowtie \begin{array}{r} 7 \\ +3 \\ \hline 10 \end{array}$$

$$6 + 0 = 6$$
$$0 + 6 = 6$$

1. $\begin{array}{r} 7 \\ +5 \\ \hline \end{array}$	**2.** $\begin{array}{r} 5 \\ +7 \\ \hline \end{array}$	**3.** $\begin{array}{r} 0 \\ +7 \\ \hline \end{array}$	**4.** $\begin{array}{r} 7 \\ +0 \\ \hline \end{array}$	**5.** $\begin{array}{r} 9 \\ +3 \\ \hline \end{array}$
6. $\begin{array}{r} 3 \\ +9 \\ \hline \end{array}$	**7.** $\begin{array}{r} 4 \\ +3 \\ \hline \end{array}$	**8.** $\begin{array}{r} 3 \\ +4 \\ \hline \end{array}$	**9.** $\begin{array}{r} 0 \\ +8 \\ \hline \end{array}$	**10.** $\begin{array}{r} 8 \\ +0 \\ \hline \end{array}$

11. $\begin{array}{r} 5 \\ 3 \\ +2 \\ \hline \end{array}$	**12.** $\begin{array}{r} 6 \\ 2 \\ +7 \\ \hline \end{array}$	**13.** $\begin{array}{r} 4 \\ 0 \\ +8 \\ \hline \end{array}$	**14.** $\begin{array}{r} 2 \\ 3 \\ +6 \\ \hline \end{array}$	**15.** $\begin{array}{r} 7 \\ 1 \\ +8 \\ \hline \end{array}$	**16.** $\begin{array}{r} 3 \\ 6 \\ +1 \\ \hline \end{array}$	**17.** $\begin{array}{r} 4 \\ 2 \\ +6 \\ \hline \end{array}$

18. $4 + 2 + 7 = $ ▨   **19.** $5 + 1 + 7 = $ ▨   **20.** $6 + 8 + 0 = $ ▨

21. $8 + 2 + 5 = $ ▨   **22.** $1 + 1 + 9 = $ ▨   **23.** $7 + 2 + 4 = $ ▨

24. $7 + 2 + 3 = $ ▨   **25.** $9 + 0 + 5 = $ ▨   **26.** $3 + 8 + 7 = $ ▨

Problem Solving: A 5-Step Plan *(pages 6–7)*

Use these five steps to solve each problem.

1. **Read**
   There were 7 cars in the school parking lot. Then 5 more cars were parked. How many cars were parked in all?

2. **Plan**
   7 cars and 5 cars
   $7 + 5 = $ ▨

3. **Do**
   $$\begin{array}{r} 7 \\ +\ 5 \\ \hline 12 \end{array}$$

4. **Answer**
   There were 12 cars parked in the lot.

5. **Check**
   $$\begin{array}{r} 5 \\ +\ 7 \\ \hline 12 ✓ \end{array}$$

1. Mrs. Gladstone gave her class 3 worksheets to do in the morning. In the afternoon she gave them 2 more. How many worksheets did they do in all?

2. Marty did some work at home. He received $3 one day, $4 another day, and $5 the third day. How many dollars did he earn in all?

3. Leroy read 8 pages of his homework. After lunch he read 6 more pages. How many pages did he read in all?

4. The Chung family has 4 trees in their front yard, but only 2 trees in their back yard. How many trees do they have in all?

5. Joe dumped 4 bags into the trash container. Sally dumped 5 bags. How many bags did they dump?

6. Miriam wrote 3 poems, Bill wrote 2 poems, and Janet wrote 6 poems. How many poems did they write in all?

Subtraction Facts *(pages 10–11)*

Subtract.

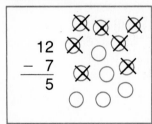

$$\begin{array}{r} 12 \\ -\ 7 \\ \hline 5 \end{array}$$

1. $\begin{array}{r} 8 \\ -\ 2 \\ \hline \end{array}$
2. $\begin{array}{r} 11 \\ -\ 9 \\ \hline \end{array}$
3. $\begin{array}{r} 5 \\ -\ 1 \\ \hline \end{array}$
4. $\begin{array}{r} 12 \\ -\ 5 \\ \hline \end{array}$
5. $\begin{array}{r} 14 \\ -\ 9 \\ \hline \end{array}$

6. $\begin{array}{r} 13 \\ -\ 6 \\ \hline \end{array}$
7. $\begin{array}{r} 10 \\ -\ 6 \\ \hline \end{array}$
8. $\begin{array}{r} 9 \\ -\ 4 \\ \hline \end{array}$
9. $\begin{array}{r} 16 \\ -\ 7 \\ \hline \end{array}$
10. $\begin{array}{r} 18 \\ -\ 9 \\ \hline \end{array}$

11. $\begin{array}{r} 3 \\ -\ 2 \\ \hline \end{array}$
12. $\begin{array}{r} 15 \\ -\ 8 \\ \hline \end{array}$
13. $\begin{array}{r} 9 \\ -\ 6 \\ \hline \end{array}$
14. $\begin{array}{r} 10 \\ -\ 1 \\ \hline \end{array}$
15. $\begin{array}{r} 6 \\ -\ 5 \\ \hline \end{array}$
16. $\begin{array}{r} 5 \\ -\ 2 \\ \hline \end{array}$
17. $\begin{array}{r} 12 \\ -\ 4 \\ \hline \end{array}$

18. $17 - 8 = $ ▨   **19.** $13 - 8 = $ ▨   **20.** $7 - 4 = $ ▨

Subtraction Properties *(pages 12–13)*

Subtract. Use addition to check your subtraction.

$$\begin{array}{r} 8 \\ -\,8 \\ \hline 0 \end{array} \qquad \begin{array}{r} 4 \\ -\,0 \\ \hline 4 \end{array}$$

$$\begin{array}{r} 15 \\ -\,7 \\ \hline 8 \end{array} \times \begin{array}{r} 8 \\ +\,7 \\ \hline 15 \end{array} \checkmark$$

1. $\begin{array}{r}9\\-8\\\hline\end{array}$	**2.** $\begin{array}{r}5\\-5\\\hline\end{array}$	**3.** $\begin{array}{r}14\\-9\\\hline\end{array}$	**4.** $\begin{array}{r}10\\-4\\\hline\end{array}$	**5.** $\begin{array}{r}8\\-0\\\hline\end{array}$
6. $\begin{array}{r}5\\-2\\\hline\end{array}$	**7.** $\begin{array}{r}13\\-7\\\hline\end{array}$	**8.** $\begin{array}{r}6\\-6\\\hline\end{array}$	**9.** $\begin{array}{r}17\\-8\\\hline\end{array}$	**10.** $\begin{array}{r}9\\-4\\\hline\end{array}$
11. $\begin{array}{r}3\\-0\\\hline\end{array}$	**12.** $\begin{array}{r}16\\-8\\\hline\end{array}$	**13.** $\begin{array}{r}11\\-7\\\hline\end{array}$	**14.** $\begin{array}{r}7\\-7\\\hline\end{array}$	**15.** $\begin{array}{r}12\\-3\\\hline\end{array}$

16. $12 - 6 = \blacksquare$ **17.** $10 - 2 = \blacksquare$ **18.** $5 - 0 = \blacksquare$ **19.** $9 - 9 = \blacksquare$

Problem Solving: Uses of Subtraction *(pages 14–15)*

Use the five steps to solve each problem.

1. Read
Bill has 4 pencils. Maria has 6 pencils. How many fewer pencils does Bill have?

2. Plan
To find how many fewer, subtract.
$6 - 4 = \blacksquare$

4. Answer
Bill has 2 fewer pencils.

3. Do
$$\begin{array}{r}6\\-4\\\hline 2\end{array}$$

5. Check
$$\begin{array}{r}2\\+4\\\hline 6\end{array} \checkmark$$

1. Jefferson School's chess club has 15 members. The math club has 9 members. How many more members does the chess club have?

2. Ms. Starr needs 17 scissors for her class's art project. She finds 9. How many more scissors does she need?

3. Carlos has 8 crayons in his box. He takes some out. 5 crayons are left. How many crayons did he take out?

4. Karen has 10 marbles. 3 of the marbles are red. The rest are not red. How many marbles are not red?

5. A school has 10 buses parked on its lot. Only 7 buses are used. How many buses remain on the lot?

6. A museum has 8 history and 11 science activities. How many fewer history than science activities are there?

Problem Solving: Choosing the Operation *(pages 16–17)*

Lynne bought 6 cards. She wants to send 11 cards.
How many more cards does she need?

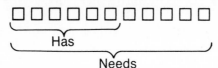

Has

Needs

Subtract. 11 − 6 = ▧   11 − 6 = 5

Lynne needs 5 more cards.

1. Barbara has $4 in her bank. She puts in some more and then has $7. How much more did she put in?

2. There are 17 chairs in Mr. Fuller's classroom. Some are taken out and 8 are left. How many chairs are taken out?

3. Jason collects baseball pennants. He has 5 green ones and 12 red ones. How many fewer green ones does he have?

4. Karl planted 3 bean seeds one day and 5 bean seeds the next. Then he planted 2 more. How many seeds did he plant in all?

5. Robert bought 10 postcards. 7 were black and white. How many were not black and white?

6. Manuel had $5 in his bank. He put in $9 more. Then how much did Manuel have?

Fact Families *(pages 18–19)*

Complete the number sentences.

| 6 + 7 = 13 |
| 7 + 6 = 13 |
| 13 − 6 = 7 |
| 13 − 7 = 6 |

1. 0 + 9 = ▧
    9 + 0 = ▧
    9 − 0 = ▧
    9 − 9 = ▧

2. 14 − 8 = ▧
    6 + 8 = ▧
    14 − 6 = ▧
    8 + 6 = ▧

3. ▧ + 3 = 10

4. 8 + ▧ = 13

5. 2 + ▧ = 8

6. 7 + ▧ = 12

7. ▧ + 9 = 9

8. 0 + ▧ = 7

Write the members of these fact families.

9. The two addends are 5 and 9.

10. The two addends are 0 and 6.

UNIT 2: Place Value

Hundreds   *(pages 26–27)*

Write the standard numerals. Then tell what each digit means.

> nine hundred forty-eight: 948 → 9 hundreds, 4 tens, 8 ones

1. one hundred thirteen

2. eight hundred forty-two

3. four hundred sixty

4. two hundred twenty-seven

5. seven hundred ten

6. seven hundred one

For each numeral tell what digit is in the hundreds place.

7. 269   **8.** 405   **9.** 813   **10.** 500   **11.** 690   **12.** 314

Comparing Whole Numbers   *(pages 28–29)*

Write >, <, or = for ●.

> 602 < 620

1. 343 ● 342   **2.** 117 ● 92

3. 762 ● 763   **4.** 530 ● 529   **5.** 301 ● 299   **6.** 908 ● 994

7. 223 ● 212   **8.** 898 ● 921   **9.** 95 ● 103   **10.** 523 ● 523

11. 799 ● 801   **12.** 101 ● 110   **13.** 101 ● 11   **14.** 410 ● 409

Rounding Numbers   *(pages 30–31)*

833 is nearer 830 than 840.
833 rounds down to 830.

Round to the nearest ten. Use the number line if you need help.

1. 838   **2.** 830   **3.** 839   **4.** 840   **5.** 835   **6.** 831

Round to the nearest hundred or nearest dollar. Use a number line if needed.

7. 870   **8.** 823   **9.** 850   **10.** $3.29   **11.** $3.85   **12.** $3.40

13. 809   **14.** 875   **15.** 839   **16.** $3.45   **17.** $3.50   **18.** $3.55

Thousands *(pages 34–35)*

**For each standard numeral name the place of the digit 4.
Then tell what the digit 4 means.**

> 483,620
> 4 is in the hundred-thousands place.
> 4 means 4 hundred-thousands.

1. 14,392   **2.** 340,500

Write the standard numerals. Tell what digit is in the thousands place.

3. four thousand sixty-nine.

4. thirty-five thousand seven hundred forty.

5. three hundred thousand five hundred.

6. eight thousand one hundred ninety-two.

7. five hundred eighty thousand fifty.

8. one hundred six thousand two hundred thirty-five.

9. seventy thousand seventy.

10. two hundred thousand two.

Tell what each digit means.

11. 7,824

12. 136,275

Comparing Larger Numbers *(pages 36–37)*

Compare. Use > and < to write two statements.

> 5,769   6,340 > 5,769
> 6,340   5,769 < 6,340

1. 76,104
  76,041

2. 328,098
  328,101

Write >, <, or = for ●.

3. 98 ● 106

4. 702 ● 698

5. 3,402 ● 908

6. 76,320 ● 76,328

7. 14,301 ● 14,310

8. 527,435 ● 527,345

9. 942,462 ● 942,471

10. 629,312 ● 629,312

11. 473,231 ● 473,213

12. 8,991 ● 9,990

13. 39,529 ● 39,418

14. 492,009 ● 550,418

Millions *(pages 38–39)*

**For each standard numeral name the place of the digit 6.
Then tell what the digit 6 means.**

> 263,470,518
> 6 is in the ten-millions place
> 6 means 6 ten-millions

1. 16,385,274

2. 615,348,920

Write the numerals. Tell what digit is in the millions place.

3. six hundred twenty million four hundred fifty thousand.

4. one million three hundred fourteen thousand five hundred twenty-four.

5. twenty million two hundred thousand four hundred.

6. fifty million fifty thousand fifty.

Tell what each digit means.

7. 1,286,547

8. 92,158,764

Compare. Use > and < to write two statements.

9. 29,762,031
29,762,013

10. 460,000,900
460,008,000

11. 91,486,213
109,338,456

Problem Solving: Too Much Information *(pages 40–41)*
Use the table on page 41 to solve the problems below.

> A team traveled from Atlanta to Philadelphia. Did the team travel
> more than 1,000 kilometers?
>
> Look down ↓ to Atlanta and across → to Philadelphia.
> 1,260 > 1,000
>
> The team traveled more than 1,000 kilometers.

1. How far is the drive from Philadelphia to Denver?

2. How far apart are Jacksonville and Philadelphia?

3. If Mr. Horton drives from Los Angeles to Philadelphia, will he drive more than 4,500 km?

4. Which distance is greater: Dallas to Jacksonville or Dallas to Atlanta?

5. What is the distance between Jacksonville and Dallas? Round this distance to the nearest hundred.

6. On her vacation Ms. Turner drove from Los Angeles to Dallas. Round this distance to the nearest hundred.

UNIT 3: Addition and Subtraction

Adding 2-digit Numbers *(pages 48–49)*

Add.

$$\begin{array}{r} {\scriptstyle 1} \\ 64 \\ +18 \\ \hline 82 \end{array}$$

1. $\begin{array}{r} 23 \\ +16 \\ \hline \end{array}$
2. $\begin{array}{r} 17 \\ +54 \\ \hline \end{array}$
3. $\begin{array}{r} 65 \\ +14 \\ \hline \end{array}$
4. $\begin{array}{r} 38 \\ +47 \\ \hline \end{array}$
5. $\begin{array}{r} 66 \\ +21 \\ \hline \end{array}$

6. $\begin{array}{r} 19 \\ +72 \\ \hline \end{array}$
7. $\begin{array}{r} 46 \\ +29 \\ \hline \end{array}$
8. $\begin{array}{r} 38 \\ +59 \\ \hline \end{array}$
9. $\begin{array}{r} 63 \\ +35 \\ \hline \end{array}$
10. $\begin{array}{r} 15 \\ +48 \\ \hline \end{array}$

11. $61 + 38 =$ ▨   **12.** $69 + 11 =$ ▨   **13.** $35 + 32 =$ ▨

Larger Sums *(pages 50–51)*

Add.

$$\begin{array}{r} {\scriptstyle 1} \\ 56 \\ +\ 69 \\ \hline 125 \end{array}$$

1. $\begin{array}{r} 98 \\ +\ 5 \\ \hline \end{array}$
2. $\begin{array}{r} 27 \\ +82 \\ \hline \end{array}$
3. $\begin{array}{r} 63 \\ +27 \\ \hline \end{array}$
4. $\begin{array}{r} 49 \\ +72 \\ \hline \end{array}$
5. $\begin{array}{r} 8 \\ +93 \\ \hline \end{array}$

6. $\begin{array}{r} 77 \\ +35 \\ \hline \end{array}$
7. $\begin{array}{r} 46 \\ +55 \\ \hline \end{array}$
8. $\begin{array}{r} 34 \\ +98 \\ \hline \end{array}$
9. $\begin{array}{r} 65 \\ +23 \\ \hline \end{array}$
10. $\begin{array}{r} 87 \\ +59 \\ \hline \end{array}$

11. $98 + 67 =$ ▨   **12.** $93 + 9 =$ ▨   **13.** $65 + 42 =$ ▨

Adding 3-digit Numbers *(pages 52–53)*

Add.

$$\begin{array}{r} {\scriptstyle 1\ 1} \\ 739 \\ +\ 684 \\ \hline 1{,}423 \end{array}$$

1. $\begin{array}{r} 712 \\ +244 \\ \hline \end{array}$
2. $\begin{array}{r} 316 \\ +\ 47 \\ \hline \end{array}$
3. $\begin{array}{r} 434 \\ +\ 94 \\ \hline \end{array}$
4. $\begin{array}{r} 932 \\ +918 \\ \hline \end{array}$

5. $\begin{array}{r} 628 \\ +549 \\ \hline \end{array}$
6. $\begin{array}{r} 524 \\ +165 \\ \hline \end{array}$
7. $\begin{array}{r} 247 \\ +581 \\ \hline \end{array}$
8. $\begin{array}{r} 746 \\ +862 \\ \hline \end{array}$

9. $\begin{array}{r} \$6.63 \\ +\ 1.33 \\ \hline \end{array}$
10. $\begin{array}{r} \$4.70 \\ +\ 5.50 \\ \hline \end{array}$
11. $\begin{array}{r} \$4.89 \\ +\ 2.38 \\ \hline \end{array}$
12. $\begin{array}{r} \$8.36 \\ +\ 6.44 \\ \hline \end{array}$
13. $\begin{array}{r} \$7.85 \\ +\ 4.69 \\ \hline \end{array}$

14. $953 + 218 =$ ▨   **15.** $87 + 787 =$ ▨   **16.** $\$2.98 + \$1.05 =$ ▨

Adding 4-digit Numbers *(pages 54–55)*

Add.

$$\begin{array}{r} {}^{1}{}^{1} \\ 4{,}728 \\ +\ 6{,}543 \\ \hline 11{,}271 \end{array}$$

1. $\begin{array}{r} 7{,}615 \\ +\ \ \ 483 \\ \hline \end{array}$

2. $\begin{array}{r} 9{,}445 \\ +1{,}372 \\ \hline \end{array}$

3. $\begin{array}{r} 8{,}501 \\ +2{,}599 \\ \hline \end{array}$

4. $\begin{array}{r} \$52.34 \\ +\ 61.34 \\ \hline \end{array}$

5. $\begin{array}{r} 9{,}999 \\ +\ \ \ \ 12 \\ \hline \end{array}$

6. $\begin{array}{r} 3{,}826 \\ +4{,}578 \\ \hline \end{array}$

7. $\begin{array}{r} 1{,}384 \\ +\ \ \ 726 \\ \hline \end{array}$

8. $\begin{array}{r} \$29.65 \\ +\ 83.49 \\ \hline \end{array}$

9. $8{,}813 + 492 =$ ▧   **10.** $5{,}235 + 5{,}325 =$ ▧   **11.** $\$19.95 + \$\ 9.98 =$ ▧

12. $5{,}673 + 4{,}856 =$ ▧   **13.** $927 + 1{,}091 =$ ▧   **14.** $\$47.16 + \$39.27 =$ ▧

Rounding to Any Place *(pages 56–57)*

Round to the nearest ten. To the nearest hundred.

5,364

5 3 ⑥ 4	4 < 5	5 ③ 6 4	6 > 5
↓	Keep ⑥.	+ 1	Add 1.
5 3 6 0		5 4 0 0	

1. 607   **2.** 7,384   **3.** 2,597   **4.** 14,082   **5.** 27,996

Round to the nearest thousand; to the nearest ten-thousand.

6. 35,196   **7.** 72,804   **8.** 49,671   **9.** 108,723   **10.** 659,984

Estimating Sums *(pages 58–59)*

Find each sum. Then estimate to check your sum.

$$\begin{array}{r} {}^{1}\ {}^{1}{}^{1} \\ 3{,}486 \\ +\ \ \ 738 \\ \hline 4{,}224 \end{array} \qquad \begin{array}{r} 3{,}④86 \longrightarrow \\ +\ \ ⑦38 \longrightarrow \\ \hline \end{array} \begin{array}{r} 3{,}500 \\ +\ \ \ 700 \\ \hline 4{,}200 \end{array}$$

4,224 is near 4,200.
The answer is
reasonable.

1. $\begin{array}{r} 327 \\ +\ 79 \\ \hline \end{array}$

2. $\begin{array}{r} 1{,}395 \\ +\ \ \ 711 \\ \hline \end{array}$

3. $\begin{array}{r} 3{,}407 \\ +\ \ \ 789 \\ \hline \end{array}$

4. $\begin{array}{r} 3{,}122 \\ +2{,}878 \\ \hline \end{array}$

5. $\begin{array}{r} 5{,}166 \\ +2{,}736 \\ \hline \end{array}$

6. $388 + 7{,}413 =$ ▧   **7.** $9{,}201 + 2{,}876 =$ ▧   **8.** $4{,}032 + 1{,}905 =$ ▧

9. $\$17.49 + \$23.68 =$ ▧   **10.** $\$4.35 + \$7.48 =$ ▧   **11.** $\$26.39 + \$9.65 =$ ▧

Adding 5-digit Numbers *(pages 60–61)*

Add. Check your answers by estimating.

$$
\begin{array}{r}
\overset{1}{}\ \overset{1}{}\ \\
76{,}349 \\
+\ 8{,}526 \\
\hline
84{,}875
\end{array}
\qquad
\begin{array}{r}
7\,⑥{,}349 \longrightarrow \\
+\ ⑧{,}526 \longrightarrow \\
\hline
\end{array}
\begin{array}{r}
76{,}000 \\
+\ 9{,}000 \\
\hline
85{,}000
\end{array}
$$

84,875 is near 85,000.
The answer is
reasonable.

1. 84,305 +12,931	**2.** 87,317 +23,977	**3.** 59,304 +42,289	**4.** 43,692 + 9,686	**5.** 92,300 + 7,621
6. 73,105 +58,965	**7.** 68,024 +97,961	**8.** 21,399 + 6,589	**9.** $706.47 + 89.68	**10.** $256.27 +378.56

11. $30{,}708 + 7{,}489 = \blacksquare$ **12.** $\$96.49 + \$273.79 = \blacksquare$

13. $\$483.27 + \$93.09 = \blacksquare$ **14.** $49{,}593 + 8{,}752 = \blacksquare$

Adding More Than Two Numbers *(pages 62–63)*

Add. Check your answers by estimating.

$$
\begin{array}{r}
\overset{2}{}\ \overset{1}{}\ \overset{2}{}\ \\
4{,}②63 \longrightarrow \\
⑦35 \longrightarrow \\
1{,}⑨26 \longrightarrow \\
+\ 2{,}⑧39 \longrightarrow \\
\hline
9{,}763
\end{array}
\begin{array}{r}
4{,}300 \\
700 \\
1{,}900 \\
+2{,}800 \\
\hline
9{,}700
\end{array}
$$

9,763 is near 9,700. ✓

1. 319 204 +728	**2.** 3,513 4,678 + 902	**3.** 35,779 3,104 +12,667
4. 627 1,483 904 +2,165	**5.** 4,136 7,528 11,738 +14,251	**6.** $ 5.19 13.64 19.95 + 8.07

7. 69 248 583 + 74	**8.** 7,629 14,813 9,564 +21,045	**9.** 27,400 16,700 43,200 +36,500	**10.** 64,128 17,954 36,041 + 9,867	**11.** $410.36 175.63 97.82 + 250.16

12. $13 + 305 + 16 + 75 = \blacksquare$ **13.** $4{,}567 + 735 + 3{,}982 + 425 = \blacksquare$

14. $5{,}763 + 2{,}573 + 938 = \blacksquare$ **15.** $29 + 78 + 16 + 43 + 62 + 50 = \blacksquare$

Subtracting 2-digit Numbers *(pages 66–67)*

Subtract. Use addition to check.

$$\begin{array}{r} {\scriptstyle 5\,12} \\ \cancel{62} \\ -25 \\ \hline 37 \end{array} \qquad \begin{array}{r} {\scriptstyle 1} \\ 37 \\ +25 \\ \hline 62 \end{array}$$

1. $\begin{array}{r}44\\-13\\\hline\end{array}$	**2.** $\begin{array}{r}65\\-22\\\hline\end{array}$	**3.** $\begin{array}{r}78\\-58\\\hline\end{array}$	**4.** $\begin{array}{r}99\\-36\\\hline\end{array}$
5. $\begin{array}{r}74\\-16\\\hline\end{array}$	**6.** $\begin{array}{r}32\\-\ 7\\\hline\end{array}$	**7.** $\begin{array}{r}87\\-19\\\hline\end{array}$	**8.** $\begin{array}{r}54\\-39\\\hline\end{array}$
9. $\begin{array}{r}80\\-68\\\hline\end{array}$ **10.** $\begin{array}{r}71\\-17\\\hline\end{array}$	**11.** $\begin{array}{r}63\\-27\\\hline\end{array}$	**12.** $\begin{array}{r}64\\-64\\\hline\end{array}$	**13.** $\begin{array}{r}50\\-16\\\hline\end{array}$ **14.** $\begin{array}{r}42\\-33\\\hline\end{array}$

15. $83 - 67 = $ ▦   **16.** $40 - 23 = $ ▦   **17.** $87 - 79 = $ ▦

Subtracting 3-digit Numbers *(pages 68–69)*

Subtract. Use addition to check.

$$\begin{array}{r} {\scriptstyle 12} \\ {\scriptstyle 5\,2\,14} \\ \cancel{634} \\ -286 \\ \hline 348 \end{array} \qquad \begin{array}{r} {\scriptstyle 1\ 1} \\ 348 \\ +286 \\ \hline 634 \end{array}$$

1. $\begin{array}{r}542\\-\ 17\\\hline\end{array}$	**2.** $\begin{array}{r}767\\-184\\\hline\end{array}$	**3.** $\begin{array}{r}813\\-608\\\hline\end{array}$	**4.** $\begin{array}{r}703\\-611\\\hline\end{array}$
5. $\begin{array}{r}\$9.95\\-\ 1.17\\\hline\end{array}$	**6.** $\begin{array}{r}835\\-107\\\hline\end{array}$	**7.** $\begin{array}{r}629\\-513\\\hline\end{array}$	**8.** $\begin{array}{r}940\\-160\\\hline\end{array}$
9. $\begin{array}{r}883\\-566\\\hline\end{array}$ **10.** $\begin{array}{r}\$7.76\\-\ 6.95\\\hline\end{array}$	**11.** $\begin{array}{r}416\\-124\\\hline\end{array}$	**12.** $\begin{array}{r}712\\-547\\\hline\end{array}$	**13.** $\begin{array}{r}\$8.07\\-\ 3.14\\\hline\end{array}$ **14.** $\begin{array}{r}\$6.00\\-\ 5.40\\\hline\end{array}$

15. $412 - 258 = $ ▦   **16.** $307 - 285 = $ ▦   **17.** $813 - 497 = $ ▦

Zeros in Subtraction *(pages 70–71)*

Subtract. Use addition to check.

$$\begin{array}{r} {\scriptstyle 9} \\ {\scriptstyle 2\,10\,15} \\ \cancel{305} \\ -187 \\ \hline 118 \end{array} \qquad \begin{array}{r} {\scriptstyle 1\ 1} \\ 118 \\ +187 \\ \hline 305 \end{array}$$

1. $\begin{array}{r}900\\-\ 35\\\hline\end{array}$	**2.** $\begin{array}{r}702\\-415\\\hline\end{array}$	**3.** $\begin{array}{r}907\\-478\\\hline\end{array}$	**4.** $\begin{array}{r}701\\-135\\\hline\end{array}$
5. $\begin{array}{r}\$4.01\\-\ .99\\\hline\end{array}$	**6.** $\begin{array}{r}523\\-158\\\hline\end{array}$	**7.** $\begin{array}{r}431\\-\ 95\\\hline\end{array}$	**8.** $\begin{array}{r}901\\-888\\\hline\end{array}$

9. $671 - 392 = $ ▦   **10.** $\$2.00 - \$.75 = $ ▦   **11.** $\$4.05 - \$3.68 = $ ▦

Subtracting Larger Numbers *(pages 72–73)*

Subtract.

$$\begin{array}{r} {\scriptstyle 14} \\ {\scriptstyle 7\ \not4\ 12} \\ 7,8\not5\not2 \\ -3,564 \\ \hline 4,288 \end{array}$$

1. $\begin{array}{r}4,135\\-2,917\\\hline\end{array}$	**2.** $\begin{array}{r}5,507\\-3,718\\\hline\end{array}$	**3.** $\begin{array}{r}6,351\\-2,148\\\hline\end{array}$	**4.** $\begin{array}{r}\$99.95\\-\ \ \ 7.98\\\hline\end{array}$
5. $\begin{array}{r}55,315\\-\ \ 7,219\\\hline\end{array}$	**6.** $\begin{array}{r}72,400\\-36,200\\\hline\end{array}$	**7.** $\begin{array}{r}85,312\\-84,412\\\hline\end{array}$	**8.** $\begin{array}{r}52,354\\-\ \ \ \ 365\\\hline\end{array}$

9. $76.50 - $45.75 = $ ▨

10. $84,312 - 13,907 = $ ▨

11. $772.20 - $390.04 = $ ▨

Subtracting Across Many Zeros *(pages 74–75)*

Subtract.

$$\begin{array}{r} {\scriptstyle 12\ 9\ 9} \\ {\scriptstyle 4\ \not2\ 10\ 10\ 14} \\ 5\not3,0\not0\not4 \\ -16,287 \\ \hline 36,717 \end{array}$$

1. $\begin{array}{r}9,007\\-8,998\\\hline\end{array}$	**2.** $\begin{array}{r}12,000\\-\ \ \ \ 239\\\hline\end{array}$	**3.** $\begin{array}{r}55,003\\-49,123\\\hline\end{array}$	**4.** $\begin{array}{r}\$300.00\\-\ \ \ 19.95\\\hline\end{array}$
5. $\begin{array}{r}4,030\\-1,974\\\hline\end{array}$	**6.** $\begin{array}{r}8,000\\-3,016\\\hline\end{array}$	**7.** $\begin{array}{r}\$201.40\\-\ \ \ 76.83\\\hline\end{array}$	**8.** $\begin{array}{r}20,000\\-16,031\\\hline\end{array}$

9. $6,007 - 4,174 = $ ▨ **10.** $50,703 - 7,030 = $ ▨ **11.** $100.00 - $99.95 = $ ▨

12. $3,000 - 2,843 = $ ▨ **13.** $6,040 - 3,970 = $ ▨ **14.** $403.04 - $87.93 = $ ▨

Estimating Differences *(pages 76–77)*

Subtract. Use estimation to check.

$$\begin{array}{r} {\scriptstyle 10\ 14} \\ {\scriptstyle 5\ \not0\ \not4\ 13} \\ \not6\not1,5\not3\not6 \\ -\ \ 7,782 \\ \hline 53,754 \end{array} \qquad \begin{array}{r} 6①,536 \rightarrow 62,000 \\ -\ ⑦,782 \rightarrow -\ 8,000 \\ \hline 54,000 \end{array}$$

53,754 is near 54,000
The answer is
reasonable.

1. $\begin{array}{r}3,629\\-1,847\\\hline\end{array}$	**2.** $\begin{array}{r}49,146\\-17,423\\\hline\end{array}$	**3.** $\begin{array}{r}602\\-\ 58\\\hline\end{array}$	**4.** $\begin{array}{r}2,736\\-\ \ 918\\\hline\end{array}$	**5.** $\begin{array}{r}19,732\\-\ 8,274\\\hline\end{array}$

6. $7,283 - 4,721 = $ ▨ **7.** $83,049 - 37,642 = $ ▨ **8.** $20,000 - 7,905 = $ ▨

9. $106.00 - $48.27 = $ ▨ **10.** $18,435 - 6,298 = $ ▨

11. $483.16 - $267.84 = $ ▨

Problem Solving: Estimates as Answers *(pages 78–79)*

Solve each problem by estimating the sum or difference.

> The Rodriguez family spent $8.83 for lunch and $19.77 for dinner. About how much more was spent for dinner?
>
> To find about how much more was spent for dinner, *use estimation.*
>
> $19.77 → $20.00   They spent
> − 8.83 → − 9.00   about $11.00
> $11.00   more for dinner.

1. 3,112 cars passed a busy intersection before noon. After noon 4,931 cars passed. About how many cars went by all day?

2. Airfare to Midland is $229.50. By bus the trip costs $89.95. About how much is saved by taking the bus?

3. An airplane picked up 129, 72, and 38 people at three stops. About how many people did it pick up in all?

4. Sam travels 2,930 km by car and 1,215 km by train. How far does he travel in all?

Problem Solving: Finding Information *(pages 80–81)*

Use the picture or the table on page 81 to solve these problems.

> On Monday how many fewer basketball than football tickets were sold?
>
> To find how many fewer tickets were sold, *subtract.*
>
> 2,749
> − 1,801
>   948
>
> 948 fewer tickets were sold.

1. How much more than a basketball ticket does a football ticket cost?

2. How many football and basketball tickets were sold altogether on Friday?

3. How many more basketball tickets were sold on Monday than on Thursday?

4. How many fewer football tickets were sold on Wednesday than on Thursday?

5. Ms. Hays had $20.00. She bought a football ticket. How much money did she have left?

6. On which days were more football tickets sold than basketball tickets?

407

UNIT 4: Multiplication and Division

Multiplying by 2 or 3 *(pages 88–89)*

Multiply.

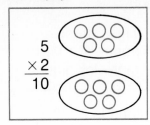

1. 2 ×3   **2.** 5 ×3   **3.** 2 ×2   **4.** 7 ×2   **5.** 7 ×3   **6.** 3 ×3

7. 1 ×3   **8.** 4 ×2   **9.** 8 ×3   **10.** 9 ×3   **11.** 1 ×2   **12.** 4 ×3

13. 2 × 9 =   **14.** 3 × 6 =   **15.** 2 × 8 =

Multiplying by 4 or 5 *(pages 90–91)*

Multiply.

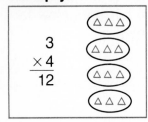

1. 5 ×4   **2.** 9 ×5   **3.** 1 ×4   **4.** 1 ×5   **5.** 6 ×5   **6.** 2 ×4

7. 3 ×5   **8.** 7 ×4   **9.** 4 ×4   **10.** 4 ×5   **11.** 8 ×4   **12.** 5 ×5

13. 4 × 9 =   **14.** 5 × 8 =   **15.** 4 × 6 =

Multiplying by 6 or 7 *(pages 92–93)*

Multiply.

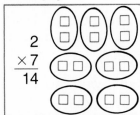

1. 2 ×6   **2.** 1 ×7   **3.** 3 ×7   **4.** 6 ×6   **5.** 9 ×2   **6.** 8 ×7

7. 6 ×4   **8.** 5 ×6   **9.** 7 ×7   **10.** 4 ×6   **11.** 1 ×6   **12.** 7 ×4

13. 9 ×6   **14.** 7 ×2   **15.** 7 ×6   **16.** 7 ×5   **17.** 6 ×2   **18.** 8 ×6   **19.** 5 ×7   **20.** 9 ×7

21. 7 × 4 =   **22.** 2 × 3 =   **23.** 5 × 2 =

24. 6 × 3 =   **25.** 3 × 7 =   **26.** 7 × 6 =

Multiplying by 8 or 9 *(pages 94–95)*

Multiply.

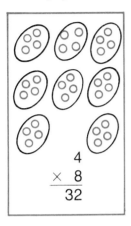

$$\begin{array}{r} 4 \\ \times\ 8 \\ \hline 32 \end{array}$$

1. $\begin{array}{r} 6 \\ \times 8 \end{array}$ **2.** $\begin{array}{r} 1 \\ \times 9 \end{array}$ **3.** $\begin{array}{r} 5 \\ \times 9 \end{array}$ **4.** $\begin{array}{r} 1 \\ \times 8 \end{array}$ **5.** $\begin{array}{r} 7 \\ \times 5 \end{array}$ **6.** $\begin{array}{r} 7 \\ \times 8 \end{array}$

7. $\begin{array}{r} 8 \\ \times 8 \end{array}$ **8.** $\begin{array}{r} 7 \\ \times 9 \end{array}$ **9.** $\begin{array}{r} 8 \\ \times 4 \end{array}$ **10.** $\begin{array}{r} 8 \\ \times 9 \end{array}$ **11.** $\begin{array}{r} 7 \\ \times 3 \end{array}$ **12.** $\begin{array}{r} 6 \\ \times 9 \end{array}$

13. $\begin{array}{r} 3 \\ \times 9 \end{array}$ **14.** $\begin{array}{r} 5 \\ \times 8 \end{array}$ **15.** $\begin{array}{r} 3 \\ \times 8 \end{array}$ **16.** $\begin{array}{r} 9 \\ \times 2 \end{array}$ **17.** $\begin{array}{r} 4 \\ \times 9 \end{array}$ **18.** $\begin{array}{r} 9 \\ \times 9 \end{array}$

19. $8 \times 2 = $ ▧

20. $3 \times 9 = $ ▧

21. $5 \times 9 = $ ▧

22. $8 \times 9 = $ ▧

23. $6 \times 9 = $ ▧

24. $9 \times 2 = $ ▧

Multiplication Properties *(pages 96–97)*

Multiply.

$$6 \times 4 = 24$$
$$4 \times 6 = 24$$

$$\begin{array}{r} 7 \\ \times 0 \\ \hline 0 \end{array} \qquad \begin{array}{r} 0 \\ \times 7 \\ \hline 0 \end{array}$$

$$\begin{array}{r} 5 \\ \times 1 \\ \hline 5 \end{array} \qquad \begin{array}{r} 1 \\ \times 5 \\ \hline 5 \end{array}$$

1. $\begin{array}{r} 8 \\ \times 5 \end{array}$ **2.** $\begin{array}{r} 5 \\ \times 8 \end{array}$ **3.** $\begin{array}{r} 0 \\ \times 0 \end{array}$ **4.** $\begin{array}{r} 0 \\ \times 2 \end{array}$ **5.** $\begin{array}{r} 1 \\ \times 9 \end{array}$ **6.** $\begin{array}{r} 9 \\ \times 1 \end{array}$

7. $\begin{array}{r} 7 \\ \times 1 \end{array}$ **8.** $\begin{array}{r} 1 \\ \times 7 \end{array}$ **9.** $\begin{array}{r} 0 \\ \times 1 \end{array}$ **10.** $\begin{array}{r} 1 \\ \times 0 \end{array}$ **11.** $\begin{array}{r} 6 \\ \times 9 \end{array}$ **12.** $\begin{array}{r} 9 \\ \times 6 \end{array}$

13. $\begin{array}{r} 5 \\ \times 0 \end{array}$ **14.** $\begin{array}{r} 1 \\ \times 2 \end{array}$ **15.** $\begin{array}{r} 2 \\ \times 1 \end{array}$ **16.** $\begin{array}{r} 0 \\ \times 3 \end{array}$ **17.** $\begin{array}{r} 3 \\ \times 0 \end{array}$ **18.** $\begin{array}{r} 1 \\ \times 1 \end{array}$

19. $1 \times 6 = $ ▧

20. $4 \times 0 = $ ▧

21. $0 \times 9 = $ ▧

22. $8 \times 3 = $ ▧

23. $0 \times 4 = $ ▧

24. $1 \times 8 = $ ▧

25. $3 \times 8 = $ ▧

26. $1 \times 4 = $ ▧

27. $8 \times 0 = $ ▧

28. $6 \times 0 = $ ▧

29. $0 \times 6 = $ ▧

30. $0 \times 8 = $ ▧

Problem Solving: Multiplying with Money *(pages 98–99)*

Ted bought 4 T-shirts for $3 each. How much did the T-shirts cost in all?

4 sets of 3

$$\begin{array}{r} \$3 \\ \times\,4 \\ \hline \$12 \end{array}$$

Shirts cost $12 in all.

1. There are 8 pictures on each of 9 pages. How many pictures are there in all?

2. Mr. Olney bought 6 new books for $8 each. How much did the 6 books cost all together?

3. Ms. Haynes bought 7 second-hand books for $4 each. How much did she pay for the books in all?

4. On one page in Juan's math book there were 4 rows of exercises. Each row had 6 exercises. How many exercises were there on that page?

5. A travel book cost $9. A novel cost $8. Ms. Kane bought one of each. How much did she spend?

6. Each box holds 8 books. How many books in all can be packed into 5 of these boxes?

Missing Factors *(pages 100–101)*

Find the missing factors.

$\blacksquare \times 5 = 35$

$5 \times 5 = 25$
$6 \times 5 = 30$
$7 \times 5 = 35$

$$\begin{array}{r} 8 \\ \times\,\blacksquare \\ \hline 48 \end{array} \rightarrow \begin{array}{r} 8 \\ \times\,6 \\ \hline 48 \end{array}$$

1. $\blacksquare \times 7 = 14$ 2. $\blacksquare \times 3 = 24$ 3. $\blacksquare \times 8 = 24$

4. $8 \times \blacksquare = 72$ 5. $5 \times \blacksquare = 0$ 6. $\blacksquare \times 5 = 40$

7. $\blacksquare \times 8 = 56$ 8. $1 \times \blacksquare = 3$ 9. $\blacksquare \times 9 = 27$

10. $\blacksquare \times 6 = 24$ 11. $\blacksquare \times 6 = 54$ 12. $6 \times \blacksquare = 36$

13. $\blacksquare \times 7 = 49$ 14. $8 \times \blacksquare = 0$ 15. $9 \times \blacksquare = 81$

16. $\begin{array}{r} 4 \\ \times\,\blacksquare \\ \hline 20 \end{array}$ 17. $\begin{array}{r} \blacksquare \\ \times\,1 \\ \hline 8 \end{array}$ 18. $\begin{array}{r} 3 \\ \times\,\blacksquare \\ \hline 18 \end{array}$ 19. $\begin{array}{r} \blacksquare \\ \times\,7 \\ \hline 63 \end{array}$ 20. $\begin{array}{r} 6 \\ \times\,\blacksquare \\ \hline 30 \end{array}$ 21. $\begin{array}{r} 8 \\ \times\,\blacksquare \\ \hline 72 \end{array}$

Dividing by 2 or 3 *(pages 104–105)*

Divide.

$14 \div 2 = \blacksquare$
$\blacksquare \times 2 = 14$
$6 \times 2 = 12$
$7 \times 2 = 14$

1. $3\overline{)6}$ **2.** $2\overline{)6}$ **3.** $3\overline{)18}$ **4.** $3\overline{)24}$ **5.** $2\overline{)12}$

6. $3\overline{)12}$ **7.** $2\overline{)16}$ **8.** $3\overline{)21}$ **9.** $2\overline{)10}$ **10.** $3\overline{)27}$

11. $3\overline{)15}$ **12.** $2\overline{)8}$ **13.** $3\overline{)3}$ **14.** $2\overline{)14}$ **15.** $2\overline{)4}$

16. $9 \div 3 = \blacksquare$ **17.** $2 \div 2 = \blacksquare$ **18.** $18 \div 2 = \blacksquare$

Dividing by 4 or 5 *(pages 106–107)*

Divide.

$\blacksquare$
$4\overline{)20}$
$\blacksquare \times 4 = 20$
$4 \times 4 = 16$
$5 \times 4 = 20$

1. $4\overline{)16}$ **2.** $5\overline{)10}$ **3.** $4\overline{)4}$ **4.** $5\overline{)35}$ **5.** $2\overline{)18}$

6. $5\overline{)15}$ **7.** $4\overline{)32}$ **8.** $2\overline{)12}$ **9.** $5\overline{)45}$ **10.** $4\overline{)24}$

11. $5\overline{)30}$ **12.** $4\overline{)36}$ **13.** $5\overline{)20}$ **14.** $3\overline{)15}$ **15.** $4\overline{)8}$

16. $12 \div 4 = \blacksquare$ **17.** $5 \div 5 = \blacksquare$ **18.** $28 \div 4 = \blacksquare$

19. $25 \div 5 = \blacksquare$ **20.** $24 \div 3 = \blacksquare$ **21.** $40 \div 5 = \blacksquare$

Dividing by 6 or 7 *(pages 108–109)*

Divide.

$\blacksquare$
$7\overline{)35}$
$\blacksquare \times 7 = 35$
$5 \times 7 = 35$

1. $6\overline{)42}$ **2.** $6\overline{)12}$ **3.** $7\overline{)28}$ **4.** $6\overline{)30}$ **5.** $7\overline{)7}$

6. $7\overline{)49}$ **7.** $5\overline{)40}$ **8.** $6\overline{)6}$ **9.** $7\overline{)42}$ **10.** $6\overline{)24}$

11. $7\overline{)56}$ **12.** $6\overline{)36}$ **13.** $3\overline{)21}$ **14.** $7\overline{)14}$ **15.** $6\overline{)54}$

16. $18 \div 6 = \blacksquare$ **17.** $36 \div 4 = \blacksquare$ **18.** $21 \div 7 = \blacksquare$

19. $63 \div 7 = \blacksquare$ **20.** $18 \div 2 = \blacksquare$ **21.** $48 \div 6 = \blacksquare$

Dividing by 8 or 9 *(pages 110–111)*

Divide.

$$9\overline{)45} \quad 5$$

$$\blacksquare \times 9 = 45$$

$$5 \times 9 = 45$$

1. $9\overline{)18}$ 2. $8\overline{)8}$ 3. $6\overline{)48}$ 4. $9\overline{)63}$ 5. $7\overline{)63}$

6. $6\overline{)54}$ 7. $9\overline{)36}$ 8. $8\overline{)24}$ 9. $8\overline{)72}$ 10. $9\overline{)72}$

11. $8\overline{)40}$ 12. $7\overline{)56}$ 13. $9\overline{)9}$ 14. $8\overline{)32}$ 15. $8\overline{)56}$

16. $27 \div 9 = \blacksquare$ 17. $16 \div 8 = \blacksquare$ 18. $64 \div 8 = \blacksquare$

19. $48 \div 8 = \blacksquare$ 20. $81 \div 9 = \blacksquare$ 21. $54 \div 9 = \blacksquare$

Division Properties *(pages 112–113)*

Divide.

$$6 \times 1 = 6$$
$$\text{so } 6 \div 1 = 6$$

$$1 \times 5 = 5$$
$$\text{so } 5 \div 5 = 1$$

$$0 \times 4 = 0$$
$$\text{so } 0 \div 4 = 0$$

1. $3\overline{)0}$ 2. $1\overline{)5}$ 3. $4\overline{)32}$ 4. $1\overline{)8}$ 5. $8\overline{)8}$

6. $1\overline{)2}$ 7. $6\overline{)0}$ 8. $9\overline{)54}$ 9. $7\overline{)56}$ 10. $8\overline{)56}$

11. $7\overline{)7}$ 12. $1\overline{)1}$ 13. $1\overline{)4}$ 14. $4\overline{)4}$ 15. $9\overline{)0}$

16. $1\overline{)9}$ 17. $2\overline{)8}$ 18. $7\overline{)0}$ 19. $5\overline{)5}$ 20. $1\overline{)0}$

21. $0 \div 8 = \blacksquare$ 22. $7 \div 1 = \blacksquare$ 23. $9 \div 9 = \blacksquare$

Division with Remainders *(pages 114–115)*

Divide. Draw dots if necessary.

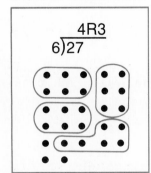

$$6\overline{)27} \quad 4R3$$

1. $6\overline{)35}$ 2. $3\overline{)11}$ 3. $7\overline{)40}$ 4. $4\overline{)19}$ 5. $9\overline{)29}$

6. $7\overline{)29}$ 7. $7\overline{)62}$ 8. $4\overline{)21}$ 9. $5\overline{)24}$ 10. $6\overline{)48}$

11. $4\overline{)30}$ 12. $2\overline{)13}$ 13. $7\overline{)32}$ 14. $5\overline{)47}$ 15. $8\overline{)60}$

16. $6\overline{)21}$ 17. $9\overline{)72}$ 18. $3\overline{)20}$ 19. $7\overline{)12}$ 20. $4\overline{)32}$

Long Division (pages 116–117)

Divide.

```
      4R2
  5)22
    20
     2

Think:
  ■ × 5 = 22
  2 × 5 = 10
  3 × 5 = 15
  4 × 5 = 20
  5 × 5 = 25
        Too big!

Use 4.
```

1. 3)11 **2.** 2)9 **3.** 4)19 **4.** 2)13 **5.** 3)18

6. 4)22 **7.** 3)16 **8.** 5)20 **9.** 2)17 **10.** 5)36

11. 2)11 **12.** 4)32 **13.** 3)23 **14.** 5)29 **15.** 4)29

16. 5)29 **17.** 3)8 **18.** 2)7 **19.** 5)17 **20.** 3)15

21. 5)33 **22.** 2)16 **23.** 4)39 **24.** 3)13 **25.** 5)40

26. 3)13 **27.** 5)22 **28.** 2)15 **29.** 4)26 **30.** 3)26

31. 4)17 **32.** 5)23 **33.** 2)19 **34.** 5)7 **35.** 3)17

More Long Division (pages 118–119)

Divide. Check your answers.

```
      8R4
  6)52
    48
     4

Think:
  ■ × 6 = 52
  8 × 6 = 48
  9 × 6 = 54
        Too big!

Use 8.

     6
   × 8
    48
   + 4
    52 ✓
```

1. 7)11 **2.** 6)50 **3.** 3)24 **4.** 8)53 **5.** 4)33

6. 3)23 **7.** 2)12 **8.** 5)48 **9.** 8)44 **10.** 5)22

11. 9)44 **12.** 6)58 **13.** 7)61 **14.** 8)17 **15.** 3)17

16. 6)52 **17.** 2)9 **18.** 7)29 **19.** 4)29 **20.** 8)65

21. 7)50 **22.** 4)18 **23.** 8)54 **24.** 8)40 **25.** 6)52

26. 9)77 **27.** 5)44 **28.** 6)42 **29.** 9)83 **30.** 9)60

31. 6)43 **32.** 8)49 **33.** 9)75 **34.** 6)23 **35.** 7)47

36. 7)53 **37.** 9)65 **38.** 7)32 **39.** 8)48 **40.** 6)31

Problem Solving: Another Use of Division *(pages 120–121)*

> Maria had 17 toys. She gave the same number to each of 5 children. How many toys did each child get? How many were left over?
>
> How many in each set? Divide.
>
> $$\begin{array}{r} 3R2 \\ 5\overline{)17} \end{array}$$
>
> 3 toys for each child.
> 2 toys left over.

1. Jamie packed 63 records. Each box held 8 records. How many boxes were filled? How many records were left over?

2. Maria won 6 prizes at each of 9 contests at the school fair. How many prizes did she win in all?

3. 9 stamps fill a page. Jo had 80 stamps. How many pages could she fill? How many stamps are left over?

4. Jay put 48 nails into 8 equal piles. How many nails did he put in each pile?

5. Laura put 36 books in 4 boxes, with the same number in each box. How many books did she put in each box?

6. David put 28 sheets of paper in 4 stacks, with the same number of sheets in each. How many sheets were in each stack?

Problem Solving: Labeling Answers *(pages 122–123)*

> Lisa paid $15 for 5 scarves. Each was the same price. How much did each cost?
>
> How much for each? Divide.
>
> $$\begin{array}{r} 3 \\ 5\overline{)15} \end{array}$$
>
> The cost of each scarf was $3.

1. A can of racquetballs cost $4. Jackie has $12. How many cans of racquetballs can she buy?

2. Mr. Baker sold 8 pairs of ice skates. Each pair cost $9. How much did they cost all together?

3. Akiko bought 8 model cars. They cost $16 in all. How much did each car cost?

4. 24 puppets are to be put on 3 shelves. How many puppets can be put on each shelf?

5. Len had $20 and bought 3 records. Each record cost $6. How much did he spend? How much was left over?

6. Karla had $30 to buy books. Each book cost $7. How many books could she buy? How much money would be left over?

UNIT 5: Money, Time, Measurement

Money *(pages 130–131)*

Use a dollar sign to show the amount.

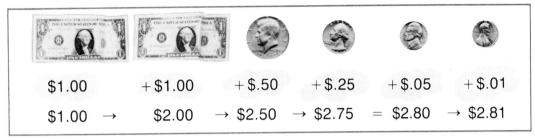

$1.00	+ $1.00	+ $.50	+ $.25	+ $.05	+ $.01
$1.00 →	$2.00	→ $2.50	→ $2.75	= $2.80	→ $2.81

1.

2. 3 dollars, 2 quarters, 3 dimes, 1 nickel, 4 pennies

3. 3 quarters, 2 dimes, 3 nickels, 5 pennies

4. 8 dollars, 6 dimes, 12 pennies

5. 4 dollars, 1 quarter, 4 nickels

6. 12 dollars, 5 quarters, 3 nickels

7. 2 quarters, 7 dimes, 8 nickels

Problem Solving: Using Money *(pages 132–133)*

Name the fewest bills and coins you could use.

Millie bought a bag of oranges and paid $1.41.

$1.00	+ $.25	+ $.10	+ $.05	+ $.01
$1.00	→ $1.25 →	$1.35 →	$1.40	→ $1.41

1. The cash register showed that Paco should get $1.37 in change.

2. Ms. Hanson bought stamps for $3.17.

3. Alan owes Juan $1.23.

4. Kurt has 46¢ in his pocket.

5. Mr. Romano spent $2.44 for lunch.

6. Linda is buying a calculator for $4.98.

415

Problem Solving: Two-Step Problems   *(pages 134–135)*

Which problems require two steps? Solve all problems.

> Mark bought a pencil for $.29 and a tablet for $.48. He gave the clerk $1.00. How much did he get back?
>
> **Step 1** Find what he spent.   → $.29 + $.48 = $.77
> **Step 2** Find what he gets back. → $1.00 − $.77 = $.23
>
> Mark gets back $.23 from the clerk.

1. Larry bought a tablet for 62¢ and a pencil for 29¢. He gave the clerk $1.00. How much change should the clerk give Larry?

2. Ms. Horn bought 2 tickets. Each ticket cost $7. She gave the clerk $20. How much money should she get back?

3. Lou bought a shirt for $17.95. He paid with a $20-bill. How much money should he get back?

4. Jane gave the cashier $5.00 for a meal costing $3.57. How much change should she receive?

5. Alice bought a notebook for 42¢ and an eraser for 26¢. She gave the clerk $1.00. How much change should Alice receive?

6. Ms. Gorky had $7.20. She spent $1.25 and 98¢ for two items. How much money did she have left?

Telling Time   *(pages 136–137)*

Read each clock.

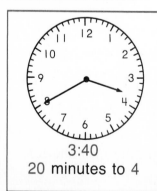

3:40
20 minutes to 4

1.

▨:▨
▨ minutes to ▨

2.

▨:▨
▨ minutes past ▨

When would you do these? A.M. or P.M.?

3. Go to bed.

4. Eat breakfast.

5. Do homework.

6. See sun set.

Problem Solving: Using Time (pages 138–139)

Joan's school day started at 8:00 A.M. and ended at 3:00 P.M. How long was Joan in school each day?

4 hours to noon

4 + 3 = 7

7 hours

1. José started painting the house at 8:00 A.M. He worked for 6 hours. What time did he stop?

2. Sally stopped working at 3:00 P.M. She had worked for 8 hours. When did she start work?

3. A truck left the warehouse at 6:00 A.M. It arrived at the store at 3:00 P.M. How long did the trip take?

4. George took his motorcycle for repairs at 10:00 A.M. It was ready at 2:00 P.M. How long did the repairs take?

5. The Weiss family left at 5:00 A.M. on a trip which takes 11 hours. What time did they end the trip?

6. Helen planned a hike to Spring Camp. The hike takes 9 hours. At what time should she start to be at Spring Camp by 4:00 P.M.?

Problem Solving: More on Using Time (pages 140–141)

Fernando eats breakfast 30 minutes before he leaves for school at 7:45 A.M. When does he eat breakfast?

7:45

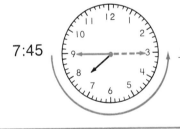

```
  45
- 30
  15
```
Fernando eats breakfast at 7:15 A.M.

1. Heather went skating at 10:45 A.M. She skated for 45 minutes. At what time did she stop skating?

2. Maria and a friend listened to records for 45 minutes. They stopped listening at 1:15 P.M. When did they start?

3. Gladys left at 3:45 P.M. She returned 30 minutes later. At what time did she return?

4. Fred practiced his guitar from 7:30 P.M. to 8:15 P.M. How long did he practice?

5. Jim ate lunch from 11:45 A.M. to 12:15 P.M. How long was his lunch period?

6. Amy started playing her flute at 7:00 P.M. She practiced for 30 minutes. When did she finish?

417

Centimeter *(pages 144–145)*

Measure to the nearest centimeter.

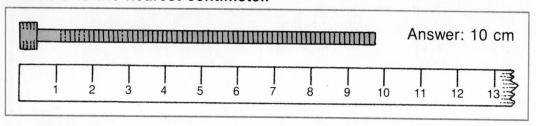

Answer: 10 cm

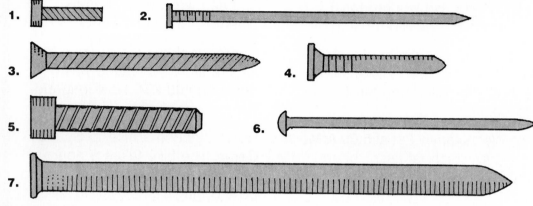

1.
2.
3.
4.
5.
6.
7.

Draw each.

8. a pencil that is 12 cm long

9. a can that is 10 cm high

Estimate and then measure to the nearest centimeter.

10. the distance across a quarter

11. the height of a pencil sharpener

Meter and Kilometer *(pages 146–147)*

Use cm, m, or km to complete each sentence.

> A couch is about 2 __m__ long.

1. the height of a room is about 3 ____.

2. A soup can is about 12 ____ high.

3. A card table is about 1 ____ wide.

4. An outdoor track is about 400 ____ around.

5. A hand-held calculator is about 14 ____ long.

6. The air distance between Chicago and Los Angeles is about 2,800 ____.

7. The air distance between New York and London is about 5,600 ____.

8. The length of a city block is about 200 ____.

9. The distance between goal posts on a football field is about 110 ____.

Other Metric Units   *(pages 148–149)*

Use L, mL, g, or kg to complete each sentence.

> The mass of a small box of
> gelatin is about 85 _g_ .

1. A tall drinking glass holds
   about 400 _____ of water.

2. A raisin has a mass of about
   1 _____.

3. A lawnmower holds about
   2 _____ of gasoline.

4. A textbook has a mass of about
   1 _____.

5. A bottle of perfume holds about
   90 _____.

6. The mass of a professional
   football lineman is about 125 _____.

7. A household hot water tank
   holds about 120 _____ of water.

Problem Solving: Finding Needed Facts   *(pages 150–151)*

**What fact must you know to solve each problem? Solve the problem
if you can.**

> Carol runs 5
> kilometers each day.
> How far does Carol
> run each week?
>
> Must know the number
> of days in 1 week.
> 1 week = 7 days
> 7 × 5 = 35
>
> Carol runs
> 35 km each week.

1. Eddie is allowed to watch TV
   for 1 hour on school days. He
   has watched TV for 15 minutes.
   How many more minutes can
   he watch?

2. Juanita bought 1 kilogram of
   potatoes, 400 grams of
   radishes, and 450 grams of
   carrots. What was the total
   mass of the items she bought?

3. John had a board 1 meter in
   length. He used a piece 75
   centimeters long for a project.
   How long was the piece that
   was left?

4. Kerry poured 1 liter of water
   into a fish bowl. He used 450
   milliliters of water to water a
   plant, and he drank 250
   milliliters of water. How many
   milliliters of water did he use?

5. Ralph's mass is 10 kilograms
   greater than the mass of his
   brother Jim. What is Jim's
   mass?

6. The distance across the lake is
   1 kilometer. Sue waded 350
   meters and swam the rest of
   the way across. How far did
   Sue swim?

419

Inch, Half-Inch, Quarter Inch   *(pages 152–153)*

Measure to the nearest inch; to the nearest half-inch; to the nearest quarter inch.

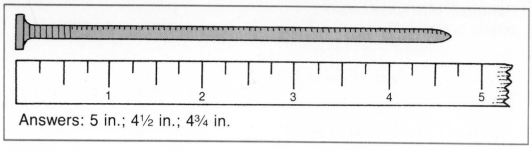

Answers: 5 in.; 4½ in.; 4¾ in.

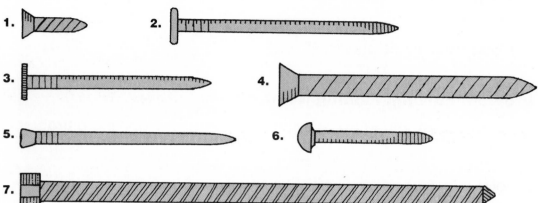

Estimate and then measure to the nearest quarter inch.

8. the distance across a quarter

9. the height of a pencil sharpener

Foot, Yard, and Mile   *(pages 154–155)*

Use in., ft, yd, or mi to complete each sentence.

A couch is about 6 __ft__ long.

1. the height of a room is about 9 ____.

2. A hallway is about 1 ____ wide.

3. The road distance from Detroit to Chicago is about 280 ____.

4. A book is about 7 ____ wide.

5. A student is about 4 ____ tall.

6. The air distance between Chicago and Los Angeles is about 1,750 ____.

7. The air distance between New York and London is about 3,450 ____.

8. The length of a household room is about 20 ____.

9. The distance between goal posts on a football field is 120 ____.

Cup, Pint, Quart, and Gallon *(pages 156–157)*

Select the answer that seems reasonable.

> A milk carton sold at a lunch counter contains __c__ of milk.
> **a.** 1 qt   **b.** 1 pt   **c.** 1 cup

1. A lawnmower holds ___ of gasoline.
   a. 2 qt   **b.** 20 gal   **c.** 200 qt

2. A cream pitcher holds ___ of cream.
   a. 1 gal   **b.** 1 qt   **c.** 1 cup

3. A cereal bowl holds ___ of milk.
   a. 1 pt   **b.** 1 qt   **c.** 1 gal

4. A bucket holds ___ of water.
   a. 2 cups   **b.** 2 gal   **c.** 20 gal

5. A household hot water tank holds about ___ of water.
   a. 30 gal   **b.** 3 gal   **c.** 3 qt

6. A tall drinking glass holds about ___ of water.
   a. 1 cup   **b.** 1 pint   **c.** 1 qt

7. An aquarium holds about ___ of water.
   a. 5 gal   **b.** 5 pt   **c.** 5 cups

8. The fuel tank of a compact auto will hold about ___ of gasoline.
   a. 12 qt   **b.** 12 gal   **c.** 2 gal

9. A tea kettle holds about ___ of water.
   a. 2 cups   **b.** 2 qt   **c.** 2 gal

Other Customary Units *(pages 158–159)*

Select the answer that seems reasonable.

> A textbook weighs __b__.
> **a.** 2 oz   **b.** 2 lb   **c.** 20 lb

1. A pencil case weighs ___.
   a. 7 oz   **b.** 70 oz   **c.** 7 lb

2. An adult cat weighs about ___.
   a. 1 oz   **b.** 10 oz   **c.** 10 lb

3. A newborn baby weighs ___.
   a. 7 oz   **b.** 7 lb   **c.** 70 lb

4. A professional football lineman weighed ___.
   a. 200 oz   **b.** 100 lb   **c.** 270 lb

5. A small box of gelatin weighs ___.
   a. 3 oz   **b.** 30 oz   **c.** 3 lb

6. I went swimming when the temperature was ___.
   a. 9°F   **b.** 90°F   **c.** 900°F

7. I went ice skating when the temperature was ___.
   a. 20°F   **b.** 70°F   **c.** 100°F

UNIT 6: Multiplying by Ones

Multiplying 2-digit Numbers (pages 166–167)

Multiply.

$$\begin{array}{r} 43 \\ \times\ 2 \\ \hline 86 \end{array}$$

1. $\begin{array}{r} 22 \\ \times\ 2 \\ \hline \end{array}$ **2.** $\begin{array}{r} 54 \\ \times\ 0 \\ \hline \end{array}$ **3.** $\begin{array}{r} 22 \\ \times\ 3 \\ \hline \end{array}$ **4.** $\begin{array}{r} 12 \\ \times\ 4 \\ \hline \end{array}$ **5.** $\begin{array}{r} 11 \\ \times\ 5 \\ \hline \end{array}$

6. $\begin{array}{r} 41 \\ \times\ 2 \\ \hline \end{array}$ **7.** $\begin{array}{r} 20 \\ \times\ 4 \\ \hline \end{array}$ **8.** $\begin{array}{r} 23 \\ \times\ 2 \\ \hline \end{array}$ **9.** $\begin{array}{r} 92 \\ \times\ 1 \\ \hline \end{array}$ **10.** $\begin{array}{r} 4 \\ \times 22 \\ \hline \end{array}$

11. $13 \times 3 =$ ▨   **12.** $3 \times 32 =$ ▨   **13.** $11 \times 8 =$ ▨

14. $4 \times 21 =$ ▨   **15.** $12 \times 3 =$ ▨   **16.** $2 \times 34 =$ ▨

Multiplying with Saving (pages 168–169)

Multiply.

$$\begin{array}{r} ① \\ 23 \\ \times\ 4 \\ \hline 92 \end{array}$$

1. $\begin{array}{r} 36 \\ \times\ 2 \\ \hline \end{array}$ **2.** $\begin{array}{r} 13 \\ \times\ 6 \\ \hline \end{array}$ **3.** $\begin{array}{r} 38 \\ \times\ 2 \\ \hline \end{array}$ **4.** $\begin{array}{r} 87 \\ \times\ 0 \\ \hline \end{array}$ **5.** $\begin{array}{r} 12 \\ \times\ 7 \\ \hline \end{array}$

6. $\begin{array}{r} 29 \\ \times\ 3 \\ \hline \end{array}$ **7.** $\begin{array}{r} 45 \\ \times\ 2 \\ \hline \end{array}$ **8.** $\begin{array}{r} 93 \\ \times\ 1 \\ \hline \end{array}$ **9.** $\begin{array}{r} 3 \\ \times 25 \\ \hline \end{array}$ **10.** $\begin{array}{r} 2 \\ \times 46 \\ \hline \end{array}$

11. $7 \times 14 =$ ▨   **12.** $2 \times 27 =$ ▨   **13.** $17 \times 4 =$ ▨

14. $2 \times 32 =$ ▨   **15.** $18 \times 5 =$ ▨   **16.** $6 \times 16 =$ ▨

Larger Products (pages 170–171)

Multiply.

$$\begin{array}{r} ⑦ \\ 29 \\ \times\ 8 \\ \hline 232 \end{array}$$

1. $\begin{array}{r} 62 \\ \times\ 4 \\ \hline \end{array}$ **2.** $\begin{array}{r} 51 \\ \times\ 5 \\ \hline \end{array}$ **3.** $\begin{array}{r} 64 \\ \times\ 6 \\ \hline \end{array}$ **4.** $\begin{array}{r} 29 \\ \times\ 3 \\ \hline \end{array}$ **5.** $\begin{array}{r} 76 \\ \times\ 7 \\ \hline \end{array}$

6. $\begin{array}{r} 84 \\ \times\ 8 \\ \hline \end{array}$ **7.** $\begin{array}{r} 93 \\ \times\ 8 \\ \hline \end{array}$ **8.** $\begin{array}{r} 76 \\ \times\ 6 \\ \hline \end{array}$ **9.** $\begin{array}{r} 9 \\ \times 87 \\ \hline \end{array}$ **10.** $\begin{array}{r} 38 \\ \times\ 7 \\ \hline \end{array}$

11. $5 \times 68 =$ ▨   **12.** $38 \times 9 =$ ▨   **13.** $3 \times 73 =$ ▨

14. $85 \times 4 =$ ▨   **15.** $6 \times 17 =$ ▨   **16.** $5 \times 47 =$ ▨

Multiplying 3-digit Numbers *(pages 174–175)*

Multiply.

③②
176
×   4
704

1. 193 × 5	**2.** 227 × 4	**3.** 109 × 8	**4.** 135 × 7	**5.** 115 × 8
6. 107 × 9	**7.** 152 × 6	**8.** 209 × 4	**9.** 453 × 2	**10.** 3 ×329

11. $7 \times 141 = $ ▦   **12.** $120 \times 8 = $ ▦   **13.** $2 \times 239 = $ ▦

14. $5 \times 142 = $ ▦   **15.** $315 \times 3 = $ ▦   **16.** $7 \times 128 = $ ▦

Larger Products *(pages 176–177)*

Multiply.

③②
274
×   5
1370

1. 517 × 4	**2.** 308 × 5	**3.** 642 × 8	**4.** 739 × 6	**5.** 451 × 9
6. 346 × 8	**7.** 787 × 5	**8.** 458 × 7	**9.** 683 × 9	**10.** 6 ×948

11. $4 \times 758 = $ ▦   **12.** $954 \times 9 = $ ▦   **13.** $738 \times 2 = $ ▦

14. $8 \times 193 = $ ▦   **15.** $7 \times 309 = $ ▦   **16.** $3 \times 952 = $ ▦

Multiplying 4-digit Numbers *(pages 178–179)*

Multiply.

①③⑤
5,147
×   8
41,176

1. 3,009 × 3	**2.** 6,479 × 7	**3.** 5,217 × 5	**4.** 8,407 × 9	**5.** 9,318 × 6
6. 6,720 × 5	**7.** 3,412 × 2	**8.** 2,605 × 8	**9.** 5,172 × 4	**10.** 6 ×4,082

11. $5 \times 476 = $ ▦   **12.** $9 \times 4,520 = $ ▦   **13.** $1,842 \times 4 = $ ▦

14. $7 \times 1,382 = $ ▦   **15.** $2,714 \times 3 = $ ▦   **16.** $9 \times 2,816 = $ ▦

Changing Metric Units (pages 180–181)

Find the missing numbers.

7m = █ cm
7m = 7 × 1m
= 7 × 100 cm
= 700 cm

1. 5 kg = █ g

2. 6 L = █ mL

3. 4 km = █ m

4. 8 kg = █ g

5. 3 m = █ cm

6. 9 km = █ m

7. 3 L = █ mL

8. 7 kg = █ g

9. 6 m = █ cm

Solve the problems.

10. A ham has a mass of 2 kg. What is its mass in grams?

11. Harold can long-jump 3 m. How many centimeters is this?

12. 5 L of orange juice is how many milliliters?

13. Randy ran 2 km. How many meters did he run in all?

Problem Solving: Too Much Information (pages 182–183)

Find the facts you need. Solve each problem.

Ms. Howe had $100. She bought 9 tapes as gifts. Each tape cost $7.49. How much did she spend?

You do not need to know Ms. Howe had $100.

$7.49
× 9
$67.41   Ms. Howe spent $67.41.

1. Ginny had $50.00. She spent $14.50 for 3 records. How much money did she have left?

2. Carlos had $40.00. He bought 4 records for $5.98 each. How much did he spend in all?

3. Mr. Edmund had a 35 mm camera. He bought 5 rolls of film for $4.89 each. How much did he spend in all?

4. Alice spent $8.85 for 3 books and $.75 for 2 cards. How much did she spend in all?

5. Joe bought 8 small cards at $.35 each. Pens cost $.95 each. How much did Joe spend?

6. Eric earned $14.95 one week. He earned $26.75 another week. How much did he earn in all?

UNIT 7: Dividing by Ones

Reviewing One-Step Division *(pages 196–197)*

Find the quotients and remainders.

$$\begin{array}{r} 8R3 \\ 5)\overline{43} \\ 40 \\ \hline 3 \end{array}$$

Think:
■ × 5 = 43
7 × 5 = 35
8 × 5 = 40 ✓
9 × 5 = 45

Use 8.

1. $6)\overline{19}$
2. $2)\overline{15}$
3. $7)\overline{9}$
4. $4)\overline{38}$
5. $8)\overline{65}$

6. $7)\overline{42}$
7. $6)\overline{53}$
8. $9)\overline{49}$
9. $8)\overline{35}$
10. $9)\overline{81}$

11. $4)\overline{19}$
12. $6)\overline{35}$
13. $3)\overline{22}$
14. $8)\overline{45}$
15. $7)\overline{27}$

16. $5)\overline{35}$
17. $2)\overline{9}$
18. $9)\overline{32}$
19. $4)\overline{26}$
20. $5)\overline{29}$

Two-Step Division *(pages 198–199)*

Divide.

$$\begin{array}{r} 34R1 \\ 2)\overline{69} \\ 6 \\ \hline 09 \\ 8 \\ \hline 1 \end{array}$$

Think:
■ × 2 = 6
3 × 2 = 6
Use 3.

■ × 2 = 9
4 × 2 = 8 ✓
5 × 2 = 10
Use 4.

1. $3)\overline{69}$
2. $2)\overline{27}$
3. $5)\overline{55}$
4. $8)\overline{89}$
5. $4)\overline{87}$

6. $4)\overline{88}$
7. $3)\overline{98}$
8. $2)\overline{68}$
9. $6)\overline{56}$
10. $7)\overline{79}$

11. $2)\overline{45}$
12. $4)\overline{49}$
13. $6)\overline{69}$
14. $2)\overline{28}$
15. $5)\overline{58}$

16. $4)\overline{84}$
17. $3)\overline{36}$
18. $2)\overline{86}$
19. $9)\overline{99}$
20. $3)\overline{66}$

21. $3)\overline{67}$
22. $5)\overline{57}$
23. $8)\overline{87}$
24. $2)\overline{67}$
25. $6)\overline{59}$

26. $7)\overline{71}$
27. $6)\overline{67}$
28. $4)\overline{85}$
29. $4)\overline{47}$
30. $5)\overline{43}$

More Two-Step Division *(pages 200–201)*

Divide.

$$\begin{array}{r} 15R4 \\ 5)\overline{79} \\ 5 \\ \hline 29 \\ 25 \\ \hline 4 \end{array}$$

1. $4)\overline{47}$
2. $6)\overline{85}$
3. $5)\overline{81}$
4. $3)\overline{25}$
5. $6)\overline{96}$

6. $5)\overline{93}$
7. $2)\overline{85}$
8. $8)\overline{97}$
9. $7)\overline{85}$
10. $8)\overline{90}$

11. $3)\overline{83}$
12. $2)\overline{57}$
13. $5)\overline{65}$
14. $3)\overline{42}$
15. $4)\overline{75}$

16. $2)\overline{78}$
17. $7)\overline{94}$
18. $4)\overline{94}$
19. $2)\overline{90}$
20. $6)\overline{71}$

Zero in the Quotient *(pages 202–203)*

Divide.

```
      40R1
  2)81
      8
      01
       0
       1
```
  ▤ × 2 = 8
  Use 4.

  ▤ × 2 = 1
  Use 0.

1. 3)61
2. 2)40
3. 6)65
4. 4)81
5. 5)47

6. 4)43
7. 3)92
8. 5)56
9. 7)75
10. 8)86

11. 6)80
12. 4)80
13. 2)60
14. 9)95
15. 5)72

16. 3)62
17. 2)81
18. 3)90
19. 2)21
20. 7)70

21. 3)32
22. 4)41

Dividing 3-digit Numbers *(pages 206–207)*

Divide.

```
    156R3
 6)939
    6         ▤ × 6 = 9
    33        Use 1.
    30        ▤ × 6 = 33
    39        Use 5.
    36        ▤ × 6 = 39
     3        Use 6.
```

1. 5)786
2. 4)864
3. 2)642
4. 9)999

5. 6)791
6. 3)694
7. 6)846
8. 5)986

9. 7)798
10. 8)889
11. 5)808
12. 7)947

13. 2)374
14. 4)732
15. 8)985
16. 3)547

2-digit Quotients *(pages 208–209)*

Divide.

```
     64R5
 6)389
    36        ▤ × 6 = 38
    29        Use 6.
    24        ▤ × 6 = 29
     5        Use 4.
```

1. 3)295
2. 5)483
3. 2)373
4. 7)691

5. 9)803
6. 4)396
7. 9)856
8. 7)651

9. 8)895
10. 6)573
11. 4)274
12. 5)828

13. 3)227
14. 7)532
15. 2)153
16. 6)434
17. 9)261
18. 7)507

19. 5)238
20. 9)832
21. 5)338
22. 4)548
23. 3)176
24. 8)435

Zeros in the Quotient *(pages 210–211)*

Divide.

```
    209
4)836
    8
    03
     0   0 × 4 = 0
    36
    36
     0
```

1. 4)417
2. 2)605
3. 5)549
4. 3)619

5. 9)972
6. 3)546
7. 8)872
8. 4)803

9. 6)660
10. 7)776
11. 3)451
12. 6)641

13. 4)243
14. 3)920
15. 2)561
16. 8)964

17. 7)720
18. 5)702
19. 9)908
20. 6)963

21. 515 ÷ 5 = ▧
22. 900 ÷ 2 = ▧
23. 318 ÷ 3 = ▧

24. 408 ÷ 4 = ▧
25. 360 ÷ 9 = ▧
26. 800 ÷ 2 = ▧

Dividing 4-digit Numbers *(pages 212–213)*

Divide.

```
   1,415R2
6)8,492
  6
  24
  24
   09
    6
   32
   30
    2
```

1. 5)6,525
2. 3)6,930
3. 7)7,216
4. 2)1,604

5. 6)3,695
6. 4)4,824
7. 9)8,190
8. 7)2,814

9. 8)8,075
10. 9)3,610
11. 7)4,587
12. 2)6,315

13. 4)3,462
14. 3)7,500
15. 8)6,700
16. 6)7,212

17. 8)2,730
18. 4)5,729
19. 9)1,916
20. 5)1,735

21. 7)9,263
22. 2)5,248
23. 9)5,280
24. 3)4,000

25. 5,700 ÷ 6 = ▧
26. 4,600 ÷ 4 = ▧
27. 1,758 ÷ 3 = ▧

28. 8,300 ÷ 5 = ▧
29. 8,000 ÷ 2 = ▧
30. 9,325 ÷ 5 = ▧

Problem Solving: Finding Averages *(pages 214–215)*

Mary scored 147, 172, and 158 points in 3 games of bowling. What was her average score?	Average score = Total score ÷ Number of games 147 172 + 158 ――――― 477 total score	$$\begin{array}{r} 159 \\ 3\overline{)477} \end{array}$$ Mary's average score was 159.

Use the graph on page 215. Find the average score.

1. Games 1, 4, and 6   2. Games 2, 5, and 6   3. Games 5 and 6

4. Games 1, 3, and 5   5. Games 1 and 4   6. Games 3, 4, and 5

7. Games 2, 4, and 6   8. Games 2, 3, 5, and 6   9. Games 2 to 6

Problem Solving: Dividing Dollars and Cents *(pages 216–217)*

Solve the problems.

Mr. Thorn paid $99.25 for 5 shirts. Each shirt cost the same amount. How much did each shirt cost?	Cost of each = Total cost ÷ Number of shirts ▓ = $99.25 ÷ 5 $19.85 = $99.25 ÷ 5 The cost of each shirt was $19.85.

1. Julio bought 8 books for $31.60. Each book cost the same. How much did each cost?

2. Henry bought 33 balloons for 99¢. Each balloon cost the same. How much did each cost?

3. Roberta spent $4.50 when she bought 6 goldfish. How much did each goldfish cost?

4. Stanley sold 9 magazines. He collected $7.65. How much did he get for each magazine?

5. Each pair of socks cost $1.28. Walter bought 4 pairs. How much did he spend?

6. Janet bought 3 music stands for $27.12. How much did each stand cost?

UNIT 8: Fractions

Fractions   *(pages 224–225)*

Write a fraction for the shaded part of each object.

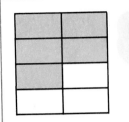
5 of 8 pieces are shaded

$\frac{5}{8}$

1.

2.

3.

4.

5.

6.

Write a fraction for the shaded part of each set.

7.

8.

9.

10.

Mixed Numerals   *(pages 226–227)*

Give a fraction for the number of boxes filled. For 1 or greater, also give a mixed numeral or standard numeral.

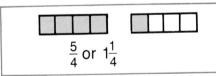
$\frac{5}{4}$ or $1\frac{1}{4}$

1.

2.

3.

4.

5.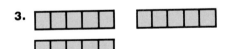

6.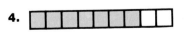

7.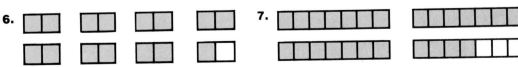

429

Finding Mixed Numerals (pages 228–229)

Give a mixed numeral or standard numeral for each.

$$7\overline{)39} \quad 5\tfrac{4}{7}$$
$$\underline{35}$$
$$4$$

$$\frac{39}{7} = 5\tfrac{4}{7}$$

$$8\overline{)461} \quad 57R5$$
$$\underline{40}$$
$$61$$
$$\underline{56}$$
$$5$$

or

$$8\overline{)461} \quad 57\tfrac{5}{8}$$
$$\underline{40}$$
$$61$$
$$\underline{56}$$
$$5$$

1. $\frac{28}{3}$ 2. $\frac{39}{4}$ 3. $\frac{27}{2}$ 4. $6\overline{)53}$ 5. $4\overline{)872}$ 6. $7\overline{)96}$

7. $\frac{46}{5}$ 8. $\frac{36}{3}$ 9. $\frac{43}{6}$ 10. $3\overline{)89}$ 11. $5\overline{)362}$ 12. $9\overline{)175}$

13. $\frac{74}{9}$ 14. $\frac{59}{7}$ 15. $\frac{96}{8}$ 16. $6\overline{)258}$ 17. $2\overline{)139}$ 18. $7\overline{)108}$

Equivalent Fractions (pages 230–231)

Write two equivalent fractions for the shaded part of each.

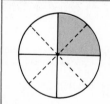 Counting s, $\frac{1}{4}$ is shaded.

Counting s, $\frac{2}{8}$ is shaded.

1.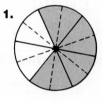

2. 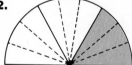   3. 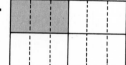   4.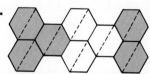

Use the fraction rulers on pages 230 and 231 to complete.

5. $1 = \frac{\blacksquare}{2}$ 6. $\frac{1}{3} = \frac{\blacksquare}{6}$ 7. $\frac{8}{12} = \frac{\blacksquare}{6}$ 8. $1 = \frac{\blacksquare}{6}$

9. $\frac{8}{12} = \frac{\blacksquare}{3}$ 10. $\frac{1}{3} = \frac{\blacksquare}{12}$ 11. $\frac{2}{10} = \frac{\blacksquare}{5}$ 12. $\frac{3}{5} = \frac{\blacksquare}{10}$

13. $\frac{8}{10} = \frac{\blacksquare}{5}$ 14. $1 = \frac{\blacksquare}{10}$ 15. $\frac{2}{5} = \frac{\blacksquare}{10}$ 16. $0 = \frac{\blacksquare}{8}$

Dividing to Find Equivalent Fractions *(pages 232–233)*

Divide to find an equivalent fraction.

$$\frac{12}{18} = \frac{12 \div 6}{18 \div 6} = \frac{2}{3} \qquad \frac{18}{24} \overset{18 \div 6}{\underset{24 \div 6}{=}} \frac{3}{4} \qquad \frac{14}{35} \overset{14 \div 7}{\underset{35 \div 7}{=}} \frac{2}{5}$$

1. $\dfrac{12}{20} = \dfrac{12 \div 4}{20 \div 4} = \dfrac{\blacksquare}{\blacksquare}$

2. $\dfrac{8}{16} = \dfrac{8 \div 4}{16 \div 4} = \dfrac{\blacksquare}{\blacksquare}$

3. $\dfrac{10}{40} = \dfrac{10 \div 5}{40 \div 5} = \dfrac{\blacksquare}{\blacksquare}$

4. $\dfrac{20}{32} = \dfrac{20 \div \blacksquare}{32 \div 4} = \dfrac{\blacksquare}{8}$

5. $\dfrac{18}{27} = \dfrac{18 \div 3}{27 \div \blacksquare} = \dfrac{6}{\blacksquare}$

6. $\dfrac{10}{12} = \dfrac{10 \div \blacksquare}{12 \div 2} = \dfrac{\blacksquare}{\blacksquare}$

7. $\dfrac{6}{12}$
8. $\dfrac{15}{20}$
9. $\dfrac{20}{24}$
10. $\dfrac{10}{16}$
11. $\dfrac{24}{30}$
12. $\dfrac{16}{28}$

13. $\dfrac{35}{55}$
14. $\dfrac{27}{45}$
15. $\dfrac{4}{12}$
16. $\dfrac{40}{48}$
17. $\dfrac{9}{18}$
18. $\dfrac{56}{63}$

19. $\dfrac{16}{22}$
20. $\dfrac{24}{32}$
21. $\dfrac{40}{56}$
22. $\dfrac{24}{27}$
23. $\dfrac{20}{30}$
24. $\dfrac{33}{45}$

Lowest Terms Fractions *(pages 234–235)*

Give the lowest terms fraction for each. For 1 or greater, also give a mixed numeral or standard numeral.

$$\frac{14}{42} = \frac{7}{21} = \frac{1}{3} \qquad \frac{28}{10} = \frac{14}{5} \rightarrow 5\overline{)14}\,^{2\frac{4}{5}} \qquad \frac{20}{5} = \frac{4}{1} = 4$$

1. $\dfrac{10}{12}$
2. $\dfrac{9}{24}$
3. $\dfrac{6}{15}$
4. $\dfrac{3}{12}$
5. $\dfrac{4}{18}$
6. $\dfrac{4}{14}$

7. $\dfrac{9}{3}$
8. $\dfrac{3}{18}$
9. $\dfrac{20}{32}$
10. $\dfrac{20}{12}$
11. $\dfrac{54}{6}$
12. $\dfrac{28}{35}$

13. $\dfrac{12}{18}$
14. $\dfrac{45}{10}$
15. $\dfrac{10}{15}$
16. $\dfrac{22}{4}$
17. $\dfrac{24}{28}$
18. $\dfrac{88}{32}$

19. $\dfrac{16}{24}$
20. $\dfrac{21}{21}$
21. $\dfrac{35}{14}$
22. $\dfrac{16}{40}$
23. $\dfrac{56}{8}$
24. $\dfrac{30}{24}$

25. $\dfrac{24}{40}$
26. $\dfrac{32}{18}$
27. $\dfrac{12}{8}$
28. $\dfrac{22}{6}$
29. $\dfrac{14}{18}$
30. $\dfrac{38}{4}$

Addition: Common Denominators *(pages 236–237)*

Add.

$$\boxed{\frac{4}{11} + \frac{5}{11} = \frac{9}{11}}$$

1. $\frac{3}{5} + \frac{1}{5} = \blacksquare$ **2.** $\frac{5}{8} + \frac{4}{8} = \blacksquare$ **3.** $\frac{1}{7} + \frac{4}{7} = \blacksquare$

4. $\frac{4}{7} + \frac{5}{7} = \blacksquare$ **5.** $\frac{1}{9} + \frac{8}{9} = \blacksquare$ **6.** $\frac{3}{10} + \frac{5}{10} = \blacksquare$ **7.** $\frac{7}{8} + \frac{5}{8} = \blacksquare$

8. $\frac{8}{12} + \frac{3}{12} = \blacksquare$ **9.** $\frac{1}{10} + \frac{7}{10} = \blacksquare$ **10.** $\frac{3}{4} + \frac{3}{4} = \blacksquare$ **11.** $\frac{4}{15} + \frac{8}{15} = \blacksquare$

12. $\frac{3}{11} + \frac{8}{11} = \blacksquare$ **13.** $\frac{5}{6} + \frac{5}{6} = \blacksquare$ **14.** $\frac{12}{15} + \frac{10}{15} = \blacksquare$ **15.** $\frac{9}{12} + \frac{11}{12} = \blacksquare$

16. $\frac{5}{9}$ **17.** $\frac{4}{6}$ **18.** $\frac{5}{9}$ **19.** $\frac{2}{12}$ **20.** $\frac{6}{10}$ **21.** $\frac{7}{15}$
$+\frac{3}{9}$ $+\frac{3}{6}$ $+\frac{8}{9}$ $+\frac{5}{12}$ $+\frac{4}{10}$ $+\frac{0}{15}$

Subtraction: Common Denominators *(pages 238–239)*

Subtract.

$$\boxed{\frac{9}{13} - \frac{4}{13} = \frac{5}{13}}$$

1. $\frac{5}{6} - \frac{1}{6} = \blacksquare$ **2.** $\frac{6}{7} - \frac{3}{7} = \blacksquare$ **3.** $\frac{9}{10} - \frac{3}{10} = \blacksquare$

4. $\frac{8}{9} - \frac{2}{9} = \blacksquare$ **5.** $\frac{7}{11} - \frac{2}{11} = \blacksquare$ **6.** $\frac{6}{8} - \frac{1}{8} = \blacksquare$ **7.** $\frac{8}{10} - \frac{5}{10} = \blacksquare$

8. $\frac{9}{12} - \frac{3}{12} = \blacksquare$ **9.** $\frac{13}{15} - \frac{8}{15} = \blacksquare$ **10.** $\frac{3}{5} - \frac{0}{5} = \blacksquare$ **11.** $\frac{5}{6} - \frac{3}{6} = \blacksquare$

12. $\frac{7}{8} - \frac{3}{8} = \blacksquare$ **13.** $\frac{9}{10} - \frac{7}{10} = \blacksquare$ **14.** $\frac{11}{12} - \frac{5}{12} = \blacksquare$ **15.** $\frac{4}{4} - \frac{1}{4} = \blacksquare$

16. $\frac{7}{8}$ **17.** $\frac{11}{12}$ **18.** $\frac{5}{6}$ **19.** $\frac{5}{5}$ **20.** $\frac{11}{15}$ **21.** $\frac{4}{9}$
$-\frac{5}{8}$ $-\frac{7}{12}$ $-\frac{5}{6}$ $-\frac{3}{5}$ $-\frac{2}{15}$ $-\frac{0}{9}$

More Addition and Subtraction *(pages 240–241)*

Add or subtract.

$$\begin{array}{r} \frac{7}{8} \\ \frac{5}{8} \\ + \\ \hline \frac{12}{8}, \frac{3}{2}, \text{ or } 1\frac{1}{2} \end{array}$$

$$\begin{array}{r} \frac{5}{4} \\ \frac{3}{4} \\ - \\ \hline \frac{2}{4} \text{ or } \frac{1}{2} \end{array}$$

1. $\frac{5}{6} + \frac{5}{6} = \blacksquare$ **2.** $\frac{4}{9} + \frac{2}{9} = \blacksquare$ **3.** $\frac{7}{8} - \frac{3}{8} = \blacksquare$

4. $\frac{7}{9} - \frac{2}{9} = \blacksquare$ **5.** $\frac{7}{10} + \frac{9}{10} = \blacksquare$ **6.** $\frac{20}{7} - \frac{6}{7} = \blacksquare$

7. $\begin{array}{r} \frac{11}{12} \\ + \frac{7}{12} \\ \hline \end{array}$ **8.** $\begin{array}{r} \frac{13}{8} \\ - \frac{5}{8} \\ \hline \end{array}$ **9.** $\begin{array}{r} \frac{7}{4} \\ + \frac{5}{4} \\ \hline \end{array}$ **10.** $\begin{array}{r} \frac{9}{16} \\ + \frac{15}{16} \\ \hline \end{array}$ **11.** $\begin{array}{r} \frac{19}{6} \\ - \frac{5}{6} \\ \hline \end{array}$

12. $\begin{array}{r} \frac{17}{10} \\ - \frac{9}{10} \\ \hline \end{array}$ **13.** $\begin{array}{r} \frac{5}{3} \\ + \frac{1}{3} \\ \hline \end{array}$ **14.** $\begin{array}{r} \frac{11}{12} \\ - \frac{7}{12} \\ \hline \end{array}$ **15.** $\begin{array}{r} \frac{15}{7} \\ + \frac{5}{7} \\ \hline \end{array}$ **16.** $\begin{array}{r} \frac{31}{9} \\ - \frac{13}{9} \\ \hline \end{array}$

Problem Solving: Using Circle Graphs *(pages 242–243)*

Use the circle graph to solve the problems.

What part of the students in all walk to school or ride a bicycle to school?	Part walk + Part use bike = Part walk or bike $\frac{9}{16} + \frac{2}{16} = \frac{11}{16}$ $\frac{11}{16}$ of the students walk or bike

1. What part of these students in all walk to school or take a school bus?

2. What part more take a bus to school than ride in a car?

3. What part of the students in all ride a bicycle, take a school bus, or get to school in "other" ways?

4. What part more walk to school than ride a bicycle?

Ways of Getting to School

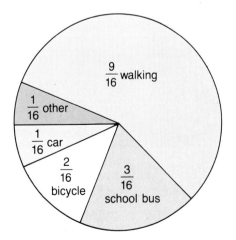

433

Multiplying to Find Equivalent Fractions   *(pages 246–247)*

Copy and complete.

$$\frac{5}{6} = \frac{5 \times 3}{6 \times 3} = \frac{15}{18}$$

1. $\frac{1}{8} = \frac{1 \times \blacksquare}{8 \times 7} = \frac{\blacksquare}{56}$

2. $\frac{7}{9} = \frac{7 \times \blacksquare}{9 \times 4} = \frac{\blacksquare}{36}$

3. $\frac{5}{4} = \frac{5 \times \blacksquare}{4 \times 8} = \frac{\blacksquare}{\blacksquare}$

4. $\frac{2}{3} = \frac{2 \times \blacksquare}{3 \times 9} = \frac{\blacksquare}{\blacksquare}$

5. $\frac{3}{10} = \frac{3 \times \overset{5}{\blacksquare}}{10 \times 5} = \frac{\blacksquare}{\blacksquare}$

Multiply each numerator and denominator by 2, 3, 4, 5, and 6 to find equivalent fractions.

6. $\frac{1}{2}$ **7.** $\frac{4}{7}$ **8.** $\frac{6}{1}$ **9.** $\frac{4}{3}$ **10.** $\frac{7}{12}$ **11.** $\frac{7}{8}$ **12.** $\frac{8}{5}$ **13.** $\frac{9}{10}$

Comparison   *(pages 248–249)*

Write $>$, $<$, or $=$ for ●. Use the lists of equivalent fractions on page 248, or use your own lists.

$$\frac{3}{4} \bullet \frac{4}{5}$$
$$\downarrow \qquad \downarrow$$
$$\frac{15}{20} < \frac{16}{20}$$

1. $\frac{5}{13} \bullet \frac{8}{13}$ **2.** $\frac{2}{3} \bullet \frac{5}{6}$ **3.** $\frac{9}{6} \bullet \frac{4}{6}$ **4.** $\frac{1}{2} \bullet \frac{2}{5}$

5. $\frac{5}{6} \bullet \frac{7}{10}$ **6.** $\frac{3}{8} \bullet \frac{2}{5}$ **7.** $\frac{8}{8} \bullet \frac{11}{8}$ **8.** $\frac{3}{10} \bullet \frac{4}{15}$

9. $\frac{3}{5} \bullet \frac{5}{6}$ **10.** $\frac{7}{9} \bullet \frac{8}{15}$ **11.** $\frac{3}{2} \bullet \frac{11}{8}$ **12.** $\frac{7}{10} \bullet \frac{3}{4}$ **13.** $\frac{8}{15} \bullet \frac{7}{12}$

Addition: Unlike Denominators   *(pages 250–251)*

Add. Use lists of equivalent fractions.

$$\frac{3}{8} + \frac{1}{3} = \blacksquare$$
$$\downarrow \qquad \downarrow$$
$$\frac{9}{24} + \frac{8}{24} = \frac{17}{24}$$

1. $\frac{3}{4} + \frac{1}{6} = \blacksquare$ **2.** $\frac{2}{3} + \frac{7}{9} = \blacksquare$ **3.** $\frac{1}{2} + \frac{1}{12} = \blacksquare$

4. $\frac{3}{5} + \frac{1}{2} = \blacksquare$ **5.** $\frac{2}{3} + \frac{5}{6} = \blacksquare$ **6.** $\frac{3}{8} + \frac{1}{5} = \blacksquare$

7. $\begin{array}{r} \frac{3}{5} \\ + \frac{1}{6} \\ \hline \end{array}$ **8.** $\begin{array}{r} \frac{1}{4} \\ + \frac{3}{4} \\ \hline \end{array}$ **9.** $\begin{array}{r} \frac{5}{9} \\ + \frac{2}{12} \\ \hline \end{array}$ **10.** $\begin{array}{r} \frac{1}{4} \\ + \frac{3}{5} \\ \hline \end{array}$ **11.** $\begin{array}{r} \frac{1}{2} \\ + \frac{1}{4} \\ \hline \end{array}$ **12.** $\begin{array}{r} \frac{5}{6} \\ + \frac{1}{6} \\ \hline \end{array}$

Subtraction: Unlike Denominators *(pages 252–253)*

Subtract. Use lists of equivalent fractions.

$\frac{9}{5} - \frac{11}{20} = $ ▨

$\frac{36}{20} - \frac{11}{20} = \frac{25}{20}$

$25 \div 5$

$\frac{25}{20} = \frac{5}{4}$

$20 \div 5$

$\frac{25}{20} = \frac{5}{4}$ or $1\frac{1}{4}$

1. $\frac{11}{12} - \frac{1}{4} = $ ▨ **2.** $\frac{1}{2} - \frac{1}{6} = $ ▨ **3.** $\frac{}{8} - \frac{1}{4} = $ ▨ **4.** $\frac{5}{6} - \frac{2}{3} = $ ▨

5. $\frac{4}{3} - \frac{5}{8} = $ ▨ **6.** $\frac{13}{18} - \frac{1}{6} = $ ▨ **7.** $\frac{9}{10} - \frac{4}{15} = $ ▨ **8.** $\frac{11}{12} - \frac{1}{2} = $ ▨

9. $\begin{array}{r} \frac{3}{4} \\ -\frac{1}{6} \end{array}$ **10.** $\begin{array}{r} \frac{11}{15} \\ -\frac{2}{5} \end{array}$ **11.** $\begin{array}{r} \frac{3}{2} \\ -\frac{3}{8} \end{array}$ **12.** $\begin{array}{r} \frac{3}{4} \\ -\frac{1}{10} \end{array}$ **13.** $\begin{array}{r} \frac{7}{4} \\ -\frac{1}{3} \end{array}$ **14.** $\begin{array}{r} \frac{7}{6} \\ -\frac{1}{8} \end{array}$

15. $\begin{array}{r} \frac{9}{10} \\ -\frac{5}{6} \end{array}$ **16.** $\begin{array}{r} \frac{7}{9} \\ -\frac{1}{12} \end{array}$ **17.** $\begin{array}{r} \frac{5}{6} \\ -\frac{4}{15} \end{array}$ **18.** $\begin{array}{r} \frac{3}{2} \\ -\frac{7}{10} \end{array}$ **19.** $\begin{array}{r} \frac{8}{15} \\ -\frac{3}{10} \end{array}$ **20.** $\begin{array}{r} \frac{3}{4} \\ -\frac{5}{12} \end{array}$

Finding Parts of Numbers *(pages 254–255)*

Find:

$\frac{3}{4}$ of 52

$\begin{array}{r} 13 \\ 4\overline{)52} \\ \underline{4} \\ 12 \\ \underline{12} \\ 0 \end{array}$

1 of 4 equal parts

$\begin{array}{r} 13 \\ \times\ 3 \\ \hline 39 \end{array}$

$\frac{3}{4}$ of 52 is 39

1. $\frac{1}{6}$ of 30 **2.** $\frac{1}{3}$ of 54 **3.** $\frac{1}{7}$ of 42

4. $\frac{1}{2}$ of 96 **5.** $\frac{1}{5}$ of 75 **6.** $\frac{1}{4}$ of 64

7. $\frac{5}{8}$ of 24 **8.** $\frac{2}{5}$ of 35 **9.** $\frac{4}{7}$ of 28

10. $\frac{3}{4}$ of 80 **11.** $\frac{2}{3}$ of 51 **12.** $\frac{3}{5}$ of 65

13. $\frac{1}{9}$ of 63 **14.** $\frac{1}{8}$ of 104 **15.** $\frac{7}{9}$ of 36

UNIT 9: Multiplying by Tens and Ones

Reviewing Multiplying by 1-digit Numbers (pages 262–263)

Multiply.

$$\begin{array}{r} ② ② \\ 8,716 \\ \times \quad 4 \\ \hline 34,864 \end{array}$$

1. $\begin{array}{r} 7,219 \\ \times \quad 2 \\ \hline \end{array}$ **2.** $\begin{array}{r} 4,826 \\ \times \quad 3 \\ \hline \end{array}$ **3.** $\begin{array}{r} 387 \\ \times \quad 9 \\ \hline \end{array}$ **4.** $\begin{array}{r} 8,479 \\ \times \quad 4 \\ \hline \end{array}$ **5.** $\begin{array}{r} 5,327 \\ \times \quad 8 \\ \hline \end{array}$

6. $\begin{array}{r} 967 \\ \times \quad 5 \\ \hline \end{array}$ **7.** $\begin{array}{r} 7 \\ \times 6,324 \\ \hline \end{array}$ **8.** $\begin{array}{r} 8,974 \\ \times \quad 6 \\ \hline \end{array}$ **9.** $\begin{array}{r} 6,974 \\ \times \quad 9 \\ \hline \end{array}$ **10.** $\begin{array}{r} 841 \\ \times \quad 7 \\ \hline \end{array}$

11. $6 \times 5,679 =$ ▨   **12.** $8 \times 2,468 =$ ▨   **13.** $5 \times 2,317 =$ ▨   **14.** $3 \times 1,907 =$ ▨

Multiplying by 10 (pages 264–265)

Multiply. Use the pattern.

$$\begin{array}{r} 647 \\ \times \quad 10 \\ \hline 6,470 \end{array}$$

1. $\begin{array}{r} 23 \\ \times 10 \\ \hline \end{array}$ **2.** $\begin{array}{r} 52 \\ \times 10 \\ \hline \end{array}$ **3.** $\begin{array}{r} 367 \\ \times \ 10 \\ \hline \end{array}$ **4.** $\begin{array}{r} 409 \\ \times \ 10 \\ \hline \end{array}$ **5.** $\begin{array}{r} 91 \\ \times 10 \\ \hline \end{array}$

6. $\begin{array}{r} 763 \\ \times \ 10 \\ \hline \end{array}$ **7.** $\begin{array}{r} 540 \\ \times \ 10 \\ \hline \end{array}$ **8.** $\begin{array}{r} 836 \\ \times \ 10 \\ \hline \end{array}$ **9.** $\begin{array}{r} 40 \\ \times 10 \\ \hline \end{array}$ **10.** $\begin{array}{r} 200 \\ \times \ 10 \\ \hline \end{array}$

11. $10 \times 301 =$ ▨   **12.** $10 \times 35 =$ ▨   **13.** $10 \times 950 =$ ▨   **14.** $10 \times 75 =$ ▨

Multiplying by Multiples of 10 (pages 266–267)

Multiply 36 by 40.

$$\begin{array}{r} 36 \\ \times 40 \\ \hline 0 \end{array} \qquad \begin{array}{r} ② \\ 36 \\ \times 40 \\ \hline 1,460 \end{array}$$

1. Multiply 40 by 10.

2. Multiply 251 by 50.

3. Multiply 300 by 90.

Multiply.

4. $\begin{array}{r} 67 \\ \times 50 \\ \hline \end{array}$ **5.** $\begin{array}{r} 87 \\ \times 70 \\ \hline \end{array}$ **6.** $\begin{array}{r} 406 \\ \times \ 30 \\ \hline \end{array}$ **7.** $\begin{array}{r} 563 \\ \times \ 20 \\ \hline \end{array}$ **8.** $\begin{array}{r} 79 \\ \times 60 \\ \hline \end{array}$ **9.** $\begin{array}{r} 498 \\ \times \ 80 \\ \hline \end{array}$

10. $\begin{array}{r} 379 \\ \times \ 70 \\ \hline \end{array}$ **11.** $\begin{array}{r} 658 \\ \times \ 50 \\ \hline \end{array}$ **12.** $\begin{array}{r} 96 \\ \times 40 \\ \hline \end{array}$ **13.** $\begin{array}{r} 654 \\ \times \ 90 \\ \hline \end{array}$ **14.** $\begin{array}{r} 1,000 \\ \times \quad 10 \\ \hline \end{array}$ **15.** $\begin{array}{r} 458 \\ \times \ 70 \\ \hline \end{array}$

Multiplying by 2-digit Numbers   *(pages 268–269)*

Multiply.

```
   52
 × 43
 ─────
  156   ← 3 × 52
 2080   ← 40 × 52
 ─────
 2,236  ← 43 × 52
```

1. 33 × 32

2. 21 × 48

3. 62 × 32

4. 61 × 56

5. 81 × 83

6. 92 × 23

7. 31 × 89

8. 82 × 43

9. 91 × 87

10. 71 × 67

11. 54 × 12

12. 71 × 89

13. 52 × 24

14. 82 × 33

15. $13 \times 73 =$

16. $70 \times 90 =$

17. $53 \times 41 =$

18. $10 \times 87 =$

19. $42 \times 72 =$

20. $20 \times 68 =$

21. $94 \times 31 =$

22. $49 \times 71 =$

23. $38 \times 73 =$

24. $97 \times 43 =$

25. $27 \times 56 =$

26. $48 \times 62 =$

Saving in One Step   *(pages 270–271)*

Multiply.

```
   82
 × 25
 ─────
  410   ← 5 × 82
 1640   ← 20 × 82
 ─────
 2,050  ← 25 × 82
```

1. 14 × 42

2. 61 × 86

3. 72 × 39

4. 74 × 42

5. 34 × 26

6. 31 × 87

7. 84 × 92

8. 43 × 62

9. 92 × 54

10. 72 × 72

11. 93 × 63

12. 57 × 91

13. 29 × 17

14. 83 × 53

15. $37 \times 53 =$

16. $27 \times 64 =$

17. $64 \times 62 =$

18. $73 \times 43 =$

19. $29 \times 73 =$

20. $71 \times 47 =$

21. $14 \times 65 =$

22. $82 \times 34 =$

23. $52 \times 94 =$

24. $35 \times 82 =$

25. $93 \times 42 =$

26. $41 \times 68 =$

27. $34 \times 23 =$

28. $42 \times 83 =$

29. $91 \times 46 =$

30. $47 \times 24 =$

Saving in Two Steps (pages 272–273)

Multiply.

```
        ②
        ⊗
        56
      × 47
       392   ←  7 × 56
      2240   ← 40 × 56
     2,632   ← 47 × 56
```

1. 27 × 25	2. 29 × 73	3. 79 × 68	4. $.37 × 34
5. 49 × 89	6. 91 × 38	7. 43 × 56	8. 36 × 74
9. $.47 × 84	10. 38 × 97	11. $56 × 28	12. 59 × 52	13. 84 × 32	14. 85 × 17

15. $36 \times 67 =$ ▨   16. $26 \times \$.62 =$ ▨   17. $64 \times 96 =$ ▨   18. $75 \times 92 =$ ▨

19. $42 \times 92 =$ ▨   20. $57 \times \$.75 =$ ▨   21. $99 \times 99 =$ ▨   22. $83 \times 43 =$ ▨

23. $73 \times 48 =$ ▨   24. $\$.75 \times 79 =$ ▨   25. $83 \times 49 =$ ▨   26. $56 \times 97 =$ ▨

Multiplying Larger Numbers (pages 276–277)

Multiply.

```
       ①③
       ⊗⊗
       526
      × 64
      2104   ←  4 × 526
     31560   ← 60 × 526
    33,664   ← 64 × 526
```

1. 243 × 27	2. 305 × 35	3. 709 × 19	4. 675 × 63
5. 342 × 62	6. $2.39 × 46	7. 213 × 38	8. 796 × 71
9. $2.43 × 82	10. 704 × 54	11. 800 × 86	12. 869 × 81	13. 413 × 52	14. $256 × 72

15. $70 \times \$3.96 =$ ▨   16. $42 \times 534 =$ ▨   17. $74 \times 786 =$ ▨

18. $80 \times 400 =$ ▨   19. $27 \times \$9.38 =$ ▨   20. $84 \times 512 =$ ▨

21. $97 \times 911 =$ ▨   22. $90 \times 900 =$ ▨   23. $97 \times 749 =$ ▨

Estimating Products (pages 278–279)

Find each product. Then estimate to check your product.

<table>
<tr><td></td><td>Estimate</td><td>Exact</td></tr>
<tr><td>(7)36 →</td><td>700</td><td>736</td></tr>
<tr><td>× (5)8 →</td><td>× 60</td><td>× 58</td></tr>
<tr><td></td><td>42,000</td><td>42,688</td></tr>
</table>

42,688 is near 42,000.
Your answer is reasonable.

1. 83
× 7

2. 483
× 5

3. 6,134
× 8

4. 63
×26

5. 92
×53

6. 98
×64

7. 365
× 74

8. $7.29
× 4

9. $19.83
× 6

10. $1.89
× 12

11. $7.05
× 18

12. $3.89
× 48

Estimate.

13. 76
×13

14. 5,263
+8,798

15. 26,384
− 7,419

16. $7.14
× 9

17. 18,256
+ 6,684

18. 9,384
−2,936

19. 427
× 68

20. $48.65
+ 9.37

21. $2.65
× 45

22. $784.69
−277.28

Problem Solving: Order Forms (pages 280–281)

Use the catalog page on page 280.
Complete an order form for each order.

Item No.	Description	Quantity	Price		Total Price	
9A	Invitations	20	$	.15	$ 3.	00
9B	Napkins	4	1.	45	5.	80
9D	Favors	12	1.	25	15.	00
9E	Balloons	3	.	39	1.	17
		TOTAL PRICE OF ORDER →			$ 24.	97

1. 2 packages of napkins, 4 streamers, and 2 bags of balloons.

2. 7 candles, 5 streamers, 10 horns, and 10 party hats.

3. 12 invitations, 3 packages of napkins, 4 favors, and 8 party hats.

4. 16 horns, 10 candles, 8 streamers, and 16 party hats.

UNIT 10: Dividing by Tens and Ones

Reviewing 1-digit Divisors *(pages 288–289)*

Divide.

$$\begin{array}{r} 407\text{R}4 \\ 7\overline{)2{,}853} \\ \underline{28} \\ 05 \\ \underline{0} \\ 53 \\ \underline{49} \\ 4 \end{array}$$

1. $4\overline{)89}$ 2. $2\overline{)673}$ 3. $6\overline{)98}$ 4. $5\overline{)365}$

5. $9\overline{)91}$ 6. $3\overline{)2{,}569}$ 7. $6\overline{)516}$ 8. $5\overline{)4{,}312}$

9. $8\overline{)738}$ 10. $7\overline{)2{,}347}$ 11. $7\overline{)1{,}043}$ 12. $3\overline{)900}$

13. $2\overline{)5{,}216}$ 14. $6\overline{)800}$ 15. $4\overline{)8{,}140}$ 16. $9\overline{)3{,}265}$

17. $4\overline{)493}$ 18. $5\overline{)6{,}732}$ 19. $7\overline{)8{,}932}$ 20. $8\overline{)4{,}537}$

Dividing by Multiples of 10 *(pages 290–291)*

Divide.

$$\begin{array}{r} 24\text{R}3 \\ 40\overline{)963} \\ \underline{80} \\ 163 \\ \underline{160} \\ 3 \end{array}$$

1. $20\overline{)876}$ 2. $10\overline{)453}$ 3. $40\overline{)800}$ 4. $90\overline{)99}$

5. $60\overline{)723}$ 6. $30\overline{)690}$ 7. $90\overline{)643}$ 8. $50\overline{)871}$

9. $70\overline{)267}$ 10. $80\overline{)573}$ 11. $30\overline{)162}$ 12. $60\overline{)379}$

13. $50\overline{)480}$ 14. $70\overline{)850}$ 15. $20\overline{)600}$ 16. $80\overline{)975}$

Using Tables of Multiples *(pages 292–293)*

Use your tables of multiples of 13 and 21 to help you divide.

$$\begin{array}{r} 58\text{R}6 \\ 13\overline{)760} \\ \underline{65} \\ 110 \\ \underline{104} \\ 6 \end{array}$$

1. $13\overline{)90}$ 2. $21\overline{)93}$ 3. $21\overline{)895}$ 4. $13\overline{)176}$

5. $13\overline{)493}$ 6. $21\overline{)567}$ 7. $13\overline{)300}$ 8. $21\overline{)615}$

9. $21\overline{)785}$ 10. $13\overline{)794}$ 11. $21\overline{)400}$ 12. $13\overline{)926}$

13. $1{,}222 \div 13 =$ 14. $1{,}344 \div 21 =$ 15. $1{,}131 \div 13 =$ 16. $1{,}554 \div 21 =$

17. $117 \div 13 =$ 18. $756 \div 21 =$ 19. $168 \div 21 =$ 20. $611 \div 13 =$

Rounding the Divisor *(pages 296–297)*

Round 74 down to 70.	Round 59 up to 60.
$$\begin{array}{r} 3 \ \text{R19} \\ 74\overline{)241} \\ \underline{222} \\ 19 \end{array}$$	$$\begin{array}{r} 13 \ \textbf{R8} \\ 59\overline{)775} \\ \underline{59} \\ 185 \\ \underline{177} \\ 8 \end{array}$$

Divide.

1. $23\overline{)345}$ **2.** $49\overline{)599}$ **3.** $31\overline{)978}$ **4.** $78\overline{)987}$ **5.** $55\overline{)139}$

6. $57\overline{)756}$ **7.** $62\overline{)992}$ **8.** $73\overline{)879}$ **9.** $86\overline{)959}$ **10.** $94\overline{)289}$

Trial Quotients: Rounding Up *(pages 298–299)*

Round 29 up to 30.		
$$\begin{array}{r} 7 \ \text{R6} \\ 29\overline{)209} \\ \underline{203} \\ 6 \end{array}$$	*Think:* ▦ $\times 30 = 209$ Try 6.	*Do:* $\begin{array}{c} 29 \\ \underline{\times \ 6} \\ 174 \end{array} \rightarrow \begin{array}{c} 29 \\ \underline{\times \ 7} \\ 203 \end{array} \rightarrow \begin{array}{c} 29 \\ \underline{\times \ 8} \\ 232 \end{array}$ $232 > 209$ **Use 7.**

Divide.

1. $18\overline{)176}$ **2.** $35\overline{)642}$ **3.** $65\overline{)376}$ **4.** $27\overline{)874}$ **5.** $89\overline{)534}$

6. $56\overline{)863}$ **7.** $29\overline{)880}$ **8.** $79\overline{)475}$ **9.** $16\overline{)130}$ **10.** $26\overline{)806}$

Trial Quotients: Rounding Down *(pages 300–301)*

Round 23 down to 20.				
$$\begin{array}{r} 35 \ \text{R5} \\ 23\overline{)810} \\ \underline{69} \\ 120 \\ \underline{115} \\ 5 \end{array}$$	*Think:* ▦ $\times 20 = 81$ Try 4.	*Do:* $\begin{array}{c} 23 \\ \underline{\times \ 4} \\ 92 \end{array} \rightarrow \begin{array}{c} 23 \\ \underline{\times \ 3} \\ 69 \end{array}$ $69 < 81$ **Use 3.**	*Think:* ▦ $\times 20 = 120$ Try 6.	*Do:* $\begin{array}{c} 23 \\ \underline{\times \ 6} \\ 138 \end{array} \rightarrow \begin{array}{c} 23 \\ \underline{\times \ 5} \\ 115 \end{array}$ $115 < 120$ **Use 5.**

Divide.

1. $33\overline{)621}$ **2.** $93\overline{)918}$ **3.** $35\overline{)596}$ **4.** $41\overline{)203}$ **5.** $43\overline{)371}$

6. $62\overline{)982}$ **7.** $92\overline{)548}$ **8.** $52\overline{)725}$ **9.** $14\overline{)512}$ **10.** $74\overline{)711}$

Changing Customary Units *(pages 302–303)*

Find the missing numbers.

10 ft = ▦ in.
1 ft = 12 in.

10 ft ⟷ 10 sets of 12 in.

10 × 12 = 120
10 ft = 120 in.

1. 11 yd = ▦ ft   **2.** 14 qt = ▦ pt

3. 80 oz = ▦ lb   **4.** 20 gal = ▦ qt

5. 7 ft = ▦ in.   **6.** 34 cups = ▦ pt

7. 12 pt = ▦ qt   **8.** 8 yd = ▦ ft

9. 24 pt = ▦ qt   **10.** 42 ft = ▦ yd   **11.** 52 qt = ▦ gal

12. 7 lb = ▦ oz   **13.** 6 pt = ▦ cups   **14.** 84 in. = ▦ ft

15. A bookcase is 72 inches high. What is the height in feet?

16. A pork roast weighs 48 ounces. What is its weight in pounds?

Problem Solving: Comparison Shopping *(pages 304–305)*

Find the prices per package. Which is the better buy?

48¢ per package or 6 packages for $2.70.	$ .45 6)$2.70 2 4 30 30 0	$.45 is less than $.48 6 packages for $2.70 is the better buy.

To find the cost per package, divide

1. 43¢ per package or 5 packages for $2.10

2. 63¢ per package or 4 packages for $2.48

Find the prices per ounce. Which is the best buy?

3. 9 oz for $2.07, 15 oz for $3.15, or 22 oz for $4.84

4. 8 oz for $3.92, 10 oz for $4.80, or 20 oz for $9.40

5. 12 oz for $1.44, 16 oz for $1.76, or 24 oz for $2.16

6. 18 oz for $3.60, 30 oz for $4.80, or 48 oz for $8.64

UNIT 11: Geometry

Solids and Their Parts *(pages 312–313)*

Tell whether each object is a rectangular prism, cube, cylinder, sphere, cone, or pyramid.

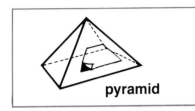
pyramid

1.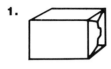

2.

3.

4.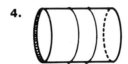

5.

What figures would you get by tracing the flat faces for the solid in:

6. Exercise **1**   **7.** Exercise **3**   **8.** Exercise **4**   **9.** Exercise **5**

Polygons *(pages 314–315)*

Which of these plane figures are polygons?

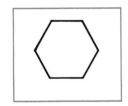

1.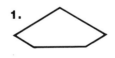

2.

3.

4.

Which of these plane figures are:

5. triangles?   **6.** quadrilaterals?   **7.** pentagons?   **8.** hexagons?
9. octagons?

a.

b.

c.

d.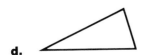

e

f.

Line Segments and Lines   *(pages 316–317)*

Give 2 names for each line segment in each figure.

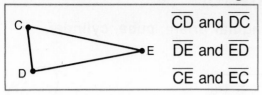

$\overline{CD}$ and $\overline{DC}$

$\overline{DE}$ and $\overline{ED}$

$\overline{CE}$ and $\overline{EC}$

1.

2. 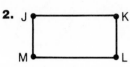   **3.** 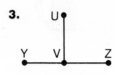   **4.**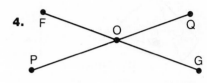

5. Give 6 names for this line.

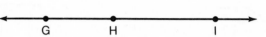

Write *intersecting* or *parallel* to describe each pair of lines.

6. 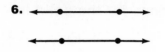   **7.** 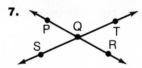   **8.**

Rays and Angles   *(pages 318–319)*

Name 2 rays with endpoint Y. $\overrightarrow{YX}$ $\overrightarrow{YZ}$

1. Name the angle shown.

2. Name the vertex of the angle.

3. Name all the angles of this quadrilateral.

4. Which angles look like right angles?

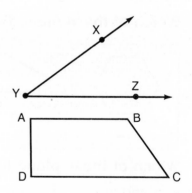

Special Quadrilaterals   *(pages 320–321)*

Which of these figures are:

1. parallelograms?   **2.** rectangles?   **3.** squares?

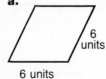

5 units

5 units

9 units

parallelogram

a. 6 units / 6 units

b. 7 units / 7 units

c. 3 units / 8 units

Lines of Symmetry *(pages 322–323)*

How many lines of symmetry does each figure have?

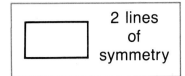 2 lines of symmetry

1.

2.

3.

4.

5.

6.

7.

8.

9.

Copy each figure on graph paper. Complete each so that the heavy line is a line of symmetry.

10.   **11.**   **12.**   **13.**   **14.**

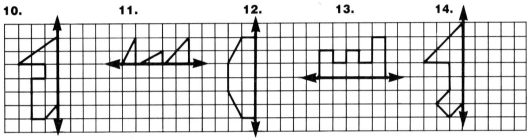

Perimeter *(pages 326–327)*

Find the perimeter of each polygon.

8 cm, 15 cm, 17 cm   Perimeter = 8 + 15 + 17 = 40 cm

1.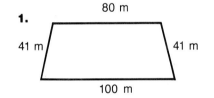
80 m, 41 m, 41 m, 100 m

2.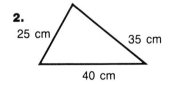
25 cm, 35 cm, 40 cm

3.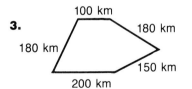
100 km, 180 km, 180 km, 150 km, 200 km

4. A square with one side of length 75 cm

5.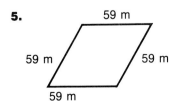
59 m, 59 m, 59 m, 59 m

6.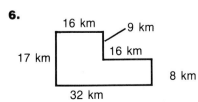
16 km, 9 km, 16 km, 17 km, 8 km, 32 km

7. A rectangle with
length: 38 m
width: 13 m

445

Area *(pages 328–329)*

Use the grid squares as square units. Find the area of each figure.

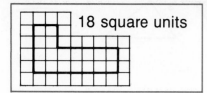 18 square units

1.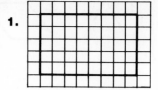

2.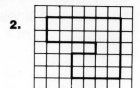

3.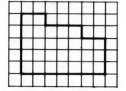

4.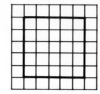

5.

6.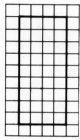

7.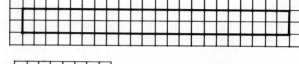

8.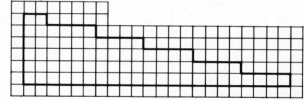

Multiplying to Find Area *(pages 330–331)*

Find the area of each rectangle.

length: 65m	65
width: 42m	$\times 42$
	130
	2600
	2730

Area = 2,730 m²

1.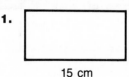
7 cm
15 cm

2. A square with one side of length 15 m

3. length: 78 m
width: 45 m

4. length: 40 cm
width: 8 cm

5. length: 95 m
width: 30 m

6. A square with one side of length 49 cm

7.
28 m
80 m

8. length: 64 m
width: 52 m

9. A square with one side of length 25 m

Volume *(pages 332–333)*
Find the volume of each rectangular prism.

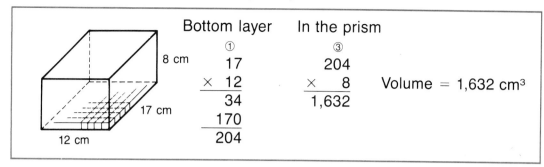

Bottom layer

①
17
× 12
34
170
204

In the prism

③
204
× 8
1,632

Volume = 1,632 cm³

1.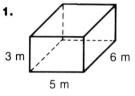

2.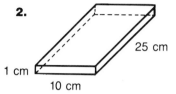

3. length: 20 m
width: 15 m
height: 25 m

4. length: 17 cm
width: 17 cm
height: 10 cm

5. length: 11 m
width: 11 m
height: 11 m

6. length: 30 cm
width: 20 cm
height: 50 cm

Using Customary Units *(pages 334–335)*
Find the area of each bottom and the volume of each box.

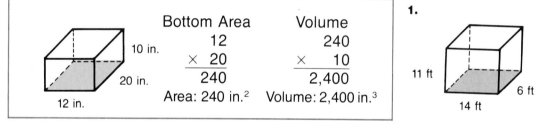

Bottom Area

12
× 20
240
Area: 240 in.²

Volume

240
× 10
2,400
Volume: 2,400 in.³

1.
11 ft · 6 ft · 14 ft

2.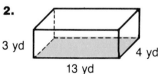
3 yd · 4 yd · 13 yd

3. length: 35 in.
width: 18 in.
height: 14 in.

4. length: 15 ft
width: 9 ft
height: 12 ft

Solve the problems.

5. A filing cabinet is 3 ft long, 2 ft wide, and 5 ft high. What is the volume of the cabinet?

6. A rug is 2 yd wide and 3 yd long. What is the area of the rug? What is its perimeter?

7. A photograph is 5 in. wide and 7 in. long. What is its area? What is its perimeter?

8. A birthday card is 9 in. long and 7 in. wide. What is its area?

447

UNIT 12: Decimals

Tenths   *(pages 342–343)*

Write a decimal to tell how much is shaded. Then name the place of each digit.

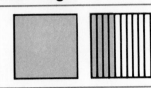
1.4
1 is in the ones place
4 is in the tenths place

1.

2.   **3.**   **4.**

Write decimals that mean:

5. 9 ones 3 tenths

6. 4 tenths

7. 1 ten 8 ones 1 tenth

Write a decimal for each.

8. sixty and three tenths

9. zero point two

10. fourteen point zero

Hundredths   *(pages 344–345)*

Write a decimal to tell how much is shaded. Then name the place of each digit.

.46
4 is in the tenths place
6 is in the hundredths place

1.

2.   **3.**

Write decimals that mean:

4. 4 ones 5 tenths 7 hundredths   **5.** 5 tens 7 ones 3 tenths 2 hundredths

Write a decimal for each.

6. two and sixty-five hundredths   **7.** four hundredths

448   **Workbook**

Comparing with Decimals (pages 346–347)

Write >, <, or = for ●.

4.2 ● 4.03
4.2
4.03
2 > 0 so
4.2 > 4.03

1. .79 ● .9   **2.** 103.8 ● 130.8   **3.** 1.0 ● 9

4. 56 ● 6.3   **5.** 7.3 ● 7.31   **6.** .9 ● .09

7. .80 ● .8   **8.** 2.01 ● 2.0   **9.** 3.06 ● 3.6

Write in order from greatest to least.

10. .09; 2.1; 4   **11.** 5; 3.09; 4.8   **12.** .20; .22; .02; 2.0

Adding with Decimals (pages 350–351)

Add.

13 + 4.9 = ■
13.0
+ 4.9
17.9

1. 33.9 + 8.7   **2.** 76.07 + 86.42   **3.** 17.44 + 27.3   **4.** $1 + .96

5. $71.48 + 46.87   **6.** 84.7 + 75   **7.** 16.4 + 25.38   **8.** 69 + 18.4

9. $1.95 + $.74 = ■   **10.** 12.46 + 7.6 + 8 = ■   **11.** 36 + .07 + 19.7 = ■

12. 1.97 + 14.2 = ■   **13.** 3.2 + .9 + 6 = ■   **14.** 4.2 + .09 + 32 = ■

Subtracting with Decimals (pages 352–353)

Subtract.

$9 − $1.67 = ■
$9.00
− 1.67
$7.33

1. 7.3 − 1.2   **2.** 23.04 − 18.66   **3.** 2.15 − 2.08   **4.** 12.4 − 11.8

5. 18.5 − 8.97   **6.** 43 − 5.8   **7.** $300 − 96.75   **8.** 7.1 − 7.03

9. 38.26 − 21.75 = ■   **10.** 10.5 − 9.9 = ■   **11.** $5 − $.49 = ■

12. 25 − 8.6 = ■   **13.** $57.75 − $56 = ■   **14.** 4.1 − 4.01 = ■

Rounding and Estimating (pages 354–355)
Round to the nearest tenth. To the nearest one.

13.74	13.⑦4 ↓ 13.7	4<5 Keep ⑦.	1③.74 + 1 ——— 14	7>5 Add 1.

1. 4.73   2. 3.46   3. 8.12   4. 5.97   5. 7.02   6. 9.05

7. 10.62   8. 9.45   9. 4.94   10. 2.16   11. 0.54   12. 19.96

Find the sum or difference. Use estimation to check.

13. $\begin{array}{r} 7.63 \\ +8.28 \\ \hline \end{array}$
14. $\begin{array}{r} .74 \\ -.31 \\ \hline \end{array}$
15. $\begin{array}{r} 5.18 \\ +.95 \\ \hline \end{array}$
16. $\begin{array}{r} 4.07 \\ -.69 \\ \hline \end{array}$
17. $\begin{array}{r} .86 \\ +2.75 \\ \hline \end{array}$
18. $\begin{array}{r} 5.3 \\ -1.57 \\ \hline \end{array}$

19. $13 - 7.8 = $ ▩   20. $.42 + 1.6 + 2 = $ ▩   21. $1.97 - .48 = $ ▩

Problem Solving: Using Decimals (pages 356–357)
Use this table to solve the problems.

	Team A			Team B		
Name	Amy	Jay	Phil	Toni	Carlos	Raul
Distance run	3.6 km	2.1 km	9.8 km	6.3 km	5.2 km	2.9 km

Who ran farther, Jay or Raul? How much farther?

Raul ran 2.9 km

Jay ran 2.1 km   ?

How much farther? Subtract.
$2.9 - 2.1 = .8$

Raul ran 0.8 km farther.

1. How far did the six runners go all together?

2. Who ran farther, Amy or Toni? How much farther?

3. Who ran farther, Phil or Raul? How much farther?

4. Find the total distance run by Team A.

5. Find the total distance run by Team B.

6. Which team ran farther? How much farther?

Tables of Measure

TIME

1 minute = 60 seconds
1 hour = 60 minutes
1 day = 24 hours
1 week = 7 days
1 year = 12 months

CUSTOMARY

Length
1 foot (ft) = 12 inches (in.)
1 yard (yd) = 3 feet
1 mile (mi) = 1,760 yards = 5,280 feet

Weight
1 pound (lb) = 16 ounces (oz)

Liquid volume
1 pint (pt) = 2 cups
1 quart (qt) = 2 pints
1 gallon (gal) = 4 quarts

Temperature
At 32 degrees Fahrenheit (°F), water freezes.
At 212 degrees Fahrenheit (°F), water boils.

METRIC

Length
1 centimeter (cm) = 10 millimeters (mm)
1 meter (m) = 100 centimeters
1 kilometer (km) = 1,000 meters

Mass
1 kilogram (kg) = 1,000 grams (g)

Liquid volume
1 liter (L) = 1,000 milliliters (mL)

Temperature
At 0 degrees Celsius (°C), water freezes.
At 100 degrees Celsius (°C), water boils.

Glossary

Addition An operation on two or more numbers that tells how many in all or how much in all. Addition exercises are written in vertical or horizontal form.

$$5 \longleftarrow \text{addend}$$

plus $\longrightarrow$ $+7 \longleftarrow$ addend $\frac{1}{9} + \frac{4}{9} = \frac{5}{9}$

$$12 \longleftarrow \text{sum}$$

Addition is used to solve *put together* story problems.

Angle A figure formed by two rays with the same endpoint. ∠DEF is a right angle.

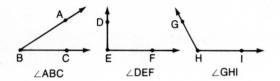

Area The number of unit squares it takes to cover the inside of a figure. Square inch, square foot, square yard, square centimeter, and square meter are standard units for measuring area.

Basic Facts Additions, subtractions, multiplications, or divisions with two of the three numbers 9 or less:

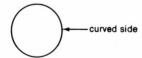

A set of related addition and subtraction facts, or multiplication and division facts, forms a *fact family:*

$7 + 5 = 12$ $12 - 5 = 7$ $8 \times 9 = 72$ $72 \div 9 = 8$
$5 + 7 = 12$ $12 - 7 = 5$ $9 \times 8 = 72$ $72 \div 8 = 9$

Circle A flat figure shaped like this.

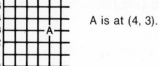

Coordinate Grid A picture of lines that cross at right angles and regular intervals. The lines are numbered so that positions can be located on the picture.

A is at (4, 3).

Common Denominator Two fractions that have the same denominators are said to have a common denominator.

Computer Literacy Knowledge of what computers can and cannot do, how computers operate, how to communicate with computers, and how to use computers to solve problems.

Cone An object that looks like this.

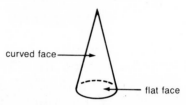

Counting Numbers Any of the numbers, 1, 2, 3, . . . , 58, 59, 60, . . . , 144, 145, 146, . . . , used in counting.

Cube A special kind of rectangular prism. Each face of a cube is a square.

Curve A path that can be drawn without lifting the pencil.

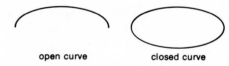

open curve   closed curve

Points can be inside, outside, or on a closed curve.

Customary Measurement System A measurement system that uses inches, feet, yards, and miles as units of length; cups, pints, quarts, and gallons as units of liquid volume; ounces and pounds as units of weight; degrees Fahrenheit (°F) as units of temperature; and minutes and hours as units of time.

Cylinder An object shaped like this.

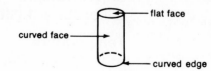

The flat faces of cylinders are circles.

Decimal A place value numeral that includes tenths, or tenths and hundredths.

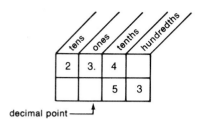

decimal point

Digit Any of the symbols 0, 1, 2, 3, 4, 5, 6, 7, 8, or 9.

Distance The distance between two points is the length of the straight path joining the points.

Division An operation on two numbers that tells how many sets with the same number of objects can be formed from a given number of objects, and how many objects are left over.

quotient $\longrightarrow$ 7 R1 $\longleftarrow$ remainder
divisor $\longrightarrow$ 5)$\overline{36}$ $\longleftarrow$ dividend

Division also tells how many objects in each set and how many left over when a given number of sets of the same size are formed from a given number of objects.

When 0 objects are left over, a division exercise can be written as:

$$\frac{5\,R0}{7)\overline{35}} \qquad \frac{5}{7)\overline{35}} \qquad 35 \div 7 = 5$$

Division is used in story problems to answer the questions "How many sets?" and "How many in each set?"

Equal (is, =) Exactly the same.

Even Numbers Any of the whole numbers 0, 2, 4, 6, 8, . . .

Equivalent Fractions Two or more fractions that name the same part of an object or set.

Expanded Form A form showing the meaning of a standard numeral as a sum.

Standard numeral	Expanded numeral
256	200 + 50 + 6
3,040	3,000 + 40

Fraction A symbol such as $\frac{1}{2}, \frac{1}{3}, \frac{2}{3}, \frac{1}{4}, \frac{3}{4}$ that names part of an object or set.

numerator $\rightarrow$ 1 $\leftarrow$ number of equal pieces in
— the part named
denominator $\rightarrow$ 2 $\leftarrow$ number of equal pieces in
the whole object or set

Graph A picture used to show data. Types of graphs are bar graphs, line graphs, pictographs, and circle graphs.

Greater Than (>) One of the two basic relations for comparing numbers that are not the same. *See Also* Less Than (<).

$$7 > 5 \qquad \frac{2}{3} > \frac{1}{3}$$

Intersecting Lines Lines that have a common point.

Length The measure of an object from end to end. To determine the length of an object, compare it with a unit object. The length of this pencil is 5 paper clip units.

Inch, foot, yard, mile, and centimeter, meter, and kilometer are standard units for measuring length.

Less Than (<) One of the two basic relations for comparing numbers that are not the same. *See also* Greater Than (>).

$$5 < 7 \qquad \frac{1}{3} < \frac{2}{3}$$

Line (straight) The figure that results from extending a line segment in both directions.

$\overleftrightarrow{AB}$, or $\overleftrightarrow{BA}$, names this line. The arrowheads indicate that it goes on forever in both directions.

Line Segment The straight path from one point to another.

$\overline{AB}$ and $\overline{BA}$ name the line segments with endpoints A and B.

Line of Symmetry A line that separates a figure into two parts that will fit exactly on each other.

453

Liquid Capacity The amount of liquid a container will hold.

Liquid Volume The number of unit containers a given amount of liquid will fill. Cup, pint, quart, gallon, and milliliter and liter are standard units for measuring liquid volume.

Lowest Terms Fraction A fraction with numerator and denominator having no common factor greater than 1.

Metric Measurement System A measurement system that uses centimeters, meters, and kilometers as units of length; milliliters and liters as units of liquid volume; grams and kilograms as units of mass; degrees Celsius (°C) as units of temperature; and minutes and hours as units of time.

Mixed Numeral A symbol for a number greater than 1, formed using a standard numeral and a fraction.

$$4\frac{2}{3} \qquad 1\frac{5}{6} \qquad 12\frac{1}{2}$$

Multiples Multiples of a number are formed by multiplying the number by whole numbers.

Multiplication An operation on two numbers that tells how many in all when one number is the number of sets and the other number is the number in each set. Multiplication exercises are written in vertical or horizontal form.

$$\begin{array}{r} 4 \\ \times 3 \\ \hline 12 \end{array}$$
$$4 \longleftarrow \text{factor}$$
$$\text{times} \longrightarrow \times 3 \longleftarrow \text{factor} \qquad 3 \times 4 = 12$$
$$12 \longleftarrow \text{product}$$

Multiplication is used to solve *set of sets* story problems.

Number Line A line showing numbers in order.

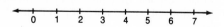

Number Sentence A completed exercise written in horizontal form.

Numeral A symbol for a number. For example:

Standard numerals: 1, 63, 159, 428

Fractions: $\frac{1}{2}$, $\frac{4}{5}$, $\frac{11}{3}$

Mixed numerals: $3\frac{2}{3}$, $5\frac{1}{6}$

Decimals: .03, 2.61

Odd Number Any of the whole numbers 1, 3, 5, 7, 9, . . .

Ordinal Number The number that tells which position an object has in a given order.

Parallel Lines Lines in a plane that never meet.

Parallelogram A quadrilateral with opposite sides parallel and equal in length.

Parentheses ( ) Symbols of grouping. Parentheses tell which operation is to be performed first.

Perimeter The sum of the lengths of the sides of a figure.

Place Value The value given to the place in which a digit appears in a numeral.

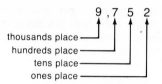

thousands place
hundreds place
tens place
ones place

Plane A flat surface.

Points Capital letters are used to name points. The pictures show points A and B.

A ●————————● B

Polygon A plane figure with *sides* that are line segments. Each pair of sides meets at a *vertex*. Triangles, quadrilaterals, pentagons, hexagons, and octagons are polygons.

Probability A number, 0 through 1, that tells how likely it is that something will happen.

Pyramid (square-based) An object shaped like this.

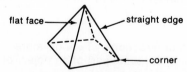

flat face — straight edge — corner

Four of the faces of a pyramid are triangles; one face is a square.

Quadrilateral Any plane closed figure with four straight sides and four angles.

Ray The figure that results from extending a line segment in one direction. A ray has one endpoint and goes on forever in one direction.

$\overrightarrow{AB}$ names the ray with endpoint A. $\overrightarrow{BA}$ names the ray with endpoint B.

Rectangle A quadrilateral with four right angles. Opposite sides of a rectangle are parallel and equal in length.

Rectangular Prism An object with square corners shaped like a box.

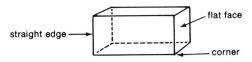

Each face of a rectangular prism is a rectangle.

Regroup Use 10 ones to form 1 set of ten, or use 1 set of ten to form 10 ones. You can also regroup tens as hundreds and hundreds as tens, hundreds as thousands and thousands as hundreds, and so on.

Roman Numerals The symbols I, V, X, . . . , that the Romans used to name whole numbers.

I = 1	V = 5	X = 10
IV = 4	VII = 7	XXIX = 29

Rounding Replacing a number by the nearest multiple of ten, hundred, thousand, etc.

3,529 rounded to the nearest ten is 3,530.
3,529 rounded to the nearest hundred is 3,500.
3,529 rounded to the nearest thousand is 4,000.

Ruler An object marked off in units that is used to measure length. Each numeral on a ruler tells how many units that point is from the end.

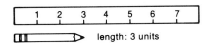

Skip Count Count by twos, threes, fours, ...

By twos: 2, 4, 6, 8, . . .
By threes: 3, 6, 9, 12, . . .

Sphere An object shaped like this.

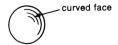

Square A rectangle with all sides the same length.

Standard Numeral A numeral for a whole number formed using the digits 0-9 and a place value system. Any whole number can be expressed by writing a digit 0-9 in the ones place for the number of ones, in the tens place for the number of tens, ...

Statistics A part of mathematics that includes describing, picturing, and drawing conclusions from sets of information, or data.

Subtraction An operation on two numbers that tells how many are left when some are taken away, or how much is left when some is taken away. Subtraction exercises are written in vertical or horizontal form.

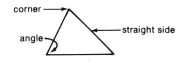

$$\frac{5}{9} - \frac{1}{9} = \frac{4}{9}$$

Subtraction is used to solve *take away* and *comparison* story problems and to answer the question "How many more are needed?" in story problems.

Triangle A figure with three straight sides.

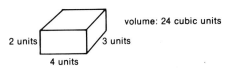

Vertex Corner point of a figure.

Volume The number of unit cubes that would fit inside an object if it were hollow.

volume: 24 cubic units
2 units 3 units 4 units

Whole Number Any of the numbers 0, 1, 2, 3, 4, . . . , 47, 48, 49, . . . , 170, 171, 172, . . .

455

Index

457

the true founder of Trinity. Young was in Westminster, with others, to witness Redman's answers to questions put to him by the young Alexander Nowell, a future dean of St Paul's and author of the Catechism, but at this time master of Westminster School. What Young heard was a series of protestant affirmations on all the salient points in controversy. Later, when questioned further about the doctrine of the real presence in the eucharist by Richard Wilkes, master of Christ's (and some time Perne's colleague at Queens'), Redman, with some of his last breath, revealed that his once firm convictions on that matter had been shaken. Wilkes, a firm Protestant, recorded what was said next:

> I am glad sayde I Mayster Doctor to heere you saye so ... Then after a little whyle pawsing sayd I, Mayster Doctoure yf I shulde not truble you, I wolde praye you to knowe your mynde in transubstantiacion. Jesu Mayster Wilkes sayeth he wyll you aske me that? Syr, sayde I, not yf I shulde trouble you, no, no. I wyl tel you sayth he.

Later on that same day, Young told Wilkes that he was no longer sure what to believe. 'A man shall knowe more and more by proces of tyme and readinge and hearinge of others.' Even what he had just heard from Dr Redman's lips had caused him to think again. For Redman was not so much a weathercock as a compass, pointing towards the magnetic pole of orthodox belief. And where he pointed, others were inclined to follow. After all, the oracle who had uttered in his death throes was one of the six authors of the King's Book of 1543, the core of conservative Henricianism.[13]

The inchoate theological situation reflected in these exchanges had by this time been clarified and even polarised by the presence in Cambridge as regius professor of the Strasbourg Protestant leader Martin Bucer, who taught the doctrines of the Reformation, said even one of his devotees, *ad*

---

[13] *A reporte of Maister Doctor Redmans answers to questions propounded him before his death concerning certaine poyntes of religion and now beyng with many in controversey* (1551). I owe this reference to Colin Armstrong, who also told me about Redman's co-authorship of the King's Book. John Foxe used *A reporte of Maister Doctor Redmans answers* for an account of Redman's dying opinions which he made a counter-foil to Bishop Stephen Gardiner, 'being inferior in no respect to the said Gardiner'. *The Acts and Monuments of John Foxe*, ed. S.R. Cattley, vi (1838) [henceforth *A. & M.*], pp. 266-8. On Redman, see V.H. Stanton, *Some Masters of Trinity College* (Cambridge, 1898). However, Stanton attributes some of Young's answers to Wilkes to Redman, a mistake easily made since the binding of gathering Sig. B in the Cambridge University Library copy of *A reporte* (Syn. 8.55.40) is confused. A further account of Redman's deathbed confessions is contained in an undated letter from Thomas Lever, master of St John's College, to Roger Ascham, *Original Letters Relative to the English Reformation*. ed., H. Robinson, i, Parker Society (Cambridge, 1846), pp. 150-2. Lever's account strengthens the impression that Young's Catholic orthodoxy was indeed wavering at this time, as does Young's own report, sent to Sir John Cheke, 3 November 1551. Foxe printed this letter in the original Latin ('as I received it written by his own hand ... the copy which he himself neither hath nor can deny to be his own') in the 1563 edition of *Acts and Monuments* and in translation in subsequent editions. (*A. & M.*, vi, pp. 271-4.)

nauseam.[14] At first, Bucer found most of the university opposed to him. Andrew Perne joined with John Young and Thomas Sedgwick, soon to be his rival for the mastership of Peterhouse, in disputing against the great Alsatian reformer on such fundamental points of Protestantism as the all-sufficiency Scripture, the unreliability of the church's *magisterium,* and the true order of justification and sanctification.[15] But resistance presently crumbled. Redman preached in the university church on the day after Bucer's funeral and some months later, as he lay dying at Westminster, declared that 'he dyd repent him that he had so much strived against iustification by only fayth'.[16] Yet Young served as regius professor under Mary and Redman's conservative, Henrician writings were posthumously published.[17] McKitterick has found the hand of Perne annotating his copy of Redman's *De iustificatione,* published at Antwerp in 1555, whereas Perne's copy of Bucer's book with the same title (1562) is without any marginalia.

Whether Perne had ever embraced justification by faith in the stark, paradoxical form in which Luther taught it seems doubtful. If Philip Melanchthon had accepted the regius chair, which we know was offered to him in 1553, that might have stabilised his mind and those of others on the basis of a more balanced and accommodating version of Protestantism.[18] As it was Perne's mind and conscience were to be stabilised on quite a different basis.[19] Yet he had long since discarded belief in transubstantiation, as early

[14] C.H. Smyth, *Cranmer and the Reformation under Edward VI* (Cambridge, 1926), pp. 163-4. For Bucer in Cambridge, see my 'The Reformer and the Archbishop: Martin Bucer and an English Bucerian',*Journal of Religious History,* 6, pp. 305-30; reprinted, Patrick Collinson, *Godly People: Essays on English Protestantism and Puritanism* (1983), pp. 19-44; idem, *Archbishop Grindal, 1519-1583: The Struggle for a Reformed Church* (1979), pp. 49-56.

[15] The original record of this disputation is in Corpus Christi College Cambridge, MS 102, no. 1. This is followed (no. 2) by 'Epistola (Buceri ad quendam episcopum) de dogmate Magr. Yunge circa justificationem'. Cf. Martin Bucer, *Scripta Anglicana* (Basle, 1577), pp. 797ff. See also *A. & M.,* vi, pp. 335ff.

[16] *A reporte,* sig. Avii.

[17] *Ioannis Redmani Angli sacrae theologiae professoris de iustificatione opus* (Antwerp, 1555). In his preface, Redman's uncle Bishop Tunstal claimed that if he had lived Redman would himself have published this treatise: 'Si vixisset, omnibus edere decreverat, sed non poterat morte praeventus.' A Marian publication even more damaging to the continuing interests of the Edwardian Protestant establishment was *A compendious treatise called the côplaint of grace compiled by the most notable clerk mayster Jhon Redman,* dedicated to the queen herself (1556?). For the preface, this series of bitter recriminations about the effects of Edwardian doctrine was said to have been written 'not verie longe before he left this transitory lyfe, which was 1551'.

[18] B.L. Beer, 'Philip Melanchthon and the Cambridge Professorship', *Notes and Queries,* n.s., 34 (1978), p. 185. I owe this reference to Mr Colin Armstrong.

[19] A complete account of conservative views known to have been entertained by Perne in these confused years would have to include his position in the controversy on the descent of Christ into Hell, where in a 1552 disputation he defended a literal understanding of that portion of the Creed, which was later associated with Roman Catholicism. (Christopher Carlile, *A discourse concerning two divine positions: The first effectually concluding, that the sowles of the faithfull fathers, deceased before Christ, went immediately to heaven* (1582), fos. xiv-xv.) On the other hand, the story, often repeated and

continued

as the Edwardian visitation of the university in 1549, when he argued publicly against it.[20] 'Show us one place, or one doctor, who saith that it remaineth not bread after the consecration.' 'We deny nothing less than his corporal presence, or the absence of his substance in the bread.' Thereafter Perne may have been reckoned by the Edwardian regime to be 'one of us'. He was included among the six royal chaplains who were to divide their time between the court and preaching in the country and in October 1552 he was approached, as one of these six, for his comments on a draft of the Forty-Two Articles of Religion.[21] A letter about university business was sent to three Cambridge figures with influence about the Court: Edmund Grindal and John Ponet, both soon to be made protestant bishops – and Perne.[22] This is of critical importance in helping to explain how Perne was regarded by Protestants less ambivalent than himself, after the Marian reaction.

At the first Convocation of Mary's reign, Perne again spoke against transubstantiation, and with exceptional boldness, earning a reproof from the prolocutor for adopting a position contrary to the formal subscription which he had made a few days earlier. The future Elizabethan bishop of London, John Aylmer, sprang to his defence, insisting that the Lower House of Convocation was 'a house of free liberty for every man to speak his conscience'.[23] This may have been the first as it was certainly the last occasion on which Perne appeared in the role of free-speaking dissident. Presently he made his peace with the new order of things, formally subscribing to articles which included a very explicit endorsement of transubstantiation. Bishop Stephen Gardiner evidently found him sufficiently reliable to be his preferred candidate for the mastership of Peterhouse, preferred that is to Thomas Sedgwick whose conduct under Edward VI's heretical government had been, on the face of it, more impeccable.[24]

And now Perne became an active suppressor of dissent, as vice-chancellor serving on a royal commission to enquire into heresy and suspicious behaviour indicative of heresy, which in 1557 met every Friday morning,

continued
canonised by Sir Sidney Lee in the *Dictionary of National Biography*, that the inconstant Perne recanted in the London church of St Andrew Undershaft his earlier doctrine that it was good to worship the pictures of Christ and the saints arose from confusing Perne with William Peryn, a former Dominican and popular London preacher. I owe both these points to Colin Armstrong.

[20] *A. & M.*, vi, pp. 320-9.

[21] *The Chronicle and Political Papers of King Edward VI*, ed. W.K. Jordan (1966), p. 101; PRO, S.P. 10/15/28, fols 60 r-5 v. I owe the latter reference to Colin Armstrong.

[22] Cambridge University Archives, MS Lett, 1, fol. 128 r. The letter was dated '16 Calen Junii' and the date of 1552 has been suggested. But this is too late, since 'M Poynt' was appointed bishop of Rochester on 6 June 1550.

[23] *A. & M.*, vi, p. 405; John Strype, *Life of Aylmer* (Oxford, 1821), p. 146.

[24] *A Collection of Letters, Statutes, and Other Documents from the MS. Library at Corpus Christi College Illustrative of the History of the University of Cambridge*, ed. John Lamb (1838), pp. 172-5; J.A. Muller, ed., *The Letters of Stephen Gardiner* (Cambridge, 1933), pp. 467-8.

mostly in Cambridge Guildhall.[25] It seems to have been the style of this
tribunal, as it was Perne's personal style, to deal severely with relatively
minor offences, as minor as the eating of a piece of black pudding at Olney
on the vigil of St Andrew. A parishioner of St Michael's who was careless
about coming to church was imprisoned during the pleasure of the
commissioners and fined the large sum of ten shillings, 'for ensampyle and
to the terror of other lyke wyse to offend'. However, this was a terror which
didn't actually hurt. There is no evidence that anyone was burned alive as
the result of this commission's activities and one may reasonably infer that
it set about its work in order to prevent burnings, not to promote them.
Unlike Oxford, Cambridge witnessed only one martyrdom, when John
Hullier of King's was burned on Jesus Green.[26] Young was among Hullier's
judges but there is no evidence of Perne's involvement. Nor was it a
physically painful experience to be burned at the stake six years after your
death: which brings us back to Martin Bucer and to the most celebrated and
bizarre sequence of events in the entire career of Andrew Perne.

   Bucer in Edwardian Cambridge had been something more than a
professor and teacher of reformed doctrine. He had exerted a profound
and personal influence, not unlike that of William Perkins, Charles Simeon
and John Henry Newman in other times and places. The late Professor
Gordon Rupp, critical as he was of Bucer's diffuse prolixity, admitted that
he was a 'great character'.[27] The famous model household which Bucer had
assembled in Strasbourg, stirring his fellow reformer Peter Marytr Vermigli
to rhapsodise about the revival of primitive episcopacy, was reconstituted
in Cambridge, where it seems to have served as the hub of a kind of holy
club, which included three future archbishops, Parker, Grindal and Sandys,
as well as the charismatic figure of the martyr John Bradford who was
especially intimate with Bucer, 'right familiar and dear unto him', according to another member of the circle.[28] I think that Perne too must have been
one of the club. In his farewell to Cambridge, Bradford exclaimed:
'Remember the readings and preachings of God's true prophet and true

[25] Cambridge University Library, Ely Diocesan Records, MS D/2/4. I am grateful to Mr John
Craig for alerting me to the existence of this register of the commission's activities. The cases cited
are at fols. 11 r and 1 v.

[26] C.H. Cooper, *Annals of Cambridge*, ii (Cambridge, 1843), pp. 103–4.

[27] Gordon Rupp, in what the sixteenth century would call a familiar letter to the author, 1979.
After Bucer's death the university assured Edward VI: 'Ex cuius vita et voce quantum ceperimus
utilitatis, quantum honestissime voluptatis.' (Undated letter to Edward VI from the university,
'D. M. Bucero clariss. Academiae lumine extincto', Cambridge University Archives, Lett. 1. 120 v.)

[28] 'Formula vivendi prescripta familiae sue A. M. Bucero et propria manu revisa', printed by
François Wendel in 'Un document inédit sur le séjour de Bucer en Angleterre', *Revue d'histoire et de
philosophie religieuses*, 34 (1954), pp. 223-33. See my 'The Reformer and the Archbishop', in *Godly
People*, pp. 30-2.

The 'pageant' of the burning of the bones of the Protestant reformers Martin Bucer and Paul Fagius in Cambridge market place on 16 February 1557, vividly represented for the benefit of Elizabethan readers of John Foxe's 'Book of Martyrs'. Andrew Perne, who played a central role in these proceedings, possessed the 1576 edition of Foxe. Martin Marprelate suggested, in the year of Perne's death, that he knew a way to get him out of the Book of Martyrs. (*Cambridge University Library*)

preacher, Martin Bucer!' And then, a few lines on: 'O Perne, repent!' 'O turn you now and convert!'[29]

Perne was to turn and convert, and more than once, but not quite in the manner that Bradford intended. When the Marian commissioners came to Cambridge in 1557 on visitation, they laid a solemn interdict on Great St Mary's for the offence of housing Bucer's bones, together with neighbouring St Michael's, where Bucer's Strasbourg colleague Paul Fagius had been buried. This set in motion a macabre process which ended with the burning of the two coffins on Market Hill, together with their contents. These events were written up and published in Strasbourg, translated into English early in the following reign, and incorporated into John Foxe's *Acts and Monuments*, the 'Book of Martyrs', an account which exploited to the full their excellent value as black comedy.[30] The country people in the market laughed at the chains designed to secure the corpses, 'for it was not to be feared that they would run away!'

The vice-chancellor who presided over this pageant (as the narrative calls it) was Andrew Perne, and he delivered a kind of anti-eulogy, railing against Bucer so shamefully 'that it is not possible to defame a man more than he did'. These words were deleted from all editions of the Book of Martyrs after the first. But what was never censored out was the story that immediately after delivering his speech, or even before it, Perne was seen by his friends in the privacy of his own lodging to strike his breast, 'in manner weeping', wishing with all his heart that he might be with Bucer in heavenly bliss: so that he stood condemned by his own conscience. A copy of *Acts and Monuments* recording this incident was in Perne's own library (it is there still)[31] and on the incriminating page a small hole has been burned, as if by someone poring over it with a lighted candle.

With the renewed settlement of Protestantism under Queen Elizabeth, Cambridge made amends to whatever was left of Bucer and Fagius. In 1560 a grace was passed and another ceremony held in which the two rehabilitated reformers were restored to all their degrees and honours. Sitting in his chair listening to a denunciation of the extraordinary cruelty and obscenity of what had been done three years earlier was the vice-chancellor for that year, who was once again Andrew Perne.[32]

---

[29]   *The Writings of John Bradford*, ed. A. Townsend (Parker Society, Cambridge, 1848), p. 445.

[30]   *Historia de accusatione, condemnatione, exhumatione, atque combustione excellentissimorum theologorum D. Martini Buceri et Pauli Fagii Anno Dom. MDLVI*, in *Scripta Anglicana*, pp. 915ff; translated by Arthur Golding as *A briefe treatise concerning the burnyng of Bucer and Phagius at Cambridge* (1562); and incorporated in *Acts and Monuments of Foxe*, viii, pp. 258-86. See also the account (by J. Mere) printed in Lamb, *A Collection of Letters*, pp. 201-10. What Foxe chose not to remember was that there was a precedent for this 'pageant' in the treatment meted out to the bones of St Thomas à Becket at Canterbury in 1538.

[31]   Perne Library, Peterhouse, E.11.17. Since the copy in question is of the 1576 edition we must presume that Perne acquired it many years after these events.

[32]   The Grace restoring Bucer and Fagius to all their degrees and honours is in Cambridge

continued

This act of rehabilitation did nothing to revive Perne in the estimation of his old colleague Edmund Grindal, who having spent Mary's reign in Bucer's Strasbourg now returned to succeed both 'Bloody Bonner' as bishop of London and John Young as master of Pembroke. Grindal was jealous for the canonisation of Bucer's memory and for the preservation of his English writings, and he achieved both objects.[33] In 1564 the queen paid a celebrated state visit to the university.[34] Although Grindal was one of a small committee in charge of the arrangements, he was unable to prevent the choice of Perne to preach a learned Latin sermon before Elizabeth. On the very eve of the visit he wrote to Secretary Cecil saying that while it was clearly too late to prevent the sermon being preached, he hoped that Perne would not receive 'too goode a Cowntenance', 'his apostasye being so notoriouse'. To treat such a man with any honour would be to comfort 'all dissemblers and neutralls and discourage the zealowse and syncere'. Perne's only way back to favour should be by public acknowledgement of his 'defection'.[35]

All to no avail. Perne's sermon was a great success. Preached on Romans 13:1, 'Let every soul be subject unto the higher powers', and in that temple dedicated to the ultimate glorification of the Tudor dynasty, King's College Chapel, it could hardly have been a failure and the Queen made her pleasure manifest.[36]

But later in the week, Perne took part in a disputation before the royal

continued

University Archives, Grace Book Δ, fol. 55 v. See *Historia de restitutione organorum Dei D. Martini Buceri et Pauli Fagii temporibus restitutae religionis in Anglia Anno MDLX*, in *Scripta Anglicana*, pp. 935-59.

[33] Collinson, *Archbishop Grindal*, p. 51.

[34] 'Commentarii hexemeri rerum Cantabrigiae actarum cum serenissima Regina Angliae Elizabeth in Academiam Cantabrigiensem advenerat AD 1564 die Aug 5; Collector N. Robinsono', Washington DC, Folger Shakespeare Library, MS V.a. 176 (Reel 8 of the English Literary MSS from the Folger Shakespeare Library, Harvester Microform). See also John Nichols, *The Progresses and Public Processions of Queen Elizabeth I* (1823), pp. 151-89.

[35] Grindal to Cecil (holograph), 3 August 1564, BL Add. 35831, fol. 184. A small problem remains. How had Perne been chosen in the first place? And why was Grindal unable to block the appointment? It was Grindal himself who on 15 July alerted the vice-chancellor and other members of the university to the impending royal visit. The university despatched the proctors and one bedell to confer with Cecil, Grindal, Dr Walter Haddon, the master of requests, and Gabriel Goodman, dean of Westminster. 'And in conclusion had put in wrightynge by the sayd master secretory all such orders as should be observed', including the orders for the sermon *ad clerum*, Cambridge University Archives Misc. Collect., 4, fol. 63, printed, *Records of Early English Drama, Cambridge*, ed. Alan H. Nelson (Toronto 1989), i, pp. 232-3. A memorandum on 'the receyvyng of Queen Elyzabethe at Cambryge' records: 'Secretory Cicill Chauncelor ... had conference with theym of theyre sermon ad clerum, disputacions, tragedies, and who should be theyre prechere, disputors etc.' (Cambridge University Library, MS Ff.5.14, fol. 87, printed, *Records of Early English Drama: Cambridge*, i, p. 230.)

[36] A minor mystery contained in the future Bishop Robinson's account of the royal visit (Folger MS) is how the full text of Perne's sermon (preceded by an epitome) should be included in what appears to be Perne's own hand; Folger Shakespeare Library, MS V.a.176, fos. 20-32 v; Nichols, *Progresses*, iii (1835) pp. 52-9.

party which went badly wrong, at least for him. The subject might have
been designed to flush out such an unreconstructed Catholic as Perne may
have been: 'Maior est scripturae quam ecclesiae authoritas.'[37] Scripture has
a greater authority than the Church. According to a partisan, Protestant
account of the occasion, not only Perne but all the old popish guard, the
unreconstructed Marian heads of houses, were drawn into the lists by this
proposition, Hawford of Christ's, currently vice-chancellor, Pory of
Corpus, Baker of King's. Confronting them in the chair was a leader and
symbol of the new order, Bishop Richard Cox of Ely. Apparently in the
perception of Cambridge this, rather than the abortive disputation at
Westminster Hall in April 1559, was the crucial occasion when Protestantism might yet meet its intellectual nemesis. 'The men of darkness had crept
forth from their lairs.' And Perne was their most vigorous champion.
Politics, of course, predetermined a different outcome. Perne and the other
conservatives would proceed to paint themselves into a corner from which
there was no escape. But Perne, of course, would survive, whereas Baker
of King's would presently face deprivation.

As to whether the disputation was deliberately staged in order to have this
effect, and by whom, we can only speculate. But according to Perne himself,
he came to the task without adequate preparation, 'absque magna praemedi-
tatione'. And what he delivered was not so much a formal exercise as
'tumultaria quadam oratio', a somewhat improvised speech.[38] What tends
to favour this possibility is that Perne's principal opponent in the disputation was Matthew Hutton, regius professor of divinity and a future
archbishop of York whom Archbishop Sandys would later accuse, half
jocularly, of Puritanism. ('If I be a papist, thou be puritan.'[39]) For Hutton
was a close friend and protégé of Grindal and Grindal's successor as master
of Pembroke Hall. Hutton provoked Perne's *tumultaria oratio* by denouncing the church in the sense of the Church of Rome as 'a shameless whore',
'impudentissima meretrix', typologically Eve and a fallen Eve at that. When
Perne questioned this typology he was asked in the words of John,

---

[37]   Robinson's (edited) transcript of the disputation survives in Folger Shakespeare Library, MS
V.a.176, fos. 69-77 v and in British Library, MS Harley 7037 (a Baker MS), pp. 214-31. The Folger
MS is evidently the source for the printed text in Nichols, *Progresses*, iii, pp. 106-17. Both MSS also
contain a highly partisan, Protestant account of the disputation which is hostile to Perne. There is
a further polemically Protestant summary in BL, MS Add. 46398. (I am profoundly grateful to Dr
Elisabeth Leedham-Green for locating some of this evidence and for her transcriptions and
translations.) All this, with Perne's letter to Parker, suggests the intense excitement which the event
aroused. This theological 'act', occupying the fifth day of the royal visit, was preceded on the third
day by the 'political' act, in which the thesis 'monarchia est optimus status Reipub[licae]' was
confuted by the future presbyterian (and republican?) Thomas Cartwright.
[38]   Andrew Perne to Archbishop Matthew Parker (holograph), 25 October 1564, Inner Temple
Library, MS Petyt 538/47, no. 284, fos. 522-3.
[39]   Peter Lake, 'Matthew Hutton – A Puritan Bishop?', *History*, 44 (1979), p. 189.

chapter 3: 'Art thou a teacher in Israel and knowest not these things?' In this contest the knives were razor sharp, the gloves well and truly off.

In his response, Perne did not exactly call Hutton a heretic, a charge which he later strenuously denied. But he did say that if his opponent did not hold to the same fundamental articles of the faith as were retained by the Roman Church he would be anathematised by all Christians. Consequently the academic and ecclesiastical world had it that Perne had indeed denounced as a heretic his colleague and fellow head of house.[40] Hutton's vividly apocalyptic vision of Rome as Babylon was destined to become an almost consensual position in the Elizabethan church and less remarkable than Perne's contrary opinion that it was a true and valid church, although not devoid of heinous error. So in the circumstances it was no mean achievement for Perne to force his opponent to admit that this identification was a piece of rhetoric which was not necessarily well-founded theologically. He had, said Hutton, described Rome as meretricious thoughtlessly, 'nimis inconsiderate'. On consideration, he would not repeat the charge.

This issue lent to this remarkable debate its acrimonious and sensational flavour. But the ostensible subject was whether Scripture had an authority superior to that of the church. On the status of Scripture, Perne was not over-respectful, joining the ranks of those critics of Protestantism who accused it of deifying a written text, making the Bible the object of idolatry. Not Scripture but the church was the final court of appeal in all matters of controversy, whereas Hutton took his stand on Christ's words to the tempter: 'It is written . . .' But it was the authority of the church which the combatants in this controversy most hotly disputed. Their differences turned on certain celebrated pronouncements of the great church father Tertullian (*Adversus Praxeam* and *Adversus Marcionem*) that antiquity would always prevail over novelty: 'Quod aliquid prius existat, eo melius habetur, quo vero posterius, tanto deterius.' In the context of this debate, Perne understood Tertullian to prefer the authority of the church to that of Scripture, since it was anterior to Scripture and underwrote it with its own authority, rather than conversely receiving its authority from the Bible. 'Longe igitur antiquior est ecclesiae quam sacrae scripturae authoritas multoque sublimior' – far more sublime. Moreover Perne found no difficulty in equating 'the church' with the Roman Church, or at least with deriving it through a uniquely Roman succession. With the great eastern churches fallen into apostasy and Turkish captivity, of all the apostolic sees only Rome survived, and Cyprian had rightly called it the first of the churches. 'Sola igitur ex hiis omnibus habemus romanam ecclesiam ... quam Ciprianus appellat principalem.'

---

[40] Inner Temple Library, MS Petyt 538/47, no. 284, fol. 522.

Perne charged Hutton with totally ignoring Tertullian's aphorism. That was as unfair as most of the hand grenades lobbed in this piece of intellectual trench warfare But like Bishop John Jewel in his officially inspired *Apologia Ecclesiae Anglicanae*, Hutton understood the principle of antiquity to condemn the Roman Church and its novelties out of hand and to justify the protestant churches in their abandonment of Rome in order to restore the primitive, apostolic standard.[41] In a memorable statement of this polemical position, Hutton insisted that if, as was the case, Rome had shifted from its foundations, it was better to return to these footings than to take shelter among these ruins, 'in ruinis delitescere'. 'Tempus ergo fuit ut exiremus ne ruina nos opporimeret.' It was high time to depart before the tottering ruins collapsed upon them.

But Perne turned Tertullian, according to Jewel's and Hutton's readings of these texts, on his head. In all essential respects, it appeared that Rome was equivalent to antiquity. Admittedly the Roman Church was not faultless. Yet it was from Rome that the creeds and even the Holy Scriptures themselves had been received, as well as the eucharistic liturgy and other ancient prayers which the Church of England still entertained. Far from a meretricious whore, Rome was the apostolic mother, 'apostolica et matrix ecclesia'.

The contrast with Hutton's sturdy Protestantism could hardly have appeared more stark. Hutton said that he esteemed the Roman bishops no less highly than he esteemed Annas and Caiaphas. Rome for him was equivalent to the ecclesiastical establishment of Jerusalem which had nailed Christ to the cross. It is indeed hard to see, on the principles stated by Perne in this disputation how he could have justified the schism of the Protestant Reformation. For all his acknowledgement of Rome's errors, he declared that it was a condition of salvation to remain within a church which he derived unreservedly from the sole surviving apostolic church. 'In eadem [ecclesia] igitur tibi manendum est.'

In the very presence of their supreme governor, Hutton and Perne scarcely bothered to conceal the fact that this was a confrontation between a Protestant and some kind of Catholic. Perne had explained in the first sentence of his opening speech that he believed sincerely in those theses which he was about to advance, while a hostile account of his performance conveys something of its vehemence. So we cannot dismiss what was said as an artificial academic exercise. Commenting with acidity on the claim that the Anglican communion service was derived in all essentials from the Roman mass, Hutton said that Perne should know. He, Hutton, had never

[41] *An Apology of the Church of England by John Jewel*, ed. J.E. Booty (Ithaca, NY, 1963), esp. p. 121, where *Adversus Praxeam* is cited. See also John Booty, *John Jewel as Apologist of the Church of England* (1963), and W.M. Southgate, *John Jewel and the Problem of Doctrinal Authority* (Cambridge, MA, 1962).

celebrated mass, thank god.[42] Perne's retort was witty. 'Nos missam quam te nunquam celebrasse tantopere gloriaris, missam faciamus.' 'As for the mass which you boast so much of never having celebrated, let's give it a miss.' But Perne's thinly disguised loyalty to the old religion was not so lightly dismissed. Presently he felt obliged to write to his friend and patron Archbishop Parker discounting the dangerous rumours which had sprung up in the aftermath of his performance. He had not called Hutton a heretic. He was far from whitewashing the Church of Rome, knowing how many shameful errors, 'multi turpissimi errores', had been introduced by sundry popes. His reading as he prepared for the disputation confirms, as we should expect, that he continued to regard transubstantiation as just such an error.[43] Yet he continued to insist that to reject Roman Catholicism totally and indiscriminately would be as arrogant as to approve it in all respects with a blanket endorsement. In his letter, as in his disputation, Perne left it by no means clear whether the Roman Church itself was to be repudiated, on account of its corruptions, or only those corruptions themselves. But it appears certain that Perne, for his part, would not have proposed the schism which we know as the English Reformation.

Was this why Perne escaped preferment to a bishopric? According to an account of the disputation which is admittedly biased against Perne, the queen continually intervened to signal her endorsement of Hutton's arguments against his. So Grindal having lost a battle may have won the war. Apparently it was soon after this that Perne was removed from the list of court preachers.[44] In the eighteenth century, it was said that he wrote

[42] Cf. the admission allegedly made by Hutton's friend and patron Bishop Grindal to a group of Puritan Londoners: 'I have said mass; I am sorry for it.' *The Remains of Edmund Grindal*, ed. W. Nicholson, Parker Society (Cambridge, 1843), p. 211.

[43] Inner Temple Library, MS Petyt 538/47, no. 284, fos. 522-3. Perne's marginalia in his copy of Heinrich Bullinger, *De origine erroris* (Zurich, 1539), with particular reference to transubstantiation, were made in about 1563, which can be established from his method of dating: e.g., 'transubstantiatio definita ante annos 502 sub leone p. 9' (fol. 233 v) 'lateranense ante annos 427 sub grego. 7' (fol. 234 v), 'Consilium lateranense sub innocentio 3° ante annos 348' (fol. 236).

[44] Parker wrote to Cecil on 26 February 1565(/6), apropos of Lenten preachers at court: 'I have altered but a few of your first bill, but removed Mr Perne, and appointed either my lord of Ely, or Peterborough to occupy one day.' *Correspondence of Matthew Parker*, ed. J. Bruce, Parker Society (Cambridge, 1853), p. 261. This is evidently the basis of Thomas Cooper's statement, *Athenae Cantabrigienses*, ii (Cambridge 1861) p. 46, that Perne was dropped altogether as a court preacher, which is possible. But Cooper's account of the offence offered by Perne in his disputation is inaccurate and seems to have misled T.A. Walker. Perne was supposed to have warmly pressed the church's power of excommunication. But that would have been in the debate on the question 'an civilis magistratus auctoritatem habeat in rebus ecclesiaticis?' (Nichols, *Progress*, i, p. 166) in which, if Folger Shakespearce Library, MS V.a.176 is to be believed, Perne took no part. But this error is more excusable than that of successive cataloguers of the Petyt MSS, including Conway Davies, *Catalogue of MSS in the Library of the Inner Temple* (1972), ii, p. 880, who misread Parker's endorsement of Perne's letter to Archbishop Parker as if Perne apologises for '*not* [my italics] disputing personally before the queen'. Perne may well have wished that that had been the nature and extent of his transgression.

'several Treatises in defence of the Reformed Religion and of Queen Elizabeth's Title and Right to the Crown of England.'[45] Perhaps that was done, if it was done (no such treatises survive), to recover court favour, but without success.

II

The ten years which followed Elizabeth's royal visit were a time of exceptional turbulence in the history of Cambridge University.[46] Superficially, this turbulence had to do with items of academic and liturgical costume, the surplices and square caps which became a symbol for the lukewarm, halfway Reformation which, in the perception of the hotter sort of Protestants, had been foisted on the Church of England within the terms of the Elizabethan Settlement.[47] Presently this emotive sense of abortive or incomplete Reformation extended to embrace questions of ministry and church order, as Thomas Cartwright's Lady Margaret lectures of 1570 called hierarchy into question on presbyterian grounds which were said to derive from New Testament texts.[48] But for the university this was also a constitutional crisis, as the principle of aristocracy in the persons of the heads in what was now an entirely collegiate university collided with the measure of democracy built into the government by the regent masters, who were young graduates of up to three years' standing. Not for nothing did one vice-chancellor of this stormy decade speak of Cambridge as 'this busy commonwealth'.

But the eye of the hurricane was Dr Perne and all that he stood for, or had failed to stand for. Unlike Oxford, Elizabethan Cambridge had not been purged.[49] The top men were Marian conformists and even collaborators: besides Perne, Baker of King's (until his deprivation, in effect for popery, in 1569), Pory of Corpus, Hawford of Christ's and Perne's fellow Norfolk man Dr Caius of Gonville and Caius, a kind of lightning conductor in this thunderous atmosphere whose own colleagues accused him of popery and atheism.[50] In a sense the Reformation had not so far impacted, not as a convulsive moment of insubordination and iconoclastic protest. So

[45]   BL, MS Add. 4223, fol. 135.

[46]   H.C. Porter, *Reformation and Reaction in Tudor Cambridge* (Cambridge, 1958), part II; and documents published in Lamb, *A Collection of Letters* and *Cambridge University Transactions during the Puritan Controversies of the 16th and 17th Centuries*, ed. J. Heywood and T. Wright (1854), i.

[47]   Patrick Collinson, *The Elizabethan Puritan Movement* (1967); John H. Primus, *The Vestments Controversy: An Historical Study of the Earliest Tensions within the Church of England in the Reigns of Edward VI and Elizabeth* (Kampen, 1960).

[48]   A.F. Scott Pearson, *Thomas Cartwright and Elizabethan Puritanism, 1535-1603* (Cambridge, 1925).

[49]   Penry Williams, 'Elizabethan Oxford: State, Church and University', in *The History of the University of Oxford*, iii, *The Collegiate University*, ed. James McConica (Oxford, 1986), p. 414.

[50]   Christopher Brooke, *A History of Gonville and Caius College* (Woodbridge, 1985), chapter 4.

now Cambridge was to pass through an experience which, like 1968 in our own memories, or Peking in 1989, was both unprecedented and unrepeatable. This was the meaning of those otherwise inexplicable spectacles in St John's, with the fellows and even the master plucking off their surplices in chapel. For it was to make the university safe for dissemblers and neutrals like Perne that the popish clerical costume had been so insensitively imposed: or so it seemed to those now beginning to be called Puritans. Conversely, conformity symbolised for Perne that firm, top-down management in which he believed, perhaps more ardently than he believed in many other things.

Symbolic of a kind of counter-reformation and constitutionally its instrumental engine were the new university statutes of 1570, which were to endure until 1853;[51] and the heart and essence of the statutes lay, as Cooper states, in their constitution of the heads as 'a distinct and separate estate in the government of the university',[52] an estate which under the statutes took to itself powers previously wielded by the generality of the regents, including the effective power to elect the vice-chancellor. In a letter of 1564 which pointed towards this major reactive reform, Perne and other seniors had asked of Sir William Cecil, their chancellor: 'Howe can the youngest men be thought mete to have the whole election for the highest officer of all under your Honour?' It was high time to 'bridle the untamed affections of yonge Regentes'.[53]

The 1570 Statutes are usually attributed to the future Archbishop Whitgift, partly because almost the first use to which they were put was to crush Whitgift's opponent, the Presbyterian Lady Margaret professor, Thomas Cartwright; and because the campaign to defeat the statutes was subsequently mingled with agitation on behalf of Cartwright, at a time when Whitgift and Cartwright were preparing to write books against each other.[54] But there is probably some truth in a separate tradition which links the new constitution primarily with the more senior figure of Perne. My predecessor, the first Regius Professor of Modern History, recorded in the eighteenth century that by a decree of the senate, Perne's family arms were displayed in the university consistory, 'where they remain to this day, in memory of the compiler [of] their present Body of Lawes.'[55]

---

[51] Lamb, *A Collection of Letters*, pp. 315-54; Heywood and Wright, *Transactions*, i, pp. 1-45.

[52] Cooper, *Annals of Cambridge*, ii, p. 258.

[53] The vice-chancellor 'and certen others of the universitie of Cambridge' to Cecil, 18 January 1563(/4), MS Lansdowne 7, no. 70, fol. 161.

[54] The bulk of the 'Admonition Controversy', but lacking Cartwright's *A second replie* (Heidelberg, 1575) and *The rest of the second replie* (Basle, 1577) is contained in *The Works of John Whitgift*, 3 vols., ed. J. Ayre, Parker Society (Cambridge, 1851-3). There is an unsatisfactory digest in *The Admonition Controversy*, ed. D.J. McGinn (New Brunswick, 1949). See Peter Lake, *Anglicans and Puritans? Presbyterian and English Conformist Thought from Whitgift to Hooker* (1988), chapter 1, 'What was the Admonition Controversy About?'

[55] BL, MS. Add. 4223, fol. 135.

Perne was Whitgift's *éminence grise*, unless it was a case of vice-versa. Theirs was an old relationship. It began in Peterhouse, where Whitgift held a fellowship, but it can hardly have been built on a shared outlook in religion, or not at first. As a schoolboy in London Whitgift had been sent back to his native Grimsby by a landlady who dared not shelter such a flagrant heretic under her roof. As an undergraduate at Pembroke Hall, Whitgift was a pupil of that same Bradford who had called upon Perne to repent. His doctoral thesis asserted that the pope was Antichrist, which was never Perne's view. In Mary's reign, Perne is supposed to have saved the skin of this future archbishop by telling him to keep his protestant mouth shut. In Strype's words, Whitgift escaped martydom 'by the secret conniv-ance of Dr Perne', who also nursed him through a grave illness.[56]

The vestiarian excitement of the mid sixties found Perne and Whitgift still on opposite sides of the argument. In a cynical but accurate letter, Perne told Archbishop Parker: 'Mr Whitgyvt saythe in wordes that he had rather have spent xl[li] [£40] than for to have had surplesis in Peter howse, but nayther he nor any of his will lose in dede v[id] [sixpence] for the waringe of a surples, as sume of them reporteth, but will rather weare iii surplesis.'[57] It is not clear that on this evidence we should relegate Whitgift to the loony left. He was already Lady Margaret Professor of Divinity and his views on surplices were shared by four heads of houses, including Perne's 1564 opponent, Hutton of Pembroke, and Whitgift's predecessor as master of Trinity, Robert Beaumont.[58] Parker had these misguided seniors in mind when he wrote darkly of 'a fewe Catylyns who be suffrance will enfect the holl'. 'I see ther is strange deling amongst the wiser sort: men be men.'[59]

That was how otherwise responsible men were liable to behave in a university run by a popular assembly of the younger dons. Hence the need for new statutes. But one precondition for the statutes was Whitgift's defection, which was now duly contrived, it appears by Parker, Cecil and Perne. In 1567, after only four months as master of Pembroke Hall, the crown (Cecil in reality) elevated Whitgift to Trinity. He wrote to ask the Secretary: 'What or who am I, that you should be so careful for me?'[60] Edward Dering of Christ's put Perne in the forefront of his complaints against the statutes and spoke of him as an enemy of the Gospel. But he attacked Whitgift from a different angle: 'D. Whitgifte is a man whome I have lovyd, but yet he is a man, and God hath suffred [him] to fall into great

---

[56] George Paule, *The Life of John Whitgift* (1610), 1699 edn, pp. 3-6; Strype, *Whitgift*, i, pp. 8-12.

[57] Andrew Perne to Archbishop Matthew Parker (holograph), 11 January 1565(/6). Lambeth Palace Library, MS 2002, fol. 119; printed and discussed in Patrick Collinson. 'The "Nott Conformytie" of the Young John Whigift', *Journal of Ecclesiastical History*, 15 (1964), pp. 192-200, and reprinted in Collinson, *Godly People*, pp. 325-33.

[58] Porter, *Reformation and Reaction in Tudor Cambridge*, p. 124.

[59] Parker to Cecil (holograph), 13 December (1565?), BL, MS Lansdowne 8, no. 49, fol. 144.

[60] Whitgift to Cecil, 17 June 1567, PRO, S.P. 12/43/8.

infirmities. So froward a minde against M. Cartwright and other suche bewrayeth a conscience that is full of sicknes. His affections ruled him and not his learninge when he framed his cogitations to get moe statutes.'[61]

With a clear majority of the regents in revolt, Whitgift and Perne were pilloried together in a slanderous libel posted on the door of the Schools.[62] It was said that 'the old compacte of twoe or three, and those especially which penned the newe statutes, worke what theie liste'.[63] Nowhere else in sixteenth-century England do we find the issue of *glasnost* so frankly confronted. The populists complained that under Statute 45 they were no longer free to denounce the established religion, nor to 'speake against any office, degree, estate or dignity within the realme'. Just so, replied Whitgift and Perne. There is not and ought not to be any such liberty.[64] It was Statute 45 which was deployed to deprive Cartwright of his chair and to drive him out of the university, and with him such lesser fry as John Millen of Christ's, who had said in a sermon that the ministry of the Church of England was 'a horrible confusion'.[65] And so Cambridge was dragged back, struggling, into the repressive later sixteenth century where it belonged, to become a kind of Venetian Republic on the banks of the Cam, stable but stifled. Perne was doge of this republic from time to time: vice-chancellor for a fourth term in 1574–5 and for a fifth in 1580-1. Was that evidence of a thirst for power? Probably not. There is no reason to suspect the sincerity of the heads when they protested that they did not covet the office of vice-chancellor, 'which is so paynfull and troblsome.' 'The masters of colleges which have had yt be so weary of yt.'[66] One has heard similar affirmations more recently from professorial heads of department. However it was rarely a necessity under these statutes to elect a vice-chancellor who was not a head of a house.

IV

It is time to take a less pejorative and more detached and appreciative view of Andrew Perne, first as a religious man and then as university politician and statesman. What looked to his critics like inconstancy and even treachery mellowed into theological latitude, a latitude reflected in the best

[61] Edward Dering to Cecil, 18 November 1570, BL, MS. Lansdowne 12, no 86, fol. 190 v.

[62] Heywood and Wright, *Transactions*, i, p. 124.

[63] Lamb, *A Collection of Letters* and, following Lamb, Heywood and Wright, *Transactions*, print from a Corpus Christi MS a schedule of 'Objections Against the Statutes', 'Answers to the Objections' and 'Reply to the Answers'. The passage cited occurs in another and fuller (collated and digested) vesion of these documents, Westminster Abbey Muniments, MS Book 14, fol. 80. I am indebted to Dr Anthony Milton for alerting me to this MS.

[64] Westminster Abbey Muniments, MS Book 14, fos. 82-4.

[65] Porter, *Reformation and Reaction in Tudor Cambridge*, p. 141.

[66] Heywood and Wright, *Transactions*, i, pp. 82, 85.

evidence we have for the contents of his mind, the great library which even in the principles of its organisation seems to imply an openness to conflicting tendencies, past and present.[67] The conservative position with respect to the Roman Church adopted in the 1564 disputation and defended in the subsequent letter to Parker, with so many patristic citations, is consistent with the well-used volumes of the Fathers on his shelves, which are annotated more copiously than any of his other books. Studying his Tertullian, Perne noted: 'Christianus debet credere credita sive tradita'; and also the principle of establishing true doctrine 'ab antiquitate et consensu et successione episcoporum'.[68] In a constructive exchange of views with John Feckenham, the deprived abbot of Westminster and a distinguished Catholic internee, with whom Bishop Cox of Ely had lost all patience, Perne suggested that Feckenham could hardly find fault with the Prayer Book without condemning his own mass book and other Catholic liturgies, since these were its sources.[69]

This evidence is not inconsistent with the covert Catholicism with which the Jesuit John Gerard credited Perne.[70] Very possibly he was what might nowadays be called a closet papist. Alternatively, although nobody had yet thought of so defining it, his religion may be thought to have displayed many features of what would later be called Anglicanism, high Anglicanism. Was his divinity merely a massive pile of theological rubble, so many ruined fragments of the monuments of the past, held together with bits of modern jerry-building? Or did it amount to a new and internally consistent Anglican synthesis? Since Perne wrote, or at least published, almost nothing, apart from a minor contribution to the Bishops' Bible,[71] it is not possible to say whether he had something like Richard Hooker's *Laws of Ecclesiastical Polity* already composed in his head, although that is possible. Thomas Aquinas sits on his shelves in many volumes, but without any marks or annotations to the text, which is not to say that he did not read St Thomas. If he did read the schoolmen, *how* did he read them, and for what purpose? We cannot say, but must hope that it will not be long before a more profound investigation of Perne's mental world and scholarly habits will provide some answers to these questions.

However, we can credit Perne with more charity than there was in Hooker, whose measured arguments fail to conceal an intensely polemical

[67] Perne's shelf categories include 'Catholici', 'Lutherani' and 'Alii Mixti'; *Books in Cambridge Inventories; Book-Lists from the Vice-Chancellor's Court Probate Inventories in the Tudor and Stuart Periods*, ed. E.S. Leedham-Green (Cambridge, 1986), i, pp. 419-79.

[68] Perne's marginalia in his copy (Perne Library) of *Opera Q. Septimi Florentis Tertulliani Carthaginensis* (Paris, 1545), occurring at fos. 8 r and 38 v.

[69] Perne to Lord Burghley, 11 May 1578, BL, MS Lansdowne 27, no. 20, fos. 36 r-7 r; 'A trewe note of certen articles confessed and allowed by M.D. Feckenham', BL, MS Royal 7.B.XII, fol. 2.

[70] John Gerard: *The Autobiography of an Elizabethan*, tr. Philip Caraman (1951), pp. 18-19.

[71] He is credited with the translations of Ecclesiastes and 'The Ballett of Balletts', sc. the Song of Songs or Song of Solomon, comprising, apparently, his sole printed publication.

purpose;[72] and some of that eclecticism attributed in the seventeenth century to Bishop John Williams: 'He that is discreet will make his Profit out of every side, or every Faction, if you like to call it so.'[73] In his old age, Perne wrote a quaint letter to the politician Sir Christopher Hatton, quaint because of the conceit it entertains of a recipe for a 'celestiall quintessence', which was a cure for the gout: but not so much a physical ailment as a kind of public gout afflicting Hatton in his exercise of the great office of lord chancellor. The third of three ingredients or 'spices' for the distillation of Perne's medicine was that Hatton should determine all cases according to strict equity: 'without any respect of person high or lowe, riche or poore, ffrend or foe, of this or that profession, protestant, papiste or puritante': the legendary three Ps of the Peterhouse weathercock.[74] There was latitude too in the bequest made to Perne's two brothers of 'a inglishe bible of the lardge volume', for that signifies the Geneva Bible.[75] One of the most learned of early seventeenth-century Calvinists, Andrew Willet, was proud of his connection with Perne, who was his godfather and gave him his name. Willet put Perne's many pious benefactions on the Protestant side of a ledger of Christian charity.[76]

But it may have been in all innocence that Perne extended his sense of fair play far beyond all normal limits to embrace that mysterious and much maligned sect, the Family of Love. In 1565 he had acquired the rectory of Balsham, a village a few miles to the south of Cambridge, and we must presume that he paid this little place some intermittent attention, not forgetting the poor of the parish when he came to compose his will.[77] In 1575 Perne was obliged to visit Balsham to investigate reports that it harboured a conventicle of the Family of Love. A number of villagers assembled, together with the vicar of a neighbouring parish, to swear blind that their beliefs were orthodox and their private religious meetings innocent, a harmless alternative to Sunday evenings spent in the pub, gaming and drinking. Butter would not melt in their mouths, as it seldom did in the mouths of Familists. However, from the recent researches of Dr Felicity Heal and Dr Christopher Marsh we now know that the men of Balsham, including some of the leading men, were indeed members of the Family of Love and continued to adhere to that obscure sect, at least until

---

[72] Lake, *Anglicans and Puritans?*, chapter 4, 'Richard Hooker'.

[73] Quoted, Collinson, *Religion of Protestants*, p. 82.

[74] Andrew Perne to Lord Chancellor Hatton, 30 June 1587 (autograph and endorsed in Archbishop Whitgift's hand 'dr perne to the L. Chauncellor'), Westminster Abbey Muniments, MS Book 15, fol. 86 v.

[75] *Andrew Perne*, p. 91.

[76] Andrew Willet, *Synopsis Papismi; Or, A General View of the Papacy: With Confutations of Romish Errors*, ed. J. Cumming (1852), ix, pp. 337–8. I owe this reference to the kindness of Dr Anthony Milton.

[77] BL, MS Add. 4223, fol. 135.

the early years of the following century.[78] The Family was notable for elevating the practice of cryptic deception (which Calvin had called Nicodemism) to a high and conscientious art. At this art the Balsham Familists excelled. They even had the nerve to solemnly declare that 'we thinke it unlawfull and ungodly to speake one thinge with the mouthe and think the contrarie with the hart, as the Libertines doe.' Had Perne met his match? Did the Balsham Familists outfox even that old fox? Probably not. Their confession was endorsed by Archbishop Parker, to whom it was sent, 'Subscription by certeyn of the Family of Love before Dr Pearne'.[79] But in that Perne subsequently did little or nothing about Balsham we must presume that he was complacent, content to be pastor to a sect of well-camouflaged heretics of the most radical kind.

That makes a bizarre and more or less irrelevant footnote to the spiritual odyssey of Andrew Perne. It would be more than a footnote to the history of the Church of England if we could work out what, if anything, the anti-Calvinist reaction in late Elizabethan Cambridge may have owed to Perne. There is evidence that he was a patron of the proto-Arminian theologian, the Frenchman Peter Baro, who as Lady Margaret Professor brought on the cyclonic theological weather which set in in the 1590s.[80] And he did what he could to impede the progress of Baro's opponent, the pope of Cambridge Calvinism, William Whitaker.[81] Perhaps someone may be able to demonstrate that Lancelot Andrewes and John Overall owed their theological orientation to the influence of Perne and of his library. Rather later, Robert Shelford, a Peterhouse man who in the 1630s made himself a spokesman for a rather extreme version of Laud's doctrine of the beauty of holiness, placed himself in a succession deriving from Perne.[82] And yet the stock of an alternative Anglican divinity seems to have grown not so much from the crypto-catholic traproot which was Andrew Perne as from the contrary, Calvinist beginnings which can be attributed to some at least of its luminaries, including Hooker and Andrewes.[83]

Such was Perne's religious temper and it looks more admirable from where many of us stand than it did to most of his contemporaries. Such also

---

[78] Alastair Hamilton, *The Family of Love* (Cambridge, 1981); B. Rekers, *Benito Arias Montano (1527-1598)* (London and Leiden, 1972); Felicity Heal, 'The Family of Love and the Diocese of Ely', in *Schism, Heresy and Religious Protest*, Studies in Church History, 9, ed. D. Baker (Cambridge, 1972), pp. 213-22; Christopher Marsh, '"A Gracelesse, and Audacious Companie"? The Family of Love in the Parish of Balsham, 1550-1630', in *Voluntary Religion*, Studies in Church History, 23, ed. W.J. Sheils and Diana Wood (Oxford, 1986), pp. 191-208.

[79] Inner Temple Library, MS Petyt 538/47, fos. 492-3.

[80] Strype, *Whitgift*, i, pp. 188-9.

[81] Ibid., pp. 453-8. See Peter Lake's discussion of this 'subtly derogatory letter' in his *Moderate Puritans and the Elizabethan Church* (Cambridge, 1982), pp. 62-3, 170.

[82] Robert Shelford, *Five pious and learned discourses* (Cambridge, 1635), epistle. I owe this reference to David McKitterick.

[83] I owe this suggestion to Dr Peter Lake.

was the temper of the college over which he presided, where Papists, Protestants and Puritans all contrived to coexist without any of the factional turmoil which periodically distracted St John's and some other colleges. However, not all Peterhouse men, let alone others, will derive as much comfort as did T.A. Walker from the fact that Peterhouse's Catholic martyrs were hurried to the scaffold by Peterhouse judges after their interrogation by Peterhouse inquisitors.[84]

V

In spite of that immense library in which a scholar could so easily lose himself for ever, it is likely that university and college affairs mattered most to Perne: more even than divinity and certainly more than Ely Cathedral. According to Gabriel Harvey, Perne resided at Ely and kept a grudging kind of hospitality there for one month of the year.[85] This tends to be borne out by orders of the dean and chapter made in August 1565 which are very explicit about the emoluments owing to the dean or any of the canons who were non-resident (and in 1561 only one canon had been resident); and which also licensed the dean to keep six bullocks and twelve sheep in the paddock called the Vineyard, for the purpose of hospitality.[86] Otherwise the record of Perne's time as dean is too meagre to permit us to confirm or discount Harvey's allegation. Such evidence as there is implies his presence at the annual audit, which took place in late October, and perhaps more occasionally at midsummer and at Christmas; but very infrequently if at all at the regular meetings of the chapter for the sealing of leases and patents.[87] It would not have been in Perne's character to have neglected his formal responsibilities in respect of Ely, or to have allowed that vast fabric to fall into extreme disrepair. But although he kept part of his library there, one gathers no sense of any particular affection for what Bishop Cox called 'that unsavoury isle with turves and dried up loads' (which may suggest that Cox saw it more often in the summer than the winter!).[88] Cambridge was where Perne belonged and it was Cambridge that he served with exceptional distinction for more than forty years.

Perne kept no don's diary and it is impossible even to hazard a reconstruction of what a typical week, or month, or year, may have consisted of. What mostly survives, like the sticks and stones left scattered after the melting of a giant snowball, is piecemeal evidence of his relentless vigilance

---

[84] Walker, *Biographical Register of Peterhouse Men*, i, p. 178.

[85] *Works of Gabriel Harvey*, ii, p. 310.

[86] Cambridge University Library, Ely Dean and Chapter Records, 1/E/2; *Correspondence of Matthew Parker*, p. 151.

[87] Cambridge University Library, Ely Dean and Chapter Records, Order Book 1550-1643, EDC/2/1/1.

[88] John Strype, *Annals of the Reformation* (Oxford, 1824), ii, pt ii, p. 177.

in defence of the liberties and privileges of the university and of his college, under their respective charters and statutes: a series of almost Pavlovian reactions to external stimuli which it would be a grave mistake to dismiss as petulant and childish, since what was at stake was the perpetuation of a free academic community and the learned pursuits proper to it. This part of Perne's experience, most of all, the modern university community can relate and respond to sympathetically.

The local community, in the shape of both town and county, as often as not proved adversarial. At the beginning of Elizabeth's reign, Perne was one of four senior members of the university appointed to the commission of the peace for the shire, perhaps with the intention of easing relations between the university and the world beyond its walls. But this experiment, which must have been Cecil's, lasted for only two years.[89] Thereafter, there was continual tension over such underlying issues as the reluctance of successive mayors of Cambridge and sheriffs of Cambridgeshire to take an oath to respect the jurisdictional rights of the university; and innumerable specific squabbles arising from the insistence of the university on the exercise of those rights within a five-mile radius of Great St Mary's church, or from particular invasions of its jurisdiction.[90] Such quarrels could be as momentous as the long-running contention over who should have the profit and responsibility of managing Stourbridge Fair, the major event in the commercial calendar of medieval and early modern Cambridge. For Perne it was a long, tough fight to prise the fair out of the hands of the courtiers and politicians who had privatised it, and then to ensure that the university benefited from its return to local control.[91] The cases could also be very petty but no less complicated for that, as intricate as the matter of the town illegally impounding the hogs of a certain college servant of Jesus, with Perne coming to the rescue of the impounded hogs;[92] or the *cause célèbre* of the petty government official who improperly arrested a man at Clayhithe (just within the five mile limits) for trying to smuggle fish (pike to be precise) out of Cambridgeshire under cover of night. The queen's household and her purveyors had claims upon those pike but they were otherwise within the university's jurisdiction, Perne's jurisdiction as vice-chancellor, who consequently found himself at legal odds with the Court of Green Cloth.[93]

[89] E.J. Bourgeois II, 'A Ruling Elite: The Government of Cambridgeshire, circa 1524-88' (unpublished Cambridge Ph.D. thesis, 1988), pp. 229, 233, 240.

[90] BL, MS Add. 5852, pp. 178-9 (fos. 91 v-2 r).

[91] Cooper, *Annals*, ii, pp. 466-75; Perne to Burghley, 21 November 1574, BL, MS Lansdowne 19, no. 20, fos. 38-9; Perne to Burghley, 18 March 1586, BL, MS Lansdowne 51, no. 62, fol. 144. The interval of eleven years between these two letters is evidence in itself of the protracted nature of the Stourbridge Fair business.

[92] BL, MS Lansdowne 54, no. 13, fol. 31.

[93] Cooper, *Annals*, ii, pp. 324–5.

In 1579 the eternal soap opera of town and gown took the form of soccer hooliganism, with the townsmen of Chesterton challenging the students to a Shrove Tuesday football match with the intention of ambushing them. Weapons were concealed in the church porch and at a cry of 'staves!' the attack was launched. Heads were broken and some students had to swim across the river to escape. (Since swimming was strictly forbidden under the 1570 statutes one wonders whether they all knew how.) On this occasion the high constable, Thomas Paris, signally failed to keep the peace. Having played in the match himself, he accused the students of provoking the violence. Fortunately, the assize judges happened to be in town at the time and they duly tried and imprisoned Paris, Perne sitting with them at the Dolphin.[94] (After this students were restricted to playing football within their own colleges, although Trinity was allowed the use of the small green between the college and the river, Garret Hostel Green.)[95]

Two years later Paris and his brother brought bear-baiting to Chesterton. Paris said that the students would arrive in strength, which they did, and in sermon time, that the proctors would intervene, which they also did (none other than Thomas Nevile being proctor), but that Paris would ensure that nothing unpleasant should happen to the bearwards. In the ensuing scuffle it was the university bedell who suffered unpleasantness. He was thrust into the very arms of the bear.[96] More judicial proceedings followed, in which Perne, yet again vice-chancellor, was again centrally involved. This case came to the attention of Cecil, Lord Burghley, as chancellor, who complained bitterly about being troubed 'for every such trifling cause ... being otherwise greatlie charged with matters of much more moment'. At the time such 'matters' included the courting of his sovereign by the French duke of Anjou, or rather the beginning of the end of that perplexing affair. Yet Perne on his side was entitled to his share of bitterness. Four times he had been wrong-footed and hauled up to London to confront the privy council, fighting tooth and nail for the privileges of Burghley's university which sheriffs and mayors and their inferior officers ignored with impunity.[97]

And in truth central government, the court, was the greatest of all headaches. The political establishment was potentially and often actually friendly and supportive, but it was also too much inclined to use the university for its own convenience. More than once Perne had to make the

[94] BL, MS Lansdowne 33, nos. 34, 35, fos. 67, 69.

[95] Cooper, *Annals*, ii, p. 382.

[96] BL, MS Lansdowne 33, nos. 31, 32, 33, fos. 62–6; MS Add. 5843, pp. 445–6 (fol. 218).

[97] Burghley to Perne, 20 May 1581, Cambridge University Archives, Collect. Admin., 5; Perne to Burghley, n.d., copy in BL, MS Add. 5852, pp. 178–9 (fos. 91 v-2 r). *Records of Early English Drama, Cambridge*, i, pp. 297–305; pp. 1222–3 in the second volume of the Cambridge *R.E.E.D.* supply numerous references to other cases involving Thomas Paris who was involved in many legal skirmishes with the university.

point that Peterhouse fellowships were not so many convenient bits of court patronage.[98] It was fortunate in many ways that the prime minister of the day, William Cecil, Lord Burghley, was also chancellor of the university. Of the thirty Perne letters which (to my knowledge) have survived, no less than twenty-four were written to Burghley. They are formal and deferential with no suggestion of friendship, which indeed did not exist between the two men.[99] But on one occasion Perne was downright sycophantic, praising Burghley's undergraduate son Robert Cecil as 'ane example of godly diligence' and 'a worthie and godly monument of your lordships good will towarde thadvansement of lerning'.[100]

But even Burghley was resisted when resistance was called for, and on one occasion Perne rather pointedly sent the chancellor copies of the charter and statutes of his own university, so that he might 'have them present allwaies'.[101] University autonomy (an autonomy in which Burghley as Chancellor had a legitimate interest and share) had to be defended at all costs. In 1573 there was the extreme embarrassment of a head of house, Thomas Aldrich of Corpus, declaring himself to be a radical Puritan.[102] It was embarrassing for Archbishop Parker, who had appointed Aldrich, and Parker decided to turn the miscreant over to the tender mercies of the High Commission for Causes Ecclesiastical. But the Ecclesiastical Commission had no business to intervene in the affairs of the university, not only in the perception of Aldrich, who refused point blank to appear before it, but in Perne's as well. It was Perne who led the university in a firm but subtle and successful démarche to ensure that the case was dealt with internally, if necessary by the chancellor, but not in any circumstance by the High Commission.[103]

[98] Perne to Burghley, 11 May 1578, BL, MS Lansdowne 27, no. 20, fos. 36 r, 37 r; Perne to Burghley, 25 July 1583, BL, MS Lansdowne 39, no. 1, fol. 2; Perne to Burghley, 1 September 1585, BL, MS Lansdowne 45, no. 58, fol. 125. And see also and especially the hostile memorandum 'Manifest reasons and argumentes that Mr Doctor Pearne denieth to admytt Richarde Bettes to a felowshippe in Peterhouse uppon her Majesties lettres of his own accorde without the assent of the whole nomber of fellows to whom her highnes lettres were also directed and without any just cause and that he might and ought to have accomplished her Majesties pleasure.' (PRO, S.P. 12/151/67, 68.)

[99] Two letters, of 1 September and 18 October 1585, are evidence of distinct ill-feeling, occasioned in part by Burghley's suspicion that Perne was interfering in the affairs of his own college (and Perne's), St John's, with the intention of frustrating the election as master of William Whitaker, Burghley's preferred candidate. (BL, MS Lansdowne 45, no. 58, fol. 125; no. 61, fol. 130. See Lake, *Moderate Puritans*, pp. 62–3).

[100] Perne to Burghley, 9 July 1581, PRO, S.P. 12/149/65.

[101] Perne to Burghley, 21 September 1582, PRO, S.P. 12/155/47.

[102] Porter, *Reformation and Reaction in Tudor Cambridge*, pp. 148–55.

[103] One of the more notable of Perne's holographs in the University Archives is the hasty note (Lett. 9 (C.6c)) written to the vice-chancellor in the midst of the affair, 'to have furder consyderation of our priviledges'; which is followed by a formal letter from the vice-chancellor and heads to the chancellor, insisting that to deliver Aldrich to the ecclesiastical commissioners would be 'agaynst the privilege of this universitie.' (BL, MS Lansdowne 17, no. 69, fol. 149.)

On his deathbed, Parker complained of Burghley and of his brother-in-law Lord Keeper Bacon (the two men who had made him archbishop), as the chief procurers of the spoil of the church, and he decided to put his complaints into a letter to the queen. Perne, who was present, strongly advised against doing any such thing. But the letter was written nevertheless, and John Whitgift, silly man, wrote to Burghley with the whole story.[104] Perne kept any such thoughts strictly to himself. When he read in his great folio edition of St Ambrose about uncharitable parsimony, he wrote in the margin in large letters; 'R. Eliz.' – but for his eyes only.[105] Although one would hardly guess it, Perne probably believed in the liberty of the Church as well as in that of the university and the college. Like his old enemy, Parker's successor as archbishop, Edmund Grindal, he read the spirited letters written by Ambrose to the emperors Theodosius and Valentinian, and like Grindal he noted in the margin of that same volume of Ambrose these words in particular: 'Ad imperatorem palatia pertinent, ad Sacerdotem Ecclesia.'[106] Palaces belong to emperors, churches to the clergy. But it would not have occurred to Perne to act as Grindal acted and to put that ancient artillery into action against Elizabeth Tudor. He would never have written the fatal Ambrosian letter in which Grindal advised the queen to leave the church to its own leadership and reminded her of her ignorance, fallibility and mortality: the letter which led to the archbishop's sequestration and downfall.[107]

So far Perne has appeared as a kind of fighting cock in a mortar board, albeit with corks on his spurs. But now it must be emphasised that he was also a very practical man, a good manager, and far-sighted. When plague came to Cambridge in his fourth term as vice-chancellor, the public health measures taken, including quarantine, were in line with the most enlightened practice known to the sixteenth century.[108] Plans and maps were sent to Burghley which contained the gist of the scheme later implemented as Hobson's Conduit, to bring water from Trumpington Ford down into the fetid King's Ditch, a project which Perne supported with a substantial legacy of £20 when he came to write his will.[109] This was to put into action some of those other lively intellectual interests which Mr McKitterick is able to illustrate from Perne's library: medicine, cartography, civil engineering.

[104] John Strype, *Life of Archbishop Parker* (Oxford, 1821), ii, pp. 430–1.

[105] Marginal note occurring on p. 20 of Perne's copy (Perne Library) of *D. Ambrosii episcopi Mediolanensis opera*, i (Basle 1555).

[106] Ibid., marginalia occurring at p. 130. See Collinson, *Archbishop Grindal*, pp. 242–3. See also idem, 'If Constantine, Then Also Theodosius: St Ambrose and the Integrity of the Elizabethan *Ecclesia Anglicana*', *Journal of Ecclesiastical History*, 30 (1979) pp. 205-29; reprinted, Collinson, *Godly People*, pp. 109-33.

[107] Idem, *Archbishop Grindal*, chapters 13, 14, 15.

[108] Perne to Burghley, 21 November 1574, BL, MS Lansdowne 19, no. 28, fos. 38-9, BL, MS Add. 4223, fol. 135.

[109] *Andrew Perne*, pp. 110-11.

The flow of water down the two sides of Trumpington Street is something which still offers minor benefits, unless we happen to be cyclists. But it seems probable that Perne was the architect, or at least an architect, of a project of far greater value, securing the continued solvency of the colleges of both Cambridge and Oxford at a time when their assets were threatened by the insidious erosion of price inflation. This measure of relief was found in an act of parliament of 1576 which required that in all leases of college property one third of the rent should be payable in kind, a combination of wheat and malt barley.[110] Whether these comestibles were consumed by their members in the form of bread and beer or taken to market, the colleges stood to gain considerably. At the valuation which the act placed on these corn rents, they not only made an effective hedge against inflation but created an instant surge in college incomes, what Gerald Aylmer has called 'a striking increase in the gross annual receipts'.[111]

The credit for this major landmark in the evolving fortunes of the collegiate system has usually been given to that great intellectual and statesman of the mid Tudor decades, Sir Thomas Smith, and Smith is said (on evidence not hitherto disclosed) to have introduced the same leasing policy at Eton in his time as provost.[112] But a mid seventeenth-century commemoration sermon for Perne claimed that the scheme was in truth his brainchild.[113] We know that Perne and Smith were friends and sometime contemporaries as fellows of Queens'. And we can also discover that the register of Peterhouse leases records some experimentation with corn rents between 1565 and 1576 (four out of nine leases containing a corn component) and the adoption of corn rents as a standard feature of all agricultural leases as soon as the 1576 act reached the statute book. For example, land at Fulbourn was leased in 1578 for twenty-one years (and that was the regular form of lease in Peterhouse by this date, and good leasing policy) at a rent of £4, plus three quarters of 'good and marchauntable whete, swete, clene, and well dressed' and four quarters of 'good and marchauntable malt'.[114] Dr Aylmer's resolution of the problem of responsibility, with advice from Sir Geoffrey Elton, is judicious: 'All in all, the likeliest course of events is that the bill originated with Perne and Smith, was pushed by Smith in the

---

[110] G.E. Aylmer, 'Economics and Finances, c. 1530-1640', in *History of the University of Oxford*, iii, pp. 535-43; G.R. Elton, *The Parliament of England, 1559-1581* (Cambridge, 1986), p. 226.

[111] Aylmer, 'Economics and Finances', p. 536.

[112] Mary Dewar, *Sir Thomas Smith: A Tudor Intellectual in Office* (1964), pp. 185-6.

[113] J. Clark, *The Faithfull steward, briefly described in a sermon preached at Cambridge on the commemoration of Dr Andrew Perne*, in *Two sermons preached at Cambridge* (Cambridge, 1655), p. 29. All suggestions that Perne was the originator of the corn rents scheme, including Thomas Baker's notes to the original edition of Strype's *Annals*, printed in the 1824 edition (iv, p. 609), are traceable to Clerk who (apart from the evidence of the Peterhouse leases) remains the only authority for this allegation.

[114] Peterhouse Archives, 'Old Register' of Leases, consulted for the years 1546-1587, passim.

commons and enjoyed Burghley's blessing in the lords.'[115]

It was with specific reference to the matter of corn rents, sufficiently technical as it was, that that celebrated Elizabethan, the London lawyer and parliament man Thomas Norton, had this to say about Perne's steward-ship: 'I think there is not a better Master for the helpings of his house, the advancement of learning, and the cherishing of toward students, and especially in divinitie and true religion, than Dr Perne.'[116] This endorse-ment is all the more remarkable in that Norton was a fierce Protestant whose prescriptions for university reform (the context of his comments on Perne) were otherwise aimed at a thorough purge of both open and secret papists. It is not surprising that when a vacancy in the mastership of St John's occurred in 1577, a majority of the fellowship of this, the second house in size, hoped for a localised Cambridge brain drain. Would the master of a college which was ninth in size out of fourteen choose to tear up roots which were a quarter of a century deep, to return to his undergradu-ate home?[117] He would not. Perne remained at Peterhouse.

We have come close to crediting Dr Perne with the constitution which governed Cambridge for 183 years and for finding a formula which made the collegiate system, the guts of that constitution, financially workable. (Whether he was also the inventor of Anglicanism is less certain.) If these claims are sustainable they ought to constitute Perne's main claim to fame. What is more clearly demonstrable is that he spent much of his time building up the University Library: putting markers on other notable libraries, working on that scholarly bibliophile Archbishop Parker, plotting to ensure that Lord Lumley's books should not all go to Oxford.[118] As for Perne's own library, which is anatomised in Mr McKitterick's essay, the first Regius Professor of Moden History called it 'a curious collection of Books', which strikes an appropriate note. For with its boxes and cases of coins and medals, its many maps and pictures, this was a library to arouse curious admiration, the interest even of tourists (referred to in Perne's will as 'any nobleman or learned stranger').[119] It is significant that Perne spoke of the 'singular beauty' of the books which Archbishop Parker had given to the university, 'to the great delectation of the eye'.[120] There were those among Perne's contemporaries who spoke of that eye as of its very nature

[115] Aylmer, 'Economics and Finances', pp. 542-3.

[116] BL, MS Add. 48023, fol. 47. For Norton's 'Devices', where these remarks occur, see my 'Puritans, Men of Business and Elizabethen Parliaments', above, p. 76.

[117] Thomas Ithell to Burghley, 3 June 1577, PRO, S.P. 12/114/3.

[118] Oates, *Cambridge University Library*, i, pp. 93-5.

[119] David McKitterick, 'Andrew Perne and his Books', in *Andrew Perne*, pp. 35-61.See Cambridge University Archives, Stokys' Book (Misc. Collect. 4), fol. 88 v, which records from August 1571 the visit of the French ambassador 'to peter howse to see dr pearnes studdie or librarie supposed to be the worthiest in all england.'

[120] Perne to Archbishop Parker, 22 November 1574 (Thomas Baker's transcript), Cambridge University Library, MS Gg.IV.8, p. 212.

idolatrous.[121] Perne was notable in an age of rampant iconoclasm verging on iconophobia for retaining and exercising a notably iconic sense, reflected, for example, in his evident love of richly illustrated books. It was, however, a restrained sense, the restraint nowadays called good taste; for, as David McKitterick explains, Perne's books were cased in practical rather than unduly lavish bindings.

VI

And so the mellowing figure of Perne, the elder academic statesman, ought to have descended towards an unsullied and honourable grave. In his last years he lived with Archbishop Whitgift at Lambeth and Croydon (others were looking after Peterhouse and the university was looking after itself) and it was at Lambeth that he died, four hundred years ago. According to the Jesuit John Gerard (by no means an impartial witness) his private advice in life had been to live, comfortably, in the established, Elizabethan religion; but not to die in it. 'Die in faith and communion with the Catholic Church, that is, if you want to save your soul.' But Perne himself died suddenly, after dinner, without a moment for repentance, in Gerard's perception forfeiting his soul.[122] Gerard is one piece of evidence that Perne's posthumous reputation remained tarnished. Another is the odd fact that Cooper in his *Annals of Cambridge* failed to record the passing of such a human monument, whereas he obituarised in the same year Alderman William Foxton, a very minor benefactor.[123] But most of the tarnish was applied by Gabriel Harvey. It was a piece of historically mordant justice that the man who had exhumed Bucer so many years before should now be himself exhumed, in the angry book published by Harvey in 1593 and called *Pierces Supererogation*.[124]

To understand why Perne should have been the object of literary vilification, four years after his burial, we have to travel back to another funeral, in Essex in the summer of 1577, Sir Thomas Smith's funeral, where Perne preached. Also present was Harvey, Smith's relation, his neighbour at Saffron Walden and an admirer and client. Harvey, a great bibliophile whose library may have rivalled that of Perne, had persuaded Smith's widow to give him some of her late husband's manuscripts, which ought to have gone to the University Library, or perhaps with Smith's printed books

---

[121] Patrick Collinson, *The Birthpangs of Protestant England: Religious and Cultural Change in the Sixteenth and Seventeenth Centuries* (1988), chapter 4; *From Iconoclasm to Iconophobia: The Cultural Impact of the Second English Reformation* (Reading, 1986).

[122] Caraman, *John Gerard*, pp. 18-19.

[123] Cooper, *Annals*, ii, p. 477.

[124] *Pierces supererogation, or a new prayse of the old asse* (1593); in Grosart, *Works of Harvey*, ii. Much of the passage relating to Perne is reproduced in E.G. Harman, *Gabriel Harvey and Thomas Nashe* (1923).

to Queens', his old college and Perne's. So Perne called Harvey a fox: to which the younger man retorted that he might be called a cub but was too young to be a fox, 'especially in his presence'. And then there was a frozen moment in time, a snapshot taken by Harvey in perfect focus. 'He smiled, and replyed after his manner with a Chameleons gape, and a very emphaticall nodd of the head.'[125] (And of course everyone knows what chameleons do when they are not gaping.)

A year later, in July 1578, Queen Elizabeth was at Audley End at the start of a politically significant summer progress into East Anglia which would determine that that rich and sensitive region was to subject itself for a century to come to protestant government, an enlightened but severe regime of godly magistracy and ministry.[126] As the university prepared to go down to Audley End to pay its respects, Lord Burghley advised on the gifts to be presented: a book for the queen, but not bound, in the manner of country bookbinders, in lavender-scented leather (scented with 'spike'), since this above all things the high-brow queen detested. (Who, one asks, would have known more about the Cambridge bookbinders than Andrew Perne, for once not vice-chancellor at this moment?) Gloves and accompanying verses should be prepared for the great courtiers: but don't bother about any gloves for me, said Burghley.[127] Harvey, a son of Saffron Walden and so on his native heath (Audley End is three miles from Walden), not only disputed before the queen like a scholar but dressed up to play the courtier, in Thomas Nashe's caustic description 'ruffling it out huffty tuffty in his suite of velvet'. Elizabeth said that he looked 'something like an Italian' and she allowed him to kiss her hand.[128] A few weeks later, as the Court made its way back to London through Hertfordshire, Harvey presented himself again and put in the queen's hands his anthology of

[125] John Strype, *Life of Sir Thomas Smith* (Oxford, 1820); Grosart, *Works of Harvey*, ii, pp. 313-14. Soon after the funeral, Harvey published an elegy in Latin verse, *Smithus, vel musarum lachrymae* (1578). In a letter he called Smith 'sutch a patron, or rather a father'. On the relationship of Harvey and Smith, see Lisa Jardine and Anthony Grafton, '"Studied for Action": How Gabriel Harvey Read his Livy', *Past and Present*, 129 (1990), pp. 30-78. On the marginalia and Harvey more generally I am reliant on Virginia F. Stern, *Gabriel Harvey: His Life, Marginalia and Library* (Oxford, 1979). Dr Stern's suggestion that Harvey's library may have contained over 3,500 titles as early as 1596 (thirty-four years before his death) looks rather inflated. (*Gabriel Harvey*, pp. 249-53.)

[126] Diarmaid MacCulloch, 'Catholic and Puritan in Elizabethan Suffolk: A County Community Polarises', *Archiv für Reformationsgeschichte*, 72 (1981), pp. 237-40; idem, *Suffolk and the Tudors: Politics and Religion in an English County, 1500-1600* (Oxford, 1986), pp. 195-7.

[127] Burghley to the vice-chancellor, Richard Howland (holograph), 15 July 1578, Cambridge University Archives, Lett. 9 (B.13a). Other letters relating to the progress are at B.13b, B.13c.

[128] Thomas Nashe, *Have with you to Saffron Walden*, in *The Works of Thomas Nashe*, ed. R.B. McKerrow, revised F.P. Wilson (Oxford, 1958), ii, pp.73-8; Stern, *Gabriel Harvey*, pp. 39-47. See also G.C. Moore Smith, *Gabriel Harvey's Marginalia* (Stratford-upon-Avon, 1913), p. 19. However it appears that Moore Smith's Harvey ('with all his great qualities, he was his own worst enemy', p.20) is seen too much through the eyes of Nashe.

laudatory verses, *Gratulationes Valdinenses*. It must be said that Nashe's account of these events trivialises aspirations to enter the public service which were no more absurd than they had been in the case of Sir Thomas Smith, and which were well supported by Harvey's intellectual talents and useful political contacts.[129] He was, says Dr Virginia Stern, a man 'who systematically and assiduously shaped and trained himself for greatness'. Prospects may have appeared particularly rosy in this summer of 1578, with the progressive, Leicestrian Protestantism which Harvey espoused in the ascendant and the French marriage project which threatened that cause heading for the rocks.

But Nashe implies that Perne observed Harvey's 'foppish' antics with a jaundiced eye. Henceforth he was that phenomenon, not utterly unknown in Cambridge at other times in its history, a formal friend but inward enemy. Presently, Harvey was an unsuccessful candidate for the post of public orator, victim of a 'slye practise' on the part of Perne, whom he proceeded to abuse in an open letter to his friend Edmund Spenser, the Pembroke poet. Perne was 'a morning bookworme' but 'an afternoone maltworme' a 'right lugler, ... who often telleth me, hee loveth me as himselfe, but out lyar out, thou lyest abhominably in thy throat'.[130] Perhaps after this Dr Perne no longer felt bound to say that he loved Mr Harvey. Harvey made Perne a fleshly symbol of a university which had fallen into decadence since the bliss of that dawn which had been the sixties. 'No more adoe aboute *Cappes* and *Surplesses:* Maister *Cartwright* nighe forgotten.' Modern languages were now all the rage; Latin and Greek neglected. 'All inquisitive after Newes, newe Bookes, newe Fashions, newe Lawes, newe Offices.'[131] So a veteran of the 1960s might complain of the academic climate of the 1980s. But Perne was happy, writing at this time to Burghley: 'All other things are verie well and in good order in thuniversitie both for thexercise of learninge and also for comlynes in apparell and manners of schollers as yt was this xx^tie yeres.'[132]

[129] Stern, *Gabriel Harvey*, p. 259. This assessment is also in debt to the work of Professor Jardine and Dr Grafton.

[130] Gabriel Harvey, *Three proper, and wittie, familiar letters: lately passed betweene two universitie men: touching the earthquake in Aprill last, and our English refourmed versiying* (1580) (Grosart, *Works of Harvey*, i, pp. 28-107). In this publication (which was far from 'proper' in our modern sense, as Harvey admitted in *Foure letters and certaine sonnets*, 1592) Perne was not named but referred to as 'youre old Controller', sc. the 'old controller' of Harvey's correspondent, 'Immerito', assumed to have been Edmund Spenser, who (it is thought) may have been disciplined by Perne as vice-chancellor. Harvey's remarks were misconstrued by some as having a more political orientation, perhaps as an attack on 'Mr Controller', Sir James Croft, and it was said that he spent time in the Fleet Prison in consequence, a circumstance which Harvey categorically denied. Harvey subsequently explained in *Foure letters* that Perne had been the target and it was here (p. 17) that he explicitly complained that his hopes of the office of public orator had been 'peltingly defeated, by a slye practice of the olde Fox'. (Stern, *Gabriel Harvey*, pp. 53, 92 n.4; Moore Smith, *Gabriel Harvey's Marginalia*, pp. 29-34.)

[131] Harvey, *Three proper letters*, pp. 27-30.

[132] Perne to Burghley, 29 April 1581, BL, MS Lansdowne 33, no. 30, fol. 60.

Since 1578, Harvey had been a fellow of Trinity Hall and had made a serious study of Civil Law, the discipline to which that college was principally committed. When the mastership became vacant in 1585, Perne was one of four heads who passed over Harvey in favour of Thomas Preston of King's, who had 'allwayes shewed himself voyd of faction', Trinity Hall being 'not altogether free from that inconvenience'.[133] Although Harvey held Preston in high regard and was not so utterly devastated by this disappointment as the legend created by Nashe would suggest,[134] it was in these circumstances that Perne became his Dr Fell. No doubt Perne blighted many a promising career in his time. He certainly had the power to do so. Whether he really had it in for Harvey or whether the vendetta existed mainly in the imagination of the man from Saffron Walden we cannot say. Nor can we say that Perne was wrong in his negative assessment of Harvey, who was impetuous if not factious. All that we know is that four years after Perne's death Harvey composed a prodigious satirical 'character' of the late master of Peterhouse, a parodic anti-encomium of five thousand words, amounting to one of the most elaborate caricatures of any public figure in the sixteenth century, comparable in scale to Skelton's poems against Cardinal Wolsey.[135]

As to what we should make of such furious 'flyting', 'frequent quarrels over nothing', Lucien Febvre wrote wise words many years ago. 'A disagreement was a godsend to people who had nothing to say ... Theirs was the sincerity of the actor who throws himself into his part.'[136] That may apply more appropriately to the Harvey-Nashe flyting than to the posthumous assult upon Perne, which was not about 'nothing'. But, as with Skelton, the literature of hyperbolic denunciation usually proves to be of limited evidential value, apart from what it may tell us about the author's resentment, and even that may prove to have been synthetic.[137] We should not entertain the illusion that Harvey reveals the true and essential Perne, or tells us many things that we should not otherwise know. His rhetorical ammunition was standard issue, the long-established tradition of the beast fable, with Perne cast as the fox.

[133] Stern, *Gabriel Harvey*, pp. 48-78; Moore Smith, *Gabriel Harvey's Marginalia*, pp. 48-9.

[134] I owe these points to Profesor Jardine and Dr Grafton. Presently, Harvey would leave Cambridge for a not unprofitable legal career in London, to which his literary diversions and entanglements were incidental. A long and comfortable retirement at Saffron Walden followed (Stern, *Gabriel Harvey*, p. 130.)

[135] Greg Walker, *John Skelton and the Politics of the 1520s* (Cambridge, 1988); Alistair Fox, *Politics and Literature in the Reigns of Henry VII and Henry VIII* (Oxford, 1989). Perne was not, of course, Harvey's only enemy and victim. He had pursued an earlier vendetta against Thomas Nevile, the future master of Pembroke, of some 8,000 words. (Stern, *Gabriel Harvey*, pp. 17-24.) Both quarrels were eclipsed by the great 'flyting' with Robert Greene and Thomas Nashe.

[136] Lucien Febvre, *The Problem of Unbelief in the Sixteenth Century: The Religion of Rabelais*, tr. B. Gottlieb (Cambridge, MA, 1982), pp. 20, 26, 99.

[137] Walker, *John Skelton*. See, e.g., the question posed by Dr Walker on p. 3: 'Does Skelton actually believe what he appears to be saying?'

In Protestant polemics, foxes represented covert and hypocritical pop-ery, wolves a more naked and honest version of the same threat.[138] It was a commonplace, repeated by Harvey's friend Spenser in the *Shepheardes Calender*, that there were no wolves in England, but by the same token all the more foxes.[139] Such a fox was Perne. Harvey indulged in the extrava-gance that all the foxiest characters in history could learn a trick or two from Dr Perne: Pisistratus, Ulysses, Proteus, King Louis XII of France and his cunning statesman, Philippe de Commines. Bishop Stephen Gardiner and Macchiavelli were a pair of cubs in comparison with Perne. (Did Harvey know that Gardiner, the arch-fox of the mid-sixteenth century, had commended Perne for the mastership of Peterhouse in 1553?)[140] 'For his pleasure' Perne once kept a fox cub in his lodgings, as other men might keep a pet bird or squirrel. (Did Harvey mean that literally or was this a snide reference to Whitgift?) Macchiavelli and Proteus: foxes could change their shape. 'The Clergy never wanted excellent Fortune-wrightes' (we should say, vicars of Bray). 'But what Byshop, or Politician in England, so great a Temporiser as he whom every alteration founde a newe man; even as new as the new Moone?' In his manuscript marginalia, Harvey wrote: 'Erasmus and Dr Perne will teache a man to Temporise and Localise at occasion.'[141] Harvey had seen various animals cleverly contrived in the sugar sculptures which decorated the table at feasts; ' but to this day never saw such a standing-dish of sugar-worke as that sweet-tongued Doctor; that spoke pleasingly whatsoever he thought; and was otherwise a fayre

[138] See, in particular, the series of mid Tudor Protestant pamphlets in which John Bale and William Turner collaborated: *Yet a course at the romyshe foxe* (Antwerp, 1543); *The huntyng and fyndyng out of the romyshe foxe* (Antwerp, 1544?); *The rescuinge of the romishe fox* (Bonn, 1545); *The huntyng of the romyshe vuolfe* (Emden, 1555?); *The hunting of the fox and the wolfe* (1565). See John N. King, *English Reformation Literature: The Tudor Origins of the Protestant Tradition* (Princeton, 1982), p. 446.

[139] See 'September', lines 152-6:

> Never was Woolfe seene many nor some,
> Nor in all Kent, nor in Christendome:
> But the fewer Woolues (the soth to sayne,)
> The more bene the Foxes that here remaine.

(*The Works of Edmund Spenser*, variorum edition, *The Minor Poems*, i, ed. Edwin Greenlaw et al. (Baltimore, 1943), p. 89.) Catholics too could deploy the wolf-fox trope. See *De lezebellis Angliae parricidio poemata Latina et Gallica* (Antwerp, 1587):

> Anglois vous dites qu'entre vous
> Un seul Loup Vivant on ne trouve:
> Non, mais vous avez unde Louue
> Pire qu'un milion de Loups

The 'Louue' was, of course, Queen Elizabeth I.

[140] Walker, *Biographical Register of Peterhouse Men*, i, p. 127. What Harvey could not know was that Gardiner was, in all probability, the author of the so-called 'Machiavellian Treatise', which drew liberally on the *Discorsi* in order to counsel Queen Mary's consort Philip on the conduct of his newly acquired kingdom. (See *A Machiavellian Treatise by Stephen Gardiner*, ed. and tr. P.S. Donaldson, (Cambridge 1975).)

[141] Moore Smith, *Gabriel Harvey's Marginalia*, p. 138.

Prognosticator of fowle weather ... He was ... the precisest practitioner of that soft, and tame Rhetorique that ever I knew in my dealings ... If ever there were Hypocrisy incarnate, it was he ...'

This was damaging, even damning. But there was already in print a more notable literary monument to Harvey's resentment in the shape of the *Shepheardes Calender*, written by Garvey's intimate friend Edmund Spenser and inspired by shared interests of a kind typical of young men with literary pretensions and political ambitions: and by a shared hostility to Perne. There seems little doubt that the interlocutor Palinode in the May Eclogue of the *Calender* was intended for Perne: Palinode, whose very name means recantation, whom Spenser's commentator 'E.K.' identifies as a 'Catholique' but whom modern critics see as a type of the conforming cleric; Palinode, complacent about country disorders (that was unfair to Perne, the veteran of Barnwell and Chesterton wars), Palinode, the careless, non-resident pastor, Palinode who is made to listen to the salutary political fable of the Fox and the Kid. Later, Martin Marprelate was to call Perne 'old Father Palinode'.[142]

Perne was unfortunate to live on the very edge of the late Elizabethan age of satire and to die in the midst of the extraordinary public furore aroused by the Martin Marprelate tracts, Puritan satire which consisted of scurrilous and circumstantial-anecdotal attacks on the bishops and any other senior ecclesiastics who happened to be within firing range. Perne himself was pilloried in the tracts in sixteen separate places and under various pseudonyms. 'the Fox', 'the old Turner', 'Andrew Ambo', 'Old Andrew Turncoat'.[143] Archbishop Whitgift was said to have been his 'boy', who carried his

[142] The closest Cambridge approximation to the country pastimes reprehended in the May Eclogue was provided by the Whitsuntide plays and games at the Gog Magog Hills, which the university authorities relentlessly opposed. Lord North, who in 1579 was accused of licensing these activities, wrote to John Hatcher as vice-chancellor: 'Sir I do so mutche mislike thes vaine and ydell toies; as I will consent to none of them and do utterly mislike any assembly of people; without the servis of God; or hir maieste.' (*Records of Early English Drama: Cambridge*, i, pp. 270-1, 292-3.) Palinode is identified as Perne in J.J. Higginson, *Spenser's Shepherd's Calender in Relation to Contemporary Affairs* (New York, 1912), pp. 72f, 89, 181-4. On the other hand, Paul E. MacLane's more perverse *Spenser's Shepheardes Calender: A Study in Elizabethan Allegory* (Notre Dame, IN, 1961) unaccountably contains no reference to Perne. Nor does Nancy Jo Hoffmann's *Spenser's Pastorals* (Baltimore, 1977). Not all Higginson's readings are now acceptable and the entire enterprise of decoding Spenser is no longer fashionable. A.G. Hamilton has said; 'What is so perverse about this effort to identify historical allusions is that Spenser has laboured so carefully to conceal them.' See 'The Argument of Spenser's *Shepeardes Calender*', in *Spenser: A Collection of Critical Essays* (Englewood Cliffs, NJ, 1968), p.30. But it will take more than that to put a good historian off the scent and in the case of Palinode Higginson seems to me to have had a good nose. On the vexed question of Spenser's politico-religious alignment, see, most recently, John N. King, 'Was Spenser a Puritan?', *Spenser Studies*, 6 (1986), pp. 1-31 and his *Spenser's Poetry and the Reformation Tradition* (Princeton, 1990). King makes no mention of Perne.

[143] *The Marprelate Tracts, 1588, 1589*, ed. W. Pierce (1911), pp. 38, 86, 170, 412. See p. 82 for the reference to 'old Father Palinode'.

cloakbag, and that was to hint at the unmentionable.[144] The Widow Twanky figure of 'Dame' Dorothy Lawson, the'shrew of Paul's Gate', the London Puritan termagant, was said to know a way to get Perne out of the Book of Martyrs'.[145] Martin Marprelate was a clown whose comic stock in trade derived from the comedian Tarlton and the repertoire of the public and popular theature. Presently the Anti-Martinist pamphlets, a somewhat dubious defensive strategy, were translated into popular entertainment on the stage. Dame Lawson trod the boards as a kind of pantomime dame and it is not impossible that Perne too was given a part in these conservative farces, which were staged not long before his death and may, for all we know, have precipitated it.[146] For the Harvey onslaught was a kind of subplot in the avalanche of satirical pamphleteering released by Martin, followed by Antimartin, and even Anti-Antimartin. Harvey being an Anti-Antimartinist, flyted with the Antimartinist, Thomas Nashe. If it were not for the Marprelate affair, Perne might have been left quietly in his grave, instead of which Archbishop Whitgift and Bishop Bancroft had to issue an order, ten years after the demise of his most notable victim, that Harvey's books (and Nashe's) were to be confiscated and never printed thereafter.[147]

It is a good question whether Perne would have appeared in the tracts but for Harvey's vendetta; or would have become to all posterity a symbol for opportunistic inconstancy but for Martin and Harvey. It is possible that the impression which these most pejorative of sources create of a Perne for ever and notoriously in the public domain of slanderous gossip was spurious: an old polemical trick. In a Puritan dialogue published in 1589 he is described as 'the notablest turnecoate in all this land', and it is alleged that 'every boy hath him in his mouth', saying of a coat that had been turned that it was 'Pearned'.[148] But that may have been written by Job Throckmorton, who in all probability was Martin himself.[149]

In spite of all this, Harvey's caricature is not worthless as descriptive characterisation. Good caricatures seldom are. What we find beneath the surface of *Pierces Supererogation* is some fascination with and even reluctant admiration for Perne's unfathomable worldly wisdom. 'He was an old soaker indeede: and had more wit in his hoary head, then six hundred of these floorishing greene heads, and lusty curled pates.' That was to say that

---

[144] Ibid., p. 69. See also p. 367: 'Doctore Perne, thou knowest, was thy joy, and thou his darling.' Dr Harry Porter is more prepared than I would be to mention the unmentionable. See his *Puritanism in Tudor England* (1970), p. 207-8.

[145] *The Marprelate Tracts*, p. 31.

[146] John Lyly(?), *A whip for an ape; or Martin displaied* (1589), sig. A2. See Leland H. Carlson, *Martin Marprelate Gentleman: Master Job Throkmorton Laid Open in his Colors* (San Marino, CA 1981), pp. 72-4.

[147] Moore Smith, *Gabriel Harvey's Marginalia*, p. 70

[148] *A dialogue, wherein is plainly laide open, the tyrannicall dealing of L. bishoppes against Gods children* (1589), Sig. D1 v.

[149] Carlson, *Martin Marprelate*. But note, with some of his reviewers, the somewhat circular arguments of Dr Carlson's study.

Perne, the old Henrician, had nothing to learn in sophistication from the clever wits of the late Elizabethan *fin de siècle*. 'No man could beare a heavy injury more lightly: or forbeare a learned adversary more cunningly.' He had such a Patience, as might soften the hardest hart.' Harvey's rash attempts to be cheeky had been met with 'the picture of Socrates or the Image of S. Andrew'. Consequently, Harvey confessed, 'I still reverence the honourable remembraunce of that grave, and most eloquent Silence, as the sagest lesson of my youth.'[150]

Moral ambivalence we have found, in plenty. But a fourth centenary is an occasion for celebration, to praise Perne, not to bury him, still less to exhume him and burn him at some metaphorical stake. And we may acknowledge that those dubious qualities which Gabriel Harvey accurately observed, at once Socratic, Macchiavellian and Erasmian, were in many respects admirable in a public man, and served his university very well through a period of sustained danger to its very existence. Indeed, as Macchiavelli himself might have said, in those circumstances it was better to be feared, and by some hated, than to be loved. Thomas Nashe was not out of order when he rebuked Harvey for his posthumous hunting of the old Cambridge fox. 'Few men liv'd better, though, like *David* or *Peter*, he had his falls, yet the Universitie had not a more careful Father this 100 yeare',[151] or, as we may well add, this four hundred years. I think that on balance we must agree with Thomas Hearne, who wrote in 1720 that Perne was 'a Person of very great Merits, notwithstanding he hath been traduc'd by some, who were much inferiour to him on all accounts'.[152]

Postscript (1993)

What, one wonders, was the intended message of the Peterhouse weathercock? In 1562, Bishop Latimer's secretary and editor Augustine Bernher attacked 'false periured hypocrites ... beyng readye lyke weather cockes to turn at all seasons as the wynde doth carry you', 'those waveryng and periured weathercockes'. (Latimer, *The Seven Sermons* (1562), Epistle.)

---

[150] Grosart, *Works of Harvey*, ii, pp. 295, 302.

[151] McKerrow, *Works of Nashe*, iii, p. 137.

[152] Thomas Hearne, *A Collection of Curious Discourses Written by Eminent Antiquaries upon Several Heads in Our English Antiquities* (Oxford, 1720), p. lxvii. This was said in commendation of Perne as a numismatist. But the implication seems to be that a man who did so much for the preservation of ancient coins could not be all bad.

that I have deſerved hell, yet will I ſtedfaſtly hope in gods infinite mercy, knowing that he hath heretofore pardoned many as great ſinners as my ſelf, whereof I have good warrant ſealed with his ſacred mouth, in holy writ, whereby he pronounceth that he is not come to call the juſt, but ſinners.

" Item, I John Shakſpear do proteſt that I do not know that I have ever done any good worke meritorious of life everlaſting: and if I have done any, I do acknowledge that I have done it with a great deale of negligence and imperfection; neither ſhould I have been able to have done the leaſt without the aſſiſtance of his divine grace. Wherefore let the devill remain confounded; for I doe in no wiſe preſume to merit heaven by ſuch good workes alone, but through the merits and bloud of my lord and ſaviour, jeſus, ſhed upon the croſe for me moſt miſerable ſinner.

VII.

" Item, I John Shakſpear do proteſt by this preſent writing, that I will patiently endure and ſuffer all kind of infirmity, ſickneſs, yea and the paine of death it ſelf:

wherein if it ſhould happen, which god forbid, that through violence of paine and agony, or by ſubtility of the devill, I ſhould fall into any impatience or temptation of blaſphemy, or murmuration againſt god, or the catholike faith, or give any ſigne of bad example, I do henceforth, and for that preſent, repent me, and am moſt heartily ſorry for the ſame: and I do renounce all the evill whatſoever, which I might have then done or ſaid; beſeeching his divine clemency that he will not forſake me in that grievous and paignefull agony.

VIII.

" Item, I John Shakſpear, by virtue of this preſent teſtament, I do pardon all the injuries and offences that any one hath ever done unto me, either in my reputation, life, goods, or any other way whatſoever; beſeeching ſweet jeſus to pardon them for the ſame: and I do deſire, that they will doe the like by me, whome I have offended or injured in any ſort howſoever.

IX.

" Item, I John Shakſpear do heere proteſt that I do render infinite thanks to his divine majeſty for all the benefits that I have received as well ſecret as manifeſt, & in particular, for the benefit of my Creation, Redemption, Sanctification, Conſervation, and Vocation to the holy knowledge of him & his true Catholike faith: but above all, for his ſo great expectation of me to pennance, when he might moſt juſtly have taken me out of this life, when I leaſt thought of it, yea even then, when I was plunged in the durty puddle of my ſinnes. Bleſſed be therefore and praiſed, for ever and ever, his infinite patience and charity.

X.

" Item, I John Shakſpear do proteſt, that I am willing, yea, I doe infinitely deſire and humbly crave, that of this my laſt will and teſtament the glorious and ever Virgin mary, mother of god, refuge and advocate of ſinners, (whom I honour ſpecially above all other ſaints,) may be the chiefe Executreſſe, togeather with theſe other ſaints, my patrons, (ſaint Winefride) all whome

I invocke and beſeech to be preſent at the hour of my death, that ſhe and they may comfort me with their deſired preſence, and crave of ſweet Jeſus that he will receive my ſoul into peace.

XI.

" Item, In virtue of this preſent writing, I John Shakſpear do likewiſe moſt willingly and with all humility conſtitute and ordaine my good Angel, for Defender and Protectour of my ſoul in the dreadfull day of Judgement, when the finall ſentance of eternall life or death ſhall be diſcuſſed and given; beſeeching him, that, as my ſoule was appointed to his cuſtody and protection when I lived, even ſo he will vouchſafe to defend the ſame at that houre, and conduct it to eternall bliſs.

XII.

" Item, I John Shakſpear do in like manner pray and beſeech all my dear friends, parents, and kinsfolks, by the bowels of our Saviour jeſus Chriſt, that ſince it is uncertain what lot will befall me, for fear notwithſtanding leaſt by reaſon of my ſinnes I be to paſs and ſtay a long while in purgatory, they will vouchſafe to aſſiſt and ſuccour me with their holy prayers and ſatisfactory workes, eſpecially with the holy ſacrifice of the maſſe, as being the moſt effectuall meanes to deliver ſoules from their torments and paines; from the which, if I ſhall by gods gracious goodneſſe and by their vertuous workes be delivered, I do promiſe that I will not be ungratefull unto them, for ſo great a benefitt.

XIII.

" Item, I John Shakſpear doe by this my laſt will and teſtament bequeath my ſoul, as ſoon as it ſhall be delivered and looſened from the priſon of this my body, to be entombed in the ſweet and amorous coffin of the ſide of jeſus Chriſt; and that in this life-giveing ſepulcher it may reſt and live, perpetually incloſed in that eternall habitation of repoſe, there to bleſſe for ever and ever that direfull iron of the launce, which, like a charge in a cenſore, formes ſo ſweet and pleaſant a monument within the ſacred breaſt of my lord and ſaviour.

XIV.

" Item, laſtly I John Shakſpear doe proteſt, that I will willingly accept of death in what manner ſoever it may befall me, conforming my will unto the will of god; accepting of the ſame in ſatisfaction for my ſinnes, and giveing thanks unto his divine majeſty for the life he hath beſtowed upon me. And if it pleaſe him to prolong or ſhorten the ſame, bleſſed be he alſo a thouſand thouſand times; into whoſe moſt holy hands I commend my ſoul and body, my life and death: and I beſeech him above all things, that he never permit any change to be made by me John Shakſpear of this my aforeſaid will and teſtament. Amen.

" I John Shakſpear have made this preſent writing of proteſtation, confeſſion, and charter, in preſence of the bleſſed virgin mary, my Angell guardian, and all the Celeſtiall Court, as witneſſes hereunto: the which my meaning is, that it be of full value now preſently and for ever, with the force and vertue of teſtament, codicill, and donation in cauſe of death; confirming it anew, being in perfect health of ſoul and body, and ſigned with mine own hand; carrying alſo the ſame about me; and for the better declaration hereof, my will and intention is that it be finally buried with me after my death.

" Pater noſter, Ave maria, Credo.
" jeſu, ſon of David, have mercy on me.
Amen.*"*

This document, discovered in the roof of Shakespeare's family home in Henley Street, Stratford-upon-Avon, and published in the eighteenth century, was not fully explained or understood until modern research revealed that in it Shakespeare's father had put his name to a 'testament' composed by St Charles Borromeo and widely circulated in England by Jesuits and seminary priests.

8

William Shakespeare's
Religious Inheritance and Environment

The world into which William Shakespeare was born was fragmented, with, in John Donne's telling phrase, all coherence gone. Shakespeare and countless others of his generation did not know what to believe or, if they did, could not tell when they might be called on to believe contrary things. Like all human systems, the medieval church had been wracked with strife and occasionally plunged into constitutional crisis. Head and members were chronically discordant, and for forty years in the late fourteenth and early fifteenth centuries there had been two and even three heads. But apart from a handful of heretics who put themselves outside society there had been an underlying unity of belief, which, if anything, was strengthened by diversity and debate among the theological schools and tendencies.

The major conflict of the sixteenth century was sufficiently deep-seated and complex to shatter the unity of Western Christendom irreparably because it concerned matters of belief that either were fundamental or were perceived to be fundamental, especially by Martin Luther. This German Augustinian canon boasted that whereas others before him had assaulted the corrupt life of the church (and none more recently or devastatingly than Erasmus of Rotterdam), he was the first to attack church doctrine. Luther did so first in the private agony of his religious and theological consciousness as a monk, a pastor of souls and a university professor at Wittenberg in Saxony; later, in public challenges to the prevailing schools of systematic theology; and finally, in questioning the principle and abused practice of granting indulgences, whereby the pope offered to reduce the penalties of sin, not only temporally but eternally – at a price. This protest, articulated in the Ninety-Five Theses of October 1517, sparked the conflagration of the Reformation, for it drew Luther ever deeper into controversy that sharpened the edge of his own critical convictions, deepened the gulf separating him from the *magisterium* of the church, and aroused immense public interest and sympathy.

At a debate in Leipzig in June and July 1519, Luther set the individual conscience grounded in Scripture above pope and council. In 1520, in *De captivitate Babylonica ecclesiae praeludium* (*The Babylonian Captivity of the Church*, to which Henry VIII of England wrote a rejoinder), he denounced as a conspiracy and a fraud the entire sacramental scheme of attaining grace. Excommunicated, he burned the papal bull that banned him and added the canon law to the flames. In 1521 he refused to recant before the emperor at Worms, a moment that the nineteenth century saw as the most pregnant in human history. At an imperial diet in 1529, a formal protest (the *Protestatio*) by Luther's supporters among the German princes gave rise to the new designation *Protestant*. The next year, the new Lutheran theology was codified by Luther's orderly colleague Philip Melanchthon in the Augsburg Confession. When Rome responded to the challenge by convening the Council of Trent, which met intermittently between 1545 and 1563, Catholicisim agreed with Luther that the differences between them were past healing and paid him the compliment of defining itself by a series of confutations of what was now known as Protestantism.

At the heart of Protestantism was Luther's conviction, which he equated with the Gospel itself, that man is justified in the sight of God not by any virtue inherent in himself or by any striving on his part but by God's unmerited grace, made available by Christ's death and appropriated by faith, understood as a deeply trustful commitment to God's mercy of the whole being, itself an act of which man was incapable until enabled by the Holy Spirit and enlightened by the Word of God contained in the Bible. Justification was an instantaneous transaction. Thereafter, the justified man, still burdened with his sinful nature but seen by God as just, served God and his neighbour, not slavishly in order to gain a reward but in a spirit of free thanksgiving. The strong stress of Luther's dialectic excluded any compromise of these evangelical principles. The Reformation slogans were 'Grace alone', 'Faith alone', and 'Scripture alone'.

The immediate effect on those who responded to this theology was the destruction of the motivation with which almost all pious acts, individual and corporate, had been undertaken. Salvation was not to be earned through continual attendance at mass, by the daily sacrifice of Christ's body and blood at the altar, in pilgrimage and prayers to saints, or least of all in the ascetic disciplines of the monastic life. There was no room in Protestant-ism for the spiritual rule of a priestly hierarchy that controlled these things and claimed a special competence in them. The church was now to consist of a listening people, a flock, as Luther once said, that hears its shepherd's whistle. The place occupied in Catholic worship by the altar, half-hidden from the congregation by a screen, was now taken by the Bible on a lectern and by the pulpit. Ears and voices were exercised rather than eyes.

Protestants retained the two sacraments of the Lord's Supper and baptism, and Luther invested them with great material value, as the means by which God ratifies and even conveys himself to the believer. Luther is often said to have taught 'consubstantiation' rather than the 'transubstan-tiation' of Roman Catholicism. In fact he eschewed all philosophical explanations of the real presence of Christ's body in the sacrament and simply asserted it as a mysterious fact, to the offence not only of Catholics but of other Protestant reformers for whom it was a merely spiritual and symbolic presence. For in the secondary reformations that sprang up in Switzerland and South Germany, initially under the inspiration of the Zurich preacher Huldreich Zwingli, the spiritual, invisible properties of God and his service were strongly emphasised and a more drastic, inconoclastic approach to traditional images and forms was taken. This 'best reformed' branch of Protestantism developed in theological and geographical isolation from the Lutheran, or 'Evangelical', branch and was set in order, doctrinally and institutionally, by John Calvin in the model of a Christian society that he built up in Geneva and in his great theological work *The Institutes of the Christian Religion* (1536).

The English church would eventually veer toward, and even anchor itself in, the Calvinist, or 'Reformed', tradition, but only after many changes of course. In the 1530s, in the midst of a dynastic and political crisis, it was detached from Rome by Henry VIII and his minister Thomas Cromwell and placed under royal supremacy , but without at first committing itself doctrinally or liturgically to Protestantism. That followed in the reign of the boy king Edward VI (1547–1553), when the Swiss model began to prevail, especially in the second version of the new English service book, the Book of Common Prayer of 1552. The English Reformed Church received its confession of faith in the Forty-Two Articles of Religion of 1553, revised in the reign of Elizabeth as the Thirty-Nine Articles, but an attempt to revise the canon law of the church in a reformed sense in the *Reformatio legum* was abortive. In the reign of Edward's elder half sister Mary (1553–1558) there was virtually a complete reaction and Catholic restoration, accompanied by active persecution of Protestants of all persuasions. But on 17 November 1558, Mary died, to be succeeded by Elizabeth (1558–1603), who was the child of her father's breach with Rome.

II

In 1564, the year of Shakespeare's birth, the bishop of the diocese in which Stratford-upon-Avon lay wrote, 'The right waie to Stablishe a kingedome is first to rectifie religion: where god is trulie Sought, there is greate Safetie'.[1] The Catholic Mary would not have dissented. But Mary had been dead for five years, and Bishop Sandys' advice was now to be understood in a contrary sense. Queen Elizabeth's Act of Uniformity of 1559 required the clergy to make exclusive use in all ministrations of the 1552 Book of Common Prayer, with a few stipulated changes, and further required 'all and every person and persons inhabiting within this realm' to resort to their

---

[1] Mary Bateson, ed., 'A Collection of Original Letters from the Bishops to the Privy Council, 1564', in *Camden Miscellany*, 9, Camden Society, new series, 53 (1893), p. 2.

parish church on Sundays and holy days 'and then and there to abide orderly and soberly during the time of the common prayer, preachings, or other service of God'.

The statute invoked sanctions as severe as life imprisonment for obstinate and persistent refusal to use the Prayer Book or for denouncing it, while those neglecting to come to church and having no valid excuse for absence were subject to ecclesiastical censure and pecuniary fine. Yet in the second parliament of the new reign the lord keeper, Sir Nicholas Bacon, complained that the act was not in force: 'How commeth it to pass that the common people in the country universally come so seldom to common prayer and divine service?'[2]

The Preface to the Prayer Book declared its intention to 'appease' diversity of practice so that 'all the whole realm shall have but one use'. In principle, at a certain hour on a Sunday morning, the entire population should have been occupied in the same action, hearing and repeating the same words. It is often said (Francis Bacon said it first) that Queen Elizabeth had no desire to open windows in men's souls. However, the Elizabethan formularies imply a uniformity of mentality no less than of behaviour. Notorious and extreme heretics were still occasionally burned at the stake, while Catholics and some extreme Protestant dissenters were executed for reasons hard to disentangle from their sectarian beliefs. Lesser heterodoxies, even those disclosed in casual speech, were dealt with in the ecclesiastical courts.

Yet, after the queen had reigned for more than forty years, the West Country was reported by its bishop to be very far from the godly uniformity that the law envisaged: 'Few or none come to church to pray to God for her Majesty, and for the good estate of the realm; but they will follow rattle headed preachers from town to town.' Rank atheism was on the increase: 'A matter very common to dispute whether there be God or not.' In contempt of religion, a goose and a gander were profanely married. At Launceston a horse's head was baptised, and in another place a whole dead horse was brought to receive the sacrament. 'Every day complaints are made by ministers who are railed on and shrewdly beaten by lewd persons. A minister was made to kiss the bare hinder parts of a man'.[3]

These sound more like fictions than sober fact. Scholars debate whether it was possible, in the sixteenth century, to be an atheist in any philosophical sense. Yet the historian of Tudor England who supposes that the Act of Uniformity was effectively and universally in force has failed to cross the *pons asinorum* of his subject, which is to grasp that the statute book is

[2] *Proceedings in the Parliaments of Elizabeth I*, ed. T.E. Hartley, i, *1558–1581* (Leicester, 1981), p. 82.
[3] HMC, *Calendar of the MSS of the Marquis of Salisbury*, x (1904), pp. 450–1.

evidence of the aspirations of government, not a record of social reality. One has no sure means of knowing how uniform in religious practice Shakespeare's generation was. As for religious knowledge and experience, that is retrievable only for a tiny, well-documented minority. It may be that the York citizen who in the late 1570s crossed himself (and was in trouble for it) indicated thus that he still believed what Catholics believe about the pope, the saints, the Mass; on the other hand, it may just have been an old habit. Since the publication in 1971 of Keith Thomas' ambitious reconstruction of early modern mentalities, *Religion and the Decline of Magic*, it has been clear that an adequate account of Elizabethan religion must include the beliefs and practices associated with witchcraft, and the many forms of magic and astrology that both competed with 'religion', in the modern sense, and were coexistent with it. But the extent and influence of this not yet demystified world view is strictly immeasurable.

The only available record of the religious sentiments of large numbers of Shakespeare's contemporaries is found in the preambles to wills. But such statements were copied from formularies or were contributed by the scribe who wrote the will.[4] Shakespeare's own will is no exception to this rule. There is abundant testimony of Shakespeare's religious knowledge, of his familiarity with both Bible and Prayer Book, of his capacity to turn to dramatic effect the common themes of religion and morals. Yet his use of these resources was eclectic and aesthetically controlled, so that recent scholarship has declared his private religious views 'inaccessible', and the evidence 'simply inconclusive'.[5]

III

An anthropologist whose task was, as it were, to take a snapshot of the religious dimension of Elizabethan civilisation at a given moment would face formidable difficulties. But the historian has a more daunting job to do, for he must trace across a century complex changes in religion and the concomitant alterations in other aspects of life. In a formal sense, England became a Protestant church and realm when the new services came into legal use on Saturday, 24 June 1559. The Act of Supremacy of 1559 had removed England from papal jurisdiction, subjecting the church to the monarch as 'Supreme Governor' and to no other power on earth. The Act of Uniformity enforced church services that were vehicles of the Protestant

[4]   There is a considerable modern literature devoted to the interpretation of sixteenth-century will preambles, an undertaking which stands in some such relation to English reformation studies as the manufacture of subsidiary working parts bears to the production of finished motor cars. For a recent and somewhat sceptical account of the use of this evidence, see Eamon Duffy, *The Stripping of the Altars: Traditional Religion in England, 1450–1580* (New Haven and London, 1992), pp. 504–23.

[5]   Darryl J. Gless, '*Measure for Measure*': *The Law and the Convent* (Princeton, 1979), p. xiii; Roland M. Frye, *Shakespeare and Christian Doctrine* (Princeton, 1963), p. 3.

doctrines of grace, faith, works and sacraments, which in 1563 were to be explicitly articulated in the Thirty-Nine Articles of Religion. This version of Protestantism approximated more closely to the Swiss and South German model, which claimed to be 'best reformed', than to Lutheranism. (Shakespeare was to make Anne Boleyn a 'spleeny' Lutheran.' [6] To put it a little too crudely, the Church of England was now to favour Calvinism. Only in respect of ecclesiastical organisation and government was the religion of England not thoroughly reconstructed in the early years of Elizabeth's reign or, indeed, subsequently. But at first few Elizabethan Protestants found episcopacy anomalous. Many early Elizabethan bishops were themselves Protestants of an advanced reformed persuasion and had spent Mary's reign in Strassbourg, Zurich or Geneva.

Beginning in the summer of 1559 with a royal 'visitation' (or tour of inspection), the newly established religion was taught and enforced by 'injunctions', royal and episcopal; by the catechism; by officially sanctioned sermons, or 'homilies'; and by the more spontaneous word of the sermon itself, although preachers were still scarce. The legal enforcement of the official religion was entrusted in part to the Court of High Commission (or the Ecclesiastical Commissioners), a mixed tribunal of clerics and lay magistrates that exercised the powers of the royal supremacy directly. The new ways were defended against their Catholic detractors at the famous pulpit of Paul's Cross in London and in such polemical publications as Bishop John Jewel's *Apologia Ecclesiae Anglicanae* (1562), the defence of a faith allegedly not new at all but primitive and apostolic. In the anonymous interlude *New Custome* (*c.* 1571), a character of that name repudiates her title and insists that she be called Primitive Constitution.

But none of this activity could convert England overnight into a Protestant nation. The full internalisation of Protestantism was to have very far-reaching implications – negative in the abandonment of belief in religious 'works', the mediation of the saints, the pains of purgatory and related pious practices and institutions, many of which centred on the mass and on pilgrimage to the shrines and images of saints. Protestants who were more than formal in their profession would relinquish the ingrained habit of punctuating their speech with the old familiar oaths 'By the mass' and 'By God's body'. Outwardly, a good Protestant would be identified by his 'conscionable' attachment to 'godly exercises' and by regular reading of the Bible in the version prepared by English exiles in Geneva. Almost the entire Reformation process might be summarised as the reception of the English Bible by a population previously denied any direct encounter with Scripture. John Foxe's *Actes and Monuments of These Latter Perilous Days* (1563, popularly known as *The Book of Martyrs*), which carried the sacred story of God's dealings with his people into the recent past, was read 'throughly'

[6] *Henry VIII*, III. ii. 99.

and 'as a book of credit'. [7] The godly man sought out sermons and, as he went to and from them, sang psalms with his family. Inwardly, such a life was sustained by a settled belief in Providence and by that alert and anxious 'walking in God's ways' commonly recorded in some of the earliest English diaries.

Communities in which the Protestant religion was taken seriously were strict observers of Sunday, the Christian Sabbath. Traditonal ways of passing time on that day were reprehended. So it was that absorption of the full implications of the new faith led to a withering of the rich culture of 'Merrie England', with the gradual disappearance of dancing, maypoles and church ales. In Coventry it was decreed in 1591 that maypoles should never be set up again. But at Stratford the issue was not confronted until 1619.

Meanwhile, the medieval urban drama, consisting of mystery, miracle and morality plays and having close ties to both religion and the social order, was coming to an end. At Coventry an exceptionally rich dramatic tradition was all but dead by 1591, although the young Shakespeare may have borrowed from some of the later performances the idea in *Hamlet* of 'out-Heroding Herod'. The Chester plays, which were staged for the last time in 1574, were said by a local chronicler to be of no use 'excepte it be to showe the Ignorance of oure forefathers'. In early Elizabethan York the great Corpus Christi cycle was first stripped of the more offensive plays concerning the Virgin Mary and then replaced by a more homiletical piece, the Creed Play. But even this was declared inadmissible by the dean of York and future archbishop, Matthew Hutton: 'Ffor thoghe it was plausible 40 yeares agoe, and wold now also of the ignorant sort be well liked: yet now in this happie time of the gospell, I knowe the learned will mislike it and how the state will beare with it I know not'. Presently, the York mysteries, in spite of their popularity, were finally suppressed by Archbishop Edmund Grindal, who also stopped the Wakefield plays.

As the religious drama was stifled, its place was taken by shows of a more secular character at midsummer and by the performances of troupes of strolling players. But the city fathers of York soon turned against the players; while at Chester, where the magistrates were 'exclaimed upon' from the pulpit for tolerating them, citizens were even fined for going elsewhere to witness such 'obscene and unlawful' entertainments. The players visited Stratford regularly in the years of Shakespeare's youth; but by the end of the century they were no longer welcome, and seven years after the poet's death they were paid to go away. By that time the itinerant drama had changed its character. The interludes brought to Elizabethan country towns seem to have been moralities, which would have reinforced

---

[7]   See 'The Veracity of John Foxe's Book of Martyrs', above, pp. 151-77.

municipal godliness, but now the frank secularity of the stage seemed to its critics 'filthy'. In spite of his coauthorship of *Gorboduc*, Thomas Norton thought theatergoing 'unnecessarie and scarslie honest'.

So it was that a mimetic civilisation of image and myth, symbol and ritual, gave way to a more patently moralistic culture of the printed and authoritatively pronounced word. The records of the last days of the old ceremonies suggest the gulf separating old from new: in Coventry payments were recorded 'to Pilate 4s. 8d.' and 'to God 16d.'; in Chester, the cost of 'guildinge of litle Gods face'; in York, an explanation that the nuts distributed by the figures of Yule and Yule's Wife in their annual procession were 'in rememberance of that most noble Nut our sauiors blessed body'. 'Most noble Nut' indeed! In 1572 the Ecclesiastical Commissioners terminated this 'very rude and barbarouse custome'. In Chester in 1599, the mayor cleaned up the midsummer show, causing the 'giants' who used to go in procession to be broken and substituting the martial figure of a knight for the traditional 'dragon and naked boys'. The divines had complained. But later the giants came back and, with them, the devils attending men in women's costume, 'to the greate dislike of them which are well disposed'.[8]

IV

When can it be said that England had become a predominantly Protestant, rather than some kind of Catholic, society? The question is much debated, some authorities believing that the Reformation happened quickly by political imposition from above. Others agree on an early date but give more credit to social and genuinely religious forces, or reformation from below. Another school of thought believes that the Reformation was forced on a reluctant populace, but not effectively before the reign of Elizabeth; while others identify the 'real' Reformation with Elizabethan Puritanism, a popular and irrepressible movement, equivalent to the internalisation of Protestant religious values in some sections and levels of society.[9]

The question seems to turn on the reign of Mary. If Mary had lived, would Catholicism have stuck as both the legally enforced and willingly professed religion of most Englishmen? According to both Scarisbrick and

---

[8]   These paragraphs summarise some of the argument and supporting material in Patrick Collinson, *From Iconoclasm to Iconophobia: The Cultural Implications of the Second English Reformation*, The Stenton Lecture 1985 (Reading, 1986); and idem, *The Birthpangs of Protestant England: Religious and Cultural Change in the Sixteenth and Seventeenth Centuries* (1988), chapter 4, 'The Cultural Revolution'. They draw upon various volumes in the Toronto series 'Records of Early English Drama': *York*, 2 vols., ed. Alexander F. Johnston and Margaret Rogerson (1979); *Coventry*, ed. R.W. Ingram (1981); *Chester*, ed. Lawrence M. Clopper (1979); and on Edgar I. Fripp, ed., *Minutes and Accounts of the Corporation of Stratford-upon-Avon and Other Records, 1553–1620*, 4 vols., Dugdale Society (Oxford, 1921–9).

[9]   Christopher Haigh, 'The Recent Historiography of the English Reformation', in *The English Reformation Revised*, ed. C. Haigh (Cambridge, 1987), pp. 19–33.

Haigh, there was no reason for it not to have stuck.[10] Does our impression of a popular revulsion from the Marian burnings depend entirely on John Foxe's power as a grand historical mythmaker? Perhaps. Yet it was not Foxe but W. Cunnyngham's *1564: A New Almanack* – the almanac was the most popular form of Tudor literature – that, a year after Foxe was first published in England, attributed the recent outbreak of the plague to the blood of God's martyrs crying out for revenge. And J.R. Green, in his *History of the English People* (1876), thought it was only in the period between the middle of Elizabeth's reign and the Civil War of 1642–1652 that 'England became the people of a book, and that book was the Bible'. He adds, 'No greater moral change ever passed over a nation'.[11]

The question cannot be answered without recourse to local and regional history, for the lack of synchronization in the process of Protestantisation is very marked. Many places in Essex and East Anglia were precocious in their acceptance and practice of the new religion, as was the Suffolk cloth town of Hadleigh by the reign of Mary.[12] The same stage was probably not reached anywhere in the north until a full half-century or more later, while far into the seventeenth century a large tract of Lancashire remained frontier territory, hostile to Protestantism. And the extreme north west and much of Wales seemed impervious to any stirring and evangelistic religious influence, whether Protestant or Catholic. Such 'dark corners of the land' were of active concern to the Long Parliament in the mid seventeenth century.

If broad regional distinctions can be drawn, it is equally necessary to recognise that local differences of environment and occupation influenced, perhaps even determined, the response to Protestant evangelism of parishes and of individuals and groups within parishes. Just as literacy was very unevenly distributed through the social hierarchies (for example, thatchers and fishermen were almost generally illiterate; tailors and yeomen, partially literate; and printing workers, wholly literate), so it appears likely that skilled craftsmen and cloth workers responded more readily to a religion of Bible-reading and sermons than peasants and agricultural labourers. And woodland and highland zones, with their patterns of scattered settlement, diverse livelihoods, and absence of close social surveillance, provided a more fertile soil for forms of religious independence than corn-growing villages, which lived under the watchful eye of squire and parson.

In tracing and measuring the acceptance of the reformed religion, one may make a rough-and-ready distinction between, on the one hand, the

[10] And see now Duffy, *The Stripping of the Altars*, pp. 524–64.

[11] J.R. Green, *A Short History of the English People* (1888 edn), p. 460.

[12] Or so Reformation historians, following Foxe, have supposed. Doubt is cast on this tradition by a recent study of the early reformation in Hadleigh. See John S. Craig, 'Reformation, Politics and Polemics in Sixteenth-Century East Anglian Market Towns' (unpublished Cambridge Ph.D. thesis, 1992), chapter 5 'Conflict: Hadleigh, 1530–1560', pp. 137–57.

almost imperceptible penetration of the language of Bible and Prayer Book as heard and absorbed in parish worship by a majority of the population, and, on the other, a more deliberate, active, instructed response to the propositions of preachers and other evangelists and to the Bible read at first hand. The first kind of exposure and response can be located in church and attributed to the reading ministry of the bulk of the clergy, disparaged by Puritans as a 'bare' reading ministry without saving force, rather than to the 'powerful' and 'edifying' sermons of the preachers. After 1568 what was heard in church was a revision of Miles Coverdale's 'Great Bible' (1539) known as the Bishops' Bible, since the episcopal bench and its chaplains shared the labour of preparing this authorised version. The more energetic response of thoroughly indoctrinated Protestants, which in many cases is describable in terms of religious conversion, was nourished as much in the home as at the parish church. 'His house he endeavored to make a little church', wrote John Geree in *The Character of an Old English Puritane* (1646). It was a commonplace.

Recently, historians have increased their interest in what may be termed Prayer Book Protestantism or parish Anglicanism – the habitual, relatively unexacting religion probably characteristic of the majority of Jacobean Englishmen. To devote too much attention to the strident minorities at both religious extremities may exercise a false sense of historical priority. Moreover, there is impressive evidence from the seventeenth century of massive public resistance to religious innovations – 'Arminian' or 'Laudian' in the 1630s, Puritan and Presbyterian in the 1640s – which argues for deep attachment to the Prayer Book and to all that it symbolised and safeguarded in the traditional scheme of things. Yet relatively low levels of religious commitment are not in practice easy to penetrate, and it is understandable that the history of the Elizabethan church should have been written very largely with respect to the minorities, Catholic and Puritan, which stood on either side of the official via media.

V

Virtually no public proponent of religion in Elizabethan England believed in, or found it possible to approve of, a state of religious pluralism. It was assumed to be dangerous and unnatural for more than one religion to be tolerated within one commonwealth. Sir Nicholas Bacon, the lord keeper, voiced a common fear when he spoke of the danger that 'religion, which of his own nature should be uniform, would against his nature have proved milliform, yes, in continuance nulliform'.[13] If anything, the Tudor state, having eliminated all duality from government by placing authority over both church and state in the same royal hands, laid a greater and more

---

[13] *Remains of Edmund Grindal*, ed. W. Nicholson, Parker Society (Cambridge, 1843), p. 471.

practically enforceable stress on religious unity than had been associated with the medieval Catholic polity.

Yet the fact could not be avoided that there was more than one religion in the realm that Elizabeth inherited in 1558. One writer accurately described the church of the Elizabethan settlement as a 'constrained union' of papists and Protestants. It was not possible by 'one blast of Queen Elizabeth's trumpet', as another critic wrote, to turn lifelong Catholics into faithful gospellers. Neither was that necessarily Elizabeth's immediate aspiration. Insofar as the settlement of religion was based on a coherent plan, the strategy of the queen herself and her closest advisers (and this, as will be shown, is a matter still in dispute) was to comprehend the entire nation in a church somewhat of the middle way, essentially Protestant but not so nakedly Protestant as to alienate confused Catholics, of whom there were many.

A philosophical and ethical principle was implied, a version of the Aristotelian via media or golden mean, first adumbrated in the apologies for the Henrician Reformation of the 1530s made by humanists and destined to become, in a somewhat different guise, the hallmark of the Church of England in its maturity, the essence of what would later be called, but was not yet known as, Anglicanism. The via media lay between having too much, as in too great an exuberance of religious ceremony, and having too little, a denuded and degraded religion. In George Herbert's words, it was 'A fine aspect in fit array, / Neither too mean, nor yet too gay.' It was also a ground on which those whose opinions were in fact divergent could in some measure agree, at least in an outward harmony. When Sir Nicholas Bacon, in a closing speech at the 1559 parliament, defended the settlement that had just been made, he warned off its detractors with these words: 'Amongst thease I meane to comprehende aswell those that be to swifte as those that be to slowe, those I say that goe before the lawe or beyond the lawe as those that will not followe'.[14]

For those reluctant to follow, the Elizabethan settlement contained some encouragement. The words with which the sacrament of the altar was communicated to the faithful were not hostile to belief in the real presence of Christ's body in the elements, thus making of this rite more than a Protestant communion for those who wished so to regard it. The queen's intention was that the form of the thing communicated should be an unleavened wafer thicker than heretofore and without the impressed marks of the passion, but otherwise not unlike the 'singing cakes' of the recent past, whereas most Protestants preferred to use common bread. The sacrament should, in the queen's view, be celebrated at a kind of altar, adorned with a cross – or so the example of her own royal chapel suggests. A clause in the Act of Uniformity, with a corresponding rubric in the Prayer

---

[14] Hartley, *Proceedings*, i, p. 51.

Book, required the clergy to wear vestments and other attire that tended
to align them with the massing priesthood of Catholicism rather than with
the Protestant ministry of Switzerland and south Germany. The queen
wished her clergy to remain celibate, a desire she shared with many old-
fashioned people; and while most Elizabethan clerics were in fact married,
the law took only grudging cognisance of the fact.

Those 'reluctant to follow', for whom such concessions were intended,
were very numerous. Whereas virtually all the surviving Marian bishops
refused to endorse the new settlement and were removed from their
positions, their example was not followed by the great majority of the
inferior, parochial clergy. Most early Elizabethan parishes were therefore
served by former Marian priests, accustomed to the old Latin service. Even
Bishop Grindal had to say on one occasion, 'I have said mass. I am sorry for
it.'[15] Many were not sorry. And if the early Elizabethan church contained
so many clerics who were still Catholic priests at heart, why should one
suppose that the laity was any differently disposed? The likelihood is that
a majority of those in the church of Shakespeare's infancy were 'church
papists', as they were commonly called. If not 'rank papists', wrote the Essex
preacher George Gifford, such people retained 'still a smack and savour of
popish principles'.[16] Yet the expectation was that such 'survivalists', as A. G.
Dickens has called them, would in the course of time be absorbed into a
broadly Protestant consensus.[17]

Although it was something that Queen Elizabeth could scarcely admit,
the success of her religious settlement depended on the preparedness of
her subjects to limit the depth of their religious commitment. The paradoxically counterproductive effect of a more aggressive Protestant evangelism and apologetic, which was asserting itself even in the relatively
unenthusiastic 1560s and to greater effect in the 1570s, was to stiffen the
resolve of those who were still Catholic in sympathy and to inspire these
stalwarts to stand up and be counted as recusants; they refused to attend
Protestant services and, by this act, indicated their rejection of the queen's
religion. As an enthusiastic form of Protestantism gathered strength, so by
a polarising process an authentic, resistant Catholicism began to flex its
muscles. As Arnold Oskar Meyer remarked, the Reformation and Counter-
Reformation coincided in Elizabethan England as mutually exacerbating
forces.

The lines had been drawn in the 1560s in a battle of the books between
Protestant apologists, notably John Jewel, and exiled Catholics, such as

---

[15] *Remains of Grindal*, p. 211.

[16] George Gifford, *A briefe discourse of certaine pointes of the religion, which is among the common sort
of Christians, which may be termed the Countrie Divinities.* (1598), p. 61.

[17] Some of the relatively conventional perspectives reflected in these paragraphs are challenged
and newly refracted in Alexandra Walsham, *Church Papists: Catholicism, Conformity and Confessional
Polemics in Early Modern England*, Studies in History, 68 (1993).

Oxford scholars like Thomas Harding, himself a former Protestant. These hostilities were on such a massive scale that they have been called the Great Controversy. Nevertheless, the real watershed was later and political. In 1569 the conservative affinities of the northern aristocracy rose, albeit without marked enthusiasm and unsuccessfully, in open revolt against the Elizabethan regime. They were encouraged by the presence in England since 1568 of the captive Scottish queen, Mary, a plausible claimant to the English throne, and by their reading of certain international signals. In the bull *Regnans in excelsis* (1570), Pope Pius V excommunicated Elizabeth and forbade her subjects to obey her laws. These were perplexing developments for English Catholics, who had hoped that it might prove possible to reconcile their faith to their political obligations as Englishmen.

Practically, the papal sentence of deposition was a futile gesture, for it did little but increase the insecurity of English Catholics. Yet from 1570 on, the well-informed knew that the pope required that they continue to profess their religion at all costs, a religion not to be confused with what went on in the queen's churches, even if this ran counter to their ordinary duty as the queen's subjects. Within four years the English Catholic seminary founded at Douai, France (then the Spanish Netherlands), by William (later Cardinal) Allen began to dispatch into England priests charged with a mission 'for the preservation and augmentation of the faith of the Catholics'. Later, other missionaries would arrive from Rome itself, where the English pilgrim hospice had been converted into another college. The capture of this institution by the Society of Jesus and its way of life under the Jesuits were matters shared with a fascinated and duly horrified English public by Anthony Munday in *The English Romayne Life* (1582): 'After supper, if it be in wintertime, they go with the Jesuits and sit about a great fire talking, and in all their talk they strive who shall speak worst of Her Majesty.'[18] The English Counter-Reformation, so long delayed, had begun.

According to the brilliant thesis advanced by John Bossy in *The English Catholic Community, 1570–1850*, that community has no history, only a prehistory before the watershed of 1570. The death of the medieval English church was a principal condition for the emergence of a new kind of Catholicism, one practiced by a minority community in a non-Catholic England. But, in the view of Bossy's critics, this idea has been allowed to run out of control. The history of the Catholics for many decades after 1570 must take account of an untold but far from insignificant number of church papists who were not recusant and did not necessarily identify with a self-consciously isolated 'community'. The most often quoted description of a church papist, that composed by John Earle for his *Microcosmographie* (1628), is cited as if it provides a firsthand description of the religious

---

conditions prevailing in the 1560s, but Earle wrote six decades later. Moreover, both the survival of church papists and the existence and health of a community of separated, recusant Catholics in good standing with their church depended on perceived continuities with the past history of the church in England and on links with the Catholic Continent. To be fair to Bossy, he is by no means unaware of the paradox that brought out of these wider connections in space and time a somewhat insular and withdrawn religious community.

Important though the church papists were, it is inevitable that historians of post-Reformation Catholicism should have focused their attention on individuals, households and other groups whose practice of Catholicism was relatively complete and coherent, not merely the debris of redundant folk beliefs. Bossy has created a rich landscape of a hidden world, describing the disciplines, the calendar, and the social rhythms of feast and fast that characterised the larger Catholic households. There is much more of this in the contribution made by local historians of the subject. Yet the most certain means of identifying Catholics in Elizabethan England has always been negative: their refusal to attend Protestant services in the parish church, or at least to receive the Protestant communion. And the historian remains very dependent on the recognition of that refusal by the authorities, their application of the label *Recusant*, and their punitive responses to it.

The responses of the authorities were not universally or uniformly energetic. Like all processes of Tudor government, they arose from personal initiatives and motives and from intermittent governmental pressures prompted by events and contingencies. The two decades following the papal excommunication and deposition witnessed a great increase in missionary activity, as exiles trained in the English seminaries abroad made their reentry, and as the Society of Jesus took a belated interest in the conversion of England with the well-publicized arrival of the Jesuit fathers Robert Parsons and Edmund Campion in 1580. These years also saw a worsening of the international situation and the intensification of threats to the security of the Elizabethan regime. At last, in the late 1580s, came open war with Spain, whose king, Philip II, was thought by English Protestants to vie with the pope himself as the archenemy of their queen and their religion. These two lines of development were woven together in the public mind. While the earl of Leicester lived (he died in 1588), it was later remembered, it went for current that papists were traitors, either in action or in affection. The earl personified a strong political commitment to a robustly anti-Catholic Protestantism.[19]

[19] See Patrick Collinson, 'Letters of Thomas Wood, Puritan, 1566–1577', in *Godly People: Essays in English Protestantism and Puritanism* (1982), esp. pp. 58–82; and Simon Adams, 'A Godly Peer? Leicester and the Puritans', *History Today*, 40 (Jan. 1990), pp. 14–19.

The consequences are reflected in the statute book. Parliament had already passed the Treasons Act of 1571, which made it treasonable to follow the dicates of the papal bull and which imposed severe penalties for importing such bulls or other objects of devotion. In 1581, to convert or suffer conversion to Catholicism with the intent of withdrawing allegiance from the queen became treason, and the fine for nonattendance at church rose to £20 a month, with provision for the sequestration of the estates of those failing to pay. This last measure was aimed at the Catholic landed gentry, whose patronage and social and political support were all but essential to the survival of the old faith and who were numerous, not only in the north but in such southern counties as Hampshire and Sussex.

By an act of 1585, a Jesuit or seminary priest apprehended in England was by definition a traitor, and those harbouring or assisting such traitors were themselves liable to execution. One such harbourer, the York housewife Margaret Clitherow, was crushed to death for refusing to plead at her trial. The fate of 123 priests (making up two-thirds of the total of Elizabethan martyrs) was the equally fearful death of hanging, drawing and quartering. In 1593, parliament debated, but failed to pass, a bill that would have deprived Catholics of virtually all legal rights. The statute actually passed in that year reduced the penalties for being a priest or Jesuit but confined all recusants to within five miles of their homes. However, many priests and most lay Catholics seem to have escaped the full rigours of this ferocious penal code, only a very few recusants paying their fines in full. In Essex more than half the money collected came from the pockets of one individual, the unfortunate Ferdinando Paris.[20]

For centuries, the victims were celebrated by the historians of one tradition as blessed martyrs and saints, but by those of the other as political offenders who were not unjustly punished for activities that were a threat to the state at a moment of acute danger. The rights and wrongs of these contrary points of view have dominated the literature. More recent studies have benefited from the broadening scope of modern social, cultural and religious historiography and have acknowledged that the topic of Elizabethan Catholicism transcends the limited themes of both hagiography and political history. The matters of most abiding and absorbing interest to Catholics were peculiar to themselves; only at moments of danger were Catholics absorbed in their relations with the government. Thus, the serious differences that divide English Catholics toward the end of the sixteenth century, which were gathered up in a *cause célèbre* known as the Appellant, or Archpriest, Controversy, were once interpreted as a dispute about the political obligations of Catholics, the problem of allegiance. But for Bossy, this was 'an ecclesiastical, not a political argument', having to do

[20] For the Catholicism of the Paris family, see Andrezji Bida, 'Papists in an Elizabethan Parish: Linton, Cambridgeshire, *c.* 1560 – *c.* 1600', unpublished Cambridge Diploma Dissertation, 1992 (Seeley Library, Cambridge).

with questions of internal organisation and authority. This is not to deny that the tensions between the Jesuits and their opponents, and between the clerical and lay points of view, which were near the heart of it, were cleverly exploited by the government, which encouraged the anti-Jesuit party of the Appellants to advance its cause by a policy of pragmatic cooperation with the authorities.

Nevertheless, the question of allegiance was inescapable and critical to the survival of the Catholic community. Usually it has seemed to historians that most Catholics were politically quiescent. The bull of 1570 was canonically and procedurally a dubious document, and in 1580 Pope Gregory XIII declared it to be for the time being practically inoperative, although binding in conscience. Catholics might be feared as a potential fifth column, but in spite of occasional scares such as the Babington Plot (1586), there is little evidence of their readiness to rise in support of England's foreign enemeies, not even in 1588.

Bossy has provided this analysis with a sociological dimension. Noting that the most significant dividing line in Catholicism is normally that which separates priests and laity, he has proposed two ideal types: on the one hand, the gentleman, pragmatic, antiheroic, old-fashioned in his politics; on the other, the missionary priest, an advanced, radical intellectual, idealist and activist, capable (as the gentleman was usually not) of political as well as spiritual adventures. The Jesuit Robert Parsons answers most closely to this second type. But Parsons' career was a failure. Given the dependence of the mission on its lay patrons (an inevitable dependence according to Bossy, a preferred and avoidable dependence in the hyper-critical view of Haigh), the gentleman had the last word over the devoted priest. The final chapter of Elizabethan Catholicism, like its first, was a story of inertia.

More recently, Peter Holmes has doubted some parts of this scenario. Study of the casuistry of Elizabethan Catholics suggests that a greater number were prepared to contemplate political resistance to the queen than historians have supposed. There were no lifelong, consistent 'Catholic loyalists' and few matters on which priests and laymen are known to have differed. Resistance was the cause not of particular groups or kinds of Catholics but of particular moments in their history. There was a 'chrono-logical rhythm' to the development of the political ideology of Elizabethan Catholics. In the 1580s the prospect of a successful political intervention against the regime appeared good and seems to have aroused a wide interest. It is hardly surprising that after 1588 interest diminished. Two years after the Armada, the Northamptonshire gentleman Sir Thomas Tresham (often cited as a typical loyalist and the most articulate of lay Catholic spokesmen) wrote fulsomely to the Privy Council of God's benefits bestowed 'under the government of so Christian a prince and council'. But there is reason to believe that Tresham's loyalty was more expedient than sincere.[21]

Expediency of many kinds was a way of life for persons as exposed and subject to contradictory pressures as the Elizabethan Catholics. Bossy has written of 'the optimum line', which provided the maximum in self-determining capacity and the minimum in destructive isolation. Haigh has described – and censured – that expediency which led many priests to neglect the fruitful mission fields of the north and far west, where the greatest numbers of retrievable church papists were to be found, in order to enjoy the protection and patronage of Catholic gentry in less remote regions. Priests were not immune to the Elizabethan craving for 'civility', even when they mentally prepared themselves for the ultimate incivility of death by hanging and drawing. In the north of England one-fifth of all the Catholic clergy in England ministered to two-fifths of the detected recusants. In 1580 half the missionaries deployed in England were in Essex, London and the Thames Valley, where only a fifth of recusants were to be found. Cumbria and much of Wales were to prove total and perhaps unnecessary losses. The gentry expected to hear mass daily. Their social inferiors would be lucky to have it monthly.

Whether or not it is possible to imagine a different kind of mission, living precariously among the people and nourishing a more popular, resistant, and Irish type of Catholicism, there is no disagreement among historians that the mission as it operated in fact, and as they must therefore describe it, had a different character and different consequences. It sustained a distinct religious community numbering perhaps 200,000, or some 5 per cent of the population. As an authentic product of the Counter-Reformation, this community was faithful in the seriousness of its religious commitment and the regularity of its practice. It was also productive in the early, heroic years of a rich alternative culture nourished by Counter-Reformation piety, notably the fervent poems of the martyred Robert Southwell ('Tender my suite, clense this defiled denne,/Cancell my debtes, sweete *Jesu*, say Amen') and the poignant music of William Byrd and many other Catholics among the composers of English music's golden age.

The community grouped itself around the great houses of Catholic nobility and gentry and was sometimes hard to distinguish from the servants and tenants of these magnates. The lay leaders were in principle

---

[21] John Bossy, 'The Character of Elizabethan Catholicism', *Past and Present*, 21 (1962); Christopher Haigh, 'The Continuity of Catholicism in the English Reformation', *Past and Present*, 93 (1981); idem, 'From Monopoly to Minority: Catholicism in Early Modern England', *Transactions of the Royal Historical Society*, 5th series, 31 (1981), pp 129–47; Peter J. Holmes, *Resistance and Compromise: The Political Thought of the English Catholics* (Cambridge, 1982). To this scholarship and these debates is now added the sensitivity of Alexandra Walsham to the polemical and pastoral significance of labels, categories and stigmas in her *Church Papists* and her forthcoming *Past and Present* article, '"The Fatal Vesper": Providentialism and Anti-Popery in Late Jacobean London'.

and often in practice totally excluded from the public offices normally attendant on their dignities, such as university positions and many others that might have drawn them toward the mainstream polite society. Their children were sent to foreign schools and convents. Yet only occasionally, as in the late 1630s and 1680s, did a minority of these outsiders entertain the political ambition of overcoming the disadvantages that were the penalty of their faith. And although an elaborate and apocalyptic mental fabric of anti-Catholicism became almost a world view in its own right for Protestant England in the seventeenth century, it was only from time to time that this form of collective paranoia became a physical threat to English Catholics. More typically, it served as an ideological stiffener against foreign threats and foreign tyrannies, real and imagined.

VI

Puritan was a term of stigmatisation, which in Shakespeare's England was bandied about freely and loosely as a weapon against a certain kind of excessive religiosity and scrupulous morality. The mayor of Chester who in 1600 reformed the midsummer pageants was called 'a godly, over-zealous man' and might well have been called a Puritan. Such 'busy controllers' were 'precise fools', 'saints and scripture men', 'curious and precise fellows who will allow no recreation'. 'It was never merry world since that sect came first among us.' In the same spirit Chaucer's contemporaries had exclaimed against 'Lollards', and Henry VIII's subjects against 'you fellows of the new trickery'. Only in the mid seventeenth century would *Puritan* be owned and acknowledged by the godly themselves as an honourable flag under which to sail – 'the good old English Puritans'.

It follows that there is little profit in attempting to invest such a loosely pejorative term with exact definitional meaning and not much more in debating whether a certain individual was or was not a Puritan. Stigmas tell us more about the stigmatiser than the stigmatised, or rather they tell us about the entire dynamic and stressful situation that gave rise to the stigma.[22] In the later years of Elizabeth, when the stigma became a topic for sophisticated investigation, on the stage as well as in literature and

---

[22] The following references encompass recent debate between Patrick Collinson and Peter Lake on 'Puritan' as substance or polemical shadow: Patrick Collinson: *English Puritanism*, Historical Association General Series Pamphlet 106 (revised edn, 1986); *The Puritan Character: Polemics and Polarities in Early Seventeeth-Century English Culture*, William Andrews Clark Memorial Library Paper (Pasadena, CA, 1989); 'Ecclesiastical Vitriol: Religious Satire in the 1590s and the Invention of Puritanism', in John Guy, ed., *The Reign of Elizabeth I* (Cambridge, 1994); Peter Lake: *Moderate Puritans and the Elizabethan Church* (Cambridge, 1982); 'Puritan Identities', *Journal of Ecclesiastical History*, 35 (1984), pp. 112–23; *Anglicans and Puritans? Presbyterianism and English Conformist Thought from Whitgift to Hooker* (1988); 'Defining Puritanism – Again?', in Frank Bremer, ed., *Puritanism: Transatlantic Perspectives on a Seventeenth-Century Anglo-American Faith* (Cambridge, MA, 1994).

commonplace books, the question of definition became in itself a kind of game and a means of heightening the polemical voltage: 'Long hath it vexed our learned age to scan/ Who rightly might be termed a Puritan.' It is somewhat in this vein that Maria in *Twelfth Night* says of Malvolio, 'sometimes he is a kind of Puritan' (II. iii. 128). A popular jest assumed the form of a mock definition, accentuating the hypocrisy that, in literary treatments of the subject, became Puritanism's outstanding feature: 'A Puritan is such a one as loves God with all his soul, but hates his neighbor with all his heart.' Historians engaged in their own struggles to delineate Puritanism have not always understood the point of these by no means disinterested satires.[23]

Perennial though the qualities attributed to it were, it is unlikely that the term *Puritan* would have been invented but for a set of specific historical circumstances arising from the Elizabethan religious settlement. The ideal content of Puritanism is elusive, but its meaning within these circumstances perfectly clear. In the perception of the Puritans themselves, the church had been 'but halfly reformed' by the legislation of 1559. Things having proceeded 'but halfly forward and more than halfly backward,' there was need for 'further reformation'; and it was in promotion of this concept that Puritan publicists, politicians, and preachers laboured. Two radical Puritan preachers, John Field and Thomas Wilcox, issued the manifesto *An Admonition to the Parliament* (1572), which complained that 'we in England are so fare of, from having a church rightly reformed, according to the prescript of Gods worde, that as yet we are not come to the outwarde face of the same'. But the authors thought better of what they had written and altered *not* in this statement to *scarce* – 'scarce come to the outwarde face of the same'. The space between *not* and *scarce* was the space occupied and exploited by Elizabethan Puritanism.

The Church of England exhibited the marks of a true church, rightly reformed. It professed sound, biblical doctrine, its sacraments were pure, and so it was not to be lightly rejected as a false church. Some extreme Puritans in extreme circumstances would from time to time reject the church and separate. Their cause was reformation 'without tarrying'. These were, toward 1580, the 'Brownists', followers of Robert Browne, who was to give his name to Separatism for a hundred years, and, toward 1590, the new wave of schism called 'Barrowist' after Henry Barrow, which transplanted from London to Amsterdam a separatist colony that, surrounded and beset as it was by splinters of further secession, came to be known as the 'ancient church' of the separatist way. But Separatism or Brownism pursued its own course, and except for later denominations that

[23] All references in the paragraphs which follow can be traced through my *The Elizabethan Puritan Movement* (1967) and many of the items in *Godly People*, including 'A Mirror of Elizabethan Puritanism: The Life and Letters of "Godly Master Dering"', and 'John Field and Elizabethan Puritanism'.

trace their origins from it and for American Christianity, to which it made an important contribution, it was of minor importance for the immediate future.

It was almost of the essence of Puritanism to remain within the national church. But the marks of a true chuch were barely exhibited, and in practice little was being done to teach and instill the doctrines and principles of a reformed church in the population at large. Thus, the Puritans seemed a race apart, isolated by their dissatisfaction with things as they were and by their full and enthusiastic participation in Protestant religion and its concomitant morals and habits. A distinct and peculiar subculture in an England that still expected a high degree of social conformity, they were almost a church within the church.

Puritans found objectionable in the Elizabethan church precisely those features that Anglicans later proudly celebrated as the virtues of the via media, notably its form of worship, which in overall structure and many specific details retained a strong measure of continuity with the services of the Roman Catholic Church. One extreme critic, the London preacher John Field, spoke of the Prayer Book as encapsulating 'a certaine kynde of Religion, framed out of mans owne braine and phantasie farre worse then that of Poperie (if worse may be), patched and peeced owte of theirs and ours together'. Among as many as a hundred points, or 'dregs', of popery allegedly retained in the Prayer Book, the Puritans took exception to the provisions for ecclesiastical vestments, including the white linen surplice, which was the standard attire for all Elizabethan ministers; the sign of the cross in baptism; and the giving of the ring in marriage.

More fundamentally, Field objected to what he called the 'general inconvenience' of the book, to its liturgical character. The constitution of the church, which was episcopal and hierarchical and retentive of the elaborate and still unaltered infrastructure of its Catholic constitution (episcopal courts, archdeacons, cathedral churches and their deans and chapters), was equally hard for many Puritans to stomach. More generally, the Puritans thought of the church as coming into being by means of the preaching of the lively word of the Gospel, which literally 'edified' its membership in an authentically Pauline sense; that is, the church was a building composed of living stones. But the church in a non-Puritan perception, which we may attribute to the queen for one, was an institution already complete, a legacy of the past, requiring only repair to some parts of its fabric. Under the broad and accommodating roof of this structure, *edification* meant nothing more than the process of instructing the people in their religious duties, the program of the official sermons known as the *Homilies*. Puritanism was a religious dynamic contained within a rather static set of values.[24]

[24] For this point, see the neglected book by John S. Coolidge, *The Pauline Renaissance in England: Puritanism and the Bible* (Oxford, 1970).

The character of the Elizabethan settlement, which provided the Puritan movement with its agenda for further reformation, was determined by political motives and even by political forces. Traditionally, the critical decisions that led to a decisive but moderate commitment to Protestantism have been ascribed to the queen herself and to her secretary of State, William Cecil, and lord keeper, Nicholas Bacon. In making the settlement, parliament proceeded on a governmental blueprint designed to establish Protestantism but in a form not too offensive to Catholic consciences.

In 1950 John Neale reexamined the sparse evidence and argued that the true story of 1559 was different. Elizabeth had not intended to legislate a Protestant prayerbook, at least not in this first parliamentary session. One of the factors that persuaded her to change her mind was the obstructive pressure exerted by advanced Protestants (or Puritans) both within and without the membership of the House of Commons, led by recently returned religious exiles. These political tactics won for the radical Protestant interests less than they had desired but more than they would have secured without them. Neale saw the long-running political contest between the queen and the Puritans in later Elizabethan parliaments as arising from the inconclusive round fought in 1559. The Puritans believed that the strategy that had won some ground on that occasion could win still more. But Elizabeth, who had been forced to yield more than she was originally willing to concede, turned that defeat to advantage by digging into a position from which she was never subsequently dislodged.

Recently doubts have been cast on the plausibility of Neale's account of the parliamentary religious settlement. It appears likely after all that the queen obtained the settlement that she and her advisers had originally intended and that only the opposition of Catholics, especially in the House of Lords, had posed any serious threat to her policy. Be that as it may, two things are not in doubt. First, the queen, while committed by birth, education and policy to Protestantism, was more conservative in her Protestantism than many of her subjects. The single fact that she was not well disposed to a preaching ministry and considered three or four preachers sufficient for a shire is enough to establish that. Secondly, more advanced Protestants, having no sense that a permanent and irrevocable settlement had been made, continued to press for progressive reform, regarding each new parliament as an opportunity to renew the campaign.[25]

It is important not to attribute every religious bill introduced into the House of Commons to a highly organised Puritan high command. Further religious legislation was favored by a broad and loose coalition of interests, including highly placed politicians and public servants and many of the early Elizabethan bishops, whose outlook on many matters was not

---

[25] See 'Windows in a Woman's Soul: Questions about the Religion of Queen Elizabeth I', above, pp. 87-118.

different from those labelled as Puritans. But there was tension between the regime, certainly in the person of the queen, and these interests, and it was out of that tension that the stigma of the term *Puritan* arose. Moreoever, we need not doubt that it was in the character of the Calvinist form of Protestantism, in England no less than in other parts of Europe, to convey to its adherents a sense of involvement in a movement and a cause, the cause of 'the godly', or God's cause.[26]

Puritanism assumed a more definite profile as a movement of nonconformity, protest and political pressure as it became clear that Elizabeth had no plans to complete the limited settlement of 1559 but rather intended to exact a strict conformity to every detail of the settlement as made. In 1565 she demanded that any cleric who did not wear the prescribed vestments (often, it appears, on the insistence of the 'simple gospellers' in their congregations, who in the aftermath of the Marian persecution were deeply offended by 'the pope's attire') was to be disciplined. According to a fashionable doctrine of the time, which became the ideological basis of Elizabethan conformism and Anglicanism, articles of clerical attire such as the surplice and square cap were *adiaphora* ('things indifferent'), which had no doctrinal value and which in their neutrality were legitimately ordered by the political authority of the queen, as governor of the church. The episcopal constitution of the church was originally viewed in the same light, not as a divine ordinance.

The first Puritans (for it was in the context of this controversy that the term appeared) either doubted whether such things were indifferent at all or held that if they were indifferent, then the individual conscience was at liberty to use them or not, according to its own sense of what was consistent with the biblical revelation of God's will. St Paul had said that all things were lawful to him, but not all things were expedient. Certainly to impose things indifferent with legal sanctions was to deprive them of any indifference they might have had.

Matthew Parker, the first Elizabethan archbishop of Canterbury and a moderate and scholarly divine who had not joined the Marian exile, proved capable of the disciplinary measures that the queen's policy required; he composed and published in 1566 a new code of conduct, the 'Advertisements', and persuaded his more radically evangelical colleagues to follow his lead. In the couse of the ensuing 'Vestiarian Controversy', some parts of which had been anticipated in the Edwardian church and in the churches of the Marian exile, ministers were suspended from duty and even deprived of their livings; books and pamphlets were published on both sides; and in London lay Puritans reverted to meeting in conventicles as

[26] 'Puritans, Men of Business and Elizabethan Parliaments', above, pp. 60–86, addresses these issues with reference to the relevant arguments in G.R. Elton, *The Parliament of England, 1559–1581* (Cambridge, 1987).

they had done in Mary's time and found themselves in prison, the victims of a new 'popish tyranny'. A sectarian fault line had opened into a narrow crack, later to become a chasm and destined never to close over in subsequent centuries.

All agreed that the surplice was not itself a matter of great moment. But as a character in Trollope reminds us, 'Wars about trifles are always bitter, especially among neighbours'. In the years after the Vestiarian Controversy, some Puritans, especially the younger men, were encouraged by the bitterness and by the train of their own thinking to call greater things in question. On the Continent, the embattled Calvinist movement was assuming a more rigid and intolerant attitude toward everything that appeared to deviate from its own understanding of the mandates of the New Testament. Any bishops who lorded it over their fellow pastors were now condemned by the leading Geneva minister, Theodore Beza, as instruments of the devil and so not acceptable for the exercise of that godly 'discipline' which Beza instead insisted on as a necessary mark of the church. In Cambridge in 1570 these 'Presbyterian' principles were explored in the lecture hall by a young professor of divinity, Thomas Cartwright. In London they justified the harsh judgment now pronounced on the English church by the even younger Field and Wilcox, authors of the *Admonition*. In a private letter, Field complained that the godly had hitherto confined their attention to the 'shells and chippings of popery' while neglecting 'that which beareth up Antichrist chiefly'.

Not all those who were dissatisfied with the extent of the reforms already achieved in the Elizabethan church agreed with Cartwright and Field in their drastic diagnoses of its structural faults. Only a minority were hard-line Presbyterians. The first priority of many and perhaps of most was to establish universally a learned, godly preaching ministry in every parish and so to make the church in reality what in principle it already was – a godly people. Edward Dering, the model and prototype of the Puritan divine, complained: 'Scarce one of a great many can give an account of their fayth ... A very small number have tasted of the beginnings of the Gospell of Christ.' To pray 'thy kingdom come' and to do nothing about the scandal of the ignorant ministry was to 'speak like parrots'. So Dering shared the indignation of the Presbyterians, but he suspected that their preoccupation with structure was to mistake the shadow for the substance of reformation. He also doubted whether their pessimistic alarmism was justified. Many bishops were godly and sympathetic. And religion had still more powerful friends in high places, including the earls of Bedford, Huntingdon and Warwick, and above all Warwick's brother, the extremely powerful favourite of the queen, Robert Dudley, earl of Leicester.

Among churchmen, Edmund Grindal was the most able and respected. As bishop of London (1559–1570) he had coerced the Puritan clergy with great reluctance. As archbishop of York (1570–1575) he had begun an effective programme of Protestantisation in the north. When this notable father of the English Reformation was transferred to Canterbury on Parker's death, it seemed to be a time to call a truce in 'civil wars of the Church of God'. But within little more than a year, a confrontation occurred between Grindal and his royal mistress that led to his effective suspension from office, the greatest of all setbacks to progressive Protestantism. The queen had declared her dislike of the preaching conferences held in provincial towns and known, somewhat misleadingly, as exercises of 'prophesying' (a term borrowed from St Paul writing to the Corinthians). She now demanded their suppression and proposed a general curtailment in the number of preachers. This was to put the Reformation into reverse; and in a courageous letter, which proved fatal to his career, Grindal told the queen that he could have no part in such a policy.[27]

On his death in 1583, Grindal was succeeded by John Whitgift, who in the 1570s had engaged Thomas Cartwright in a running battle of the books arising from the *Admonition*. Whitgift was a more than willing instrument in repressing not only acts of nonconformity but the Puritan conscience, from which such acts arose. The entire clergy was required to subscribe, on pain of suspension and ultimate removal, to a schedule of three articles that included an affirmation that the Prayer Book contained nothing contrary to God's Word. Resistance to this demand became a common cause for Puritans of all complexions and so played into the hands of Presbyterian extremists. John Field, as secretary of a Puritan cell in London, aspired to play the same role nationally. Ministers in the country were exhorted to resist subscription, to group themselves in conferences, or 'classes', which already resembled the constituent units of a Presbyterian, non-episcopal church, and to maintain an active liaison with their friends among the parliamentary gentry.

These internal developments coincided with a period of acute danger, as it was perceived, to religion, the queen's life, and the Protestant establishment from its Catholic enemies, internal and external. In the Netherlands, William the Silent fell victim to an assassin's bullet in 1584. The members of the English parliament of 1584 went to it committed to applying lynch law to the person most likely to benefit by their queen's violent death – Mary Stuart. Their speeches complained of the untimeliness of the archbishop's onslaught against the godly preachers and dwelt on the deplorable condition of the clergy at large. In this mood, many were willing in this and the following parliament to give a hearing to bills that would have dismantled the existing constitution of the church at a stroke, replacing it with a form of Presbyterianism.

---

[27] Patrick Collinson, *Archbishop Grindal, 1519–1583: The Struggle for a Reformed Church* (1979).

It was not to be. Elizabeth stood in the gap, and presently the Presbyterian moment passed. After the defeat of the Armada in 1588 there was some shift in public attitudes. The great patrons of Elizabethan Puritanism were dead or dying, Leicester among them. Puritan extremism reached its limits, so far as literary exchanges were concerned, in the virulently antiepiscopal pamphlets known as the Martin Marprelate tracts of 1588–90, which were almost certainly written by Job Throckmorton, a Warwickshire gentleman and member of parliament. Marprelate provoked a severe reaction in the form of an exemplary Star Chamber prosecution of Thomas Cartwright and other notorious Presbyterians (but not Field, who, like Leicester, had died in 1588). In the 1590s, Richard Hooker elevated anti-Puritan polemics to philosophical heights previously unknown in his *Laws of Ecclesiastical Polity* (1593–97). He defended the existing constitution of the church not on the rather weak grounds of the *adiaphora* but as broadly consistent with the intentions of the Apostles and of Christ Himself and as inherently reasonable. Meanwhile, Puritanism as an organised, political movement lay low, waiting for a better day.

That day seemed to dawn with the accession in 1603 of King James I. Unlike Elizabeth, whose motto, especially in matters ecclesiastical, was *Semper eadem* ('Always the Same'), James was prepared to envisage change where he was convinced that it was called for; and as a well-informed Calvinist Protestant, he was in sympathy with at least some parts of the agenda of moderate Puritanism. In particular, he needed no persuasion that the ministry of the church ought, as a matter of course, to be a learned preaching ministry. And, like the church's Puritan critics, James perceived that its pastoral effectiveness was gravely damaged by the alienation, or 'impropriation', of the revenues of thousands of parishes into lay hands and sought, albeit unsuccessfully, a remedy. Consequently the Millenary Petition (so called because a thousand ministers were said to have put their hands to it) and the many other addresses that greeted the new king were not entirely unrealistic.

However, as a veteran campaigner against hardline Presbyterianism, which in his Scottish kingdom was the principal political problem with which he had to contend, James was an even more resolute opponent of the Puritan threat to royal supremacy than was the old queen. The mere fact that the Puritans were capable of organising and applying political pressure rendered them odious and dangerous in the king's perception, regardless of the content of their programme.

These two sides of James's mind on ecclesiastical questions were displayed at the Hampton Court conference that the king held with the bishops and a small group of Puritan spokesmen in January 1604. This was a kind of round-table conference in which the king was willing to explore, with an open mind and with a variety of points of view represented, remedies for acknowledged ecclesiastical abuses and failings. But in other episodes the conference was made an occasion for James to issue a public warning to the Puritans that if they maintained a posture that implictly defied his royal prerogative in matters of religion, he would 'harry them out of the land, or else do worse'. In the event, the conference was not very productive, except that the Authorised, or King James, Version of the Bible (1611) came out of an idea floated at Hampton Court.[28]

Whitgift was succeeded as primate by Richard Bancroft, who had built his career on the literary and forensic exposure of Martin Marprelate and other Puritan extremists. Bancroft proceeded to codify the canon law of the Church of England and, with the king's endorsement, to impose the canons by a subscription campaign that had a far more devastating effect than the one conducted by Whitgift twenty years earlier. Some Puritans were driven out of the church altogether into a separatist exile in the Netherlands. Many more toed the line and ceased to be Puritans, at least in the original and most proper sense of that elastic term. Historians used to see in this profound reaction the origins of the 'Puritan Revolution', their term for the great political crisis and Civil War of the mid seventeenth century. According to S.R. Gardiner, the greatest of the modern historians of these events, what Charles I reaped, his father had sown at Hampton Court. 'James went his way, thinking little of what had done.' The Puritans were to have a terrible revenge.

The perspective implied in that analysis is so foreshortened as to be false. Although the Puritans were endlessly frustrated in their hope of political satisfaction in the shape of a new religious settlement, many of their ends were well on the way to achievement by the time of James's death. Most of the more able and energetic of the Jacobean bishops were the children of Grindal rather than of Whitgift or Bancroft: Calvinists, firm in their detestation of Catholicism, promoters of the godly preaching ministry, and often regular preachers themselves. Under George Abbott of Canterbury and Tobias Matthew of York, both primatial sees were for long held by churchmen of this calibre. The formal qualifications of the clergy had by now so far improved that in many dioceses more than half were licensed preachers. By the 1620s the great majority of those ordained and instituted to livings in all dioceses were university graduates.[29]

---

[28] Patrick Collinson, 'The Jacobean Religious Settlement: The Hampton Court Conference', in Howard Tomlinson, ed., *Before the English Civil War* (1983); Kenneth Fincham and Peter Lake, 'The Ecclesiastical Policy of King James I', *Journal of British Studies*, 24 (1985), pp. 169–207.

[29] On all this see now Kenneth Fincham, *Prelate as Pastor: The Episcopate of James I* (Oxford, 1990), which corrects some of the judgments entered into here. For example, Fincham regards the preaching, pastoral, evangelical Jacobean bishops as children of Bishop John Jewel rather than as 'Grindalians'. And he finds that the extent to which the clergy of the Church of England had become a graduate clergy by the 1620s has been exaggerated.

As for society at large, in many parts of England it had now advanced some distance along the road of moral change traced by J.R. Green. Jacobean provincial life was often dominated by the twin commanding figures of godly ministry and grave magistracy, those two 'optic pieces' of the commonwealth, as one preacher put it. Shakespeare was expressing his misgivings about this overtly and excessively righteous kind of government when he drew the figure of Angelo in *Measure for Measure*. In the towns, sermons drove out plays and other 'obscene' entertainments, and the 'rude multitude', the 'base rabble', was obliged, however reluctantly, to knuckle under to a bleakly Sabbatarian regime. In printed form, the kind of divinity known as 'practical' sold briskly, as the increasingly literate middle classes warmed to its edifying themes. Hooker and Shakespeare were not the best-selling authors of Jacobean England; far more popular were the physicians of the soul, Richard Rogers, John Dod and William Gouge, and above all William Perkins and Lewis Bayly (*Practice of Pietie*).[30]

In all this there were seeds of future conflict. 'The war was begun in our streets', wrote the great divine Richard Baxter, 'before the king and the Parliament had any armies.' But it is not likely that that 'war' would have breached the outward casing of Protestant provincial society if power had not passed, in the disastrous reign of Charles I, into the hands of an ecclesiastical party whose policies were detrimental not only to Puritanism but also to the religious values of a moral majority of Protestants, values that in the years of Shakespeare's maturity had not been much questioned but that were now, in a revival and extension of the old stigma, denounced as puritanical by the new men in power. This party – sometimes labelled Arminian after Jacobus Arminius, the Dutch proponent of a theology of grace divergent from the doctrine of double predestination taught by strict Calvinists, and sometimes Laudian after Archbishop William Laud – set itself against the 'orthodoxy' of the prevalent Calvinism, promoted unwelcome 'innovations' in ritual and ceremony, gave new and disturbing emphasis to the exalted status of the clergy and its material rights and claims, and seemed to be prepared to betray the Reformation and England itself into the hands of its Romish enemy. But these developments, with their catastrophic consequences for the Church of England, extend beyond the lifetime of Shakespeare and the scope of this essay.[31]

---

[30] Patrick Collinson, *The Religion of Protestants: The Church in English Society, 1559–1625* (Oxford, 1982); idem, 'The Protestant Town', in *Birthpangs of Protestant England*; David Underdown, *Fire from Heaven: Life in an English Town in the Seventeenth Century* (1992).

[31] A swiftly-moving debate has outstripped and undermined the over-confident judgments of this paragraph. See Nicholas Tyacke, *Anti-Calvinists: The Rise of English Arminianism, c. 1590–1640* (2nd revised edn, Oxford, 1990); Peter White, *Predestination, Policy and Polemic: Conflict and Consensus in the English Church from the Reformation to the Civil War* (Cambridge, 1992); Julian Davies, *The Caroline Captivity of the Church: Charles I and the Remoulding of Anglicanism* (Oxford, 1992); Kevin Sharpe, *The Personal Rule of Charles I* (New Haven and London, 1992).

VII

My final aim is to investigate the local and particular impact of religious change in Warwickshire, in Stratford-upon-Avon and in William Shakespeare's immediate family circle. A report made to the privy council by the bishop of Worcester in the year of Shakespeare's birth says that of forty-two justices of the peace and other officers resident in his Warwickshire jurisdiction, twenty-one were 'adversaries of true religion'. Only eight were identified as 'favourers of true religion'. According to an earlier bishop of Worcester, that founding father and martyr of the English Reformation, Hugh Latimer, Stratford lay at the 'blind end' of his diocese. So although Edgar Fripp thought that in Mary's reign the town was 'a protestant stronghold' and was 'encircled by the martyr fires', this seems most unlikely. Latimer's editor, Augustine Bernher, may well have had Stratford in mind when he wrote from the south Warwickshire town of Southam of 'great Parishes and market Townes ... utterly destitute of God's word'.[32]

The early corporation records of Stratford contain none of the telltale clues to the precocious Protestant enthusiasm found in the annals of Ipswich, Leicester, or indeed Coventry, within a day's ride of Stratford. Almost no payments or gifts of wine for visiting preachers are listed, no expressions of anxiety about church attendance or Sabbath observance. Evidently violent affrays, unregulated muck hills, and stray dogs troubled the magistrates more than sin. Only in 1564, with the departure from the town of the influential Catholic Clopton family, were the images defaced and the rood loft taken down in the guild chapel, the principal religious edifice in the town of Stratford. These measures should have been taken in 1560, and in southeastern England they generally were.[33]

In 1566 the curate composed a will for an alderman in which he bequeathed his soul to God 'to be in joy with our Blessed Lady and with all the Holy Company of Heaven'. It is probable that most members of this community were church papists. John Bretchgirdle, the vicar who baptised Shakespeare, was a learned man who left behind him a distinguished little library. It was the library of a humanist but not necessarily that of a convinced Protestant. His successor fell under suspicion at the time of the Northern Rebellion and lost his position, while both the curate and the schoolmaster left town at the same time and evidently under the same cloud.[34]

---

[32] Bateson, 'A Collection of Original Letters', pp. 7–8; *Sermons and Remains of Hugh Latimer*, ed. G.E. Corrie, Parker Society (Cambridge, 1845), p. 384; Edgar I. Fripp, *Shakespeare Man and Artist* (Oxford, 1938), i, pp. 21–2; it is significant that Bernher's words occur in a passage added to his Preface to Latimer's *Sermons* between 1562 and 1578; Latimer, *Frutefull Sermons* (1578), sig. * v.

[33] Fripp, *Minutes and Accounts*, i.

[34] Idem, *Shakespeare Man and Artist*, i, pp. 37–42, 48; S. Schoenbaum, *William Shakespeare: A Documentary Life* (New York, 1975), pp. 20, 53.

The next vicar to be installed, Henry Heycroft, was not a cryptopapist. Yet not until the mid 1580s are there any signs of a watershed in the religious culture of Stratford or evidence of any local influence that could have brought about such a conversion. Simon Hunt, the schoolmaster who must have taught Shakespeare, withdrew to Douai in 1575, moved on to Rome and became a Jesuit. One of Hunt's pupils and Shakespeare's schoolfellow, Robert Dibdale, took the same route. He reentered England as a priest in 1580 and died on the scaffold in the aftermath of the Babington Plot in 1586. So the evangelical credentials of early Elizabethan Stratford are anything but convincing. Bishop Bayly's *Practice of Pietie* continued through countless editions and as far away as Hungary (where it was translated) to indict Stratford as a town meriting God's visitational wrath for profaning the Sabbath and 'contemning his Word in the mouth of his faithful ministers'.[35]

In 1586, as part of the groundwork for the presentation of petitions and bills for further reform in the House of Commons, the organised Puritan movement mobilised its supporters in the country to draw up surveys of the condition of the parish clergy at a time when Archbishop Whitgift and the High Commission were continuing to harry with subscription and suspension the minority of 'faithful' and 'sufficient' ministers. In Warwickshire this undertaking was very likely inspired by two local Puritan notables, Thomas Cartwright, installed by the earl of Leicester as master of his hospital in Warwick, and Job Throckmorton of Hasely, the future Martin Marprelate.

Doubts have often been cast on the value of the Warwickshire survey as sober historical evidence. Yet comparison with an episcopal inquiry of about the same time in which the clergy were required to assess themselves suggests that it is factually accurate. The Puritan surveyors found the vicar of Warwick to be 'unsound in some pointes of christian religion' and 'verie much subject to the vice of good fellowshippe'. The curate of the Shakespeares' ancestral parish of Snitterfield was a nonpreacher, conceded to be 'honest' but 'far unfit for the ministerie'; 'he teacheth to plaie on instrumentes and draweth wrought workes'. A pluralist who held three livings, including Henley-in-Arden, was encouraged by the prospect of a French and Catholic royal marriage to shave off his Protestant beard. The incumbent at Honiley 'could not one daie reade the commandementes for want of his spectacles' – a touch worthy of Marprelate. At Grafton the vicar, John Frith, was an aged Marian survivor, 'unsound in religion.' 'His chiefest trade is to cure hawkes that are hurt or diseased, for which purpose

Documentary Life (New York, 1975), pp. 20, 53.

[35] Lewis Bayly, *The practice of pietie* (1632 edn), p. 432. Stratford's punishment was to be 'twice on the same day twelvemoneth (being the Lords Day) almost consumed with fire'. Bishop Bayly does not explain how so much of Elizabethan Stratford survived this double calamity, still less how Sunday could occur on the same date in two successive years.

manie do usuallie repaire to him.' This is the man who is thought to have
married Shakespeare and Anne Hathaway, and he is sometimes linked with
the figure of Friar Laurence in *Romeo and Juliet*, a herbalist who corresponds
to the popular stereotype of the 'massing' priest as 'conjurer'.[36]

At Stratford, the Puritan surveyor had high praise for the newly installed
vicar, Richard Barton: 'a preacher, learned, zealous, and godlie, and fit for
the ministerie. A happie age yf our Church were fraight [with] manie such'.
Barton had been visited on the town by the godly earl of Warwick, and with
his advent in 1585, Stratford at last embarked on the first steps of J.R.
Green's path of moral transformation, which would reach its climax, in a
sense, in the magistrates' decision in 1623 not to entertain the visiting
players. In 1591 the corporation was anxious lest the poverty of the living
would mean that 'the word' would be taken from them and 'able and
learned' ministers discouraged from accepting the cure. Barton had been
offered more money as an inducement to stay. Their anxiety was ground-
less. Barton was the first of a line of zealous preachers, rarely interrupted.
In 1587 and 1588 Cartwright himself preached at Stratford, accompanied
by Throckmorton, the town marking these notable visits by gifts of wine and
sugar.[37]

Ecclesiastical life in Stratford was self-contained and self-sufficient to an
unusual degree. The tithe income was enjoyed by the corporation, which
paid the vicar an annual stipend of £20. In 1591 the town petitioned for the
right of appointing to the vicarage, which was vested in the crown. In one
respect, Stratford already approximated to the model of ecclesiastical
organisation and discipline desired by Cartwright and Throckmorton.
Instead of the normal oversight of its faith and morals by bishop and
archdeacon, the town was ecclesiastically a 'peculiar', subject in the first
instance to the jurisdiction of its own vicar, who sat in judgment over his
parishioners in his own court of correction.[38]

Much of the business of this little tribunal resembled that of archdeacons'
courts elsewhere – the detection and punishing of sexual and marital
offences, which explains their familiar title of 'bawdy courts'. (At Stratford,
Thomas Faux 'scandalised' the court by calling it the bawdy court.) There
are several recorded instances of the court's provoking a spirited resistance
to its discipline by the townspeople. On 1 October 1595, Elizabeth Wheeler
'brawled' in the court itself – crying out, 'Goodes woondes, a plague of God
on you all, a fart of ons ars for you' – and was excommunicated. On 26
March 1616, Shakespeare's son-in-law Thomas Quiney was ordered to do
public penance for copulation with Margaret Wheeler (perhaps the daugh-

[36] *A Seconde Parte of a Register*, ed. Albert Peel (Cambridge, 1915), ii, pp. 165–74; *Ecclesiastical Terriers of Warwickshire Parishes*, ii, ed. D.M. Barrett, Dugdale Society, 27 (Oxford, 1971).

[37] Fripp, *Minutes and Accounts*, iii, pp. 160–1; iv, pp. 17, 31, 127.

[38] E.C.R. Brinkworth, *Shakespeare and the Bawdy Court of Stratford* (1972).

ter of the impenitent Elizabeth?), who had died in childbirth with her baby eleven days earlier. This is a most intriguing episode, for Quiney had married Judith Shakespeare (irregularly according to church law, as it happens) on 10 February. Had Margaret died because she refused to tell the midwives until it was too late who the father of her child was? It was understandable that so recent a bridegroom as Quiney should have asked to have the humiliation of public penance commuted to a payment of five shillings into the poor box.[39]

From the late sixteenth century, the records of Stratford's bawdy court document a creeping Sabbatarianism. In 1590 the court ordered the churchwardens and constables to go through the inns and alehouses in time of divine service to detect those engaged in gaming and tippling. Presentments for such offences subsquently occur with regularity. In 1622 Thomas Canning admitted to playing at ball on the Sabbath, said that it was the first time that he had done so, and promised that it should be the last. In the same year, two parishioners were interviewed for the offence of striking noisy children in church who were disturbing the sermon. They were told that they ought to have complained to the magistrate, who would have had the children whipped. On the same occasion, four morris dancers and 'the Maid Marion' were in court. Two years later Stephen Lea was in trouble for singing 'profane and filthie songs' and for deriding ministers and the profession of religion. In 1619 a rather unsatisfactory vicar, John Rogers, was squeezed out of office by the corporation to make way for a stirring preacher in the Puritan mould, Thomas Wilson. *A Satire to the Chief Rulers in the Synagogue of Stratford* was scattered in the streets, complaining against the dominant Puritan oligarchy: 'Stratford's a town that doth make a great shew,/But yet it is governed but by a few.../Puritants without doubt'. Here was 'the war in our streets' referred to by Baxter.[40]

And what of the Shakespeares? It has been argued that the family tradition was conformable and Anglican, that it was crypto-Catholic if not fully recusant, and that it was Puritan. Of these incompatible theories, the suggestion that Shakespeare's father was a Puritan, even an extreme Puritan and Separatist, is the most implausible and weakly supported. It

[39] Ibid., pp. 153, 128, 143; Edgar I. Fripp, *Master Richard Quyny, Bailiff of Stratford-upon-Avon and Friend of William Shakespeare* (Oxford, 1924). Fripp makes no mention of this embarrassing affair in his account of Thomas Quyny's marriage to Judith Shakespeare, although he remarks (p. 205): 'Thomas Quyny, as Shakespeare probably foresaw, did not prove a satisfactory husband.'

[40] Fripp, *Shakespeare Man and Artist*, ii, pp. 838–45; C.J. Sisson, *Lost Plays of Shakespeare's Age* (Cambridge, 1936), pp. 193–6. For the cultural and social context of libellous ballading, see David Underdown, *Revel, Riot and Rebellion: Popular Politics and Culture in England, 1603–1660* (Oxford, 1985); Underdown, *Fire from Heaven*, pp. 27–32; Adam P. Fox, 'Aspects of Oral Culture and its Development in Early Modern England' (unpublished Cambridge Ph.D. thesis, 1993), chapter 4 'Ballads and Libels'.

rests on deeply mistaken and anachronistice perspectives of Elizabethan religious life.[41] Those writers who regard John Shakespeare as a conformable citizen who, as a chamberlain (treasurer) of the Stratford corporation, willingly presided over the Protestansation of the guild chapel believe that his withdrawal from all civic responsibilities after 1576 contains no suspicious circumstances but was prompted by genuine business and financial embarrassment. It was reported in 1592 that he (and some others) stayed away from church only 'for fear of process for debt', and many authorities believe that this was the simple truth.[42]

I agree with De Groot that some explanation of John Shakespeare's withdrawal from public life must be found other than in business failure and that the reason is likely to have been religious. Shakespeare's father was most probably an unreconstructed Catholic of the old sort who was a potential and perhaps an actual 'convert' of the missionary priests who had penetrated to the vicinity of Stratford by 1580. He had had no formal schooling and whether or not he was literate is an old controversy. The family into which he married, the Ardens, had many links with recusancy; and it is not unlikely that Mary Arden, the poet's mother, was more consistent in her Catholicism than her husband, a common and understandable state of affairs. That John Shakespeare was a municipal officer when the guild chapel was Protestantised proves nothing. Indeed, the fact that the great doom painting was whitewashed over rather than destroyed suggests the kind of crypto-Catholic conduct of which Puritans often complained.[43]

In 1583 the extended family to which Shakespeare belonged was placed in great jeopardy when their cousin John Somerville was arrested on his way to London to assassinate the queen. The response of Warwickshire Catholics was to clear their houses 'of all shows of suspicion'. So it was probably at this time of danger that John Shakespeare concealed in the roof of his house in Henley Street the copy of St Charles Borromeo's 'Last Will of the Soul' to which he had apparently set his name, article by article, fourteen in all, making it the personal confession of 'John Shakespear, an unworthy member of the Holy Catholik religion'. This document bemused scholars when it was discovered by chance two centuries later. The Jesuits Campion and Parsons are known to have asked for thousands of copies of this little classic of Counter-Reformation piety to distribute in England, and in 1580 Campion stayed in a house only twelve miles from Stratford. There

[41] Thomas Carter, *Shakespeare:Puritan Recusant* (1897); Fripp, *Shakespeare Man and Artist*.

[42] Henry S. Bowden, *The Religion of Shakespeare* (1899); George Wilson Knight, *Shakespeare and Religion* (1967); Schoenbaum, *William Shakespeare: A Documentary Life*, pp. 34–40; J.S. Smart, *Shakespeare: Truth and Tradition* (1928).

[43] J.H. de Groot, *The Shakespeares and 'The Old Faith'* (1946); Peter Milward, *Shakespeare's Religious Background* (1973); Heinrich Mutschmann and Karl Wentersdorf, *Shakespeare and Catholicism* (New York, 1952).

is no conclusive evidence of John Shakespeare's Catholicism, but this is very nearly conclusive.[44]

As for William Shakespeare himself, the late seventeenth-century report of Richard Davies that Shakespeare 'died a Papist' is unsubstantiated. Yet since the dramatist avoided all parochial office and responsibility, in both Stratford and London, failed to receive the communion in Southwark (on the surviving evidence of the distribution of communion tokens),[45] and is only assumed to have attended church in that he was never presented for recusancy, he may well have leaned in that direction. The plays themselves contain no reliable pointers to the dramatist's private religious convictions, tastes or prejudices; although there is a persistent and well-informed use of Catholic terminology and imagery (as there is in the thoroughly Protestant Edmund Spenser), which is a little intriguing, unless Shakespeare employed them for the mere sake of artistic authenticity. The point has often been made that he did not exploit the stories of either King John or Henry VIII as a robustly Protestant dramatist (such as John Bale) would have exploited them. Again, while not a virulently anti-Puritan dramatist, Shakespeare made use of some features of the stage Puritan in constructing two of his least appealing characters, Malvolio and Angelo, and always represented the parish clergy of the Elizabethan church as figures of fun. But it is to Ben Jonson's *Bartholomew Fair* and *The Alchemist* and to Thomas Middleton's *The Family of Love* that we must turn, not to Shakespeare, to find unambiguous Puritan parodies.[46]

Shakespeare's plays are replete with points of religious reference and resound with echoes of the Bible, Prayer Book, and Homilies, texts with which he was thoroughly familar. No less than forty-two biblical books are refracted in his dramatic corpus. But whereas proponents of Shakespeare's supposed bias toward Puritanism suggest that the poet learned the Bible in the Genevan version at his mother's knee, this seems most unlikely. Richmond Noble thought it 'reasonable to doubt that Shakespeare was grounded in the Bible in his home'.[47] Some biographers believe that his knowledge was of the kind acquired almost by a process of osmosis, as Bible and Prayer Book were heard again and again, in church. A. L. Rowse has remarked: 'The rhythms of the majestic phrases of the Bible and Prayer Book, heard all the days of one's youth, enter into the blood-stream: one

[44] The intriguing question of the Borromeo implant is fully discussed by Schoenbaum, pp. 41–6, for whom, however, with no doubt admirable conservatism, it is not 'very nearly conclusive'.

[45] Jeremy Boulton, 'The Limits of Formal Religion: The Administration of Holy Communion in Late Elizabeth and Early Stuart London', *London Journal* (1984), pp. 135–54.

[46] For the early appearances of the stage Puritan and the development of the character, see my 'Ecclesiastical Vitriol', in Guy, ed., *The Reign of Elizabeth I*. For a view different from that expressed in this paragraph, see now Donna B. Hamilton, *Shakespeare and the Politics of Protestant England* (1992).

[47] Richmond Noble, *Shakespeare's Biblical Knowledge and Use of the Book of Common Prayer*; A.L. Rowse, *William Shakespeare: A Biography* (1963), pp.41–7.

cannot get them out of one's head, even if one would.' Even if atheism or agnosticism lies ahead, it is an atheism or agnosticism nourished and made tolerable by those mighty words. So 'a tale told by an idiot' derives from the Psalmist: 'We bring our years to an end, as it were a tale that is told.' Henry VI declares, 'Blessed are the peacemakers' (*2 Henry VI*, II.i.34), and Marcus in *Titus Andronicus* quotes, 'To weep with them that weep' (III.i.244). [48]

But Noble points out that the Bible was not yet so resonant with this generation and argues that Shakespeare's knowledge was so accurate and so aptly applied that it could have been acquired only by reading. 'It is sufficiently clear that Shakespeare read the Bible in adult life and it may be that he did so fairly frequently.' This may underestimate the capacity of the memory in a culture that was still more aural than literate. As the Bible itself puts it, 'Faith cometh by hearing'. The fact that the Bishops' Bible is the version most heard in the earlier plays and the Geneva Bible is more frequently echoed in the later suggests that it was only in his maturity that Shakespeare owned a Bible and read it at first hand. This is precisely what the general historical picture would lead us to expect. There is also interesting evidence that Shakespeare appreciated and borrowed from one of the greatest of the godly preachers of the Elizabethan church, Henry Smith, called by Thomas Nash 'silver-tongued'.[49]

So Shakespeare may have been himself part of that creeping 'moral change' which Green located within his lifespan, the complicated tract of which this essay has attempted to traverse. Shakespeare's father was probably a Catholic of the old stamp, whereas the more respectable of the poet's two sons-in-law, the successful physician John Hall, was an impeccable Jacobean Protestant whose published casebook bears the motto 'Health is from the Lord'.[50] As for Shakespeare himself, we cannot say.

---

[48] Milward, *Shakespeare's Religious Background*.
[49] Rowse, *Shakespeare the Man*, pp. 28–31.
[50] Fripp, *Shakespeare Man and Artist*, ii, pp. 881–92.

Index